# POLITICS AND SOCIETY IN ISRAEL
## Studies of Israeli Society
### Volume III

# POLITICS AND SOCIETY IN ISRAEL
## Studies of Israeli Society
### Volume III

*Editor:* **Ernest Krausz,** Bar-Ilan University
*Assistant Editor:* **David Glanz,** Bar-Ilan University

*Publication Series of the Israel Sociological Society*

Transaction Books
New Brunswick (U.S.A.) and Oxford (U.K.)

Sponsored by the Schnitzer Foundation for Research on the Israeli Economy and Society—Bar-Ilan University.

Library of Congress Catalog Number: 79-93045
ISBN: 0-88738-012-3 (cloth), 0-87855-969-8 (paper)

Printed in the United States of America

**Library of Congress Cataloging in Publication Data**

(Revised for vol. III)
Main entry under title:

Studies of Israeli society.
    Vol. 2: Editor, Ernest Krausz; assistant editor, David Glanz.
    Includes bibliographies.
    v. 1. Migration, ethnicity, and community—v. 2. The sociology of the kibbutz—v. 3. Politics and society in Israel.
    1. Israel—Social and conditions—Collected works.
2. Israel—Emigration and immigration—Collected works.
3. Israel—Ethnic relations—Collected works.
4. Kibbutzim—Collected works. 5. Israel—Politics and government—Collected works. I. Krausz, Ernest. II. Glanz, David.
HN660.A8S83      306'095694      79-93045
ISBN 0-87855-369-X (v. 1)

# Contents

# Preface

The object of this series, as defined in the previous two volumes, is to identify the major themes of sociological research on Israeli society, and to gather the best material that has appeared in international scholarly journals and books in English. Such a selection of previously published articles, accompanied by original integrative essays, is intended to provide a review process of sociological research in the field, and to generate discussion, reassessment, and further research.

The selection of the topic for each volume has been guided by two principal criteria: (1) that the subject should be of considerable interest both for Israeli society and for social science, and (2) that a critical mass of literature on the topic be available, to provide a comprehensive view of "the state of the art," and to facilitate a better understanding of Israeli society.

The current volume not only meets these desiderata but goes beyond that. A sociological view of political life in Israel demonstrates the links with other institutional facets of Israeli society, such as the class and ethnic factors at work; the ideological and religious dimensions in politics; the military variable; and so on. Since Israeli politics is of very wide interest, the special contribution of a sociological analysis is that it clarifies the important processes of change that have occurred in Israeli political life in the last decade, marked by the "political upheaval" (*mahapach*) of 1977; the Begin era; and the break in the national consensus since the 1982 war in Lebanon. This volume appears before the significance of the July 1984 election will be fully analyzed by social scientists. Nonetheless, we are confident that the volume will be useful in analyzing future developments in Israeli political life.

The volume contains a comprehensive bibliography, the first of its kind on the subject of politics and society in Israel, including some 500 items. We hope that this bibliography will serve as a significant resource for readers interested in studying the topic in greater depth.

The preparation and publication of this volume would not have been possible without the help of a number of organizations and individuals. First and foremost we are most grateful to the Schnitzer Foundation for Research on the Israeli Economy and Society, Bar-Ilan University, for its generous support in sponsoring this volume. We also wish to express our gratitude to the Sociology and Anthropology Department of Tel-Aviv University, which has provided the excellent facilities of the Israel Sociological Society. We wish to express our appreciation to members of the Editorial Board and especially to two individuals who invested a considerable amount of time and effort in the preparation of this volume—Professor Elihu Katz (chairman of the Editorial Board) and Ruth Bokstein (secretary of the Israel Sociological Society). We thank Professor Yonathan Shapiro (chairman of the Israel Sociological Society), who wrote an original introductory essay, and whose guidance in the review and selection process of material for this volume was invaluable. We were also fortunate that two distinguished scholars—Professor Karl W. Deutsch and Professor S.N. Eisenstadt—agreed to write the introduction and the epilogue respectively. Finally, we gratefully acknowledge the kind cooperation we received from the authors and publishers who permitted us to reprint their articles.

# Acknowledgments

We also wish to gratefully acknowledge the following journals and publishers for permission to use previously published material:

"Authority without Sovereignty: The Case of the National Centre of the Jewish Community in Palestine," *Government and Opposition,* Vol. 8, No. 1 (1973):48-71. ©Government and Opposition Ltd.

"Israel's Compound Polity," in *Israel at the Polls,* ed. Howard R. Penniman, 1979, pp. 1—38. ©American Enterprise Institute for Public Policy Research.

"The Reopening of the Frontiers, 1967-82," in *Zionism and Territory,* by Baruch Kimmerling, 1982, pp. 147-82. ©Institute for International Studies.

"Ideological Dimension," in *The Origins of the Israeli Polity,* by Dan Horowitz and Moshe Lissak, 1978, pp. 120-56. ©The University of Chicago.

"The Primarily Politicial Functions of the Left-Right Continuum," *Comparative Politics,* Vol. 15, No. 2 (1983):139-58. ©The City University of New York.

"Change and Continuity in Zionist Territorial Orientations and Politics," *Comparative Politics,* Vol. 14, No. 2 (1982):191-210. ©The City University of New York.

"The Dilemma of Reconciling Traditional Cultural and Political Needs: Civil Religion in Israel," *Comparative Politics,* Vol. 16, No. 1 (1983): 53-66. ©The City University of New York.

"Political Legitimacy in Israel—How Important Is the State?" *International Journal of Middle East Studies,* Vol. 10, No. 2 (1979):205-24. ©Cambridge University Press.

"Israel's Right-Wing Jewish Proletariat," *The Jewish Journal of Sociology,* Vol. 24, No. 2 (1982):87-97. ©The Jewish Journal of Sociology.

"The Ethnic Lists in Election 1981: An Ethnic Political Identity?" in *The Election in Israel, 1981,* ed. Asher Arian, 1983, pp. 113-38. ©Ramot Publishing Company.

"The NRP in Transition—Behind the Party's Electoral Decline," in *The Roots of Begin's Success,* ed. D. Caspi, A. Diskin, and E. Guttman, 1983, pp. 141-68. ©Croom Helm Ltd.

# 1

# Introduction

## Karl W. Deutsch

The reality of Israel is presented in this book in many different ways. Israel is seen as a collection of successive waves of immigration, of traditions and ideologies, of ethnic groups, of social strata and classes, of basic themes of cultural orientation, or of stages of historical development. The authors are good at their jobs, and each chapter is written with professional mastery.

What do all those different perspectives add up to? One result could have been utter confusion, compounded by the length of the book. This the editors have avoided. Or it could have become a coherent work, full of light and depths and color, richer in content than a single author's work could be. This the editors have achieved.

It is hard to characterize this book in a few words. One might call it a treasury of information, an armory for future arguments, or a tool chest for analysis. It is a bit of all of these, but when read through, the whole book is more than the sum of its parts. Above all, it is a work of serious sociological research. Its scholarship is thorough, and the level of professional competence is high. Many of the authors are young, and their work proves that sociology is alive and well in Israel.

What do they tell the world about their country, and what are they telling their own countrymen?

### Changes in Ideology

The authors are telling their countrymen, and indirectly the world of social scientists, that Israel has changed tremendously. The political changes that surfaced in the late 1970s and early 1980s, they tell us, had their roots in social, psychological, and ideological changes that occurred during the preceding twenty years. The generations of pioneers that led the country between 1925 and 1955 came in many cases out of the socialist and labor movements of Eastern and Central Europe. They hoped to create in

Israel a new kind of society and a new kind of human being. The results in many ways have been less new than expected, apart from one fundamental achievement that the authors take for granted. Israel has given millions of Jews for the first time in more than two millennia the chance to live free from discrimination, oppression, and the threat of physical and cultural extermination. It has given them pride and at least temporary military security, and it has worked a miracle in creating a common modern language and culture for millions of people from many countries, whose ancestors had spoken many languages for many centuries.

But this is not what the authors talk about, since they know it so well. The free upright walk of young Israelis is noticed by a foreign visitor who remembers the way many Jews used to walk in the countries and epochs of their persecution; in Israel many of the memories of the Diaspora are gone, and are a matter for a great museum or for drastic political simplification. These sociologists are talking about how the ideologies of socialism—of a new society and a new type of human being—have lost much of their power, how largely the motivations for economic effort and political behavior of most Israelis have become much like those of most people in other industrial countries. As elsewhere, Israelis center on the search for security, opportunity, better material standards of living, and higher social status, even to the detriment of their less-favored countrymen. The chapters by Dan Horowitz and Moshe Lissak, Daniel Elazar, Asher Arian, and Michal Shamir impressively document this change.

## Change in Ethnic Composition

At the time of the establishment of the State of Israel the majority of the Israelis were European Jews, with small additions from the United States and Canada. By the late 1970s, a majority of the now larger Jewish population were immigrants from Africa and Asia and their descendants. Despite this Oriental majority, the Western Ashkenazic minority remained economically, socially, and culturally dominant.

The authors know that Israel offers its people one of the most highly developed welfare-state systems in the world, but they report in detail on the many disadvantages and slights—social, economic, cultural, and psychological—that Sephardic Jews of Oriental background, although now a numerical majority in Israel, are still suffering, often after more than a generation, much as people of "non-Western" backgrounds are suffering in other industrial countries formally and informally dominated by Western culture. The political awakening of this Sephardic majority and its large support since 1977 for the Likud coalition of the right-of-center parties is another one of the great changes that have occurred in Israel.

## A Blind Spot with Changing Boundaries:
## Israeli Perceptions of the Arabs

In the early stages of Zionism, until the mid-1920s and even into the 1930s, Arabs in Palestine and in adjacent territories, we learn in this volume, were most often seen as a nonpeople. They seemed politically apathetic under Turkish and later British rule, most of them scattered in their villages like so much human dust. A writer spoke of the Jews as "a people without land" who had found in Palestine "a land without people." Arab nationalistic activity was ascribed merely to the machinations of a handful of landowning *effendis* and reactionary Muslim clerics. After 1933, under the increasingly deadly threat of Nazism, Arab nationalism was seen mainly as an extension of Nazi penetration without any authentic existence of its own.

These fateful misperceptions of the 1930s and 1940s were enhanced by a decisive political error of many Arab leaders and their followers who during World War II openly sided with Hitler's Germany, as did the Mufti of Jerusalem and the Iraqi nationalist leader El Geilani. Other Arabs, including an Egyptian government, declared themselves neutral in that war, and most Palestinian Arabs opposed the immigration of Jews fleeing for their lives. The United States and other Western powers in those years acted similarly by granting immigration to their countries only on a fatally small scale, claiming that they did more by avoiding the rise of anti-Semitism at home and fighting to defeat Nazi Germany on the battlefield—a contention that today weighs less than the memory of 6 million Jewish men, women, and children brought to death by the actions of the Nazi government.

It is necessary to recall these events because they have left, to this day, three lasting impressions in the minds of many Israelis of all ages: all or most Arabs are pitiless enemies; no other nation or group of nations in the world can be relied on to aid Israel in an hour of need; and no country or group of countries would offer shelter to 3.5 million Israelis—as distinct from a few individuals or small groups—if they should have to leave Israel.

These memories, often unspoken, still have an impact. They overshadow, to this day, in the minds of most Israelis any concern about the human, civic, economic, and cultural concerns of their Arab neighbors within Israel and in the territories that are occupied and administered by the Israeli armed forces, as well as in the rest of the Arab world. Within Israel, as Sammy Smooha shows, Arab affairs are not dealt with at the Cabinet level, but are usually left to special Arab affairs sections or departments, headed by Israeli "Arabists," charged in substance with maintaining the status quo or changing it in favor of Israeli settlers and land-use projects. In the occupied territories, army rule has similar effects.

Even the present volume, excellent and thoughtful as it is, illustrates Smooha's thesis. It contains not a single chapter by a social scientist of Arab background. Even if all Arabs should refuse any dialogue, their published views could be studied. Among the many references in the volume there is no appreciable number of citations from Arab newspapers, books, or scholarly papers, nor from the speeches and writings of Arab political leaders within Israel and the occupied territories, nor are even many names of such leaders to be found. So far as Israel's Arab citizens or subjects are concerned, Israeli sociological research still is at a stage where it resembles the work of an honest and hardworking veterinarian whose patients do not talk.

Difficulties of language cannot be a lasting excuse. If Israeli social scientists of high quality such as the authors of the present volume had no time to learn to read Arabic, translations could have been used. So far, a white patch has remained in the map of *Politics and Society in Israel,* to which this volume is dedicated. This is one major unfinished task for Israeli sociology; I trust that the high intellectual quality, realism, competence, and dedication of Israeli sociologists will fulfil it some day with distinction.

Even so, the authors already report changes. The Arabs are now seen as a real and permanent part of the political landscape, who will neither emigrate nor give up their language, culture, and Muslim or Christian religion. The same holds for the much larger Arab populations in the occupied territories of the West Bank and the Gaza Strip. Their military occupation since 1967 can still be prolonged, but it can hardly be expected to last forever. Baruch Kimmerling presents important materials on this question in his second article.

## Other Changes

Linked to the major changes discussed so far, smaller but politically significant changes are reported. Menahem Friedman analyzes the numerical decline of the National Religious Party (NRP) from more than 9 percent of the vote in the national elections of 1977 to less than 5 percent in 1981. He finds that after the victory of the rightist Likud coalition in 1977, many NRP voters of that and earlier elections no longer felt the need for a special party to protect their religious and traditionalist concerns against a secularized government, and hence felt free to shift their vote to other parties, expressing their interest about other issues.

Even earlier, as Charles Liebman and Eliezer Don-Yehiya show, a part of the religious tradition—divided as it was between the militant one of the Bible and the more passive one of the Diaspora—has been reinterpreted by the government, the educational system, and the media in the direction of what the authors call a new "civic religion," in which the contrasts between religious tradition and secular nationalism have become reduced, so as to end earlier periods of confrontation.

Yael Yishai reports the rise of a right-wing Jewish proletariat, recruited mainly from Sephardic Jews who feel disadvantaged and exploited as mere wage workers in the enterprises of the collectives—the kibbutzim in which they are denied full membership—and of the labor union organization—the Histadrut—both dominated by members of the major Labor Party—Mapai. The same workers often feel neglected and discriminated against in the new development towns, which appear to some of them as ghettoes. Their political response has aided Likud's rise to power, and it may influence the political landscape of Israel for years to come. Their protest has found a channel in one of the two major parties, and increasingly also in the other one. Hanna Herzog describes how ethnicity has served in other cases as well as a tool for political bargaining and thus, in the end, has aided in integrating various ethnic groups within a common Israeli political system.

Despite the authors' emphasis on change, they also show how much has remained permanent in Israel. The new language and culture are here to stay. The reinterpreted Jewish tradition is still a recognizable tradition. Almost all Israelis continue to face Arab hostility with calm courage, although aware of some changes in it. The great influence of the armed forces has remained, too, and has even grown. But these and other elements of continuity form a background against which the many changes stand out.

What is the upshot of it all? Perhaps this: Israel has changed decisively in many ways during the last twenty years; hence her probable future may be no longer what it used to be; and these studies by Israeli sociologists offer the best overview of these changes that one could hope to find.

Israel is more than just a country of a people. It is a crucible and, in spite of its uniqueness, a representative exemplar of the world. Social scientists from many countries owe its sociologists a debt of gratitude for having analyzed so many of its problems so well.

# 2

# Political Sociology in Israel: A Critical View

*Yonathan Shapiro*

The papers assembled in this volume represent the best selection of studies on political sociology in Israel available to date. As such, this volume both summarizes and reflects the functionalist approach, which has been dominant until recently, and the efforts of the authors to come to grips with the changes in political life in Israel. My essay uses this volume as a point of departure for a critique of this hitherto dominant school of thought. According to the functionalist view, the major problem Israel has faced since its establishment can be analyzed in terms of the processes of adjustment in the existing system, seen best in the acculturation and integration of the new masses of immigrants. Within this functionalist paradigm the developing relations between the immigrant groups and the establishment have not been seen as creating a class problem. Yet it is this emerging process of stratification in Israeli society and its exploitation in populist politics that appears to be central for the understanding of the more recent developments. Hence, although it may seem somewhat unusual, the aim of this essay is not only to criticize this theoretical framework, but at the same time to suggest an alternative approach to the study of politics in Israeli society.

Israeli politics has not been, until recently, the subject of much research among Israeli sociologists. They preferred subjects such as immigrant absorption or the study of the kibbutz, areas dealt with in the first two volumes of the *Studies of Israeli Society* series. This lack of interest is despite the fact that Israeli society is thoroughly politicized, with political parties and organizations affecting every aspect of life. Indeed, Israel was founded by political organizations that recruited their members for immigration to Palestine and raised funds for the establishment of the economic and cultural infrastructure of the new society. It was the Zionist Organization and its respective parties that created a new society and revolutionized the way of life and thinking of the Jews who came to Palestine. The Jews, who had been a persecuted minority for 2,000 years, established there a sovereign state with a Jewish majority. The Jewish community in Palestine considered itself the inheritor of the ancient Jewish culture, identified itself with millennia-old Jewish history, and revived the ancient Hebrew language, making it the everyday language of Israel.

Perhaps this very politicization of Israeli society is the reason for the hesitation of sociologists to study its political system. The Zionist revolution took place in this century and Israel was only founded in 1948. Some of the founding revolutionaries are still living among us. Apparently Israeli sociologists are not yet capable of demystifying this revolution, an inevitable result of sociological research. In discussing the Israeli political scene, Israeli sociologists tend to sound very apologetic. Although signs of a more critical approach can be discerned, in general they prefer to focus on minor flaws and ambiguities in Israeli society and its political culture rather than to question its basic assumptions.

However, political events of the last few years have shaken the political system and raised basic questions about its core values, which heretofore were regarded as sacrosanct and unshakeable. These events began with the Six-Day War in 1967, which transformed Israel into an occupying power. Soon after, the Social-Democratic Party—Mapai (since 1968 the Labor Party)—began to decline. Mapai was the dominant party in Israel from its establishment—and even earlier in the Jewish community in Palestine (the *yishuv* as it was called)—and during the formative period of the new society. The 1973 Yom Kippur War brought in its wake the transfer of control in the Labor Party from the founding fathers, East-European born, to the first Israeli-born generation. Three years later, in 1977, this party fell from power. Its place was taken by a government headed by rightist parties (the Likud), at whose core was the Herut Party, founded and headed by leading members of the Irgun Zvai Leumi, a right-wing military underground which operated against the British during the *yishuv* period. In those years and during the first years of statehood, these groups were excluded from any influence on the political, economic, and cultural system of Israeli society.

All the essays in this volume were written after the Six-Day War; many after the downfall of the Labor Party and the rise of the Likud, an event referred to in Israeli political jargon as the *"mahapach"* (upheaval). This event was instrumental in stimulating new thinking about Israeli politics. A more critical approach among Israeli sociologists can be discerned in this book, which is a fairly representative sample of research in the area of Israeli political sociology in recent years. However, this collection is composed exclusively of papers and book chapters which have appeared previously in English only. A scholarly quarterly devoted to politics and international relations has begun to appear in Hebrew recently, and a number of important books on the subject, published in Israel, have not yet been translated into English.

Most of the studies of Israeli politics gathered here still exemplify the unwillingness, and perhaps the inability, of the authors to criticize the basic assumptions of their society. At the core of these assumptions is the belief that Israel is a pluralist democracy, and that in the formative period of the Jewish society before the establishment of the state, the founding fathers succeeded to a large extent in building a society in accordance with their socialist-Zionist ideology. They achieved this despite the fact that, as a result of the democratic pluralistic structure of the political system and the lack of political sovereignty, they had to reach compromises with various other social groups in the Jewish population. This political reality forced Social-Democratic leaders, who wished to lead the entire community, to mobilize maximum support for their socialist-Zionist ideology. Achieving a broad consensus in the community was of paramount importance. The achievement of such a consensus in turn, scholars argue, institutionalized the democratic process in the new society.

The theoretical sociological orientation adopted by scholars who support this interpretation of the history and the sociology of Israeli society is functionalism. Dan Horowitz, in an article published in 1983 in Hebrew, correctly observes that "the dominant school in macro-sociological research in general, and in political society in particular, in Israel, was structural-functional."[1] This theoretical approach in the analysis of Israeli politics is epitomized by Moshe Lissak and Dan Horowitz in their important book *The Origins of the Israeli Polity,* a chapter of which is included in this volume.

Many scholars, following in their footsteps, seem completely oblivious to the fact that functionalism has been discredited among most sociologists in Europe and the United States in recent years. The explanation for this discrepancy between Israeli sociologists and the international sociological community seems to be the Israeli sociologists' identification with the national interest. They prefer a theory that treats society as a unified social system, each part of which contributes to the maintenance and stability of the system as a whole. Functionalism seeks continuity and not change; it deals with social integration and views negatively social processes and social organizations and institutions that do not contribute to such stability and integration.

Israeli sociologists are particularly enchanted with the functionalist idea which views the cultural values accepted by the majority of members as the core of any viable social system. The value consensus provides its axis. This idea sustains the assertion, already mentioned, that there was maximum agreement with the dominant socialist-Zionist orientation during the *yishuv* period, a position accepted by almost all the contributors to this volume. All of them note the strength of ideology during the *yishuv* period. Only in contemporary Israeli society, they admit, has the power of ideology waned. It no longer mitigates the conflict of interests and the power struggles for political power, economic resources, and social prestige. But these sociologists have no convincing answer as to how or why this change took place. Most attribute it to the establishment of the sovereign Jewish state. In every sovereign state, they argue, there are conflicts between interest groups and contests over power and material resources. The Jewish society went through a process of "normalization" after the establishment of the state, and today it is a state like all others. Political parties must contend for votes; then national leaders must build coalitions based on pragmatic arrangements that allow them to keep the voters' support and loyalty. In this process particularist interests of various groups in society become more influential in national politics while the influence of collectivist ideology weakens.

This explanation is not very convincing. It is surprising that most of the political sociologists in Israel, when studying their own society, ignore the rich tradition of political sociology that deals with informal political structures, with the covert activities of elites, and with the oligarchies that control ostensibly democratic political parties. They pay little attention to the political activity that goes on in informal meetings and in secret consultations, the covert operations of pressure groups, or the systems of interpersonal relations of politicians and its influence on their policies. The scholars prefer to discuss the formal structure of politics: official agreements between parties, party platforms and public statements of leaders, and public opinion surveys. This is not a lack of sophistication on their part, but an unwillingness to deal with the shady side of politics. We are still too close to the revolutionary generation, and our respect for them and their achievements prevents a critical analysis of their methods of operation and rule—the sort of analysis that is current among our colleagues in other democratic countries.

Nevertheless, there can be seen in recent years the beginning of a change in the attitudes of political sociologists to the study of Israeli politics. Yoram Peri's essay on the relationship between the army and politics exemplifies this new approach. Peri points to the system of informal relations between the heads of the Labor Party and high-ranking army officers, which made possible the control of the army by the dominant party, and the changes that have been taking place following the decline of the Labor Party.

Lately we have witnessed a growing debate among political sociologists in

Israel. This debate has developed mainly between those sociologists loyal to the notion that Israel is democratic, liberal, and pluralistic, and those who attempt to present the controlling elites, party oligarchies, and pressure groups as powers interfering in the formal democratic process and distorting it. The first group includes Moshe Lissak and Dan Horowitz, two of whose essays are included here. In their book, mentioned earlier, they made use of David Riesman's model of the autonomous veto groups in American politics in order to explain Israeli politics. They ignore the fact that Riesman used the veto groups as proof of the inability of the American political system to provide the United States with direction and leadership, while they assert that our politicians did succeed in leading Israeli society to political independence.[2] Another writer, Peter Medding, who studied the Social-Democratic Party from the establishment of the State of Israel up to 1969, concluded that its manner of functioning negates the iron law of oligarchy of Robert Michels.[3] In Medding's opinion, the Israeli party mediates between the various social groups and the Israeli political system. Its control is based on the agreement of many groups within the population. Its power is therefore consensual power, Medding determines, rather than the rule of a party oligarchy.

Other scholars, including me, do not accept these theses. I believe Israel was governed until recently by a ruling elite that, with the help of the dominant Social-Democratic Party, gained control of the Histadrut (Israeli federation of labor), which had gathered under its control most of the trade unions and many industrial and financial enterprises that together made up about 20 percent of the Israeli economy. It should be remembered that the intervention of the state in economic life in Israel is greater than in any other noncommunist state.[4]

Many of the scholars who argue that Israel is a democratic pluralistic state based on consensus and on the ability of many groups in the population to influence government policy, adopted the consociational theory. According to this theory, consociational democracy arises in societies divided into groups that succeed in enlisting maximum loyalty of their members, usually religious or ethnic groups. A democratic regime that wishes to preserve integration and stability must permit the various groups maximum autonomy and even veto power over the decisions of the central government. In a democracy of this sort the government is composed of broad coalitions based on compromises and understandings reached by the leaders of the various groups.[5]

Attempting to include the Jewish society of the formative *yishuv* period in the family of divided political societies, these Israeli scholars claim that the Jewish community in that period was divided into religious and secular groups, and within the secular camp into a labor movement and a bourgeoisie. The antagonisms between the groups were so sharp that only a consociational democracy was able to preserve the unity of the *yishuv*. A consociational democracy is so pluralistic that it lacks a real political center. And what, in the eyes of loyal democrats, could be better than extreme pluralism? It is difficult to accept this claim with regard to the political system during the *yishuv* period. There were conflicts between religious and secular groups, and between socialists and conservatives, which found expression in the various political parties. But there were no separate and autonomous communities of a cultural, ethnic, or religious nature with crystallized leaderships.

In the period of statehood a new differentiation developed among the Jewish population that was perhaps more meaningful than those existing in the *yishuv* period. The mass *aliyah* (immigration) following the establishment of the state brought to Israel many immigrants from Asian and African countries. The current distinction in Israel between immigrants from Asia and Africa (Sephardim) and those from Europe (Ashkenazim) is based on religious and historical differences between these communities, which have existed for hundreds of years. Cultural and social differences between European countries and Asian and African countries sharpened the differences between the two populations in Israel.

Relations between Ashkenazim and Sephardim were the central subject of sociological research in Israel after the establishment of the state. It became clear that to the cultural and historical differences that had existed previously between the two populations, a class distinction was added, with the Asian-African immigrants constituting the lower strata and those from Europe the higher ones. But an analysis based on class distinctions is not accepted among Israeli sociologists, just as it is not accepted among their American colleagues: A class analysis is likely to lead sociologists to deal with conflict and change rather than stability and consensus. In studying relations between the two populations, Israeli scholars prefer to deal with cultural and ethnic aspects rather than class. As for the differences between ethnic communities, the sociologists permit themselves to be very critical of their society, for the same reasons that American sociologists are critical of ethnic discrimination in the United States. The upper strata of those of European descent in Israel have experienced a dilemma of the sort Myrdal uncovered among members of the White majority in their attitude toward the Black minority in the United States. This dilemma results from the contradiction between the principle of equality of all citizens, which is a supreme value accepted by all in American culture, and the prevalent discrimination against the Blacks.[6] In Israel, in addition to the value of equality, there is another core value: the absorption and integration of all immigrants. It sharpens further the contradiction between the agreed-upon values of society and the social reality that made those of Asian-African descent into a stratum of low prestige and inferior economic status. Because of this contradiction between values and social reality, criticism of discrimination and of prejudice toward the Oriental Jews is expected and accepted among the Israeli sociologists.

In recent years the study of relations between Sephardim and Ashkenazim has assumed an important place in Israeli political sociology, as evident in this volume. This is because the relations between the two populations became a major factor in party politics in Israel. In the 1960s and 1970s, Sephardic vote began to move away from the Labor Party to the Likud. The explanations for this phenomenon center on the feelings of discrimination and deprivation of the Sephardim, which led them to oppose the dominant party and to support the Likud opposition. Scholars also claim that as a result of their religious and cultural traditions, the Sephardim are more attracted to the nationalist ideology of the Likud than to the democratic and humanistic socialism of the Labor Party. Their higher birth rate made the Sephardim the majority within the Jewish population during the 1970s, and their support of the Likud brought it into power.[7]

There are those who attribute the fall of the Labor Party mainly to internal developments,[8] but there is no doubt that the support of the Likud by the Sephardim was an important cause of the change of government in Israel. To understand the changes in the voting behavior of the Sephardic Jews, the class dimension must be added to the analysis of Israeli politics, even though this approach is not, as I have said, favored by most Israeli sociologists.[9]

To understand the class structure in Israel, it is necessary to note that most of the immigrants who arrived before World War II were from Eastern Europe, where they were part of the petite bourgeoisie. In Palestine these immigrants split into two groups. There were those who continued their petit-bourgeois activities as storekeepers and small businessmen, while others, who called themselves pioneers (halutzim), aspired to become manual laborers. For the latter, Zionism was a national and a social revolution at the same time. They believed that physical labor had a central role in the process of liberating the Jew from his Diaspora mentality and creating a new Jew. With their labor they hoped to prepare the country for the absorption of more immigrants, and to establish a "workers' community" in Palestine.

This personal transformation was difficult for the young people who arrived in Israel. Their social-class background abroad did not prepare them for this; and most of them did not persevere in this aim for long. Despite their revolutionary fervor and their belief in the socialist-Zionist idea, which necessitated their transformation into a proletariat, they preferred nonphysical work. The *yishuv* period was one of constant immigration and of great mobility among the immigrants. Many, even those who had no aspirations of this kind, began their careers as laborers, but in a few years moved to positions of office work and management in the public bureaucracy—Zionist and Histadrut—which developed rapidly. Large amounts of capital imported into the country as donations were turned over to the political leadership. The economic needs of a developing society undergoing rapid processes of urbanization and industrialization coincided with the interest of the politicians who aspired to establish an organizational bureaucratic machine that would strengthen their control of the new society, and the desire of many pioneers to become free of their wearisome physical labor.

A class of managers and clerks was thus created in Israel. This class, which is also developing rapidly in all European industrialized countries, is termed by Ralf Dahrendorf, following scholars of the Austro-Marxist school, a "service class." I prefer to call it a "bureaucratic class." The values, behavior norms, and life style of this class, says Dahrendorf, are formed under the influence of the bureaucratic-hierarchical structure in which they operate. This structure causes those operating in such a framework to be preoccupied with problems of promotion and prestige. "Status for the service class" says Dahrendorf, "is not a static notion. Hierarchy always implies the possibility of promotion; social mobility and the service class belong inseparably together."[10]

The bureaucratic class in Israel continued to grow, and its values and life style became the dominant culture in Israel, just as has occurred in Europe, in Dahrendorf's view. Moreover, since Israel contained many immigrants who began their working lives as laborers at the bottom of the occupational ladder and after a short time, became clerks and managers, there developed an interesting though paradoxical situation. Despite the dominant socialist-Zionist ideology, workers became bureaucrats, and a class-conscious proletariat never developed. This rapid mobility from manual labor to clerical and managerial positions increased even more in the early years of the state. During the first three years the population had almost tripled and with it the public bureaucracy. These clerks and managers were mainly recruited from among the veteran immigrants from Europe and their children.

Thus, the dominant Social-Democratic Party in the *yishuv* period, provided not only employment for the immigrants and assistance in housing, health, and welfare services; its policy permitted and encouraged rapid social mobility from manual labor to office work and management. This veteran population consolidated the culture of the bureaucratic class.

For those coming with the very large wave of immigration immediately after the establishment of the state, the reality was different. In the years during which these immigrants and their children underwent the process of socialization and absorbed the dominant bureaucratic culture of their new society, bureaucratic growth slowed down. This change inevitably created two distinct populations: (1) the old-timers and their children of European descent, who joined the bureaucratic class, and (2) the immigrants from Asia and Africa and their children, who, while absorbing the culture of the bureaucratic class, remained mainly manual laborers.

One of the results of this new social reality was the transformation of Israel into what Randall Collins calls "the credential society."[11] In order to move up in society, i.e. in the bureaucracy, it was necessary to attain academic degrees, and here the veterans of European origin had a decided advantage over the immigrants. The acquisition of university education and academic degrees required much preparation and the foregoing of immediate rewards for an extended period. Most immigrant families from Asia and Africa were not able to do this. Their economic situation did not allow it, nor did their culture prepare them for it. At the same time, they were not absorbed by a class-conscious proletariat, since such did not exist in Israel; instead they absorbed the values of the bureaucratic class, while access to it was closed to them. This situation brought about feelings of alienation from the dominant culture and estrangement from the establishment. This reaction found expression in the 1960s and 1970s in their political behavior. They voted in increasing numbers for the Likud opposition and against the Social-Democratic Party, which was identified with the establishment.

The dialogue that ensued between the Likud leaders and large strata of Asian-African immigrants brought the Likud to power in 1977, and resulted in a meaningful change in the political system and in the political culture in Israel, i.e, the crystallization of the populist political structure. In the case of Israel, it was a democratic populism, in which a populist leadership gained power through democratic elections.

Populism is composed of a distinct political ideology and a political structure.[12] Populism is not an ideology of social change. It is designed for groups that feel deprived and cut off from the dominant culture and the political center, and are nurtured by their hate for the establishment. It promises these groups liberation from their feelings of estrangement and deprivation. A populist movement produces from its midst leaders able to create a mystic tie with the masses, giving them the feeling of participation in decision making and giving expression to their longings, something that the parties and parliament representing the establishment cannot provide. Thus, populism is against the establishment, not against the state.

The support for populism in Israel came from different groups than in Europe; it came mainly from the members of the petite bourgeoisie who felt themselves abandoned and cut off in a capitalist society. The European working class was organized in labor unions and political parties that represented it and bestowed on their members an ideological orientation which made clear to them their role and position in the social and political system. As a result they were class conscious and proud of their class affiliation, and populism did not attract them. In Israel, as noted above, the immigrants who became laborers were not absorbed into a class-conscious working class. This reality strengthened their feelings of alienation and estrangement, feelings which grew greater among their children who were born and educated in the country, and served in the army. Many of them became attracted to the populist movement and its leaders.

Israeli populism crystallized after the Likud rose to power. Menachem Begin, its leader, looking for a formula to consolidate his rule and give it legitimacy, nurtured and developed its Israeli version. The spiritual baggage Begin and his comrades acquired as they matured in Eastern Europe before World War II, directed their adaptation to the new situation, but Israeli populism entailed for them a new way of operating the political system. The populist formula in Israel was created at the end of the 1970s and emerged in the process of the new leaders' adaptation to the reality they found when they came to power. Menachem Begin created an emotional tie with the masses in mass meetings in the town squares, and his associates have tried to follow his example. They based their appeal on the hatred of the masses for the establishment and its various institutions. The populists claimed that they were the real representatives of the masses because they exemplified the nation's will, identified with its aims, and worked to enhance and glorify it. They made use of a national mystique, giving all members of the nation a feeling of partnership, with no differences of status. This is a common formula in populist movements.

As every other populist movement, Israeli populism adhered to formulas suited to the culture in which it operated. Thus Begin adapted his slogans to the Jewish cultural tradition, a tradition which expressed both feelings of fear and inferiority, mixed with ethnic pride and arrogance. Begin and his associates, as proud Jewish leaders, encouraged the Jewish people to hold their heads high against those who wished to demean and even destroy them, promising a glowing future to the nation which had known great suffering and persecution.

Populist regimes are considered by scholars to be unstable and unable to continue in power for long periods. The vague promises of the populists to establish a society in which the whole population can participate raises expectations among their supporters that cannot be met by the leaders. The feelings of belonging and identification with the nation through unmediated contact with the leaders cannot, in the long run, substitute for solving social and economic problems. One can therefore predict further changes in the political system of Israel, and we can only hope that they will not adversely affect the democratic framework of Israeli society.

## Notes

1.    Dan Horowitz, "The Yishuv and Israeli Society—Continuity and Change: The Yishuv as a Political Community in a Two-Community System," *Medinah, Memshal v'Yachasim Beinleumiim* 21 (Spring 1983):33 (Hebrew).
2.    Dan Horowitz and Moshe Lissak, *The Origins of the Israeli Polity* (Chicago: University of Chicago Press, 1978).
3.    Peter S. Medding, *Mapai in Israel* (Cambridge: Cambridge University Press, 1972).
4.    Yonathan Shapiro, *Democracy in Israel* (Tel Aviv: Massada, 1978); Nadav Halevi and Ruth Klinov Malul, *The Economic Development of Israel* (New York: Praeger, 1972).
5.    Arend Lijphart, *Democracy and Plural Societies* (New Haven: Yale University Press, 1977).
6.    Gunnar Myrdal, *An American Dilemma* (New York: McGraw-Hill, 1944).
7.    Such explanations are scattered throughout this book in various essays. In addition see Asher Arian, ed., *The Elections in Israel, 1977* (Jerusalem: Jerusalem Academic Press, 1980); idem, *The Elections in Israel, 1981* (Tel Aviv: Ramot, 1983).
8.    Yonathan Shapiro, "The End of a Dominant Party System," in Asher Arian, ed., *The Elections in Israel, 1977,* pp. 23-28.
9.    The following paragraphs of this article are based on my book, Yonathan Shapiro, *An Elite without Successors* (Tel Aviv: Sifriat Hapoalim, 1984 [Hebrew]).
10.    Ralf Dahrendorf, "Recent Changes in the Class Structure of European Societies," in *A New Europe,* ed. Stephen Graubard (Boston: Houghton Mifflin, 1963), pp. 291-336.
11.    Randall Collins, *The Credential Society* (New York: Academic Press, 1979).
12.    In this essay, the facts regarding the Israeli experience are based on a symposium on populism, held in London in 1968. The papers from the symposium were published by Ghita Ionesco and Ernest Gellner, eds., *Populism: Its Meaning and National Characteristics* (London: Weidenfeld & Nicholson, 1969).

# Part I

# HISTORICAL DEVELOPMENT

# 3

# Authority without Sovereignty: The Case of the National Center of The Jewish Community in Palestine

## Dan Horowitz and Moshe Lissak

THE PROCESS WHICH CHARACTERIZED THE POLITICAL SYSTEM OF THE Jewish community in Palestine was a process of the formation of a non-sovereign political centre which progressively increased its authority through the exercise of control over the mobilization and distribution of resources. The bearer of this process was a power conscious elite – oriented on the formation of an institutionalized national centre. The mobilization of resources outside of the system enabled this centre to allocate more resources than it had to extract from its periphery. Thus, a dynamic equilibrium was created in which progressively increasing demands were balanced by an increased mobilization of resources. The operation of the system was dependent upon a division of functions between an evolving coalitionary national centre and various particularistic sub-centres. The lack of sovereignty paradoxically contributed to the development of 'rules of the game' which made the resolution of conflicts possible within a quasi-parliamentary framework.

The pre-independence Jewish community in Palestine has often been called 'a state in the making' or 'a state within a state'. Despite its being a minority community within a wider political system, the Jewish community, or the *Yishuv*[1] as it was called, developed political institutions which enjoyed a large degree of authority, as well as mechanisms for the settlement of political conflicts which resembled those of a sovereign state.[2]

[1] The Jewish community in Palestine was called the *Yishuv*. The ordinary meaning of the word is settlement, but it is used also to describe an ethnic community living in a certain territory.

[2] For general historical, sociological and political surveys see the following publications: (a) historical, sociological and political surveys: Alex Bein, *The Return to the Soil: A History of the Jewish Settlement in Israel*, Youth and Hechalutz

The phenomenon of a national minority under foreign rule developing an elaborate and semi-autonomous political system raises questions of both historical and sociological significance. The most important of these questions are: first, what were the circumstances that enabled the central political institutions of the *Yishuv* to consolidate its quasi-state power and maintain a large degree of authority in spite of the limitations consequent upon its lack of sovereignty? Secondly, how did the central political institutions resolve the problem that arose from the existence of rival political centres operating within the same territorial framework, i.e. the Mandatory government and the leadership of the Arab community? Thirdly, what kind of interaction developed between the Jewish community in Palestine and the Jewish communities overseas which constituted the former's main source of demographic growth, economic aid and political support? Fourthly, how were political conflicts among social groups, ideological movements, political parties and economic interest groups resolved in the absence of those sanctions available to a sovereign state?

These questions may be tackled from several angles. One aspect, which emphasizes the ideology of Jewish colonization in Palestine, has been thoroughly explored by several authors.[3] However, little

---

Department of the Zionist Organization, 1952. Shemuel N. Eisenstadt, *Israeli Society*, Basic Books, New York, 1968. Bernard Joseph, *The British Rule in Palestine*, Public Affairs Press, Washington, 1948. Dov Weintraub, Moshe Lissak, Yael Azmon, *Moshava, Kibbutz and Moshav: Patterns of Jewish Rural Settlement and Development in Palestine*, Cornell University Press, Ithaca and London, 1969. Leonard J. Fein, *Politics in Israel*, Part I, Little Brown & Company, Boston, 1967. Esco Foundation for Palestine, *Palestine: A Study of Jewish, Arab and British Policies*, Vol. 2, Yale University Press, 1947. *Palestine Royal Commission Report*, Cmd. 5479, July 1937. Government of Palestine, *A Survey of Palestine, Prepared for the Information of the Anglo-American Committee of Inquiry on Palestine*, 2 Vols., Jerusalem, 1946. (b) economic surveys: David Horowitz and Rita Hinden, *Economic Survey of Palestine*, The Jewish Agency, 1938. Robert Nathan, O. Gass and D. Creamer, *Palestine: Problems and Promise*, Public Affairs Press, Washington, 1946. Robert Szereszewski, *Essays on the Structure of the Jewish Economy in Palestine and Israel*, Falk Institute, Jerusalem, 1968. Ruth Malul-Klinov and Nadav Halevi, *The Economic Development of Israel*, published in co-operation with the Bank of Israel by F. D. Praeger, New York, 1968. (c) demographic and other statistical data: Government of Palestine, Office of Statistics, *Statistical Abstract of Palestine*, Jerusalem 1937–1943. David Gurevich and Aaron Gertz, *Statistical Handbook of Jewish Palestine*, Jewish Agency for Palestine, Jerusalem, 1947.

[3] See for example, S. N. Eisenstadt, *op. cit.* V. D. Segre, *Israel: A Society in Transition*, Oxford University Press, London, 1971, Chaps. 3–4. Israel Kolat,

attention has been paid as yet to other aspects of the issues concerned, in particular the characteristics of the power structure of the Jewish community and its political centre and the manner in which the latter controlled the relationships between individuals and groups within the Jewish community on the one hand, and external political entities such as the Mandatory authorities, the Arab community and the Zionist movement in the Diaspora on the other hand.

The following analysis focuses on these specific aspects. Accordingly, its point of departure is the following inter-related propositions: (a) the political institutions of the *Yishuv* gradually increased their authority by extending their control over the mobilization and allocation of resources. The formation of an autonomous political centre was aided by the tendency of the *Yishuv* to expand and separate itself from the bi-national Palestinian society.

(b) The allegiance of ideological movements, political parties and economic interest groups to the emerging national political institutions was secured through a division of functions between the central political institutions and the various particularistic groups, which enabled the latter to retain considerable control over their own resources. Consequently, it became possible for various social groups to mould new patterns of social, economic and spiritual life without directly exposing themselves to the intervention of other groups.

(c) The national centre controlled many of the channels through which resources flowed into the system. Consequently, it was able to allocate those resources, not originating in the *Yishuv* itself, and thus meet the demands presented by various groups within it. In this respect, the process of accumulation of power was analogous to a levy imposed on the use of the services of the centre which acted as a provider of resources.

(d) A pragmatic attitude on the part of the dominant elite, the adoption of the principle of political representation as a basis for the allocation of resources and the coalitionary structure of the central institutions all enabled the evolving political centre to mitigate the impact of social and political conflict on the fragile integrity of the *Yishuv*'s political system.

---

'From a Community of Workers to a Nation-State', *Lamerchav*, 15 January 1971 and 22 January 1971. Dan Horowitz, 'Between Pioneer Society and Normalization', *Molad*, Vol. 19, No. 146–7, October 1960, pp. 413–31. Martin Seliger, 'Positions and Dispositions in Israeli Politics', *Government and Opposition*, Vol. 3, No. 4, Autumn 1968, pp. 465–84.

## THE EVOLUTION OF CENTRAL POLITICAL INSTITUTIONS

One of the main features of Jewish colonization in Palestine from the last quarter of the 19th century was the aspiration to create the distinct communal entity associated with Zionist ideology. In spite of the marked national consciousness which characterized the new settlers who emigrated to Palestine in the last decades of Ottoman rule, the Jewish community failed to develop autonomous and authoritative political institutions until the end of the first world war.[4] Only with the establishment of British rule and the arrival of new immigrants, inspired by the Balfour Declaration, did the Jewish community succeed for the first time in giving an institutionalized meaning to its yearning for separate political and social identity. From the 1920s onwards, two main political institutions played the role of a political centre for the Jewish community: (a) The Jerusalem Office of the World Zionist Organization (WZO);[5] and (b) The National Council (*Havaad Haleumi*) of the Jewish community organized in the framework of the Jewish Assembly (*Knesset Israel*).[6] These two bodies enjoyed a legal status under the British mandate. The Zionist Executive, whose main functions in Palestine were transferred in 1929 to the Jewish Agency for Palestine (*Hasochnut Hayehudit*), derived its legal authority from Article 4 of the Mandate according to which 'an appropriate Jewish Agency shall be

---

[4] There were a few attempts to establish central political institutions of the Jewish community before the first world war. All these attempts failed. Worth mentioning in this context is the initiative of the Zionist leader Menachem Ussishkin who convened in 1903 an 'Assembly of the *Yishuv*' in Zichron Yaakov which formed the central organization which existed for less than a year. There was also the 'Palestine Office' of the World Zionist Organization established in 1908, headed by Arthur Ruppin. The 'Palestine Office' and its director played a crucial role in the development of agricultural settlements in Israel, in particular the establishment of the first *Kibbutzim*.

[5] The main office of the WZO was in London, the location of the Executive of the WZO, headed for many years by Prof. C. Weizmann.

[6] The term National Institutions refers to the World Zionist Organization (WZO) Executive (in a later period to the Jewish Agency Executive) and to the National Council of *Knesset Israel* (The Community Organization of the Jewish Population in Palestine). For a detailed description of these institutions see: Moshe Burstein, *Self Government of the Jews in Palestine since 1900*, Hapoel Hazair, Tel Aviv, 1934. The Jewish Agency for Palestine, *The Jewish Case before the Anglo-American Committee of Inquiry on Palestine*, Jerusalem, 1947. Moshe Attias, *Knesset Israel in Palestine: Its Foundation and Organization*, Havaad Haleumi, Department of Information, Jerusalem, 1944.

recognized as a public body for the purpose of advising and cooperating with the Administration of Palestine in such economic, social and other matters as may affect the establishment of the Jewish National Home and the interests of the Jewish population in Palestine, and, subject always to the control of the Administration, to assist and take part in the development of the country.'[7] On the other hand, the National Council, which was founded in 1920, operated without legal status until the late 1920s when it derived its authority from the Religious Community Order of 1926 and the Jewish Assembly Regulation based on this Order.[8]

The National Council was elected by the Assembly of Representatives which in turn was elected in general elections by all adults in the Jewish community.[9] With regard to the Zionist Executive and later the Jewish Agency the situation was more complicated. The Zionist Executive bodies were elected on the basis of the results of the elections to the Zionist Congresses whose electorate consisted of all those affiliated to organized Zionist movements in the Diaspora as well as in Palestine. The establishment of the Jewish Agency was aimed at widening the basis of support for Jewish colonization by co-opting non-Zionists into the bodies that supervised it. These two political institutions, which were also known as the 'National Institutions' (*Hamosadoth Haleumiim*), operated on the basis of a division of labour between themselves. The Jewish Agency dealt mainly with immigration and settlement while the National Council was responsible for education, welfare and religious services. Both institutions fulfilled representative functions *vis-à-vis* the British authorities. As from the 1930s, the Jewish Agency also supervised unofficially the

[7] See Palestine Royal Commission, *op. cit.*, Article 4, p. 35.

[8] The activities of the *Vaad Leumi* on the other hand were based on: (1) Article 83 of the 1923 order in Council in which it was said that 'each religious community shall enjoy autonomy for the internal affairs of the community subject to the provisions of any Ordinance or Order issued by the High Commissioner'. See Robert H. Drayton, *Laws of Palestine*, Waterlaw, London, Vol. III, 1934, p. 2588; (2) on the 1926 Religious Communities (organization) Ordinance. This provided that 'if any religious community in Palestine makes application under this Ordinance, the High Commissioner may, with the approval of a Secretary of State, make rules for its organization as a religious community and its recognition as such by the Government of Palestine'. See R. H. Drayton, *op. cit.*, p. 1292.

[9] The elections were based on proportional representation and consequently there was a proliferation of competing political parties and *ad hoc* candidates' lists which took part in the elections. Elections were held in 1920, 1925, 1931 and 1944.

illegal defence organization of the Jewish community – the *Hagana*.[10] The Jewish Agency was the stronger and more influential of the two 'National Institutions' since it controlled the national funds and even subsidized many of the activities of the National Council, particularly in the field of education.

Many of the political and social activities of the Jewish community did not take place in the framework of the central political institutions but in that of the particularistic institutions formed by political movements. The strongest among them was the General Federation of Jewish Workers (the *Histadruth*) which was established by the political parties of the labour movement in 1920. This organization did not confine its activities to conventional trade union functions but also operated both as the provider of health and other welfare services and as an economic entrepreneur. The *Histadruth* had no counterpart in the non-labour sector which was less organized and more fragmented than the labour sector in its political, economic and social activities.

The institutionalization of political roles within the Jewish community consolidated its separate national identity and enabled it to achieve the implementation of its common national goals more effectively.

## CENTRIFUGAL AND CENTRIPETAL TENDENCIES

The evolution of a stateless political system was made possible through the attempt, exceptional in the history of the settlement by European emigrés of areas inhabited by native populations, to establish an immigrant society alongside, and not superimposed on, the existing social structure. The Jewish settlers did not follow the patterns of white settlement in South Africa, Rhodesia and Kenya where the settlers became a privileged foreign upper class based on native labour. Guided by an ideology of an evolving national centre for the Jewish people, the *Yishuv* built a new stratificational structure alongside the local Arab society.[11]

---

[10] For a detailed description of this underground military organization see: Ben-Zion Dinur *et als.* (eds.), *The History of the Hagana*, Vol. 2, Part 2, Maarachot Publication House, pp. 1053–72. See also Y. Bauer, 'From Cooperation to Resistance – the Haganah 1938–1948', *Middle Eastern Studies*, Vol. 2, 1966, pp. 182–210.

[11] Moshe Lissak, 'Patterns of Change in Ideology and Class Structure in Israel' in S. N. Eisenstadt, Rivkah Bar-Yosef and Chaim Adler (eds.), *Integration and Development in Israel*, Israel Universities Press, Jerusalem, 1970, pp. 141-61. S. N. Eisenstadt, 'Israel Society', *op. cit.*, pp. 143-53. Josef Ben-David,

The formation of an economic structure characterized by a stratum of employers of European origin and cheap local labour was prevented by two factors:[12] first, the formation of a stratum of Jewish manual workers; and, secondly, the partly successful attempt to ensure a monopoly status for the Jewish worker in the Jewish sector. The process of separation between the two economies depended on the exercise of ideological and political pressure on Jewish employers. This pressure, exerted mainly by the organized Zionist labour movement,[13] was supplemented by a counter-tendency towards separation on the part of the Arabs.

The striving for separation met with opposition both from the Mandatory government and from within the *Yishuv* itself. The latter was inspired by sectors within it which were unwilling to accept the ruling on the separation of the *Yishuv* economy and all that it implied – including expensive 'Jewish labour' and 'Jewish produce'. The separation of the Jewish and Arab economies actually led to the formation of two different levels of wages, capital investment, organization and technology within one territorial framework.[14]

'Professions and Social Structure in Israel', *Scripta Hierosolymitana*, Vol. 3, The Hebrew University, Jerusalem, 1959.

[12] On the attitude of the National Council to Jewish labour see Moshe Attias, *The Book of Documents of the National Council of Knesset Israel: 1918–1948*, Jerusalem, 1953, pp. 139, 178, 203, 204. Z. Sussman, *The Policy of the Histadrut with Regard to Wage Differentials: A Study of the Impact of Egalitarian Ideology and Arab Labour on Jewish Wages in Palestine*, PhD Dissertation, The Hebrew University, Jerusalem, 1969, Chap. 3. D. Ben-Gurion, *The Renovated State of Israel*, Vol. 1, Am-Oved, Tel Aviv, 1969, pp. 41–6. Moshe Berslavsky, *The Labour Movement in Palestine*, Vol. II, Hakibbutz-Hameuchad, Tel Aviv, 1954, pp. 28–32. Zvi Rosenstein (Even-Shoshan), *The History of the Labour Movement in Palestine*, Am Oved, Tel Aviv, 1955, pp. 75–83, 147–54, 246–7. Esco, *op. cit.*, pp. 559–62.

[13] The labour movement embraced several Zionist-socialist workers parties which co-operated within the *Histadruth* (The General Federation of Jewish Labour), which was established in 1920. The *Histadruth* functioned not only as a trade union but also as an economic entrepreneur which eventually established some of the biggest enterprises in Palestine. In addition to it the *Histadruth* provided comprehensive health and welfare services for its members. The biggest party in the 1920s was *Achdut Haavodah* (The United Labour Party). This party united a smaller party—*Hapoel Hatzair* (The Young Worker) in 1930 and established *Mapai* (Palestine Jewish Labour Party).

[14] On the differences between the Jewish and Arab economies see for example: Nathan, Gass and Creamer, *op. cit.*, Chap. 12. Z. Sussman, *op. cit.*, Chap. 3. D. Horowitz, *The Development of the Palestine Economy*, Bialik Institution, Tel Aviv, 1954, pp. 9–12, 117–18, 165–76. Zeev Abramovitz and Itzchak Gelfat, *The Arab Economy in Palestine and the Mediterranean Countries*, Hakibbutz Hameuchad, Tel Aviv, 1944, pp. 98 ff.

Employers, investors and consumers were called to sacrifice their economic expediency for the sake of a broader national interest which in many respects corresponds with the interests of the organized labour movement.

As a matter of fact, the need to exert political pressure in order to secure the employment of Jewish workers, many of whom were newcomers to the country, was one of the main causes for the development of organized political parties in the early stages of the *Yishuv*'s development (at the beginning of the 20th century). It was not a coincidence that labour parties were the first to consolidate their organization and institutionalize their political activities. However, the activities of these parties were not confined to attempts to induce Jewish employers to employ Jewish labour. They also promoted, by means of national capital, the establishment of economic enterprises controlled by the labour movement and by the workers themselves.

This endeavour was carried out in two stages. During the 1920s, the labour movement concentrated on developing its organization and submitting the workers' demands to the central political institutions of the Jewish community and the Zionist movement. In the 1930s, on the other hand, the political orientation of the labour movement's leading party – *Mapai* – underwent a change which expressed itself in the struggle for the key positions in the executive bodies of *Knesset Israel* and the Jewish Agency. The political change was complemented by a shift in the ideological outlook of the majority of the labour movement – from 'class to nation'.[15] The shift in the focus of the labour movement's activities from internal institution building to an effort to assume responsibility for the policy-making of the 'National Institutions' may be regarded as an expression of centripetal tendencies within the Jewish community.

However, this *centripetal* movement took place almost simultaneously with a *centrifugal* movement in the right wing of the *Yishuv* and the Zionist movement, which brought about the estrangement of the non-labour Revisionist Party from the national centre. This party eventually withdrew from the Zionist movement and set up the 'New Zionist Organization'.[16] Centrifugal tendencies during the

[15] This expression is taken from the title of D. Ben-Gurion's book. See D. Ben-Gurion, *From Class to Nation*, Tel Aviv, 1933.
[16] The 'New Zionist Organization' is the splinter body established by Vladimir Jabotinsky in 1935 after the revisionists' dissent from the WZO. They aimed to become an alternative to the WZO, but failed to attain this objective. After the

1930s and 1940s were not confined to the revisionists. More moderate right-wing parties also strove to reduce dependency on the national centre though they did not go as far as withdrawal from the framework of the 'Organized *Yishuv*'.[17] Under these circumstances the spheres of authority of the centre were flexible and potentially redefinable. Yet, on the whole, it can be said that centripetal tendencies were stronger than centrifugal ones during the 1930s and 1940s.

The success of the labour movement in its struggle for power during the 1930s and the 1940s may be attributed among other things to the future oriented and collectivist ideology of its elite.[18] This orientation was embodied in the pioneering ideology that emphasized the harnessing of the individual to the needs of the collective and the readiness to postpone immediate gratification for the sake of realizing goals in the future. The pioneering sector considered itself a select group which was entitled not only to the esteem of all, but also to positions of leadership in the society. Accordingly, political militancy on the part of members of the labour movement was sanctioned and its mobilization capacity increased. Nevertheless, the future oriented ideology and the collectivist tendencies had disadvantages too. They gave rise to a tendency among the elite group towards splinter groups based on the various views held concerning the nature of the future desired. The splinter tendencies, which were not confined to the labour movement, accounted for the plurality of organized groups which developed their own institutional frameworks. These included, for example, the various *Kibbutz* and *Moshav* movements; the religious and revisionist independent labour organizations; and the three underground military organizations, the *Haganah*, the *Irgun Zvai Leumi* and *Lochamei Heruth Israel* (The Stern Group).[19]

---

second world war they returned to the WZO and took part in the elections to its 1946 Congress.

[17] The 'Organized *Yishuv*' was an expression used to define all the political groups which abided by the authority of the National Institutions. The 'Organized *Yishuv*' did not include non-Zionist groups, the extreme orthodox *Agudat-Israel* and the communists on the one hand and the revisionists dissenters from the organized Zionist movement on the other hand.

[18] S. N. Eisenstadt, 'Israeli Society', *op. cit.*, pp. 7–58. Dan Horowitz, 'Between Pioneer Society and Normalization', *op. cit.* Israel Kolat, *Ideology and Reality in the Jewish Labour Movement in Palestine*, PhD Thesis, The Hebrew University, Jerusalem, 1964.

[19] David Niv, *Battle for Freedom: The Irgun Zvai Leumi*, Vols. 1–3, Klosner Institute, Tel Aviv, 1967.

## MOBILIZATION OF RESOURCES

The process of this *Yishuv*'s transformation into a viable entity could not have been achieved by political participation alone. Mobilization of resources on a large scale was also required for this purpose.[20] This involved a continuous flow of monetary means to finance Zionist colonization and the activities of the organizational bodies promoting it. The inflow of private capital laid the foundation for the privately-owned economic sector, while the importation of national capital enabled the ideologically pioneering oriented groups to develop economic patterns based on self-labour. The inflow of capital was thus a necessary though insufficient condition for the growth and development of the Jewish community in Palestine. The variety of capital sources accounted for the fact that the Jewish economy in Palestine developed into a pluralistic economy in which there co-existed private, public and co-operative sectors each of which was subdivided into varied forms of economic organization. This pluralism also mitigated class conflict in the *Yishuv* society.

The reduction of class tension was thus made possible by the inflow of public capital which enabled the workers to increase their share of the national income without necessarily doing so at the expense of the middle class. Since the inflow of public capital was controlled by the central political institutions of the *Yishuv*, the labour leadership regarded the challenge of the main political rival, the revisionists, as a more acute threat to its position than that of its rivals in the economic sphere, the moderate bourgeois groups known as *Ezrachim*.[21] In fact, many of the latter groups co-operated with the labour movement in the executive bodies of the Jewish Agency and

---

[20] For the analysis of the role of mobilization in economic and social development see K. W. Deutsch, 'Social Mobilization and Political Development', *The American Political Science Review*, Vol. LV, September 1961, pp. 493–514. S. N. Eisenstadt, 'Modernization and Conditions of Sustained Growth', *World Politics*, Vol. XVI, No. 4, July 1964, pp. 576–95. A. Etzioni, 'Mobilization as a Macro-Sociological Conception', *British Journal of Sociology*, Vol. XIX, No. 3, September 1968, pp. 243–53. David E. Apter, *The Politics of Modernization*, The University of Chicago Press, 1969, Chaps. 10, 11. J. P. Nettl, *Political Mobilization*, Basic Books, 1967.

[21] The term *Ezrachim* (civilians) is commonly used to refer (1) to groups outside the labour movement, usually to centrist and rightist parties and (2) to non-party (or movement) members. The origin of the term came from an attempt made in 1919–20 to establish a political organization of the right under the name of The Citizens Association. The term has a similar connotation as that of bourgeois in France although not identical with it.

*Knesset Israel.* The co-operation between the bulk of the organized labour movement and the moderate non-labour parties created a favourable climate for the evolution of a political system based on voluntary participation.

The voluntary nature of the *Yishuv*'s political organization led first to the formation of a coalitionist regime in the executive bodies of the *Yishuv* institutions. A coalescent political climate thus evolved, based on mutual tolerance and co-operation within the framework of the so-called 'Organized *Yishuv*'. This political climate stood in sharp contrast to the marked tendency towards intolerance which characterized the relationships between the parties of the organized labour movement and those groups which refused to accept either the consensus embodied in the policy of the National Institutions or the rules of procedure relating to the determination of this policy. This lack of tolerance was most apparent in the attitude of the labour movement towards the communists on the 'left' and the revisionists on the 'right'. It follows, therefore, that the tendency towards political tolerance in all matters relating to social and economic cleavages, did not apply to conflicts over the legitimization of the National Institutions' authority and the acceptance of their decisions as binding. It is noteworthy that the issues over which problems of authority and secession arose were generally not those relating to the distribution of resources, but rather to differences of opinion over the attainment of collective goals.

The multiplicity of interest groups, each of which demanded its share of resources allocated by the central institutions of the *Yishuv* and the Zionist movement, led to highly developed processes for the articulation of interests. Apart from demands for financial means, demands for immigration certificates, jobs and sites for settlements were prominent. The National Institutions played an important role in handling these interests and translating them into political decisions. They were able to accede to the majority of these claims because the importation of capital released them from the dilemma that every government faces in having to extract more and more resources from society in order to meet increasing demands.

A further factor which reduced the burden on the *Yishuv* was, paradoxically, the very lack of sovereignty of the National Institutions. The existence of the Mandatory government meant that the National Institutions were not responsible for those essential services which even a *laissez-faire* regime was obliged to provide. However, the limited scope of the Mandatory government's services could not

have satisfied the needs of a population with relatively high expectations, such as the Jewish population of Palestine. Thus the *Yishuv*
found itself increasingly in need of means to finance its health,
welfare and education services. In addition, the *Yishuv* had to allocate
means for security as a result of the Arab reaction to Jewish settlement. A gap thus developed between the increasing demands of the
*Yishuv* and the limited willingness on the part of the Mandatory
government to accede to these demands. This gap widened when,
besides the demands for services, further demands were presented,
deriving from the national interests of the Jewish community as a
consequence of the political conflict with the Arab majority.


THE STRUGGLE FOR POWER

The vulnerability of the authority of the central political institutions which originated in their lack of sovereignty, increased the
importance of the qualifications of the labour elite which manned
the key positions in these institutions. One of the characteristics of
this elite was an inclination to prefer rewards of power to economic
rewards, which gave it some advantage over other elite groups both
in the *Yishuv* itself and in its immediate environment. Thus, for example, it was possible to allocate positions of high prestige but of
limited power to representatives of the Zionist movement in the
Diaspora. The power orientation also eased the relationships of the
labour movement elite with the elites of the *Ezrachim* groups. The
members of the latter groups tended to concentrate on economic
rather than political activities.[22] Thus, they in fact relinquished opportunities to translate their economic achievements into political
power and contented themselves with a secondary role in the political
leadership of the *Yishuv*.

A more extreme example of concentration on non-political activities was that of some economic and social elites which actually withdrew from active political participation in the formation of the
national centre. In certain cases, such as that of the extreme orthodox
Jews in Jerusalem, the withdrawal was total and permanent while in
other cases, such as that of the traditional *Sephardic* notables, it was
partial and temporary. The relative positions of the various elite
groups with respect to the striving for priority on the one hand and

[22] See Dan Giladi, 'Private Entrepreneurship, National Capital and the
Political Consolidation of the Right', in S. N. Eisenstadt *et als.* (eds.), *The Social
Structure of Israel*, Academon, Jerusalem, 1956, pp. 85–7.

FIGURE I

Preference for Acquiring
Political Power

|  | A<br>The Labour movement | B<br>The Revisionists |  |
| --- | --- | --- | --- |
| The<br>'Organized<br>Yishuv' | | | Groups<br>outside<br>the<br>'Organized<br>Yishuv' |
|  | Civilian right-wing<br>and religious parties<br><br>C | Economic and social<br>elites apathetic to<br>the formation of<br>the national centre<br>D |  |

Preference for Economic
and Social Rewards

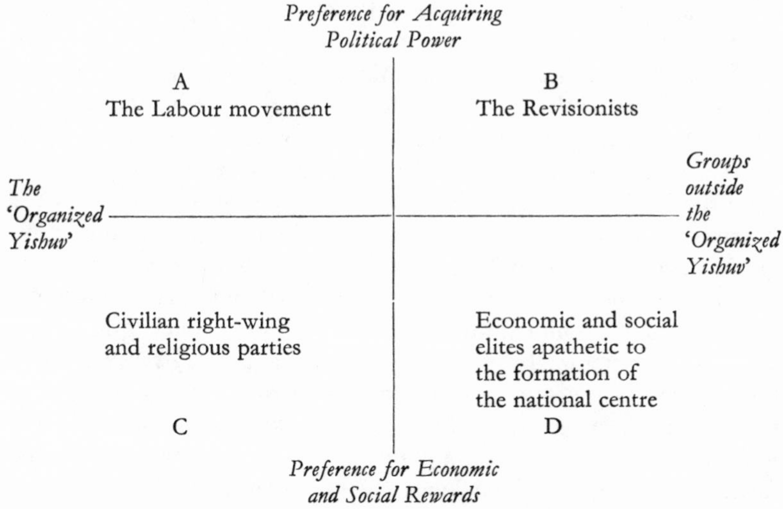

the attitude to the individual system of the 'Organized Yishuv' on the other hand, is presented schematically in Figure 1.

The evolving political institutions of the Jewish community maintained a complex and ramified system of mutual relationships with the various groups within the Yishuv on the one hand and with the Mandatory government, the Arab majority and the Zionist movement in the Diaspora on the other. These relationships involved an exchange of resources which enabled the political centre of the Yishuv to gain power through the bargaining process associated with exchange relationships. In this context, the particularistic nature of power relationships in general and the existence of different exchange rates with each of the partners to the bargaining process both enabled the dominant elite to convert symbolic and material resources into resources of power and vice-versa.[23] Within the exchange system the

[23] For a theoretical discussion of exchange relationships and types of power see Peter M. Blau, *Exchange and Power in Social Life*, John Wiley and Sons, 1966. S. N. Eisenstadt, *Essays on Comparative Institutions*, Part III, John Wiley and Sons, 1965. Karl W. Deutsch, *The Nerves of Government*, The Free Press, 1966, Chap. 7. Talcott Parsons, 'On the concept of Power' in Reinhard Bendix and Seymour M. Lipset (eds.), *Class, Status and Power*, Routledge and Kegan Paul, London, 2nd edn., pp. 240–65. R. L. Curry Jr. and L. L. Wade, *A Theory of Political Exchange: Economic Reasoning in Political Analysis*, Prentice Hall, Englewood Cliff, N.J., 1968. Peter Bachrach and Marton S. Baratz, 'Two Faces of Power', *The American Political Science Review*, Vol. LVI, No. 4, December 1962, pp. 947–52. Amitai

main effort was directed to the acquisition of power both in the form
of autonomy in decision-making and control over inputs and outputs
of material and symbolic resources.[24]

The significant input by the Mandatory government into the
political centre of the *Yishuv* was its recognition of the National Institutions as the authorized representatives of the *Yishuv* and of world
Jewish interest in the National Home in Palestine. This recognition
gave the National Institutions, first and foremost, control over the
distribution of immigration certificates in accordance with the immigration quotas determined by the Mandatory government. This control implied the possibility of selecting those potential immigrants
who suited the political and colonizing criteria which guided the
policy of leadership. In exchange, the 'Organized *Yishuv*' remained
loyal to the Mandatory government for many years, although its
loyalty was at times conditional. The loyalty was terminated only
when the Mandatory government imposed severe restrictions on the
further development of the Jewish National Home.

The relationships of the central political institutions of the *Yishuv*
with the Arab sector of the population were primarily of an economic
nature. In these relationships the *Yishuv* converted current assets into
fixed assets by exchanging money for land. The agent in these trans-
actions was not the unstable centre of the Arab community, but
elements in the Arab periphery which acted contrary to the declared
policy of the Arab leadership. Economic relationships existed between the Arab and Jewish peripheries too and their scope varied with

---

Etzioni, *The Active Society*, The Free Press, 1968, pp. 313–81. Edward W. Leh-
man, 'Toward a Macro-Sociology of Power', *The American Sociological Review*,
Vol. 34, No. 4, August 1969, pp. 453–64.

[24] The dominant elite was fully conscious of the manipulative value of the
control of resources and its impact on the authority of the central National
Institutions. This consciousness is illustrated in David Ben-Gurion's letter to his
daughter and son of 7 September 1935. 'The World Zionist Organization is not
a state, it has no real governmental authority, no power to coerce, no taxation,
and no ability to impose membership on anyone. This is an organization of
volunteers founded on discipline based on free will, rather than on coercion.
This organization, however, has a considerable capital – two funds, banks, settlements etc. It has political rights as well: representation before the Mandatory
Government and the League of Nations and the allocation of immigration
certificates. The Zionist Organization speaks for the nation and mobilizes the
masses. But if two parties will be ousted from the Executive they will be also
removed from any position of real influence on the direction of the organization's
activities. They will also be denied of any rewards that can be derived from the
Executive.' David Ben-Gurion, *Letters to Paula*, Am Oved, Tel Aviv, 1968, p. 98.

political changes. In these exchanges, the Jewish economy made use of both Arab labour and produce. In this way, some of the imported Jewish capital found its way to the Arab economy and thus brought about a rise in the Arabs' standard of living.[25] The exchanges also led to tensions between the social, economic and political separatist tendencies which characterized the policies of the *Yishuv* leadership, and the instrumental use of cheap Arab labour and agricultural produce in the *Yishuv* periphery. Thus a conflict emerged between the approach of the dominant political elite and that of the groups which were not prepared to accept economic segregation.

The exchange relationships of the *Yishuv* with the Jewish Diaspora in general and with the Zionist movement in particular were characterized by an almost entirely one-way flow of both material and manpower resources from the Diaspora to Palestine. The outputs of the *Yishuv* to the Zionist movement consisted mainly of cultural and symbolic values. The institutions of the *Yishuv* derived power from their control of resources including manpower flowing into the country from the Diaspora. Since the quotas of immigrants[26] were limited, discrimination against dissenting political groups in this respect was one of the most effective sanctions exercised by the parties controlling the National Institutions. The dissenting groups were thus denied reinforcement from the ranks of their supporters in the Diaspora. The tendency towards the political manipulation of manpower resources was not confined to the question of the distribution of certificates, it was part of a more general phenomenon of manpower control by political groups which ensured a reservoir of manpower attached to them ideologically and organizationally. Centres for the ideological and vocational training of potential settlers abroad functioned as mechanisms for the political socialization of young people wanting to immigrate to Palestine. The fact that immigration was organized in groups meant that potential immigrants became attached to the political movements that organized them and later cared for their economic, social and cultural absorption in Palestine.

[25] The Jewish Agency for Palestine, *The Jewish Case Before the Anglo-American Committee of Inquiry on Palestine. Statements and Memoranda, op. cit.*, pp. 351–9.

[26] The schedules of immigration certificates issued by the Mandatory government and allocated by the Jewish Agency were of several different categories: (a) persons of independent means; (b) persons of religious occupation, students and orphans whose main maintenance was assured; (c) people with prospect of employment in Palestine (The Labour Schedule); (d) dependents of permanent residents or immigrants belonging to the former categories.

## FOCI OF CONFLICT

In spite of the power orientation of the elite which constituted the social bearer of the nation-building processes, it did not regard the accumulation of power as an end in itself. The self-image of this elite was rather that of pioneers who were laying the political and ideological foundations of an autonomous Jewish society in Palestine. Moreover, national aims were interwoven with social aims based on the various ideologies, each of which proposed a different model for the desired society. Under these circumstances, ideological programmes were turned into the bases of political organizations and became sources of conflict between groups with different ideological commitments. The formation of the national centre was therefore not only an institutional process, but also a value based process in which the accumulation of power was conceived as being subjected to the realization of collective goals.

The consolidation of the Jewish *Yishuv* in Palestine as a political system striving for autonomy, was thus a threefold process which involved three dimensions: (a) the institutionalization of a political centre with authority but without sovereignty; (b) the regulation of the exchange and distribution of resources; (c) the moulding of the value ideological character of the society.

Each of these three dimensions contained the seeds of conflict among the various political and social elite groups. Thus from the moment that one elite group, that of the labour movement, achieved a position of priority in the National Institutions, it was faced with the problem of preventing the disintegration of the political framework as a result of these conflicts.

The dominant elite was thus forced to create mechanisms for binding political decision-making and the resolution of political conflicts. The manner in which this challenge was met affected the diverse relationships of the dominant elite with other elites, both within and outside the framework of the 'Organized *Yishuv*'. The nature of these relationships of conflict and co-operation was determined by the multifaceted nature of the conflict element, its intensity and the amount of disagreement over the rules governing the resolution of conflicts within the system's framework.

The concept of the multifaceted nature of the conflict relates to the number of dimensions around which the conflict focused. The notion of intensity of conflict refers to the extent to which the subject of the conflict was a central issue, the degree of involvement of the parties in the conflict and the nature of the means used in the political struggle or, as Dahrendorf put it, 'the energy expenditure and degree of involvement of conflicting parties'.[27] Disagreement over the rules for the resolution of conflict was reflected in the denial of the quasi-parliamentary authority of the National Institutions, and the refusal to accept their decisions as binding.

Data indicating a multifaceted and intensive conflict and a lack of agreement over the mechanism for its resolution reflect a maximal gap between the parties involved in the conflict and a minimal chance of that gap being bridged. This is exemplified in the varieties of relationships between the dominant elite associated with the *Mapai* party and other elite groups (see Table 1).

The data show that the dominant elite maintains a variety of political relationships expressing different levels of conflict with other elite groups, both within and outside the 'Organized *Yishuv*'. The fact that a parallel was found for every hypothetical combination of criteria is characteristic of the wide range of political conflicts and the complexity of the mutual relationships between the various political and social groups in the *Yishuv*.

## RESOLUTION OF CONFLICTS

The regular functioning of the *Yishuv*'s political system was secured through the continued attempt to achieve the widest possible consensus within the pluralistic and coalescent political framework. The political centre was thus a coalitional system composed of sub-centres each of which maintained a high degree of autonomy in everything pertaining to its authority over its respective members. The central political institutions were obliged to concede several of their functions, mainly of a social and economic but sometimes also of a political nature, to these sub-centres (the most prominent of which was the *Histadruth*). The political parties themselves were, at one and the same time, both participants in the coalitional national centre and separate entities which tended to extend their sphere of activity on the sub-centre level. Thus, they engaged in providing economic, social and cultural services which went far beyond the function of mobilizing political power so as to influence decisions on the national level. In fulfilling quasi-governmental functions while participating in the coalitional system, the parties in a way became agencies of the national centre for the provision of public services mainly of the

[27] Ralf Dahrendorf, *Class and Class Conflict in Industrial Society*, Stanford University Press, Stanford, 1967, p. 211.

TABLE I

| Relationships between Mapai and: | Multifacetedness of the conflict | Intensity of the conflict | Disagreement over rules[28] |
|---|---|---|---|
| Revisionists | + | + | +· |
| Right wing, conservative and religious[29] | + | + | − |
| Liberal and religious centre[30] | + | − | − |
| Ethnic groups[31] | − | − | − |
| 'Assimilating' elites[32] | − | − | + |
| Communists | − | + | + |
| Extreme orthodox Jewry[33] | + | − | + |
| Zionist left wing in the Histadruth[34] | − | + | − |

type that characterize the modern welfare state.[35] Moreover, the parties also played the role of the main arbitrators between the citizen and the national centre. Because of the lack of official channels for presenting claims against the centre, the indirect party-controlled channels were used for this purpose.

The adoption of democratic rules facilitated the settlement of conflicts through political compromises or, when this did not seem

[28] The use of (+) to note disagreement with the rules of the game is intended to adjust the third criterion to the first two criteria so that the three (+) will indicate the highest level of conflict.

[29] This category includes the right wing of the General Zionists, *Hamizrachi* and the Farmers Association.

[30] This category includes the left wing of the General Zionists, the *Hapoel Hamizrachi*, the *Alia Hadasha* (New Immigration Party) representing mainly new immigrants from Germany.

[31] This category includes the Sephardic and Yemenite organizations.

[32] This category includes some non-political notables who were socially involved with the British and Arab officials of the Mandatory government and demonstrated their reservation with regard to the activities of the so-called 'Organized *Yishuv*'.

[33] This category includes the *Agudat Israel* and other extreme orthodox elements especially in Jerusalem.

[34] This category includes *Hashomer Hatzair* and a small Zionist-Marxist party called *Poalei Zion Smol*, and since 1944 also the *Hatenua le-Achdut Avoda*, which split from *Mapai*.

[35] Benjamin Akzin, 'The Role of Parties in Israeli Democracy', in S. N. Eisenstadt, Rivkah Bar-Yosef and Chaim Adler (eds.), 'Integration and Development in Israel', *op. cit.*, pp. 13–18.

possible, the approval of majority decisions. The political system of the *Yishuv* was oriented to *ad hoc* decisions on pragmatic questions whose impromptu solution was called for at the time. In this respect, limited sovereignty was, in a way, an advantage since the institutions were able to evade those issues which a sovereign government would have been obliged to solve. Thus, for example, it was possible to avoid making decisions of a constitutional nature for the establishment of norms with value implications. This situation eased the relationships between the religious and secular parties in particular. The resolution of conflicts by compromise applied only to those groups which recognized the authority of the central national institutions and not to splinter groups such as the revisionists which were subjected to various social, economic and political sanctions, including, at times, the use of force.

The second dimension of the resolution of conflicts derived from the problem of the regulation of exchange processes and allocation of resources. The characteristic arrangement for handling the allocation of resources among those groups affiliated to the 'Organized *Yishuv*', was the institution of the 'party-political key'.[36] This unique method carried the principles of proportional representation and coalitional participation, on which the democratic system of the *Yishuv* was based, to their extreme. The balance of power between the parties, as reflected in political representation on quasi-parliamentary and executive bodies, was expressed in the allocation of budgets, the granting of immigration certificates and appointments to national and public institutions. This principle had far reaching implications for the stability of the political balance of power among the parties constituting the 'Organized *Yishuv*'. The political parties were transformed into agencies for the allocation of resources, a function which could then be exploited for purposes of mobilizing political support. The 'party-political key' thus helped to maintain the internal political *status quo*, since the ability to gain additional support depended to a large extent on the amount of resources at the disposal of the political parties which, in turn, was a function of their power at the time. Moreover, the conversion of parties into agencies

[36] The 'Party-Political Key' is a principle which dominated the allocation of budgets, immigration certificates, settlement sites, administrative jobs and other employment. According to this principle such resources were allocated in proportion to the relative strength of the parties and other political groups in the representative bodies of the central National Institutions. By these kinds of agreements the outcome of political elections had an impact on many spheres of life which are not considered political in the narrow sense of the word.

controlling a more or less defined part of the resources distributed by the centre, tended to reduce the potential floating vote in the *Yishuv*. The internal stability of the system created a strong impetus for individuals and groups to identify with some political party in order to benefit from the attendant advantages. In view of their control over the allocation of administrative posts in the National Institutions, for example, the parties could use the system of co-optation, based on particularistic criteria, to absorb potential political activists and thus maintain control by the party leadership over the selection of persons for public positions.

Left wing and right wing, religious and secular, did not necessarily hold opposing views on the arrangements for the resolution of political conflict in the *Yishuv*. On both the left and right wings there were coalescent elements which accepted the institutionalized pluralism as the basis for achieving consensus or at least *modus vivendi*. Similarly, on both sides there were elements which strove for party and sectoral exclusivity which, in fact, meant dissensus. Four primary types of parties may therefore be distinguished on the basis of their ideological position on the one hand and their attitude towards the resolution of conflict on the other (see Figure 2).

The national centre constituted a common institutionalized framework for the moderate left and right wings, which represented the decisive majority of the Jewish community in Palestine. A series of political institutions formed a point of contact between the left and right elements of the 'Organized *Yishuv*'. They included, among others, the National Institutions, economic institutions which operated on public capital, the *Hagana* and the local authorities. The *Histadruth* was the institutional framework in which the moderate and extreme left wing met (although the communists, in particular, were not always permitted to take part in the *Histadruth* elections). Local authorities and economic organizations such as those of traders, farmers and industrialists constituted the institutional frameworks within which the meeting between right-wing groups of the 'Organized *Yishuv*' and those outside of it took place.

The third dimension of the conflicts which the centre had either to resolve or at least to reduce was the ideological dimension. The fact that co-operation existed between various ideological groups in the *Yishuv* entailed a paradox of a kind. Acceptance of the idea of ideological pluralism and tolerance was not apparently consistent with zealous adherence to ideological programmes. Thus, the effective functioning of the central political institutions of the *Yishuv*

FIGURE 2

*Pluralistic and Coalescent Orientation*

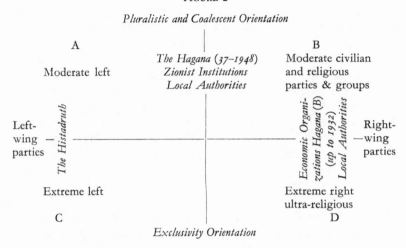

| A | | B |
|---|---|---|
| | The Hagana (*37–1948*) | Moderate civilian |
| Moderate left | Zionist Institutions | and religious |
| | Local Authorities | parties & groups |

Left-wing parties — *The Histadruth* ———————————— Economic Organizations Hagana (B) (*up to 1932*) Local Authorities —— Right-wing parties

Extreme left    Extreme right ultra-religious

C    D

*Exclusivity Orientation*

*Type A* includes most of the Zionist left-wing parties (*Mapai, the Achdut Ha-avoda Movement* and *Hashomer Hatzair*).

*Type B* includes the moderate *Ezrachim* and religious parties (General Zionists A and B, *Hamizrachi* and *Hapoel* Hamizrachi).

*Type C* includes the communists and *Paolei Zion Smol*. (The latter only in the 1920s and early 1930s).

*Type D* includes the extreme right-wing (*revisionists* and *Irgun Zvai Leumi*) and the ultra-religious (*Agudat Israel* and *Ha-eda Hacharedit*) parties.

required the curbing of the ideological tensions existing between the various political groups. There were three mechanisms which made this curbing possible:

(1) The emphasis of the common ideological bases of the 'Organized *Yishuv*'s' political parties which was reflected in the consensus over basic Zionist aims. On the other hand, the attitude towards those movements which were not a party to this consensus was uncompromising and intolerant.

(2) The National Institutions' tendency to avoid ideological dilemmas in their discussions and decisions and to concentrate on 'practical issues' which could be resolved in a practical manner. This tendency could be clearly discerned in the avoidance of a definition of Zionism's final aim as well as in a readiness to compromise on all matters relating to the status of religion in the organized public life of the *Yishuv*. Political decisions were taken on a *tactical* rather than a *strategic* level, and the short rather than the long term was emphasized.

(3) The canalization of ideological zeal into 'movement' oriented 'enclaves' or 'sub-centres'. The *Histadruth*, settlement and youth movements, organized religious bodies, etc., provided the framework for ideologically-based social initiative and the fostering of particularistic group values. It was under these conditions that the social experiments which characterized the *Yishuv*, such as the *Kibbutz*, the *Moshav* and the *Histadruth*'s economic enterprises, developed. Each of these unique forms of social organization reflected the desire to translate ideological theory into organized social action. However, within these ideologically oriented enclaves prevailed an atmosphere of intolerance towards political deviation.

## DISCUSSION

The aim of the foregoing analysis of the *Yishuv* society is not to construct a model applicable to other cases of developing societies: too many unique features exist in the case history concerned to allow us to indulge in such an attempt. Nevertheless, it is worthwhile relating the features of the *Yishuv*'s political system to more generalized concepts which may serve as criteria for comparative analysis. One of the models which, in spite of its shortcomings, appears to be suitable for our purpose is Shils's model of 'Centre and Periphery'.[37] This model was found to be useful since the formation of an authoritative political centre was essential for the evolution of the *Yishuv* as a semi-autonomous political entity. Moreover, the notions of central and peripheral conceived as representing a continuum rather than a dichotomy enable us to refer to the position and the self-image of the various sub-centres within the community in relation to the fundamental process of centre formation. A systematic analysis of this kind, however, is beyond the scope of this paper. Nevertheless, the reader would do well to note certain problems associated with the application of the centre-periphery model to the case under discussion. Particularly worthy of mention are two elementary questions. The first concerns the extent to which the political centre was indeed 'central'; the second – the extent to which the periphery was 'peripheral'. These questions arise from the nature of the Jewish community's evolution in Palestine, since in its development the

---

[37] See Edward A. Shils, 'Centre and Periphery' in *The Logic of Personal Knowledge*, Routledge & Kegan Paul, London, 1961. S. N. Eisenstadt, 'Prestige, Participation and Strata Formation', in J. A. Jackson (ed.), *Social Stratification. Sociological Studies 1*, Part I, 1968.

*Yishuv* had no dominant centre with recognized authority. The absence of such a centre was particularly apparent under Ottoman rule. Even in the early years of the British Mandate, the extent of the evolving centre's authority was rather limited. It was threatened by the simultaneous evolution of various institutionalized sub-centres which themselves enjoyed a considerable degree of authority. Some of these sub-centres, such as the *Histadruth* which served as a focus of identification for the Jewish worker might indeed have developed into alternative centres. However, such a development was avoided because of the shift which occurred in the orientation of the labour movement from 'class to nation' in the early 1930s.

The question of the centrality of the centre revolved around its ability to enforce its rules without the ultimate authority possessed by a sovereign state whereas the question of the extent to which the periphery was 'peripheral' was mainly one of the definition of the status of the sub-centres and their spheres of autonomy. These sub-centres could not actually be considered peripheral in the full sense of the term since they did not passively receive instructions and opinions from the centre. In fact, the sub-centres were to a large extent autarchic enclaves whose evolution was related to their attempt to shape the image of society or at least the way of life of those inspired by them. In this respect, the centre was not an exclusive source of charisma in the sense that Shils uses the term; a considerable amount of charisma actually crystallized in each of the sub-centres.

The growth and consolidation of the centre depended on the readiness of the most powerful sub-centres to forego their aspiration to exclusiveness and recognize the authority of the centre in certain spheres whilst, at the same time retaining their own autonomy in other spheres. In this respect, the coalitional structure of the centre was a reflection of the pluralism expressed by the multiplicity of sub-centres.

The question of the extent to which the periphery was 'peripheral' is also related to the historical background of the evolution of the *Yishuv* in Palestine. In contrast to most developing societies which freed themselves from colonial rule, the *Yishuw* was not a traditional society in the process of modernization. Socio-political groups with innovatory orientations often operated independently of the national centre; furthermore, not only were they not moulded by the centre, but, on the contrary, they participated actively in the moulding of the centre.

Nevertheless, the term 'periphery' is not totally without relevance to the development of the *Yishuv*. Three factors may be noted which give the concept such relevance: (a) the existence of groups which had no affinity to the sub-centres and groups which played a passive role in the crystallization of the national centre; (b) the existence of a differential degree of acceptance of the 'peripheral condition' among the various sub-centres as a result of different aspirations with regard to the interpretation and renewal of values; (c) the existence of a differential degree of ability on the part of the various sub-centres to influence the national centre.

A systematic analysis in terms of Shils's model would probably take the form of an attempt at locating the different ideological movements, political parties and economic interest groups along the centre-periphery continuum. However, the position of different groups along this continuum changes as a result of centrifugal and centripetal trends. Therefore a comparison of the different groups along the continuum at different points of time may reflect the impact of the time factor on the political structure and this would mean introducing a historical dimension into a sociological analysis.

# 4

# Israel's Compound Policy

*Daniel J. Elazar*

On May 17, 1977, the Israeli electorate voted to turn out a sitting government for the first time since the establishment of the state. Indeed, it was the first serious setback for Labor since the struggle between the Labor camp and its opponents in the late 1920s had led to the ascendancy of the former, culminating in the Labor party victory in the 1931 elections for the Jewish national assembly in Mandatory Palestine. It is not unfair to say that this defeat symbolized the end of the first generation of Israeli statehood. That generation, which had witnessed the founding moments of the state between 1947 and 1949, reached the peak of its power in the Six-Day War of 1967 and entered its final period with the Yom Kippur War in 1973.

The electoral history of the country has paralleled this generational rhythm. The all-inclusive governing coalition that established the state in 1948 gave way to a Labor dominated government in the first elections in 1949. Labor's position was nearly undermined in the 1951 elections as a result of mass immigration, but the Labor camp, using the resources at its disposal and under David Ben-Gurion's leadership, managed to resurrect itself and in the 1955 elections established the clear dominance that it maintained for the next twenty-two years. Beginning in the 1965 elections, however, the groups that were later to become the backbone of Likud support began to defect from the Labor electorate, and by the 1973 elections, in the immediate aftermath of the Yom Kippur War, Likud was moving toward ascendancy. Thus the 1977 electoral results were not simply a fluke or the result of immediate campaign issues but reflected a long-term trend within the Israeli body politic.

This trend is one manifestation of the transition from a polity based on ideological divisions to one in which the expression of public interests is more complex. The initial momentum for the creation of Israel could only have come from people with strong ideological motivations; indeed, in the early years ideological divisions permeated the political structure to the point where politics and the benefits thereof were rooted in a system of ideological movements-cum-parties that had coalesced in the 1920s. But Israel's continued existence depends upon a process of "settling in." More and more, this seems to mean adaptation to the exigencies of territorial democracy.[1] In this respect, Israel's development parallels that of other new societies.

## Israel as a New Society

Israel is one of the handful of "new societies" in the world, in the select company of the United States, Canada, the Republic of South Africa, Australia, and New Zealand.[2] Therein lies the beginning of an understanding of the politics of the Jewish state. New societies are those founded "from scratch" as a result of migrations to virgin territories (that is, territories essentially uninhabited or perceived to be so by the migrants) since the beginning of the modern era in the mid seventeenth century. Their settlers underwent a frontier experience as a major part of the process of settlement, and each in its own way was from its very beginning a modern society. These new societies stand out in sharp contrast to both traditional societies and those that have undergone modernization, whether from a traditional or a feudal

---

[1] The term territorial democracy was first used by Orestes Brownson in *The American Republic* (1866) to describe noncentralized, American institutions in contrast to centralized, Jacobin ones. It is used in this context as the form of political organization in which the principal expressions of politics and political interest are articulated through territorial political units (for example, states, counties, cities, or towns); territorial political structures (for example, electoral districts); and territorial political organizations (for example, the county medical association, the regional planning society) that possesses real power or influence in the shaping of public policy. See Russell Kirk, "The Prospects for Territorial Democracy in America," in Robert A. Goldwin, ed., *A Nation of States* (Chicago: Rand McNally, 1974), 2nd ed. for one view of territorial democracy. I have elaborated on his definition of the concept in my forthcoming book, *Federal Democracy*, and have applied it to Israel in *Israel: From Ideological to Territorial Democracy* (New York: General Learning Press, 1971).

[2] The concept of "new societies" is based in part on the work of Louis Hartz, *The Founding of New Societies* (New York: Harcourt, Brace & World, 1964). At least some of the Caribbean and Latin American countries, which in some ways meet the primary objective criteria used in determining which are the world's new societies, may have to be added to this list. Though the surface evidence is mixed, I have strong reservations about including them. It bears noting that Israel is the only new society whose founders did not come, in the main, from the British Isles or Northern Europe. The great majority of Israel's settlers came from Asia or Eastern Europe, the Near East and North Africa, bringing with them very different cultural baggage.

base. The key to their birth as modern societies lies in the migration of their founders to frontier environments where they were able to create a social order with a minimum amount of hindrance from entrenched traditional or feudal ways or from existing populations needing to be assimilated.

Traditional or feudal societies are built upon what are generally accepted as organic linkages among tribes, communities, or estates whose origins are lost in history. New societies, in contrast, are constructed upon conscious (and usually historically verifiable) contractual or covenantal relationships among individuals and groups; the sense of common purpose that bound their founders together continues to bind subsequent generations. In almost every case, the dominant founders of a new society—those who set its tone—were motivated by a common sense of vocation based on ideologies or commitments they brought with them and which they tried to apply in the creation of new political and social institutions. In the process of nation building, they forged a sense of vocation that continues to serve as a shared mystique, a future-oriented myth, to inspire or justify the efforts of their heirs.[3] The actual creation of these civil societies was almost invariably manifested through some kind of constituting act, usually one that was expressed in documentary form. Even if no single compact or constitution was involved, the political organization of each new society is based on many "little" compacts necessitated by the realities of having to create new settlements and institutions "overnight" on virgin soil.

While the founders of each new society brought with them a cultural heritage derived from their societies of origin, their motive in migrating was almost invariably a revolutionary one. They sought to create a better society than the one they had left, believing it impossible to do so in the lands of their origin. As part of their efforts, they took what they believed to be the most significant ideas and institutions from their homelands and transplanted them, with appropriate adaptations.

Though Palestine in the nineteenth century was not as empty as North America in the early seventeenth century, for the Zionist pioneers it was effectively empty in that they did not expect to model the society they intended to build upon any indigenous social order,

---

[3] For an examination of mystique as future-oriented myth, see John T. Marcus, "The World Impact of the West: The Mystique and the Sense of Participation in History," in Henry A. Murray, ed., *Myth and Myth Making* (New York: George Braziller, 1960), pp. 221–239.

Arab or Jewish.[4] Even the "old *yishuv*"—the Jewish settlements that antedated the Zionist efforts and did not share the same sense of political vocation, although they, too, sought to build new societies of their own—was strictly off limits as a model. The goal of the pioneers was to replace its way of life, based as it was on traditional Judaism, with a new one that, while in harmony with the highest Jewish ideals, would be fully modern—whether socialist, liberal democratic, or religious.

The Zionist pioneers explicitly and consciously intended to build the kind of society advocated for their countries of origin by their European revolutionary peers, who shared the same modern ideologies. But the very essence of Zionism was that Jews could only build their new society by leaving the lands of the Diaspora and migrating to a new land or, more accurately, by returning to their "old-new land."[5] In the process of implanting their settlements and institutions in the new territory, the Zionist pioneers shaped a sense of national vocation that has become the Israeli mystique.[6] While Zionist theories were based on the ideas of organic nationhood common in nineteenth-century Europe, the organizations and settlements of the pioneers themselves were quite literally based on compacts or covenants linking the dedicated individuals who took upon themselves the burdens of creating the new society.

The construction of the modern Israeli polity began in the last generation of the nineteenth century. The first modern Jewish agricultural settlements were established in the 1870s. By World War I, when that generation came to an end, the well-known second *aliya* (literally, "ascent"—the term used to describe migration to the country) of

---

[4] Early Zionist literature makes few references to an indigenous population in Palestine that would have to be dealt with on a continuing basis. Moreover, in making this assumption about the "emptiness" of the land, the Zionists merely reflected common European notions about non-European populations in that period. See Rufus Learsi, *Fulfillment: The Epic Story of Zionism* (New York: World, 1951); Arthur Hertzberg, ed., *The Zionist Idea* (New York: Doubleday, 1959); and Walter Z. Laqueur, *History of Zionism* (New York: Holt, Rinehart & Winston, 1972).

[5] The term "old-new land" was used by Theodor Herzl himself as the title for his utopian novel (*Altneuland* in the original German), which describes his vision of life in a restored Jewish state. For a broad picture of Zionist thought as a modern ideological system, see Hertzberg, *The Zionist Idea*.

[6] Horace M. Kallen delineates the relationship between Israel and its mystique in *Utopians at Bay* (New York: Theodor Herzl Foundation, 1958). For an Israeli view of the mystique see, for example, David Ben-Gurion, *Rebirth and Destiny of Israel* (New York: Philosophical Library, 1954); Ronald Sanders discusses the development of the mystique in contemporary Israel in *The View from Masada* (New York: Harper & Row, 1966).

1903–1914 had brought in the most important of the future founders of the state who created the first of the institutions that were to give the state its tone.[7] The founders were for the most part imbued with contemporary socialist ideologies; hence, their covenants and compacts were oriented toward a cooperative, rather than an individualistic, model of social and political organization. Later they were to acquire a strong collectivist tinge. This orientation was reinforced by the Jewish political culture of the founders. As a result, when the state of Israel was established as an outgrowth of the Jewish *yishuv* of the pre-state period, it assumed very extensive responsibilities within the polity. Today Israeli society is permeated by governmental activity. Israel may be the only new society developed on the basis of socialist principles.

On another level, Israel is heir to the first identifiable "new society" in history, that of the Jewish people, who, in the ancient Israelite migration to Canaan and settlement there under the aegis of the Abrahamic and Sinai covenants, represented a similar phenomenon approximately three millennia before the opening of the modern era.[8] The biblical account of their experience offers a paradigm of the new society model set forth here. Both the covenantal nature of Jewish political organization and the future-oriented mystique of the Jewish people were institutionalized within ancient Jewish society and, after passing through various permutations in the Land of Israel and in the Diaspora, reappeared in new form in modern Israel.[9] One consequence

---

[7] Laqueur, *History of Zionism.*

[8] There is now reasonable historical evidence to confirm this whether the biblical account is exactly accurate or not. Perhaps more important, the Israelite experience as it is described in the Bible is paradigmatic of all subsequent new societies. Indeed, in its explanation of the origins of the Jewish people the Bible devotes considerable space to discussing and emphasizing precisely those elements that are here identified as being essential to the definition of new societies. The use of covenant forms to create political relationships was an ancient Near Eastern practice as George E. Mendenhall has pointed out in "Covenant Forms in Israelite Tradition," *Biblical Archeologist*, vol. 17, no. 3 (July 1954), pp. 50–76. The Israelites transformed the covenant principle from one used for quasi-feudal purposes between rulers or polities into one used for federal purposes within polities. See, for example, S. J. Mackenzie, *Faith and History in the Old Testament* (New York: Macmillan, 1963), pp. 40–53; and John Bright, *A History of Israel* (Philadelphia: Westminster Press, 1956).

[9] While no one has directly discussed ancient Israel as a new society, Yehezkel Kaufman has laid the groundwork for such a discussion in his monumental *Toldot Ha-Emunah Ha-Yisraelit* [History of the faith of Israel] 4 vols. (Jerusalem and Tel Aviv: Bialik and Dvir, 1937–1960); also available in an abridged English version as *The Religion of Israel* (Chicago: University of Chicago Press, 1960), selected and translated by Moshe Greenberg. See also Henri Frankfort, et al., *Before Philosophy* (London: Pelican Books, 1949) and Harry M. Orlinsky, *Ancient*

of this was that even those Jews who came from distinctly premodern environments had, to some degree, internalized a political culture with "new society" characteristics that, however latent, could be made manifest upon their resettlement in the new territory under new political and social conditions.

Consequently, an understanding of Israel's political and social system is not to be found in the study of modernization. Instead, the crucial questions to be confronted are those revolving around the actualization of a new society: the problems of political and cultural continuity and change, of how the particular cultural baggage brought by Jews returning to their old-new land was subsequently modified by the experience of nation building in the new territory; the impact of the new territory and the confrontation with it (what in the United States has been called "the frontier experience"); and the constitutional problems (in Israel's case, problems of reconstitution) that necessarily accompany the creation of a new society.[10]

Israel has an emergent political culture composed of a number of different elements that exist in somewhat uneasy tension with one another. This tension is evident in a great gap between the formal institutional structure of the polity (which is an expression of European statism) and the actual political behavior and informal institutional arrangements that make it work. Formally, Israel is a highly centralized, hierarchically structured, bureaucratic state on the model of France. In fact, the state and its institutions function on the basis of myriad contractual agreements—actual and tacit—which assume widespread power-sharing on a noncentralized basis. These are enforced through a process of mutual consultation and negotiation in which every individual party to an agreement must be conciliated before action is taken.

---

*Israel* (Ithaca: Cornell University Press, 1954). Lincoln Steffens offers some suggestive if unusual confirmations of this hypothesis in "Moses in Red," reprinted in Ella Winter and Herbert Shapiro, eds., *The World of Lincoln Steffens* (New York: Hill & Wang, 1962). Some Zionist thinkers, beginning with Moses Hess, the best of them, did see ancient Israel as the first "nation" in the modern sense, thus coming close to the concept suggested here. Hertzberg, *The Zionist Idea*, discusses them in his introduction. See also Hans Kohn, *The Idea of Nationalism* (New York: Macmillan, 1944), Chapter 1. For a discussion of the continuity of the Jewish political tradition in this respect, see Daniel J. Elazar, *Covenant as the Basis of the Jewish Political Tradition* (Ramat-Gan: Bar-Ilan University and Center for Jewish Community Studies, 1977) and "Kinship and Consent in the Jewish Community," *Tradition*, vol. 14, no. 4 (Fall, 1974), pp. 63–79. See also Salo W. Baron, *The Jewish Community*, 3 vols. (Philadelphia: Jewish Publication Society, 1942).

[10] Daniel J. Elazar, *Israel: From Ideological to Territorial Democracy* (New York: General Learning Press, 1971).

Because Israel is still an emergent society, the precise political-cultural synthesis cannot yet be forecast. So, for example, in 1975 the proportional-representation, party-list electoral system, which has been a feature of modern Israel since the beginning of the Zionist effort was modified to provide for the direct election of mayors independently of their city councils and to endow them with a modest veto power over council actions. This radical departure represents a step away from continental European parliamentarianism, at least on the local plane, and toward a separation of powers model which is more consonant with Jewish political culture.

Finally, Israel is an exceptional phenomenon in the world of modern territorial states in that it is intimately linked to the Jewish people, an entity with political characteristics not confined to a particular territory. Israel itself has still-undetermined boundaries, a condition which is presented to the world as a product of momentary circumstances but which has been characteristic of the polities in the Middle East since the dawn of recorded history. Moreover, a great part of its political life is and will continue to be rooted in confessional, consociational, and ideological divisions that are far more permanent than boundaries have ever proved to be in the Middle East. With all the trend toward territorialization within Israel, territory remains only one of the dimensions which its people and institutions use in organizing space and time for political purposes.

## The Compound Structure of the Israeli Polity

For those familiar with Western European, and most particularly American, institutions (where polities are territorially based, where government is organized fairly simply on two or three levels or planes, and where the greatest complexity is found in the overlapping of local governments), the Israeli situation is complex indeed. For those familiar with the American federalist theory of the compound republic, it is of particular interest to note that the Hebrew word used to describe the organization of a polity or government, *leharkiv*, means "to compound."[11] The same word is used to describe complexity, offering etymological testimony to the expectations inherent in the environmental and cultural matrix in which the Jewish people always have been embedded and in which Israel functions today. The fundamentally contractual character of Jewish political life is reflected in the idea that bodies and polities are compounded from different

11 Vincent Ostrom, *The Political Theory of a Compound Republic* (Blacksburg: Virginia Polytechnic Institute Center for the Study of Public Choice, 1971).

entities that retain their respective integrities in the larger whole.[12] Thus the state of Israel can be seen as a republic compounded in a variety of ways.

In formal terms, Israel is a parliamentary democracy in which the 120-member Knesset is the repository of state sovereignty. The Knesset is elected on the basis of proportional representation with the country serving as a single constituency. Parties submit lists of candidates in rank order and voters cast their ballots for an entire party list. Each party is awarded the number of seats equivalent to its percentage of the total valid vote, with excess votes above the number required per seat distributed by a formula designed to reduce the chances of very small parties to obtain a seat or two in the legislature. As a result, Israel has a multiparty system, with no party ever having won a majority of the Knesset seats since statehood; all cabinets, known in Israel as governments, have been formed by coalition. Customarily, the party winning the largest number of seats in the Knesset takes the lead in coalition formation. Until the elections under consideration here, the Labor party or its predecessor, Mapai, had formed every government since the establishment of the state, in every case relying upon a coalition.

The Knesset is elected at least once every four years. While it can be dissolved earlier, this has rarely occurred, and the tendency is for a Knesset to fill out its full term. The government is responsible to the Knesset and sits as long as it enjoys the confidence of the Knesset. Only the prime minister must be a member of the Knesset, although in practice well over half of the ministers usually are. As in other parliamentary democracies in the twentieth century, the government tends to dominate the Knesset rather than vice versa, although the Knesset has developed some means of exerting influence within the government-dominated system, particularly through its standing committees.

The Knesset elects a president for a six-year term to serve as head of state. His powers are quite limited and are in the main symbolic. His principal governmental role is to initiate the coalition-building process so that a government may be formed after the elections.

Israel has an independent judiciary, whose independence is jealously guarded. In accordance with the political doctrine of parliamentary systems, the Knesset is the repository of political sovereignty in the state (a matter not altogether in accord with

---

[12] Elazar, "Kinship and Consent."

Israel's political culture: significantly, the term "sovereignty" is never used in Israeli law) and formally the High Court has no power of judicial review over the constitutionality of Knesset acts. Nevertheless, it has extended its powers of judicial review as far as possible in that direction, at times ruling legislation unenforceable because of procedural inadequacies.

Israel did not adopt a written constitution upon the attainment of statehood. Instead, those who sought one and those who opposed it compromised, agreeing to enact piecemeal a series of basic constitutional laws which would, in the end, amount to a constitutional document. These basic laws require a minimum of sixty-one votes, or half the total Knesset plus one, for enactment, amendment, or repeal, but otherwise there is relatively little distinction between basic laws and ordinary legislation.

The elections for the Knesset are the only countrywide elections in which all Israeli citizens are entitled to participate. Permanent residents as well as citizens may vote in local elections for mayors and councilmen. Until 1975, local councils were elected on a party list basis and the mayor was number one on the leading list; since then, direct election of mayors has been instituted, while councils are still elected on the basis of party lists.

This formal structure can at best serve as a benchmark for understanding Israeli politics. It is perhaps most accurate in matters pertaining to Israeli electoral politics, primarily because its fixed electoral requirements are those most fully implemented as written in law. Even so, their meaning is dependent upon the way in which the Israeli polity is compounded.

**The Compound of Ideological Parties.** In the first place, the political system of Israel is a compound based upon federal and consociational connections between different Zionist parties or movements. Various groups of socialist Zionists, each with its own ideology, erected their own settlements and institutions in the country, as did Zionists with a liberal (in the European sense) ideology and others whose primary ideology was derived from traditional religion. The latter groups ranged from religious socialists, who based a modern collectivist ideology on ancient religious sources, to the religious right, who saw no reason to allow any kind of secular thinking or behavior in the state to be.

Each of these movements sought to create as comprehensive a range of institutions as it could, a kind of nonterritorial state of its own, but within the framework of the overall Zionist effort. Since they also wanted the overall effort to succeed, they federated to form various umbrella organizations and institutions through which they could pursue the common objective of a Jewish homeland, even while contesting with one another over the shape of the state to come and the vision that would inform it. This federation of movements became the basis for the present Israeli party system. In many respects, it conforms to the models of consociationalism put forth by Lipjhart, Daalder, and others.[13]

Today, as in the past, the country divides into three "camps": labor, liberal or center (the Hebrew term translates as civil) and religious).[14] Contrary to the conventional wisdom, the three camps do not relate to each other on a left-right continuum but stand in something like a triangular relationship to one another, portrayed in Figure 1–1. For a long time, preoccupation with European modes of political thought prevented students of Israeli politics from seeing this, even though there never was a time when Israel was not organized on this basis. What each has staked out for itself is a particular vision of what the Zionist enterprise and its creation, the Jewish state, are all about. At times that vision has taken on ideological form, and at times it has been nonideological. The camps themselves divide into parties, some of which are quite antagonistic to one another within the same camp; it is within the camps that left-right divisions do exist. The size of each camp is not fixed, either in relation to the total Jewish population or in relation to the others, but whatever the fluctuations, the camps themselves persist. Their persistence is reflected in the general stability of Knesset elections in Israel and in the division of offices within the World Zionist Movement.

A governing coalition is formed when major shares of two of the camps can be combined. Until the most recent election, government coalitions generally consisted of some two-thirds of the labor camp, plus two-thirds of the religious camp, plus a small crossover element from the civil camp. In the Begin-led government coalition, the same principle operated but in reverse: virtually the entire civil camp, except for Independent Liberal Gideon Hausner, joined forces with the entire religious camp. This coalition was joined by a significant element from the Labor camp, the Democratic Movement for Change. This, more than any mathematical formula, explains the basis for coalition formation in Israeli politics.

---

[13] K. D. McKae, ed., *Consociational Democracy: Political Accommodation in Segmented Societies* (Toronto: McClelland and Steward, 1974).

[14] S. N. Eisenstadt, *Israeli Society* (London: Weidenfeld & Nicolson, 1967), and Leonard J. Fein, *Politics in Israel* (Boston: Little, Brown, 1967).

## Figure 1–1
## THE THREE ZIONIST CAMPS

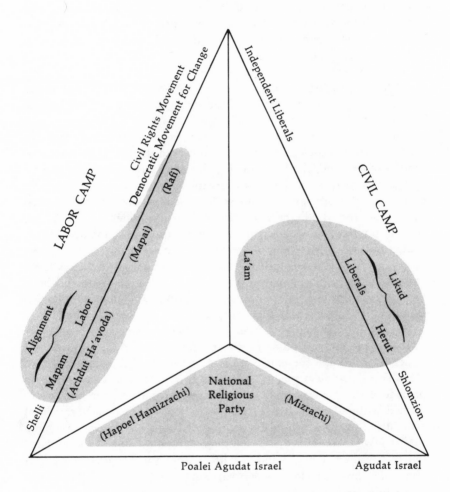

RELIGIOUS CAMP

NOTE: This figure shows the left-right position of the major Israeli parties within the three Zionist camps. Shaded areas show the major party federations for the 1977 elections; in parentheses are the names of important groupings no longer in existence as separate parties. The placement of a party's name on an inside line of the big triangle indicates its ideological affinity with the adjoining camp; thus Hapoel Hamizrachi was ideologically close to the labor camp, Mizrachi to the civil camp. The Democratic Movement for Change, though most of its leaders and supporters came from the labor camp, eventually joined the Likud government. SOURCE: Author.

As the ideologically based party or "movement" federations became institutionalized, they became tighter and more all-embracing. They developed their own settlements, their own newspapers and journals, their own cultural institutions, their own educational systems, their own banks, their own industries, and even their own armies. In pre-state days this was particularly functional, not only as a way of mobilizing energy for the pioneering tasks but as the basis for organizing the incipient Jewish commonwealth within the political context of the British Mandate. The colonial authorities, recognizing that the fundamental aspirations of the Jewish pioneers ran counter to their interests in most respects, did not wish to relinquish any serious governmental powers to the Jewish community. On the other hand, the Palestine in which the pioneers were building their new structure had long been organized on the basis of the millet system, a form of political and social organization that has existed throughout the Middle East for centuries, if not millennia. The millet system provided for the maintenance of quasi-autonomous ethnic communities organized on the basis of ethno-religious (here understood as a form of ideological) ties within the framework of whatever empire was in power at any particular time. This system made it both easy and natural for the colonial authorities to allow the Jewish community to function as what was, in effect, the Jewish millet.[15]

Since imperial policy under the millet system was to severely limit the internal activities of the ruling power and to allow each millet to determine the extent of local services to be provided to its members, the system made it possible for the Jewish community to provide such governmental or quasi-governmental services as it wished without too much reference to the formal governmental structure. Every Jew, simply by virtue of being Jewish, was assigned to the Jewish community as a matter of "citizenship" and was required to adjust himself and his life within the framework of that community, just as Muslims and various Christian groups did in their respective communities.[16]

The ideological basis of the federation of parties was functional in yet another way. The overwhelming majority of the Zionist pioneers came from the countries of Eastern Europe where socialist

---

[15] Eisenstadt, Israeli Society.

[16] The status of the Jewish community in Palestine was formalized in law in this manner under both the Ottoman and British regimes. The Palestine Orders in Council of 1922, 1923, and 1939 and the Jewish Communal Ordinance of 1927 set the framework for the internal autonomy of the yishuv under the mandatory regime.

and other movements dedicated to radical social change flourished in an atmosphere of the most extreme ideological intensity. Hence they brought with them a strong predisposition toward making ideology the measure of all things and a tendency toward ideological hairsplitting. Indeed, so intensely ideological were they that it is possible to argue that only their common Jewishness, which led them to certain perceptions about the necessity for unity at some point and which gave them a useful cultural inheritance for the promotion of the requisite unity, kept them from going the divisive or repressive way of their non-Jewish peers from the same East European milieu.

Understood in this context, Israel's adoption of the proportional-representation system was quite appropriate. Voters cast their ballots for party lists, and seats in the legislature or on the local councils were distributed among the parties in proportion to the votes they received; thus each constituent unit in the federation of parties was provided with representation according to its strength as a unit. This was no different, in essence, from other kinds of federal arrangements in which the territorial units are represented as such in the federal legislature, but in which the choice of the representatives is left to the units to make internally. As long as all potential citizens could find a home within one of the parties, this system was able to adequately represent the *yishuv*, provide a proper arena for bargaining among the various interests within it, and promote the adoption of policies and courses of action appropriate to the needs of the overall community.

This was the situation inherited by the new state in 1948. The essence of the constitutional history of Israel since then has been a growing conflict between the original ideological basis of Israeli civil society and the new demands of a post-statehood generation. The Israelis' growing perception of the need to modify the existing political order is a response to a convergence of forces that have greatly weakened the degree of commitment to the specific ideologies of the pre-state period while increasing the functionality of territorial units at the expense of existing ideological institutions.

The federation of parties was perpetuated even during the period of mass immigration following the establishment of the state (1948–1951) and subsequently. New immigrants were "allocated" among the various parties for integration purposes in proportion to the parties' existing strength. Each party was given responsibility for settling an appropriate percentage of the new arrivals and integrating them into the life of the country. Each supplied its immigrants in the temporary settlement camps with leaders who provided access to the country's institutions and served as the conduit for transferring state assistance in the settlement process. In return, the immigrants became enmeshed in the parties' own institutional structures and became faithful voters for "their" party in Knesset elections more often than not, thus contributing to the virtually undeviating record of electoral stability that Israel maintained for a generation. Their loyalty also contributed to insuring the perpetuation of the status quo in public policy making, usually by allowing the same people to remain in office for long periods of time and discouraging the introduction of young people (or new faces of any age, for that matter) into the higher levels of political decision making.[17]

Furthermore, because of most of the immigrants' lack of familiarity with popular government, their willingness to conform to the models set before them contributed to the growth of the power of the party professionals. Even in the years before statehood, the parties and their subsidiary institutions had been growing more centralized, partly because of the exigencies of the objective situation in which the pioneers found themselves and partly because of their original socialization into the political life of Eastern Europe where centralization of power was the norm. Still, in those years, when the *yishuv* was small and relatively homogeneous and face-to-face interpersonal relations were still possible among most party members, the impact of the centralizing tendencies was substantially reduced.

Mass immigration changed the scale of political organization in the country and opened up new possibilities for professional politicians to concentrate party decision-making powers in their own hands. For most of the first two decades of statehood, their success in doing just that was virtually unlimited. Thus, within their respective spheres, the parties remained the basic decision makers, and decision making was increasingly concentrated in the hands of the national party leaders.

On the other hand, the role of the parties or their institutional agents (including the Histadrut, the General Federation of Labor, which embraced virtually the entire work force prior to 1948 and continues to embrace the overwhelming majority of both urban and rural workers) in the provision of normal public services was progressively reduced. Though they continued to provide some services that in other political systems are provided by governments, the

---

[17] In turn, the larger parties have introduced a limited system of ethnic "ticket balancing" in the composition of the party lists, which determine who is actually elected to the Knesset once the party's proportion of the total vote is established.

transfer of other services, particularly those of military units, elementary schools, and labor exchanges, to the state had the effect of substantially reducing the dependence of the citizenry upon the parties once they had passed through the initial stages of settlement and absorption. This was particularly true in the case of urban dwellers. The parties' role in their daily lives was shifted to the management of "influence" (*protektzia*) and the distribution of jobs (particularly, but not exclusively, in the public services); the control of ostensibly neutral enterprises (housing projects, industries, and business enterprises, in particular) and government departments was the key to their power.[18] As the parties lost direct control over certain public services, they strengthened their control over public nongovernmental institutions and organizations in compensation, thereby maintaining their overall power even under the changed circumstances.

With the passing of the period of mass immigration, the divergencies between the political and social structures of the country began to develop in earnest. While party governments of the old style remained dominant, especially at the state level, the parties themselves began to lose their meaning. Not only were they losing responsibility for functions, but their ideological bases were deteriorating. The decline in importance of rural pioneering, the changes in the world situation (particularly the growing antagonism of the Soviet Union and its satellites toward Israel and the concomitant increase in Israeli ties with the United States), the disappointments with socialist orthodoxies at home and abroad growing out of their evident disfunctionality for development purposes and their frequent antidemocratic manifestations, combined to move all but the most hardened ideologues out of old grooves.[19] Only in the religious camp do the ideological justifications remain sufficiently strong to create demands as intense as in the early days. These are accommodated by maintaining parallel general and religious institutions in many fields.

Moreover, the great bulk of the population was becoming more or less settled and was developing ties both to the land and to the state that were independent of those fostered by the parties and their ideologies. This was particularly true among the young, whether native-born or reared from early childhood in the country. To them, the land of Israel was "home" in a way that it could not be to their

---

[18] Nadav Safran describes the shift of party control from direct to indirect services in *The United States and Israel* (Cambridge, Mass.: Harvard University Press, 1967), Part 3.

[19] The political aspects of this are discussed in Fein, *Politics in Israel*.

immigrant parents.[20] In this respect, the situation in Israel today parallels that of other new societies when the initial ideology of the founders ceased to be all encompassing. Nevertheless, the importance of the compound of parties remains great because it is so highly institutionalized.

**The Compound of Economic Sectors.** Another means by which Israeli society is compounded is through the division of public activity into what are known in Israel as "sectors": governmental, cooperative, and private along one plane and urban and rural along another. It is not surprising that most enterprises in a government-permeated society like Israel exist by virtue of government assistance, either through direct investment, loan guarantees, or simple sponsorship with appropriate tax benefits, favorable foreign exchange rates, and the like. While the Israeli government has veered sharply away from the strongly socialistic position of its leadership at the beginning of statehood, this has not meant any movement toward laissez-faire. Government's role remains as great as ever in promoting state-permeated social capitalism within a mixed economy. It is enhanced by the fact that Israel's precarious security situation and narrow economic base give political decisions priority over economic ones in most cases.

If the government sector is invariably the strongest, the cooperative or workers' sector is the oldest and most hallowed. It emerged in the 1920s, when the various small collectives of Jewish pioneers were brought together to create the Histadrut[21] and the Hevrat Ovdim (Workers' Society), which was to be the means through which the Labor Federation could establish and maintain its own complex of economic activities. While the cooperative sector has diminished greatly in importance since the establishment of the state, it remains the biggest nongovernmental owner and operator in the country. The largest industries, including the largest conglomerate in the country, are under its ownership. The internal public transportation companies, with the exception of the state railroads and the minuscule internal airline which provide very limited service, are workers' cooperatives. The kibbutzim and moshavim are integral parts of the cooperative sector.[22] The largest department store chain is Histadrut-owned. The

---

[20] Alan Arian (Asher Arian in Israel—the author of Chapters 3 and 11 in this book) has documented and analyzed this in *Ideological Change in Israel* (Cleveland: Case Western Reserve University Press, 1968).

[21] For a fuller discussion of the organization and role of the Histadrut in present-day Israel see Appendix A.

[22] On the kibbutzim and moshavim see below, pp. 17–19.

Histadrut operates Kupat Holim (the Workers' Sick Fund), the largest health maintenance organization in the country, which serves over two-thirds of the population, and through it controls a network of hospitals and old-age and rest homes—in other words, the complete apparatus of a socialized health system. In addition, the Histadrut is the great comprehensive labor union in the country.

The Histadrut has become considerably bureaucratized over the years, so that, while it has sought to serve the Zionist mission of rebuilding the state and the public good as interpreted by its leaders, it has also become at least as distant from its own members as the government is from the man in the street, if not more so. This needs to be emphasized so as to gain proper perspective on the workings of that sector.

3)     Finally, there is the private (meaning capitalist and small business) sector, which is growing after having been the weakest of the sectors for many years. Although there has always been private enterprise within the Zionist effort, because the overwhelming majority of the pioneers were socialists, private business was not a very acceptable form of pioneering activity. Only in recent years has the importance of a healthy private sector, both as a countervailing power to the other two sectors and as an element of the economy in its own right, come to be recognized and even encouraged by the government. It is typified by the range of private entrepreneurial activities characteristic of all modern Western societies.

By and large, these three sectors have not developed on a competitive basis; rather, they tend to cooperate with each other as could be expected in a small country with a relatively weak economy and a political culture which emphasizes partnership. Many enterprises have been jointly developed by two or all three sectors. Efforts on the part of private investors—usually from overseas—to "buck" these arrangements have generally come to naught since, unless the government's attitude is favorable, it is very difficult to succeed in any economic enterprise in Israel. What is particularly important is that the government, which is generally assumed to be in the business of providing services, also has a strong economic stake in the society, while the general labor association, which in other countries would be an interest group, plays an even more important role as a supplier of services on a "retail" as well as "wholesale" basis and as an economic developer.

The division between urban and rural sectors is equally important. The rural sector tends to be self-contained in many respects, because almost all agricultural production and rural life are embraced within the framework of the kibbutzim and moshavim. Moreover, the special place which the kibbutzim and moshavim occupy in the Zionist enterprise makes them the arbiters of the rural sector. (The original Zionist vision placed heavy emphasis on Jews' returning to the soil, where they would redeem themselves through cooperative toil in a natural setting.)

Not only are the kibbutzim highly integrated political, social, and economic units, the exact antithesis of fragmented urban society, but in many respects they are more modern than Israeli cities in their culture, behavior, and technological development. Every kibbutz is organized as a cooperative society in which all except the most personal items of property are legally held in common. Social life is necessarily intimate, with a common dining hall and other facilities to enhance the already great likelihood of high social integration that exists in any community of a few hundred to a few thousand people.

The moshav is more individualistic than the kibbutz. In the moshav every family has its own farm and private life, with some work and all major purchasing and marketing done in common. This makes for a cooperative rather than a collectivized atmosphere, but since the moshav is small (usually much smaller than the kibbutz), it tends to be a highly integrated social unit. Like the kibbutz, the moshav is both a cooperative society with shared economic functions and a municipal unit with its own general meeting and local committee.

The particular character of rural settlement in Israel is such that even family farms are concentrated in villages with their own local institutions; the 728 rural settlements that enjoy local governmental autonomy have an average population of under 800. Moreover, rather than confining themselves to limited local government tasks, as those serving populations that small in the United States would do, the kibbutzim and moshavim provide comprehensive economic and social services as well as traditional municipal functions on a level that far exceeds almost anything known among Western local governments. Services which they cannot properly provide are often provided by the regional councils, the federations of settlements to which they belong, which are themselves relatively small, ranging in population from 678 to 20,378, with only four over 10,000.[23]

Because these rural settlements can bring to bear a full range of options—political, economic, social, and commercial—to confront any problem, they are the most autonomous local governments in the

---

[23] Yosef Criden and Saadya Gelb, The Kibbutz Experience (New York: Herzl Press, 1974).

country and also the ones with the most effective cooperative arrangements with one another and with the state authorities. The greater internal diversity of the cities and their more limited corporate purposes prevent them from functioning nearly as well. Moreover, since cities are considered to be mere byproducts of the Zionist movement, which, as a back-to-the-land movement, was in many respects anti-urban, they do not have the same claim on the resources or respect of the state that the rural settlements do.[24]

The cities are open to greater permeation by the external society —including the institutions of the state and the cooperative sector— in every respect. While the kibbutzim and moshavim are closely integrated within the cooperative sector, as the elite elements of that sector they can manage their relationships with it. Cities, on the other hand, are often dependent upon decisions taken by the cooperative sector at the higher echelons of its bureaucracy, over which they have minimal influence.

**Ethnoreligious Pluralism in Israel.** On another level, the state of Israel is compounded of a Jewish majority and several different ethnoreligious minorities: Muslim Arabs (344,000); Christians, mostly Arab (77,300), divided into various churches; Druse (38,000); and small communities of Bahai, Circassians, and Samaritans—each with its own socioreligious structure and legal status. Following the Middle Eastern pattern, all of these groups seek to preserve their corporate identity, and Israel has granted them a legal status and institutional framework through which to do so. Under Israeli law, there is no Israeli nationality as such, only Israeli citizenship. Individuals are Jewish or Arab or Armenian or whatever by nationality.

While the legal status and institutions of each group are adapted to its particular situation, with Muslim Arabs having the most comprehensive among the minorities and Circassians the least, all have certain basic institutions and government support for their activities as corporate entities as well as the normal services provided to all citizens. Since, in Israel, matters of personal status are by law the province of the religious communities (this, too, is a common Middle Eastern pattern), every person must be a member of some religious community if he or she hopes to get married, divorced, or buried. Of course, while an individual may choose to use only these minimal services from his or her religious community, the communities provide many more services and are expected to do so by their faithful.

---

[24] Eric Cohen, *The City in Zionist Ideology* (Jerusalem: Hebrew University Institute of Urban and Regional Studies, 1970).

Each religious community has its own religious courts, whose judges are supported by the state, hold commissions from the state on the basis of qualifications determined by each religious community, and are selected by the appropriate bodies of each religious community under procedures provided for by state law.[25] These courts administer the religious laws of their communities—each of which has its own legal system for matters within its competence. Religious laws stand in relationship to the secular legal system in Israel roughly as state laws stand in relationship to federal law in a federation with a dual legal system.

The principal administrative organs of the religious communities vary from community to community. The Christian communities have no separate administrative bodies other than the church hierarchies, which also handle matters of religious law, because they are essentially in the Catholic tradition; they also play a more limited role in the lives of their citizens. The religious functions of the Muslim communities are administered through the *wakfs*, the Muslim religious trusts; and in the Jewish communities, every locality with a Jewish majority has a local religious council consisting of laymen and rabbis elected through a complex formula and jointly supported by the state and local governments. All of these bodies are, in some respects, subject to oversight by the Ministry of Religions, whose minister is a member of the cabinet and which is the channel through which state funds reach the various religious groups.

Because of the pattern of settlement common in the rural Middle East, where villages are either ethnically homogeneous or shared by perhaps two ethnic groups, local government becomes a major vehicle for the expression of these corporate interests. The Israeli government has made great efforts to encourage villages housing these minorities to acquire full municipal status and to utilize the instrumentalities of local government not only to provide local services but also to express the cultural personalities and values of the groups within them. This represents a partial adaptation to the realities of what was known as the millet system under the Ottoman Empire, whereby every ethnic group was constituted as a millet with its own internal autonomy.[26]

---

[25] M. Jaffe, "The Authority of the Rabbinate in Israel," *Public Administration in Israel and Abroad* (Jerusalem: Israel Institute of Public Administration, 1966).

[26] It must be emphasized that the separations which result are by choice and not by law. While Arabs may go to any school in Israel, they prefer to maintain their own schools, in which the principal language of instruction is Arabic rather than Hebrew and the curriculum reflects Arabic culture and either Muslim or Christian religious beliefs and practices.

From the point of view of the state, these religious groups obtain their powers through state law. From the perspective of each of the religious communities, however, their powers flow directly from heaven and their law represents the divine will. As far as they are concerned, the state has only a minimal role in determining their existence and certainly no legitimate role in determining their powers other than that to which they are willing to acquiesce.[27]

Each of the several communities represents a further compound within its ranks. Every Arab locality is a compound of extended families—really clans—so much so that voting and political office holding, not to speak of decision making and the distribution of political rewards, are dependent upon competition or cooperation among the extended families in each locality. Every so often a group of young people emerges to challenge this arrangement, and it is said that the Arabs are modernizing and will no longer be bound by this kind of familial loyalty. However, all but the most radical of the young usually end up following the lead of their families in these matters. One consequence is that Arab voting patterns originally reflected agreements between each clan and one of the Israeli political parties, based upon political trade-offs rather than principle. This, too, has begun to change. As a result of the radicalization of sectors of the Arab population, increasingly the clans are voting for the Israeli Communist party, more as an expression of Arab identity than for ideological reasons.

**Israel as a Jewish State.** While by law Israel has no established religion, it is, by self-definition, a Jewish state. This means not only a state with a Jewish majority, but one in which the Jewish people as a corporate entity can express its particular culture, personality, and values and which seeks to foster the expression of that triad as, perhaps, its principal task. It is in this respect that many Israelis, including the leadership, consider the state a part of a larger entity known as the Jewish people. Israel is the only politically "sovereign" state within that entity and, as such, occupies a unique position. It is also, for certain purposes, a Jewish community and maintains relationships with other Jewish communities on what could be considered a federal basis. The Jews of Israel, particularly the most politically conscious among them, see the fostering of this relationship as one of the tasks of the state.

---

[27] It would not be incorrect to estimate that as many as one-third of all Israelis hold the religious law of their respective communities in higher regard than the law of the state, including a small group of Jews (perhaps several hundred) who reject state law altogether.

The principal institutional manifestations of this special relationship between Israel and the Jewish people are found in the "national institutions" functioning within the state's territory. These institutions are so named because they are considered to belong to the entire Jewish people (or nation, in Zionist terminology) and not to the state of Israel alone. Among these are the Jewish Agency and the World Zionist Organization (wzo), which are responsible for Jewish immigration, land settlement, and vital social and educational projects in Israel, and the Zionist education of Jews in Israel and outside; the Jewish National Fund (jnf), which is responsible for land purchase and reclamation throughout the country; and the Keren HaYesod (Foundation Fund) which is responsible for fund raising throughout the world except in North America.[28] Constitutionally, they are linked with the state by special compacts affirming this unique relationship.[29]

The country's universities are also national institutions. The Hebrew University is formally designated as such by law. Its library is the national library and is so named. All other universities in the country have the same status, de facto, since they have the same arrangements for governance and funding. The universities' boards of governors are drawn from the Jewish community worldwide; some two-thirds of their budgets come from world Jewish sources and only 10 percent from the funds of the state of Israel. Budgeting and policy-making powers are shared by the state's Council for Higher Education, the university's "national" governing board, and the academic senate (roughly the equivalent of state, federal, and local bodies, if one were to translate them into modern political terminology). Even the political parties themselves are technically national rather than state bodies tied in with party branches as in other countries. (For example, ex-Foreign Minister Yigal Allon was recently named chairman of the "national," or worldwide, Labor party while Shimon Peres, the head of the opposition, remains chairman of its Israeli "branch.") Although the reality is that officials of the state dominate

[28] Lands purchased by the Jewish National Fund are deemed to be the permanent possession of the entire Jewish people for whom the jnf serves as trustee. They cannot be alienated through sale but only through long-term lease to those who work them or who develop them for useful purposes. Virtually all Jewish agricultural settlements, including the kibbutzim and moshavim, are located on jnf land which they hold by lease. The terms of the leases include social provisions with regard to proper land use and require the observance of the Sabbath in matters connected with the property on the part of the leaseholder (many of the latter provisions have proved legally unenforceable but retain some moral authority).

[29] See Eisenstadt, *Israeli Society*, p. 299.

the national institutions when they care to (and this is invariably the case with the parties), it does not change the theoretical basis upon which they are structured and which does influence their operations.

Since 1967, these fine points of political theory have taken on a new reality and a new concreteness—so much so that they are now clearly major factors in determining the direction of Israeli political development. A small minority that wishes to dejudaize Israel continues to exist. Far more significant, however, for the mainstream of Israeli political development is the way in which figures such as Moshe Dayan, Yigal Allon, and Yitzhak Rabin—the first sabra generation of leaders—have embraced the idea of Jewish peoplehood, not to speak of the revival of the discussion of the matter of Israeli Jews' connection to both their Diaspora brethren and to Jewish religious tradition that can be found across the length and breadth of the land.[30] Menachem Begin, who is firmly rooted in this sense of Jewish peoplehood and tradition, has become a major articulator of both dimensions and has invariably received a favorable response from his public.

Granted, the aforementioned developments can lead to very serious theoretical, conceptual, and practical problems for Israelis, other Jews, and people attempting to study the Israeli political system. Unfortunately, reality frequently has that effect. What is clear is that Israelis and their institutions are no more (or less) capable of dealing with reality in this regard, or better equipped to do so, than are Diaspora Jews or social scientists.

Finally, the Law of Return, which guarantees every Jew (except those fleeing criminal prosecution of one kind or another) the right of entry into Israel and more rapid naturalization than non-Jewish immigrants, in effect obligates the state and local governments of Israel to provide services to every Jewish immigrant from the moment of his or her settlement in the country.[31] In fact, because of the domi-

---

[30] Since June 1967, *Midstream* has regularly printed speeches and statements by these men and others affirming their reconsideration of this question. Published examples of the Israelis' rediscovery of their Zionist and Jewish connections are cited in Daniel J. Elazar, "The Rediscovered Polity: Selections from the Literature of Jewish Public Affairs, 1967–1968," *American Jewish Year Book*, vol. 70 (Philadelphia: The Jewish Publication Society of America, 1969), pp. 132–237.

[31] There is a great deal of misunderstanding regarding the Law of Return. Israel has immigration laws similar to those of other Western countries, with permits issued upon application and naturalization following in due course. However, since Israel is considered the state of the Jewish people, Jews enter almost as if they were engaging in interstate migration in the American manner. It should be noted that similar laws hold true in other countries with regard to those considered nationals even if born outside their borders.

nant political culture, such services and benefits are extended immediately to all those accepted as residents of the state, without regard to ethnic, national, or religious distinctions.

Some have suggested that Israel is also compounded on the basis of the country and region-of-origin groups within the Jewish population. Certainly these groups exist within the body politic, but because none of them seek to perpetuate themselves as separate groups, except for limited cultural, religious, or filio-pietistic purposes, they lack the legitimacy of the other elements out of which Israel is compounded. Israeli politics does take these groups into consideration in more or less subtle ways. Overt efforts to give group ties political expression, however, have been discouraged by members of the groups themselves. Thus, since the early days of the state, no ethnic lists have been successful as such in state elections or, except for a few peripheral cases, in local ones. On the other hand, there are definite efforts to balance tickets, particularly in local elections, and to provide representation for different groups on tickets in the Knesset elections. Moreover, some local lists, while claiming to be of a general orientation, in fact represent predominantly one country-of-origin group or another. Thus, while the shared ideology of Jewish Israel is highly integrationist, in fact something akin to what is known as ethnic politics in the United States exists under the surface.

The tendency toward "ethnic" politics (the term is misleading in the Israeli context since all Jews are of the same *ethnos* or people) increasingly overlaps with issue areas since a very large majority of the least successful families in Israel, from a socioeconomic point of view, are Jews from North Africa (Morocco, Algeria, Tunisia, Libya, and Egypt) and West Asia (Iraq, Iran, Syria, Lebanon, Turkey, Afghanistan, India, and the Soviet Asian Republics) who came to the country after the establishment of the state. These are the so-called Oriental Jews, who now form a majority of the state's population. These Jews are from families that never left the Middle Eastern culture areas, who have lived within the Islamic world since the rise of Islam, and whose customs reflect that world just as those of Northern European Jews reflect their world. It should be noted that most of the Oriental Jewish immigrants have done well enough, but, at the same time, the bulk of those who have not are drawn from their ranks. As these have-nots and their advocates have become more militant in demanding government assistance to improve their lot, their militancy has taken on "ethnic" overtones.

## Manifestations of Territorial Democracy

If ideological democracy places a premium on doctrinal faithfulness (or what passes for it) in the attainment of true citizenship and political influence, territorial democracy places a premium for their attainment on simply living in a particular *place* by right. Territorial democracy has two faces. It can be used as a means for specific communities to secure political power or influence by occupying specific territories or it can be used in a very neutral way to enable any groups that happen to be resident in a particular area at a particular time to secure a voice in the political process. What is common to both is the role of territorial units as the basis for organizing power.

Territorially based polities of the first kind began to develop as a matter of course when the pioneers settled in and staked claims to "turfs" of their own. The first of these were explicity territorial: the moshavot (private, as distinct from cooperative, farming villages), the kibbutzim, and the moshavim, which came to conceive of themselves as virtually autonomous communities in the pre-state days. Israel's cities, the embodiment of the second face of territorial democracy, began their development at essentially the same time as the first agricultural settlements. The first of them, the "new city" of Jerusalem (that is, the settlement outside the walls of the "old city"), begun in the 1860s, was founded as a synthesis of the two faces, consisting as it did of neighborhoods created as virtually antonomous communities within the city by like-minded householders contracting together to found new settlements within an urban context.

The first city consciously founded as an urban settlement without an ideological base other than the general ideology of Zionism was Tel Aviv—significantly enough, founded in the same year as the first kibbutz, 1909. Tel Aviv represented, from the first, territorial democracy in its most neutral sense. Whoever settled within the city limits was entitled to the rights of local citizenship and could participate in political life to the extent and in the way he desired (within the context and opportunities offered by the political system in general) without having to subscribe to any particular ideological or religious doctrine or formula. One result of this was that Tel Aviv, for years, went counter to the countrywide trend toward socialism; it became a stronghold of the General Zionists (the present Liberals), though as the city grew larger its population became more mixed and diversified and the city lost any particular ideological tinge it might have had.

Tel Aviv became at one and the same time the paradigm and the caricature of the Israeli city as a neutral, democratic, territorial political unit. In the 1920s and 1930s and then at an accelerating rate after 1948, other cities followed its lead. As the country's Jewish population expanded, many of the original moshavot, which had been founded as agricultural colonies in preideological days became citified and were transformed into just such neutral territorial units. After 1948 these were supplemented by more than twenty new towns founded to absorb the new immigrants. Taken together, these cities, which by 1967 encompassed 65.3 percent of the country's total population, have become the major vessels for the assimilation of the waves of mass immigration that came into the country beginning in the 1930s.[32]

Today Israel's cities (which embrace over 85 percent of its population) provide the principal opportunities for nonideological participation in Israeli political life; hence, they are the entry points through which immigrants from Oriental countries and their children have gained political power. Two points illustrate this trend. First, one of the most frequently noted phenomena of politics in Israel is the disproportionately large percentage of leaders drawn from the Russian-Polish-Rumanian groups, particularly from the kibbutzim. Oriental immigrants and their children are particularly notable by their small numbers in the Knesset, the cabinet, and the ministries. This is emphatically not the case at the local level. Slightly more than 50 percent of the Jews of Israel are from North Africa or West Asia by birth or by descent. Approximately 47 percent of the political leaders and public officials (taken together) at the local level are drawn from those groups. Moreover, many have become mayors or deputy mayors (already 37 percent of the total in 1965), giving them concomitant political and social advancement.[33]

The development of nonideological politics within nominally

[32] *Statistical Abstract of Israel, 1968* (Jerusalem: Central Bureau of Statistics, 1968). In a significant number of cities and towns, territorial neutrality has led to the development of ethnic neighborhoods, which, however, under the present electoral system, are unable to obtain direct local representation. Perhaps as a result, ethnic ticket-balancing is even more pronounced on the local level than in Knesset elections.

[33] Szewach Weiss, *Hashilton Hamkomi B'Yisrael*, [Local government in Israel: a study of its leadership] (Tel Aviv: Am Oved, 1972), Chapter 10. It should be noted that the recruitment and advancement of Sephardic and Oriental Jews is not spread evenly throughout the system of local government. The older and larger cities have disproportionately fewer officeholders from those backgrounds, while the new towns with their mainly "new immigrant" populations have disproportionately more.

ideological parties has already spread to higher political echelons as well, partly in response to new voter interests as registered by party leaders with their fingers on the public pulse and partly in response to objective conditions that have consistently demanded pragmatic rather than ideological solutions to unanticipated problems. In this way, at least, objective conditions have functioned to reinforce the local consequences of territorial democracy, thereby mitigating the possibilities of conflict inherent in its pressures upon the older ideologically based system.

The precise nature of this movement of Oriental Jews and others who do not fit into the present party establishment into the larger arena of the Knesset and the supralocal party organizations will depend to no little extent on the fate of proposals for electoral change that are presently under consideration as part of the overall movement from ideological to territorial democracy. While electoral reform is far from certain, it is clear that most Israelis are quite eager for changes in the voting system that will introduce territorially based representation, at least to some extent.[34] It is equally clear that the parties themselves are either reluctant or hostile to the idea. They have attempted to blunt the reform effort by broadening the territorial basis of representation within their respective party organizations. Should they succeed in this effort, the federation of parties would no doubt survive more or less intact and even gain new strength. Should electoral reform come about, the present system would indeed undergo adjustments.

Whatever the results of the electoral reform effort, all indications are that Israel's political order is at the beginning of a period of change induced by the continuing process of "settling in" in a new society. While the trend right now is away from the ideological patterns of the first generations of pioneers and toward political participation on a territorial basis, in the last analysis, democracy in Israel, as in the other new societies, must develop out of a synthesis between the ideological, territorial, and ethnoreligious dimensions. By their very nature, such societies require the maintenance of a national mystique (with its ideological overtones) as the basis for the consensus that

---

[34] Of the several proposals for district elections under consideration in Israel at the present time, the two most prominent are: the proposal to establish single-member constituencies as in the United Kingdom, which is likely to substantially alter the present party system; and the proposal to elect eighty members from sixteen five-member districts which, with the election of another forty members at large, would guarantee the continued existence of the present party system. On electoral reform, see Chapter 2 in this book.

holds them together, while, simultaneously, the sheer passage of time tends to promote the expression of certain aspects of that mystique through other channels.

## The Conflict of Cultural Inheritances

The political culture of contemporary Israel is compounded of a number of elements that have yet to merge into an integrated whole. Three major political cultural strands can be isolated.[35] The most visible of these was imported from Eastern and Central Europe by the majority of the pioneering generation and built into the state's institutions at every turn. Its salient elements, for our purposes, are: a strong statist-bureaucratic orientation, a perception of public officials as standing in a superior relationship to the general public by virtue of their role as servants of the (reified) state, an acceptance of heavy state involvement in the economic and social spheres as normal and even desirable, and a strong tendency toward encouraging the centralization of power wherever power is exercised. Political organization is expected to be centralized, hierarchical, and bureaucratic in character.[36]

The second political cultural strand was also imported. While primarily associated with Jewish immigrants from West Asia and North Africa, it can be found among those European Jews who came to Israel directly from the *shtetl* (the Yiddish term for the East European townlet where the average Jew lived at the turn of the century) or a *shtetl*-like environment and were not previously acculturated to the larger European environment. While this political culture also perceives the governing authority as a powerful force existing outside and independent of the people, it sees government as both more malevolent and more limited, the private preserve of an elite, functioning to serve the interests of that elite. Government is perceived in very personal terms as a ruler with whims rather than as the comprehensive

---

[35] The concept of political culture is discussed in Gabriel A. Almond and Sidney Verba, *The Civic Culture* (Princeton: Princeton University Press, 1963); Lucian Pye and Sidney Verba, eds., *Political Culture* (Princeton: Princeton University Press, 1965); Daniel J. Elazar, *American Federalism: A View from the States* (New York: Thomas Y. Crowell, 1966), Chapter 4; and *Political Culture, Working Kits No. 1 and 2* (Philadelphia: Center for the Study of Federalism, Temple University, 1969). Fein, *Politics in Israel*, presents one picture of Israel's political culture in Chapters 2 and 3.

[36] See Gabriel A. Almond, "Comparative Political Systems," *The Journal of Politics*, vol. 18 (1956), pp. 391–409, for suggestive comments on the political culture of continental Europe. An expanded exposition of his thesis can be found in Almond and Verba, *The Civic Culture*.

and reified state of the first political culture. Individuals imbued with this political culture have no concept of political participation, perceiving themselves as subjects not citizens. Indeed, they perceive the subject's task as being to avoid contact with the government or anyone associated with it, insofar as possible, for safety's sake. When they have to deal with government officials, they generally take a petitionary approach, humbly requesting consideration of their needs and recognizing the superior power of the official without necessarily endorsing his authority. The state is definitely not looked upon as a vehicle for the provision of services or for social improvement. Rather, the hope is that its role will be as limited as possible so that it will interfere in the lives of its subjects as little as possible.[37]

The third political cultural strand grows out of the indigenous political experience of the Jewish people in their own communities. It is civic and republican in its orientation and views the polity as a partnership of its members, who are fundamentally equal as citizens and who are entitled to an equitable share of the benefits resulting from the pooling of common resources. This culture combines the expectation of a high level of citizen participation with that of a clear responsibility on the part of governing authorities to set the polity's overall direction. The concept of the reified state does not exist in this Jewish political culture, nor does the notion of a ruler ruling by whim. Rather, the community is perceived as constituted by its citizens, reflecting the character of the Jewish people as a new society. Individual responsibility to the community is perceived to be of prime importance, and members of the community are held to have civic obligations to fulfill by virtue of their association with it. At the same time the leaders of the community are perceived to be responsible to the community in two ways: to its constitution, which gives it shape as a community, and to its members, who give the leaders their authority. The role of the community in dealing with human needs is perceived to be substantial but never all-embracing. That is, politics is not conceived as the be-all and end-all of life or as its architectonic principle. Rather, politics is perceived as an important means for creating the good society, necessary for living the good life, both of which are defined in other (traditionally religious) terms. Whereas the first two political cultures see authority and power as hierarchical, Jewish political culture sees it as federal, that is, as the product of a series of covenants (or partnership agreements) derived from the great

---

[37] Almond and Verba, in *The Civic Culture*, discuss this. See also Edward Banfield, *The Moral Basis of a Backward Society* (New York: Free Press, 1958).

covenant that created the Jewish people and reaching down to the immediate compacts that create specific communities within the Jewish body civic or politic that affirm the essential equality of the partners as well as the authority of the institutions they create.

Though the origins of this strand are as old as the Jewish people itself, the circumstances of Jewish political life since the destruction of Jewish independence some 2,000 years ago, and most particularly since the rise of the modern nation-state in the last 200 years, were such that Jewish communities were not in a position to preserve their own political autonomy unadulterated. Consequently, the Jewish strand is frequently more latent than manifest. At the same time, every Jewish community did maintain an internal political organization of its own, to a greater or lesser extent, which even when not conceived to be political by its members did serve to socialize them into certain specific patterns of political behavior vis-à-vis one another and the community as a whole.

This strand is spread across virtually the entire Jewish population of Israel to a greater or lesser extent, which means that, more than any of the others, it provides common points of reference and possibilities for communication among Jews from widely varying Diaspora environments. While the character and content of Jewish political culture have been less well explored than either of the other two strands, in recent years studies of Jewish political behavior over time have brought us to the point where we can begin to extrapolate certain patterns that seem to be endemic to it.[38]

To some extent, Israeli civil society is already an amalgam of the three strands, with different institutions reflecting one strand more than the others. In other respects, the three stand in tension and even conflict. Thus the Israeli bureaucracy is very European in style as well as in structure, while the army—the most fully Israeli institution in the whole country—comes far closer to the model of authoritative relationships rooted in Jewish political culture.[39] The subject strand,

---

[38] The study of Jewish political culture is still in its infancy. The materials by this author cited above offer a good starting point for examining the subject. More specifically, see Baron, The Jewish Community; Irving Agus, "The Rights and Immunities of the Minority," Jewish Quarterly Review, vol. 45, pp. 120–129; Gedalia Alon, Mehkarim B'toldot Yisrael [Studies in the history of Israel] (Tel Aviv, 1957–1958), vol. 11, pp. 58–74; and Jacob Katz, Tradition and Crisis (New York: Free Press, 1961), Chapters 1–5.

[39] Fein, Politics in Israel, Chapter 5, describes the bureaucracy. An excellent description of the federal (in its social sense) character of the army is provided by S. L. A. Marshall, "Israel's Citizen Army," in Swift Sword (New York: American Heritage, 1967), pp. 132–133. See also Amos Perlmutter, Military and Politics in Israel (Totowa, N.J.: Frank Cass, 1969).

whose legitimacy is in doubt everywhere, is particularly visible in the development towns.

Yet underneath all of these, the upward thrust of the previously latent Jewish political culture is becoming increasingly evident, albeit far from unilinear in its progress. Take the role of the Supreme Court in relation to the Knesset. Following European models, the Knesset is formally the highest repository of authority or sovereignty in the state, with its supremacy both specified in law and taken for granted in practice. Parliamentary systems do not give their supreme courts power to declare acts of parliament unconstitutional. Accordingly, Israel makes no formal provision for judicial review of legislative acts of the Knesset.[40]

At the same time, courts have always held very authoritative positions within the framework of Jewish political life, and Jewish political culture has emphasized judicial decision making as being of the highest importance. The Supreme Court of Israel has taken its obligations very seriously and, beginning in 1969, has, in effect, asserted a limited power of judicial review, effectively declaring an act of the Knesset to be unconstitutional by holding that it was unenforceable (98169 *Berman* v. *Minister of Finance and State Comptroller*). Israel's *Marbury* v. *Madison* came about by the action of an individual citizen who filed suit against the implementation of a Knesset act to finance election campaigns out of public funds on the grounds that the act was discriminatory on behalf of existing parties and against new seekers of Knesset seats. The court held that even though Israel's written constitution is not complete, the article dealing with elections had been adopted properly and could be held to be of constitutional validity and that under its terms the act was indeed discriminatory and hence unconstitutional. It enjoined the minister of finance from paying out any funds under the act's provisions. The Knesset accepted the court's ruling and in response passed a revised act designed to accommodate its constitutional objections, thereby effectively affirming at least a limited power of judicial review as part of the country's constitutional mechanism and moving the country a step away from the European models and closer to a model indigenous to the Israeli situation.[41]

---

[40] See Yehoshua Freudenheim, *Government in Israel* (New York: Oceana Publications, 1967). The situation in classic parliamentary democracies is portrayed in John C. Echlke and Alex N. Dragnich, eds., *Government and Politics* (New York: Random House, 1966).

[41] Amnon Rubinstein discusses this question in "Supreme Court vs. The Knesset," *Hadassah Magazine*, vol. 51, no. 7 (March 1970).

Though a common political culture is still in its formative stages, certain elements within it can already be identified. First, there is the strong sense of national unity—one might say embattled national unity—which pervades the country, the effect of Israel's immediate security position and the whole history of Jewish isolation in the larger world. Since the former is simply a continuation of the latter in a particular context, this element is rooted very deeply in the psyches of Israeli Jews.

Similarly, a common sense of vocation is inherited from the larger Jewish political culture. Until the 1950s this sense of vocation was clearly manifested through the Zionist vision of rebuilding Israel to redeem the Jewish people. Since then its precise character has become somewhat less explicit as it has become ideologically simplified and intellectually broadened. The revival of elements of the Zionist mystique after 1967 has given it new life.

The federal element (in the social even more than the political sense) is an important component of Israel's emergent political culture. We have already noted the use of federal principles in the foundation of the state's institutions. These institutional arrangements are simply the most visible manifestions of the federal principles that permeate Israeli society and its political culture from its congregational religious organization to its system of condominium housing, even though it has no acknowledged federal structure. Contractual government, the constitutional diffusion of power, and negotiated collaboration are all elements of the Jewish political culture that are finding expression, albeit imperfectly, in the restored Jewish state.[42]

Constitutionalism, republicanism, and desires for self-government are also deeply rooted in the emergent political culture of Israel. Whatever the problems faced by the country, threats to constitutional legitimacy or the republican form of government are not among them. Indeed, it is precisely because such threats are virtually unthinkable that we know that cultural rather than simply strategic or expediential supports for constitutionalism and republicanism are involved.

---

[42] There is good reason to believe that the federal element is present in all of the new societies, derived, at least in part, from their origins as contractual partnerships. This is true even in those societies where no visible federal structure is involved. Contractural government, the constitutional diffusion of power, and negotiated collaboration seem to be characteristic of their polities. See Daniel J. Elazar, *Studying the Civil Community* (Philadelphia: Center for the Study of Federalism, 1970) and "Federalism" in the *International Encyclopedia of the Social Sciences* (1968).

In other matters, the shape of the emergent Israeli political culture is more equivocal. Impressionistic observation seems to reveal that a change is taking place in the relationship between the bureaucracy and the public. While the bureaucrats may not be becoming more efficient, they are becoming less officious, accepting their role as public servants rather than officials of the state.

The same equivocal situation prevails in regard to the role of the citizens. It is generally assumed that citizens should be concerned with civic matters, and citizen participation in elections as voters is particularly high. At the same time, attempts to develop a widespread "participatory" outlook run into difficulties because of the nature of the party system, where centralized control and adherence to the ideological symbols and forms of an earlier generation act to discourage participation by those who are not "political" in Israeli parlance (that is to say, those who do not make politics the overriding concern in their lives).

In this connection, it is important to note the first signs of the emergence of the "citizen" or "amateur" in politics. The first manifestation of this phenomenon was the abortive attempt by certain former members of the Rafi party (originally founded by Ben-Gurion and his followers in 1965 and subsequently merged with Mapai and Achdut Ha'avoda as the Labor party) in 1969 to reestablish their political coalition through the mobilization of "amateurs." The reform movements stimulated by the Yom Kippur War extended this effort, and the Democratic Movement for Change (DMC), which won fifteen seats in the 1977 elections, represents its most extensive manifestation to date. The difficulties that confront the effort are fully reflected in the organizational problems of the DMC and its history since the election. In addition, local efforts to create similar coalitions occur from time to time and from place to place. All these represent the difficult beginnings of what could become an important trend.

By the same token the public's expectations of politicians are reasonably high. The people demand a high standard of behavior on the part of those they entrust with power, without necessarily being concerned with devising ways to impose sanctions if they do not live up to that standard. Prime Minister Rabin's resignation over his foreign bank account is one reflection of this. Indeed, the question of political morality in this sense was a major issue in the 1977 elections. Here, too, there has been no crystallization of political-cultural patterns, as the events of the past year have revealed.

## Political Response

As Israel enters its second generation of statehood and its fifth of pioneering, its political system is still in the process of responding to the demands of state building. This response can be viewed through at least three dimensions: the developing structure of Israel's constitution, the character of republican government in Israel, and the quality of Israeli democracy.

**Constitutionalism.** We have already noted how the covenant idea, with its underlying premise that civil society is really a partnership among the contracting individuals who form it, is basic to Israel both as a new society in the modern sense and as the heir to the Jewish political tradition. The unbroken line from the Israelite tribal federation through the *kehilot* (the organized Jewish communities) of the Diaspora to the kibbutzim of modern Israel has yet to be established by research, but such probings as have taken place give every indication of revealing its existence. Certainly, what is common to all is the idea of constitutional legitimacy flowing from contractual consensus.

Israel is committed theoretically to the adoption of a formal written constitution and made an initial effort to write one in 1949. The first Knesset was actually elected as a constituent assembly. The series of compromises involved in the decision to postpone the writing of a constitution need not concern us here. Suffice it to say that a reluctance growing out of just those problems of creating a new political-cultural synthesis indigenous to the new society described above lay at the root of the decision. The problems of religion and state, the precise forms of political institutions, the degree of governmental centralization, and the extent to which individual rights needed constitutional safeguards were basic constitutional questions deemed worth deferring on that account.

Instead, a standing Constitutional, Legislative, and Judicial Committee was established as part of the Knesset's committee structure and charged with the responsibility of drafting Basic Laws on a chapter by chapter basis for submission to the Knesset, where approval by an absolute majority (at least sixty-one votes) would give them constitutional status. In line with the political theory under which the state operates, the final document will continue to be called a Basic Law and not a constitution (the latter term apparently is reserved for use by the Jewish people as a whole, whether one takes a religiously orthodox or a secularist approach to the constitutional problem of Jewish peoplehood). By 1978, five Basic Laws, recognized as constitutional in character, had been enacted. They and other materials deemed to have a substantial bearing on constitutional questions have been interpreted by the government and the courts to create the basis of a constitutional tradition in the state.[43] The High Court of Israel has also moved to transform Israel's Declaration of Independence into a constitutional document or to affirm its status as such.[44]

**Republicanism and Democracy.** In Israel, as we have seen, representative government was originally conceived to be government through representative institutions (that is, parties and movements) rather than representative men. And, as we have also seen, this approach is now under some attack in a developing struggle over the means of representation and the constitution of the institutions themselves.

Republicanism as originally introduced in Israel rested on European models, which meant that its parliamentary institutions were structured as if the ideal were undivided responsibility of the governors to the governed through the legislature. What has emerged, in fact, is a growing concern with and a continuing, if halting, trend toward separation of governmental powers. The government (that is, the cabinet) has taken on an existence increasingly independent of the Knesset and vice versa, even though most members of the government continue to sit in the Knesset.

The ability of the government to achieve independence is not difficult to fathom. Indeed, the central problem in parliamentary systems all over the world is how to make cabinets responsible to their parliaments rather than simply converting the parliaments into routine ratifiers of cabinet proposals. While Israel has not solved this problem, it has developed and institutionalized certain techniques that aid the Knesset in preserving some independence of its own—within the limits dictated by the parliamentary system—and it has also given it real opportunity to help shape government proposals into better legislation. The Knesset has done this by using a very unparliamentary device: standing committees with functional areas of responsibility somewhat akin to the American model and strikingly opposed to the classical parliamentary one. These standing functional committees include representatives of all the party factions sitting in the Knesset. Meeting behind closed doors, they allow members from the opposition

---

[43] Amnon Rubinstein, *Ha-Mishpat Hakonstitutioni Shel Medinat Yisrael* [The constitutional law of the state of Israel] (Jerusalem: Schocken, 1969).

[44] Ibid., Chapter 1. Kallen, *Utopians at Bay*, pp. 15–22 offers a most suggestive analysis of the Declaration of Independence as a statement of the political theory undergirding the state from this perspective.

parties or the minority parties in the government to influence legislation by the use of their talents as individuals in a way that would be impossible if they had to act openly in an arena where their suggestions would be judged on a partisan basis. Thus the opposition parties are able to make substantial contributions to the legislative process through the committee system, where their more able members can participate as individuals rather than simply as spokesmen for their parties, opposing and subject to public opposition from the ruling coalition at every turn.[45]

In this connection, the expansion of the bargaining arena has to be considered another aspect of republicanism in Israel. As befits a society whose origins lie so heavily in contractual arrangements, bargaining and negotiation are important features of Israel's political process, though, as befits a society torn between formal institutions representing the statist-bureaucratic political culture and tendencies reflecting the others, much of the bargaining is conducted despite the formal structure rather than in harmony with it. The Knesset committee system is simply one way in which it has been institutionalized without overt political change. For most matters, the government itself is hardly more than a coalition of ministries, each of which has been delegated broad powers by the Knesset so that it can virtually legislate in its own field. These ministries negotiate with their clients, their local government counterparts, the prime minister, each other, and the corresponding Knesset committees to implement their programs.

Most of the Jews who have settled in Israel came after the state was established and not as pioneers. In general, they had very low expectations regarding government services and even lower expectations regarding their ability to participate in or even influence the shape of government policies. The expectations of the Arabs, on both counts, were even lower. At the same time, many of the Jews were ambivalent in that they saw the new state as a messianic achievement and hence expected its government to solve personal problems of housing and employment in a very paternalistic way.

As the population acquired an understanding of democratic government, their demands intensified; some groups, once passive, became almost unrestrained in their insistence on having their way. With this escalation of demands came an escalation of complaints about the way in which services were delivered. Individuals would seek to influence those responsible for service delivery in specific cases affecting them, relying heavily on personal contacts to do so, but saw

---

[45] Author's interviews with members of the Knesset, 1968–1969.

no general role for themselves as participants in the political process. This is now slowly changing, as more and more native-born Israelis reflect the socialization process of the school system and what we have come to associate with middle-class values in the political sphere.

By and large, there has been no systematic effort on the part of the public or spokesmen for the public to articulate and aggregate public preferences into collective choices that become the expression of demand. Except in a few areas of immediate concern that are tacitly understood as such, matters in Israel have not much passed the grumbling stage.

By the same token, it would be hard to say that there is a conscious effort to organize in response to such demands. That is obvious enough since the demands themselves are hardly felt to exist. Much of what does exist in this regard is a result not of internal pressures in Israel but of the leaders' being cognizant of the trends in the Western world in this direction and seeking to find echoes of them, or perhaps to anticipate such echoes, within their country.

With that initial understanding, it is possible to identify two major sources of the articulation and aggregation of demands. Protest groups have emerged from among the disadvantaged members of Israeli society, that is to say, those immigrants from Oriental countries and their children who have been left behind in the general upward mobility of the population. They have made substantial claims, particularly in the areas of education and housing, upon all the authorities of the state on the grounds that they are suffering from discrimination and lack of equal opportunity. Their demands have followed traditional lines of protest and are only beginning to lead to systematic efforts to transform the present situation.

The other group consists of members of the academic community whose business it is to study policy problems and make recommendations for their resolution. These people have been tempted to follow conventional Western European and American thinking on the subject, accepting the management-oriented reformism of the twentieth century West. However, virtually all of those who have been in responsible positions have, whether for reasons of political prudence or intellectual skepticism, refrained from pursuing those ideas as far as they have been pursued in the West. In general, little attention is paid to them by the government.

Whether these forces are sufficient to overcome bureaucratic inertia and the natural preferences of a people who have grown accustomed to a hierarchical system is an open question. What is clear is that the political culture of Israel acts as a strong bulwark against changes in the present system—a system that balances formally hierarchical and centralized institutional structures against a myriad of implicitly contractual arrangements, with all the bargaining and negotiation that accompany such arrangements and actually inform the system. Perhaps as the Israeli political culture takes on a more consistent and harmonious character, this will prove to be dysfunctional and one aspect or the other will undergo serious modification.

## Conclusion

While there has been considerable continuity in the Israeli government despite the election-induced changes, there are already strong signs that the new government is trying to respond to the demands of Israel's second generation of statehood and is attacking certain sacred cows of the Labor camp in an effort to liberate the Israeli citizenry from many of the restraints of the previous generation. In part, this is a reflection of the liberal economic orientation of the Likud. In part, it reflects its political liberalism, which is committed to limiting government intervention into the lives of the citizenry. The Likud's steps to reduce economic regulation and subsidization generally have been well received by a public that seeks greater freedom in these spheres. The new government has also taken some modest steps to recognize the pluralistic character of Israeli society. At the same time, Prime Minister Begin has emphasized the fundamental linkage between Israel and Jewish culture and tradition. All these initiatives reflect trends in the development of Israeli society that are likely to continue to gain strength in the coming generation.

# 5

# The Reopening of the Frontiers, 1967-82

## Baruch Kimmerling

In May 1967 Egypt violated two of the tacit agreements which had provided the basis for the *status quo* between Israel and Egypt since 1957: it concentrated forces in the Sinai Desert near the cease-fire line with Israel (at the same time expelling the UN Emergency Force stationed there as part of the 1957 settlement for Israeli withdrawal), and it closed the Straits of Tiran. From the Israeli perspective, each of these acts constituted a *casus belli*.\* On 5 June Israel attacked the Egyptian forces in the Sinai and in Egypt itself. On the same day, Jordan and Syria entered the war in support of Egypt. The results of the war are well known. Israel defeated the three Arab states in what became known as the Six-Day War, and gained control of the Sinai Peninsula, the west bank of the Jordan, and the Syrian Golan Heights. As a consequence, Israel controlled additional territories totalling about 26,158 square miles, including about 23,166 square miles in the Sinai Desert—an area more than three times as large as its total territory prior to the 1967 War. Israel immediately annexed the eastern part of Jerusalem and unified the city, which had been divided since 1949. Along with the additional territories, more than a million Arabs fell under Israel's administration.†

---

\*In 1964, Shimon Peres (*Bemaarachot*, 146, p. 3) listed three possible circumstances which would be cause for war: (1) the blockage of navigation to Eilat, (2) the conquest of Jordan, or (3) the concentration of forces in such proximity to Israel as to threaten its existence.

†After the waves of flight of Arabs from the captured territories died down, the Central Bureau of Statistics undertook a census (1967, 1968). In the West Bank, 598,687 inhabitants were reported (compared to about 730,000 under Jordanian rule); in the Gaza Strip and Northern Sinai there were 356,261 inhabitants (compared to a previous 450,000—an Egyptian estimate, probably inflated); in East Jerusalem there were 66,857 inhabitants (compared to 75,800

The acquisition of these extensive territories had not been anticipated, and stemmed in part from the war's outcome and in part from a constellation of international circumstances favorable to the Israelis. Israeli society adjusted very rapidly to the new situation, which significantly enhanced its self-image and had far-reaching effects on its actions in various spheres and many different directions. The purpose of this chapter is, *inter alia*, to describe the process of adjustment to the new situation and analyze some of its effects. We will discuss how the situation was perceived by various social and political groups, how it affected the struggles among them, and how these struggles influenced the Arab-Israeli conflict.

As soon as the new territories were acquired, the ambivalent attitude of the Israeli sociopolitical system toward them became apparent along four dimensions:

*A. The Dimension of Collective Symbols.* Until 1948, Judea and Samaria had always been an integral part of the Land of Israel (*Eretz Israel*). During the periods of the First and Second Temples, the Jews lived in the mountain area rather than in the coastal plain where most of modern Israel is located. Many Jewish symbols were linked to this area. Almost every place which was captured was the site of graves of the forefathers of ancient Israel and stirred recollections of biblical places about which every Israeli child had learned. This depth of feeling was expressed by Moshe Dayan immediately after the war when he declared that "We have returned to our people's holy places, to Shiloh and Anatot,* and we will never leave them." Religious sentiments were heightened by the interaction between the feelings aroused by the war and the encounter with places which were the cradle of Jewish mythology. This encounter also had negative effects: it challenged the consensus which had been arrived at through the first nineteen years of the Jewish state's existence. Ideological debates on basic questions of the Zionist

under Jordanian rule); and in the Golan Heights, there were 6,396 inhabitants (previous number unknown). Today this Arab population is estimated to be more than 20 percent larger because of the high rate of natural increase (close to 3 percent annually) and because Israel has permitted many residents who fled during the 1967 War to reunite with their families.

*Shiloh was a political-religious center at one period at the beginning of the Jewish nation, while Anatot was a village of priests near Jerusalem and the birthplace of the prophet Jeremiah.

movement were renewed, such as the demographic composition of the Jewish state, the extent of land needed for its existence, and especially the right of the Jewish people to settle in Israel.* The resolution of this issue would help to determine the attitude to be adopted toward the Palestinians. Did a Palestinian nation exist? (Did the Israelis want it to exist?) If it did exist, was a new explanation required for the persistence of the Jewish-Arab conflict?

*B. The Demographic Dimension.* The issue of the demographic composition of Israeli society arose because this time—in contrast to 1948/49—the vast majority of the Arab population did not abandon the occupied territories and did not aid in their "de-Arabization."† Had Israel claimed sovereignty over the West Bank territories, it would have had to accept—along with the territories—an Arab population which would constitute a very large minority. The inclusion of this minority in the collectivity, while preserving its democratic character, would have transformed it into a de facto bi-national state, which would severely threaten its basic self-image as a primarily Jewish society. Thus was created an internal conflict between demands to "open up the fatherland" by absorbing some of the new territories and the fear of threatening the collective identity and its societal boundaries if these demands were met.

In order to compute the "demographic threat" to the collectivity, estimates were published which showed the composition of Israel's population between 1990 and 2010 depending upon, variously, (1) how many and which territories were annexed to Israel, (2) three different growth rates of the Jewish population (level of fertility), and (3) three different rates of Jewish immigration to Israel (see Table 6.1).

From these estimates it is clear that if Israel annexed all the occupied territories and the average annual rates of Jewish immigration were low (the pessimistic view), then in thirty years the country's Arab population would be almost half of the total population, while if Israel did not annex any of the territories (excluding East

---

*For a comprehensive discussion of this issue, see Chapter 7.

†In fact it seems that, as a complement to the guerilla actions of the Palestinian organizations, which were undertaken mostly outside the boundaries of Israel and the occupied territories, the patriotic Arabs remained in the territories to prevent the type of de-Arabization which occurred in 1947.

Table 6.1

ESTIMATED PERCENTAGE JEWISH POPULATION
OF ISRAEL IN 1990, 2000, AND 2010
BASED ON VARIOUS TERRITORIAL,
IMMIGRATION, AND FERTILITY ASSUMPTIONS

| Territorial and Immigration Assumptions | Level of Jewish Fertility[a] | | |
|---|---|---|---|
| | Low Fertility | Medium Fertility | High Fertility |
| Israel returns to pre-1967 boundaries, annexing only East Jerusalem | | | |
| | | *Year 2000* | |
| | 77.3% | 78.0% | 78.8% |
| Israel annexes West Bank, Gaza Strip, and Golan Heights | | | |
| | | *Year 1990* | |
| Zero immigration | 54.0 | 54.7 | 55.0 |
| 20,000 annual immigration | 57.2 | 57.9 | 58.5 |
| 40,000 annual immigration | 59.9 | 60.6 | 61.2 |
| | | *Year 2010* | |
| Zero immigration | 45.0 | 48.4 | 50.2 |
| 20,000 annual immigration | 50.6 | 53.9 | 55.6 |
| 40,000 annual immigration | 55.0 | 58.0 | 59.6 |

*Sources*: Central Bureau of Statistics (1981); Friedlander and Goldscheider (1979: 197).

[a]Medium fertility level assumed for the Arab population throughout.

Jerusalem, which is already annexed), the Arab population would only be about 21 percent of the total if Jewish fertility rates were high and 23 percent if Jewish fertility rates were low. The demographers Friedlander and Goldscheider (1979) calculated that if Israel annexed all the conquered territories and the rates of Jewish immigration were low or nil, the Jews would constitute 45-55 percent of the state's population in 2010, whereas if Jewish immigration were above average (40,000 immigrants annually) and Jewish fertility high, the Jewish population would constitute 60 percent of the total population. On the other hand, if Israel annexed only East Jerusalem, and Jewish immigration and fertility were both high, in 2010 the Jews would constitute 79 percent of the population of Israel (Central Bureau of Statistics, 1981).

*C. The Dimension of Central Interests.* The perceptions of interests involved in Jewish control of the territories were also widely varied. (1) All the territories captured in the 1967 War were perceived as drastically improving Israel's strategic position. The Suez Canal and the Sinai Desert gave the country a sense of security by creating a buffer zone between it and its most powerful enemy—Egypt. The Jordan River and the Jordan Valley provided a much more defensible boundary than the tortuous armistice line of 1947, while control of the Golan Heights also meant control of the lion's share of water sources essential to Israel.* (2) Some of the lands—especially the unsettled areas—were perceived by political leaders as valuable frontier essential to Israel's continued development and the absorption of new immigrants. This perception was a carryover of the agrarian views of the traditional Zionists. (3) The territories brought control of such additional resources as minerals in Sinai (e.g., manganese, uranium), relatively cheap manpower from Judea and Samaria,† and, as noted, water in the Golan Heights.

---

*The main border clashes with Syria from the beginning of the 1960s until the 1967 War grew out of Syria's attempts to divert the path of the Jordan River and its flow to the Negev through the Israeli pipeline. For several years the United States attempted to help the two sides reach an agreement on a just division of the Jordan's waters (the Johnston Plan).

†Within a short period, tens of thousands of workers from the occupied territories streamed to Israel in the wake of a postwar economic boom. These unskilled or semiskilled workers were concentrated mainly in the service and construction industries.

Later, oil fields were found in Sinai that, until 1977, supplied about one-fourth of Israeli oil consumption. (4) The control of the occupied territories brought to Israel a sense of change of status from a *tiny* state to one comparable in size to other *small* states—more in keeping with its social development, its international political role, and its level of technological and scientific advancement. (5) However, all these other interests were perceived as only of secondary importance when compared with the hope aroused in the Jewish community that the Israeli-Arab conflict might be resolved through negotiations over these territories. In the immediate postwar period it was widely felt both inside and outside Israel that the Arabs would be willing to acknowledge Israel's right to exist in exchange for the return of some or all of the conquered territories. However, it is important to emphasize that from the beginning there were many who were opposed to any such return, either because they saw symbolic gains or other interests as more important than peace, or because resolution of the Israeli-Arab conflict did not seem to them to be possible. (6) The interests involved in Israel's orientation to the occupied territories extended to its ties with other countries, especially the United States, whose policy of political and economic support is perceived as a cardinal Israeli interest.

D. *The Perception of the Direction of the Action of Time.* During the Mandatory Period, the Arabs sought to preserve the existing power relations—the status quo—while the Jewish community was interested in changing them in order to gain strength for a future showdown. From this perspective, time was perceived as favoring the Jewish side, so long as it undermined the status quo. To a certain extent, the situation was reversed between 1949 and 1967. The Arabs perceived of Israel as destined to continue its territorial expansion at their expense, so that they sought to gather strength to achieve their goal of destroying Israel (see Harkabi, 1972). Israel simultaneously strove to achieve two goals: first, in the long run, to gain Arab recognition of Israel's right to exist; second, in the short run, to prevent the Arabs from achieving their goal. Dan Horowitz (1971), in analyzing the Jewish-Arab conflict, concluded that

The Israeli approach (which granted priority to the attainment of short-range goals even at the expense of the long-range goal)

stemmed from the assumption that existence *per se* takes precedence over peaceful existence. According to this assumption, the chances for peace are always doubtful, while the destruction of Israel in the event of military defeat is certain. From this stemmed the Israeli tendency to grant priority to short and middle-range security considerations over long-range political considerations, including those long-range goals linked with the chance of realizing Israel's declared ultimate goal. From the standpoint of Israel's long-range goal, it should have acted *to promote peace [i.e. the recognition of its legitimate existence]* whether the prognosis for this was optimistic or pessimistic. In reality, though, whenever a conflict emerged between the promotion of peace and Israeli-Arab power balance considerations ... Israel gave priority to doing away with the immediate danger (1971:7).

After 1948, Israel sought to preserve the status quo and the Arabs to undermine it. The effect of the time element was clear: time was perceived as working in the Arab's favor as long as the power relations—military, political, and social—were changing but as working in Israel's interest to the extent that her legitimated existence within the 1949 boundaries became institutionalized.

Between 1967 and 1973—with Israel administering the extensive captured territories—the view was strengthened on both sides that time was clearly operating in favor of the Israeli strategy of preserving the new territorial status quo.* Actually, Israel was pursuing the strategy of preservation of the status quo while creating *faits accomplis* in the territories to strengthen its position (1) inasmuch as it felt it would be unable to translate its war gains into Arab recognition of its existence and (2) inasmuch as chauvinistic trends were nurtured by the Arab refusal to recognize Israel. Nevertheless, the Israeli political system still had to decide whether to grant priority to the long-range goal—that is, to leave the territories available for possible exchange for Arab recognition—or to favor secondary goals, such as preserving maximum territory to ensure immediate security.

Israel's control of the territories created a much more complex conflict with the Arabs than before and confronted the system with

*It seems that the Egyptian belief that time was working in favor of Israel was a major factor in the initiation of war against Israel by the Egyptians (and the Syrians) in October 1973.

additional cross-pressures and internal cleavages.* The high degree of consensus which had prevailed in Israeli society between 1949 and 1967 on matters of national defense declined.† Some of the divisions led to the creation of political factions and parties as the conflicts concerning the captured territories cut across the political and ideological orientations which had been dominant in Israeli society.

In most of the controversies over defense policy, the future of the conquered territories and their inhabitants, and relations with the Arab states, the antagonists were divided into two camps, referred to colloquially as "hawks" and "doves." In broad outlines, the "doves" (a) were willing to relinquish all or most of the territories captured in 1967 in exchange for "some sort of peace,"** (b) wanted more active peace initiatives by the Israeli government toward the Arab states, (c) opposed the establishment of *faits accomplis* in the territories because they limited future options for peace, and (d) acknowledged the Palestinians' rights to parts of Palestine.

The elements common to the "hawks" view are less easily summarized: (a) they demanded annexation of all the territory acquired in the 1967 War to achieve strategic depth and easily defensible boundaries; (b) they sought to resolve the problem of the existence of large Arab populations in some of the territories by

---

*The situation after June 1967 was similar in complexity and type of problems to that before the "simplification" which had come about in 1948/49 with the de-Arabization of the country (see p. 133n above).

†During this period, security was a central concern in Israeli society. Any action linked to it became a sort of sacred rite (see Eisenstadt et al., 1972:205). Not only was it perceived as a vital need, but it was linked to the "prophetic" leadership of Ben-Gurion (see, for example, Brecher, 1972). The emphasis on security had far-reaching institutional effects: (a) the military became highly autonomous, since it lay beyond the political system's control; (b) there were attempts to convert military power and prestige to economic and political power, such as the attempt of the ruling party—Mapai—to gain votes in the 1955 elections by claiming credit for a technological-military achievement or the attempt to stifle criticism of the government on the grounds that it was damaging to the state's security. This abuse of the concept of national security was referred to as "defensism."

**The nature of the settlement for which the doves were willing to surrender territories is a subject of controversy. Some demanded nothing less than "real peace" as a condition, while others were willing to accept less on the grounds that one could not demand a total and immediate revolution in Arab attitudes.

granting Israeli citizenship, with all its rights and obligations, to all residents of the territories "who would so desire"; (c) they wanted to make it possible for agents of the government and private entrepreneurs to acquire Arab lands in the occupied territories to facilitate the de-freezing of ownership of these lands and permit the establishment of Jewish settlements in the territories—the first step toward establishment of sovereignty over the area.

There were only marginal attempts at building political groups and parties based on these opposing views. While an integral part of the nationalist right-wing program of the Gahal party (see Glossary)— and later the Likud (see Glossary), which succeeded it—was the idea of "no re-division of the land," this was only one of a series of opposing positions whose radicalism varied according to the times. After the 1967 War there were new parties which opposed Gahal, their very existence based on their opposition to retreat from the territories. One such party was that of Dr. Israel Eldad (right-wing leader and one-time major ideologue of the Lehi) in the 1969 Knesset elections. (It failed to win even one seat.) In addition, a Movement for a Whole Israel was established, lasting until September 1973, when it joined the Likud. The Thiya party (see Glossary) split from the Likud after the Camp David agreement. But the most salient hawkish sociopolitical movement in this period was the Gush Emunim (see below).

There were also several groupings of doves on the fringes of Israeli politics. One was Uri Avneri's party—Haolam Hazeh—which favored withdrawal from all the territories and Israeli peace initiatives "in exchange for territories." There were two other small parties in the Israeli parliament which favored withdrawal from all the territories. These were the Communist parties—one of which would have made withdrawal conditional on the achievement of a settlement, while the other favored unconditional withdrawal.* (The first of these merged with Avneri's party in 1977 to form the Zionist Sheli party.) Prior to the 1969 elections, a Peace List was organized by several professors (mostly from the Hebrew University) and intellectuals, who sought to pressure the government to adopt

*In 1965 the Israeli Communist Party split into two factions—an Arab faction and a Jewish faction. The Arab faction adopted a pro-Soviet policy, while the Jewish faction supported Israeli national interests (as perceived by them). Before the 1973 elections the Jewish faction united with leftist Zionist groups.

a more flexible position on territorial questions. Two other extra-parliamentary groups—Siah (the Israeli New Left) and Matzpen (see Glossary)—adopted extreme leftist positions on Israel-Arab relations and demanded unconditional withdrawal from the territories. (Siah defined itself as Zionist, while Matzpen was known for its anti-Zionist position.) Two parties in the government coalition—the National Religious Party and the Independent Liberal Party—generally adopted opposing positions, the first being hawkish and the second moderately dovish. After the Sadat visit to Jerusalem, a movement known as Shalom Akhshav [Peace Now] was formed, which tried to accelerate the peace negotiations with Egypt by encouraging the Israeli leadership to offer more concessions and be more flexible, mainly in regard to the Palestinian problem.

PRESSURES FROM THE PUBLIC

From the standpoint of this study, the most interesting early postwar grouping was that of the Hebron/Kiryat Arba settlers, which succeeded in forcing the government to include a large area in the map of Israeli presence in the territories.

As a densely populated Arab center, the city of Hebron had been outside the initial Israeli "settlement map." On the other hand, Hebron is part of the Jewish mythological past: it is the location of the graves of some of the Jewish forefathers and until 1929 the site of an ancient Jewish community, some of whose members were killed in the riots of that year, which completely destroyed the community. The destruction of Hebron was a traumatic event for the Jews of Palestine, which provides the background for the initiative of the Hebron settlers and the government's reaction to it.

Prior to Passover of 1968, a religious group led by a young and unknown rabbi (M. Levinger) came to Hebron claiming that it wished to celebrate the holiday there. The group rented a hotel near the center of town and prolonged its stay. For the time being, the military government was ordered "neither to help nor to hinder them" (*Maariv*, 6/5/73), but three months later the military agreed to ensure the group's safety on condition it would leave the hotel and move to a nearby area under military supervision. In effect, the government had recognized the group in order to control it. Later the group members were promised a place to live, and under pressure of the right-wing opposition (principally the National Religious Party in the coalition), the government was forced to acknowledge the "fact" of a Jewish quarter near Hebron/Kiryat Arba.

There were several reasons for the government's change of policy in response to the group's pressure. First, the group based its struggle on two principles of great potency in Israeli society: personal fulfillment through pioneering and the return to a place perceived as belonging to the collectivity in terms of both the recent past and Jewish mythology. Second, the group was seeking very diligently the fulfillment of the collectivity's central task of continuing direct conflict with the Arabs without threatening the government's power to control the conflict in other spheres. Third, the collectivity's goals were not clearly defined, and the action of the Hebron settlers had the political and material support of some of the hawkish components of the government and public. Finally, the group's militant action was perceived as in accordance with legitimate norms and values, and it is very difficult for a political establishment to counter radical groups claiming to be more effectively pursuing legitimate goals. (Later on, the patterns of activities and symbols employed by this group would provide a model for another militant movement—Gush Emunim.)

THE STRUGGLE WITHIN THE GOVERNMENT

The most significant struggle over the occupied territories occurred within the ruling parties—the Labor Party and the parliamentary Maarach (Alignment) which it maintained with Mapam (the United Workers' Party), which included a very broad range of territorial conceptions—from extreme hawkish to moderate dovish. (See "Alignment" and "Mapam" in Glossary.) Within the Alignment, which essentially determined Israeli policy, the controversy over the occupied territories was interwoven with internal power struggles, both in the party and in the state.

In the Labor Party, between 1967 and 1973 there were three dominant streams of thought concerning occupied territories. One stream was led by Pinhas Sapir, Secretary of the Treasury, considered the party strongman and controller of its *apparat*, in addition to having a major role in economic decision-making (Salpeter and Elitzur, 1973); another stream was led by Defense Minister

Moshe Dayan, whose charismatic personality made him attractive to many; a third stream, less established as a pressure group, was led by the Minister of Education and Vice Premier Yigal Allon. Each of these streams had interests extending beyond the problem of the territories, but they generally preferred to frame their conflicting interests and struggles for power in terms of an ideological struggle over the fate of the territories. The power struggle focused on the determination of the next Prime Minister. The adoption of the position of one stream's policy concerning the territories would be seen as a gain in the power struggle for the post of Prime Minister. This is not to say that the conflict over the territories was secondary, but rather that in addition to all the other factors noted, Israeli policy on the territories' fate was conditioned by power struggles within the Israeli political system (see *Maariv*, 8/4/72).

Sapir, though he made few public statements on the subject of the territories, was considered to be the main representative of the dovish approach to the Labor Party and the Israeli government. His arguments tended to be pragmatic and to emphasize that Israel should not annex territories whose population would radically change the country's demographic balance. In addition, he wanted the creation of a proletariat of Arab manual workers supervised by Jewish skilled workers and "managers," which Zionism had always opposed. Arie Eliav was considered the ideologue of this stream, and he argued both in terms of the traditional values of part of the Labor Movement (such as Jewish labor and universalistic egalitarianism) and of the rights of the Palestinians to part of the land of Palestine:

> The path Israel should take is to declare her readiness in principle ... to return to the Palestinian Arabs most of the territories of the [West] bank and the Gaza Strip so that they may establish on them and in the territories of the east bank of the Jordan an independent and sovereign state of their own.... The Jews have full historical rights ... over the whole of Israel ... but it must be said: on this very piece of land, on the very same square kilometers ... there are national-historical rights for the Palestinian Arabs who live there as well. Who will delude himself and say that these Arabs, natives of this piece of land, are "passersby"? These "passersby" have been living here for more than 1300 years (1972: 153-54).

On the other hand, Moshe Dayan (in a speech delivered on 27 June 1973) argued that the Palestinians had lost their right to political self-determination when they chose to join the Hashemite Kingdom and reject the Partition Plan. They remained refugees primarily because the other Arab countries did not grant recognition to the population "transfer" between them and Israel and did not absorb the refugees. Their leaders wished to turn back the hands of the historical clock and to establish the State of Palestine instead of the State of Israel (*Haaretz*, 6/29/73). Thus, according to Dayan, the Palestinians' right to territorial lands had been nullified because (a) they had relinquished their right in the past, (b) a population transfer had been made, and (c) the claims of the Palestinians were irreconcilable with Israel's right to exist. Conclusions as to the Palestinians' territorial rights can be derived from Eliav's view, but not from Dayan's thesis, since he also acknowledges a "Hashemite entity" with claims to the territories. Dayan's position on the territories can be seen as an attempt to annex the maximum amount political conditions would allow by establishing settlement facts in the tradition of practical Zionism. He sought to solve Israel's demographic problems and the problems of political representation of the territorial populations by formulating a type of dual governance whereby the inhabitants would live on territory administered by Israel (in the future possibly under Israeli sovereignty) while they would have political representation in Jordan (BBC interview, 5/14/73). In the case of the Sinai, Dayan was prepared for an Israeli withdrawal from all the territories "essential to Egypt, for its day-to-day life and security" (*Time*, 7/24/73)—i.e., from the Suez Canal and the Suez Bay—in exchange for a settlement. His approach was anchored in the basic conviction that time is working in Israel's favor and thus the political/military status quo should be preserved.*

In addition to the basic hawk and dove approaches in the ruling party, a third, compromise view was formulated by Yigal Allon—known as the Allon Plan—whose basic points were advanced as early as July 1967. The fundamental principle underlying the Allon Plan†

---

*From the same interview: "For the next ten years Israel's boundaries will remain as they are now, but no large-scale war will take place . . . [!] "

†The plan is summarized here on the basis of Y. Cohen (1972) and an address by Allon to a conference on the implications of the 1967 War for Israeli society published in *Yediot Achronot*, 6/4/73.

was *selective annexation* of territories so that (a) the main centers of Arab population would not be included within the territories annexed to Israel, (b) defensible boundaries incorporating most of the strategically important areas (such as the Jordan Valley, Sharm-al-Sheikh, and the Golan Heights) would be assured, (c) the major places considered sacred to Judaism (such as Jerusalem and Hamakh-pela Cave near Hebron) would be included within the annexed territories, and (d) no areas would be annexed which were essential to the Arabs and whose annexation would stand in the way of any future settlement with them. The plan was formulated in very flexible terms, leaving open the options of a settlement with the Hashemite Kingdom and/or with any Palestinian entity. It had two parts—the programmatic part described above and the operative part, which included concrete suggestions for the establishment of areas of Jewish settlement beyond the armistice lines of 1949. These settlements, in accordance with the conception prevalent between 1937 and 1947, would independently determine the physical boundaries of Israel.

The Allon Plan was never accepted by the Israeli government, but its operative part seems to have served as a working consensus for the political system until the May 1977 elections. The plan was not even submitted for formal approval because its acceptance would have disturbed the equilibrium within the ruling party, would have damaged Israel's relations with friendly nations (especially with the United States), and would not have satisfied either the doves or hawks.* However, the operative part of the plan (the settlement of the territories) provided a common ground for doves and hawks: the opponents of annexation saw in it a framework for a future political settlement, while the proponents of annexation viewed it somewhat favorably because it did not bar partial or total annexation. Above all, the plan was seen as having the advantage that "It can be enacted immediately and does not leave a vacuum because of the lack of any Israeli presence" (*Davar*, 12/22/68). The plan's

---

*At the time the plan was presented, a "national unity government" was in power in which the right was participating. This government had been established before the 1967 War but was dissolved on 5 July 1970 in the wake of Gahal's suspicion that it was about to accept a proposal by the U.S. Secretary of State (William Rogers) for a settlement which would entail Israeli withdrawal from most of the territories.

operative part was accepted as a compromise between the ruling party and Mapam, and it acted as a balance within the government coalition between the religious parties, on the one hand, and the moderate Independent Liberal Party, on the other. The actions taken by the government in accordance with the plan placed it midway between the extreme demands of the right for immediate annexation of Judea and Samaria, the Golan Heights, and large parts of Sinai, and the demands of other parties and groups to leave most of the territories free of Jewish population—or even for immediate retreat from some or all of the captured territories without any political compensation from the Arabs.* Thus the operative part of the Allon Plan became, between 1967 and 1977, a sort of balance point for the system as a whole.

The two main implications of selective Jewish settlement in the captured territories for the Jewish-Arab conflict were: (a) it served to create a new territorial status quo while leaving room for future negotiation; (b) it refocused the conflict on the struggle between the Jewish and Palestinian peoples—a struggle which had steadily declined in significance between 1949 and 1967.† Between June 1967 and May 1977 seventy-six settlements were established in the territories captured by Israel in the 1967 War (see Table 6.2).

The balance in the political system achieved by the fulfillment of the operative part of the Allon Plan was only temporary, and with the passage of time, public attitudes moved in a "hawkish" direction. Thus, during the formulation of the Alignment's political platform in October 1969, proposals were made (largely under pressures exerted by the Defense Minister) for demanding a more intensive Israeli presence in the territories. In the election campaign, however, only general statements were included in the platform to the effect that "the country's boundaries must be strategic defense boundaries as needed to ensure the State's unchallenged existence, the defense of its peace and the prevention of any future attempts at attack" and "the establishment of security settlements and per-

---

*For example, the Histadrut's Secretary-General, Y. Ben-Aharon, called for a withdrawal from part of Sinai to show "good intentions."

†The refocusing of the conflict on the Palestinian Arab problem was a result not only of Israeli settlement activities, but also of the growth of autonomous Palestinian political institutions and guerilla organizations whose political successes intensified their activities.

Table 6.2

NEW JEWISH SETTLEMENTS IN THE OCCUPIED TERRITORIES,
1967-1979

| Region | June 1967-May 1977[a] | | June 1977-July 1979[b] | | Total Number | Percentage of All Settlements |
|---|---|---|---|---|---|---|
| | Number | Percent of Total | Number | Percent of Total | | |
| Golan Heights | 25 | 86% | 4 | 14% | 29 | 24% |
| West Bank | 28 | 41 | 40 | 59 | 68 | 55 |
| Sinai and the Gaza Strip | 23 | 92 | 2 | 8 | 25 | 20 |
| Total | 76 | 62 | 46 | 38 | 122 | 100 |

Sources: (1) M. Drobless, Settlement Department, The Jewish Agency, Press conference, 7/25/79; (2) Y. Galili, Zu Haderekh, 8/20-8/27/80; (3) Haaretz, 9/14/79.

[a]Period of the Labor government

[b]Likud government

manent settlements should be speeded up" (Maariv, 8/5/69). However, an appendix was attached to the platform which was known informally as the "oral Bible." It stated the Alignment position on territorial aspirations and security needs in specific terms:

Israel views the Jordan River as its eastern security boundary [that is—a boundary west of which foreign military forces may not cross]; the Golan Heights and the Gaza Strip will remain under our exclusive control, and free navigation from Eilat and southward will be assured by independent Israeli forces which will control the area of the Straits. This area [the eastern coast of Sinai] will be attached to Israel by a territorial continuum.*

But this document was not binding and left room for manipulation by the party's factions, each of which could accept or reject it or interpret it as the members saw fit.

*Personal letter from Minister Galilee to the Prime Minister, 7 August 1969; published in Maariv, 4/15/71.

The 1973 election campaign (which was postponed due to the war) also focused on an attempt to intensify Israeli presence in the occupied territories. The Minister of Defense proposed the certification of land purchases in the territories by both institutions and individuals (i.e., treating the territories as a frontier).* This would legitimize what had been occurring since the end of 1972, when Jewish entrepreneurs, along with government and "national" institutions, began to purchase considerable tracts of land, particularly in the West Bank.† The process began when:

It became clear that in reality the attitude of the Arab population had taken an interesting turn. While in the past there was nothing more distasteful than the sale of land to Jews, and Israelis were forced to purchase land under the name of unknown companies in Lichtenstein, the ban has been lifted. Some Arabs are willing to sell land to Jews openly and the purchasers come with the seller to his Arab neighbors in order to receive a written certification from them stating the boundaries of the sold area (*Haaretz*, 3/27/73).

This process of the defreezing of lands in the occupied territories was almost identical to the process of the defreezing of Arab lands in the Mandatory Period (see Chapter 2). The flow of capital—both from the national authorities and public institutions, and from the private entrepreneurs and speculators—caused a sharp rise in land prices,** but also stimulated more and more Arabs to convert

*Dayan also proposed the establishment of a city (Yamit) and deep-water port in the Rafah Approaches. Establishment of a city at this site would, in the long run, require setting the border deep in Sinai—a deviation from the Allon Plan (*Haaretz*, 8/17/73).

†The official basis of these purchases was Order 25, issued by the Military Government in Judea and Samaria on 18 June 1967: "Any land transaction, whether direct or indirect, is to be undertaken only by permission of the certified authority" [*that is, the military government*]. Official permits were granted to four civilians allowing them to purchase lands in the territories, but no more permits were granted after the matter became a subject of public controversy (see W. Weinstein, *Maariv*, 4/6/73).

**One of the arguments against permitting private purchases was that it would lead to speculation. At first it was possible to purchase land for £P 3-5 per square meter, but the price rose quickly to £P 20 per square meter (*Maariv*, 4/6/73).

land to capital despite the community pressures against sales to Jews. In the West Bank a national committee was established for the purchase of Arab lands which were liable to be sold to Jews (*Maariv*, 4/8/73), and "Jordan's religious leaders announced . . . that anyone selling his land to Israelis is a traitor to Islam and the Arab nation" (*Haaretz*, 4/9/73). The General Manager of the Jewish National Fund was forced to acknowledge that "Since the beginning of the public debate over land purchases in Judea and Samaria, the supply of lands for sale has been reduced" (*Haaretz*, 4/10/73).

Let us assume that the supply of lands for sale grew as Israeli control of the territories was seen as permanent both by landowners and purchasers (who were prepared to invest more as the risk of loss declined and chance for profits increased). After the 1973 War this trend seems to have been reversed. Thus Dayan was in favor of legalizing land purchases to achieve (a) additional defreezing of land by encouraging investment by private individuals, (b) the intensification of Israeli presence in the territories, being aware that changes involving land in the Jewish-Arab conflict are generally irreversible, and (c) enhancement of his political prestige by demonstrating his power to influence policy. For a time it seemed that with the support of the Prime Minister, Golda Meir, Dayan's approach would be accepted by a majority. But Mrs. Meir changed her mind "in the wake of the international uproar" the proposal aroused (*Haaretz*, 4/9/73). She also wanted to prevent speculation by private entrepreneurs: in response to a question by Menahem Begin in the Knesset, the Prime Minister said that when she saw the list of requests for land purchases—requests for acquisition of 50,000 dunams, 15,000, 5,000, 2,000, etc.—she realized that what was involved was land purchase for speculation (*Haaretz*, 4/11/73). However, the matter was raised again in the elections of 1974, and the struggle regarding settlement in the new territories began anew. A compromise was finally arrived at in an agreement known as "The Galilee Document" (named after its author, Israel Galilee, a prominent figure in the Labor Movement), in which Dayan received approval for speeding up the rate of settlement and the construction of a deep-water port "south of Gaza." In the matter of land purchase, the agreement altered the status quo only slightly. Primacy was again granted to a national authority—the Israel Land Authority—in the purchase of lands. (Most of the public land acquisitions were made through a subsidiary company of the JNF—Himnuta—which is registered as a European corporation.) But purchases of land by private entrepreneurs were permitted in cases in which "the Israel Land Authority cannot purchase it or is not interested in purchasing it" (*Maariv*, 8/10/74). In practice, this agreement could not be put into effect before the outbreak of the 1973 War.

Settlements were established on four different types of land. The first type was government lands, owned by the Jordanian and Egyptian governments. In many cases, Arab inhabitants cultivated these lands or claimed the right to them and de facto ownership of them. Until 1973 about 57,000 dunams of this type of land were fenced off in the Raffah area. When the Bedouins living there were evicted in 1972, it became a controversial matter in Israel. Of the 360,000 dunams in the Gaza Strip, more than 55 percent of the lands were registered in the name of the British High Commissioner; this was transferred to the Egyptian military command and later to the State of Israel (*Yediot Achronot*, 3/17/72). The second type of land was acquired—in exchange for payment or for government lands—from Arab owners.* The third type was abandoned lands, particularly in the Golan Heights, where about 35 villages (totalling 70,000 dunams) were abandoned, and in Judea and Samaria, where 37,500 dunams defined as "abandoned" were given over to Jewish settlement. The fourth type was taken by order of the military after the Arab owners refused to sell. Such were the lands given to the settlers of Kiryat Arba (Hebron) and Nahal Gittit. In Akraba (a small village in the West Bank), the agricultural produce was destroyed in order to pressure the owners to sell their lands (*Maariv*, 7/14/72), which also became a subject for controversy. In such cases, the military could keep the area closed to the original owners for as long as it wished in exchange for yearly damage payments.

In East Jerusalem, which was immediately annexed to the State of Israel, the expropriation of lands was undertaken. By August 1970, about 17,000 dunams had been transferred to Israeli ownership—about 25 percent of the total territory (70,000 dunams) annexed to the Israeli city of Jerusalem. The new territories were about half the area of Israeli Jerusalem prior to 1967 (37,000

---

*About 50,000 of 52,000 dunams of land purchased by the Israel Land Authority in the occupied territories were exchanged for government lands (*Maariv*, 4/6/73).

dunams) and almost three times the size of Jordanian Jerusalem before 1967 (6,000 dunams). According to the original plans, between 100,000-150,000 persons would be settled on these lands. These actions, as well as intensive building activities, were undertaken to establish *faits accomplis* according to Benbenisti (1973:98-288), who until 1971 was in charge of affairs relating to the eastern part of the city. Land expropriation and the other settlement activities in Jerusalem and the other captured territories were undertaken in an almost clandestine manner. In an article entitled "Wall and Tower—1973 Version," a reporter described the settlement of Nahal Gittit as follows: "[They] came to the Akraba lands at night, and prepared and fenced the camp of tents by the next morning. It was worthwhile remembering that the 'wall and tower' period ended 35 years ago" (*Haaretz*, 8/20/73). (See Chapter 4.)

During this period, a new form of settlement was begun—the *mizpe* (lookout)—to strengthen the Jewish presence in the Galilee, where there had always been an Arab majority. Consisting of a small number of families at a selected location (usually on a hilltop which has strategic control of the surrounding area), these settlements do not have infrastructures of schools, medical dispensaries, stores, etc., but are dependent on nearby city or village centers for these services. From this point of view they are extensions of city suburbs. It is still too early to see in which directions the *mizpim* will develop, or how long they will last.

Thus, between 1967 and 1977, when the various governments were in doubt about the fate of the newly acquired territories, they resorted almost ritualistically to patterns of action from the past. These patterns of action were employed because the system's goals were vague and sometimes conflicting (for example, seeking security and peace at the same time), and because of cross-pressures from various groups and components of the system. Between 1967 and 1977 these were constraints to the development of a policy which would (1) freeze the political status quo created after the 1967 War, while (2) promoting Israeli presence by means of settlement, and (3) achieving selective ownership of territories on the assumption that time was operating in favor of the Israeli side. It seems then that the inability to obtain sovereignty was the result of both internal and external constraints.

## THE NEW REGIME AND THE PEACE TREATY WITH EGYPT

In May 1977, as a result of the general elections, Israel for the first time ever had a change of government. The reins were transferred to the Likud, a coalition headed by the Herut party (see Glossary), the direct descendant of the Revisionist Zionist party.* There was a general expectation that the new government would harden the Israeli position toward the Arabs—especially in regard to territorial disputes. After all, the Revisionist Party motto was "Both sides of the Jordan—both this side and that belong to us" (from a song composed by Jabotinsky), and it not only did not recognize Arab rule over the western side of the Jordan (i.e, the West Bank), but until 1965 had not accepted the fact that Trans-Jordan had been detached from the territory of Palestine in 1922. The badge of the youth movement of the party—Beitar (see Glossary)—carried a map of "Greater Israel" which included all the territory of Palestine before the first partition.† The Revisionist Party had a clearly defined place in the Zionist spectrum: it was considered an elitist movement with a distinctly right-wing, anti-socialist stand, which gloried in the primordial symbols of Homeland, Blood, Race (in the pre-fascist era), and a single flag.** The leaders of this movement, and especially its founder (Jabotinsky), laid great importance on military bearing and discipline, and they supported a militant underground movement which competed with the semi-legal army of the Yishuv, actively opposing both the British and the Arabs. After the State of Israel was proclaimed, this underground movement accepted democratic principles and became one of the political

---

*In spite of the general movement rightward within the Israeli political system beginning with the War of 1967 and leading eventually to the change of government in 1977, it appears that it was not the platform of the Likud which brought it victory, but a protest vote against the Labor Party's misman-agement of the 1973 War and the corrupt practices of various party members which had recently been exposed. This protest brought about the establish-ment of a new party—the Democratic Movement for Change—which entered into a coalition with the Likud and the National Religious Party, changing the Israeli political map.

†The badge was changed in 1978 after the Likud came to power.

**The Revisionists opposed the two-flags approach of the left, which carried a red flag to symbolize social progress as well as the blue-and-white national flag.

parties. For many years its leadership, headed by Menahem Begin, was composed of the former leaders of the underground—the Irgun Zvai Leumi—and it began receiving the votes of the new immigrants who had come from the Middle East (i.e., the Oriental Jews), who were on the periphery of the social and political system. Herut was thus a social protest party, in spite of its nationalistic stress. The ideology of the leaders and the aims of the constituents were linked through a number of populist appeals, with ties to the land being central. On the other hand, Revisionist Zionism did not consider "creating facts" (or what we have referred to as presence) as important to the achievement of territorial aims as did the predominant sector of the Zionist movement.

It was expected that soon after the Likud took over the government, Israel would announce the annexation of all the territories, or most of them, or—at the very least—the areas referred to in the Bible as Judea and Samaria (i.e., the West Bank), in accordance with its election platform and its official ideology. The government did not announce any immediate annexation, however, or even any such intention,* though at the very beginning it took steps which meant the rejection of the Allon Plan (selective settlement of the West Bank) and the intention of creating facts by means of presence even in areas densely populated by Arabs.

It is hard to imagine what would have happened had there not been an unusual combination of events. First, almost immediately after the Likud came to power, Egypt announced its willingness to make peace with Israel in exchange for the evacuation of lands conquered in 1967; second, in the last year of the term of office of the Likud, it seemed very likely that the Likud would not be reelected, which meant that the Alignment would be returning to power.† These two developments influenced the policy of the Likud toward the territories.

---

*The non-annexation of the territories, as long as negotiations were in progress, was a condition laid down by Moshe Dayan for joining the Likud government. Only after the 1981 elections did the Likud government extend Israeli rule to the Golan Heights.

†This was the forecast of all the public opinion polls in 1980. It was primarily due to serious failures in the economy, which had brought Israel an annual inflation rate of about 130 percent, and the image of a government which could not function, especially after it had suffered a number of major setbacks.

Peace with the Arabs or, to be more precise, obtaining recognition and legitimation of the existence of a Jewish state in the Middle East was always a central desideratum in Israeli society (see Chapter 7), and it was one of the most basic aims of the Zionist movement, especially after the State of Israel was proclaimed. The longer the period that elapsed from the War of 1947/48 without peace with the Arabs, the more that aim began to appear as semi-utopian, or for future generations only, to much of the population. But it is one of the central beliefs of those who are dovish that it is possible to achieve peace, and that Israel can influence the Arabs to agree to it.

When President Sadat arrived in Jerusalem (19-21 November 1977) and proposed peace, his proposal could not be opposed (in terms of public policy) either externally or internally. Added to this was a belief, widely shared among the Israeli leadership, that Egypt was primarily interested in the return of its territories (the Sinai Peninsula and possibly the Gaza Strip), and would be willing to accept a formula which would permit the continued control by Israel of the West Bank (and possibly the Golan Heights), provided that a degree of political independence was given to the inhabitants of these areas. This was the background for the formulation of Israel's proposal of Palestinian autonomy which was agreed upon at Camp David. It appears that that agreement was sufficiently vague to satisfy both the Israeli and Egyptian interpretations. The Israelis understood autonomy to mean self-rule in internal matters (education, health, welfare, employment, etc.), while land, water, and internal and external security would all be under Israeli supervision. This would apply for the transitional period of five years; no indication was given as to what would occur after that. The Egyptian interpretation, on the other hand, of the words "establishing the elected self-governing authority . . . in order to provide full autonomy for the inhabitants" included the establishment of an Arab Palestinian state in the West Bank and Gaza Strip within the transitional period.* The contradiction between these two interpre-

*See "Letters Accompanying the Peace Treaty" from Menahem Begin and Anwar Sadat to Jimmy Carter, *Treaty of Peace between the Arab Republic of Egypt and the State of Israel*, 26 March 1979. Washington: US Department of State, Bureau of Public Affairs, 1979.

tations is clear, but each side hoped that time would eventually work for its view. The Egyptian side hoped that the internal dynamic created with the establishment of a self-governing authority in the West Bank and Gaza, coupled with international pressure, would force Israel to recognize a sovereign Palestinian state (or one with a federative tie with Jordan). On the other hand, the Israeli leadership hoped that during the transition it would be able to so entrench the Israeli presence in these territories that political control would have to remain in its hands. In other words, Israel hoped to exchange control of Sinai for greater Israeli control over the West Bank, an area to which the Jewish collectivity is attached by deep sentiment (see Chapter 8).

From the pinnacle of popularity it attained in March-April 1979 as a result of signing the peace treaty with Egypt, the Likud's popularity rating fell drastically, and by the middle of 1980 it seemed that in the coming elections there would probably be a change of government, with the control returning to the Left, which does not share the Likud's views regarding the territory in the West Bank. Despite the results of the polls of early 1980, the Likud won the elections, but at that period it was afraid that its whole territorial conception, upon which it based the Israeli agreement to the Camp David accord (whereby it relinquished control over the entire Sinai peninsula and accepted a peace settlement which seemed to carry a high price tag) would collapse. From that time on, the government began acting differently. But to understand the processes involved, we must analyze an additional phenomenon within the Israeli sociopolitical system.

### GUSH EMUNIM: FROM SETTLERS TO INHERITORS*

Gush Emunim came onto the Israeli political map on 26 July 1974, when a group of about a hundred people, accompanied by about 2,500 supporters, camped in an old railroad station—Sebastia—in an area densely populated by Arabs and considerably beyond the territory the Allon Plan had envisioned for Jewish settlement. After three days of deliberation, the government decided to forcibly evacuate the place (which by then had been renamed *Elon Moreh*

*This analysis is based mainly on Raanan (1980), Sprinzak (1981), O'Dea (1978), and conversations with Gideon Aran, who prepared a Ph.D. thesis on this subject at the Hebrew University.

in Hebrew). The settlers offered passive resistance. During 1975 the members of Gush Emunim tried on five occasions to return, but the military government again and again evicted them. They tried again on the festival of Hanukkah at the end of 1976, accompanied by about 2,000 supporters. This time there were also voices of support from the activist left and from a number of Jewish leaders throughout the world. The government negotiated with the settlers, and reached a compromise under which thirty families, including about fifty children, plus another twenty singles were transferred to a nearby army base. There they began building a settlement, using private funding. In May 1977, Prime Minister Begin visited the base and announced that "there will be many more Elon Morehs." But the establishment of the settlement was delayed (meanwhile the government had begun its peace talks with Egypt), and the group again began a series of protest actions. In June 1979 the government resolved to establish a permanent settlement in a nearby area, but a number of local residents appealed to the Supreme Court, claiming that parts of the settlement would be located on their land. The Supreme Court restricted itself to deciding if the location of the settlement was based on security considerations or was politically motivated.* The Court decided that the site selection was politically motivated and ordered the area evacuated within thirty days. A short while later the settlement was moved to another location. Elon Moreh was the symbol for the struggle of Gush Emunim to change the map of Israeli presence on the West Bank, and, since 1977 a total of thirty-three settlements, which the settlers refer to as *hitnahluyot* ("inheritances"), have been set up. The establishment of another forty-four settlements in the area is planned by the middle of 1981 (either close to or within areas densely populated by Arabs), with a total of about 25,000 Jewish residents (*Haaretz*, 2/2/81). Not all these settlements belong to the Gush Emunim (the *Amana* settlement movement), but Gush Emunim is

---

*According to the Hague Convention, a conquering power is forbidden to make any changes in captured territory prior to the signing of a peace treaty except for security reasons. Israel claimed that the various settlements served its defense needs, but in this case the Court ruled against it. (As regards the West Bank, Israel does not consider itself a conquering power because it did not recognize the legitimacy of the annexation of the West Bank by Jordan.)

clearly the driving force in this settlement process and in applying political pressure.

## WHAT IS GUSH EMUNIM?

The Gush Emunim movement began its development in the 1950s within a Jerusalem *yeshiva* (a senior institution for Jewish studies)— Merkaz Harav—which belonged to the Zionist-Nationalist wing of the religious sector. The students, on the whole, came from established middle-class families, and they sensed a dissonance between their religious commitment and their elite family backgrounds. In Israeli society, in spite of its many religious elements (see Chapter 7), the major social decisions were made by people who were secularists. While there were religious political parties (the Zionist Mizrahi and non-Zionist Agudat Israel), they concerned themselves primarily with maintaining the religious sector and meeting its needs. They usually did not become involved in other political questions dealing with foreign policy or internal affairs. Thus the religious sector remained on the periphery of the society, which deeply affected the national-religious middle-class youth.

The first important step by this group to enter the mainstream was to serve in the Israeli army. Defense and service in the armed forces are central components of Israeli society (see Horowitz and Kimmerling, 1974), and combining military service, primarily in the elite forces (paratroopers and armor), with Talmudic studies kept the group together while bringing it into a more central place in Israeli society (see Kimmerling, 1979a). Military service also gave the group organizational skills, contact with the subculture of non-religious Israeli youth, experience in handling the mass media, etc. which would later be useful in its political struggle (see Raanan, 1980 and Sprinzak, 1981). This step was taken at about the same time as the encounter of the Israelis with Judea and Samaria. If this confrontation was a shock to the secular population of Israel, for the religious population it was "divine guidance." They summoned up all the references in Jewish religious literature to the sanctity of the land and the responsibility of Jews to redeem it and safeguard it from non-Jews. With the active pressure of Gush Emunim (led by a group of rabbis headed by the dean of the Merkaz

Harav yeshiva) the Israeli political system became mired in theological arguments which paralyzed its ability to make decisions.

As a result of the 1973 War, Gush Emunim became a political force independent of the National Religious Party, under whose aegis it had operated since 1967. It emerged as part of a general protest against what was perceived as the failure of the political leadership to foresee the coordinated Arab attack on Israel and to lead the nation in a time of crisis. Also contributing to the formation of Gush Emunim was the new balance of forces revealed in the 1973 War, which brought about a reevaluation by most of the community in Israel of Israel's capacity to retain the land conquered in 1967 (see below). Gush Emunim reacted along two planes: (1) ideological and (2) political.

On the ideological plane, it formulated a policy which stressed that no land should be surrendered within the boundaries of the land promised to Abraham ("from the River Euphrates ... in the north to the river of Egypt [the Nile] in the south, and from the Great [Mediterranean] Sea in the west to the desert in the east"). While the Jewish religion has never had universal agreement on the validity of these boundaries or the time period in which they will be achieved, the leaders of Gush Emunim (and some of the leaders of the National Religious Party) translated these verses to political demands in the here and now (Raanan, 1980:81). Even more, they saw the unity of the land as part of the unity of the cosmic order, and a necessary condition for the final redemption, while most others saw Israel as acquiring these lands as a result of the final redemption. Thus surrendering any land became a violation of religious law, while preventing the surrender of land became a religious commandment, which completely ignored the realities of the political situation and relied on the hope that somehow all the problems could be solved by some miracle. The escape from reality was accompanied by a rejection of Western culture, which was blamed for the Holocaust and all the Israeli troubles, including the pressures for Israel to retreat from the occupied territories. The immediate Arab environment was seen in xenophobic terms, including rejection and hatred.

On the political plane, the members of Gush Emunim began to "create facts" of Jewish presence in areas of the West Bank—primarily in those areas with a dense Arab population where they feared land might be returned under the Allon Plan. This followed the classic Zionist practice of pioneering settlements, used in setting up the Jewish quarter of Kiryat Arba near Hebron. As in the case of Hebron, the Jewish community found it difficult to withstand pressures from such settlements.

Thus from 1977 there was a combination of (1) a nationalistic right-wing government, with a reservoir of populist supporters, which annulled the settlement policies of the left, and (2) a messianic religious group which was rapidly becoming politicized, and which had adopted the tactics of the Zionist left and the central symbols of pioneering, asceticism, and settlement in an openly conflictual context. This combination brought about a marked pioneering movement in the occupied territories. It was no longer referred to as settlement, however, but rather as *hitnahlut*, with the implication that this was a form of "inheriting" the land in accord with the divine promise made to the Children of Israel. This new terminology was soon widely accepted and became part of the standard political lexicon.*

"PEACE NOW"

A political group which was formed immediately after the visit of President Sadat to Jerusalem and the beginning of peace negotiations between Egypt and Israel was the Peace Now movement. Its leaders and activists were very similar in background to those of Gush Emunim—that is, young men and women of the middle class and upper middle class elite, most of whom were academics, college students, and officers in the Israeli army reserve who had served in elite units in the 1973 War. They began organizing after the publication of an open letter from a number of reserve officers to the Prime Minister which demanded that the territory conquered by Israel in 1967 be returned for the sake of peace. Their motto was "Peace [*shalom*] is preferable to the whole [*shelema*] of Israel."

Within a short time this group was able to bring out tens of thousands of people for demonstrations of unprecedented size in

---

*Gush Emunim was a major participant in the movement for halting the withdrawal from Sinai, and in the violent clashes with the authorities during the evacuation of the settlements of Raffah Approaches and the town of Yamit in March-April 1982.

Israel, which were a counterbalance to the pressure of Gush Emunim and the other political extremists. Peace Now saw itself as a continuation of protest groups which had emerged as a result of the 1973 War and had brought about the resignation of Golda Meir. The program of Peace Now was phrased in vague terms so that it could attract all the dovish elements in the country, and it took no stand whatsoever on two central issues of the Arab-Israeli dispute: control over East Jerusalem and recognition of the Palestine Liberation Organization (PLO). After the signing of the peace treaty with Egypt in 1979, the activities of Peace Now died down to a large extent, and by the 1981 elections its leaders were split up among several political parties. Peace Now's activities were renewed during the Lebanese war of 1982, demanding the immediate withdrawal of the Israeli armed forces from Lebanon.

PUBLIC OPINION

A detailed breakdown of Israeli attitudes concerning territorial concessions from 1968 to 1979 is provided in Figure 6.1, from which four broad generalizations can be drawn. (1) In general, there was a tendency not to return the land conquered in 1967. Those who wished to return *all* the territories were always a distinct minority in comparison to those who wished to return only part or none of the territories. (2) Public opinion made differentiations between territories. Thus, for example, while only one percent was willing (in February 1968) to return the Golan Heights in exchange for peace, 41 percent was willing to return the Sinai peninsula. (3) Public opinion was subject to extremely sharp swings. Thus, for example, while only 6 percent of the population was willing to return the whole of Sinai in July 1973, 60 percent was willing to do so in November 1977—a dramatic change by any measure! (4) There was a tendency to be more willing to return territories (on a selective basis) as time went on.

This increasing willingness to return territory stemmed primarily from (a) the 1973 War and (b) the visit of President Sadat to Jerusalem, where he announced his readiness to make peace with Israel. Several turning points are evident in Figure 6.1. Immediately after the Six-Day War (1968), a substantial minority of the people were ready to return the territory in the Sinai, while keeping the

Figure 6.1

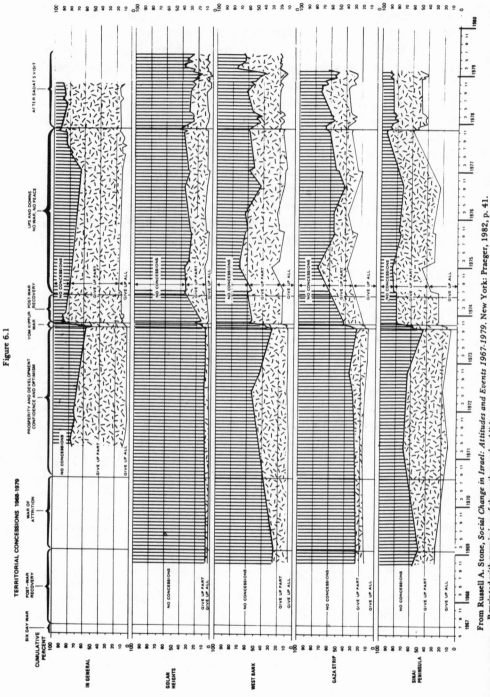

From Russell A. Stone, *Social Change in Israel: Attitudes and Events 1967-1979.* New York: Praeger, 1982, p. 41.

other areas. When it was seen that peace was not a realistic hope, this readiness declined. At all times thereafter (except July 1973), however, there was readiness by most of the population to return all or part of the Sinai peninsula. As a result of the 1973 War, those who stated that none of the West Bank should be returned declined from 67 to 42 percent, while those who were willing to return the entire West Bank went up from 8 to 18 percent. This tendency continued, so that by February 1975 those wholly opposed had decreased to less than a third of the population. But the percentage favoring no return went up again, reaching 57 percent by September 1976.

The visit of President Sadat did not change public opinion in regard to the West Bank and the Golan Heights: Egypt's readiness to make peace with Israel changed only the feelings about the Sinai peninsula. There was least change of position in regard to the Golan Heights. Up to the 1973 War, 90 percent of the population believed that nothing should be returned. As a result of the war there was a moderate increase in those favoring partial return, with those believing that nothing should be given back ranging from 65 to 75 percent. As for the West Bank, there was always a sizable element which believed in selective annexation.

How can these changes in public opinion best be explained? After the 1967 War, when Israel had won a decisive victory, it did not appear to be logical to forego any territories. Not only was the cost of keeping them low and the gains to be derived from keeping them obvious (as time went on, becoming even more evident)* but also Arab behavior, as expressed in the Khartoum Declaration,† offered no incentive for Israeli concessions. Figure 6.1 shows the lack of national consensus as regards Israeli control of the West Bank, the "holy places," the "original homeland," etc. The readiness to make territorial concessions varied among the members of the different Israeli governments (including that of the Likud), which had a significant impact on the national consensus, since public opinion is influenced to a great extent by the messages the government

---

*As detailed at the beginning of this chapter.

†In September 1967 the leaders of the Arab world, meeting in Khartoum on the invitation of President Nasser, resolved "three noes": "no peace, no negotiations, and no recognition of Israel."

transmits to the populace—both direct (declared policy) and indirect (the decisiveness of policy and the extent of agreement within the government). But it is difficult to make a sharp differentiation between public opinion and the opinion of the government because, to a large extent, they are exposed to the same reality and share the same basic values.

CHANGES IN TERRITORIAL POLICY: 1979-1982

For the first two years, the new regime which came to power in 1977 acted in quite a different manner than had been expected. It negotiated a peace treaty with Egypt and signed an agreement for complete withdrawal from the Sinai peninsula. In this agreement it also recognized that the Palestinians have "rights" (without defining what these rights are)—a basic change in some of the components of the Arab-Israeli territorial conflict. But the regime did not make any concessions which would hinder efforts to increase Israeli control over the territories of Judea and Samaria. To some extent as a result of the pressure of Gush Emunim and in reaction to changes in Israeli public opinion, but primarily because it believed that its time was running out, the Likud government moved rapidly to create facts of Israeli presence in the territories which would make it more difficult to withdraw from parts of "the whole Israel" and perhaps prevent any implementation of the Allon Plan (see map, p. 240). What were the main points of these actions?

First, there was a drastic change in priorities in order to strengthen Jewish presence on the West Bank. An estimated 8 percent of the 1980-81 national budget was allocated for the maintenance and development of hitnahluyot,* but if one adds the supports not included in the budget, such as tax exemptions for those living in development regions, the salaries of government workers who deal primarily with the settlement of these areas, subsidies for transportation, etc., this figure rises to 12 to 15 percent of the national budget (excluding interest on loans and military expenditures, which represent about half the total budget), and probably even higher. The fact that this amount was spent at a time of economic crisis during which cuts were made in welfare services shows that the government was willing to bear the political costs of allocating major

*See Zvi Shuldiner, "The Real Cost of the Hitnahlut," Haaretz, 7/25/80.

resources for aims on which there was no public consensus. In Jerusalem and other places in November 1979, there were demonstrations demanding that funds be allocated for meeting social problems (primarily a shortage of housing for young couples) instead of investing them in the hitnahluyot.*

Second, there were drastic changes in policy in regard to retaining control over the territory of the West Bank. Lands which had belonged to the government of Jordan were seized. The area of these lands was about 700,000 dunams, or one-eighth of the area of the West Bank.† Apart from these lands registered in the name of the Jordanian government, up to 1967 only about one-half of the rest of the territory had been legally registered. The remaining land was available for bargaining between the government and individuals because proving ownership was very difficult in most cases. In addition, about half the land legally registered was registered to absentee owners, and its administration had been transferred to custodians. Much of this land, primarily of that classified as belonging to the government, was awarded to the hitnahluyot. Between October 1980 and February 1981, 20,605 dunams of land were seized for this purpose (*Haaretz*, 2/26/81). Until 1979 only large tracts had been taken, creating a certain territorial continuity, but from then on any land which could be obtained was seized, even if it was surrounded by land under private Arab or communal Arab ownership, and an attempt was made to demonstrate presence on it (*Haaretz*, 2/11/81).

Third, beginning in March 1981, some hitnahluyot were awarded the status of local authorities, and courts were established in some of them. Based on the traditions of Mandatory Palestine, local authorities have considerable authority over local matters, and some of the *mitnahlim* (lit., "inheritors"—the settlers in the hitnahluyot) tended to interpret this as partial Israeli sovereignty over those areas under their control.**

*See *Haaretz*, 11/23/79. In response, the government tried to combine social needs with its ideological aims by offering extremely cheap housing in the West Bank (*Haaretz*, 9/14/79), but the demand for housing was greatest in settlements near the cease-fire lines of 1948/49, which were seen as safest from return to Arab control.

†See *Haaretz*, 10/26/79; based on research by Arie Eliav.

**Yehuda Litani, "The Territories Have Already Been Annexed,"*Haaretz*, 3/8/81.

At the same time, something quite different occurred which could have major implications for the future. As a result of the peace treaty with Egypt, the government was forced to take down Israeli settlements which had been set up in Sinai, along the entire Gulf of Aqaba (to Sharm-el-Sheik), and in the Raffah area. These settlements were not closed down without serious internal strife among the settlers and their supporters. Those settlers who were evacuated were granted compensation exceeding the real value of their property,* which made them accept the evacuation without a major political struggle. However, this evacuation had far-reaching significance—for the first time in the history of Jewish settlement, Jewish presence was seen to be reversible. One assumes that the students of the school of Jabotinsky, who did not see settlement as the practical expression of Zionism, found it far less difficult to take such a step than did the members of the Labor parties. A precedent was created which puts into question the effectiveness of the Israeli government's efforts in this period to bolster Jewish presence on the West Bank.

Fourth, in the beginning of 1982 the Israeli government asserted the extension of Israeli rule over the Golan Heights, which meant the annexation of the area to Israel. The main reasons for this step and its timing seem to have been: (a) it was the last stage of the withdrawal from Sinai, and the unprecedented evacuation of the Israeli settlements (especially the towns of Yamit) created a more favorable international atmosphere for such an action. (b) the Likud government needed to demonstrate to its constituency that it had not betrayed the hard line in the Jewish-Arab conflict; (c) there was relatively high public support for the Golan Heights annexation (as indicated in Figure 6.1 above). The only real opposition to the annexation came from the sparse Druse population of the area (about 8,000 people in five villages), who were primarily concerned about

---

*The high rate of compensation was intended to serve as a precedent, but in the event the next government wishes to evacuate settlers, it will not be able to afford to do so, because the Sinai peninsula and the Gaza Strip included a few hundred families, while the West Bank includes thousands of families who have become mitnahlim. The compensation for the territories evacuated at this point is equal to about half of what Israel is spending on welfare! It has aroused great anger and stirred public debate, and those leaving the settlements have been labelled "peace profiteers" (see *Haaretz*, 12/23/80).

their possible compulsory enrollment in the Israeli armed forces and the confiscation of their lands and water sources for new Jewish settlements.

SUMMARY

In the relatively short period of time between 1967 and 1982, a great number of very dramatic changes occurred in the territorial context of the Arab-Israeli conflict. The Israelis acquired control over vast new areas of land, some of which were densely populated and others of which were desolate. At the beginning of this period it was hoped that it would be possible to convert most of these territories in exchange for recognition of the legitimacy of the State of Israel by the Arabs—to trade land for peace. As these hopes dwindled, the readiness to give up these lands decreased—especially those areas for which there were strong sentiments derived from Jewish mythology and Zionist ideology. Because these sentiments were strong from the very beginning with respect to Old Jerusalem, it was annexed immediately by Israel.

But the conquest of these new lands stirred up a dispute in Israel in regard to their degree of frontierity—i.e., the degree to which they were a resource for territorial expansion. Taking into account the political constraints, to what degree could control of these lands be increased by adding a settlement presence and ownership (public and/or private) to the military presence, so that thereafter sovereignty could be imposed upon them? The major obstacle to Jewish control over these territories was the dense Arab population in the West Bank and Gaza Strip. The dispute about the degree of frontierity of these lands to some extent broke down the national consensus which had existed in regard to the management of the Arab-Israeli conflict, but there was general agreement concerning the strategic-defensive value of these territories.

As a result of the 1973 War, the Arabs' opposition to Israel's continued occupation of these territories was strengthened, and they were prepared to pay a high price to gain control of these lands, which meant that Israel might have to pay a high price to retain them. The cost-benefit balance of keeping these territories was no longer so favorable for the Israelis. In response to the Egyptian readiness to exchange peace and recognition of Israel for territory, the Israeli government tried a different approach: to obtain peace and recognition by exchanging territory (the Sinai) for territory (continued control over the West Bank). In the process, it was willing to create a precedent of the reversibility of settlement presence.

Considerable quantities of land on the West Bank passed to Israeli control, but it is very difficult to determine how much was involved. Based on an estimate by the government of Jordan of February 1979, 27.3 percent of the lands of the West Bank passed to Israeli control,* but this appears to be highly exaggerated and includes the area of Jerusalem annexed by Israel.

With this background, factional rivalries in Israel were intensified. A radical, fundamentalist group—Gush Emunim—appeared which was largely divorced from political reality and rejected the values of Western culture. In its efforts to strengthen Jewish control over territory, it managed to move the entire system to a certain extent in its direction. As a result of its initiative, and with the economic and political support of the government, the extent of control in the occupied territories was raised considerably by means of presence, and the new area began to become more and more regarded as a frontier.

From June 1982, following the Lebanese War, the prestige as well as the effective social and political control of the PLO collapsed in the West Bank. One of the consequences is that large tracts of land which were frozen have begun to be sold by Arab owners, mainly to private investors. The frontierity of the West Bank has risen sharply, and many private land purchasing and development companies have begun to supply large settlement projects in the area, competing with the governmental projects. They promise housing and a high quality of life, not far from the metropolitan centers, at relatively low prices. According to some estimates, by the end of 1982 about 200,000 dunams will have been purchased or expropriated by governmental agencies, and an additional 20,000 to 100,000 dunams by private investors (*Haaretz*, 12/17/82).

But the struggle within the Jewish community in these matters is far from decided, and it is possible that it will only be decided as a result of the intervention of external forces.

---

*See "Research Material," *Journal of Palestine Studies* 32: 95. In testimony before a committee of the U.S. Congress, the estimate was even higher, and was set at about one-third of the land of the West Bank (Ruedy, 1978).

# Part II

# POLITICAL CULTURE AND IDEOLOGY

# 6

## Ideological Dimensions

### *Dan Horowitz* and *Moshe Lissak*

In the study of the Zionist movement and
the Yishuv, it is common to overemphasize
the importance of ideological debates and
of changes occurring over the years in the
ideological positions of the various Zionist
parties and movements. Thus, there is a
tendency to reduce the history of Zionism
to an account of the realization of ideology
and tension between imperatives of ideology and the limitations imposed by reality.
Although this approach results in a lop-
sided image of the history of Zionism, it
is accurate in that it reflects the central
position of ideology in the consciousness
of the political elite of the Yishuv. The
history of the Yishuv was indeed marked
by intensive ideological controversies and
debates, and idealistically inspired attitudes
were actually conceived as legitimate criteria to assess the success or failure of
political and social endeavors.

The preoccupation with ideological issues and controversies is related to the fact
that the Yishuv as a society with its own
distinct collective identity arose out of an
ideological impulse. Zionist immigration to
Palestine was propelled by ideolog'cal motivation. The tendency of the Yishuv to
segregate itself to the point where it became an autonomous social entity also
arose out of ideological imperatives. Even
the common cultural basis of the Yishuv

Reprinted from Dan Horowitz and Moshe Lissak,
*The Origins of the Israeli Polity,* Chicago, The
University of Chicago Press, 1978, pp. 120-56.
©The University of Chicago.

—the Hebrew language—emerged as a modern spoken language not through a gradual process of evolution, but through a deliberate process of cultivation itself ideologically motivated. One definition of ideology states it is a set of "ideas by which men posit, explain, and justify ends and means of organized social action with the aim to preserve, amend, uproot or rebuild a given reality."[1] If we accept this definition, then the uniqueness of the Yishuv lies in that the fact that its very existence was the outcome of "organized social action" aimed at a deliberate transformation of reality.

This approach can also clarify the relation between ideology and the institutional organization of the Yishuv. For the most part, this organization was not the product of the social and historical heritage of an established community, but the outcome of conscious action on the part of different movements which joined on a common ideological basis. The most comprehensive ideological framework was the concept of "Zionism" in its broadest sense: the drive to establish a national center for the Jewish people in the Land of Israel through a process of immigration and settlement, and to form an autonomous community possessing its own political and cultural distinctiveness. Beyond this broad consensus, Zionism split into a number of political and ideological movements which differed from one another regarding "minimalist" or "maximalist" approaches, different visions of the new Jewish society to be created, and different views about the appropriate means for the realization of Zionist goals. The fact that the fulfillment of Zionism depended upon the construction of a new society made Zionism an ideology of radical change, although its adherents included conservatives. It also explains the importance of ideological factors in determining the balance of political forces in the Yishuv and the extent to which different groups in the Yishuv could be considered as central or peripheral.

This connection may be further elaborated by applying the distinction between two dimensions of ideology, the fundamental and the operative. The fundamental dimension refers to the principles which determine the final goals and grand vistas in which the ideology is to be realized, while the operative dimension concerns the principles which guide concrete political action.[2] The creation of a new society from its very foundations could not possibly have been guided by an ideology which placed one-sided emphasis on the fundamental dimension. In this respect Zionism differed from Messianic movements in Jewish history which possessed the characteristics of millenarian movements.[3] Zionism, unlike such movements, was modern from its inception and placed a strong emphasis on the operative side. In fact, the New Yishuv owes its origins to the Hovevei Zion (Lovers of Zion) movement in Russia, whose major aim was to found Jewish agricultural colonies in Palestine without being concerned with the political dimension of Jewish independence. On the other hand, the operative dimension alone could not provide enough motivation to inspire immigration to Palestine, or to withstand the austere and difficult conditions of the pioneering way of life. In circumstances such as these, political success could be achieved only by those movements that possessed the capacity to develop a balanced ideology that did not put too much emphasis on either the fundamental or the operative dimensions. The impact on the emerging society of the Yishuv of the various ideological movements in Zionism was determined by their ideological orientations toward some fundamental attributes of social order and social action.

## Ideological Orientations

The first of these fundamental attributes of ideology was the relation to *time*,[4] of which there were three major aspects: the attitude toward past, present, and future; the appropriate tempo of change in the context of social action; and the perception of timing.

The attitude toward past, present, and future was related to the problem of historical continuity, i.e., the extent to which each variation of Zionist ideology called for a break with the past or, on the contrary, rested on traditional legitimacy. The notions past, present, and future were also related to innovative or conservative orientations in ideologically inspired action. The combination of a break with the past and a demand for change is readily perceived as consistent, but it is also conceivable that a fundamental perspective resting on traditional legitimacy would have operative goals calling for change in certain spheres. Such a combination, for example, characterized the religious Zionist movement which sought to preserve the continuity of Jewish tradition, yet advocated such innovative endeavors as immigration and settlement in Palestine, which undoubtedly required a substantial future orientation.

By its very nature, Zionist ideology in all its variations implied a considerable emphasis on an active future orientation, since it called for the creation of a new political and social system in the future. Moreover, it emphasized activity in the present to prepare the way for the establishment of an autonomous Jewish society that would fulfill national, and perhaps even social aspirations in the future. The active future orientation was particularly apparent in the ideology of the Zionist Labor movement, which included both a departure from traditions associated with the Jewish past and a pronounced accent on promoting innovations in the present to determine the shape of the future. It should be noted that within the Labor movement there were disagreements concerning the degree of emphasis on a future orientation. However, even among the more radical component of the Labor movement, a degree of ambivalence toward the past could be discerned. For example, David Ben-Gurion shared many of the sentiments of the school of thought which developed a strongly negative evaluation of Jewish existence in the Diaspora; he was a bitter opponent of Yiddish and among the early advocates of the exclusive use of Hebrew. But he frequently employed symbols drawn from the more distant Biblical past which he associated with Jewish sovereignty in the Land of Israel.[5]

It was religious Zionism that faced the most fundamental problems in confronting the issue of a future orientation. The non-Zionist ultraorthodox circles subjected religious Zionism to intense criticism, charging that it was "forcing the end" or attempting to interfere in the "divinely ordained process of history."[6] According to the traditional conception strictly adhered to by the ultraorthodox, redemption will occur only with the coming of the Messiah. The religious Zionists replied that the modern "return to Zion" was actually the "beginning" of the period of redemption mentioned in traditional sources. This mixture of modernism and Messianism notwithstanding, religious Zionists continued to urge strict observance of the traditional religious way of life; the traditional legitimation was the basis of their Zionist activity. The non-Zionist ultraorthodox circles were in a better position to perceive the inevitable contradiction between participation in a basically secular nationalist movement and consistent observance of the traditional Jewish way of life.

In any case, insofar as ideological controversies within the Zionist movement were concerned (as opposed to those between Zionism and other ideological trends within Jewry), the core of the dispute in respect to the future was not the national question, but the shape of the Jewish society in Palestine. The Labor movement was unique in its comprehensive future orientation that called both for national and social change.

The various ideological movements within Zionism also differed in their conceptions about the pace or tempo of the changes each ideology desired. The problem of the pace of change is twofold: (a) does an ideology call for slow or rapid change; and (b) is change perceived as a gradual process or as something to be accomplished by the revolutionary approach of alternating rapid radical change and slower development? A revolutionary ideology emphasizes not the "average" rate of change but the "variance" in the rate of change.

The rate of change is also related to the time range of concrete political objectives. The debate in the Zionist movement on the definition of the "final goal" of Zionism reflected these problems. The Labor movement identified with the moderate approach of Chaim Weizmann, who opposed the definition of the final goal before political conditions were sufficiently ripe, whereas the Revisionists called for immediate definition of the final goal.[7] The decision to refrain from defining the final goal implied a willingness to accept slow and gradual progress while the realization of the more far-reaching goals of Zionist colonization were deferred until a distant future time.

Adherence to a policy of selective immigration and willingness to accept a slower rate of demographic growth for the Yishuv because of the limits of the country's economic absorptive capacity were consistent with the perception of Jewish colonization as an extended and gradual process. The Labor movement shared this gradual approach with the proponents of "practical Zionism" among the Ezrahim.[8] This approach of "one more acre, one more goat" was viewed with intense aversion by the Revisionists, as they advocated rapid change and revolutionary measures. The tendency to speed up the pace of development was reflected in the ideas of "transfer" or "evacuation," which called for the rapid immigration of hundreds of thousands of Jews from Europe in the shortest possible time.[9] The desire for revolutionary action to effect immediate change of the Palestine regime was expressed in the strong emphasis the Revisionists placed on the political and legalistic aspects of international recognition of the Jewish national home. This was in effect an extension of the Herzlian concept of "charter," which implied immediate action to establish a Jewish government in Palestine even before the emergence of an economic, demographic, and ecological infrastructure.[10]

The tendency of the Labor movement to strive for a gradual realization of objectives dictated by ideology applied not only to the national political sphere but also to the social sphere. This tendency was particularly evident among members of Hapoel Hatzair, who objected to the term "socialism" mainly because it appeared to them too grandiose, and an ultimate goal relevant only to the distant future.[11] The idea of socialism could not, they felt, serve as the basis of immediate objectives of the Labor movement in Palestine. Ahdut Ha'avoda's position was more ambitious, but the major ideologists of the party, in particular Berl Katznelson and Yitzhak Tabenkin, did not welcome the slogan coined by the Labor Brigade about an all-inclusive "workers' commune." Instead Ahdut Ha'avoda adopted "constructivist socialism," which implied the creation of a socialist workers' society through the gradual construction from the ground up of a workers' economy with the aid of national capital.[12] This gradual, constructivist approach to a large extent paralleled the constructivist approach of "practical Zionism." A different approach to the problem of pace was that of the left-wing Zionist movement. Hashomer Hatzair developed the doctrine of "stages," which called for gradual constructivism in the first stage to prepare for a second stage of radical revolutionary action. This approach was criticized for urging one "to act like Ahdut Ha'avoda while speaking of the future like the left wing of the Labor Brigade."[13]

The question of the pace of development was closely related to the question of timing of initiatives in political, economic, and other spheres. The question of timing in processes of social change in general, and in modernization in developing countries in particular, is essentially the question of synchronization of differential rates of development in various spheres.[14] The accumulated experience of social change in developed as well as developing countries indicates that there is no particular social institution whose rate of development exclusively determines the rate of development in other social institutions. This experience invalidates to a considerable extent the conception of an inevitable "spillover" of economic and technological change to the sphere of political development. Predictions based on this conception —which was rooted originally in Marxism, but has had a strong impact on recent functionalist theories of modernization and European integration—proved erroneous, mainly due to lags in the rate of development in different spheres.[15] It now seems evident that the different institutional spheres do not act in conformity with the economic-technological sphere that was once perceived as the "leading sector." Newer conceptions of social change generally attribute greater importance to the persisting influence of historical traditions, political structures, and cultural factors in speeding or slowing development.

However, in the case of the Yishuv, the impact of developmental lags originating in a lack of balance between institutional spheres at the outset of the development process was limited due to the absence of rigid traditions of premodern social and political patterns of organization. Thus the pace of Jewish nation-building in Palestine was subject to a considerable degree of ideologically directed control, and the problem of synchronization could be translated into operational concepts of timing. Policy decisions and institutional initiatives could be timed according to the image of the future held by political elites.

From this perspective the most important ideological controversy focused on the question of a balanced rate of development between the political sphere and the demographic and economic spheres. The major protagonists were the "practical Zionists," who focused on immigration and settlement, and the "political Zionists," who sought above all else progress toward political autonomy in Palestine. Even within "practical Zionism" the problem of balanced development arose between the rate of demographic growth determined by immigration and the rate of economic development measured by what was termed the "economic absorptive capacity of the country." The First Immigration, identified mainly with the Lovers of Zion movement, laid the foundations of "practical Zionism" in its most extreme sense. Later expressions, such as the colonization policies of Dr. Arthur Ruppin, articulated the same conception, i.e., that the development of the Yishuv was determined primarily by economic and settlement development. The opposing idea of "political Zionism" was authored by Herzl, but its most ardent advocates were Max Nordau and Vladimir Jabotinsky. They viewed the political sphere as the "leading sector" which would prepare a short cut in economic and settlement development. Jabotinsky, therefore, refused to scale down or obscure the ultimate goals of Zionism for reasons of political timing. He rejected the contention that it was useless to make demands that were not backed up by the demographic and economic assets of the Yishuv.[16]

A conception favoring a balance between spheres of development emerged in Weizmann's "synthetic Zionism," adopted by various Zionist circles, including the majority of the Labor movement. This concept implied not only parallel political and settlement development, but also mutual reinforcement between the two spheres. Ben-Gurion's preference for balance expressed itself in his tendency to subject the timing of adopting new objectives to the requirements of political strategy. For example, he opposed raising the demand for a Jewish state in the early 1930s[17] but supported partition in 1937; formulated the Biltmore Program calling for a Jewish state in all of Palestine in 1942; and in 1946 pressed for a formula which implied a renewed acceptance of partition. The ideology of "synthetic Zionism," sensitive to the requirements of synchronization in political and settlement activities, enabled the Zionist leadership to translate national political objectives into practical imperatives aimed at the balanced construction of economic, social, and political institutions. In this way, a realistic order of priorities was created which prevented the conversion of Zionist goals into a utopia.

This approach was alien to the Revisionist spirit. The point of departure for the Revisionist leaders was the political ideal and not the realities of economics, settlement, and immigration. The Revisionists and most of the other non-Labor Zionists were also opposed to the concept of simultaneous realization of national political objectives and social objectives inherent in the ideology of constructivist socialism. They contended that the struggle over the nature of the future Jewish society in Palestine should be postponed until the national political aims of Zionism were fulfilled. Paradoxically, this position paralleled the one adopted by the "orthodox" Marxist wing of Zionism represented by the left Poalei Zion party, which maintained that the emergent Jewish society would inevitably be capitalist and the transition to socialism should be achieved in the future by means of class struggle.[18]

However, the majority in the Labor movement aspired at a synthesis between action for the good of the workers and action for the benefit of the entire Yishuv. Thus the majority adopted a conception of the synchronized development of Zionism and socialism through colonization. The adoption of this concept and the attempts at its realization gave the Labor movement a strategic advantage. The Labor movement's political strategy in internal struggles—which combined the presentation of political demands to the national center with institution-building activities and the mobilization of political support—corresponded to the strategy of "synthetic Zionism" in the external struggles of the Yishuv.

Active and Passive Perceptions of
Man-Environment Relations

The various perceptions of history and of time as a factor in social action are related to another fundamental dilemma by which we may distinguish different belief systems: the difference between active and passive perceptions of man's relation to his social and natural environment. For example, a future orientation and a perception of controllable time are both compatible with an active attitude to the environment. Zionism intrinsically possessed the active orientation implied in the basic notion of "autoemancipation," but among the ideological trends within Zionism, there were different perceptions of the range of man's freedom to change his environment and mold his future through voluntary action. The question was which social and natural limitations were perceived as obstacles to be overcome and which were perceived as permanent constraints which man cannot challenge.

The distinction between active and passive relation to the environment did not correspond with the division between left and right in the Zionist movement. Thus both the Labor movement and the Revisionists manifested a dynamic, active approach to reality, while the more conservative part of the Ezrahim manifested a more passive approach. A characteristic expression of the active approach was the attitude of the "pioneering" sector of the Yishuv to opinions and forecasts of experts who cast doubt on the ability of the Zionist movement to overcome obstacles in economic development and settlement, and later, during the War of Independence, in the military sphere as well. The standard ideological response to the pessimistic emphasis on limitations of "economic absoptive capacity" was that it was possible to overcome such obstacles by sheer will power derived from high levels of motivation and identification with collective goals. In other words, the perception inherent in the notion of "pioneering" (halutziut) upheld the possibility of evolving forces within man that could enable him to prevail over seemingly insurmountable obstacles.

Another expression of the faith in voluntary action was the emphasis placed on the qualitative human factor as a counterweight to the chronic shortage of resources of manpower, land, capital, and even weapons and equipment in times of war. The constant repetition of Herzl's saying "If you will it, it is no dream" became part of the indoctrination process that enabled a numerically small community of settlers—at first thousands, later tens of thousands, never exceeding several hundreds of thousands—to have faith in the ability of few pioneers to act as a vanguard preparing the way for millions. This perception was apparent in the ideology of the BILU movement[19] of the First Immigration and was revived on a wider scale at the beginning of the Second Immigration. Some of its most outstanding expressions in later periods were in the ideology of the Labor Brigade in the Labor movement and the Brit Habiryonim among the Revisionists.[20] Nevertheless, there was a difference between the Revisionist variant of activism and the "pioneering" variant of the Labor movement. The central motifs of "pioneering" were elitism, service to the collective, asceticism, and a total commitment to goals set by ideology. But the mission-orientation of the Labor movement was translated into practical objectives which resulted in tempering the romantic-utopian components of Zionist ideology. By contrast, the symbolization of "the way of glory, romance, and death"[21] and the stress on "social austerity" made it difficult for the Revisionists to institutionalize their activist approach as the Labor movement did.[22]

In the course of various ideological controversies and especially in disputes about the "skepticism of the economists," Labor movement spokesmen, notably David Ben-Gurion, argued that "there are no 'laws' of economics."[23] This argument, however, usually referred to economic laws as generalizations depicting average "utilitarian" human behavior rather than to those expressing physical limitations stemming from an absolute deficiency of resources. The preoccupation of most Labor movement leaders with raising funds and creating appropriate organizational instruments, as well as their constructivist and gradualist approach, confirms their underlying recognition that voluntarism and activism have limitations. A practical approach of this kind was much less apparent among the Revisionists, and was conspicuously lacking in the extreme romantic wing of this movement whose major spokesmen were the poet Uri Zvi Greenberg and the historian Abba Ahimeir.[24] Their inspiration was apparent in the early ideological positions of IZL and LHI.[25]

The activist aspiration directed at changing the natural and social environment was shared only in a limited sense by the non-Labor and non-Revisionist bourgeois circles in the Yishuv. For them activism implied mainly the act of immigration and settlement, and their vision of the future Jewish society in Palestine was that of a "normal" society "like all other nations."[26] This "normalizing" approach did not demand the high levels of motivation required for mobilizing human resources beyond what appeared to be the "normal" level of other societies. The emphasis these circles placed on profitability as a cardinal criterion of investment was rooted in their assumption that the human will cannot be expected to compensate for the absence of capital or for non-profitability in competitive market economy. This approach was sharply criticized by Labor movement spokesmen, who stigmatized it as "petty bourgeois" and opposed to the virtures of pioneering. A strictly passive approach to the social environment appeared only among the non-Zionist ultraorthodox of the Old Yishuv, whose extremist wing viewed any active effort to change reality as heresy. For them, activism implied confounding the will of God, or as they put it, an "affront to Heaven." The world view that guided the extreme ultraorthodox elements was that the redemption of the Jewish people must await the advent of the Messiah; any attempt to "force the end" was heretical in essence.

Faith in man's ability to change reality through voluntary action doubtless contributed to the high motivation of those groups of people mobilized in social movements, whether these were pioneering movements or underground military organizations. This ideologically and politically committed minority succeeded in influencing the behavior of the majority in two ways. First, mainly in times of crisis, this minority acted as an avant-garde that set behavioral norms for society as a whole. Second, the pioneering minority increased the over-all capacity of the collectivity by making significant contributions through their own efforts. Phrasing our conclusions in economic terms, we may say that the high marginal increment of output contributed by the pioneering minority raised the average level of output of the community at large. And indeed the achievements of the Yishuv in the economic, military, and settlement spheres exceeded the predictions of most experts. Branches of the economy considered unprofitable eventually stabilized on a solid economic basis, and in the War of Independence military forces that were deficient in manpower and equipment frequently overcame superior forces.

However, the far-reaching conclusions sometimes presented by ideologues who idealized the supposed superiority of what Arlozoroff referred to critically as a "heroic economy" (as opposed to a "rational economy") are not substantiated by analysis of the economic data.[27] Some of the achievements attributed to high motivational levels may be explained as the result of high levels of investment of resources originating outside the system. It is also evident that faith in the power of voluntarism in the economic sphere was, in certain cases, carried to such an extreme that it was responsible for such economic practices as barren investments, deficits, and bankruptcies. In attempting to place the faith in voluntarism in its proper perspective, it is appropriate to cite the American sociologist Talcott Parsons's response to Ben-Gurion's saying that there are no laws of economics: "The fact that a piece of paper floats in the air does not mean that the laws of gravity are invalid."[28]

### Collectivistic and Individualistic Approaches

The activist approach shared by both the left and the nationalist radical right within the Zionist movement, implied a high level of commitment to ideological goals. Commitment was not a commitment to abstract values, but a sense of service and dedication to a collectivity. This type of commitment was expressed on two levels: on the fundamental level, the collectivity was the frame of reference of the ideology —"nation," "class," or both; on the operative level, it was the movement itself that embodied the goals and needs of the collectivity as interpreted by the movement elite. From this perspective, there arises another basic dichotomy, associated with that between activity and passivity but not identical with it: the choice of collectivism versus individualism.

The perception of the individual as a bearer of collective ideals whose commitment to these ideals makes him or her subordinate to their imperatives was characteristic of both the pioneering ideology and the ideology of the national radical right. In its own way each of these movements called on the individual to sacrifice private interests and to place him or herself at the disposal of a movement that purported to serve collective goals and interests. In the Labor movement, the individual was mobilized in the service of two collectivities, nation and class. The most extreme expression of this mobilization was the Labor Brigade, which sought to prevent the formation of group interests within the collective by advocating a general "commune" for all Jewish workers in Palestine.[29] Other collectivist movements recognized the existence of subunits to mediate between the individual and the collectivity— such as the *kibbutzim*, which accepted the authority of the movement's umbrella organization and extended aid when necessary to other subunits.[30] The ceremony in which new members were inducted into the Hagana also emphasized the idea of the subordination of the individual to the authority of the collective framework: new recruits were inducted with an oath of allegiance which stated that each member becomes a party to a covenant between himself and the organization "for life."[31]

The Revisionist ideology in particular was noted for its collectivistic emphasis. The constitution of the New Zionist Organization stated that "the mission of Zionism . . . has priority over the interests of the individual and the group and class."[32] Even more extreme was the LHI position. Its founder and leader, Abraham Stern ("Yair"),[33] wrote that "we have enlisted in the cause of our entire lives; only death can release us from the ranks."[34]

In contrast to this collectivistic approach, the ideology of the parties of the center such as the General Zionists called for building the land through private initiative and political organization on the basis of common interests, rather than subordination of collective ideals. This approach was advocated in the 1920s by the "Brandeis group" of American Zionists[35] and by the Ezrahim in the 1930s and 1940s, especially the Farmers Association and other organizations of the private economic sector. The contrast between the ideological orientations of the Ezrahim groups and those of the left and the radical right help to explain the tendency among the Ezrahim to focus their public activities on the municipal or local plane. While the left and the nationalist right adopted comprehensive nationwide symbols of collective solidarity, the frameworks of solidarity of the second- and third-generation settlers in the *moshavot* and urban neighborhoods founded in the First Immigration were mostly local units.

Thus in regard to the collectivism-individualism dichotomy, as in the case of the active-passive dichotomy, there was a greater resemblance between the Revisionists and the Labor movement than between either one of them and the non-Revisionist Ezrahim. This similarity, however, concerned primarily the intensity of the commitment of the individual to the collectivity and not the scope of this commitment. In regard to the scope of commitment there was a clear-cut difference between the Labor movement and the Revisionist movement. The ideology of Revisionism was marked by a purely political and national emphasis without the intrusion of other components, such as the socioeconomic component of socialism in the Labor movement. Therefore, Revisionism tended to restrict the individual's scope of commitment to the collective to activities designated to achieve political goals. The Labor movement, on the other hand, strove in various ways to enlarge the scope of the individual's commitment to the collective, extending it to the individual's entire way of life, including spheres of activity not directly connected with the attainment of political goals. Thus the difference between Revisionism and the Ezrahim was that while both saw allegiance to the nation as superior to any other group allegiance, the Ezrahim viewed the commitment deriving from this allegiance as much less intense.

The Labor movement, on the other hand, developed an ideology of dual commitment—to nation and to class. The two commitments were considered complementary, since it was maintained that the organized "working class" was also the nation's vanguard. Thus, the Labor movement came to be perceived as mediating between the collectivity, for whose ultimate good it strove, and the individual, who was summoned to place himself at the collective's service. Allegiance to the movement per se became increasingly important from the time Mapai sought to participate in the national center. Later, when Mapai expanded its political recruitment and sought support among middle-class circles and professionals, allegiance to the movement tended to become in itself a criterion of affiliation to the pioneering sector of the Yishuv, which led to a partial shift in the meaning of pioneering roles. While at the outset these roles were perceived as open to all who wished to contribute to the common effort, with the institutionalization of the movement there was an increasing tendency to condition access to these roles (which conferred elite status on their occupants) on allegiance to the movement, so that membership in some movement umbrella organization became an almost essential requirement for occupying roles that were defined as "pioneering." In sociological terms, the shift was one from a pure universalistic achievement orientation to an orientation containing ascriptive-particularistic elements.

### Territorial Boundaries and National Identity

As we have seen above, the definition of the relation of the individual to particularistic collectivities within the over-all national collectivity was a subject of controversy in the Yishuv. A firm consensus existed, however, concerning the commitment of the individual to the national collectivity, at least as far as the Zionist parties were concerned. The question then arose as to how it was possible to maintain commitment to a national collectivity whose territorial boundaries were not clearly defined. The serious implications of this question are clear when we recall that from its inception one of the points of departure for Zionist ideology was the existence of a bond between a nation and its territory. The Zionist movement was constantly engaged in disputes with movements advocating Jewish autonomy in the Diaspora over the possibility of maintaining the autonomous institutional existence of a minority group in societies which have become secularized in the wake of the industrial and national revolutions.[36] Another controversy occurred with the territorialist movement, which advocated a Jewish territorial concentration but not necessarily in the Land of Israel. Zionism responded with fundamental arguments concerning the bond between the Jewish people and the Land of Israel and operational arguments to the effect that it would not be possible to attract Jews to a land other than Israel.[37] The efforts to create a territorial concentration and a sovereign Jewish society in the Land of Israel did not solve the ideological problem of defining the territorial boundaries of the national collectivity while this process was going on. Moreover, the concept of the unity of the Jewish people itself implied a nonterritorial definition of the boundaries of the collectivity.

This contradiction between the efforts to create an identity between nationality and territory and the recognition of the existence of a nation without a territory led to the emergence of several ideological trends that claimed that a new "Hebrew" nation was coming into being in the Land of Israel that was not identical with the Jewish nation in the Diaspora. Such a trend was the "Canaanite" movement, a marginal group whose literary and cultural impact was far more extensive than its political impact.

A problem no less critical in the fundamental sense and with more far-reaching implications in the operative sense was the existence of two national communities in Palestine. The problem of the existence of the Arab majority in Palestine became a dispute over the limits of territorial flexibility in regard to the fulfillment of Zionist goals. Until the idea of partition was broached in the 1930s, the territorial dispersion of Zionist settlement was determined by economic and other considerations related to the availability of land and not to the problem of determining the future borders of a Jewish state, the establishment of which was not deemed possible in the near future. Only in 1937 when the idea of partition was raised did the issue of territorial flexibility of

Zionism become an actual controversy, with two alternatives: *more sovereignty in less territory, or more territory at the cost of sovereignty.* In the controversy over territorial flexibility four positions crystallized. The fundamentalist position advocated full Jewish sovereignty in the "Land of Israel" on both sides of the Jordan River. This position rested mainly on the conception that the Jewish people's historical and religious rights to the "heritage of their fathers" were incontrovertible. Support for this position came mainly from the Revisionists and the Mizrahi, but it had some support in the Labor movement as well.[38] The second position, which was the province of a minority in the Zionist movement, preferred a large territorial framework rather than exclusive Jewish sovereignty. This position, known as "binationalism," was first upheld by Brit Shalom,[39] and later received its most important support from Hashomer Hatzair. The third position, which was advocated by Weizmann and Ben-Gurion in 1937, and ultimately adopted by the Zionist Organization in 1946, accepted territorial limitations on Zionist goals, at least temporarily, in order to establish a sovereign Jewish state in a part of Palestine. The supporters of this position did not entirely deny the bond between the Jewish people and the Land of Israel, but advocated flexibility in the operative goals of Zionism—at least in the short run.[40] The fourth position sought to postpone the decision on this ideological dilemma to a later time in order to permit the quantitative growth of the Yishuv to the point where a Jewish majority would exist in all of Palestine. The major political implication of this position was a perpetuation of foreign rule in Palestine until the Jews became a majority. Supporters of this position were found both in the Labor movement and among the Ezrahim.

The debate continued as long as the leadership of the Zionist movement could avoid making a final decision. However, in facing the United Nations debates of 1947, the Zionist movement could no longer evade a decision on the territorial dilemma—and it opted for partition. In the final analysis, after the establishment of the state and the flight of most of the Arab population, what emerged was a Jewish nation-state in a part of the Land of Israel.

## The Ideological Debate

The intensive ideological activity in the Zionist movement involved a wide variety of issues, but a small number of master issues can be isolated: the national question; the social question, which centered on the nature of the desired social order; the question of democracy and political pluralism; and the status of religion in society.

Positions on these substantive issues can be classified according to three patterns. The first pattern is the single-issue ideology, which emphasizes one central issue. The second is the multi-issue ideology, which formulates a position on each substantive issue separately, so that a position on one issue is not necessarily connected to positions taken on other substantive issues. The third pattern is the comprehensive ideology, in which issues are treated and positions defined from the perspective of a uniform world view reflecting the pursuit of ideological coherence.

The tendency to construct comprehensive ideologies was most apparent in the Marxist wing of the Zionist movement. But this ideological trend encountered difficulties when it attempted to include its position on the national question in the comprehensive ideological framework of Marxism. In order to do this, Marxist Zionists relied on an interpretation of the national question that differed from the prevailing doctrines of "orthodox" Marxism. Hashomer Hatzair, for example, developed the formula of a "synthesis" between Zionism and "revolutionary socialism."[41] In adopting this position, they rejected the Communists' monistic approach, the cause of their negative attitude toward Zionist ideology.[42]

The extreme ultraorthodox groups outside the organized *Yishuv* also possessed a comprehensive ideology. These groups adopted the principle of deciding all issues on the basis of *halacha* (the Jewish religious law) as interpreted by their rabbinical leaders. The Agudat Israel party even institutionalized this practice by creating a body called the Council of Sages. As their political and ideological activity was also concentrated on the religious issue, Hamizrahi and Hapoel Hamizrahi were often vague on nonreligious issues because they were reluctant to depart entirely from the Zionist consensus by forming a distinctive view on issues other than the status of religion. Their political behavior thus resembled at times that of a single-issue party.

The party closest to a "pure" single-issue pattern was the Revisionist party. Jabotinsky, the Revisionist leader, described the tendency of his movement to deal only with the national issue while leaving decisions on other issues to the future as adherence to "one flag" only. Thus he rejected any ideological commitment beyond the nationalist one.[43]

The most typical representative of the multi-issue pattern was Mapai. Mapai had a broad ideological platform which dealt with the four major substantive issues mentioned above, though in respect to some of them its ideological formulations were vague or changed over the years. Since Mapai's ideological approach was related to its pragmatic and constructivist tendencies, its positions on the social and national issues were of a moderate-center nature. On every issue except one— the conception of the Jewish worker as the dominant element in the Zionist movement—Mapai's position was closer to the center of the spectrum of political opinion than to its extremes. A similar approach characterized a large part of the Ezrahim, which from their liberal stand- point strove for conciliation and cooperation between movements pos- sessing different approaches to the problems of social order and religion. Like Mapai, the parties of the center and moderate right possessed distinctive positions of their own on each of the major substantive issues. They shunned the tendency to integrate these positions into an internally consistent ideological doctrine even more than did Mapai.

## The "National Question"

Among the central issues of ideological debate in the Yishuv, the national question was particularly salient. The New Yishuv was a product of Zionist ideology and, except for the Communists, Canaanites, and the ultraorthodox, this ideology formed the common value basis of the entire Yishuv. The existence of a considerable degree of con- sensus concerning the final goal did not however prevent dispute over whether it was better to emphasize this by making it an explicit demand, or to soft-pedal it while concentrating on middle-range Zionist demands. The disputes concerned differences of approach on the operative rather than fundamental level. Yet, over the years, the debates on middle- range goals produced a feedback which eventually influenced, at least to some extent, the formulation of the ultimate goal.

The main source of both controversy and ideological change was the need to respond to what was called "the Arab problem." Since the basic premise of Zionist ideology was the desire to create a sovereign Jewish society in Palestine, at first the presence of the Arab population was perceived mainly as an obstacle to the fulfillment of Zionist goals which ought to be dealt with primarily on the operative level. But when the conflict with the Arab national movement and its "Palestinian" offshoot focused on the issue of rights to Palestine, the question of the Arab population was raised over and over again on the fundamental level as well. Even so, the overwhelming majority of the movement continued to believe in a distinction between the "right" of the Jewish people as a whole to Palestine and the "rights" of the Arab residents in Palestine.[44]

Two opposing evaluations of the Zionist response to the Arab problem are offered by students of the history of the Yishuv and the Zionist movement. According to one interpretation, there was a tendency among the founding fathers of the Yishuv to suppress the question, albeit not to the extreme of some of the early Zionist thinkers, such as Israel Zangwill, who spoke of "a land without a people for a people without a land."[45] In contrast to this interpretation, there is incontrovertible evidence that from the early period of Zionist settlement, the Arab question arose constantly in debates, which indicates that there was a clear awareness of its implications for the realization of the Zionist idea.[46] These two interpretations can be reconciled if we keep in mind the distinction between fundamental and operative ideology. On the fundamental level there was a tendency, at least until the late 1920s, to pay little attention to the question because it was perceived mainly as a constraint on the operative level. Thus, the debate in this period on issues associated with the "Arab problem" was almost entirely operative. The first organized expression of a revised treatment of the Arab question on the fundamental level was the appearance of the Brit Shalom group. The unique character of this group was its readiness to see the conflict in terms of two *subjective* claims or rights.

It is possible to indicate different levels of perception of the Arab-Jewish conflict in the development of Zionist ideology. The lowest level was the common perception at the turn of the century (before the rise of the organized Arab national movement) which treated the question as an essentially social problem on the local level and did not consider the Arabs a political community.[47] The next level of perception recognized the Arabs as a social entity with a political will of their own, but saw the nationalistic anti-Zionist stance as a distortion of the Arabs' true self-interest. This perception interpreted the Arab position as the outcome of intrigues fostered by British imperialism or incitement by the *effendi* class. This perception was widespread in the Labor movement mainly during the 1920s and thereafter in the Marxist wing of the Labor movement.[48]

The riots of 1929 and the revolt of 1936–39 strengthened a third level of perception about the Arabs, which was in many respects close to the Revisionist position. According to this view there was an inevitable confrontation between two national movements in Palestine and only the slightest chance for a peaceful resolution of the conflict. The Arabs were thus perceived as an opponent in a "zero-sum game," i.e., a contest in which gain for one side implies loss for the other. Jabotinsky gave a concise expression of this perception when he said that "any group of native-born, whether backward or cultured, sees its land as its own 'national home' in which it wishes to live and to remain the sole masters; such a nation will not voluntarily accept new masters nor will they accept any form of joint ownership."[49] The proponents of this opinion in the Labor movement were less explicit than Jabotinsky. They were aware of the contradiction between the national awakening among the Arabs and the Zionists' desire, out of ideological and social motives, to reach a modus vivendi with the Arabs as individuals. However, as long as the conflict continued to occupy center stage, the majority of the Labor movement sided with those who refused to condition Zionist activity on Arab consent, as Ben-Gurion had said: "We have come here and will continue to come here with or without a Jewish-Arab agreement on the matter."[50]

On the fourth level we discern the influence of the feedback effect from the operative aspects of the Arab problem onto the fundamental dimension of Zionist ideology. This approach was first expressed in the idea of the binational state, as for example in the words of Dr. Arthur Ruppin (a member of Brit Shalom) before the Zionist Congress of 1929: "We seek to rid ourselves of the mistaken notion that has ruled Europe for a hundred years and has caused a world war, to wit that a state can contain only one nation."[51] The perception of the conflict as a conflict between two rights found indirect expression in the readiness to accept the idea of partition. There were leaders, such as Ben-Gurion, who at first saw partition as one stage in the process of the ultimate fulfillment of Zionist goals in their entirety; yet a new perception began to crystallize that saw partition as a form of compromise between two just claims. The tendency to perceive the Arabs not as an object of Zionist activity but as subjects with legitimate claims of their own was apparent in Weizmann's speech before the Anglo-American Enquiry Commission in which he defined Zionist demands as "to move on the line of least injustice."[52]

The only element in the Yishuv that took an unequivocal position in relation to the Arab-Jewish conflict on both the fundamental and the operative levels was the Revisionist movement, which sought a one-sided resolution of the conflict through either force or British support. The Labor movement, the religious parties, and the General Zionists continued to grapple with the Arab question, with frequent differences of opinion occurring within these parties, as for example on partition, and with leading figures in these parties, such as Ben-Gurion, occasionally changing positions.[53]

Differences between moderates and extremists were also quite definite in positions adopted toward the British. Here there were no fundamental differences in approach, except between the LHI and the Communists on the one hand, and all the other movements on the other. The LHI and the Communists viewed Britain as an enemy because it was an imperialist ruler, while the parties of the organized Yishuv, the Revisionists, and even the IZL did not reject the British Mandate in principle, so long as its goals were compatible with Zionist goals (thus, the White Paper of 1939 was considered a betrayal of the Balfour Declaration by the British government). This approach was challenged by the LHI during World War II. Its leaders saw the British as an "enemy" and the Germans only as a "persecutor"; they not only insisted on continuing the struggle against the British, but also sought ways to establish contacts with the Axis Powers. Later, during the period of the postwar "struggle" against the British, the debate in the Yishuv and the Zionist movement took the form of a dispute between "activists" and "antiactivists" and revolved around issues of tactics and strategy, those groups who took a moderate stand on the Arab question adopting a less activist approach in relations with the British and vice versa.[54]

## The "Social Question"

The point of departure for ideological debate in the social sphere was different from the departure point in the controversy over the national question. There was not even a basic consensus on the need to pursue a definitive ideological answer to the question of the desired social structure of Jewish society of the future. Among the Ezrahim and (even more) among the Revisionists, there was a tendency to deny the relevance of ideological debate over the nature of the ideal social order during the process of political realization of Zionism.[55] The dominant ideology on the Zionist left, however, stressed the mutual dependence between realizing Zionism and laying the foundation for a new and "just" society. This controversy was related to another about the place of class struggle in the Yishuv. Revisionism, for example, connected its opposition to the socialist ideology of the Labor movement with negation of the idea of class struggle. Jabotinsky described the use of the class struggle as a means to attain an equilibrium between wages and profits as "simply unthinkable since it is something that will destroy the Zionist enterprise."[56] This approach was further expressed in the efforts of the Revisionists to undermine the authority of the Histadrut, as when Jabotinsky published an inflammatory article calling on the workers to break strikes organized by the Histadrut.[57]

The issue of class struggle was also a subject of controversy in the Labor movement itself, even though most parties within the movement shared a common desire to combine the colonization process with an attempt to create a society based on equality in which organized workers would have a position of hegemony. While the extreme left—the Communists and Poalei Zion Smol—stressed the class struggle as the main path to the attainment of socialism, Mapai chose "constructivist socialism," although it did not abandon the trade union struggle as an expression of class conflict in a society where a private economic sector existed alongside the workers' sector. The experience of the Labor movement in the 1920s convinced the Mapai leaders that the controversies on the fundamental level over communism, socialism, and the class struggle, were irrelevant to the operative poblems faced by the workers in Palestine because the major problem was the creation of adequate conditions for the development of a Jewish working class.

This idea was formulated with great clarity by Chaim Arlozoroff, the brilliant young leader of the Labor movement who was assassinated in 1934. Arlozoroff contended that the three aspects of the class struggle —the political struggle for power, the social struggle over the prestige and a way of life, and the economic aspects of income distribution— did not apply in the social framework of the Yishuv. The struggle for power had no meaning in a binational society under colonial rule. The prestige aspect was irrelevant because the recognition in Zionist ideology of the need for productivization of the Jewish people and for transition to manual labor was sufficient to assure the prestige and status of the Jewish worker. The economic aspect was irrelevant because the tasks of social construction were based on external capital, in particular national capital, and this fact removed one of the class struggle's most potent motives, a redistribution of national income.[58] Even though

Mapai did not formally adopt Arlozoroff's theses in a literal sense, both Berl Katznelson's conception of "constructivist socialism" and Ben-Gurion's strategy of "from class to nation" were based on similar assumptions. Constructivism was predicated on the possibility of constructing an autonomous workers' economy by means of national capital raised through the national funds, while the strategy of "from class to nation" was based on the assumption that controlling the distribution of imported economic resources through the national institutions would do more to determine the workers' share of the national income than a class struggle or even a trade union struggle in the private economic sector.

The adoption of the "from class to nation" strategy resulted in a paradoxical shift in positions between the right and the left. In the 1920s the left was militant while the right and the center assumed a more conciliatory stance toward the workers. This posture stemmed from a mixture of paternalism and acceptance of the Zionist ideal of "productivization." In the 1930s, however, Mapai became increasingly moderate as it consolidated its leading position in the national center, while the right became more militant. This tendency was expressed in the strengthening of the Revisionist movement and radicalization of its position toward the Histadrut and the Labor movement. The shift between left and right in extent of radicalization created a situation where the positions that were dominant in the 1920s in each sector became the province of minorities. Within the Labor movement, Hashom er Hatzair became the major opposition group, stressing that "with the increasing development of the country, class conflicts will become more prominent while national solidarity will steadily diminish."[59] Among the non-Labor Zionists, Weizmann and the "A" General Zionists continued to view the workers' sector as a pioneer in the building of the country.

To the extent that debate on the "social question" centered on the issue of ownership of the means of production, a common approach crystallized among the moderate wings of both the socialist and the nonsocialist camps. This was the acceptance of a pluralistic economy in which a private sector established with private capital and initiative would exist alongside a workers' sector composed of Histadrut-owned enterprises and cooperatives of all types including the settlement movements affiliated to the Histadrut.[60] Besides the private and the Histadrut sectors, there was also a public sector in the Yishuv which included companies wholly or partially owned by the national institutions.

The prevailing support in the Labor movement for building a new society and a national home through the creation of a workers' economy caused a series of ideological disputes connected with the economic and social organization of that economy. The first centered on the choice between different organizational principles for the workers' economy: the cooperative system versus the administrative system. The "administrative system" referred to economic enterprises owned by the Histadrut or one of its subsidiaries whose managers were appointed by the central institutions of the Histadrut and whose workers were actually wage-earners whose position regarding control of the enterprise was no different from that of other Histadrut members who worked in the private or public sector. Under the cooperative system, on the other hand, the workers of an enterprise owned the means of production or leased them, in the case of land. The advantages of the administrative system were that the enterprises could be directed to serve the general interest and that the large scale of these enterprises permitted a more rational use of resources. On the other hand, there were those who argued that this system would eventually degenerate into "bureaucratism." The major advantage of the cooperative system was said to be the greater motivation and involvement of the workers, while a counter argument was raised that the cooperative system would create a tendency for the small units to attempt to free themselves from the control of the community. The position eventually adopted by the Labor movement permitted the parallel existence of both systems.

The second ideological dispute pertained only to the cooperative system and focused on the extent of cooperation in ownership and consumption in cooperative frameworks as a whole and in the Labor movement settlements in particular. Three organizational patterns prevailed in communal agricultural settlements: the *kibbutz* (and *kevutza*), the *moshav*, and the *moshav shitufi*. The issue was primarily between the first two, which were the dominant patterns. While the *kibbutz* embodied the maximum level of cooperation in production as well as consumption, the *moshav* was based on individual or family consumption with only very limited cooperation in production. The orientation of the *moshav* to the ideology of the Labor movement was expressed mainly in adherence to the idea of self-labor, and cooperation was confined almost entirely to marketing. Advocates of the *kibbutz* approach saw it as a higher level of fulfillment of socialist ideals, a more efficient instrument for the performance of pioneering tasks, and a more rational system of work organization. Partisans of the *moshav*, on the other hand, argued that the latter gave more freedom to the individual, increased the motivation to work, and strengthened the family unit—in this case the nuclear family—not only in the spheres of consumption and socialization but also in the sphere of production.[61] The wide gap between these two forms of settlement would seem to call for an intermediate type based on full cooperation in the sphere of production with consumption based on the individual and family unit, and indeed the *moshav shitufi* developed from the other two patterns, but the number of these settlements remained small. It is characteristic of the "constructivist" orientation of the workers' economy that a fourth possible type of cooperative framework did not take root in the Labor movement, the idea of "communes" based on full cooperation in consumption with the income of the group derived from the earnings of members working outside the communal framework. The Labor Brigade adopted this system in part but eventually disbanded, and subsequent efforts to establish urban "communes" on a permanent basis failed.

The third ideological dispute concerned equality of rewards. At the outset the *moshav* did not establish equality in income and consumption, but rather limited it to equality of opportunity in respect to the amount of land allotted to each family and the size of the initial investment in equipment, seed, and so on. Inequality stemming from differential productivity of units of production was recognized as legitimate. The *kibbutz*, on the other hand, instituted full equality between members in respect to economic and other instrumental rewards. Efforts were made to reduce inequality of symbolic rewards, such as prestige, by instituting the principle of rotation among occupational and administrative positions. But these attempts contradicted the need for specialization that eventually became more important as the economy and the means of production reached a higher level of development.

The fourth dispute concerned the ideal size of the socioeconomic unit, and had two facets. In the twenties, the Labor Brigade called for the creation of a "general commune" to encompass all Jewish workers in Palestine and abolish inequality not only within units of production (such as the *kibbutz*) but also between units of production. The debate on this issue ended with the disintegration of the Labor Brigade in the mid-twenties. Debate persisted, however, concerning the desired size of the communal socioeconomic unit. The advocates of large units (the "large *kibbutz*") based their arguments on economic efficiency and greater absorptive capacity, while the advocates of small units (the "small *kevutza*") emphasized the more favorable setting for interpersonal relations that would result from a smaller, more intimate group.

### The Question of Democracy

A high level of ideological commitment is apt to create a favorable climate for ideological fanaticism, particularly when the ideologies concerned are radical. Adherents of radical ideologies are inclined to present their doctrines of a priori truths and to depict their rivals' doctrines as the embodiment of iniquity and falsehood. But in a political system whose center lacked the sanctions available to a sovereign state, the only possibility for creating effective political institutions lay in the willingness of all parties to establish a pluralistic political structure based on compromise. In these conditions the issue of democracy posed both an ideological and an institutional challenge to the political movements in the Yishuv. Ideological radicalism of one kind or another was characteristic of some of the Labor movement and of the Revisionist nationalist right wing and the underground military organizations which emerged from it. Within the Labor movement the first step toward pluralism was the founding of the Histadrut. It involved a compromise between the totalistic orientation of Ahdut Ha'avoda, which sought to concentrate all the functions of the parties in the Histadrut, and the desire of the minority, headed by Hapoel Hatzair, to maintain a degree of autonomy for the various political parties of the movement. Thus, Ahdut Ha'avoda abandoned its original position and came to accept political pluralism within the Histadrut,[62] while Hapoel Hatzair complied with the idea that the Histadrut would not confine itself to purely instrumental functions. Hapoel Hatzair, however, favored the coexistence of various political and ideological trends and opposed the application of the principle of majority rule, referring to it as "majoritarianism."[63] In contrast, Ahdut Ha'avoda called for the creation of centralized institutions as the "true" expression of the concentrated will of the collectivity.

In the 1930s, as the Labor movement became increasingly integrated into the institutional frameworks of the Yishuv and the Zionist movement, there was a greater tendency within Mapai to assume a more explicit ideological stance favoring pluralistic democracy. However, the acceptance of a pluralistic political structure and democratic procedure and the emphasis on the principle of "one man, one vote" were primarily products of operative considerations, rather than of fundamental beliefs. Even by the 1940s, there remained on the fundamental level a strong residue of belief in the movement's right to resort to coercion when necessary to realize its goals, as Ben-Gurion had said: "I would not hesitate to employ coercion to realize the goals of Zionism or socialism, but there is no way for us to compel either the Yishuv or the Jewish people. We must find the way through men's hearts . . . and through agreement."[64] The conception of democracy held by the Labor movement was therefore not based on unconditional compliance with democratic "rules of the game."

As Mapai became more willing to recognize the legitimacy of political pluralism, opposition, and the presence of conflict, the opposite occurred in Hashomer Hatzair, which changed from a nonpolitical youth movement into the major spokesman of the Marxist left in the Labor Zionist camp. Hashomer Hatzair continued to participate in the institutional frameworks of the Yishuv and the Zionist movement, as well as the Histadrut; its totalistic tendencies were turned inward. The outcome was the concept of "ideological collectivism," which rejected political and ideological divisions within what was seen as the "organic" entity of its *kibbutz* movement.[65] The "doctrine of stages" developed by Hashomer Hatzair enabled it to accept democratic rules of the game within the national movement and its political institutions while the political goals of Zionism were in the process of realization. The "dictatorship of the proletariat" and all this implied for political conflict would be postponed until Zionism had achieved its political goals, when the class struggle would become the dominant factor in political life.

For the Revisionists, the question of democracy was expressed in the problem of the role of leadership. This problem was twofold. On one hand, the movement itself was perceived as a kind of political order or fraternity, based on a quasi-military discipline. On the other, in regard to the Zionist movement as a whole, the Revisionists felt that their kind of radical nationalism qualified them for exclusive leadership of the Jewish national movement. Thus, one may detect certain anti-democratic overtones in Revisionism characteristic of the European radical right in the interwar period. This tone led Labor movement spokesmen to identify Revisionism as an expression of fascism.[66] The leadership principle was indeed explicit in the code of the Revisionist youth movement, Betar, which stated that "discipline implies the submission of the masses to the authority of a leader."[67] Jabotinsky himself remained a liberal with elitist leanings who believed that leadership should mobilize the will of the masses, not through coercion, but in the manner of a "conductor who is entrusted in good faith with the command of an orchestra."[68] The antidemocratic tone was expressed by the ideological mentor of the radical Brit Habiryonim, who stated flatly that a "harmonious" society dedicated to a particular ideal does not feel the absence of freedom just as the healthy person does not notice the presence of the air he breathes and does not uphold unrestricted freedom of speech.[69] The lack of clarity within Revisionism in respect to democracy continued to be reflected within the military organizations that emerged from Revisionism, the IZL and the LHI. LHI's approach was based on denial of the democratic principle of majority rule and substitution of a revolutionary right which would be free of any conventional restraints.[70] The IZL too was prepared to defy the will of the majority during a period of nationalist struggle, but justified this mainly on the grounds that the national institutions operated on a voluntary basis. This problem arose once again in the period of transition from Yishuv to state, when Menachem Begin decided, contrary to the opinion of some of his close associates, in favor of limiting IZL activity, after the establishment of a sovereign Jewish state, to legitimate political opposition according to democratic "rules of the game."[71]

Unlike the Revisionists and the Labor movement, the parties of the center and the moderate right were free of the radicalism that made it difficult to cooperate with other parties in the framework of common institutions. However, while all the Ezrahim accepted the liberal principle of political and ideological pluralism, there were some groups among them which did not accept the principle of democratic representation according to the formula of one man, one vote. The spokesmen for part of the Ezrahim sector, particularly the leaders of the farmers of the *moshavot*, sought to create political institutions based on group representation that would reflect "qualitative" as well as quantitative considerations. Moshe Smilansky, a leader of the *moshavot* farmers, expressed the view of this group when he argued that a way should be found "to take into account not only the ballot cast by the voter but also the weight of his contribution to society." Smilansky also expressed a preference for bargaining and compromise over strict majority decision: "why should we choose to defeat instead of to persuade?"[72] he asked, expressing a position compatible with the pattern of consociational democracy.

We see, then, that the democratic element in the ideologies of most movements within the Yishuv was mainly on the operative level, while on the fundamental level most parties carried traces of a predemocratic or even undemocratic position. On the operational level, the parties were facing the problem of how to combine coalescent politics based on mutual cooperation and compromise with a desire to make a decisive impact on the shape of society as a whole. In trying to solve this problem, the Zionist Labor parties adopted the formula of "hegemony" of the Labor movement in the Yishuv. This formula served to justify the efforts of the Labor movement to attain the key positions within political institutions while preserving their coalitionary structure.

## The Status of Religion

The capacity of the political system of the Yishuv to exist as a pluralistic system was tested over the issue of religion and its role in the evolving Jewish society in Palestine. In spite of the identity between religion and nationality in Judaism, which received legal expression in the organization of the Yishuv as a religious community, the overwhelming majority of the Zionist movement was secular. Moreover, the ideologies of some of the groups within Zionism in general and the Zionist Labor movement in particular, had distinctly anticlerical overtones. These trends were the combined result of a socialist outlook and a negative attitude to the traditional Jewish way of life in the Diaspora. Even those secular ideological currents that did not wish to sever all ties with Jewish tradition found it impossible to make their ideology consistent with a religious world view—on the fundamental level, at any rate.

The point of departure of religious Zionism, which distinguished it from Agudat Israel, was the perception of the return of the Jewish people to its homeland as an act of religious significance.[73] In this sense there was more to the approach of religious Zionism than the desire to establish a society that lived according to the *halacha*. However, religious Zionism, as opposed to its secular counterparts, held, that a religious world view does not allow an authority higher than the *halacha*, which meant that acceptance of any political authority would remain conditional. Religious Zionism faced the difficulty of striving to obtain autonomy for the religious sector of the community and to create the optimal conditions for the observance of the *halacha* by individuals, while at the same time seeking to impose a religious character on the public life of the Yishuv as a whole. Religious Zionism chose to give priority to the second goal, thus distinguishing itself from Agudat Israel and the extreme ultraorthodox who tended to concentrate on developing a religious way of life for their own closed circles.

The issue of religion and its place in the political system did not assume high operative significance in the period of the Yishuv, since the absence of sovereignty relieved Zionism and the organized Yishuv of the need to reach decisions on most of the problems connected with the social role of religion. The existence of an external non-Jewish authority that recognized religious pluralism was a convenient arrangement. The legal framework of the Mandate provided positive institutional autonomy for the Jewish community in the religious sphere, expressed mainly in the assignment of all matters connected with personal status to the jurisdiction of the religious courts. This system was supported by the overwhelming majority of the Jewish community, who saw it as a factor strengthening the autonomy of Knesset Israel. The binational nature of Mandatory Palestine reduced to a minimum the possibilities of religious legislation in matters other than personal status.

The absence of a sovereign political framework meant, therefore, that the ideological conflicts over the status of religion on the fundamental level were expressed only partially on the operative level. In the Labor movement, for example, opposing opinions on the religious question never reached the stage of open confrontation since they were not connected with the actual political issues of the day. However, Labor leaders often voiced different opinions on the religious issues. While Berl Katznelson maintained that "a generation that creates and innovates does not throw the heritage of previous generations on the rubbish heap . . . but may keep the tradition by adding to it,"[74] other Labor leaders who received their political education in the Marxist atmosphere of Russian socialism tended to adopt militantly anticlerical positions. A variety of approaches to religion also characterized the Revisionist movement. Though Jabotinsky's opinions were thoroughly secularist and he was willing to accept only the national and social aspects of the Jewish tradition,[75] there were others in his movement who possessed a religious outlook, and some of them were even observant. There was a common ideological tendency among parts of the Labor movement and the Revisionists to secularize certain symbols derived originally from the religious conceptions of Messianism and redemption and to fit them into a nonreligious world view. This approach was characteristic of Ben-Gurion in the Labor movement[76] and Abba Ahimeir of the radical Revisionists. The latter, for example, spoke on the one hand of the "spiritual health" of a "harmonious religious society," and on the other of "Zionism that in its most basic sense is a secular antitheological phenomenon."[77] Similar differences in approach to the question of religion and tradition were present among the General Zionists and other Ezrahim groups, though the question of religion was not the center of their ideological concern.

## Universal and Jewish Ideological Influences

The variety and complexity of ideological positions in the Yishuv and the intensity with which ideological debate was conducted were to a large extent products of the intellectual climate in the Diaspora in which Zionism arose and developed. The Jewish society in Europe of the late nineteenth and early twentieth centuries had been exposed for at least several decades to the intense influence of ideologies and trends of thought from the non-Jewish environment. This was a period of widespread political and ideological ferment, particularly in the areas in which Zionism emerged—Central and Eastern Europe. Thus both from a chronological and geographical point of view, Zionism began at a crossroads where ideological and political movements met and clashed within the Jewish society and the wider society of which it was a part. The ideologies that animated political movements in Europe served as a source of ideas and models for the ideologies emergent in European Jewish society of the nineteenth century. Indeed, nearly all of the important ideologies in the non-Jewish environment found a parallel in Jewish society or the Zionist movement, with a stress on the particular Jewish aspect for interpretation of these conceptions.

The first ideological model with a wide impact on Jewish society was modern nationalism.[78] This model provided a common denominator not only for the various brands of Zionist ideology, but also for the territorialist and autonomist trends within Jewish society. The influence of

non-Jewish nationalist movements was selective and differential; for
example, the Revisionist political and ideological style was most heavily
influenced by the Polish national movement and the Italian *risorgi-
mento*.[79] The Zionist Labor movement, on the other hand, attempted to
find its way to a conception of nationalism through the maze of current
definitions among the left of Central and Eastern Europe. Its Marxist
wing adopted a conception of Jewish nationalism based on the teachings
of the Marxist-Zionist thinker, Dov Ber Borochov.[80] The nationality
problems of the multinational Austro-Hungarian Empire influenced the
development of Zionism, if only for the fact that many of the founders
of the World Zionist Organization, chief among them Theodor Herzl
and Max Nordau, were citizens of Austria-Hungry. In Eastern Europe,
however, populist influences were more prevalent. Many Eastern European Zionists regarded ties to the land, to territory, as the key to
nationality. This approach was reflected in the philosophy of the founders of Hovevei Zion, the most prominent of whom was the philosopher
and author of "Autoemancipation," Dr. Leon Pinsker.[81] Later this approach was apparent in the stress placed on "redeeming the land," a
motif that appeared in the Labor movement as well as among non-
socialists from Eastern Europe, such as Menahem Ussishkin. In contrast, the conception of nationalism of Ahad Ha'am (the pseudonym of
Asher Ginsberg)[82] was drawn, despite his Eastern-European origins,
from Western European and especially English sources, evident in the
special emphasis he placed on the cultural dimensions of national
identity.

The second ideological model that had a deep impact on the Zionist
movement was socialism. Marxian socialism in its two main variants—
revolutionary and reformist—was reflected in the ideology of the non-
Zionist Bund and the Zionist Poalei Zion at the turn of the century.
It is also characteristic that the split in the international socialist movement after World War I between the reformist social-democratic wing
and the "orthodox" revolutionary wing was replicated subsequently in a
split in the Poalei Zion movement. The doctrinaire character of "orthodox" communist Marxist and the anti-Zionist attitudes of its leading
exponents considerably weakened its Zionist parallel, and the majority
of Poalei Zion and its affiliated party in Palestine, Ahdut Ha'avoda,
gradually adopted a moderate social democratic interpretation of socialism. Ahdut Ha'avoda later adopted the concept of constructivist
socialism shared by the other major workers' party, Hapoel Hatzair,

whose inspiration was not Marxian socialism, but populist socialism.[83]

Populism, in its Eastern European version, was the third major ideological movement to influence Zionism. The populism of the social revolutionaries[84] and the "Narodnaya Volya"[85] which preceded them inspired the goal of skipping the stage of capitalist development in creating a productive workers' society in Palestine based on agricultural cooperatives. The social revolutionaries' influence was also felt in the ideals of voluntarism, personal example, and service to the collectivity integrated into the conception of "pioneering" (halutziut). From this point of view, the development of Hashomer Hatzair in the Labor movement in Palestine was exceptional, since at its outset it was closer to the populist approach and to Hapoel Hatzair, while later in the twenties it adopted a Marxist position closer to the intermediate groups between the social-democratic Second International and the communist Third International.

The fourth ideological model, which shared some traits with populism and which also influenced movements within Zionism, was a right-wing radicalism rooted in historical romanticism. The link with populism was the common feeling of revulsion and rejection of modern capitalism and its cultural side effects, such as the alienation from nature and the soil. In contrast to the socialist populism of East Europe, the radical right emphasized the racial and communal bases of the national collectivity and was more amenable to elitist sentiments. This ideological model influenced a trend within Revisionism whose major spokesmen were the historian Abba Ahimeir and the poet Uri Zvi Greenberg; there was an affinity between Brit Habiryonim and the European radical right, including its fascist offspring.[86] The racist elements of the radical right, which became sharply anti-Semitic with the rise of the Nazi movement, increasingly led Zionists to reject the romantic nationalist conception. Even so, traces of this ideology continued to appear in the poetry of Uri Zvi Greenberg, in the initial ideological concepts of the LHI, and in the "Canaanite" teachings of the poet Yonathan Ratosh.

A fifth ideological model that had a wide, although differential, influence on movements within Zionism was liberalism. Its impact was greatest in the English-speaking countries and in Central Europe, but thinkers such as Ahad Ha'am also drew some inspiration from it.

Besides the ideological models that originated in the non-Jewish world, intellectual and cultural currents within Judaism also had an important influence on the ideological development of Zionism and the

Yishuv. These ideas can be viewed partly as ideological models, but substantively speaking most of them were cultural rather than political. The first of these influences relevant in this context was the Jewish Enlightenment (Haskala) movement.[87] Although Zionism emerged as a reaction to that aspect of the Enlightenment movement which implied integration into non-Jewish society, Zionism, or at least its secular wing, adopted many of the social and cultural conceptions that originated with the Haskala: the attitude of intellectual openness toward the world at large, the quest for liberation from the bonds of tradition, the rejection of the ghetto mentality, and the striving for normalization and productivization. The major difference between Zionism and the Jewish Enlightenment was that Zionism rejected the call for integration into the non-Jewish society, advocating instead the building of an autonomous Jewish society in Palestine parallel to the national societies of other peoples. This aim of Zionism soon met with the obstacle of a binational reality in Palestine, where the Yishuv was a minority. Searching for a solution to this problem, all the ideological currents within Zionism drew inspiration from the ideological and cultural model that advocated autonomous Jewish organization, based on the Jewish communal structure, even within the framework of non-Jewish rule. Both Knesset Israel and the Jewish municipal frameworks within the Yishuv reflected the influence of autonomous Jewish communal organization, mainly as it existed in Poland.[88]

While the Jewish Enlightenment and autonomism had a wide impact on Zionism, the influence of cultural and ideological currents within traditional Judaism on groups and individuals in the Zionist movement and the Yishuv was more selective. The influence of Hassidism, for example, was actually less apparent in religious Zionism, whose standing among traditional Jewry was impaired by the opposition many Hassidic rabbis voiced to Zionism,[89] than in secular Zionist circles where there was a tendency of romanticize and idealize Hassidism stemming from the perception of Hassidism as a *popular* movement. This, at any rate, was the image prevalent among historians and scholars of Hassidism such as Samuel Horodetzky, Ben-Zion Dinur, and Raphael Mahler.[90] The image these writers created of the popular nature of Hassidism, its simplicity and directness, and the devotion of its adherents was absorbed by segments of the Labor movement; even a strictly secularist movement such as Hashomer Hatzair, which eventually turned Marxist, perserved a sentimental image of Hassidism. The other movement of importance among East European Jewry, the Mitnagdim, whose center of activity was in the *yeshivot* (rabbinical schools), influenced Zionism through individuals, many of whom were educated in the Volozhin *yeshiva*. This *yeshiva* was exceptional because of its Zionist-nationalistic outlook for a certain period. German Orthodoxy, the third major movement in traditional Judaism, was also predominantly anti-Zionist. But several individuals with a strong Zionist orientation emerged from this movement and took part in molding the Mizrahi and Hapoel Hamizrahi movements.

## Ideology and Social Action: The Fundamental and Operative Dimensions of Ideology

Our examination of the sources of ideological influence on the political movements in the Yishuv and Zionism has shown that these movements were influenced primarily by ideological models from the non-Jewish environment. Aspects of the political culture and political style of individuals and groups were influenced heavily by ideological and cultural models originating in the Jewish society of the Diaspora, primarily Eastern Europe. The specific contribution of the social and political system of the Yishuv itself was to translate the general principles of ideology into norms of action and means of implementation. Moreover, feedback from the attempts to implement ideologically inspired goals eventually influenced substantive aspects of the ideologies themselves. An important example of this trend was the conception of constructivist socialism, which departed from its ideological beginnings in populism and socialism. A more extreme example was the Canaanite ideology, which although it bore traces of populist and radical right ideologies, was primarily an intellectual effort to come to terms with the new cultural and national reality the Yishuv created. A completely different example of feedback effect on ideology was connected to Zionism's traumatic encounter with the facts of Arab hostility. One of the responses to this unexpected reality was the theme presented by official Zionist spokesmen which emphasized Zionism's positive role in bringing progress to a backward area. This contention has an obvious parallel to the paternalistic imperialist ideologies that stressed the "white man's burden." This parallel, however, did not derive from the direct influence of these ideologies, but from the attempt to confront the political and symbolic problem of a conflict of interests between two nations engaged in a struggle over the future of the same land. It is noteworthy that this land was ruled by an imperial power which itself assumed a paternalistic stance on numerous occasions.

Ideological consciousness played a central role as a motivating factor in immigration to Palestine and in the intensive participation in political movements. Also, ideology provided models of the ideal social order. The impact of such images was particularly strong on those movements in the Yishuv that developed ideologies with activist, collectivist, and future-oriented characteristics. The ideological currents that combined these characteristics, i.e., subordination of the present to the requirements of future goals and giving preference to collective needs over individual needs, also served to legitimate the political and social status of certain groups. The "pioneering" sector was viewed as an elect group worthy not only of general esteem, but also of positions of social and political leadership. The positions attained through the inspiration of this ideology were soon converted into a source of rewards such as power, prestige, and to a lesser extent material advantage.[91] Notwithstanding this, the future-oriented collectivist ideology created sufficient social and political pressure, in the sense of internal motivation and external social pressure, to mobilize the resources of the Yishuv and the Diaspora for efforts beyond those common to less ideologically oriented societies. Its utopian elements inspired several unique forms of social organization that became the trademarks of the Yishuv, such as the Histadrut, the *kibbutz*, and the ramified network of national institutions operating on a voluntary basis. In the final analysis, however, utopian elements of a fundamental nature could not be translated into operational imperatives except through a process of transformation in which some of their features would be abandoned or compromised. Contradictions naturally emerged between the original ideological demands and their practical political and social applications. The "pure" ideals and goals of fundamental ideology meanwhile continued to play an important role in the process of political socialization and as a focus for political identification. As a result, the political elites tended to continue paying homage to components of the original ideology that had been greatly modified or abandoned.

Two characteristic tendencies thus emerged. One was the tendency to sanctify institutional frameworks and organizational forms originally designated to represent and embody ideological values. The paradoxical but familiar phenomenon of "conservative revolutionaries" emerged. Successful in institutionalizing the values contained in their ideologies, those who effected the revolution inherent in the fulfillment of Zionist goals became increasingly concerned with the maintenance and preservation of the institutional frameworks they had created. The second tendency, related directly to the first, was expressed in a growing dissociation between these institutions and the values they were supposed to represent. As the gap steadily widened between the "pure" values of fundamental ideology and the operational values guiding social and political action, the tendency to seek ideological justifications for the distribution of individual and group rewards and for activity motivated by particularistic interests and short-term expediency grew. This gap between word and deed, ideal and reality, was the outcome not only of pressures created in the process of institutionalization, but also of compromises among parties to the exchange process which took place in the political markets of the "state in the making."

# 7

# The Primarily Political Functions of The Left-Right Continuum

## *Asher Arian* and *Michal Shamir*

### Labels and Cues

The concepts of left and right—or liberal and conservative in their American versions—are common terms in politics, in political discourse, and in political analysis. Their meaning, however, is multifaceted at best, elusive at worst, and—over time and across polities—quite divergent.

The left-right continuum in politics has been used for 200 years as a means to order a cognitive map of political and ideological relationships. Right and left make sense only if you happen to be the king of France chairing the first joint meeting of the States General on May 5, 1789, or the second meeting on June 23. There the nobility took the place of honor to the king's right, and the representatives of the Third Estate were to the king's left. In August 1789 when the Aristocrats and the Patriots met at the Tuilleries to form the Constituent Assembly in order to write a constitution, it was the Patriots who sat to the left and the Aristocrats to the right of the speaker's tribune. It was on August 26 that this group voted the Declaration of the Rights of Man, a landmark of political thought and practice.

Most often in political discourse the left-right continuum has been given economic meaning, referring to equality as opposed to inequality, government intervention as opposed to free enterprise, tolerance of change as opposed to adherence to the status quo. Political activists, commentators, and scientists have widened the scope of the terms to include the major issues of the day. Thus hawks and doves were labeled conservative and liberal in the United States, and similarly in Israel the hawks are right, the doves left. Issues such as divorce laws, abortion, foreign aid, and integration have also been subsumed under these headings.

The concept of left-right or liberal-conservative has come to be regarded as an overall ideological dimension, as a kind of "superissue," as ideology. For political savants the continuum denotes ideological content; political scientists and elites use these terms more or less consistently to reflect the political and ideological realities of the time.

Accepted wisdom not only equates the left-right continuum with ideology, but from the dominant perspective it is also regarded as exogenous, as determining the vote. Downs took this approach to the extreme.[1] He conceived of it as *the* determinant of the vote. Although later work qualified this conclusion and left-right is now regarded as one in a list of determinants, the literature still seems to reflect a conception of the continuum as a very important factor in the calculus of the voter.[2]

We shall present an argument—and data—challenging those two perspectives. The left-right concept for most people is not ideology, nor does it influence their vote. In other words, using Downs's terminology, there exists a left-right space, but it is a political space, mainly a party space, and not an ideological space. It is therefore not independent of the vote, and hence the continuum cannot determine the vote. In this sense, Stokes's criticism of Downs is irrelevant.[3] Although it may be true that Downs's model is deficient in the sense that it does not reflect the fact that politics is multidimensional, that issues and conflicts cannot be arranged along one dimension, that leaders and the public do not necessarily see the continuum in the same fashion, that the continuum is not constant but changes over time, and that many "valence issues" cannot be arrayed along a continuum at all inasmuch as there is no divergence of opinion on them, the critique loses its cogency if the continuum is not a determinant of the vote.

Left and right and liberal and conservative are political labels. They are cues given by the political system, in particular by political parties, with respect to political objects. The major political objects are of course the political parties toward which the citizen must orient himself: either approve, support, and vote for or oppose, reject, and vote against. The function is one of labeling for self- and party identification on the one hand as well as of vetoing and rejecting others' cues on the other hand. The left or right label is above all part of one's political vocabulary, of one's political education, of one's political and social adjustment. And it is learned. Such learning is reinforced as one proceeds with one's voting history, identifies with one's party, and absorbes the cues generated by those activities. In this view it is the vote that largely determines the left or right definition and not the reverse. One situates oneself on the continuum as a reflection of behavior other than voting; one's vote does not stem from the highly cerebral task of self-placement on the continuum. Although we realize that the nature of this relation is much more complex and endogenous than we have portrayed here, our argument is that for most people left and right labels are not cognitive in nature; they do not denote ideology and surely do not reflect ideological conceptualization and thinking. For some the political cues may include policy and ideological content; but on the whole, the labels and cues of left and right are party based and party related.

Two important functions that political attitudes fulfill are object appraisal and social adjustment.[4] Both are relevant to our discussion. Object appraisal is cognitive in nature and, in the context discussed here, ideological and policy oriented. Following this line, self-identification is based on issue preferences; thus the common view holds that a political label primarily reflects an orientation toward issues. Another functional version that requires lower levels of conceptualization and political information but is also cognitive in origin postulates that political labels provide individuals with shortcuts and simplifying devices for orientation and guidance in the political system. Such a need of course becomes stronger as the politics of a country becomes more complex, and here the labels may be more relevant.[5] Social adjustment is the second function of the left-right label, and we suggest that it is the more important one for a large portion of the public. It fulfills one's needs for self-identification and social acceptance by significant others and reference groups from which one learns one's political and social identification.

Indeed, much of the European and American research into the left-right continuum may be reread in this light to support our thesis. A left-right or a liberal-conservative continuum exists and is meaningful to a large portion of the electorate who can place themselves and political parties along it. Major issues correlate with this left-right continuum.[6] The terminology is well known, and the public has learned the labels and relates them to parties and to a lesser degree to issues. In all cases the relationship between party and self-location on the left-right scale is stronger than the relationship between left-right labels and ideological content.[7]

Further analysis indicates that the picture varies among groups at different levels of political cognition and education. The relationship between the left-right position and indices of policy or ideological orientation is stronger for those with high political cognition: for them the object appraisal function is most evident. But correlations with party identification change little in strength across different levels of political cognition because the social adjustment function operates for all.[8] In more complex and polarized systems, the higher salience of the left-right dimension is most noticeable, yet it should not be inferred from this finding that people have a clear—or, for that matter, any—understanding of the ideological content imputed to those terms.

That left-right labels do not denote ideologies, that people often use those terms "with little comprehension of their ideological meaning, even though 70 percent or more of the citizens in these mass electorates may use them to describe political parties,"[9] is by now well documented. Nevertheless, it seems that focusing on the individual and on the common identification of left-right labels with ideology has prevented us from drawing the right conclusions from these findings. Most American studies that followed Cambell and associates' and Converse's focused on the concepts of liberal and conservative, getting entangled in the study of ideology and preoccupied with its existence or lack thereof within the masses. In general the results were negative, although there is still controversy about the comparison of the 1950s with later periods.[10] There is no ideological thinking or conceptualization, and nothing that can be called a superissue, or ideology, for a large portion of the public: no constraint, no relationship among different issue positions held by the public, and no stability over time in the public's positions on issues. Converse introduced the term *nonattitudes*—survey responses showing that no attitude actually existed. It followed, then, that the lack of ideology or meaning for the conservative-liberal label stemmed from nonattitudes within the public.[11]

One of the methodological critiques of this literature is relevant here. Smith argues that the level of conceptualization measures used, which showed increases in the 1960s over the 1950s, actually measured the salience of the liberal-conservative labels—the respondents' knowledge and recognition of these cues—not ideological conceptualizing and thought.[12] These measures went up in the 1960s, reflecting changes in political climate and cues—the more ideological, clear, differentiated, and intense cues of the Vietnam and racial issues and, in particular, the polarizing Goldwater candidacy in 1964. When the political system made the labels more prevalent and salient, the respondents perceived the liberal and conservative labels as more prevalent and salient. Change was driven by a political motor, not an ideological one.

The learning of "ideological" cues does not occur in a vacuum. Their source is political, and it is this complementary, system-level, functional analysis that we shall pursue. Our argument is political and is focused on the political system in general and the party system in particular. The labels do not necessarily correspond to "natural" political entities: they were invented, not discovered, by political analysts for the political establishment. They are used to label and to identify the good or the bad, the right and the wrong, the desirable and the despicable. The stigma or the distinction that often accrues to each label should be understood as an artifact with political intent and content. Words, too, produce political impact. Political parties and leaders use these cues for their own ends.

The political context is a major factor that shapes the labels and their use both for the parties and the public at large. In a certain context the labels and cues are more pervasive, more emphasized, and more useful than in others, and we will demonstrate the operation of this factor in our analysis, as did Finlay and associates, who found that the labels were much less meaningful in non-Western countries.[13] Each party may choose to stress its own label, underscoring its positive connotation, or to castigate those of its rivals. Also, the degree of issue or ideological content loading in the left-right labels depends on which political actors are giving the cues and on the particular political scene: the cue givers can present and emphasize more or less of that content. The structure of conflicts and policy issues in a polity is also important:

are they "constrained" in the sense that they go together, fitting party cleavages? But even if there is a good fit of issues to the continuum, the major impact of the label would reside in its partisan, political nature and not in its ideological aspect.


## A Crucial Test

A least likely crucial case[14] for the confirmation of this thesis is a polity that is highly ideological, where ideology is widely thought to play an important role, and where ideological discourse is strong. Israel is such a political system. Israeli politics, its parties, and its public have often been described as highly ideological by political and social observers.[15] Even though this view is exaggerated and ideology has become less important than in the past, there is no question that Israelis are very much aware of political happenings and have a high interest and involvement in politics. Newspaper consumption is widespread, and the nightly television news is watched by a sizable portion of the adult population. The major issues of the day are highly salient to most, and no one would argue that such issues as the occupied territories are nonattitudes. Yet we shall show that even in such a system the left-right concept is not ideological but is primarily a label related to and probably stemming from one's party identification. Thus we shall argue that it is not the lack of issue orientation or nonattitudes that deprive the left-right notion of ideological content. Left and right definitions are profoundly political; irrespective of issue content and attitude existence, they are mainly party loaded and party linked.

Israel is an appropriate setting in which to test some of these ideas. A country with a reputation of ideological politics, influenced greatly by European political ideas (nationalism, socialism, liberal democracy) yet open to American influences, Israel's many political parties have often been arranged on a continuum from left to right in a manner similar to that used to arrange the political parties of other Western countries.

From the 1920s, the period in which the British mandate began in Palestine, through independence in 1948, until the beginning of the 1970s, Israel had a dominant party system. One party (Ahdut Haavoda, later Mapai, now Labor) was dominant in the sense that it won a plurality of the votes in elections, was essential to the forming of coalitions, created and maintained the centralized economic and political hierarchies that facilitated the perpetuation of its rule, and was dominant in a spiritual sense in that the goals and ideals of the period were associated with it and vice versa.

The dominant party enjoyed plurality support from most significant groups in the country, and so the party, including its label—left—was widely ac-

Table 1  Alignment and Likud Knesset Seats, 1965-1981

|            | 1965 | 1969 | 1973 | 1977 | 1981 |
|------------|------|------|------|------|------|
| Alignment  | 63   | 56   | 51   | 32   | 47   |
| Likud      | 26   | 32   | 39   | 45   | 48   |

Alignment included Rafi and Mapam in 1965; Likud included
State List and Free Center in 1969  and Sharon in 1977.

cepted in the society as the only legitimate ruler. The right organized late and less systematically; the centers of power were not within its reach. The Irgun Zvai Leumi, the militia headed by Menachem Begin, later formed the core of the Herut movement, which in turn became the biggest party in the Likud. In the prestate period and in the years following the founding of the state, the Irgun and the Herut were stigmatized as underground organizations outside the structure of the national institutions headed by Mapai. This view was ironic because the activities of the Hagana and Palmach were equally illegal from the British point of view, but the power to define legitimate and illegitimate was held by the leaders of Mapai. Prime Minister David Ben-Gurion placed the Irgun and the Herut in the company of the other ostracized group when he declared that all parties were candidates for his coalition government except the Communist party and Herut.

Two factors closely related to the rise of the right are the political and demographic changes that have occurred in Israel since independence. Until 1967, Herut and Begin were ostracized by the Mapai establishment on the grounds that they were outside the system of consensus prior to the formation of the state. In 1967, in the period before the Six Day War, Gahal (a combination of the Herut movement and the Liberal party) joined the National Unity Government, and Begin became a minister of the government of Israel. This legitimacy was enhanced by the fact that Gahal left the Unity government well before the 1973 Yom Kippur War, a defection that highlighted the decline of the dominant status of the Alignment. Not only were the political fortunes of the Likud and Begin picking up because the political fortunes of the Alignment were turning down, but time was working in the Likud's favor. Twenty-five years after independence, a sizable portion of the electorate did not know of the stigma that Begin had carried. The intergroup fights of the past generation busied older people and scholars but not the man on the street. His conceptual world of politics was different, and with generational change the role of the right and the Likud changed. As Table 1 clearly shows, the Likud continually gained votes and political power.

The passing of dominance from the Alignment led to a very competitive state of affairs by 1981. The two largest lists were almost even at the polls. Of the two million votes cast, the Likud and the Alignment won between them almost a million and a half votes, giving the Likud forty-eight seats and the Alignment forty-seven.

## The Growth of the Right

Observing the Israeli political system in the crucial period of transition from dominance to competitiveness allows us to consider the role of left-right labels in a political system undergoing change. It has often been observed that Israel has been moving to the right, and that is certainly so (see Table 2). In the twenty years from 1962 to 1981 the right increased more than fourfold, from 8 percent in 1962 to 16 percent in 1969 to 35 percent in 1981. Not only has identification with the right become more legitimate in the system—so, too, has the word. When the Israel Institute of Applied Social Research ran a pretest before the 1962 study, the right political trend was found to be so discredited that the institute decided to substitute the political party of the right—Herut—in the questionnaire. The final version of the question had as its extremes "Marxist left" and "Herut"; "moderate left" and "center" were the other two categories. By 1969 the problem had dissipated, and the terms *left* and *right* were used for the extreme responses. By 1981 some studies began splitting the "right" response into right and moderate right because the distribution had shifted over time.[16]

This movement to the right coincided with the strengthening of the Likud and the weakening of the Labor-Mapam Alignment, as shown in Table 1. The ideological perspective imputed to the left-right continuum would lead us to expect that as a society's orientation shifts so do its positions on political issues.[17] The fascinating finding about Israel is that although the country has moved to the right politically, the distribution of attitudes on important matters has remained basically constant (see Table 2). Hardline stands on returning the territories are about as prevalent today as they were in 1969.[18]

The samples are different, and the distribution of responses is not identical. Still, what is striking is the relative stability of the attitude in the society. In 1969, 90 percent favored returning none of the territories or only a small part, and in 1981, after most of Sinai had been returned, the figure was 92 percent.

Explaining attitudinal stability in light of the movement of the political continuum to the right appears to be more difficult because the population has

**Table 2** Left-Right Tendency, 1962-1981[a]

| | 1962 | 1969[c] | 1973 | 1977 | 1981 |
|---|---|---|---|---|---|
| **LEFT-RIGHT LABEL[b]** | | | | | |
| Left | | 6% | 3% | 4% | 4% |
| | 31% | | | | |
| Moderate left | | 19% | 19% | 14% | 13% |
| Center | 23% | 26% | 33% | 29% | 39% |
| Right | 8% | 16% | 23% | 28% | 32% |
| Religious | 5% | 6% | 7% | 6% | 6% |
| No interest in politics; No answer | 33% | 27% | 15% | 19% | 6% |
| **ECONOMY** | | | | | |
| Capitalist | 7% | 10% | | 11% | 10% |
| More Capitalist | 19% | 24% | | 18% | 25% |
| | | | not | | |
| More Socialist | 39% | 38% | | 31% | 40% |
| | | | asked | | |
| Socialist | 15% | 19% | | 25% | 20% |
| No Answer | 20% | 9% | | 15% | 5% |
| **RETURN THE TERRITORIES** | | | | | |
| None | | 38% | 31% | 41% | 50% |
| | not | | | | |
| A small part | | 52% | 52% | 43% | 42% |
| | asked | | | | |
| Most | | 5% | 10% | 7% | 4% |
| All | | 1% | 2% | 7% | 3% |
| No Answer | | 4% | 5% | 2% | 1% |
| Sample Size: | 1170 | 1314 | 1939 | 1372 | 1249 |

a. From 1962 through 1977 the surveys were conducted by the Israel Institute of Applied Social Research, the 1981 survey by the Dahaf Research Institute.
b. The question was "With which political tendency do you identify?" The first four responses were read, the last two were not.
c. The 1969 return the territories question was posed in August to a sample of 380 respondents.

**Table 3** Measures of Left-Right Label Among Alignment-Likud Voters, 1969-1981

| Date of Study[a] | Total Sample Size | Sample Size[b] | Pearson's r vote by left-right label | % Alignment/ % Likud | % Alignment giving "left" response | % Likud giving "right" response |
|---|---|---|---|---|---|---|
| Sept 1969 | 1314 | 565 | .21 | 84/16 | 45 | 42 |
| Oct-Nov '69 | 1825 | 786 | .45 | 74/26 | 55 | 55 |
| May 1973 | 1939 | 986 | .25 | 70/30 | 36 | 49 |
| Sept 1973 | 548 | 258 | .27 | 63/37 | 37 | 45 |
| March 1977 | 1372 | 516 | .44 | 54/46 | 37 | 69 |
| March 1981 | 1249 | 733 | .40 | 59/41 | 31 | 57 |
| April 1981 | 1088 | 514 | .42 | 53/47 | 49 | 68 |
| June 1981 | 1237 | 607 | .55 | 48/52 | 46 | 72 |

a.    Studies conducted by Israel Institute of Applied Social Research, except for March 1981 and June 1981 which were conducted by Dahaf Research Institute.

b.    Respondents answering vote intention question "Alignment" or "Likud" are used in the computations in this table.

not become more capitalist in economic matters, as might have been expected from the right label. As shown in Table 2, almost 60 percent of the population has consistently favored socialism. Government intervention has often been decried, and the economy has been liberalized; yet the movement to the right has not been reflected in this important economic attitude. The stability of these attitudes over time forces us to consider the sense in which the system has changed.

What we have witnessed in Israel over the last few decades is a process of political change, not ideological change. The growth of the Likud and the growth of the right must be understood as a reaction to the years of dominance of the Alignment and the left. The terms are important as labels but not necessarily as indicators of the ideological content of party programs. Likud means not only right but also non-Alignment and hence nonleft. Our argument is that the designations of left and right are more important in their labeling function than in their ability to denote ideological orientation. Beyond the aggregate stability of attitudes and the simultaneous movement to the right of party identifications and fortunes, another good example of how this labeling function acts is the very stable religious response (see Table 2), a category not offered to the respondents. A steady 5 to 7 percent of the respondents sampled over a period of two decades volunteered the religious answer when asked to identify the political label with which they identified. Those respondents are the voters of the religious parties.

The interrelations among vote, left-right labels, and attitudes provide further tests for our contention that political change—not ideological change—accounts for the shifting fortunes of political life in Israel and that left-right labels are partisan rather than ideological. The transition from a dominant system to a competitive one is shown in Table 3. It is clear from the eight surveys conducted over a twelve-year period that the Alignment has lost support and that the Likud has gained. More important, the correlation between the vote and the political label has tended to rise over time, indicating that the distribution of left-right labels became more important in a political context of competition than was the case when a plurality of most groups supported the same party.

### Left-Right, the Parties, and the Voters

We have seen that the right and the Likud have increased in strength over time and that the left and the Alignment have declined. We get a more refined picture of the process when we look at the responses of those who reported that they intended to vote for one of the two parties. Those responses indicate that both the right and the Likud have grown and that the Alignment has declined. The portion of the Alignment voters who identified themselves as left has been constant. The shrinkage of the left is a result of the decline of the Alignment; the growth of the right stems from the greater legitimacy and the increasing political power of the Likud.

That a political label serves a veto function by pointing out which party one wants to avoid is not surprising to observers who know the nature of political communications in Israel. This function was filled by the left in the prestate and early state era—the period of one-party dominance—when the left was widely considered the legitimate authority in the system. Now, because the direction of that basic understanding has changed, the label *right* serves the function of identifying the bad guys (the left) as well as of reinforcing one's sense of identification with the group that one wishes to support (the right). The prime mover behind the label is identification with one of the political parties; from that flows identification with one of the political labels.

In the analyses that follow we deal only with that part of the samples (about half—see Table 3) that reported supporting one of the two large parties. A large portion of Israeli samples (30 to 40 percent) has refrained from answering when asked about voting intention or behavior; a smaller fraction has chosen other, smaller parties. To test the set of relations that interests us, we have focused attention on the first group.

The long-term explanation for the pattern of increasing correlation between vote and label shown in Table 3 is the shift from dominance to competitiveness. In a dominant party system, the clarity of the signal of the dominant party is less crucial because most groups support it anyway. No political cues are needed; no ideological labels are necessary to identify the object of the vote. The message can remain fuzzy as long as political dominance is not at stake. The more competitive the system, the more important it is to direct attention toward the ideological labels and thus facilitate the cuing function of the campaign. This interpretation seems to fly in the face of the inherited wisdom that maintains that competitive systems, especially those in which two large parties are competing against each other, work to blur ideological messages in order to appeal to the center. In reality, no contradiction exists at all. A party competing in a two-party system does not strive for ideological clarity; instead, it endeavors to cue its supporters by using labels such as left and right to reinforce their decisions to vote for the party. The cue is important as an additional support for the voting decision, not as a correlate of ideological content. This labeling function explains why in Israel, in the long term, the correlation between the vote and the label increased as the system passed from dominance to competitiveness.

The higher levels of response over time to the left-right question, as shown in Table 2, reflect this political change. The labels have become more important for the competitive parties that need to send more of these cues, as well as for the public that receives them. Thus a much larger number of the electorate in a competitive system respond to the labels and define themselves accordingly.

There is also an evident short-term corollary. Cuing becomes more effective as election day comes closer. One of the prime functions of the election campaign is to provide the opportunity for and to legitimize the effort of political cuing. For example, the 1981 election was held at the end of June. The correlation between the vote and the left tendency rose from .40 in March to .42 in April to .55 in June. Similarly, the September 1969 survey yielded a correlation of .21; and the October-November survey, conducted just before and after the election, yielded a correlation of .45. We can be precise because we know when each interview took place. The correlation between the vote and the left-right tendency for those interviewed during the two-week period before the election in 1969—at the height of the election campaign—and during the two to three days after the election produced an $r$ of .46. The correlation declined to .42 and .43 one and two weeks after the election and to .31 two to three weeks after election day. The campaign that provided greater visibility for party names and cues facilitated the higher correspondence between the vote and the left-right label. We reject the alternative argument that because the campaign period made party positions clearer, it became easier for individual voters to identify the party closest to their political labels. In the period under consideration in Israeli politics, ideological differences among the parties diminished and campaigns became less ideological.

There is a basic sense in which all politics in Israel are ideological. Mes-

**Table 4** Pearson Correlations Among Alignment-Likud Vote, Left-Right Label, and Attitudes on Foreign Policy and the Economy[a]

| Time Period | Vote x Left-Right | Left-Right x foreign policy[b] | Left-Right x Economy | Vote x Foreign Policy | Vote x Economy |
|---|---|---|---|---|---|
| Sept. 1969 | .21 | .12 | (.03)[c] | .09 | (.00) |
| May 1973 | .25 | .22 | .10 | .23 | .17 |
| March 1977 | .44 | .24 | .21 | .26 | .23 |
| March 1981 | .40 | .26 | .20 | .26 | .16 |

a. For sample sizes, see Table 3.

b. The question used in 1969 was different from the other three time periods.  In 1969 it was "To what extent would you support a militant policy by Israel toward the Arab states?"  69% were in the two affirmative categories, 29% in the two negative ones, 2% not answering. The territories question used in 1973, 1977 and 1981 was asked in 1969 but to a small sample (see Table 2).  It was decided therefore to utilize the larger sample of 1969 at the cost of using a different -- but related -- question.

c. Correlations in parentheses are not significant at the .05 level.

sages are packaged in ideological containers; code words are frequently attached. Isms and such phrases as fascism, socialism, and revisionism, as well as the basic values of the labor movement, abounded in the 1981 campaign; yet for many of the voters they were empty sounds. The style of Israeli political communication overshadows the substance.

Another test of our contention is confirmed by the data presented in Table 4. In each case the correlation of the vote and the left-right label was higher than the correlations between the vote and attitudes and between the left-right label and attitudes. Attitudes tended to be weakly related to vote and political label and never reached the level of the correlation between the vote and the political label. The short-term factor of the election campaign evident in the correlation between the vote and the left-right label also affected attitudes: the further along in the campaign, the higher the correlations between attitudes and the vote and between attitudes and the label as well. But in no year did these correlations exceed the correlation between the vote and the label, which remains the highest correlation of all.[19]

Political parties send cues about issues and attitudes. These cues are packaged and labeled to aid the voter in making the correct voting decision. It is fashionable to dignify these cues and labels by designating them superissues or ideology, whereas in fact their basic function for the bulk of the population is to identify the party to be voted for. Consider, for example, the way this function has worked in Israel. As we have seen, the majority of the population has supported a firm stand on the territories and has approved of a socialist economy over the years. Weak relationships existed between the left-right label and the attitude on territories (.26) and between the label and the economic attitude (.20)—the two important issue dimensions of the left-right continuum. But further insight into the cuing process was gained when party preference was controlled for. Alignment voters were much more differentiated with respect to the economic issue than the territories issue, concerning which left and right lose meaning. Likud voters were more differentiated with respect to the territories issue. This finding corresponds to the cues provided by the parties and to the consensual positions. There is at work a process of filtering that determines that left-right will be important when the following conditions are met: first, when the opinion is part of the consensus that marks the political system and, second, when it is applied to the supporters of the party that generates approving cues about the issue. The left-right label contributes only marginally to the sharp focus of the picture compared to the general climate of attitudes and the positions of the parties.

In a more direct attempt to ascertain the meaning of left-right, the following question was asked: ''People talk a lot about left and right in politics. In your opinion, what are the main things that distinguish between left and right?'' First, it is important to note that 70 percent of the sample indicated nothing at all. Second, moving to the right yielded higher response rates (see Table 5). We interpret this finding to mean that the former dominant left is in retreat ideologically as well as politically and that its adherents are less equipped to confront the issue than the more assertive voters of the right. The pendulum in Israel is swinging in their favor, and the respondents of the right are prone to talk about it.

Our conclusion regarding the filtering function of the left-right continuum was reconfirmed when this open-ended question was analyzed. The ideological content of the territories increased steadily from left to right, and the content of the economy issue decreased in the same direction.[20] Each group plays to its strong suit: the right to the territories, the left to the economy. Each group plays to that issue that enjoys wide social support. Left-right does not reflect ideology; it reflects an accurate perception of the composition of social-political reality. Table 5 shows that those identifying themselves as religious are most similar to those who identify themselves as right.

Left-right has no content for most people; only 30 percent imputed to it issue meaning. When asked whether they thought left-right was meaningful in Israeli politics today, 15 percent said definitely, an additional 20 percent answered affirmatively, and 23 percent took a noncommittal center position. This distribution not only reinforces our general doubt about the potency of left-right, it also strengthens the finding regarding the right: the farther on the right respondents placed themselves, the higher the percentage who thought

**Table 5** Ideological Content by Left-Right Label for Alignment-Likud Voters[a]

|  | Left | Moderate Left | Center | Moderate Right | Right | Religious | Total |
|---|---|---|---|---|---|---|---|
| Territories | 7 | 12 | 14 | 27 | 28 | 29 | 19 |
| Economy | 13 | 12 | 12 | 4 | 4 | 5 | 11 |
| None | 80 | 76 | 74 | 70 | 68 | 67 | 70 |
| Total | 4 | 15 | 21 | 16 | 17 | 3 | N=645 |

the continuum meaningful. The ascendant right perceived these cues as more central to their growing power than did the declining left, for whom these cues were often unnecessary during the period of dominance.

The process of filtering, or the use of selective perception in handling political cues, was also evident in the results achieved from using a different approach. Using semantic differential questions, we measured over time the images of the ideal party and those of the two major parties on the right-left continuum (see Table 6). In May 1973, before the October Yom Kippur War dealt a fatal blow to the dominance of the Alignment, the ideal party was perceived to be the right, the Likud was thought of as strongly right, and even the Alignment was considered more right than left. By 1981, the passing of dominance and the advent of competitiveness had clearly emerged. Although Alignment voters perceived things much as they had in 1973 (but note how they had become smaller as a group compared to the Likud voters), Likud voters perceived the Alignment as much more left than in the past. The cue had been received. The Alignment had to be rejected. The Likud cue to its voters to strengthen their vote transmitted the signal that the Alignment had become left and therefore had to be rejected not only on political grounds but on ideological ones as well. Whereas Likud voters perceived their party as right over time, they perceived that the Alignment had moved to the left. In a relative sense, then, they too had moved to the right.

Alignment voters also picked up party cues. The ideal party was perceived as more left, or at least less right, between 1973 and 1981. They considered their ideal party more centrist than ever before. They understood that something had occurred in the party space; in a competitive system their ideal party, by moving toward the left, became stuck in the center. Although their party had moved to accommodate the shifting nature of the party system, Alignment voters themselves stayed put. Over the two time periods their distribution by left-right tendency was stationary. Likud voters, despite the static nature of the perception of their party (see Table 6), moved dramatically to the

Table 6 Left/Right Party Images by Vote, 1973 and 1981[a]

|  | Ideal | Alignment | Likud | N |
|---|---|---|---|---|
| May 1973 | | | | |
| Alignment voters | 20/48 | 33/37 | 10/76 | 708 |
| Likud Voters | 7/69 | 32/43 | 7/79 | 313 |
| Total | 15/54 | 32/37 | 9/76 | 1021 |
| April 1981 | | | | |
| Alignment voters | 24/38 | 32/33 | 10/75 | 306 |
| Likud voters | 3/76 | 53/25 | 4/82 | 208 |
| Total | 14/57 | 42/29 | 7/79 | 586 |

a.    Based on a seven-point semantic differential battery. The numbers in the table are the sum of the percentage of the sample identifying the parties with a given characteristic, with the three categories left of the center point being summed and presented left of the slash and the three categories right of the center point summed and presented right of the slash. The size of the middle category is the difference between 100 and the sum of the two reported figures. For example, on the seven point scale, 14 per cent reported in 1981 that their ideal party was either in the first, second, or third category toward the right end of the continuum, while another 57 per cent were in the three categories on the left end and 29 per cent (100 − 71) were in the fourth or middle category.

right; 45 percent of them identified themselves as right in 1973 compared with 58 percent in 1981.

If our conclusions regarding the political functions of the left-right continuum are correct, our findings should reflect these conclusions when we control for important attitudinal and social factors. And indeed they do. The higher the level of political interest, the greater the correlations between attitudes and the left-right label and between attitudes and the vote (see Table 7), as the ample literature on political interest and education leads us to believe. The ideological functions of the continuum are especially pronounced at higher levels of interest and education.[21] In addition and central to our theory, the relation between the vote and the label remains high regardless of the level of interest in politics. The cues sent by the parties bypass attitudes for the less interested but work well nonetheless. The generalizations in the literature re-

**Table 7**  Pearson Correlations of Alignment-Likud Vote, Left-Right Label, and Attitudes by Political Interest and Continent of Birth[a]

| | Territories | Economy | Left-Right Label |
|---|---|---|---|
| **High Interest (N=201)** | | | |
| Vote | .41 | .33 | .45 |
| Label | .42 | .43 | |
| **Some Interest (N=268)** | | | |
| Vote | .33 | .14 | .45 |
| Label | .22 | .14 | |
| **Little Interest (N=186)** | | | |
| Vote | .13 | (.03) | .31 |
| Label | .15 | (.01) | |
| **No Interest (N=136)** | | | |
| Vote | (.07) | (.11) | .43 |
| Label | .15 | .11 | |
| **European-American (N=329)** | | | |
| Vote | .26 | .19 | .49 |
| Label | .33 | .26 | |
| **Asian-African (N=368)** | | | |
| Vote | .24 | .17 | .33 |
| Label | .18 | .16 | |

| | Territories | Economy | Left-Right Label | Territories | Economy | Left-Right Label |
|---|---|---|---|---|---|---|
| **High Interest** | European-American (N=94) | | | Asian-African (N=80) | | |
| Vote | .38 | .34 | .52 | .44 | .39 | .35 |
| Label | .45 | .54 | | .37 | .39 | |
| **Low Interest** | European-American (N=45) | | | Asian-African (N=75) | | |
| Vote | (.05) | (.06) | .56 | (.09) | (.07) | .36 |
| Label | (.22) | (.20) | | (.20) | (.04) | |

a. From March 1981 survey. For Israeli-born, father's continent of birth. Israeli-born whose fathers were also Israeli-born were excluded from the analysis (9% of the sample).

garding interest and ideology are correct, but they overlook the political aspect of the relationship. The relationships between the left-right label and attitudes and between the vote and attitudes are indeed conditioned by the level of political interest. But not so the relationship between the vote and the left-right label. That relationship remains strong at all levels of political interest.

Although the relationship is weaker, the levels of education generate the same general pattern as the degree of political interest.[22] The higher the level of education, the more effective the left-right continuum is in cuing political attitudes; but regardless of the level of education, the political cuing function works well.

In Israel the difference between those Jews who arrived in Israel from European-American countries and those who arrived from Asian-African countries has always been great. The former was the founding group whose members possessed modern skills and higher levels of education. Closely associated with the party of dominance, the group set the tone and the norms of the developing country.

Given the general political relevance of the ethnic variable, we examined its effect on the relationships between vote, attitudes, and the left-right label. Table 7 shows that the general pattern of correlations holds: the highest correlation in both subtables is the one between the party vote and the left-right label. It is higher than the correlations between attitudes, on the one hand, and the political label, on the other. When comparing the European born with those from Asian and African countries, we found a similar magnitude of relationships between attitudes and the vote. But the correlation between the vote and the left-right label is lower for the Asian-African born, as are the correlations between the political label and the two issues. Looking further into these relationships by controlling for ethnic origin and political interest simultaneously, we found that the differences between the two ethnic groups remain with regard to the relevance of the left-right continuum but that the similarities between the ethnic groups are much more striking than the differences. At high levels of interest the correlations between attitudes, the political label, and the vote are high for both ethnic groups, and at low levels of interest relations between the vote and attitudes and between the left-right label and attitudes disappear for both groups. Only the correlation between the vote and the political label remains high—and at the level of the correlation for the high-interest group.

Age variations between the two ethnic groups may be at least a partial source for the difference between them. Jews of European origin are on the average older. When we controlled for age, we found indications of two age-related processes: with aging, the correlation between the vote and the left-right label increased—the cues are learned and learned better the older one is. But there also seems to be a generational effect: the older generation still holds the cues from the period of dominance, thus relating the cues less to party than do younger age groups (although not as little as the youngest generation). The correlations between the vote and the label are .27 for those aged eighteen to twenty-two, .36 for the group aged twenty-three to twenty-eight, .51 for those between twenty-nine and thirty-eight, and .42 for those over thirty-nine.

## CONCLUSION

Our argument is that only by reinjecting the political consideration into the analysis can the functioning of the left-right continuum be properly understood. The electorate is in need of cues, and the labeling provided by the parties helps voters make sense of the party system. Although this sense may be related to attitudes and ideology at higher levels of educational achievement and political interest, the basic relationship between party choice and left-right tendency is much stronger and equally clear at all levels of ideological conceptualization.

Reinterpreting in this light the vast amount of data that has been collected places the political party and its activity at the center of politics—where it belongs, in our opinion—and not at the receiving end of a long causal chain. The political party transmitting cues is more important than the ideological content of the label that is being transmitted. Elections are primarily contests between political organizations and competing elites and only secondarily contests between opposing ideas. Parties often try to present their appeals in ideological guise, and in some elections ideological alternatives have even been presented and debated. In Western democracies, the tendency to present political parties as representing competing ideologies is great among scholars, analysts, journalists, and politicians themselves. But in most cases the party, trying to mobilize voters and legitimize itself by stressing the correspondence between the cues and the label it transmits and the messages and symbols acceptable in a given polity, is at the center of attention.

The left-right continuum should be thought of as denoting a party space, not an ideological space, for the electorate. This conceptualization should not be construed to mean that the left-right continuum is irrelevant to politics. For much of the academic, political, and communications elite, left-right represents ideological content as well as political cues. For the "masses," the left-right continuum does not structure the vote; it defines the boundaries of the party space within which the voting choice is made. As we have shown in the case of Israel, it may be that left and right have become more important not because of increasing ideological differences but because of increasing competitiveness between parties. There is no need to forsake the use of left and right labels in politics as long as we remember the fundamentally partisan and political purpose that they serve.

### NOTES

We thank Mr. Ilan Talmud for his able assistance in communicating with the computer. The research on which this article was based was supported in part by the Pinhas Sapir Center for Development of Tel-Aviv University.

1. Anthony Downs, *An Economic Theory of Democracy* (New York: Harper and Row, 1957).

2. See the rational choice, spatial analysis school and empirical work along the line of the Michigan school, such as Arthur Miller, Warren E. Miller, Alden S. Raine, and Thad A. Brown, "A Majority Party in Disarray: Policy Voting in the 1972 Election," *American Political Science Review* 70 (1976): 753-78; J.D. Holm and J.R. Robinson, "Ideological Identification and the American Voter," *Public Opinion Quarterly* 42, no.2 (1978): 235-46; and Theresa, E. Levitin and Warren E. Miller, "Ideological Interpretations of Presidential Elections," *American Political Science Review* 73 (September 1979): 751-71.

3. Donald E. Stokes, "Spatial Models of Party Competition," *American Political Science Review* 57 (1963): 368-77.

4. C. Alan Elms, *Personality in Politics* (New York: Harcourt Brace Jovanovich, Inc., 1976).

5. See Giovanni Sartori, *Party and Party Systems* (Cambridge: Cambridge University Press, 1976); Ronald Inglehart and Hans D. Klingemann, "Party Identification, Ideological Preference and the Left-Right Dimension among Western Mass Publics," in *Party Identification and Beyond*, ed. Ian Budge, Ivan Crewe, and Dennis Farlie (London: Wiley, 1976), pp. 243-73, who make an argument similar to ours; see also Downs, *An Economic Theory*; Angus Campbell, Philip E. Converse, Warren E. Miller, and Donald E. Stokes, *The American Voter* (New York: Wiley, 1960); and Philips W. Shively, "The Development of Party Identification among Adults: Exploration of a Functional Model," *American Political Science Review* 73 (1979): 1039-54—all of whom develop the functional model of party identification.

6. See Inglehart and Klingemann, "Party Identification"; Samuel Barnes, "Left, Right and the Italian Voter," *Comparative Political Studies* 4 (1971): 157-75; Hans D. Klingemann, "Testing the Left-Right Continuum on a Sample of German Voters," *Comparative Political Studies* (1972): 93-105; Jean A. Laponce, "Note on the Use of the Left-Right Dimension," *Comparative Political Studies* 3 (1970): 481-502; and Levitin and Miller, "Ideological Interpretations."

7. Inglehart and Klingemann, "Party Identification," and Levitin and Miller, "Ideological Interpretations."

8. Hans D. Klingemann, "The Background of Ideological Conceptualization," in *Political Action*, ed. Samuel H. Barnes et al. (Beverly Hills, California: Sage Publications, 1979) pp. 255-78; and Inglehart and Klingemann, "Party Identification."

9. Levitin and Miller, "Ideological Interpretations," p. 751; see also David Butler and Donald E. Stokes, *Political Change in Britain* (New York: St. Martin's Press, 1969); Philip E. Converse, "Some Mass-Elite Contrasts in the Perception of Political Spaces," in *Social Science Information* 14, no. 3/4 (1975): 49-83; Inglehart and Klingemann, "Party Identification"; Miller et al., "A Majority Party in Disarray"; Hans D. Klingemann, "Measuring Ideological Conceptualizations," in *Political Action*, ed. Samuel H. Barnes et al. (Beverly Hills, California: Sage Publications, 1979), pp. 215-54; and Pamela Johnston Conover and Stanley Feldman, "The Origins and Meaning of Liberal/Conservative Self-Identifications," *American Journal of Political Science* 25, no. 4 (November 1981): 617-45.

10. See Norman H. Nie and Kristi Andersen, "Mass Belief Systems Revisited: Political Change and Attitude Structure," *Journal of Politics* 36 (1974): 540-91; Norman H. Nie et al., *The Changing American Voter* (Cambridge, Massachusetts: Harvard University Press, 1976); John C. Pierce, "Party Identification and the Changing Role of Ideology in American Politics," *Midwest Journal of Political Science* 14 (1970): 25-42; Gerald M. Pomper, "From Confusion to Clarity: Issues and American Voters, 1956-1968," *American Political Science Review* 66 (1972): 415-28; John O. Field and Ronald Anderson, "Ideology in the Public's Conceptualization of the 1964 Election," *Public Opinion Quarterly* 33 (1969): 380-98; Christofer H. Achen, "Mass Political Attitudes and the Survey Response," *American Political Science Review* 69 (1975): 1218-31; John L. Sullivan, James E. Pierson, and George E. Marcus, "Ideological Constraint in the Mass Public: A Methodological Critique and Some New Findings," *American Journal of Political Science* 22 (May 1978): 233-49; George F. Bishop et al., "Effects of Question Wording and Format on Political Attitude Consistency," *Public Opinion Quarterly* 42 (1978): 81-91; and Gregory G. Brunk, "The 1964 Attitude Consistency Leap Reconsidered," *Political Methodology* 5 (1978): 347-59.

11. Philip E. Converse, "The Nature of Belief Systems in Mass Publics," in *Ideology and*

*Discontent*, ed. David E. Apter (New York: Free Press, 1964), pp. 206-61; Philip E. Converse, "Public Opinion and Voting Behavior," in *The Handbook of Political Science*, vol. 6, ed. F.I. Greenstein and N.W. Polsby (Reading, Mass.: Addison-Wesley, 1974), pp. 75-170.

12. Eric R. A. N. Smith, "The Levels of Conceptualization: False Measures of Ideological Sophistication," *American Political Science Review* 74 (1980): 685-96.

13. David J. Finlay et al., "The Concept of Left and Right in Cross-National Research," *Comparative Political Studies* 7 (1974): 209-21.

14. Harry Eckstein, "Case Study and Theory in Political Science," in *The Handbook of Political Science*, vol. 7, ed. Fred I. Greenstein and Nelson W. Polsby (Reading, Mass.: Addison-Wesley, 1975), pp. 79-137.

15. Shmuel N. Eisenstadt, *Israel Society* (London: Weidenfeld and Nicolson, 1967); Emanuel Gutmann, "Political Parties and Groups: Stability and Change," in *The Israeli Political System*, ed. Moshe Lissak and Emanuel Gutmann (Tel-Aviv: Am Oved, 1977), pp. 122-70 (in Hebrew).

16. For the wording of the question, see note b, Table 2. All the surveys were based on representative samples of the adult urban Jewish population of Israel. With two exceptions, the surveys reported here were conducted by the Israel Institute of Applied Social Research. The March and June 1981 surveys were conducted by the Dahaf Research Institute. All the questionnaires were prepared by Arian.

17. Converse, "The Nature of Belief Systems in Mass Publics," and Butler and Stokes, *Political Change in Britain*.

18. The territories question was put to a small sample in August 1969 but was not repeated in subsequent surveys conducted that year. See note b, Table 4.

19. In 1969 the foreign policy question was different from the one used in the other surveys (see note b, Table 4). This difference makes questionable the comparison of the correlations over time. Disregarding this question, we observe some long-term strengthening of the weak correlations between attitudes and the vote as well as between attitudes and the left-right tendency.

20. See Conover and Feldman, "The Origins and Meaning of Liberal/Conservative Self-Identifications." They discuss similar American findings and reject the traditional bipolar conception of ideological identifications.

21. Campbell et al., *The American Voter*; Converse, "The Nature of Belief Systems"; Converse, "Public Opinion and Voting Behavior"; and Ingelhart and Klingemann, "Party Identification."

22. See Converse, "Public Opinion and Voting Behavior," for similar results.

# 8

# Change and Continuity in Zionist Territorial Orientations and Politics

## Baruch Kimmerling

The main purpose of this paper is to summarize the persistent and changing components in the Zionist ideology and political praxis that refer to territory, by using some analytical concepts that will be presented and developed. I shall analyze systematically the period beginning with the initial stage of the Jewish settlement of Palestine and ending with the preliminary consequences of the recent peace treaty between Egypt and Israel.

The major theoretical question around which the discussion will be focused is the possible causal relationships between the diverse and changing orientations or feelings toward a specific territorial expanse and the political practice (i.e., different degrees and patterns of control or desire for control) related to this space.

### Types of Orientation and Patterns of Control

The orientations toward a certain territorial expanse constitute the first dimension of territorial behavior. These orientations run along a continuum of the degree of the expressiveness (or "sentiment")[1] that peoples feel toward a tract. On one end of the continuum are the more instrumental orientations toward an expanse, which refers to the space as a source of material resources, or as a property (in which prices are determined solely according to the demand-supply rules of the market). An additional instrumental orientation should be the perception of a territorial space as a strategic asset, which relates to the environment in terms of the possibility of physical control, either from offensive or defensive perspectives. Somewhere in the middle of the continuum is located the political orientation toward a territory; i.e., the perception of the space in terms of political control. The political organizer of a space (e.g., the government) is the highest ultimate authority that determines what territory is to be allocated to which individuals, groups, and institutions.[2] On the other end of the continuum are located mainly the primordial and religious (or moral) orientations. The primordial tie is the most profound expression of feelings of belonging (usually on the basis of "blood connections" to family, tribe, or nation). Places within a space are accorded "intrinsic significance" for an individual or a collectivity because of the very fact that they serve as a common basis for the community and an integral part of its very definition. Thus, Toennies, for example, defined his conception of *gemeinschaft* society as one where the common tie of its members to the land is the basis of solidarity.[3] The moral orientation toward a territorial expanse refers to the sacred meaning of a space. This is a geographical space where the supernatural and the material unite and interact.[4] Man may therefore refer to and organize physical space by its distance from a "sanctified," or a symbol-laden place, which constitutes some kind of center, often the center of the cosmic order in its entirety. Any harm inflicted on the center violates the cosmic order.

The second dimension of socioterritorial behavior consists in the patterns of control over a defined space as exercised by a collectivity. These patterns of control relate to the orientations just as *human behavior* relates to *values*. The patterns of control are derived from various combinations of three components: sovereignty, ownership, and presence.

The concept of "presence" can include a number of phenomena, the common factor in all being existence within a given territory. Existence here represents either (1) an expression or basis for claims for possession without regard to ownership, or (2) a demonstration of ownership upon land or the putting into effect of that ownership—especially if one's claim is contested. Presence can sometimes be very limited or temporary, and it varies from the appearance of religious figures and missionaries, shepherds and adventurers—a common combination that opened the Latin American frontier for the Spaniards—to the establishment of permanent settlements such as occurred in the north of that same land mass.[5] All of these "presences" eventually brought a military presence in their wake, followed later by attempts at imposing sovereignty, or a measure of control equivalent to sovereignty. There were occasions when military control preceded any other type of presence.

In the case study presented in this paper, the concept of presence has a more univocal meaning: the existence of Jewish settlement on any tract of land. The establishment of village settlements (as well as urban ones) was indeed an aim in itself and was an integral part of the process of building the Israeli nation. But in the context of Ottoman (and later Mandatory) Palestine, these settlements had an additional, secondary role, and that was the consolidation of control over the land and the creating of a fait accompli. In the Middle East, in terms of the law and customs, not being present on land, not living on it or working it, and, even more, the presence of another person on it, put the claimant's title in peril. At a later time there was a change in the function of presence, and it became a political means in an attempt to widen the control over territory conquered by military force.

The second form of control is ownership of land. Ownership, as it is understood today, is derived from Roman private law, but it undoubtedly preceded it. In most professional literature, any mention of the ownership of land refers to the private ownership of that land. In the present case, public or institutional ownership played a decisive part in the scheme of things, and in the period before sovereignty was a substitute for, or the functional equivalent of, the concept of sovereignty, because it was only by this means that it was possible to freeze completely the land that had been transferred from private ownership within one collectivity (the Arab) to another (the Jewish).

In the first stage of Zionist settlement, when the Jewish collectivity did not have enough physical and political strength to conquer land, the only way open for the acquisition of land was through means of acquiring ownership, or, in other words, exchanging capital for land. When the Jewish collectivity achieved sovereignty and became militarily powerful, conquering land replaced buying it. But even then, as will be seen below, public ownership of land did not decrease in importance.

The third method of control over territory is sovereignty. Sovereignty is in essence the exclusive authority that the state exercises over a given territory, and is in actuality an inseparable part of the very definition of the modern state, even though historically the concept is derived from the feudal system, which granted the lord exclusive right to rule over vassals who lived on his land. Sovereignty is a notion in international law, but its appearance is a political rather than a legal act, because it is conditional on the formation of a state. For example, in the case of Ireland, De Valera argued in a letter to Lloyd George (September 13, 1921) that "Our nation has forcefully declared its independence and *recognized itself* as a sovereign State." [6] But most experts in international law are not satisfied with the self-recognition approach, and require some international legitimation. It is true that "the formation of a new State is a matter of [political] fact," as stated by Oppenheim,[7] "[but] it is through [international] recognition, which is a matter of law, that such new State becomes a subject of International Law. As soon as such recognition is given, the new state's territory is recognized as the territory of a subject of international law, and it matters not how this territory was acquired before recognition." Thus, "where a new State arises the law has looked chiefly to the emergence of the new subject rather than the incidental transfer of territory; it has looked to the sovereign, rather than the territorial, element of territorial sovereignty." [8]

These three different forms of control over territory—presence, ownership, and sovereignty—may exist independently of one another, but it is worth-

**Table 1** Patterns of Control of Territorial Expanses

| Pattern | Sovereignty | Ownership | Presence |
|---------|-------------|-----------|----------|
| a | − | − | − |
| b | − | − | + |
| c | − | + | − |
| d | − | + | + |
| e | + | − | − |
| f | + | − | + |
| g | + | + | − |
| h | + | + | + |

+ present

− absent

Source:  Baruch Kimmerling, "Sovereignty, Ownership and Presence in the
Jewish-Arab Territorial Conflict: The Case of Bir'im and Ikrit,"
Comparative Political Studies, 10 (July) 1977:38.

while to examine the interaction between them. If we limit ourselves to presenting them dichotomously and examining whether each of the three forms
exists individually, or whether more than one exists together, there are eight
possible patterns of actual or potential control over territory.

Pattern *A* is the frontier in its pristine purity: a target land that is uninhabited, or is believed to be so. In *The First Frontier*,[9] one finds those who
sailed on the Mayflower describing

> these vast and unpeopled countries of America which are fruitful and fit for
> habitation being devoyd of all civil inhabitants; wher ther are only savage and
> brutish men which range up and downe, little otherwise then the wild beasts of
> the same.

The image that the *Hovevei Zion* had of "Zion" was not much different,
except for the "affinity" they felt for the local Arabs, who appeared to them
to be "relatives," or, at least, as representing the type of life that their
forefathers had led.

Pattern *B* is actually the first stage of penetration into an uninhabited country. This consists of having some type of presence, whether this was the Pilgrims in New England (before it became a colony), or the Portuguese *bandeirantes* who came to search for gold (but who later were used by Portugal to justify political claims), or the Spanish missionaries in the north, in New Spain (Mexico), in Paraguay, or along the Amazon and Orinoco rivers.[10] In Palestine, until 1947, the Jews never used this mechanism of control by itself. After the 1967 war, on the other hand, this pattern became the most central in Zionist territorial policy, but it was accompanied by military conquest of the areas involved.

The existence of law and order, of a government and administration (even if this is not set up by the immigrants and settlers themselves), is an essential condition for the existence of ownership over land, in the Western sense of the term, and for the growth of control Pattern *C*. From the definition itself, when there is the concept of land ownership in a certain territory, this means a perceptible drop in the amount of "free land." Often there is an artificial decrease of frontier in order to ensure large estates and *haciendas*, as was the case in both North and South America,[11] by use of political, military, or economic means. Companies formed for acquiring land, for its sale and development, speculators and private entrepreneurs, whose major objective is the acquisition of land, are all institutions and social roles which play a not insignificant role in connection with frontier case studies. In conditions of land scarcity, to acquire land and to guarantee that the land which was transferred to the collectivity's ownership is then frozen by it, it is not enough simply to have sufficient money to buy the land; there must be a group of speculators and mediators on the one hand and economic and political institutions on the other, to accomplish this. These institutions, or to be more precise, one institution—the Jewish National Fund—acted to a large extent as the functional equivalent of a sovereign state. The JNF bought land for the same reason that the United States, for example, bought Louisiana from Spain in 1803, or Alaska from Russia in 1867.

Pattern *D* can appear in some of the earliest stages of the colonizing settlement process, but in the Jewish-Palestine case, it had special significance. Until the Jews acquired sovereignty in 1948, it served the Jewish collectivity as the functional equivalent of sovereignty. Territories were acquired and settled, and a territorial continuum was formed between them. By means of these two types of supervision, which in this case were complementary, an entire method of "building the nation" was developed, based primarily on the acquisition of adjacent tracts of land and "creating" social, economic, and political facts (i.e., settlement points on these). This method even became ideologized and was crystallized into a political movement known as "Practical Zionism," as opposed to political Zionism.[12] Its motto was "a *dunam* here; a *dunam* there,"[13] with the intention of combining all the *dunams* "here" and "there" into a single territorial tract.

Pattern *E* contains a new component. When it is not accompanied by the two other components (and primarily when it does not have the component of presence) it closely resembles, in our context, the concept of a "secondary settlement frontier," this being "found in nearly all countries today where attempts are being made to extend the habitable area. . . . Any state, such as Australia or the Republic of Sudan, which includes sections of desert provides examples of this situation. Special services are supplied for operation in the uninhabited areas if necessary."[14] Siberia was also a secondary settlement frontier for Russia, and the great drift of immigrants into Siberia in many ways resembled the movement to the West in the United States.[15] In regard to the Jewish case, the Negev Desert served as a secondary frontier and as a territorial reservoir for Israel, from the time that it was conquered in 1949. Its importance as a secondary frontier increased when Israel agreed to vacate the Sinai Desert as a result of the peace treaty with Egypt. Another secondary frontier is Galilee, which is an area sparsely populated by Jews.

The combination of presence and sovereignty creates pattern *F*. When a territory is not a source of contention in any way, there is no difference in principle if there is or is not presence on the land held under the sovereignty of any collectivity. There might be an economic or internal-social significance, but not a substantive one. This is not true if the territory is a source of contention in any way: in such a case, presence is *seen* as offering political support for one's sovereignty, and strengthens the claim to control over the land in that it grants additional legitimation for control. The conception of underlining this perception to some extent resembles the Spanish settlement points along the border that were a bone of contention with the United States. Thus, for example, San Francisco was a combination of a *presidio* (a frontier garrison), a mission, and a *pueblo* (town or village), and it was meant to serve as a point that "created facts" both against the Indians and against the Americans who were encroaching upon it.[16]

Pattern *G* is very similar generally to pattern *E*, and it would appear that only in the case being analyzed here would there be any significant difference between the two. The perception that sovereignty does not guarantee control over a territory, and that the territory must also be under the ownership (preferably public) of the collectivity, appears to be a perception that evolved from the development of the Jewish-Arab conflict in Palestine.

Pattern *H* is actually the one where the frontier *ends*. The land is under the political sovereignty of the collectivity, under its ownership, and settled by it. On the other hand, all the previous patterns of control showed different forms of frontiers, even though the order in which they appear in Table 1 is not even an ordinal scale of control over territories.

Let me go back now to the orientations toward spaces as described above. The interaction between the dimension of the orientation toward a territory and that of the pattern of control over it determines the degree of the centrality of a territory. Thus, spaces are within most central locations in the system when the orientation toward them is primordial or moral, or both, and the level of control over them is that of sovereignty and ownership, and preferably presence as well.

A wide spectrum of phenomena could conceivably be predicted by the extent of the collectivity's readiness to pay for the achievement of what seems to be two kinds of consistencies within the system: (1) consistency between the three components of the patterns of control of territorial expanses—ownership, presence, and sovereignty—so that the existence of one makes the others desirable; (2) consistency between the patterns of control over, or the amount of "frozenness" of, a territorial space and the orientation towards it. The less fluid a space is, the more expressive an orientation it requires, and vice versa. But within the system one or both kinds of inconsistencies can persist because there are almost always internal and external constraints that can prevent the attainment of consistency.[17]

## Change and Continuity

The span of territorial conflict directed by the Jewish social system against the Arabs can be divided into four main periods: (1) The presovereign period, when the area of control—ownership and/or presence—was very vague because the aspired borders were undefined. As time passed, the borders became more and more defined by social and political realities. (2) The period when the system achieved sovereignty (following the 1947-48 war), the frontier was totally and ultimately closed (from the point of view of the Israeli system), and the battle continued to gain recognition and legitimacy for these boundaries (from the Arab neighbor states as well as the "world"). Attempts continued to raise the level of control *within* the borders. (3) The third period (following the 1967 war) when Israelis *perceived* that the frontiers were *partially* reopened, but the "real" ability of the system to increase (complete or selective) control over the "new areas" was uncertain and ambiguous. This potential "openness" of the frontiers broke the consensus within the system as to the goals of conflict management. Some reverted to advocate gaining of optimal territory, and the security perceived as connected with territory versus the goal of achieving recognition and legitimacy. This seems to be reached at least partially in the fourth period when (4) as a consequence of the general election in 1977 a different political subculture—i.e., the Revisionist Zionists—took over the government, and the "peace deal" was signed between Egypt and Israel.

As Palestine's Jewish community attained sovereignty over some of the area, the attitude of the collectivity toward the land changed in comparison with the presovereign period, when the system was limited to struggling for ownership of territory as a temporary substitute for sovereignty. Sovereignty in this context, when once achieved, implied complete political control of the land and, seemingly, the exclusive ability to determine the "rules of the game." Under such conditions, the internal impact of the Jewish-Arab conflict was expected to disappear. However, several factors combined to ensure that the basic situation continued to be perceived and defined as a conflictual one. The system continued to act accordingly, although with an improved bargaining position. These factors were:

First, after the 1947-8 war in which the Jewish community attained sovereignty, the state of war was not replaced by peace but rather by shaky armistice or cease-fire settlements.[18] At various times military force was used by both sides. Allon[19] claimed that this state of battle, determined by the Arabs, required Israel to define itself as being in a state of active warfare. One of the derivatives of this situation was the Arab refusal to recognize Israeli sovereignty, and differential degrees of recognition by "the rest of the world" (particularly in reference to sovereignty over territories beyond the boundaries allocated to the Jewish state in the 1947 Partition Plan). The very existence of this nonrecognition, which was accompanied by expressions of extreme hostility and the use of force, demonstrated the problematic nature of Israel's sovereignty over the territories and introduced a permanent factor of uncertainty into the system. This factor brought with it the need for continued ritualistic conflictual behavior, expressed in actions aimed at demonstrating, realizing, and strengthening Israeli sovereignty over the territories included within the state's boundaries.[20]

Second, sovereignty over the territories was not clearly understood by all Israelis. This introduced an endemic state of latent legitimacy crises into the system, calling into question the collectivity's very existence. These crises operated in various spheres in contradictory ways: some strengthened the system's conflictual behavior, while others limited such reactions.

Third, despite the fact that the direct confrontation with the Arabs over land had ended, and the vast majority of the lands were transferred not only to the collectivity's sovereignty but also to its ownership, there was still an Arab agrarian population controlling and owning lands within the state. This population had previously been the "other side" in the conflict. Its very existence—despite its new definition as part of the collectivity—was a sufficient stimulus for the continuation of conflictual reaction pattern toward the Arab citizens of the state.[21]

Fourth, the transition to a sovereign state did not bring with it an immediate revolution, neither in the institutional structure of Israel's political system in comparison with the first period, nor in the basic perceptions that guided it.[22] Even changes in personnel of the political elite and the major decision makers were very slow. Under such conditions it is not surprising that, in spite of the new conditions, many patterns of reaction created and learned in the pre-sovereign period continued to exist. Of course this did not stand in the way of changes in reaction to the conflict.

In the wake of the 1967 war there was a resurgence of the direct confrontation over lands between the Arabs (Palestinians and some of the Arab states) and Israel. As a result of the political situation that was created, the collectivity's physical boundaries and the amount of territory in its hands were again perceived as fluid, after a fairly long period (since 1949) of stability, and thus subject to manipulation. Here appeared a fourth pattern of land control (in addition to sovereignty, ownership, and presence): military occupation or, put more elegantly, "administration." As a result of the war, Israel obtained military control over extensive territories. This control was perceived as being temporary because of a variety of political and social constraints stemming from factors external to the system (such as the inability to fully translate military strength into international political power), and characteristics of the system (such as the inability to absorb an extensive Arab population into Jewish society). This temporary occupation could end in different ways for different territories—either with their return to Arab control (as occurred after the short capture of Sinai in 1956) or with the de jure imposition of Israeli sovereignty on them. The temporary occupation was not perceived dichotomously, but rather as a continuum of situations that might move in the direction of permanence.

In order to transform the temporary to the permanent—until sovereignty could be imposed on the territory—again use was made of the ownership pattern of control. Before 1948, ownership had served as a substitute for sovereignty. Now, too, the ownership is reinforced by Israeli presence; that is, by the creation of established facts through settlement. Between 1967 and 1981 we are witness to a partial return to the pattern of the Jewish-Arab conflict that prevailed in the first period, as it pertained to land. This was a result of the reconversion of the territorial problem into a direct conflict with the Arab population, and a source of pressure from other nations that created a new sense of uncertainty as to the collectivity's ultimate physical boundaries. In the occupied territories, unmediated contact with a heterogeneous Arab population was taking place in the framework of political constraints yet non-sovereignty for the Arabs, which was an integral part of the conflict management strategy.

It is not surprising that a social system with strong continuity, when facing a situation similar or identical to one that it faced in the past, will perceive the problems as identical to those of the past and react to these problems in a similar way. Thus, the existence of a sovereignty vacuum in the occupied territories again aroused the "Yishuv situation" in which not only the collectivity's physical scope but also its ethnic content and political identity constituted a problem. It had seemed that this problem would not arise again—at least from the Jewish side—after the 1948 war, as a result of which most of the Arab population was uprooted from the territories captured by Jewish forces and ceased to exist as a whole society. Thus, this perception of the situation constituted a renewed stimulus for conflictual reactions already learned in the past, such as land purchase (ownership) and settlement (presence), which were central items in Zionist ideology.

Between 1967 and 1973, Israel aimed at the preservation of the territorial status quo, while both sides perceived the Arab interest as lying in its violation. Time was perceived as acting in favor of this status quo, that is, in Israel's favor. However, in the sum total of power accumulation by both sides, the effects of time were not unambiguous.

In the fourth period what seems almost a different culture (i.e., the followers of the Revisionist Zionists) took over the reins of leadership in the system and began the dramatic bargaining process between Egypt and Israel, and the system appears to have reached a new balance among the territorial orientations. As a result of the combination of the new rulers' ideology and the peace talks, the liquidity of different territorial expanses was transformed and this dimension was polarized. The less central territories became even more peripheral and liquid; the more central ones became more central and less liquid. The primordial and moral-religious orientations toward Judaea and Samaria were increased and the strategic orientations toward the Sinai decreased. The direct consequences of this new ideological emphasis in the system was that when Egypt offered peace and official recognition in exchange for all or most of the territories occupied in the 1967 war, Israel attempted to convert the less centrally located territories instead of the more centrally located expanses, to the almost total neglect of the other factors in the Jewish-Arab conflict.[23]

## The Mountain Area

The whole territorial expanse around which the Jewish-Arab conflict has focused may be divided into two areas: (1) the central mountain area and (2) the coastal plain and great valleys. Later, from 1967, a third area may be added: the Sinai peninsula. Historically, as well as recently, the major primordial symbols of the Jewish collectivity and its "holy places" have been linked to the mountain area of biblical Judea and Samaria (including the city of Jerusalem). At the same time, the mountain area was less available to the Jewish settler and the land buyer. It was densely populated and characterized by less liquid land tenure patterns; i.e., land predominantly owned collectively by many smallholders, extensively cultivated, and sometimes "consecrated to God."[24] It is not surprising that in the formative period the Jews were unable to purchase even a minimal amount of land in the mountains, and the area remained devoid of Jewish control (except for the district of Jerusalem). But until the end of the formative period, despite the lack of control over this space, it was viewed as an integral part of Palestine as a political entity. The Jewish community, as well as world Zionist leadership, could not relinquish the claim for future control over the whole territory, including the mountains.

This claim formed an integral part of the political management of the conflict. Of course, the Jewish community did not give up the religious and primordial orientations toward the central mountain area (the orientations were usually mixed), but the political orientation predominated, and the area was viewed instrumentally. This view was reinforced after the decision to accept the 1947 Partition Plan—and the more so as a result of the 1947-48 war—when the ultimately physical boundaries of the collectivity seemed to be determined and the central mountain area was excluded from even the sphere of potential control.[25] The space was located, from the system's standpoint, but not from the standpoints of several marginal groups, outside the boundaries. Except for the Old City of Jerusalem, the area was not explicitly included in the immediate system of symbols of the nation. But it did remain part of Jewish mythology overemphasized in the school curricula as a result of the intensive teachings of the Bible, and the then stigmatized right-wing attempt to transform this lost territory into a primordial symbol embracing the whole collectivity. This was an attempt to mobilize the periphery to fulfill nationalist goals, and to challenge the nation's rulers, the so-called pragmatic left. In sum, pressures were felt within the collectivity to include this area in the orientation of the collectivity, and relate it in expressive terms (primordial or moral). This lay behind the great ideological split between the "hawks" and the "doves" that occurred in Israeli society when control over this territory and its inhabitants was accidentally attained in 1967.[26]

As for the Old City of Jerusalem, where the expressive factor was highly predominant—and the political and demographic costs seemed reasonable—the system moved without delay in exercising control over this "holy place" and annexed it, at the same time expending considerable efforts to establish a dense presence and even ownership. Here control was made consistent with societal orientation. A strong consensus existed in the collectivity over these acts.

For the rest of the mountain area, however, the situaiton was different. The standstill in the phase of military—and selective settlement—presence, accompanied by a seemingly strategic (or political) orientation, was the outcome of a mixture of perceptions of external constraints (i.e., the international political arena, the demographic balance) and the contrasting orientations toward this area. The mixture created diverse political sectors, applying pressures in different directions. The "hawkish" pressure to increase the level of control was, on the one hand, directed toward the immediate translation of military power and victory into the highest level of control. This was usually justified or presented in terms of primordial and religious orientations (sometimes accompanied by strategic argumentations). On the other hand, it was also expressed in moderate and pragmatic suggestions (e.g., those of Moshe Dayan) to open the space to "private entrepreneurs" who were expected to create a flow of financial resources—and reopen the process of land accumulation, similar to the situation that prevailed in the first period of the conflict. The so-called demographic problem was supposed to be solved through a highly sophisticated differentiation between territory and population that is the basic premise of the "autonomy" proposal for the Arab Palestinian population in the fourth period, and the third period perception of a division of sovereignty between Israel and Jordan. Israelis would have the control over the territory and the population would fall under a limited self or full Jordanian rule.

The "dovish" counterpressure over time neither demanded immediate withdrawal from these territories nor denied their "emotional significance" for the collectivity. Their predominant orientation toward the territory space captured in 1967 was political—and the mountain area (excluding Jerusalem) figured in their conception of land as a convertible resource to be exchanged either for Arab recognition (i.e., peace), or for legitimacy and consolidation of the control over those territories held by the system after the 1947-48 war.[27]

While the simple "dovish" approach aimed at preparing the collectivity for a future in which the system would relinquish its control over the occupied territories, a more sophisticated approach attempted to halt the tendency toward consistency between expressive orientations to territory and the level of control over it. The argument in this case was that in a situation where two national movements held conflicting "equally legitimate" claims to a territory, the only solution is division. Both peoples could thus persist in their sentimental attachments to the whole territory, but such attachments would not bestow any legitimate rights of control to one side over the lands of the other side. For example, the Jews can feel attachment to Hebron, like the Arabs to Jaffa, without either aspiring to control the cities; thus, "attachment" and "right to control" had to be differentiated.[28] This negation of consistency between maximum expressiveness toward and maximum control over a territorial expanse seems to be a profound psychopolitical change, not just a simple redefinition of the situation.

## The Coastal Plains and the Great Valleys

In contrast to the mountain area, the coastal plain is less abundant in ancient Jewish primordial symbols. In the biblical period the coastal plain was populated more by non-Jews than by "sons of Israel." But from a historical standpoint, it was not completely excluded from the perception of the country's boundaries, and at various times, especially in the Second Temple period, some of it was under Jewish control. From the beginning of the British Mandate—if not before—the area was included as an integral part of the political entity of "Palestine," and became an object of Zionist aspirations. The major advantages of this area, as well as of the great valleys (and some parts of the southern mountain of the Galilee), were their sparse populations—which comprised primarily poor tenants or nomad Bedouin tribes—and their ownership by wealthy city-dwelling (absentee) landlords. Here were the most liquid lands in Palestine, and during the first period of the conflict many plots of land were purchased by the Jewish National Fund, by societies, and by private investors. On these lands a relatively dense network of Jewish settlements (i.e., presence plus ownership) was established,[29] producing not only a territorial continuum but also an infrastructure for a complete Jewish sociopolitical system in Palestine. Soon the area was viewed as an integral part of the very definition of the collectivity, its most central or core territory. The process of land acquisition was relatively slow, but when territory was purchased the transition from a "desired territory" to a space perceived as core was usually a rapid one. The transition from "not control" to control by ownership was the principal bottleneck because of a shortage of financial resources on the Jewish side, as well as the political and administrative barriers set up by the third parties to the conflict (the Ottomans and the British), and sometimes the tenants' resistance to the transfer of lands that they worked.

The rapid transition from instrumental orientation toward the coastal area (i.e., farming for economic profit, the usual colonizing motivation) to the idea of settling on lands that have primordial meaning, was rooted in the predisposition to relate to these lands as "homeland." This in turn came about partly because of the immense emotional and physical efforts involved in the very process of settlement. Overcoming the difficulties of "conquering" the land from nature—when "nature" included not only sand and swamp, but psychological, social, and political obstacles as well—imparts to the "conqueror" a deep expressive attachment to the "conquered lands" and a feeling of just claims to them. The "conqueror" needs this feeling in order to deny the definition of the situation as zero sum, which may be stressed by the opponent. But defining the battle as one against nature rather than against men or sociopolitical reality (i.e., the Arab community) was not only necessary in

**Table 2** Major Changes in the Outputs of Socioterritorial Behavior-Principal Spaces

| initial output | attained output | | | |
|---|---|---|---|---|
| | no-control and undesired territory | no-control but desired territory | peripheral territory | core territory |
| no-control & undesired territory | | | Sinai Peninsula (1949)[a] Golan Heights (1967) Jordan Valley (1967) Gaza Strip (1967) Sinai (1956)[a] Sinai (1967) Sinai (1979) | Negev (1948)[b] |
| no-control but desired territory | Trans-Jordan (1922) | | Mountain region (1967) | Coastal Plain (1890-1947)[d] Galilee (1890-1947)[b] |
| peripheral territory | Horan (1948) | Mountain region (1948)[c] Gaza Strip settlements (in future)[e] | | Territories attained in 1947/8 war (additional to Partition Plan of 1947) |
| core territory | The Palestinian Arab State (1947) Beit-Haarava (1947) Gush-Etzion(1948) | Hebron (1929) East Jerusalem (1948) | | |

a. returning shortly to the initial output
b. low Jewish presence and ownership
c. excluding Jerusalem and including the Jordan Valley
d. including the Great Valleys (Jezrael, Heffer and Beit-Shean).
e. according to the Peace Treaty between Egypt and Israel.

order to grant self-legitimacy to the Zionist activities, but also formed an integral part of the tactic of conflict management.

In the coastal plain and the great valleys, the combination of ownership and presence-by-settlement in the formative period constituted the functional equivalent of sovereignty. These were accompanied by self-administration (e.g., municipalities), more or less included in a territorial continuum that was a politically homogeneous entity, subordinate to a Zionist quasi-government. These processes reinforced the expressive orientation toward these areas. The gradual obtaining of control over resource in conflict, mainly by converting economic resources into land, was a necessary condition for the process of society and nation building.

So long as neither party to the conflict could achieve a decisive power position, the mountain and the coastal plain plus valley area was "naturally" divided between the belligerents well before the various partition plans attempted to grant this division political institutionalization. Neither side could achieve its "final territorial goal." The struggle continued only in order to achieve more control over marginal areas (e.g., "cleaning up" the Arab presence in the coastal area after the 1947-48 war, or the establishment of Israeli presence along the western Jordan Valley and the Gaza Strip after the 1967 war). Only in the fourth period did the Jewish side try to reopen the struggle over the mountain area.

## Changes in the Output of Socio-Territorial Behavior

A given territory may change its symbolic place in the system; that is, the collectivity may change its orientation toward a given territorial expanse, or its degree of control over it, or both.

In order to summarize, illustrate, and analyze the issue of the present paper, I shall present four basic territorial outputs; that is, the combination of the major feelings (i.e., orientations) of a collectivity toward a space, and actions (political, economic, etc.) in the space, in order to achieve control over it or to increase existing control. The territorial outputs will be: (1) those territories over which the collectivity does not have either aspirations or control; (2) territories desired by the collectivity but over which it has not actual control; (3) expanses that are under the collectivity control (at least by presence) but are perceived as having instrumental value only—peripheral territories; and (4) territories over which there is strong control combined with fundamental expressive orientations toward it—core territories.

Each of the four could be either initial territorial outputs or subsequent outputs. Thus, there are 12 logically possible patterns of change or fluctuation. Empirically, analyzing twenty-one cases, I find only ten patterns of fluctuation in outputs of socioterritorial behavior. There were no cases of change from (1) uncontrolled and undesired to uncontrolled but desired territory, nor of change from (2) core to any kind of more peripheral territory. This does not mean, of course, that such transitions are not possible, empirically or theoretically.

The second finding that emerges from Table 2 is that it is possible to convert territorial expanses from the outer region of "no-control" not only to peripheral territorial zones (e.g., Sinai three times—1948, 1956, and 1967, or the Jordan Valley) but also to core territories that Israel annexed as a result of the 1947-48 war, which were excluded from the collectivity's orientation when the 1947 Partition Plan was accepted by the Jewish community. Opposite movement is also not infrequent. Large areas moved from "control" to "no-control" zones, like the Sinai Peninsula during the implementation of the first phase of the peace treaty between Egypt and Israel. Thus, drastic transitions occurred as a result of the inner dynamics of the Jewish-Arab conflict, the chains of stimulus and response on the part of all sides involved in the conflict. These dynamics are most clearly manifested by other cases of space that moved after 1949 from the initial zone of no-control to some degree of control. In all these cases—excluding the Negev—control over the space was achieved only as a byproduct of military or political needs, with territorial expansion not being an end in itself. But after the attainment of control, there were tendencies to define the spaces as "necessary" to the existence of the collectivity (mainly in strategic terms), and/or to revive the potential expressive orientations toward them. The boundaries of expressiveness have been affected by perceived possibilities of controlling the space, in terms of domestic, social, political, and international constraints.

On the other hand, considerable territories dropped from the collectivity's orientation and desire for control, and moved toward the zone of no-control (including no-orientation). These threw the scarcity of the territorial resource claimed by both parties into relief and heightened the acuteness of the conflict.

I can cite only one case in which territorial space controlled by the system through ownership and dense settlement-presence, and perceived as an integral part of the collectivity's space, was abandoned. This was Gush-Etzion, a relatively isolated group of settlements in the mountain area destroyed in 1948 by Arab forces. What seems to be important to note in this instance is not so much that a relatively centrally located territory was abandoned as a direct result of the local power balance between the sides, but that the space was apparently for some time cognitively abandoned as well. The total irreversibility of a territory located in a semicentral zone seems thus questionable. An additional point abandoned in 1947, without any attempt to retain it despite its obvious strategic isolation, was Kibbutz Beit Haarava. These cases seem to demonstrate that the system was *not* ready to pay *any* price to maintain control over a relatively centrally located territorial space when the perceived probability of success was low. Thus it is probably injudicious to refer to fragmented central territorial spaces as "irreversible." That is to say, the system tended to pay higher (but not unlimited) costs to keep its level of control when (1) the territory was already under the control of the system, and when (2) the orientation toward it was expressive. This conclusion is, of course, appropriate only for specific and limited areas and not for the whole territory of the collectivity. I assume that for the whole territory, or a considerable portion of it, or even for expanses perceived as necessary for the very existence of the collectivity, the system, is ready to pay "any" price.

In three cases the collectivity lost control of specific areas but did not expel them from its cognitive map (orientation zone). The first occurred in 1929 when the ancient Jewish community of Hebron was destroyed and many of its members massacred. Hebron was transformed into a symbol, not only because a Jewish community (ownership and presence) was destroyed, nor because it was a holy place (near to the Cave of Machpela), but mainly because its fate was perceived as representing the fate of the whole Jewish community in the event of an Arab victory over the Jews (equivalent to the function of Deir Yassin in the Arabs' interpretation of the Jewish "intentions" and techniques of conflict management). The second case was the fall of the Jewish Quarter in the Old City of Jerusalem, and of the whole eastern part of the city, at the hands of the Arab Legion in 1948. This was the only territorial loss defined by Ben-Gurion as a "misfortune for many generations." The territory included the most holy place for the Jewish people—the Wailing Wall. Israel proclaimed West Jerusalem its capital in 1948 despite its strategic vulnerability and the political difficulties this provoked. Most nations do not recognize its status because Jerusalem was destined for internationalization, according to the Partition Plan of 1947. The system was ready to pay these costs, as it was ready to bear the costs of annexation of the eastern city in 1967. It seems that the strong expressive orientation towards this area was not sufficient to initiate measures to take control over it, but when control was accidentally gained, the system was highly predisposed, as soon as possible, to incorporate it into the core zone.

## Conclusion

On the basis of these twenty-one cases (Table 2) we may be able to provide a tentative answer to the question of the possible causal relationship between the control and the orientation aspects of socioterritorial behavior. In other words, what in the long run determines the level of control over a space when the power relations between opposing sides are held constant by (1) the level of control itself, (2) the degree of expressiveness, or (3) a previously existing orientation in the system toward the territorial expanse? In order to make the answer more meaningful, it seems necessary to consider the question in two different contexts: (1) the territory of the country as a whole, and (2) distinct spaces or regions within the country.

The expressive orientation toward "Zion was a necessary but not a sufficient condition for the creation of Zionist immigration and settlement. Neither Birobidjan nor Argentina nor Uganda—the various alternative territories proposed at different times as a national homeland to solve the so-called Jewish problem—had any effective mobilizing appeal. However, "Zion" was a vague, unspecified, and flexible territorial concept. The gap between the semi-metaphysical concept and real political boundaries left the interpreters of the concept with a great degree of freedom; e.g., the choice between the mountain area or the coastal plain, one or both sides of the Jordan River, or "from the Dan [River] to Beersheba," versus from the Litani River to Aqaba beach, two of several biblical definitions of the collectivity's boundaries. Thus, most orientations toward the future or actual "homeland" did not prescribe either a distinct territory, except Jerusalem, or a necessary level of control over it. Actual Jewish control of specific territory was attained mainly where and when the opportunities (determined by political constraints, social conditions, and financial resources) were favorable, and later when perceived instrumental (political or strategic) needs called for it. Moreover, all the presently available evidence indicates that the achievement of control over the territories captured by Israel after the 1967 war was accidental, or at least unplanned. The "sentiments" toward these distinct territorial expanses reappeared (or were expressed) only *after* control was attained. Only a free-floating predisposition of expressiveness toward them existed previously. It can be assumed that the major "function" of these expressive orientations, which clearly manifest themselves only after control over territory is attained, is to grant the system some self-legitimacy in maintaining control. More important, they are an integral part of *the absorption of the space into the collectivity's self-image*, which then reinforces control. In sum, the kind of orientation maintained toward a distinct territorial space seems to be a result of the degree of control achieved over the space; there is no evidence from this case that orientation determined the achievement of control over a defined territorial expanse, on the systemic level of analysis. But when a minimal degree of control (at least military presence or ownership) was attained, an interaction between the type of orientation—on the instrumental-expressive continuum—and the pattern of control can be observed with each tending to reinforce the other.

In the period 1967-80, with the partial reopening of the frontiers, and the greater focusing of the Arab-Israeli conflict around its territorial components, the system tended to return to the means of conflict-management characteristic of the pre-sovereign period. It concentrated on expanding presence and ownership, while postponing the "ultimate goals" of total or selective annexation of the new territories or their return to the Arabs in exchange for recognition or peace. This happened not only because of external constraints, but also because there was no consensus on the question within the collectivity. The increased salience of the conflict in general,[30] and its territorial components in particular, was in part caused by heavy Arab presence in some of these territories. This necessitated control over men, not only land. The increased awareness, plus the conflict becoming active (versus dormant) and the zero-sum qualities of that conflict, led to inconsistent feelings in the system, so that it enacted incomplete control over large territorial spaces. The feelings of inconsistency seemingly also contributed to the intensification of internal dissensus and political struggles around the territorial issues.

## NOTES

This paper is based on a concluding chapter of a forthcoming book entitled *Zionism and Territory: The Socio-Territorial Dimension of the Zionist Politics* (Berkeley: Institute of International Studies, University of California), written while the author was on his sabbatical at the Center for International Studies, Massachusetts Institute of Technology. Thanks are due to many who helped me by critical reading of diverse preliminary drafts—among many others: Moshe Lissak, Shmuel N. Eisenstadt, and Dan Horowitz (Hebrew University), Russell A. Stone (SUNY at Buffalo), Ithiel De Sola Pool (MIT), Samuel P. Huntington (Harvard), Bob Brym (Toronto), and Joel Migdal (Washington, Seattle).

1. An attempt to construct a conceptual framework for analysis of orientation toward territorial expanses was undertaken by Eric Cohen in "Environmental Organization: A Multidimensional Approach to Social Ecology," *Current Anthropology* 17 (January, 1976): 49-70. For the application of this framework to territorial conflicts, see Baruch Kimmerling, *A Conceptual Framework for the Analysis of Behavior in a Territorial Conflict: The Generalization of the Israeli Case* (Jerusalem: The Leonard Davis Institute for International Relations, Hebrew University, 1979).

2. E.W. Soja, "The Political Organization of Space, *Association of American Geographers Resource Paper* no. 8 (Washington, D.C.: American Geographers Association, 1971).

3. Ferdinand Toennies, *Community and Association* (London: Routledge and Kegan Paul, 1955).

4. Mircia Eliade, *Patterns of Comparative Religion* (London and New York: Sheed and Ward, 1958), pp. 314-319.

5. By "frontier" I mean the term as coined by Frederick Jackson Turner (in 1893); see "The Significance of the Frontier in American History," *The Frontier in American History* (New York: Henry Holt and Company, 1920), pp. 1-38.

6. Nicolas Mansegh, *The Irish Free State* (Oxford: Oxford University Press, 1934), p. 29.

7. Lassa F.L. Oppenheim, *International Law*, 8th ed., ed. H. Lauterpacht (London: Longmans, Green and Co., 1957), p. 544.

8. R.Y. Jennings, *The Acquisition of Territory in International Law* (Manchester: Manchester University Press, 1963), p. 8.

9. David Horowitz, *The First Frontier: The Indian Wars and America's Origins 1607-1776* (New York: Simon and Schuster, 1978), p. 18.

10. See Alistair Hennessy, *The Frontier in Latin American History* (Albuquerque: University of New Mexico Press, 1978), pp. 54-60; and H.E. Bolton, "The Mission as a Frontier Institution in the Spanish American Colonies," *American Historical Review* 23 (October 1917).

11. See Paul W. Gates, "Frontier Estate Builders and Farm Laborers," in *The Frontier in Perspective*, ed. Walker D. Wyman and Clifton B. Kroeber (Madison: The University of Wisconsin Press, 1957), pp. 144-163; and E. Wolf and S. Mintz, "Haciendas and Plantations in Middle America and Antilles," *Social and Economic Studies* 6 (October, 1957).

12. See Walter Laqueur, *A History of Zionism* (London: Weidenfeld and Nicolson, 1972), pp. 277-308; and Dan Horowitz and Moshe Lissak, *Origins of the Israeli Polity* (Chicago and London: University of Chicago Press, 1978), p. 126.

13. A *dunam* is a Turkish measure of land, commonly used in the Middle East. An acre is equal to about 4.5 *dunams*.

14. J.R.V. Prescott, *The Geography of Frontiers and Boundaries* (Chicago: Aldine Publishing Company, 1965), p. 35.

15. D. Treadgold, *The Great Siberian Migration* (Princeton: Princeton University Press, 1957).

16. John Francis Bannon, *The Spanish Borderlands Frontiers, 1513-1821* (Albuquerque: University of New Mexico Press, 1974), p. 233.

17. Kimmerling, "A Conceptual Framework," p. 15.

18. Fred J. Khouri, *The Arab Israeli Dilemma* (Syracuse: Syracuse University Press, 1968), pp. 180-204.

19. Yigal Allon, *A Curtain of Sand: Israel and the Arabs Between War and Peace* (in Hebrew)

(Tel-Aviv: Ha'Kibbutz Ha'Meuchad, 1968), p. 15.

20. See for example the cases of the two Arab villages Bir'im and Ikrit, as presented by Baruch Kimmerling in "Sovereignty, Ownership and Presence in the Jewish-Arab Territorial Conflict: The Cases of Bir'im and Ikrit," *Comparative Political Studies* 10 (July 1977): 155-176.

21. See for example the military government, Sabri Jiryis, *The Arabs in Israel* (Beirut: Institute of Palestinian Studies, 1969), pp. 95-116; Ian Lustick, *Arabs in the Jewish State: Israel's Control of a National Minority* (Austin and London: University of Texas Press, 1980), pp. 123-129; and Jacob M. Landau, *The Arabs in Israel* (London: Oxford University Press, 1969).

22. See Horowitz and Lissak, passim.

23. Kimmerling, "A Conceptual Framework . . .," p. 27.

24. Gabriel Baer, *Introduction to the History of Agrarian Relations in the Middle East* (in Hebrew) (Tel-Aviv: Ha'Kibbutz Ha'Meuchad, 1971), pp. 76-82.

25. R.E. Gabbay, *A Political Study of Jewish-Arab Conflict* (Geneve et Paris: Libraries E. Drot et Minard, 1959).

26. R.J. Isaac, *Israel Divided: Ideological Politics in Israel* (Baltimore: Johns Hopkins Press, 1976).

27. See N. Kaplowitz, "Psychopolitical Dimensions in the Middle East Conflict: Policy Implications," *Journal of Conflict Resolution* 20 (June 1976): 279-318.

28. See Shlomo Avineri's treatment of these two concepts in *Ma'ariv* (Hebrew daily) 5 June 1973.

29. Elhannan Orren, *Settlement Amid Struggle: The Pre-State Strategy of Settlement, 1936-1947* (Jerusalem: Yad Izhak Ben-Zvi, 1978. Hebrew).

30. Baruch Kimmerling, "Anomie and Integration in the Israeli Society and the Salience of the Arab-Israeli Conflict," *Studies in Comparative International Development* 9 (Fall, 1974): 64-89.

# 9

# The Dilemma of Reconciling Traditional Culture and Political Needs: Civil Religion in Israel

## Charles S. Leibman and Eliezer Don-Yehiya

There are two models or conceptions of the primary function of modern governments. We call one the service model. According to this model, the function of government is to provide services and to reconcile conflicting interests among different groups and individuals. David Apter uses the term reconciliation system to describe the "secular-libertarian" form of authority which generally characterizes such a state.[1] He contrasts it with what he calls a mobilization system characterized by a "sacred collectivity" form of authority. This fits, with some modification, what we call a visionary model. In this model, government has a predetermined vision or goal, and its primary function is to educate and mobilize on its behalf. The term *vision* is appropriate since the goals transcend the immediate material needs of the nation's population, which is conceived of as a moral community.

Our models stand at two ends of a theoretical continuum and are useful in distinguishing between different governments which fall closer to one or the other end. Clearly the governments of the Soviet Union or Nazi Germany or Cuba are closer to the visionary end of the continuum and Sweden or England to the service end. But the service model is not necessarily more democratic or the visionary one more authoritarian. It depends to some extent on whom the government services and who generates and shares the vision (the elite or the entire population). There is a tendency for visionary governments to adopt authoritarian means, but this tendency may be restrained by other aspects of the political culture. Robert Bellah, for example, distinguishes a liberal constitutional regime from a republic. Liberal constitutionalism (a service type model) is built on the notion that "a good society can result from the actions of citizens motivated by self-interest alone when those actions are organized through proper mechanisms." The republic (a visionary-democratic type model) "has an ethical, educational, even spiritual role. . . ."[2]

The foregoing suggests a four-celled matrix of modern nation-states.

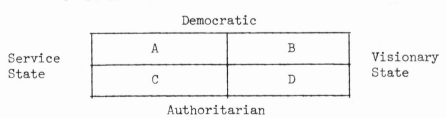

Democratic

| | A | B | |
|---|---|---|---|
| Service State | | | Visionary State |
| | C | D | |

Authoritarian

Type A, the service-democratic model, and Type D, the visionary-authoritarian model, are more common types of regimes, but Type C, the service-authoritarian model (e.g., Jordan), and Type B, the visionary-democratic model (e.g., Israel), do exist in reality as well as in theory.

One would anticipate that any visionary government would develop a highly articulated system of symbols (rituals, myths, special terminology, shrines, heroic figures, etc.) which defines the boundaries and the meaning of the *moral* community, legitimates the vision, socializes the population to the values it embodies, and mobilizes them to the efforts required for its realization. This is what we mean by the term *civil religion*.

Civil religion, in turn, can be primarily political or social in its orientation.[3] Where the orientation is primarily political, the vision is generated and imposed by an elite; the symbols point to the centrality of the state; power and national unity are emphasized; and the structure of government tends to be authoritative, although, as we shall see, even this is compatible with a democratic regime.

Where the orientation is primarily social, the vision emerges as a collective conception, and its parameters and meaning are defined by a variety of groups, each of which adds to its own nuances. The symbols point to the society and its people rather than to the state; voluntarism and pluralism are valued more than power and unity; and the structure of government tends to be democratic rather than authoritarian.

Our concern is civil religion's approach to a problem endemic to all new nations: the relationship between the needs of the nation and the tradition(s) and culture(s) from which the new nation emerged. One can construct a civil religion out of new or syncretic symbols, denying that the civil religion is connected to a past tradition. There are problems with this option. Part of the population may be deeply committed to its own tradition and perceive that tradition as bearing implications for the conduct of the nation. In addition the leaders of the new nation will want to exploit traditional symbols and values to strengthen national loyalties among this segment of the population. Furthermore, even among the more modern (secular) elements of the population, some primordial ties are likely to be retained, and the traditional culture offers the new nation a sense of continuity with the past. This may serve to legitimate the people's right to the land itself, to autonomy, and to an identity as a group distinct from others.

On the other hand, even if we assume only one tradition, some people may be ideologically as well as behaviorally non-traditional if not anti-traditional. Hence, traditional symbols may be divisive rather than integrative, delegitimating instead of legitimating. Secondly, values and behavior patterns anchored in traditional culture may hinder efforts at reorganization and change in political, economic, and social spheres.[4]

The problem is particularly acute in visionary-democratic states. Service states avoid the purposive shaping of their political culture. In the visionary-authoritarian state (all totalitarian states fall into this category), the political elite views the tradition, particularly when it is institutionalized in traditional religion, as a competitor for loyalty and an obstacle in its effort to shape the society in accordance with its values. Hence, totalitarian regimes develop new symbols which they hope will integrate and mobilize the population and legitimate their political vision. All the instruments of a modern state stand at their disposal in this effort. But under special conditions, in times of crises in particular, even totalitarian regimes may rely on traditional symbols. In that case they confront the dilemma of reconciling their political needs with the values inherent in traditional culture—a dilemma which visionary-democratic states confront most acutely, since they lack the coercive instrumentalities of the authoritarian regime. The very condition of political freedom and the possibility of cultural pluralism makes tradition an especially attractive source for symbols because of the deference in which it is held. This is especially true where the majority of the population views itself as the heirs of one tradition and that tradition speaks in one way or another to matters of national concern. The dilemma arises, as we noted, from the presence of one or more dissenting minorities but, even in their absence, from the inappropriateness of traditional symbols and values to the political needs of a modern state. Hence, the effort by democratic-visionary states to resolve the dilemma by transforming and transvaluing traditional symbols to make them more compatible to dissenting minorities and to the needs of the state. Obviously, the dilemma can never be entirely resolved since the more the symbols are transformed and transvalued to overcome one horn of the dilemma, the less "traditional" they become. Symbols are continually transformed and transvalued in traditional culture as well. The difference is in the degree and self-consciousness of the transformation and transvaluation. We distinguish three approaches or strategies of transformation and transvaluation in visionary-democratic regimes.

### Confrontation

In the first approach, the civil religion self-consciously confronts and to some degree rejects the tradition. But it forms its symbols out of this rejection. The link to the tradition is maintained by the very seriousness which is accorded to traditional symbols which are deliberately changed in order to adapt them to new needs and values.

This approach is particularly suited to culturally sophisticated people among whom the tradition is too deeply embedded to be ignored but who have rejected many of its symbols and/or their referents.

It is not easy to sustain a confrontation approach in a pluralistic-democratic polity where a considerable part of the population is traditionalist. A civil religion which is based exclusively on such an approach is likely to be a divisive rather than an integrative force in society. Hence over the long run this approach can be maintained as one variant in a civil religion which makes room for other approaches or strategies as well.

## Selectionism

The second approach, which we call selectionism, maintains that the tradition is composed of a variety of strands reflecting different sets of symbols and values. Some of these are affirmed while others are ignored, rather than confronted and rejected. Selectivity, it is argued, is quite legitimate within the context of the tradition itself. In fact, some proponents of this approach claim that the part of the tradition which they affirm is really more legitimate, authentic, or essential than that which they reject.

This approach is associated with a system of beliefs and symbols which aspires to become the common civil religion of the whole polity. Such a civil religion tends to stress the importance of that which unites the nation, such as the state and its institutions. Hence, the association between the selectionist approach and a civil religion whose orientation is primarily political rather than social.

## Reinterpretation

The third approach nominally affirms the entire tradition. The civil religion associated with this approach is characterized by the penetration of traditional symbols throughout the culture and their reinterpretation so that new values may be imposed upon them. As we observed, all religious development is characterized by reinterpretation and imposition of new values. The distinction is really the degree to which traditional symbols are reinterpreted to meet contemporary needs.

This is the least self-conscious of all approaches and is closest, in structure as well as content, to traditional religion. The attitude toward the tradition is very positive. Were the adherents of the reinterpretation approach to admit to their transvaluation of traditional symbols, they would transform them into arbitrary signs devoid of meaning and defeat the very purpose they seek to achieve: legitimating their values by linking them to the tradition. The reinterpretation approach is encouraged by a decline in the influence of modern-secular belief systems and their capacity to legitimate societal institutions and values.

## The Case of Israel

Israel is a visionary-democratic type society, and the nature of its vision provides two dimensions to the dilemma of reconciling traditional culture and contemporary political needs.

First, Zionism is the vision around which Jewish society in the Land of Israel formed itself. According to this vision, Jews, through their own efforts, will construct a Jewish society in their own land which will be the cultural and political center of all Jews. This is a basic component of Israeli civil religion in all its manifestations. In order to confirm the Jewish identity of the Israeli polity (and the polity of the *yishuv*—the modern, pre-state Jewish settlement in Palestine), Zionist civil religion required symbols drawn from traditional Jewish culture capable of expressing and fostering the historic and contemporary links between Judaism, the Jewish people, and the Israeli polity.

In view of the central role of Jewish religion in the national history and culture of the Jewish people, there is hardly a single Jewish symbol which is not loaded with religious meaning. The problem is not only the fact that broad circles in Israeli society are overtly secularist. They might simply accept these symbols as part of their historical heritage. The problem is the references and meanings to which the symbols point. The Jewish religion is God-centered. It accords ultimate power and authority in human affairs, including those of a social and political nature, to God alone. God is the only true king of Israel, its sole protector and redeemer. It is not easy to reconcile this point of view with a conception of national self-redemption, which is a central component of modern Zionism.

This can be illustrated by reference to problems involved in the celebration of Jewish holidays. Passover and Hannukah (the Feast of Lights) are among the most widely celebrated Jewish holidays. Both have explicit national-historical referents. Passover commemorates the Jewish exodus from Egypt; Hannukah, the Maccabean or Hasmonean revolt and the attainment of cultic freedom and a large measure of Jewish sovereignty in the Second Temple period.

Both these holidays, one might expect, would serve as important components in Israeli civil religion providing mythic-ritual symbols which would remind Israelis of their heroic past, of their lengthy history, their ability in the past to overcome vicissitudes, etc. The problem is that the holidays have assumed a fairly specific meaning in the Jewish tradition, and sub-symbols were developed or interpreted in accordance with this meaning. A central theme in the traditional meaning of both holidays is that success or victory was due entirely to God's miraculous intervention on behalf of the Jews and not to any action of the Jews themselves, not even of their leaders. As the traditional *haggadah* (pl.: *haggadot*) which Jews recite at the inception of Passover states: "And the Lord brought us forth from Egypt, not by means of an angel, not by means of a seraph, nor by means of a messenger: but the Most Holy, blessed be He, Himself, in His glory. . . ." The meaning of Hannukah is conveyed in the prayer which Jews are instructed to repeat three times a day and following every meal during the holiday.

> Then didst thou in thine abundant mercy rise up for them in the time of their trouble . . . thou delivered the strong into the hands of the weak, the many into the hands of the few . . . the arrogant into the hands of them that occupied themselves with they Torah.

What, according to the traditional liturgy, did the Jews themselves do? "After this, thy children came into the inner sanctuary of thy house, cleansed thy Temple . . . kindled lights . . . and appointed these eight days of Hannukah." The worldview expressed in such a prayer is hardly reconcilable with a modern movement for national liberation.

The dilemma of reconciling Zionism and the tradition acquires a second dimension in the Jewish-Israeli culture. This is the problem of the relationship between those who settled in the land of Israel and the Jewish Diaspora, both past and present. Traditional Jewish culture, the Jewish religion, is primarily the product of two thousand years of Diaspora life. It bears the unmistakable imprint of a religious conception of reality and of a people which deemed itself as powerless and homeless in material terms and compensated for this condition in symbolic terms. Zionism sought more than Jewish sovereignty in the Land of Israel and the ingathering of the Diaspora; it called for the redemption of the Jewish people from their own tradition and culture which Zionists perceived as a product of the unnatural condition under which the Jews had lived for so long. This involved a measure of hostility not only to the Jewish past but to the vast majority of Jewish people living outside the land who did not share the Zionist vision of immediate return to the Land or self-sacrifice on behalf of the establishment of national independence. Exilic Jews were seen as passive, miserable, and oppressed, and the Diaspora a source of shame and humiliation.

On the other hand, since Zionism claimed to be acting on behalf of the Jewish people and as legitimate successor to the Jewish past, it could never dissociate itself from Diaspora Jewry and Diaspora culture. Israel, its existence as a state and its culture, is meaningful and significant to most Israelis precisely because they perceive it as the great achievement in the struggle of Jewish history, the culmination of longings embedded in Jewish culture, inseparably linked to the Jewish past and the Jewish people.

In the *yishuv* and the State of Israel, there were, and are, militant Jewish secularists who insist on total separation of Israeli society and culture from any link to traditional Judaism and to Jews outside Israel. At the opposite extreme are the ultra-religious who deny the legitimacy of a so-called Jewish state which they perceive as the antithesis of authentic Judaism.

However, 94 percent of Israeli Jews affirm the attachment of Israel with Jewish peoplehood, culture, and history.[5] It is among this vast majority of Israeli Jews that one can find those who favor each of the three approaches for reconciling traditional culture and contemporary political needs and values in Israel. Among the 94 percent is a problematic group: the 12 percent who define themselves as religious and are committed to a Jewish state. Even the reinterpretation approach is not quite suitable to them. Their religious orthodoxy precludes their legitimating any transformation or transvaluation. Hence, they really stand outside Israeli civil religion. They evaluate each approach more or less sympathetically but never fully participate in any of them.

In the development of Israeli civil religion we can identify separate periods in which each approach was dominant, although one finds traces of all approaches in every period among different groups. We will associate each approach with the societal goals of the period in which it was dominant and illustrate how traditional symbols were transformed and transvalued in accordance with each approach.

Israeli civil religion has excluded the Arabs (15 percent of the total population). Their traditions (Christian-Arab, Muslim-Arab, Druze, or other) were never deemed relevant in the formulation of Israel's sacred symbols. Efforts to integrate Arabs into Israeli society have been by recognizing and legitimating their minority status with rights to partially autonomous cultures. The Jewish sector has sought to link them economically and politically but not culturally or socially to the larger society.[6]


## Confrontation and Labor Zionism

As we noted, the confrontation approach is suitable to a culturally sophisticated group deeply rooted in the very tradition whose values it opposes and whose symbols may evoke a negative resonance. Confrontation was the characteristic approach of the Labor Zionist movement which led the *yishuv* in the two decades preceding the establishment of the state. While other strategies were present in that period, confrontation was the primary mode through which Labor Zionism related to the tradition and by which it developed a symbol system which both reflected and supported its particular values and perceptions of reality.

The Labor Zionist goal included the creation of a new type of Jew and a new society. Its very image of the desirable Jew and desirable society was the mirror image of the traditional Jew and traditional Jewish society. For example, Labor Zionism's attitude toward non-Jews and toward other nations was more universalist than the dominant civil religion of any other period. It deliberately rejected the particularism and ethno-centrism of the Jewish tradition.

Confrontationalism was reflected in both old as well as new symbols. Traditional rituals and myths were deliberately inverted in order to accord with new needs and values. Whereas traditional Jews centered the celebration of the holiday of Hannukah around the cruze of oil which miraculously burned for eight days, a popular Hannukah song in the transformation period glorified the modern Zionist pioneers (really the *yishuv* itself) since "we found no cruze of oil, no miracle was performed for us."[7]

The Passover celebration begins with a Seder or festive meal at which, as we noted, the haggadah is read. The kibbutzim formulated their own *haggadot*.[8] In general, God was excised; nature, springtime, and nationalist elements were emphasized. Even evolutionary and class struggle themes found expression in the *haggadot* of the more leftist kibbutzim. A most dramatic expression, however, of the confrontation approach is the statement by Ber Borochov (1881–1917), the foremost ideologue of the Labor Zionist movement. One of the most popular sections of the *haggadah* speaks of four sons, one wise, one wicked, one simple, and one childish. The second son is called wicked because he raises questions about the very basis of the Passover ceremonial and seems to exclude himself from the community of celebrants. Borochov, however, praised the wicked son because that son wanted no part of the freedom given by God but insisted upon attaining freedom by himself. The same "wicked ones," Borochov argued, are those who today insist on attaining freedom with their own hands and thereby create "the foundation for the construction of a new Jewish life."[9]

The strategy of confrontation is applicable to *new* myths and rituals as well. A striking example is the myth of Joseph Trumpeldor.[10] The story of Trumpeldor's death and the fall of Tel Hai in 1920 assumed mythic dimensions in the *yishuv* within a year of the event. From the very outset Trumpeldor was projected as an anti-hero to the religious tradition, the archetype of the "new Jew" as opposed to the "traditional Jew." Even before his death Trumpeldor had achieved the status of a folk hero, noted for his courage. He was believed to be the first Jew appointed as an officer in the Czarist army. He was the antithesis of the traditional Jew who went to almost any lengths to avoid service in that army.

Comparison between the defenders of Tel Hai and classical Jewish martyrs led Labor Zionist spokesmen to invidious distinctions:

> The early martyrs all sought in return for their deeds . . . a place in the world-to-come—the personal pleasure which every religious Jew feels in giving his life. . . . This was not true of the martyrs of Tel Hai who did not sacrifice their lives for personal pleasure. . . . They were not concerned with whether or not they would earn pleasure in the next world. All that mattered to them was that the Jewish people should survive and the Land of Israel be rebuilt.[11]

According to another Labor Zionist spokesman, unlike Jewish heroes of the past, "Trumpeldor is not merely a victim, a passive hero; he is an active hero." Finally, in what can only be described as the adoption of anti-semitic stereotypes, Trumpeldor was described as follows: "He had not a trace of sickliness, nervousness, impulsiveness, disquietude—qualities which characterize the Diaspora Jew." Ben-Gurion declared that "for this generation"—those to whom he referred as "the comrades of Trumpeldor"—this land is more holy than for the tens of generations of Jews who believed in its historical and religious sanctity; for it has been sanctified by our sweat, our work, and our blood."[12]

Although the civil religion of Labor Zionism was the most influential system of beliefs and symbols in the pre-state period, it did not encompass the entire Jewish community. The religious sector opposed its overt secularism, and the Revisionists (ultra-nationalists) sharply criticized the socialist component of its belief system.

In a sense, there were several varieties of civil religion in the *yishuv* period, each with its own community of believers. The *yishuv* was in fact a federation of relatively voluntaristic and autonomous communities united by their common commitment to the Zionist ideal. Hence, the potential and even necessity for each to develop its own symbol system.

This changed after the establishment of the state. A politically oriented civil religion which strove to unite and integrate the entire Jewish population around the symbolism of the state now emerged. This symbol system called *mamlakhtiut* (statism) was associated with the selectionist approach although it found its earliest development among the Revisionists in the pre-state period.[13]

## Selectionism and Statism

Those traditional symbols which pointed to or could be interpreted as pointing to the centrality of the state were integrated into the civil religion; others were ignored. Ben-Gurion and his followers defined and sought to impose their version of civil religion more explicitly than any other group of leaders in any other period. In the years from 1948 to the end of the 1950s Israeli civil religion assumed a political rather than a social orientation, almost meeting the criteria of political religion as Apter defines it.[14] Apter observes that political religion is particularly attentive to the young in whom it places the hope for the creation of a new generation. It was to this group, a generation removed from firsthand encounter with the Jewish tradition and without the deep associations, memories, and nostalgia of their parents, before whom the statists projected their conception of the tradition.

Ben-Gurion affirmed his unbounded admiration for some aspects of the tradition. On the other hand, he and other statists denied significance to that part of the traditional culture which originated in the period of Jewish exile. They projected the modern settlement of the Land of Israel as the successor to the period of Jewish national independence which ended in 70 C.E. The intervening two thousand years of exile were devoid of meaning.

The result of the exile, according to Ben-Gurion, was to alienate the Jews from their greatest cultural achievement—the Bible. Post-biblical Judaism, he claimed, was apolitical, particularistic, and prone to exaggerated spiritualism. It neither understood nor properly appreciated the Bible and the biblical period with its rich harmony of spiritual and material, moral and political, Jewish and universal values. Only those who have returned to their Land and lead an independent national life can truly appreciate the Bible.[15] While Israel's first prime minister generally refrained from denigrating the rabbinic tradition, the product of the exilic period, his silence with respect to its literature, coupled with his reverence for the Bible and the biblical period, was enough. "We are consciously divorcing ourselves from the recent past," he wrote on one occasion.[16]

The Bible, in turn, was not only celebrated in the formulation of adult study circles, through the major emphasis given it in schools, in the international Bible quiz which culminated on Israel Independence Day, but in fetishistic veneration as, for example, in the creation of the Shrine of the Book which housed the Dead Sea Scrolls.[17]

The most important new symbol reflecting the selectionist approach was Independence Day. We have defined selectionism as the affirmation of one strand in the tradition at the expense of others. How can such an approach incorporate new symbols? We argue that one can identify a strategy of selectionism when the new symbol is linked to a traditional one in such a way that one aspect of the tradition is emphasized at the deliberate expense of another.

An association was drawn in the early years of statehood between Independence Day and Passover, an association facilitated by the occurrence of the former 13 days after the conclusion of the latter festival. There were many references in the first years of statehood to Independence Day, "the day of days," as a kind of culmination of the process which begins with the Passover celebration of the exodus from Egypt. Independence Day, therefore, replaced Shavuot, the holiday of the giving of the *Torah* which was traditionally linked to Passover. The traditional paradigm was exodus (physical freedom) followed by the giving of the *Torah*

(spiritual freedom). The new paradigm became exodus (freedom from foreign oppression by leaving Egypt) followed by Independence Day (achieving national
autonomy by establishing the State). The paradigm was strengthened by compari-
sons between Ben-Gurion and Joshua who led the Jews into the Promised Land in
the biblical period.

## Reinterpretation and Israel's New Civil Religion

Neither Labor Zionism and its confrontational approach nor statism and its selectionist approach maintained their dominant position in Israeli political culture. The
massive influx of traditionally oriented immigrants following the establishment of
Israel was one reason for the decline of the more secular type civil religions.
Indeed, the more secular the civil religion, the greater its difficulty in sanctifying
institutions and patterns of behavior because its symbols lack grounding in the
collective consciousness and historical culture of the people. The more tenuously
the civil religion is linked to the tradition, the more difficult it is to assert the sacred
nature of its myths and rituals. David Apter found this to be true in authoritarian
regimes.[18] It is certainly true in a democratic-visionary polity like Israel where the
political elite cannot always draw upon the support of state-controlled instruments
for socialization in order to maintain the total commitment of the population.

But the need remained for an ideational and symbolic system to legitimate the
Jewish state, mobilize internal and external support for its survival and development, and provide content and meaning to its Jewish identity. The reasons behind
the decline of Labor Zionist and statist civil religions help account for the rise to
dominance of a New Civil Religion[19] which utilizes the approach of reinterpretation
and is more receptive to traditional culture and religion than the other two approaches. The New Civil Religion reached a dominant position after 1967. The peak
of its influence came with the Likud victory in 1977 (the Likud is more closely
identified with the New Civil Religion than any other party), though its roots are to
be found in the mid-1950s with the adoption of the Jewish Consciousness Program
for Israeli schools. Its goal was to unite and integrate the society around its
conception of the Jewish tradition and the Jewish people; it no longer sought the
creation of a new Jew and a new Jewish society (Labor-Zionism) or the unification
and integration of the society around the symbols of statehood (statism). However,
the tradition and Jewish peoplehood, as we shall see, assumed a particular meaning
in the New Civil Religion.

This is the most ethno-centric of all civil religions. It affirms all Jewish history
and culture and gives special emphasis to the isolation of Jews and hostility of
Gentiles. The characteristic slogan of this period is the biblical phrase "a people
that dwells alone" or the rabbinic metaphor "Esau hates Jacob." It is, needless to
say, a civil religion especially well suited to masses who are familiar with and
attached to traditional symbols but unsophisticated concerning their explicit meaning.

The tradition is reinterpreted—gently, subtly, and unself-consciously. National motifs and a nationalist interpretation of religious symbols are omnipresent. For example, the popular army weekly publication, *In The Camp,* is intended for the average soldier and the general reader. It also devotes material to each holiday in the issue immediately preceding its onset. In a recent Passover issue the cover reproduced a drawing from an 1849 *haggadah* showing Moses and the Egyptians at the Red Sea. Of the eight articles, three related to the holiday. One treated changes in the celebration of Passover in the kibbutz, stressing that the kibbutzim were now observing more and more of the traditional rituals. A second analyzed the character of Moses (lonely and isolated: note the parallel to Israel's contemporary self-image) and observed that "the most magnificent treatment of Moses, the most human and superhuman of all, and perhaps the most faithful to the truth, is that of the Torah." (The *haggadah*, it should be observed, never mentions Moses, and the traditional reason offered is that there is only one hero in the exodus story and that is God Himself). The third article recounted the 1920 Arab riots against Jews in Palestine noting that they broke out on Passover.

By definition one cannot create a new reinterpreted symbol, but the treatment of the Holocaust illustrates how the strategy of reinterpretation deals with a symbol of recent origin. Analysis of the Holocaust symbol also provides an instructive comparison of how each of the three approaches deals with the dilemma of relating the tradition (in this case the tradition of Jewish suffering and dispersion) to the needs of a modern state.

## The Holocaust in Israeli Civil Religion

The very term Holocaust (capital H) is a symbol which points to the destruction of European Jewry. It has any number of other meanings and references according to how it is projected and interpreted. We cannot hope, in so brief an essay, to explore the problem of the development of the Holocaust symbol in Israeli society in any depth. Yet the different ways in which the symbol is projected and interpreted are so dramatic that it lends itself to summary treatment.

As acute an observer of Israeli society as Amos Elon noted that Israelis "hardly give themselves the chance to forget the Holocaust." The traumatic memory is part of the rhythm and ritual of public life."[20] In the words of the army's *Informational Guidelines to the Commander,* the Holocaust to a great extent fashions "our national consciousness and the way in which we understand ourselves and the world in which we live."[21] In contrast to these observations it is significant to note that the mode of observance of Holocaust Day was only fixed in 1959 when the Knesset was called upon to act in the face of widespread public indifference to the Day. Until then there were no visible signs of commemoration on the Israeli street. Places of entertainment operated as on any other day; there were no special radio programs. Hebrew writers simply ignored the Holocaust during the 1950s. Until the 1960s it found no expression in the school curriculum. It is true that in 1954 the Government created Yad Vashem, a public memorial to honor the memory of the Holocaust victims. This today is one of the country's two major shrines. But reading the Knesset debates surrounding its establishment one senses how problematic the whole matter was to the leaders of Israel. The Government only acted under pressure, not the least of which apparently was the fear that memorials would be established abroad challenging Israel's status as the legitimate representative of the Jewish people, authorized to speak on behalf of all Jewry, including those who died in the Holocaust.

All this hesitation and reluctance reflected the selectionist approach which chose to ignore traditional Gentile hostility. According to Ben-Gurion:

> German anti-semitism, the Dreyfus trial, . . . persecution of Jews in Rumania, . . . they represent events from the past in foreign lands, sad memories of Jews in exile, but not emotional experiences and facts of life which educate and direct us.[22]

In other words, this was part of the tradition which the statists refused to incorporate in their symbol system.

> The Jewish people erred when it blamed anti-semitism for all the suffering and hardship it underwent in the Diaspora. . . . The cause of our troubles and the anti-semitism of which we complain result from our peculiar status that does not accord with the established framework of the nations of the world. It is not the result of the wickedness or folly of the Gentiles which we call anti-semitism.[23]

According to Pinhas Lavon, a member of Ben-Gurion's cabinet and later minister of defense, the Holocaust is not without historical precedent. Jews, he said, were killed in the past. Furthermore, Nazi efforts at genocide had precedent in Turkish attempts to kill all Armenians, "and the blood of the Armenian people is no less precious to us than our own."[24]

The problem of the Holocaust symbol stemmed in part from the fact that the history of Diaspora Jewry and its condition as a persecuted minority were irrelevant for statists. A second problem stemmed from the Israeli perception of the victims' behavior as one of passivity and surrender—typical of exilic Jewry but one with which Israelis could not identify. Could one acknowledge this without reopening wounds and destroying the unity of the Jews?

The confrontation approach which we associated with Labor Zionism in the pre-state period faced this challenge squarely. The image of Holocaust victims who went "like sheep to the slaughter" was rife in the *yishuv*. According to one kibbutz *haggadah*, ". . . Hitler alone is not responsible for the death of six million—but all of us and above all the six million. If they knew that the Jew had power, they would not have all been butchered. . . ."[25]

But in the years following the end of the war, overwhelmed by the magnitude of Jewish persecution, by the presence of former concentration camp inmates and European refugees in Israel, and perhaps by their own guilt in having judged the victims so harshly while doing little to save them, a process of transvaluation began in which the Holocaust symbol now pointed to physical resistance and rebellion. In general it was the political left who remained faithful to Labor Zionist principles and a confrontation strategy whereas the Labor Zionist right wing was attracted to statism and selectionism. The former favored memorializing the Holocaust, and it was they who succeeded in imposing their symbolic model on the commemoration. What they did was to redefine the relevant behavior of the Holocaust victims to coincide with their own values so that the victims became positive rather than negative role models. The day chosen by the Knesset to honor the victims was called Memorial Day for the Holocaust and Ghetto Revolts and was associated in particular with the Warsaw Ghetto uprising. Yad Vashem's subtitle was Memorial Authority for the Holocaust and Bravery. Knesset members who favored its establishment (they included, we must add, minister of education Dinur, in other respects a leading advocate of statism) connected the heroic acts of physical resistance against the Nazis with the heroism of Israeli fighters in the War of Independence.

But the Holocaust is commemorated today in the spirit of the reinterpretation approach. One finds references to bravery and resistance, but this is not the major theme. The Holocaust is primarily a paradigm for the condition of Israel and the hostility of its enemies. In the words of the present minister of education, ". . . the Holocaust is not a national insanity that happened once and passed, but an ideology that has not passed from the world and even today the world may condone crimes against us." Contemporary values are, in retrospect, imposed upon the past so that Israelis can derive the meaning they want from the past. The dead, for example, became victims who "sacrificed" their lives purposefully. According to the former President of Israel, "Our decision is firm that the people ingathered again in its ancient homeland will preciously guard these eternal values for which a third of our people sacrificed their life." Finally, the Holocaust symbol points to the debt which the world owes to Israel. According to a Knesset member speaking at the closing ceremony for Holocaust memorial day:

> . . . even the best friends of the Jewish people refrained from offering significant saving help of any kind to European Jewry and turned their back on the chimneys of the death camps. . . . Therefore all the free world, especially in these days, is required to show its repentance . . . by providing diplomatic defensive-economic aid to Israel.

### A Final Word

Our primary concern in this essay has been to illustrate three approaches for coping with the dilemma of tradition and modernity in a new state. We noted, in the case of Israel, that each approach was consistent with a dominant value of the civil religion but we only touched upon the political-economic-social conditions and considerations which give rise to each approach. In addition, whereas the dilemma we have posed is central to the civil religion there is more to civil religion than the problem to which we have addressed ourselves. There are symbols which point to concerns that have only marginal bearing on the problem. Because the different approaches and strategies are embedded in the civil religion they are influenced by the general level of public commitment. In this respect, civil religion is quite like traditional religion. We can analyze religion in organizational, ideational, symbolic, or other terms, but we must never overlook the danger of concentrating on its formal properties and of ignoring the dimension of its acceptance, the degree of its penetration, or the level of commitment it evokes from its ostensible adherents.

## NOTES

The article is based on material gathered for the authors' forthcoming book, *Civil Religion in Israel: Traditional Religion and Political Culture in the Jewish State* (Berkeley: University of California Press, 1983). We wish to thank the Israel Foundations Trustees–Ford Foundation for their assistance.

1. David Apter, *The Politics of Modernization* (Chicago: The University of Chicago press, 1965), p. 25.

2. Robert Bellah, "Religion and the Legitimation of the American Republic," in Robert Bellah and Phillip Hammond, *Varieties of Civil Religion* (New York: Harper & Row, 1980), p. 9.

3. For a similar distinction see John Wilson, *Public Religion in America* (Philadelphia: Temple University Press, 1979).

4. Clifford Geertz, *The Interpretation of Cultures* (New York: Basic Books, 1973), pp. 238–49, has labeled this the conflict between essentialism and epochalism.

5. Charles Liebman and Eliezer Don-Yehiya, "What a Jewish State Means to Israeli Jews," in Sam Lehman-Wilzig and Bernard Susser, eds., *Comparative Jewish Politics: Public Life in Israel and the Diaspora* (Ramat-Gan, Israel: Bar-Ilan University, 1981), pp. 101–09.

6. Ian Lustick, *Arabs in the Jewish State* (Austin: University of Texas Press, 1980).

7. Ehud Luz, "On the Maccabean Myth of Rebirth," *Hauma*, 18 (December 1979), 44–52 (in Hebrew).

8. Avshalom Reich, "Changes and Developments in the Passover Haggadot of the Kibbutz Movement" (Ph.D. diss., Austin: University of Texas, 1972).

9. Cited in Eliezer Don-Yehiya and Charles S. Liebman, "The Symbol System of Zionist Socialism," *Modern Judaism*, 1 (September 1981), 121–48.

10. Yael Zerubavel, "The Last Stand: On the Transformation of Symbols in Modern Israeli Culture" (Ph.D. diss., Philadelphia: University of Pennsylvania, 1980); and Don-Yehiya and Liebman, "The Symbol System of Zionist Socialism."

11. Hebrew source cited in Don-Yehiya and Liebman, "The Symbol System of Zionist Socialism."

12. Hebrew sources cited in ibid.

13. Eliezer Don-Yehiya and Charles S. Liebman, "Zionist Ultranationalism and Its Attitude toward Religion," *Journal of Church and State*, 23 (Spring 1981), 259–73.

14. David Apter, "Political Religion in the New Nations," in Clifford Geertz, ed., *Old Societies and New States* (New York: The Free Press, 1963), pp. 57–104.

15. David Ben-Gurion: *Stars and Dust* (Ramat-Gan, Israel: Massada, 1976), p. 104 (in Hebrew).

16. Ibid., p. 134.

17. Amos Elon, *The Israelis* (London: Sphere Books, 1972), p. 294.

18. Apter, "Political Religion in the New Nations."

19. Charles Liebman and Eliezer Don-Yehiya, "Traditional Judaism and Civil Religion in Israel," *Jerusalem Quarterly*, 23 (April 1982), 57–69.

20. Elon, *The Israelis*, pp. 205–06.

21. Sources in this section, unless otherwise noted, are identified in the original Hebrew in Charles Liebman, "Myth, Tradition and Values in Israeli Society," *Midstream*, 24 (January 1978), 44–53.

22. David Ben-Gurion, "Concepts and Values," *Hazut*, 3 (1957), 8 (in Hebrew).

23. David Ben-Gurion, *In the Conflict*, vol. 4 (Tel Aviv: Hotzaat Mapai, 1949), p. 12 (in Hebrew).

24. *Knesset Protocol* (1952), p. 910.

25. Reich, "Changes and Developments in the Passover Haggadot," p. 393.

# Part III

# POLITICAL INSTITUTIONS
# AND BEHAVIOR

# 10

## Political Legitimacy in Israel:
## How Important Is the State?

### Donna Robinson Divine

Without knowing its exact dimensions, political scientists have taken government
to be the primary unit for the study of political behavior. No matter how far
modern analysis appears to be from the formalism embodied in mere descriptions
of government, political science still assumes that the institutions of government
form the major system within which political activity is embedded.[1] Government
is understood not simply as the organization ordering political activity, but also
as the foundation of the moral community within which people live. Government
not only symbolizes but also defines appropriate political behavior, proper
political associations, and, of course, legality and illegality. Government is
thought to define right by virtue of its possession of legitimacy, a power that
holds people together through their adherence to a public morality supposedly
articulated and certified through the government.[2] Political scientists attribute
legitimacy to governments when it appears that the community over which such
governments rule is cohesive. The legitimacy of government is understood as an
isomorphism of the coherence of the political community.

But if the research of anthropology, sociology, and, paradoxically, even modern
political science has pressed any powerful argument, it is that governments are
not necessarily central to the continuity of political communities.[3] Yet, political
scientists have ignored the brunt of their own arguments and discoveries about
political parties, social structure, and cultural values. Perhaps political scientists
are reluctant to carry the argument that far, because if governments are not
central, the state itself may not be the context within which the most meaningful
political activities take place. Thus the degree to which the state and the government are important structures for political activities is at least an issue open to
dispute.

That issue serves as the point of departure for this essay which questions the
assumption that the state and thus the institutions of government are necessarily
legitimate simply because the political community is intact and functions well

---

[1] Even the series of political studies inspired by Gabriel Almond and published by
Little, Brown focuses heavily on government. See especially Leonard Fein, *Politics in
Israel* (Boston: Little, Brown, 1967).

[2] This is true of such different approaches to the study of legitimacy as Richard E.
Flathman, *Political Obligations* (New York: Atheneum, 1972) and Robert E. Lane,
*Political Ideology* (New York: The Free Press, 1962).

[3] David Easton states it most forcefully in *The Political System* (New York: Alfred A.
Knopf, 1971), p. 137.

as a unit, because laws are passed and policies are made. The fact that people allow themselves to be ruled together has too long been attributed to the nature and activities of the government conducting their affairs. But to assume the existence of governmental legitimacy on the basis of political cohesion is not empirically or logically sound. Such an assumption neither fully explains nor establishes the connection between governmental legitimacy and political cohesion. When the political community coheres, it is legitimate, but that does not necessarily mean that the government is legitimate as well. Political legitimacy does not arise from the mere institution of government, nor is it necessarily generated by its operations. But what then is legitimacy if not an indicator of the acceptability of government?

Our analysis of legitimacy begins with the assumption that propriety and rightness can be ascertained in the public realm. For political legitimacy in the most general sense presupposes a judgment on society, the rightness of association, the propriety of the exercise of power, and the acceptability of its institutional agents.[4] Just how that judgment is made is unclear, and how that judgment ought to be made has been the focus of disagreement in political philosophy for as long as the study has existed.[5] Thus while legitimacy has served as the focus of many philosophical and theoretical studies, its nature has not been fully clarified. And the most common source of confusion has been the conventional and widely accepted definition of legitimacy as an attribute of governments alone.[6]

As an outgrowth of this definition, many modern political philosophers understand legitimacy to be the correlative of the obligation to obey laws made by the government.[7] Because obedience appears crucial to cohesion, this is but another way of identifying the legitimacy of government with political cohesion. But it might be argued against these philosophers that principled disobedience to the law is not necessarily a refutation of the legitimacy of government, so varied are the reasons for disobedience and so widespread the public consciousness of its implications. It follows as well that obedience itself may not depend upon agreement with respect to the legitimacy of the government.

Rather, it may be plausibly asserted that if propriety and rightness are the concepts underlying legitimacy, they should serve as tangible criteria of its existence: namely, that legitimacy must entail a demonstration of propriety and rightness in the political realm. One such demonstration takes place when the community is considered to be the common property of its citizens and when

[4] Hanna Pitkin, 'Obligation and Consent', Part II, in *Concepts in Social and Political Philosophy*, ed. Richard E. Flathman (New York: Macmillan, 1973), pp. 201–219 at p. 201.
[5] For a survey of the literature, see Richard B. Friedman, 'On the Concept of Authority in Political Philosophy,' in Flathman, *Concepts in Social and Political Philosophy*, pp. 121–146.
[6] Max Weber, *Economy and Society*, ed. Guenther Roth and Claus Wittich (New York: Bedminster Press, 1968), I, 212 ff.
[7] Pitkin, 'Obligation and Consent,' pp. 210 ff.

citizens have control over it comparable, in some respects, to the control property owners exercise over their property.[8] For if propriety and rightness have any concrete meaning in the political realm, that meaning is tied up with the notion that the political community belongs, in some way, to the citizens.

This notion of legitimacy still appears to be abstract, and stands in need of further clarification. For this purpose, we can draw upon some of the major studies of political legitimacy to help refine the concept and render it less abstract. Although no single definition of legitimacy has emerged from the works of political philosophy, typically, political philosophers have focused on the nature of man, the character of the ties binding men together and/or the particular actions of government which men feel obligated to obey or endorse.[9] Thus, at least three kinds of definitions of legitimacy have characteristically been posited. The exercise of political power is considered legitimate as a function of (1) who exercises it, (2) on what basis it is exercised, or (3) toward what end it is exercised. Most philosophers have taken one or another of these three criteria as an idea of political legitimacy.

Aristotle, for example, explained that political societies in which men ruled over other men were natural associations. Man, he asserted, is by nature a political animal inasmuch as he is born into a family unit in which power is unequally distributed. Man first becomes aware of others by virtue of his need of them, including the need to obey those who can sustain him in his infancy. Governments are natural extensions of the father, for their role in society is the analogue of the father's role in the family.[10] The nature of man demands such power structures, and those governments which meet man's basic needs for sustenance are legitimate. Modern political scientists, who assert that legitimacy is determined by the nature of man, extend Aristotle's metaphor by examining the similarity in relationships between government and citizen on the one hand, and between parents and children on the other.[11]

Other political philosophers, dissatisfied with Aristotle's approach to the problem of political legitimacy, have disputed it insofar as they find it in man's nature to rule rather than to be ruled, the family unit notwithstanding.[12] They argue that power within the family is intrinsically unstable if only because of the normal human life cycle of growth and death. For these political philosophers, political societies are not natural but unnatural units of organization that require a particular and an extraordinary effort to effect. Men create such societies by voluntarily consenting to their formation, and governments are either established simultaneously as part of a single agreement, or they are created as the first

---

[8] Ibid., p. 203.

[9] Friedman, 'On the Concept of Authority.'

[10] Ernest Barker, ed., *The Politics of Aristotle* (New York: Oxford University Press, 1962), pp. 1–9.

[11] J. A. Laponce, 'Political Community, Legitimacy and Discrimination,' *British Journal of Political Science*, 4, 2 (April 1974), 121–137 at p. 123.

[12] John Locke, *Two Treatises of Government* (New York: Cambridge University Press, 1960), pp. 345–361.

collective act of the nascent political society.[13] Hobbes, Locke, and Rousseau, typical of such political philosophers, understood legitimate power to be power created through consent.

But from the empirical perspective, a central problem of consent theory is that it has proved almost impossible to find a model of such an agreement. And where such agreements have been construed to exist, they have been so general that no explicit criteria for determining the legitimacy of particular governments can be extrapolated. Even more problematic is the status of such an agreement relative to succeeding generations. Hobbes would bind future generations to the ascribed voluntary actions of their ancestors;[14] Locke would disagree and posit that each generation decides anew, consciously or unconsciously, whether or not the present government is fulfilling the tenets of the original agreement.[15] Rousseau would take an altogether different approach and have men use the law-making process as a means of renewing the agreement in every generation and for every citizen in a legitimate political society.[16] But consent theorists, including those writing today, continue to have trouble judging the legitimacy of any specific government because of the difficulty they encounter in generating common principles which can be said to underlie all ostensible social compacts establishing societies.[17]

Last, some political philosophers would have us test the legitimacy of government by judging the content of its particular laws and policies, with special emphasis on their ultimate purpose.[18] Another way of stating this, in the language of political science, is to call this a judgment on outputs. In this sense, political legitimacy is effected through the enunciated policies and activities – or outputs – of the political authorities. Outputs influence the level of specific support for a society because they claim to serve a social purpose. Noting the importance of the purpose of policy, David Easton has observed that 'if outputs are to have any impact on support, in one or another way, they must be able to meet the existing or anticipated demands of the members of a system.'[19] Such an impact can be arranged by actually changing policies or by changing personnel to create the impression that new policies will be forthcoming. As Easton points out, it is not always clear whose needs or how many of them must be met in order to generate enough support for a political society, and quite often support stems from merely creating the impression that important needs are being fulfilled.

In spite of the substantial conceptual differences in these efforts to explain how power can be legitimized, a deep similarity exists. For all the theories try

[13] See Thomas Hobbes, *The Leviathan*; John Locke, *The Second Treatise on Government*; and J. J. Rousseau, *The Social Contract*.

[14] Thomas Hobbes, *The Leviathan* (Baltimore: Penguin, 1968), pp. 247–251.

[15] Locke, *Two Treatises of Government*, p. 386.

[16] J. J. Rousseau, *The Social Contract* (New York: E. P. Dutton, 1950), pp. 23 ff.

[17] Pitkin, 'Obligation and Consent,' p. 208.

[18] Peter G. Stillman, 'The Concept of Legitimacy,' *Polity*, VII, 1 (Fall, 1974), 32–56.

[19] David Easton, *A Framework for Political Analysis* (Englewood Cliffs: Prentice-Hall, 1965), p. 127.

to describe how a society can properly be said to belong to its citizens. Governments are considered to be the agents that symbolize the society as an integral unit. Therefore, governments have traditionally been taken to be the set of institutions that must be controlled or influenced if such ownership of society can be claimed. Such an inference is seductive and has consequently been adopted by most political philosophers, but it is not necessarily true nor does it inhere in the notion of legitimacy. Our reading of political philosophy has taught that if a society can be controlled without government, if people can feel that their society belongs to them, in circumstances where they have no influence or power over government, the society is still legitimate in some sense, and power can still be exercised legitimately, albeit by agents other than the government. Thus, legitimacy describes not obedience to the law but a sense of one's relationship to the law and society. Legitimacy is then not only an attribute of governments; it also properly attaches to society itself.

Legitimacy is a measure of the sense people have that they belong together in a political association, that the significant institutions of that association, whatever their nature, belong to them, and that their will is an important constituent in propelling the actions of that association. It is not necessary that everyone has his way on every occasion but that everyone feels that his will is somehow considered and has a chance of influencing, even if not determining, public actions or policy. It is thus crucial that needs be not systematically and consistently ignored if citizens are to identify the society as their own.

Popular participation in government need not be a necessary condition of societal legitimacy if the government has no central role in determining the actions of the community. In such cases the government is not legitimate, for it is an institution over which people have no perception of direct control. David Easton makes a similar point when he writes: 'The fact that policies recognized as authoritative for the whole society must exist does not imply or assume that a central governmental organization is required in order to make decisions and effectuate them.'[20]

Hence political philosophy has not only helped us to formulate a basis upon which to ascertain the legitimacy of political power, its three characteristic definitions can also be said to constitute standards by which to measure the legitimacy of any agent exercising political power. There can be empirical instruction in political philosophy. But it is not enough to rest an argument about the nature of political legitimacy on abstract logic. The argument itself is too important. For ultimate vindication, it must be applied to a particular case.

The political meaning of legitimacy will become more clear, then, if we consider it in a specific context where enough data can be explored to test the force of the conceptual argument. Israel, in this sense, is a most appropriate case because in a new and democratic state like Israel the issue of legitimacy is raised often and resolved visibly enough to draw a graphic picture of the nature of Israeli political legitimacy. In this context, the three typical philosophical

[20] Easton, *The Political System*, p. 137.

definitions of political legitimacy are employed as models constituting alternative ways of understanding how power is legitimized in Israeli society. Above all, this entails an examination of the extent to which the government, as a set of institutions, is legitimate, if only because in modern and cohesive societies, such institutional legitimacy is expected. But if, by applying the three models of the ways in which power is legitimized, we find that the Israeli government does not legitimize the power it is wielding, then given a legitimate political society, we can determine, by using those same three models, which agent has provided the basis for that societal legitimacy.

Specifically, it is argued that in Israel, the agent legitimizing political power was not the government but the largest political party, Mapai. (Mapai was Israel's largest political party from 1948 to 1969 when it joined with other political parties to form Mai. Mapai remains the major constituent of Mai.) Whether by virtue of the so-called nature of man, or the possible existence of a social contract, or the specific policies and collective actions of the society, the power that Mapai exercised was, as a whole, endowed with a legitimacy that the powers exercised by the parliamentary assembly or by the various ministries of state lacked. This is not to advance the claim that the policies adopted by Mapai had the same force of law as policies officially promulgated by the Israel parliament, but that the process of policy formulation within Mapai afforded more people a sense of being counted and belonging together than the similar process carried out by the offices of state alone. It is such a sense, rather than obedience, which marks legitimacy, and in Israel it was Mapai that developed that sense among people. It is possible to verify this assertion by analyzing the Mapai party and its relationship to government in Israel in terms of the various approaches suggested by political philosophers in their stipulations of the prerequisites of political legitimacy. For purposes of convenience, this analysis covers the period before Mapai joined with other political parties to form Mai.

THE ARISTOTELIAN APPROACH

If one applies Aristotle's observations in an Israeli context, then Mapai was the family of Israeli man writ large. The government, in contrast, overlaid with a heavy bureaucratic apparatus, did not resemble any of the human associations into which man is born or in which he develops.[21] The Israeli government treats citizens impersonally, and this is only partly a result of its size. The ideological basis of the state's bureaucratic apparatus intensifies the tendency to treat people not as individuals but rather in terms of the categories in which their demands or needs can be understood.[22] Mapai, however, as large as it became, always

[21] Brenda Danet and Harriet Hartman, 'Coping with Bureaucracy: The Israeli Case,' *Social Forces*, 51, 1 (September, 1972), 7–22 at p. 13.

[22] Rivkah Bar Yosef, 'The Moroccans: Background to the Problem,' in *Integration and Development in Israel*, ed. S. N. Eisenstadt, Rivkah Bar Yosef, and Chaim Adler (New York: Praeger, 1970), pp. 419–428; Shlomo Avineri, 'Israel: Two Nations?' in *Israel:*

dealt with its members and potential supporters in personal terms analogous to the family situation. Mapai met the most fundamental needs of people by distributing jobs and favors on a scale that the government, committed to a merit system, could not match.[23]

Power in Mapai belonged to those persons who could arrange favors for people by constituting themselves as effective links among members: between the center and the periphery; between the parliamentary factions, secretariat, and government ministers, on the one hand, and the branch workers, on the other. The power brokers of Mapai were the people who could harmonize the operations of its disparate parts by means of personal ties which linked all segments of the population and of the party.[24]

Unlike other political parties in Israel, the Mapai party stood for no single policy line or ideology.[25] The Mapai apparatus managed to attract and incorporate into a single political framework potential ideological rivals and erstwhile dissident political groups. The party tied them together in a number of ways. First, the party leadership enabled all groups to exercise some influence. Formally, party decisions were made arithmetically on the basis of majority rule, a process that might reinforce divergent opinions within the party and aggravate relations among groups. But informally, decisions represented compromises that did not offend any political faction.[26]

Second, all had access to important party positions. The Appointments Committee, which named one-third of the party parliamentary list, was sensitive to the party's factions and to its ideological diversity. The Committee intentionally selected members from all of the party's internal groups to avoid alienating factions of party workers.[27]

Third, the party responded to individual ambitions and interests as well as to the needs of its internal factions. In the Mapai framework, an informal, loosely organized group of party workers, called the Gush, unofficially supervised the operations of the Appointments Committee to insure its continued sensitivity to the individual variations in the party membership. The Gush tied together the central party institutions with the local party branches, the Secretariat with the regional councils, the government ministers with local party bosses. The Gush's leaders were members of the Appointments Committee and its supporters were full-time employees of the party. The Gush consisted of people whose livelihoods and political careers intertwined and whose lives were, therefore,

---

*Social Structure and Change*, ed. Michael Curtis and Mordecai Chertoff (New Brunswick: E. P. Dutton, 1973), pp. 281–305.

[23] Donna Robinson Divine, 'The Modernization of Israeli Administration,' *The International Journal of Middle East Studies*, 5, 3 (June, 1974), 295–313.

[24] Peter Y. Medding, *Mapai in Israel: Political Organization and Government in a New Society* (Cambridge: Cambridge University Press, 1972), chap. 8.

[25] The party was established by people adhering to several different ideologies and no single ideology ever emerged. Consensus was established on largely pragmatic grounds. See especially S. N. Eisenstadt, *Israeli Society* (London: Weidenfeld and Nicolson, 1967), chap. 4.

[26] Medding, *Mapai in Israel*, p. 206.        [27] Ibid., p. 156.

wholly dependent upon the continuous electoral success of Mapai, nationally and locally.[28] In addition, the Gush 'fathered' the careers of many Israeli politicians who had no local or national base of their own.[29]

The name Gush signified a set of individuals with far-reaching contacts. Allegedly, its leaders personally knew all of the Mapai membership – an exaggeration that could not be easily dismissed as Gush leaders spent their days talking in homes and businesses with the party rank and file.[30] The Gush struggled to hold on to the allegiance of all members, regardless of ideological or policy proclivities, through its influence over appointments. To effect an appointment was to meet the basic needs of people for a livelihood and to thereby impose obligations – political support in return for jobs. The obligations thus bound individuals not only to the Gush but also to the Mapai party into whose patronage net they fell. The Gush could aid the political advancement of the most dissident party members as long as the dissidents refrained from attacks on the organizational structure of the party.[31]

Thus a web of patron–client relationships was established covering all areas of the country and all sectors of the economy. One belonged to the larger community because one belonged to this network. It was said that the Gush 'would take care of its own,' but in fact, it took care of Mapai and Mapai took care of individuals in the country. And Mapai's stress on personal ties extended to its conduct of the government, where the exercise of real power by functionaries depended upon maintaining some sort of personal contact, however indirect, with the people as individuals.

Even a Ben Gurion as prime minister could not retain control over the government when he lost personal contact with the party power brokers and thus with the party membership. His influence as a ruler declined as he chose to withdraw from party activities and from the company of the Gush.[32] Note, for example, the disputes that led to the so-called Lavon Affair. Pinhas Lavon was minister of Defense in 1954 when the Egyptians uncovered an Israeli plot to complicate Egyptian relations with the West by blowing up the USIA library in Cairo. Lavon claimed that the plan was initiated without his knowledge, and he demanded that he be cleared of any responsibility for it. In 1960 Ben Gurion had insisted that the only way responsibility could be fixed for the security mishap was through a judicial inquiry, but he had to give up this demand because none of the other Mapai ministers in the government joined him.

No other Mapai party leader supported Ben Gurion because he did little personally to try to mobilize the party apparatus.[33] His call for a judicial inquiry into the Lavon Affair was symbolic of his trust in purely state institutions and

[28] Ibid., p. 148.            [29] Abba Eban's career was sponsored by the Gush.

[30] Natan Yanai, *Qera be-Tsameret* (Split at the Top) (Tel Aviv: Lewin-Epstein, 1969), p. 84.

[31] Ibid., p. 79.

[32] Avraham Avi-hai, *Ben Gurion State-Builder* (New York: John Wiley and Sons 1974), chap. 13.

[33] Yanai, *Qera be-Tsameret*, pp. 143–151.

of his neglect of the web of personal relationships supporting the Mapai party. Not only would his party not stand for such devaluation, but Israelis, in general, would not accept it. This became apparent in the election of 1961 when Ben Gurion's continued tenure was the central issue of the election, rather than the administration of justice in the Lavon Affair. Ben Gurion had obviously not convinced the public that the major problem of Israeli society was the proper attribution of responsibility for the security mishap of 1954: the key issue of that election was Ben Gurion's own leadership of the country. What is significant in the public reaction to the Lavon Affair is the extent to which the people followed the political line of the Mapai party bosses. To both bosses and citizens Ben Gurion was the chief threat because his proposals for a judicial inquiry entailed too close an examination of the operations of the political party and perhaps its disestablishment. A judicial inquiry constituted a threat to the party because it involved a judgment on the right of an official to retain an important party appointment, a right that party bosses held to be within the province of the party decision-making organization alone. Evidently, the public accepted that interpretation as attacks were directed against Ben Gurion and his ostensible dictatorship of the party.

Israelis became much more critical of Ben Gurion as he lost power in the political party. The clearest example of this weakening in his public image is suggested by another episode. In March 1963, stories appeared in the Israeli press publicizing the contributions of German scientists to the Egyptian rocket program.[34] Israelis worried about the project because of the potential military danger that such rockets posed to civilian centers. Ben Gurion reacted more strongly to the public furor than to the disclosure of the role of German scientists because he feared that public antagonism to the West German government for allowing its scientists to work in Egypt would endanger his plans for a normalization of the relations between West Germany and Israel.[35]

What makes the German normalization policy important for our purposes is that it belonged almost exclusively to Ben Gurion. In fact, one of Mapai's leaders, Golda Meir, stated that she, in principle, opposed the establishment of full diplomatic relations with West Germany.[36] But Ben Gurion ignored the opposition or the apathy of the party councils and tried to impose his policy directly upon the government. He emphasized its expected material benefits.[37] Before the parliament, Ben Gurion tried to discount the issue of the German scientists by discounting the danger of the Egyptian rockets. According to Ben Gurion, the rockets, because they lacked a pilot device, represented an insignificant challenge to Israel's security, one that did not justify irritating relations with West Germany.[38]

It was members of Ben Gurion's own party who thwarted his designs for a

[34] Ibid., p. 39.    [35] Ibid., p. 40.
[36] Ibid.    [37] Ibid., p. 42.
[38] Ibid., p. 41, and Michel Bar-Zohar, *Spies in the Promised Land* (London: Davis-Pynter, 1972), p. 273.

new German foreign policy. They inspired a cabinet committee to conclude that Ben Gurion had committed a major error in not pressuring the West German government to recall its scientists.[39] Ben Gurion was thus unable to arrange full diplomatic ties between Israel and West Germany.

The cabinet committee report struck the final blow at Ben Gurion by demonstrating the extent to which his power as ruler of the country could dwindle in the face of inattention to the party bosses. For the German policy probably failed not so much because of content as because of lack of the proper pedigree.

Although it cannot be established definitively that Ben Gurion's German policy failed because he neglected to involve the party bosses in its formulation, this neglect is a likely cause of its failure. For the next prime minister, Levi Eshkol, under similar military circumstances, was able to implement the same German policy that had eluded Ben Gurion. Significantly, Eshkol chose to include party bosses and leaders in its formation and application.[40]

Thus, Mapai more than any of the other political parties in Israel which exacted ideological or religious commitments, more than the offices of state, qua impersonal bureaucratic mechanisms, was able to substantiate its claims to rightful political leadership insofar as its leadership of the people was based on natural ties among the people. Its system of patronage permitted individuals to conduct their political and economic affairs in personal terms, for patronage is the political surrogate of family relationships. According to anthropologist Jeremy Boissevain, patronage exists because 'there is still need for protection that neither the State nor the family is able to provide.'[41] If, as Aristotle implied, such natural ties allow citizens in a society to believe that their society belongs to them, then Mapai, because of its conduct of policy, initiated this belief and, through its daily operations, reinforced it.

## THE SOCIAL CONTRACT APPROACH

If power can be legitimized through voluntary consent, then, too, Mapai, more than any other political party or institution in Israel, can claim to be the agent legitimizing political power in the state. If an agreement lies at the social basis of Israeli society, it was surely arranged under the auspices of the Mapai party.

Of all Israeli political parties that preceded the formal establishment of the state and its government, the Mapai party controlled the most expanded dimensions of political space. Whereas the typical political party in prestate Israel restricted its activities to the immediate vicinity of its members and their most central concerns, Mapai's activities covered all of the most fundamental areas of public life. Mapai organized people, albeit sometimes in small numbers, in all of the economic and social sectors of the country. In these organizations, people

[39] Yanai, *Qera be-Tsameret*, p. 44.
[40] Henry M. Christman, ed., *The State Papers of Levi Eshkol* (New York: Funk and Wagnalls, 1969), pp. 51 ff. For a general description of Eshkol's political style see Medding, *Mapai in Israel*, p. 270.
[41] Jeremy Boissevain, 'Patronage in Sicily', *Man*, I, 1 (March, 1966), 18–33 at p. 30.

stood obliged to the party for the conveniences and benefits of association which it bestowed upon them. Hence, if the social contract can be understood as a compact conferring rights and privileges, such a compact can be found metaphorically and piecemeal in the various agreements made to establish unions, cooperatives, and agricultural collectives – all sponsored by Mapai.

Even though a social contract is customarily thought to be a single instrument, there is no reason to assume that it has to be.[42] It could, in fact, consist of a series of agreements by which the contract becomes the sum of its individual parts, the parts being explicit agreements in which social, political, and moral obligations are clearly defined. It is rare that one single compact embodies the totality of an individual's common obligations, especially if we are considering the possibility that such a compact really exists in history.

The history of Mapai's organizational activities is in large part the story of the emergence of an Israeli social contract. Contractual relations existed among members of Mapai organizations whose collective aims and obligations were explicit. If a social contract provides the social foundation for the state of Israel, it consists of these voluntary agreements establishing political and economic associations during the prestate Zionist development of Palestine. To participate fully in the politics of the prestate era, to exercise power or influence legitimately, be it for or against any particular policy, meant to partake, in some way, of the parts of the social contract, which, in turn, amounted to membership in an organization affiliated with or controlled by Mapai.

It would appear unnecessary to review in detail the areas of Jewish life in Palestine whose operations were the product of agreements sponsored by the Mapai party. The pervasiveness of Mapai is self-evident from the barest historical survey of the period. Mapai provided health and welfare services, banking facilities, housing, and recreation activities. Mapai political leadership supervised the functioning of the Palestinian Jewish community, and when it did not itself appoint the head of an office, the party or group which did, did so because of an agreement with Mapai.[43] Not that Mapai had the power to dictate policy, but Mapai had to give consent to the compromises arranged in all areas of Jewish communal existence. In addition, the founding fathers of Israel were, for the most part, members of Mapai, and the constitution of Mapai serves as a source of the social contract for Israeli society, for it contains the only formal articulation of whatever social and political goals have been affirmed as national by any significant number of Israelis.[44] Mapai dominated the Palestinian Jewish polity and its domination continued as the state of Israel, which has no written constitution, took root and developed.

[42] See Rousseau on the 'clauses' of a social contract. Rousseau refers to the parts of a social contract often. For example, *Social Contract*, p. 14.

[43] Dan Horowitz and Moshe Lissak, 'Authority without Sovereignty: The Case of the National Jewish Community in Palestine,' *Government and Opposition*, 8, 1 (Winter, 1973), 48–71 at p. 55.

[44] Eisenstadt, *Israeli Society*, pp. 16 ff.

[45] Alan Arian, *The Choosing People* (Cleveland: Case Western Reserve, 1973), p. 81.

Students of Israeli politics have observed the constant predominant influence of Mapai, but have sought to explain it as, in some way, a function of the compatibility of the party's views with the shifting views and opinions of the electorate. These students have concluded that Mapai's power derived from its ability, in the words of Alan Arian 'to draw strength from all sectors of the society.'[45] Thus Professor Arian notes that this party's influence and role in Israel can be understood because it is Israel's 'dominant party,' using that term in the technical sense defined by Duverger in his classic, *Political Parties*.[46]

But the dominant party is a party type which describes rather than explains a party's hold on power.[47] The point is to account for the dominance and not simply to catalog its manifestations. Moreover, given the Israeli propensity to the formation of political parties and to participation in political movements, it seems fair to view the dominant party situation in Israel as a political anomaly. A more satisfactory account explains the dominance by virtue of its role in legitimizing political power: to feel counted in Israel, more importantly, to be counted politically, most people knew that they ought to belong to the Mapai party.

Still, to comprehend more fully how people could believe Mapai to be the sole agent arranging voluntary and collective consent to the establishment of a political society, we must clarify the nature and role of other political parties in Israel, especially with respect to Mapai. For it might be the case that other political parties are viewed as arranging social contracts for their own adherents. We must examine the extent to which Mapai is typical of all Israeli political parties. Then we must look at the relationship of all parties to government from the perspective of consent theory to determine whether it is the Mapai party, and not the institutions of government or other political parties, which is considered the guardian of the social contract.

Consent theory can help clarify the precise role of Mapai in legitimizing political power by focusing our attention on political parties not formally aligned with Mapai. Many philosophers of consent have measured the legitimacy of government by the degree to which political oppositions function in the public realm.[48] If consent theory is to be taken seriously, it suggests that opposition is to be allowed so long as it is not directed against the right of a government to exist, but instead against particular governmental actions. This argument, that consent is implied by the operation of a 'loyal' political opposition, has as its practical corollary the proposition that the operations of a political opposition signify the legitimacy of the governmental institutions within which the opposition operates. But while political oppositions often do exist in societies believed

[46] Ibid., p. 45.

[47] Maurice Duverger, *Political Parties* (London: Methuen, 1965), pp. 410, 417–418, and Giovanni Sartori, 'The Typology of Party Systems: Proposals for Improvement, in *Mass Politics*, ed. Erik Allardt and Stein Rokkan (New York: The Free Press, 1970), pp. 322–352.

[48] Extrapolated from Friedman, 'On the Concept of Authority,' p. 140, and from Michael Walzer, *Obligations* (Cambridge: Harvard University Press, 1970), p. 47.

to be founded on a social contract, their significance with respect to the legitimacy of the society's governmental institutions cannot be taken for granted. The existence of political oppositions has a direct bearing upon the legitimization of political power in a society but that bearing depends not on the context within which such oppositions formally operate but within which they effectively operate. For if power is legitimate it manifests its legitimacy by exerting control over action. There is no political power for its own sake. A closer look at political oppositions in Israel is, therefore, necessary. But it is not necessary for our purposes to conduct an inquiry into all of the political oppositions, for we are only interested in developing a model of the behavior of oppositions. Consequently, it is enough to examine the country's largest, most typical, and most vocal political opposition and its style of operation especially with respect to the institutions of government and to Mapai.

Gahal (Gush Herut-Liberalim) is commonly taken to be the most authentic political opposition in Israel, for one of Gahal's constituents, Herut, not only had never joined Mapai in a government coalition, it also had not cooperated with Mapai in any of its broad economic interest group federations before joining with the Liberals to form Gahal in 1965. Herut did not belong to the labor organization, the Histadrut, nor did it participate in the federations of agricultural settlements and cooperatives.[49] Israelis understood Herut to be the heart of the political party opposition in the country.

The fact of its existence as a political opposition in parliament was interpreted to mean that all Israelis, whether in support of or in opposition to the particular people in power, consented to their institution of government and to its general exercise of power. Indeed, the circumstances of Herut's founding and its subsequent history appeared to reinforce the Israeli perception that their government was based upon voluntary consent.

Herut was founded by people already labeled as opposition by the World Zionist Organization – revisionists, terrorists, aggressive dissidents, all of whom once disputed, almost to the point of civil war, the leadership and policies of the World Zionist Organization in its role as the quasi-government of Jewish Palestine.[50] Herut's spiritual leader was Vladimir Jabotinsky, who created the World Union of Zionist Revisionists in 1925 because of his dissatisfaction with what he called the restrained policies of the World Zionist Organization. Jabotinsky began by disputing the philosophy of the Zionist movement and ended by questioning the legitimacy of the organization that operated as its spokesman and governor. Leading the revisionists out of the World Zionist Organization in 1935 to form the New Zionist Organization, Jabotinsky, in the name of the revisionists, called for the immediate creation of a Jewish state, the encouragement of mass immigration – especially of the middle classes – and large-scale investment of private capital.[51] Because so much of the revisionist

[49] Fein, *Politics in Israel*, pp. 90–91.

[50] J. B. Schectman, 'Revisionism,' in *Struggle for Tomorrow*, ed. Feliks Gross and Basil J. Vlavianos (New York: Arts, 1954), pp. 86–100 at p. 88.     [51] Ibid., pp. 88–89.

policy seemed unrealizable, the party's most fundamental principle was simply its opposition to the social, political, and economic basis of the Zionist movement in Palestine. Thus,,if the World Zionist Organization can be taken to be one institutional expression of a social contract binding together Zionists (including those who were not members of Mapai), the revisionists, through secession, were no longer parties to that contract and were disposed of its obligations.

During the riots in Palestine in 1936, the Revisionist party rejected the official Zionist policy of restraint, and by World War II, two paramilitary groups inspired by revisionism but not formally coordinated by the party, began to assume great risks for a Jewish state, striking at the British and at the Arabs.[52] The groups cooperated neither with one another nor always with the Revisionist Party.[53] They were simply unwilling to compromise with the World Zionist Organization. But after a world war, a protracted guerilla war, and a war of independence, the revisionists and the various military forces were ready to compromise, to recognize the legitimacy of the World Zionist Organization and of a smaller Jewish state, most of whose policies they still disputed. Revisionists, members of the paramilitary organizations, established Herut as a competitive political party to vie for power in the new state.[54]

Herut thus appeared to become a full partner in the political society by proclaiming itself as a political party competing for power in the government. But the party could not divest itself of its history. Hence, in its first years it was viewed with a great deal of suspicion. One sociologist, in observing that 'the right oriented Herut, in a country dominated by social democratic philosophies, parties and institutions, was isolated and semi-ostracized . . .' went so far as to assert that 'Herut has served for the community's leaders as the symbol of an untenable position, a threat to the core values of Israel.'[55]

But this cannot be taken as an accurate description of Herut over time. Herut's political strength increased in the parliament and in local municipalities during the course of Israel's statehood. Significantly, its influence apparently increased as it cooperated more closely with Mapai at the local and at the national level.[56] Finally, as part of Gahal, Herut joined the Histadrut after having long advocated its disestablishment. And in 1967 it joined the government coalition. Thus the extent to which Gahal became a significant political opposition derived from its association in the labor federation and in national coalition with Mapai rather than from its mere membership in the Israeli parliament. That is to say, Gahal became a more acceptable political party and, hence, more legitimate, because it cooperated more extensively with Mapai. The aura of Mapai's legitimacy fell

---

[52] Ibid., p. 90.
[53] Ibid., p. 94.                                                                                    [54] Ibid.
[55] Amitai Etzioni, 'Israel's Colonial Temptations,' *West Africa Affairs*, 1 (1969), 20–23 at p. 21.
[56] Shevah Weiss, *Ha-Politikayim be-Israel* (Politicians in Israel) (Tel Aviv: Achiasaf Publishing, 1973), and Shevah Weiss, *Tipologiya Shel Nivharim ha-Lokaliyyim Ve-She'elat ha-Yitzivot be-Shilton ha-Makomi be-Israel* (Typology of Local Elections and the Question of Stability in Local Government in Israel) (Jerusalem: Akadamon, 1970).

upon Gahal as Gahal's association with Mapai appeared to imply consent to Mapai's principles and certification of Mapai's power.

It also should be stressed that the major opposition did not organize its followers into an embryonic society as did Mapai nor did it exact from them the same kind and number of mutual obligations. Herut organized to oppose a particular social foundation without proposing an alternative. That Herut claimed a Jewish state on both sides of the Jordan River did not provide social coherence because the claim was never the basis for social or economic organization; it had merely been a factor in the formation of several disparate military groups. Herut only finally endorsed a particular kind of Jewish society when, as part of Gahal, it joined the Histadrut. Herut had never elaborated its own vision of Jewish society and so its principles could never serve as a hypothetical social contract.

If a social contract and all that it entails render proper the exercise of political power, then Mapai, and no other political party or institution of government in Israel, was its trustee. But more importantly, Mapai's social contract embraced so many groups and communities that people could derive the sum total of their human political obligations through their affiliation with this political party.

POLICY CONTENT APPROACH

The character of political opposition in Israel also explains how political power is legitimized in the society when the criteria of legitimacy are determined by the consent of public legislation. The articulation of critical standards by which to judge the adequacy of policies customarily emanates from political oppositions. Political oppositions are only sometimes born in disputes over public policies, but they are always expected to speak to these issues.[57]

There are certainly good arguments to be made that political oppositions should evaluate the propriety of proposed public policy, but that they often do this as an aspect of their activity which political scientists generally overlook. Many policy disputes, in fact, constitute challenges to the rightness of policy, and it is this kind of challenge which is indicative of the way in which political power is legitimized. The precise nature of the connection between political oppositions and judgments of political legitimacy may become clearer if we remember that political oppositions cannot avoid taking a stand on a claim or even an intimation that a policy is illegitimate. Two practical, if not logical, consequences follow from the involvement of oppositions with the issues of political legitimacy. The debate over the legitimacy of any policy becomes a dialectic that can locate the various oppositions. And on the assumption that all policies that are ultimately successful passed because they were in part considered legitimate, there is a positive correlation between legitimacy and policy effectiveness. Insofar as political oppositions in a democracy exert some measure of

---

[57] Robert A. Dahl, 'Some Explanations,' in *Political Oppositions in Western Democracies*, ed. Robert A. Dahl (New Haven: Yale University Press, 1966), pp. 359 ff.

control over policies of state, an opposition becomes legitimate by virtue of its association with policies which are considered legitimate. Therefore, if our goal is to isolate the agent legitimizing political power in Israel, it is instructive to describe the forms of political oppositions there, and then to evaluate their relative effectiveness in influencing the formation of public policy.

In Israel, it is not only the political parties outside of the government which dissent from the government's policies and challenge their validity. It is possible to locate as much dissent and as much opposition within the governing parties as without, and within Mapai as much as within any other political party.[58] The extent to which policies are acceptable and legitimate in Israel turns out to be a function of their acceptability in Mapai. The political community rarely voices a serious protest that does not echo through the chambers of the Mapai party and receive reinforcement there.

The decision to go to war in June 1967 and the protests aroused by the need to make such a decision illustrate the nature of political oppositions in Israel and their manner of judging particular policies. The events preceding that prolonged and agonized decision rendered visible the positions of various political oppositions which felt compelled by the circumstances to advocate specific 'war' policies. Thus, political party activities related to that decision can serve as a means to locate the political oppositions in Israel, to measure their relative effectiveness, and in so doing to ascertain their legitimacy relative to one another.

Gahal rejected Prime Minister Eshkol's policies during the pre-1967 war period because by not immediately responding to Egyptian army mobilization in the Sinai Peninsula and to an Egyptian blockade of the Straits of Tiran, he seemed to have lost control of Israel's security.[59]

Leaders of Gahal, in the meantime, had decided that only a return to power of David Ben Gurion, Israel's long-time head of state and their former arch political rival, could extricate the country from the emergency. Eshkol appeared to Gahal too weak to be able to lead the country into a war that seemed increasingly inevitable.[60] But Eshkol ignored their suggestions to resign.

After several meetings with Ben Gurion, Menahem Begin, head of Gahal, turned to the National Religious Party to help reestablish Ben Gurion as prime minister or as minister of defense. In this examination of political oppositions, it is appropriate to look at the National Religious Party as well as at Gahal. The National Religious Party represents a different kind of political opposition from that of Gahal. Not as large as Gahal, the party has received just under 10 percent of the votes in the past several elections. Though it has almost always been a member of the government coalition, it considered itself to be an opponent of

[58] Daniel J. Elazar, *Israel: From Ideological to Territorial Democracy* (New York: General Learning Press, 1971), p. 5.
[59] Michel Bar Zohar, *Ha-Hodesh ha-Arokh be-Yotar* (The Longest Month) (Tel Aviv: Lewin-Epstein, 1968), p. 144.
[60] Ibid.

Mapai because of the National Religious Party's strict commitment to increasing religious influence over secular life.[61]

At the end of May 1967 both Gahal and the National Religious Party decided Ben Gurion's return to power provided the solution to Israel's security problems. At this time, the policy position of Ben Gurion was well known; he felt that Israel had already lost the advantage of surprise in any attack it might mount, so that it had no alternative but to wait. Ben Gurion's caution appealed to the National Religious Party, which still hoped to avoid war. Paradoxically, Gahal, too, looked to Ben Gurion, notwithstanding its contrary views on prospective foreign and military policies, because of his ability – tested in two wars – to govern the country during crises. Gahal recognized that a country increasingly disappointed with the performance of its head of state needed a strong prime minister who could provide the necessary moral leadership.[62] An editorial in the Hebrew daily *ha-Aretz* summaries the disquiet: 'Mr. Eshkol is not built to be prime minister and minister of defense in the present situation. The government as presently constituted cannot succeed in leading the state in a time of danger and they must open up places to erect a new administration.'[63]

Gahal's Menahem Begin and Moshe Haim Shapira, then minister of the interior and a leader of the National Religious Party, met with Eshkol on 27 May 1967 to suggest that Ben Gurion return to at least the ministry of defense.[64] Eshkol could not ignore the suggestions this time because of his party's long-standing ties with the National Religious Party. A comparison of the roles of the two parties in their unsuccessful attempts to bring Ben Gurion back into the government outlines the different degrees of their influence over the actions of government, for each was unsuccessful in a different sense. Gahal had much less leverage than did the National Religious Party. For a week, Gahal alone sought the return of Ben Gurion to the government and elicited no response from the Mapai-dominated government. Without the intercession and support of the National Religious Party, Gahal's plan for a new government would not have been taken seriously by Eshkol or his party. By contrast, Eshkol felt obliged to respond to the National Religious Party. Eshkol suggested that he relinquish the defense portfolio not to Ben Gurion but to Yigal Alon, a young protégé of Eshkol. The National Religious Party would have accepted and a compromise would have been arranged had Eshkol only to contend with this party's opposition.[65]

But the opposition to Eshkol had increased within Mapai, and there the demands for a change in the government were unequivocal: Mapai wanted to appoint Moshe Dayan, military hero of the Sinai War, as minister of defense.[66] Eshkol's political life could not have survived a return to power of Ben Gurion, and he considered Dayan's appointment as minister of defense only slightly less lethal a political blow. For Ben Gurion and Dayan had left Mapai to form their

[61] Ibid., p. 156.
[63] Michel Bar Zohar, *Ha-Hodesh*, p. 156.
[65] Ibid., p. 169.

[62] Fein, *Politics in Israel*, p. 94.
[64] Ibid., p. 141.
[66] Ibid.

own party in challenge to Eshkol's hegemony over Mapai. Those who seceded from Mapai in 1964 to form the political party Rafi were among the most well-known military leaders in Israel's history – Moshe Dayan, David Ben Gurion, and former director general of the ministry of defense and initiator of the Israeli-French arms deals, Shimon Peres. Their collective secession implied a rejection of Eshkol's direction of military affairs, and their party's election campaign in 1965 explicitly attacked Eshkol's management of the army and of the defense ministry.[67] Eshkol felt a special need to demonstrate his ability to handle the military and security affairs of the state personally, but he was unable to do this in May–June 1967.

Eshkol, allegedly master of consensus politics, ruled, but public confidence in his ability continued to diminish. As it diminished, opposition to his policy grew within his own party. Generals argued for war while United States officials urged restraint; cabinet ministers debated, postponing final decisions while the country, fully mobilized, waited.[68] Eshkol, bent on keeping Dayan out of the cabinet, stubbornly searched for plans to appease the dissidents in his own party. Dayan, aware of Eshkol's position, proposed that he be given a special commission to serve under the chief of staff of the army as commander of the southern front. Eshkol agreed, hoping that such an assignment for Dayan would satisfy the critics.[69]

Eshkol had underestimated the number of Dayan's supporters within his own party and their determination to have their way. Members of Mapai and of the Mapai parliamentary faction insisted in several meetings with Eshkol and with other party leaders that Dayan be made minister of defense and that a national unity coalition be formed. Powerful groups within the Mapai party – the Haifa branch, representatives of the Tel Aviv organization – (in other words the Gush), met together informally with Eshkol to convince him of the necessity of a 'wall-to-wall' coalition and of the appointment of Dayan as minister of defense.[70] Eshkol had no choice but to accept these demands because he realized that his own position as prime minister depended upon the support of these local leaders.

If the quality of an opposition is measured by its potential for influencing or blocking governmental action, then Gahal in parliament was the least effective organ of Israel's political oppositions. Gahal alone could not have secured a change in ministerial personnel or in policy. Eshkol, after all, had felt no need to respond directly to the demands of the parliamentary opposition for a new prime minister. The National Religious Party, as associate of Mapai's in the government coalition, could press harder and invoke some sort of response from the Mapai leadership. But the most effective opposition existed within the walls of the Mapai party itself.

Thus it is not necessarily in the nature of political oppositions in Israel to be outside of the established government or of the major party directing the

[67] Natan Yanai, op. cit., p. 295.            [68] Bar-Zohar, Ha-Hodesh, p. 92.
[69] Ibid., p. 175.                                        [70] Ibid.

coalition, because political opposition more often than not emanated from the dominant party itself. The efforts to change the cabinet in May 1967 rendered the various political oppositions visible and forced attention to the heart of the matter of political opposition in Israel – the oppositions within the major political party. What is surprising is not so much the strength of the internal political opposition as the progressive weakness of the party oppositions whose power derived simply from their positions in parliament or in the offices of state.[71]

It is not easy to move from the issue of effectiveness to that of legitimacy. But the activities of the various political oppositions during the weeks preceding the outbreak of war in 1967 do more than merely demonstrate that the opposition within Mapai was the most effective opposition in the country. This was true, but focussing on the policy aspect of the controversy suggests that the Mapai opposition was the most effective because it was thought to be the most legitimate. Opposition to Eshkol enjoyed widespread sympathy among many people and political parties, but the country's leadership responded to that opposition only when it emanated from parties closely linked to Mapai or from the political apparatus of the party itself. That Mapai opposition made changes within the government inevitable means that Mapai is an institution that legitimizes power by exercising it in the absence of force or violence. It legitimizes power according to our argument because in its exercise Mapai appears to be sensitive to the policy positions of the Israeli populace, leading that populace to believe that it has been considered in the determination of public policy.

CONCLUSION

Mapai's role as a legitimizing agent explains its dominance. All societies need to legitimize power for without legitimacy governments lose much of their potential power. That political power is legitimized through a political party should not be surprising in the Israeli context where the religious and the secular, the socialist and the capitalist, among many ideological types, argue over the proper shape of a Jewish state, of its government, and of its policies. In the absence of a reasonable hope that a consensus can emerge on the kind of state which is desired, the state itself is only partly finished and cannot itself demand a full political commitment. It is better to leave the state an unfinished entity and its government the bearer of only partial legitimacy exacting only partial loyalty.

This is not to deny that obligations to the state are incurred. They are. Still, the state cannot demand full and active endorsement of its political, social, and theological form, because no single form would satisfy all Israelis. Thus the public policies officially passed by the offices of state but worked out through the Mapai party apparatus were acceptable because they were more tentative

[71] In national elections the whole of Israel is constituted as a single constituency. Consequently, the members of the parties do not derive any power as constituency representatives.

than they would have been had they been fashioned completely and exclusively by the offices of state. Were they to be viewed as simply the policies of the government, the government could have claimed an absolute and total commitment to them. As it stands, all sorts of exceptions are made for people who cannot follow policies because of the dictates of their conscience.[72]

In spite of the conventional claims of political scientists, then, the legitimacy of government is not an absolute precondition for political order or even for democracy. If the Lockean notion of tacit consent makes any sense at all it is that people can be ambivalent about the legitimacy of government while continuing to obey the laws. Doubts about the legitimacy of government do not necessarily destroy social cohesion.

This is a far-reaching assertion. But the political situation in Israel testifies to its accuracy. The Israeli government exacts a loyalty sufficient to wage war, to pass and apply laws, to direct economic affairs. But it does not command the full and active consent of all of the members of the society to all of these activities. Pacifists challenge its wars, activists its efforts to establish peace; secularists oppose the incorporation of theological principles as state law while the religious exert efforts to expand the application of religious law. It is no wonder, then, that a principal concern of government is not to alienate any large segment of the population. Thus the government is satisfied with a partial commitment. But to what are the people wholly committed?

If affiliation is indicative of commitment, then a more total commitment is directed to party than to government. Consensus was formed on government actions because of Mapai's control of the government. Thus a necessary constituent of the government's operations was the Mapai party's participation and control of offices. Mapai exercised power in such a way that people felt that the power exercised was partly their own. Mapai's association with the government endowed the government with what legitimacy it possessed. For Israelis no greater affirmation of the legitimacy of political power is possible or necessary. So ambivalent a view of government in Israel, however, does not diminish the force of its political order as a state or of its democracy. If Michael Walzer has perceived the truth about the state in democracies, then Israel is but a typical example: 'while the state may well provide or seek to provide goods for all its members, it is not clear that these add up to or include the highest good. Perhaps they are goods of the lowest common denominator and only for this reason available to all, for it may be that the highest good can be pursued only in small groups. . . .'[73]

SMITH COLLEGE

NORTHAMPTON, MASS.

[72] Parties and individuals are allowed to abstain in crucial parliamentary votes if they are matters of conscience. I am treating Israel as a segmented society in the way used by Robert A. Dahl, 'Introduction,' *Regimes and Oppositions*, ed. Robert A. Dahl (New Haven: Yale University Press, 1973) and Ronald Rogowski, *Rational Legitimacy* (Princeton: Princeton University Press, 1974).

[73] Walzer, *Obligations*, p. 20.

# 11

## Israel's Right-Wing Jewish Proletariat

### Yael Yishai

THE most striking feature of the general elections for the tenth Israeli Knesset, in June 1981, was the dissociation of the workers from the Labour party (the Labour Alignment). Their allegiance to the right-wing Likud confirmed and reinforced what had seemed to be a transitory phase in Israeli politics, the Likud's ascent to power in 1977.

The defection of the proletariat from its 'natural' political affiliation is not a unique Israeli phenomenon. Those voters whom Nordlinger has called 'working-class Tories'[1] can be found in large numbers in several political systems, and especially in Great Britain. In fact, social class has been shown to be the major determinant of political affiliation only in Finland[2] and New Zealand.[3] Two principal reasons have been advanced for the right-wing tendencies of the working class. The first, the affluence hypothesis, which is grounded in psychological motivations, argues that those workers who have subjective middle-class identities will tend to vote for a Conservative party especially when they are dissatisfied with their present conditions.[4] The alternative, sociological, hypothesis focuses on other factors such as age, sex, regional diversity, and ethnicity;[5] these factors are said to erode the link between social class and political affiliation. Israel falls into this latter category, since the political behaviour of its Jewish proletariat is now largely connected with ethnic origin. That proletariat consists more than proportionately of immigrants from Asian and African countries, and their descendants, who since 1977 overwhelmingly support the Likud.

Of course, it is not easy to determine the meaning of 'right-wing';[6] but the Likud advocates free enterprise in the economic and domestic fields and hawkish nationalistic policies in foreign relations. This paper attempts to discover the reasons for the strong attraction which the Likud has for working-class voters, and for the clear rejection of the Labour Alignment. For some years before the 1977 general election, Oriental Jews had expressed feelings of resentment, dissatisfaction, and alienation; and they blamed successive Labour administrations. On the other hand, they saw the Likud as a political party which offered them the possibility of achieving power and influence; it seemed therefore logical and expedient to support the Likud and by so doing to

exact a revenge upon the Labour Alignment. Moreover, right-wing
ideologies had a special appeal for Oriental voters. The combination of
these factors has led Israeli Jewish workers to form a solid bloc of Likud
voters, a development which does not only represent a dramatic change
in electoral behaviour, but which might affect the whole structure of
Israeli politics.

## Working-class Jews in Israel

Israel is one of the more egalitarian democracies.[7] Nevertheless, the
country has a disproportionate number of Jews of Afro-Asian origin
among those who have the lowest educational achievements, whose
occupations yield the lowest income, and who live in the poorest
housing conditions. The *Statistical Abstract of Israel* shows that in 1980,
17.5 per cent of the Israel-born children of an immigrant father from
Europe or America, but only two per cent of the Israel-born children of
an immigrant father from Asia or Africa, had 16 or more years of formal
education; while 40.6 per cent of the former, but only 15 per cent of the
latter, were among academic, scientific, and professional workers.
Moreover, 35.7 per cent of those of Oriental origin, against 15.6 of those
of Western origin, were industrial skilled and unskilled workers. As for
housing, whereas less than one per cent (0.9) of households of those of
Western origin had more than three persons in a room, this was the
case for 2.6 per cent of households of the Israel-born of Oriental origin;
on the other hand, 29.1 per cent of the former against 15.3 per cent of
the latter had under one person per room. Finally, the income index per
urban employee's household of those who were themselves born in Asia
or Africa was 80.1 against 100 in the case of those born in Europe or
America. Moreover, 71.1 per cent of the Jewish population aged 14 and
above who had a maximum of four years of schooling were Orientals,
although Oriental Jews accounted for only 43.8 per cent of that age
group; 81.6 per cent of all those Jews who lived in homes with a housing
density of more than three persons per room were Orientals; and 59.7
per cent of all unskilled workers were Orientals, who constituted 42.1
per cent of all Jews gainfully occupied. As for income, Jewish
households with a head of household born in Asia or Africa constituted
32.4 per cent of all Jewish households, but accounted for 52.1 per cent
of Jewish households in the lowest decile of net income per standard
person. In 1980, the proportion of Orientals in the Israeli Jewish
population was 44.9 per cent: 19.5 per cent were born in Asia/Africa and
25.4 per cent were born in Israel and had a father born in Asia or Africa.[8]

## Voting patterns

The results of the 1973, 1977, and 1981 general elections show a
remarkable and consistent shift of the Oriental vote from the left-wing

Labour Alignment to the right-wing Likud. On the other hand, the Western Jews who had deserted the Alignment in 1977, often in favour of the Democratic Movement for Change, returned in 1981 to the Alignment. Asher Arian has noted that while 60 per cent of the Orientals supported the Likud and 30 per cent of them voted for the Alignment in 1981, precisely the reverse was true of Western Jews: 60 per cent of them voted for the Alignment, and 30 per cent for the Likud. In areas of predominantly Oriental settlement (such as Beth She'an, Kiryat Shmona, Ramla, and Rosh Ha'ain), more than half of the electorate voted for the Likud in 1981 — 56.4, 55.7, 51.7, and 57.7 per cent respectively, a notable gain in each case on 1973 and 1977.[9]

It is not the voting patterns alone which lead to the assumption that there is now a right-wing proletariat in Israel. A change in the perception of political parties might have led to a view of the Likud as a party of reform. However, a study of party images has shown that the Likud is perceived in fact as a right-wing party: 77 per cent of respondents saw the Likud as right-wing, while only 28 per cent believed the Alignment to be a party of the Right.[10] The Likud is recognized to have a right-wing ideology both in foreign relations and in domestic economic policy.

### Rejection of the Labour Alignment

RESENTMENT. The Labour Party is held responsible by most Oriental Jews for the disadvantages which they have suffered. The mass immigration within the first decade after the establishment of the State of Israel has been widely discussed and documented. The Jewish population more than doubled, from 716,700 in 1948 to 1,810,200 in 1958.[11] Most of the newcomers from Asia and Africa did not have the skills necessary in a rapidly industrializing society, and they were sent to remote development towns or to agricultural settlements. Some of them moved into the larger cities, in areas which became slums. Resentment against their living conditions grew, and some Orientals believed that there was a deliberate policy on the part of the establishment (the Labour party) to take advantage of the poor and the uneducated who could not fight back. Various remedial economic and educational measures which were implemented in order to bridge the 'ethnic gap' were only partly successful.

Resentment persisted, and it is probable that a desire for revenge was an added incentive when working-class voters supported the Likud in 1977. The Likud, if only by virtue of its having been in the opposition in the previous Knesset, could not be held responsible for the correlation between economic deprivation and Oriental origin. But four years later, in 1981, the situation of Oriental Jews had not significantly improved. On the contrary, according to various indices the poor had become poorer. The average income of a household whose head was an employee of Afro/Asian origin decreased from 82.2 to 81 per cent of the average income of a Western employee's household.[12] And the National Insurance Institute stated that the proportion of households living below the poverty line more than doubled: from 2.8 to 6.6 per cent between 1977 and 1980.[13] Finally, the percentage of households in the lower deciles of income grew from 8 per cent in 1975 to 10.3 per cent in 1980.[14] Nevertheless, working-class voters again supported the Likud in 1981, probably because the Labour Alignment was still seen as the party responsible for instituting and maintaining the ethnic gap.

DISSATISFACTION WITH THE INSTITUTIONS OF LABOUR. Many Oriental Jews view the kibbutzim and the Histadrut (the General Federation of Labour) as institutions affiliated to the Labour party[15] which in practice exploit the workers.

In 1980, the kibbutz population accounted for only 3.6 per cent of the total Jewish population of Israel: 113,977 persons in 246 kibbutzim.[16] The heirs of the legendary pioneers who made the desert bloom and lived under spartan conditions now own more than a third (35.7 per cent) of Israel's cultivated land and produce two thirds of the country's total agricultural exports. The kibbutz movement also has industrial enterprises: in 1977–79, it had 152 regional projects and 377 which were autonomously operated. Of those engaged in the latter ('pure' kibbutz projects), 40.5 per cent are paid employees — that is, not members of a kibbutz; while in the regional enterprises, 80 per cent are paid employees.[17]

Large numbers of kibbutz employees are Oriental residents of development towns. In 1978, 17 per cent of the total Jewish population of Israel lived in 29 development towns,[18] which had been planned as urban centres for the agricultural areas around them. But in many cases these towns have remained small and have not prospered; while in a few cases there are characteristic problems of social malaise, such as a high rate of juvenile delinquency. The contrast between the affluence of the kibbutzim which border on disadvantaged urban areas, and the low standard of living of the Oriental residents who are employed on kibbutz projects, has aroused a great deal of tension and hostility. Kibbutz members are employers, with the status rewards of white-collar and managerial positions; they also reap the profits of their industry. The employees, on the other hand, do not have a direct share in these benefits. By virtue of its ideology, the kibbutz is a closed, in effect almost impenetrable, society with clear boundary lines. Of course, the hiring of labour is not congruent with the principle of equality upon which the kibbutz was founded; but such a deviation has been claimed to be a response to the national need of providing employment for immigrants. Another sharp contrast between the standards of kibbutz members and of their employees is in the field of education. Kibbutz teachers are well trained, and the schoolchildren have the most advanced equipment for learning — while the educational level in the surrounding development towns is often of a low standard.

The hostility of the development towns to kibbutzim reached its peak during the 1981 general election campaign, when kibbutz members were accused in a campaign advertisement in a local newspaper of being 'bloodthirsty beasts feeding on Kiryat Shmona' (a development town).[19] On the other hand, kibbutzim have claimed that their members are engaged in voluntary work for the benefit of development towns, and that in 1978–79 there were 2,500 of their members engaged in such work in 25 development towns.[20] Far from being grateful, many of the urban residents regard such efforts as an unwelcome intrusion under the guise of philanthropic activities; and they were particularly resentful of the part played by such kibbutz volunteers during the election campaign. Oriental Jews see the co-operative settlements, and the Labour party to which they are affiliated, as symbols of economic exploitation, of the affluent 'first Israel', contrasting with the salaried workers employed in the regional enterprises of the kibbutzim. They therefore did not hesitate to express their frustration and resentment by voting against the Labour Alignment and for the Likud. This hostility did not fade after the general election. In September 1981, the Prime Minister was reported to have referred in a radio interview to members of kibbutzim as 'arrogant millionaires enjoying their swimming pools'.[21] This accusation led to a vociferous public debate, which exacerbated the existing friction and estrangement.

As for the Histadrut, it is naturally identified with the Labour Alignment as well as with the employer class. From a Federation of Labour concerned with national and social ideals, it has become transformed into a giant economic empire, with its own banking concerns as well as heavy industry and the provision of various services. In 1976, the Histadrut accounted for about 27 per cent of Israel's gross national product.[22] It is at the same time a trade union and a manufacturer, and so it must represent the interests of both workers and proprietors, employees and employers. And it is the Oriental Jews who predominate among the workers, while the managers and most senior officials are Ashkenazim — Western Jews. Admittedly, at the lower echelons of power the Histadrut has provided Oriental Jews with a channel of mobility unmatched by any other institution: in 1981, 70.5 per cent of the secretaries of local Workers Councils were of Oriental origin, while their proportion in 1977 had been 62 per cent.[23] However, in 1981 in the top positions of the Histadrut, on its Executive Committee, less than a quarter of the members were Oriental Jews — nine out of 41. Therefore, although the majority of Oriental Jews are members of the Histadrut, many of them do not see it as an organization which represents their interests. There has recently been an attempt on the part of the Likud to challenge the power of the Labour Alignment in the Histadrut by putting forward as a candidate for the office of Secretary-General the Deputy Prime Minister of Israel, who is of Moroccan origin and who grew up in a development town.

ESTRANGEMENT. Although Oriental Jews overwhelmingly supported the Labour party in the 1950s and 1960s, they did not adhere to the socialist ideals proclaimed by that party; and they were aware that they were a disadvantaged segment of Israeli society. The founding fathers of the Labour movement were mainly immigrants from Poland and Russia who came to settle in Palestine in the 1920s, and their foremost national objective was the establishment of socialism through the creation of a Jewish working class in the land of Zion. Most Oriental Jews, however, had been workers in their lands of origin, but not a working *class*. The concept of a struggle between capitalists and the proletariat as well as the development of historical materialism were totally alien to them. In their native countries, where the Muslim ethos predominated, authority was vested in an absolute ruler and his sovereignty was sanctified by the religious establishment. When they were told of Marxist-Leninist ideas, they rejected them out of hand: they were observant Jews and socialism espoused secularism; socialism advocated equality and the elimination of power structures, while they adhered to a hierarchical order with the family at the kernel but extending to all social domains. Zionist socialism represented a total upheaval, with its promotion of an 'occupational revolution' which would turn Jewish merchants and artisans into farmers and labourers. Oriental Jews respected tradition and considered toiling on the land as inferior work. Their version of Zionism was religious Messianism: coming to settle in Israel would be the fulfilment of ancient prayers and aspirations, not a deliberate rejection of one's past traditions and observances.

Oriental Jews still believe that they are a disadvantaged group. The majority of them (59 per cent), in a poll conducted in October 1981, thought they were a deprived group; but only 27 per cent of Western Israelis believed that Oriental Jews were deprived. Moreover, exactly the same proportion (59 per cent) of the Israel-born children of Oriental immigrants also thought that Oriental Jews were a deprived group in Israel; but only 34 per cent of them believed the deprivation to be intentional and manipulated by the establishment, while 46 per cent of those born in Asia or Africa were of that opinion. When asked whether they thought there would be violent clashes between Orientals and Ashkenazim as a result of the ethnic problems, 24 per cent of those born in Asia or Africa replied in the affirmative, while a slightly smaller proportion (20 per cent) of their Israel-born children were of that opinion. The immigrants from Europe and America were less pessimistic: only 12 per cent of them thought that there would be violent clashes, while 14 per cent of the Israel-born children of Western immigrants held that belief. As for the Israel-born children of Israel-born fathers (regardless of the country of origin of their grandfathers), 12 per cent of them believed there would be violent confrontations.[24]

In July 1979, two years after the Likud had won the general election of 1977, a public opinion poll enquired, 'Are you satisfied with the government's performance?' Of the respondents born in Asia or Africa, 59 per cent said they were, as did 60 per cent of Israel-born children of Oriental parentage. On the other hand, only 34 per cent of those born in Europe or America, and 39 per cent of the Israel-born of Ashkenazi parentage, were satisfied. Moreover, when asked to compare the achievements of the Likud with those of the Labour Alignment, 61 per cent of the Oriental respondents, but only 34 per cent of the Ashkenazi respondents, thought that on balance the Likud had had more successes than failures when compared with the Alignment.[25]

*The Appeal of the Likud*

UPWARD MOBILITY. Oriental Jews seem to believe that it is the Likud rather than the Labour Alignment which offers them a channel for rapid political advancement. This belief is not based on hard political facts. In the seventh Knesset (1969–73), the Labour coalition had eight members who were Oriental Jews while the Likud had three; in the eighth Knesset (1973–77), the Labour coalition had 12 and the Likud had six. In the ninth Knesset (1977–81), when the Likud achieved power, the Labour Alignment had eight Oriental MKs and the Likud had seven; and in the tenth Knesset in 1981, with the Likud having retained power, the Labour Alignment still had more Oriental MKs, 12, against the Likud's nine.

On the other hand, while the number of Oriental MKs in the Labour coalition has wavered (from eight to 12, back to eight, then up to 12), the Likud has exhibited a continuous upward trend — from three, to six, to seven, to nine. Moreover, the Likud's Oriental MKs generally enjoy greater popularity than their counterparts in the Labour Alignment do. Here it is important to note that Moroccans constitute the largest segment of Oriental Jews in Israel, and that they are a politically well organized and articulate group. A North African (mainly Moroccan) party was established under the name of Tami, the Movement for Israel's Tradition, and it won three seats in the 1981 Knesset. More than half of the Likud Oriental MKs (five out of nine) are Moroccans, while in the Labour Alignment only one third (four out of 12) are Moroccans. Furthermore, the Likud's Oriental MKs are seen as genuine representatives of the 'second Israel', who have emerged from development towns and other deprived areas to serve their people. Admittedly, the Labour Alignment can boast that one of its Oriental MKs is the mayor of a development town in the Negev; but in the view of Likud supporters, he and his colleagues have been co-opted by the Ashkenazi élite, who patronize them. Of course, it is not easy to differentiate between a 'genuine' and a 'co-opted' leader, since by the nature of Israeli politics they are both nominated by their political party.[26] Nevertheless, there appears to be a general belief that the Likud offers greater opportunities for promotion. As a result of being in power for three decades, the Labour coalition has the image of a highly institutionalized semi-oligarchic party; while the Likud expanded so rapidly that it had many vacant posts. Oriental Jews were quick to seize the opportunity of filling these posts with vigorous energy, and to point out that they achieved in the Likud positions of power and prestige which had been denied them in the Labour Alignment.

It is worth noting here that since 1969, the proportion of Israeli Jewish voters who were born in Asia or Africa has slightly but steadily declined: 47.8 per cent in 1969, 46.9 per cent in 1973, 45.9 per cent in 1977, and 44.9 per cent in 1980.[27] On the other hand, the proportion of Israel-born voters whose fathers were immigrants from Asia or Africa has increased steadily from 21 per cent in 1969, to 23.2 per cent in 1973, 25 per cent in 1977, and 25.4 per cent in 1980.[28] It is therefore obvious that Oriental Jews are still seriously under-represented in the 1981 Knesset, with 21 Oriental MKs between the two main parties, one each in four small parties (Telem, Hadash, Tehiyah, and the National Religious Party), and three in Tami — that is, 28 out of the total number of 120 Members of the Knesset.

HAWKISH PATRIOTISM. In the all-important matters of national security and foreign policy, the Likud's stance has been generally much more hawkish than that of the Labour Alignment. In its electoral platform, the Likud committed itself to the principle of a Greater Israel and to establishing settlements in the occupied territories. On the other hand, although the Alignment does have some ardent hawks, it is generally far more moderate than the Likud;[29] in its electoral platform, it promised that it would make territorial concessions in return for a lasting peace.

In spite of the Likud's Peace Pact with Egypt, that party still appears to have a popular image of greater intransigence: in a public opinion poll carried out in July 1981, 70 per cent of the respondents said that they thought the Labour Alignment would be willing to surrender some of the occupied territories, while only 30 per cent thought that the Likud might do so.[30] From its advent to power in 1977 until the general election of June 1981, the Likud in fact established 42 settlements on the West Bank (or Judea and Samaria in the official terminology). A public opinion poll, carried out by the Israel Institute for Applied Social Research in 1979, showed a larger proportion of Oriental-born than of Western-born Jews to be in favour of such settlements: 73 against 56 per cent. Moreover, the Israel-born children of Oriental Jews were almost exactly as hawkish as their parents: 72 per cent of them were in favour of the settlements. Surprisingly perhaps, the Israel-born children of immigrants from Europe and America were more hawkish than their parents: 65 per cent of them were in favour of the settlements. On the other hand, the Israel-born children of Israel-born parents were almost as moderate as the Western immigrants: only 58 per cent of them were in favour of the new settlements.[31]

It also seems that the large majority of Oriental Jews are willing to pay the price, literally, of establishing the new settlements: in 1979, 66 per cent of those born in Asia/Africa, and 77 per cent of the Israel-born of Oriental parentage, stated that they were in favour of giving priority in the national budget to the new settlements. In contrast, just under half of the Western immigrants (49 per cent), and more than half (55 per cent) of their Israel-born children, were of that opinion; and the proportion in the case of the Israel-born children of Israel-born fathers was 57 per cent.[32]

The new settlements have given rise to a great deal of international protest and censure; but the Oriental hawks do not appear chastened by these reactions. What was perhaps unexpected has been the apparent willingness of Oriental Jews to make serious economic sacrifices — for the new settlements are a costly enterprise, requiring large sums of money which would otherwise have been spent on social welfare (of which the Orientals are the main beneficiaries). Poverty in Israel has been said to be the product of a trade-off between guns and butter.[33] It seems that those who are most in need of butter are also those in favour of the acquisition of guns.

One explanation of the hawkish inclination of Oriental Israelis is that although they cling to some of the traditions of their lands of origin, they wish to show that they are patriotic Israelis and strongly hostile to Arab countries. Moreover, they claim to understand well Arab nationalism and politics, and say they have good reason to distrust Arab leaders as peace makers; they insist that Israel's enemies understand only the language of force. At the end of 1979, while nearly two thirds (63 per cent) of Western Jews stated that peace had more advantages than disadvantages, only 41 per cent of Afro/Asian Jews were of that opinion; but exactly 50 per cent of the Israel-born children of both Oriental and Western immigrants, and also 50 per cent of the second generation to have been born in Israel, expressed that belief.[34]

Another explanation for the hawkishness of Oriental Jews is their belief that such an attitude gives them enhanced prestige vis-à-vis other social groups (including Israeli Arabs), as well as demonstrating their intense patriotism. In this context, it must be remembered that the majority of the total Jewish electorate is against relinquishing the occupied territories — but would agree to returning only a small proportion.[35] Oriental Jews have simply adopted a more extreme position.

In the economic field, it seems irrational for members of the working class to favour a right-wing party such as the Likud. A closer examination of the Likud's 1977 electoral platform, however, reveals that although it advocated free enterprise and other aspects of a laissez-faire policy, it also stressed the importance of combating poverty and gave that goal as much emphasis as that of attaining peace.[36] The Labour Alignment, on the other hand, put the main emphasis on national security and peace; and it was far less committed to the enactment of a wide range of social legislation. The Likud, by challenging the existing social order, was seen as a party of the people and the slogan coined by Mr Begin, 'To Benefit with the People', reinforced the image. Of course, the electorate was aware that campaign promises are rarely fulfilled; but at least the Likud appeared to be moving in the right (as well as right-wing) direction.

*Conclusion*

The general election of 1981 reaffirmed the support which the Jewish working classes had given to the Likud four years earlier, when they had transferred their allegiance away from the Labour Alignment. Oriental Jews continued to blame the Alignment for the decades of their disadvantaged condition; they showed their enduring resentment by voting again in favour of Labour's opposition, and in that way were able to give expression to their grievances without disrupting the civic order.

Although the Likud in its first term of office did not achieve great improvements for Oriental Jews either in the economic field or in the political, an even greater proportion of them voted for that party in 1981. One probable reason for this paradoxical behaviour was that, unlike the Labour Alignment, the Likud stood for religious observance and against making greater concessions to the Arabs — both attitudes which hold great appeal for Oriental Jews. They could be proud of being observant Jews; they did not have to undergo any transformation; and, while remaining in their development towns or urban neighbourhoods, they could freely express their hostility to their Arab neighbours and their support for those Israeli Jews who became settlers on the West Bank. In that way, they were conforming to the values of the ruling party in Israel and overcoming their sense of alienation; and that was apparently more important than immediate economic improvement. Another probable reason for supporting the Likud was that it was a party which apparently held greater prospects of political advancement for Oriental Jews.

What of the future? Will the Likud retain its right-wing character or will it become a party of the workers and advocate policies geared to the needs of the proletariat? Will it retain its predominantly Ashkenazi leadership or will it transform itself into a genuine Oriental party? The present alliance between Oriental Jews and the Likud appears fairly durable. However, it may be that the establishment of yesterday (the Labour Alignment) will become the militant opposition of tomorrow and the champion of deprived groups, thus 'normalizing' the political situation by forging a link between a Labour party and the Jewish proletariat of Israel.

## NOTES

ABBREVIATIONS

I.I.A.S.R.   ISRAEL INSTITUTE OF APPLIED SOCIAL RESEARCH
S.A.I.   Statistical Abstract of Israel

[1] Eric A. Nordlinger, The Working Class Tories, Berkeley, Ca., 1967.

[2] See Pertti Pesonen, An Election in Finland, New Haven, Ct., 1968.

[3] Alan D. Robinson, 'Class Voting in New Zealand: A Comment on Alford's Comparison of Class Voting in American Political Systems', in Seymour M. Lipset and Stein Rokkan, eds., Party Systems and Voter Alignments, New York, 1967, pp. 95–119.

[4] David E. Butler and Donald E. Stokes, Political Change in Britain: Forces Shaping Electoral Choice, New York, 1969, pp. 120–37.

[5] See, for example, Robert A. Dahl, Political Oppositions in Western Democracies, New Haven, Ct., 1966.

[6] John C. Thomas, The Decline of Ideology in Western Political Parties, Beverly Hills, Ca., 1975, pp. 46–49.

[7] The Gini index of Inequality for various democratic countries is as follows: Netherlands (1967).45; Japan (1971).42; German Federal Republic (1970).39; U.S.A. (1972).39; Great Britain (1968).34; and Israel (1968–69).38. See Karl W. Deutsch, Politics and Government, Boston, 1980, pp. 126–27.

[8] See S.A.I., 1981: for education, p. 608; for occupation, p. 346; for housing density, p. 301; for income, p. 293; and for the percentage of Oriental Jews, p. 56. See also Judith Bernstein and Aaron Antonovsky, 'The Integration of Ethnic Groups in Israel', The Jewish Journal of Sociology, vol. 23, no. 1, June 1981, especially pp. 10–20.

[9] See Asher Arian, 'Elections 1981: Competitiveness and Polarization', The Jerusalem Quarterly, no. 21 Fall 1981, p. 23. See also Central Bureau of Statistics, Electoral Results, for the 1973, 1977, and 1981 Knessets.

[10] Arian, op. cit., p. 7.

[11] S.A.I., 1981, p. 30

[12] S.A.I., 1981, p. 275.

[13] National Insurance Institute, *Annual Survey* (in Hebrew) 1980, p. 146.

[14] For 1975, see *S.A.I.*, 1980, p. 274; and for 1980, *S.A.I.*, 1981, p. 292.

[15] In the 1981 general elections, the Labour Alignment won 88.5 per cent of the votes in all kibbutzim. See *Results of Elections to the Tenth Knesset*, 30.6.81, Central Bureau of Statistics, Special Series No. 680, p. 45.

[16] See *S.A.I.*, 1981, p. 39.

[17] See Moshe Sokolowski, *Haker et Hatnua Hakibbutzit*, Brit Hatnua Hakibbutzit, publication no. 148/80, Tel Aviv, 1980, pp. 9, 14, 16.

[18] Eliyahu Borukhov and Elia Werczberger, 'Factors Affecting the Development of New Towns', *Environment and Planning*, vol. 13, A, 1981, p. 421.

[19] See the report in *Haaretz*, 6 June 1981.

[20] See Sokolowski, op. cit., pp. 7–8.

[21] See *Haaretz*, 28 September 1981. This description of members of kibbutzim was rejected by half the respondents (49.9 per cent) in a public opinion poll: *Haaretz*, 20 November 1981.

[22] See the Histadrut publication, *Netunim Kalkalyim al Chevrat Ha-ovdim be-1976*, October 1977, p. 2.

[23] The information is based on the list of Secretaries provided by the Executive Committee of the Histadrut.

[24] See *Monitin* (Hebrew monthly), no. 38, October 1981, p. 31.

[25] See I.I.A.S.R., publication (S) JK/742/H, July 1979, pp. 13–14.

[26] See Giora Goldberg, 'Democracy and Representation in Israeli Political Parties', in Asher Arian, ed., *The Elections in Israel, 1977*, Jerusalem, 1980, pp. 101–18.

[27] See *S.A.I.*; 1970, p. 46; 1974, pp. 46–47; 1978, p. 57; and 1981, p. 56.

[28] See *S.A.I.*; for 1969: 1970, p. 46; for 1973: 1974, p. 45; for 1977 and 1980: 1981, p. 56.

[29] Avner Yaniv and Fabian Pascal, 'Doves, Hawks and other Birds of Feather. The Distribution of Israeli Parliamentary Opinion on the Future of the Occupied Territories, 1967–1977', *British Journal of Political Science*, vol. 10, April 1980, pp. 260–67.

[30] Pesach Adi, 'Halikud Vehamaarach Be'enei Habocher', I.I.A.S.R. Newsletter no. 54 July 1981, p. 19.

[31] I.I.A.S.R. publication (S) HL/747H, August 1979, p. 10.

[32] Ibid.

[33] Ofira Seliktar, 'The Cost of Vigilance in Israel: Linking the Economic and Social Costs of Defense', *Journal of Peace Research*, vol. 17, no. 4, 1980, pp. 340–55.

[34] See I.I.A.S.R., IL/756/H, November 1979, p. 16.

[35] Louis Guttman, *The Israel Public, Peace and Territory: The Impact of the Sadat Initiative*, Jerusalem, 1978, Table 1, pp. 8–9.

[36] Yael Yishai, 'Welfare Policy: Party Platforms During the Elections to the Ninth Knesset', *Social Security*, no. 14–15, November 1977, pp. 17–31 (in Hebrew).

# 12

## The Ethnic Lists in Election 1981:
## An Ethnic Political Identity?

### Hanna Herzog

The elections of 1981 were presented in the communications media and in some sociological analyses as standing in the shadow of ethnic polarization (*Yediot Aharonot*, 3 July 1981; *Maariv*, 10 July 1981). In view of such analyses, the question must be raised as to whether an ethnic political identity indeed exists or is developing in Israel. The present paper is an attempt to deal with this question by means of an historical examination of those lists known as "ethnic."[1] Because of considerations of space, selected examples will be presented and not an exhaustive discussion of all the lists.

In the 1981 elections five parties defined as ethnically-based participated. These five parties joined a large group of "ethnic lists" which have been part of the political scene in Israel since the renewal of Jewish settlement in modern times (the New Yishuv). Since the elections to the first Asefat Ha-Nivharim (Elected Assembly) in 1920 and up to the tenth Knesset elections (1981), there were 49 ethnic lists, counting lists that ran for more than one election separately for each appearance (see table 1 for details).

On the surface, it would appear that the increasing number of lists and the consistency of their appearance are an expression of ethnic political identity. In fact, from the standpoint of their electoral attainments, the ethnic lists have remained a marginal phenomenon on the political landscape of Israel. This marginality is most striking in view of the change in the ethnic composition of the Jewish population of Israel since the establishment of the state. In the wake of large waves of immigration from Moslem countries, the proportion of people of Asian and African origin in the Jewish population rose steadily from 22.5 percent in 1948 to 38.8 percent in 1951, 48 percent in 1957, and to 55 percent in 1975, at which point it has since remained.

The ethnic political organization which existed before the establishment of the State of Israel did not become a nucleus for political absorption of those of Oriental origin. The ethnically-based political organizations founded after the

## TABLE 1

*The Ethnic Lists in the Election Campaigns*
*to the Elected Assembly and the Knesset, 1920-1981*

| 1st Elected Assembly 1920 | No. and % of mandates | 2nd Elected Assembly 1925 | No. and % of mandates | 3rd Elected Assembly 1931 | No. and % of mandates | 4th Elected Assembly 1944 | No. and % of mandates |
|---|---|---|---|---|---|---|---|
| Sephardic Federation | 54 (17.3) | Sephardic Federation | 19 (7.2) | Sephardic Federation | 6 (4.6) | Independent Yemenite Association | 4 (2.5) |
| Yemenite List | 12 (3.9) | Yemenite Association | 20 (8.8) | Sephardic Community Workers | 3 (3.0) | Yemenite Association | 2 (0.4) |
| Young Orientals | 4 (1.3) | | | Sephardic Workers of Zion List | — (0.05) | Youth of Aden | — (0.1) |
| Young Israelis | 2 (0.6) | | | Oriental Supporters of Jabotinsky | 5 (4.2) | | |
| Bukharian Community | 5 (1.6) | | | Sephardic Borochov List | | | |
| Georgian Community | 1 (0.3) | | | Yemenite Association | 3 (3.0) | | |

(Table continued)

| | 1st Knesset 1949 No. and % | 2nd Knesset 1951 No. and % | 3rd Knesset 1955 No. and % | 4th Knesset 1959 No. and % | 5th Knesset 1961 No. and % |
|---|---|---|---|---|---|
| | National Union of Sephardis 4 (2.5) | Yemenite Association 1 (1.2) | Yemenite Association — (0.3) | Yemenite Faction — (0.2) | For Justice & Fraternity — (0.3) |
| | Yemenite Association 1 (1.0) | Sephardis and Orientals 2 (1.8) | Sons of Yemen Movement — (0.3) | Union of North African Immigrants — (0.8) | Yemenite Immigrants List |
| | | Israeli Faithful — (0.6) | Original Religious List — (0.3) | National Sephardic Party — (0.3) | |
| | | | Sephardis and Orientals — (0.8) | Union of Independent N. African Immigrants — (0.1) | |
| | | | | National Union of Sephardis & Orientals — (0.2) | |

(Table continued on next page)

(Table 1 continued)

| | 6th Knesset 1965 | | 7th Knesset 1969 | | 8th Knesset 1973 | | 9th Knesset 1977 | | 10th Knesset 1981 | |
|---|---|---|---|---|---|---|---|---|---|---|
| | No. | and % | No. | and % | No. | and % | No. | and % | No. | and % |
| Young Israel | — | (0.2) | Young Israel — | (0.1) | Yemenites List — | (0.2) | House of Israel — | (0.5) | Tami 3 | (2.3) |
| Fraternity List | — | (0.9) | | | Black Panthers — | (0.9) | Coalition of Workers and Neighborhoods — | (0.1) | The Unity Party — | (0.07) |
| | | | | | Blue-White Panthers — | (0.4) | Zionist Panthers — | (0.1) | Your People — | (0.02) |
| | | | | | Movement for Social Equality — | (0.7) | | | One Israel — | (0.19) |
| | | | | | Peoples Movement — | (0.5) | | | Tent Movement — | (0.03) |

A dash indicates that the percentage of the vote received was not enough to obtain a mandate.

Where a party is listed without indication of number and percentage of mandates, this indicates that the party took place in the election but that no details of its achievement are readily available.

establishment of the state by the new immigration did not last long and none developed into a long-term framework working among people of like origin. But despite the lack of continuity and the lack of electoral success, the phenomenon of ethnic lists is consistent and continuing. Except in the elections to the seventh Knesset (1969), there appeared in each campaign more than one ethnic list. The consistency of the phenomenon on the one hand, and on the other hand, the splits, the organizational impermanence, and the fact that new organizational foci continued to form — all these things require explanation. Do we have here proof of the existence of ethnic political identity in Israel?

## WHAT IS POLITICAL ETHNICITY?

When we discuss the ethnic lists, the fact should be noted that the title "ethnic lists" is applied in Israel only to those lists whose originators were of Asian or African origin.[2] The exclusive application of the term "ethnic" to groups whose origin was in Islamic countries, despite the fact that Israeli society is a mosaic made up of people from different countries (i.e., "ethnic groups"), reflects a social reality in which the dominant groups were identified as "Israeli society" and all the other groups as "ethnic."

The dominant principle accepted in the Yishuv was to encourage all organized groups to join Knesset Israel, a voluntary political framework, which included those groups organized along ethnic lines. Moreover, in order to widen the electoral basis of elected bodies and make them more stable, a willingness to give preferential treatment to such groups was shown. For example, providing a special election day for Yemenites (1923), or permitting voting in ethnic polling stations (1931). Simultaneously, on the ideological level, ethnicity as a legitimate basis for political organization was decried. Disapproval was generally shown in indirect ways by stigmatization of the lists and their leaders (Herzog 1983). The ethnic lists were presented as threatening the ideal of "mizug galuyot" (a blending of the Diaspora, or in colloquial language the melting pot); in other words as advocating separatism.

A study of the demands of the ethnic lists from the time of their inception in the elections to the first Asefat Ha-Nivharim reveals that the organization of ethnic lists was a means of preserving prestige and/or political power by political entrepreneurs, but not an end in itself. The ethnic lists did not have a separatist ideology and in most cases did not demand the preservation of ethnic uniqueness. Their aspiration was to become rooted in the political system of the Yishuv and later the state by adopting the rules of the game of this system.

Since the concept of ethnicity became a means of classification and

## TABLE 2
### Splits and Mergers in Ethnic Lists

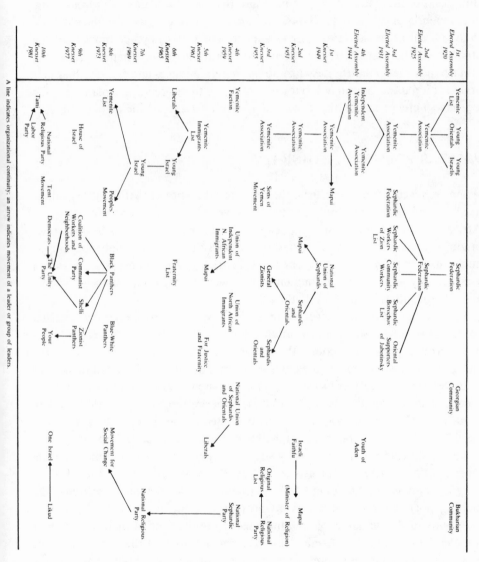

A line indicates organizational continuity; an arrow indicates movement of a leader or group of leaders.

categorization of the population and a criterion for the distribution of power and position in the political parties and organizations, political entrepreneurs of "Oriental"* origin also used it for purposes of political manipulation. In the process of bargaining over positions of power and distribution of resources between these entrepreneurs and their rivals in the political arena, political ethnicity developed and received its significance (Herzog 1981).

The processes which took place in the Israeli political arena give support to those approaches, theories, and empirical studies which indicate that ethnicity is a phenomenon which emerges and changes in the course of interaction among groups and competition for various resources (Barth 1969; A. Cohen 1974; Deshen 1974, 1976).

My claim is that rather than being an expression of ethnic political identity, the ethnic lists in Israel until now have been a tool for political bargaining, and only a temporary and conditional alliance between political entrepreneurs, just as ethnicity in itself was also presented as temporary and conditional.

## IMPERMANENCE AS AN ORGANIZATIONAL PATTERN

Table 2 is a graphical attempt to show the impermanence of ethnic lists. The table shows the political undertakings, the number of times each ethnic list faced the voters, and the wanderings of the leaders from their previous organizations to some non-ethnic parties or to new ethnic organizations. The table shows clearly that some of the leaders took part in more than one attempt at ethnic organization. Many of these leaders began their activity within ordinary political parties. It is interesting to note that only a few of them ceased political activity with the disappearance of their particular ethnic list.

The disappearance of most of the ethnic lists from the political scene after one or two election campaigns created the stereotype of lists springing up on the eve of elections (Peretz 1960), lists which are a result of short-term planning. As a matter of fact lists which formed shortly before elections and those which operated as organizations for long periods previously can be found side-by-side. For example, a National Sephardic Party headed by Sciaky (1959) was organized about two-and-a-half months before the elections, and likewise Tsedek ve-Ahvah (Justice and Fraternity) (1961) led by Yishai, or Tami (Tradition of Israel Movement) with Abu-Hatzeira at the helm (1981). On the

---

* This essay uses the term "Oriental" rather than Sephardi. See Arian and Shamir, *The Ethnic Vote in Israel's 1981 Elections*, in this volume, for clarification concerning these two terms.

other hand, Yisrael ha-Tzeira (Young Israel) was organized in 1962 and appeared in the elections of 1965, and the Black Panthers arose as a protest movement in 1971 and took part in elections in 1973. Beit Yisrael (House of Israel), an organization of people of Yemenite origin, was organized in 1972 but presented a list of candidates only in the 1977 elections. It therefore appears that the impermanence of the ethnic lists is a result less of the length of time they organized prior to the elections than of their patterns of organization and activity. All the lists, even those calling themselves parties, are not really parties in the accepted definition of the term in the social sciences.

Most scholars agree that a party is a voluntary organization for the enlistment and manipulation of political power with the aim of holding or sharing in political authority. For the purpose of achieving this aim the party maintains a permanent organization throughout the entire society, usually controlled from the center outwards, and seeks to send its representatives to central positions in various political frameworks. A party has a broad base of support, and it appeals to every citizen as such (Duverger 1972, pp. 1-2; Chambers and Burnham 1975, p. 5). According to this definition the ethnic lists are parties only in the sense that their purpose was to capture positions of power by attempting to gain a mandate in the elections. Their organization was weak, temporary, and appealed to special interests.

An examination of their modes of organization and the nature of their activity reveals that the ethnic lists were temporary alliances of political entrepreneurs, each of whom was connected with individuals and groups whose origin was the common denominator of their political activity. Most of the lists had no source of income, and no permanent organizational staff or other permanent organizational machinery. When the list failed in the elections, the alliance disintegrated.

This was the case, for example, with Ha-Ihud ha-Leumi me-Yisudam shel Sepharadim ve-edot ha-Mizrah (National Union of Sephardic and Oriental Jews) headed by Shlomo Cohen-Tzidon (1959). The Ihud Leumi did not organize itself like a party with elected bodies and a staff, although activists bore title like "chairman", "secretary", "spokesman", etc. (see various issues of *El Hamizrah*, the list's newspaper). The organization had at its disposal very limited means and its operations relied on a number of activists, each of whom collected a group around him. Some of the activists were connected with groups in organizations of immigrants from Egypt, Algeria and Iraq (*Maariv*, 7 August 1959). Others had connections in small local organizations in immigrant neighborhoods or development towns (*El Hamizrah*, 23 September 1958, pp. 7-8; Deshen 1970, pp. 56-61). Mr. Cohen-Tzidon, who had left Mapai (the Labor Party) to head the list, indicated in an interview with the writer (27

August 1978) that he had no control over his people in the various regions. Lacking a staff and an agreed method of forming the list, the movement's offices were flooded with requests to add this one or that "in a safe place" on the list of candidates, or to exclude representatives of various bodies in the list. Most of the struggles were over the place of representatives on the list (*El Hamizrah*, 11 August 1959). Attempts at combining with other ethnic lists which appeared in the same election campaign also failed because of the struggle over precedence in the list of candidates (*Maariv*, 7, 21 August 1959; 16 June 1961).

The struggle for the first place on the list was usually very sharp because the possibility of winning more than one or two mandates was very small. Without an organization or financial resources, the list could not allocate to its members any positions of authority or prestige, income, or other prerequisites, except the list itself, and therefore the struggle was concentrated on the leadership position.

A weak organizational pattern characterized most of the ethnic lists, with the ties of the activists based on personal acquaintance and loyalty. In the Black Panthers as well, a movement considered comparatively well-organized, similar organizational characteristics can be discerned. The Black Panthers, who succeeded as a spontaneous protest movement, failed when they reached the stage of political organization and institutionalization (E. Cohen 1972; Bernstein 1976; Peres 1976, pp. 160-75).

In the opinion of students of the movement the Black Panthers failed to transform themselves into a mass movement and to extend their membership beyond Jerusalem because their leaders were inexperienced and lacked organizational ability and financial resources. One of the main difficulties was the inability of the list to disconnect itself from its origin as a street gang, which created among its members an intensive particularistic solidarity not easily broadened to include other groups, who, in turn, although identifying with the aims of the Black Panthers, were unable to accept its leadership. The group was built upon the bonds among its founders, but at the same time its fate was determined by differences and rivalry among these leaders.

In an attempt to break out of the mold of "street gang", they allied themselves with Shalom Cohen, who had left the Ha-Olam Ha-Zeh Koah Hadash (This World — New Power) faction and his partner Uri Avneri in 1971, and established the Ha-demokratim ha-Yisraelim (Israeli Democrats) party. Each group was in need of the other; Cohen had a seat in the Knesset but no movement (*Haaretz*, 25 February 1973), while the Black Panthers were a movement, but had no organization or resources. In Bernstein's opinion (1976, p. 356) Shalom Cohen contributed experience, money, offices and organization to the alliance, while the Black Panthers supplied the public. Cohen's oppositionist opinions permitted the Black Panthers entrance into the political structure without their having to appear to join the political establishment (ibid., p. 365). But despite the renewed organizational deployment, the struggle over leadership continued, leading eventually to a split in the movement. Bernstein (1976, pp. 369-70) believes that the organizational changes were, in fact, more limited than they appeared on the surface. Despite the establishment of an organizational structure, the enlistment of new activists and the transfer of focus from Jerusalem to Tel Aviv and Beersheba, she claims, the basic informal absorption structure continued to operate. Thus the branches established prior to the election were not real branches but depended on a few central people who became "local" Black Panthers. Some of them were individuals who had some differences with the local authorities, and the support of the Black Panthers transformed them into local leaders. They were usually, however, not people who had roots or supporters in the place, and they did not try to cultivate any. In some cases, after achieving their aim, these "local leaders" retired from political activity. The cooperation among the branches was minimal and relied entirely on Shalom Cohen's individual efforts.

The similarity of the organizational pattern of other ethnic lists to these findings of Bernstein regarding the Black Panthers are startling. The Tami list to the tenth Knesset, which had at its disposal much greater financial and organizational resources than its predecessors, did not reveal organizational patterns basically any different. Tami as a list for the Knesset was the result of an alliance among politicians, the most important of whom were Aharon Abu-Hatzeira, Aharon Uzan, and Eli Dayan.[3] Each had a different political background and ties with a different public. For example, in not a few cases the local branches of Tami were nothing but former local branches of the National Religious Party whose members switched en masse to Tami because of personal loyalty to Abu-Hatzeira (*Maariv*, 1 September 1981).

These organizational patterns are, as have been said, inherently different from organizational patterns and activities defined as "party," but very similar to what are called political factions in social science language. Political factions are political conflict groups which do not have a formal structure. They are characterized by a complicated and unstable pattern of group interaction. The bases of this interaction are personal and individual ties between leader and followers, and among leaders. In contrast to the party system in which the organizational ties are the basis for its maintenance as a political group, the faction, lacking organizational structure, depends for its continued existence upon the leader and the nature of his ties with his supporters (Chambers 1963; Nicholas 1965, 1966; Nicholson 1972; Zuckerman 1979).

As was stated, an analysis of the organizational pattern of the various Israeli ethnic lists reveals that the organizational dimension which connects participants was indeed missing — they had no commitment to "the organization," and they were indeed conflict groups based on ties and loyalties among politicians and representatives of various kinds of groups. These ties served to connect one leader with another but were not strong or encompassing enough to create a united organization. The whole system of activity was mediated through a number of central figures, activists between whom the ties were only partial and all of whom had perhaps more salient ties with other groups. The bonds among the group's leaders were conditional, dependent on the partners' satisfaction with the place accorded him on the list of candidates, and later, on how successful the list was in the electoral struggle.

## IMPERMANENCE AS A PRODUCT OF THE POLITICAL STRUGGLE

One of the questions arising from the analysis above is why the ethnic lists did not crystallize into political parties. This question is made more salient in view of the current public notion about the existence of ethnic voting and the development of ethnic consciousness in Israel.

In other words, to put the matter into general sociological terms, what conditions foster the growth of political factions as an alternative to parties?

Chambers (1963) argues that factions are pre-party entities, a transition stage in the process of crystallization of the modern political party. Huntington (1969, pp. 412-15) refers to political factions in similar terms. He sees them as a primary stage of political organizational development in societies in the process of change and modernization, a stage characterized by a low degree of institutionalization and public participation. He considers the reports of 42 parties in Korea, 29 in North Vietnam or 18 in Pakistan as indicating factions rather than bona fide parties, similar to those cliques, factions, clubs and family groups which controlled European and American politics in the 18th and 19th centuries. A similar organizational pattern is characteristic of parliamentary cliques in countries like Nigeria today, or revolutionary cliques like the Narodniks in Russia in the 19th century. All of these are examples of small groups attempting to promote specific interests. Their power is limited, they are much divided, and those active in them change partners from time to time without increasing the total number of participants to any great extent.

To sum up, political factions are said to grow with the end of the traditional order and the beginning of modernization, accompanied by processes of industrialization, bureaucratic rationalization, and a change in traditional political patterns (Graziano 1973).[4]

In line with this view, it might be concluded that the Israeli ethnic lists are a transition stage in the political maturation of representatives of Oriental groups. The Israeli press has often expressed this view (*Maariv*, 28 September 1969; 15 May 1977). A similar approach can be discerned in Lissak (1972, p. 269), who says that ethnic or local lists sprang up just at a time when Oriental groups were politically passive. He argues that the national parties encouraged satellite ethnic lists on the local level thus gaining votes of people of particular origins who were unwilling to cooperate with others of different backgrounds, for reasons of personal conflicts or struggles for prestige. He claims that the lists gave immigrants from the east the opportunity to learn the rules of the political game in modern society.

The failure of the ethnic lists has been explained by various scholars in the spirit of these assumptions. The argument was either that the population of Asian and African origin in Israel is a population in transition and that therefore it has not yet arrived at the stage of building and institutionalizing strong organizations, or that the group is making a gradual transition from the political passivity which was characteristic of the early stage of absorption to activism arising from economic participation and political socialization. The failure of the ethnic lists is explained, in the transitory phase in which they are to be found, by insufficient knowledge of the rules of the game, lack of leadership and absence of economic resources (Bernstein 1976, pp. 104-17; Lissak 1972; Smooha 1978, pp. 207-10).

As opposed to the claim that factionalism is characteristic of transition stages, Zuckerman (1979, pp. 28-38) gives examples of growing political clientism in places which are not in the process of change or are not undeveloped industrially, such as the USSR and the USA. In his opinion, it is in the political structure that factors which encourage factionism, patron-client relationships, or norms of clientism should be sought. He discerns two factors which in his opinion support the factional pattern, uniting people around interests and exchange relations of benefits and personal loyalties: (a) the existence of a comparatively large number of positions, the achievement of which is connected with political competition; and (b) a minimum of formal limitations to the frequency of competition for these positions. It follows then, in his opinion, that it is democratization and economic development dependent on the government which strengthens the pattern of political factionalism.

Israeli society, in which there are comparatively many positions available through the political system, government intervention in many spheres, and at the same time an emphasis on democratic competition with minimum formal limitations, is a fertile ground, therefore, for the development of machinery for the encouragement of factional organization. I believe that the mechanisms in the political system of Israel which encourage short-term and amorphous organizations depending on ethnicity as a political resource can be located. In the political competition over positions of power, a special pattern of mutual ties between ethnic entrepreneurs and other party bodies became institutionalized. This pattern fostered ethnic organization, but at the same time ensured its organization in factional temporary patterns.

As was noted previously, up to now scholars tended to assume that the non-crystallization of an ethnic party pattern arose from a paucity of resources and leadership, that is that the ethnic ventures were in the stage of "political maturation." My argument is that the factional structure is not a result of political *naiveté*, but on the contrary, the result on the part of the ethnic leaders of learning to know the political system in the course of attempting to maneuver within it. The regular parties, in their attitude to the ethnic ventures, in fact strengthened the orientation to continue organizing along ethnic lines, although in a weak pattern, in the form of an alliance between leaders in order to achieve political representation. This organizational pattern reduced the electoral chances of the lists but at the same time convinced the parties that it was worthwhile to invest in the ethnic entrepreneurs.

A number of mechanisms were used in the course of the years by the various parties in their relationship to ethnic organization. These mechanisms, instead of bringing about political competition, evolved into a pattern of political exchange relations. The main mechanisms are discussed below.

*Open Support for Ethnically-Based Organizations*

The mechanism of open encouragement and support for the establishment of ethnically-based organizations was employed in order to create a tie between people of various origins and the parties, usually with the aim of dealing with problems of absorption of new immigrants and as a means of political recruitment. Such was the Tzeirei Ha-Mizrah (Young Orientals) list of people of Yemenite origin who participated in the elections to the first Asefat Ha-Nivharim (1920). The list had its origin in an organization of young people of Yemenite background founded by Hapoel Hatzair (The Young Worker, the first labor party in the pre-state period) in 1911 (Gluska 1974, pp. 96-99). Hitahdut ha-Teimanim (Yemenites' Association) founded in 1923, which participated in the elections of 1925, was the result of incentives of the settlement authorities in the country (*Hodaot Ha-Vaad Ha-Merkazi Le-Hitahdut Ha-Teimanim*, pp. 3-5).

In the early years of the state, this mechanism resulted in the founding of associated parties, that is lists which appeared independently in the election but which openly announced their ties with a "mother" party. One example was the

Sepharadim ve-edot Ha-Mizrah Vatikim ve-Olim (Sephardic and Oriental Veterans and New Immigrants) list, which appeared in the second and third Knesset elections, and was connected with the General Zionists. This pattern disappeared in the course of time in respect to Jewish ethnic lists, but still exists in the Arab sector in Israel (Landau 1981, p. 205).

The heartiest encouragement of ethnic-based organization, however, was given to groups formed actually within the general political parties and organizations, a pattern which also goes back to the days of the Yishuv as, for example, in 1923, when a Yemenite Workers' Club was formed within the framework of the Histadrut (The General Federation of Labor). Special ethnic departments were usual in most of the parties (E. Cohen et al. 1962; Zamir 1966). And it must be strongly emphasized that very often the initiative for the organization of such groups came not from the participants themselves but from the general party. Cooperation suited both the general parties and the ethnic leaders, that is both the list activists and the functionaries who directed ethnic departments within the party machinery.

*Covert Support for Ethnic Lists*

It is difficult to learn the extent of covert support for ethnic lists since neither the leaders of the lists themselves nor the bodies which supported them were interested in having this matter become known. At the same time, after elections, some facts leaked out which not infrequently corroborated the existence of such a mechanism.

For example, Ben-Shoshan, one of the leaders of the Tsfon Afrikaim Bilti Teluyim (Independent North Africans) list, which was established in 1959 in the wake of the Wadi Salib riots in Haifa, testified that the list was supported by Mapam (United Labor Party, a Marxist oriented party) (*Maariv*, 16 June 1961). Ben-Shoshan described the list as a "dummy" movement designed to snatch votes which would otherwise go to Herut (Freedom, the opposition party at that time headed by Menachem Begin) or to the dominant Mapai. This list, added to the three other ethnic lists participating in that same election, increased disunity among those competing for votes among Oriental voters. A similar splintering occurred in 1973 as a result of the covert support given to Eddie Malcha as head of a rival list to the Black Panthers (Bernstein 1976, p. 321).

Yemin Suissa was the head of the Ohalim (Tents) movement, striving for a resolution to the housing problem, which arose as a political list during the campaign of 1981. He related that before the elections he flew to Geneva to enlist the support of Nissim Gaon, the patron of all the Sephardi organizational attempts. When Gaon refused, Ohalim turned to the Labor Party which provided one million Israeli pounds (*Yediot Aharonot*, 5 October 1981). This was not enough to allow Ohalim to become large and well-organized, but served to keep it in existence temporarily and weakly.

*Co-optation of Leaders*

The use of ethnicity as a resource for political organization served political initiators as a springboard to advancement within the parties, as a result of the co-optative tactics used by the various parties in respect to activists of the ethnic lists. Readiness to absorb ethnic activists in the parties or to find positions for them has been noted in the political scene in Israel for many years (Bernstein 1976, pp. 108-109; Eisenstadt 1967, pp. 308-309). The findings of the present study show that these tactics were used mainly in respect to the heads of the lists. This readiness by the parties to absorb heads of independent ethnic lists encouraged political entrepreneurs of ethnic origin to found new lists. Despite their electoral defeat, many found their way into other parties. For example, Cohen-Tzidon, who left Mapai to stand at the head of a new list in 1959, was offered all sorts of positions if he would agree to bow out (*Maariv*, 7 August 1959). Even though the list had no electoral success, paradoxically, Cohen-Tzidon, as a representative of an "ethnic political body," found himself in a good bargaining position with the establishment of the Liberal Party before the 1961 elections, and became one of its leaders. As the party gained stability, he lost his preferential place.

Rabbi Toledano was appointed Minister of Religion in the Mapai government of 1958 because he had a history of political involvement in various ethnic frameworks both before and after the establishment of the State of Israel (*Haaretz*, 18 March 1945; 23 January 1949; 2 August 1951; 5 September 1952). The proposal to give him the appointment was made public after his name had been mentioned in connection with the organizational attempt of Ha-Ihud Ha-Leumi (*Haaretz*, 16 November 1958). Avner Sciaky, who headed an ethnic list in the fourth Knesset election campaign and later founded the Tehila Movement for educational advancement of Orientals, was appointed vice-Minister of Education by the National Religious Party (Brichta 1972, p. 96, n. 69); and the Black Panthers leaders found their way in 1977 into the Israeli leftist parties, Shelli and Rakah.

Political co-optation was often accompanied by financial aid and support, and the solution of housing and employment problems (Bernstein 1976, p. 108; *Yediot Aharonot*, 5 October 1981). For example, after the Wadi Salib riots, a representative of Mapai suggested to Ben-Harosh, who headed the protest demonstration, that he work for Mapai in Wadi Salib. According to Ben-

Harosh, the representative said: "Why not exploit the elections to the Knesset to improve your economic situation? If you don't want money, we'll give you a clubhouse and arrange employment for you" (*Haaretz*, 6 September 1959).

Various scholars have noted the way the establishment dealt with ethnic protest. Etzioni-Halevy (1975) indicates that the legitimacy of the demands was recognized and a number of committees to improve conditions were established. Brichta (1973, pp. 312, 321) says that the ethnic-based organization brought about increased ethnic representation in the general parties, while Bernstein (1976, p. 109) notes that the protest of the Black Panthers resulted in some changes bringing some improvements for the underprivileged in a few areas.

These partial achievements, added to the co-optation process and the solution of personal problems achieved by the activists, were factors which encouraged the continuation of ethnic-based organization without requiring many resources or much organizational effort. Ethnicity became a manipulatable resource in political bargaining.

*The Ethnic "Key" in Parties*

The fact that country of origin served as a guide in the allocation of positions within general parties often encouraged ethnic political activists to demand higher positions within their party. Sometimes, if the demand was not met, they left and set up independent lists. This was the case with Moshe Yishai's list Le-maan Ha-Tzedek ve-ha-Ahvah (For Justice and Fraternity) in the elections to the fifth Knesset. Yishai was the head of the Tzedek ve-Ahvah faction within the National Religious Party (NRP), and the faction demanded a "safe" place for him in the candidates' list for the elections in 1959 (*Haaretz*, 27 August 1959), but this "uprising" was put down and he was given thirteenth place. On the eve of the fifth Knesset elections Yishai revived his faction, first within the party (*Haaretz*, 7 June 1961), but he was again put in thirteenth place (*Haaretz*, 7 July 1961); and later stood as an independent (*Haaretz*, 30 July 1961).

Yitzhak Yitzhaki, who reached the ninth Knesset as second on the list of Shlomzion (Peace of Zion), which merged with the Likud (Unity — the combined party made up of Herut and the Liberal Party), was dissatisfied with the attention his proposals in the Knesset received and left to found the Yisrael Ahat (One Israel) list (*Yediot Aharonot*, 9 January 1981). He participated in the tenth Knesset campaign in this independent list. According to him, the list spent a comparatively small amount of money in the advertising campaign before the elections, depending mainly on volunteers (*Yediot Aharonot*, 3 July 1981). He thought that "thousands will follow me because I am a true friend of the shekhunot" (distressed neighborhoods) (*Yediot Aharonot*, 9 July 1981). The list did not even win enough votes to seat one member in the Knesset, and after the defeat Yitzhaki decided to return to the Likud party (*Yediot Aharonot*, 14 August 1981).

Shortly before the deadline for submitting lists for the tenth Knesset, Abu-Hatzeira, who had just been tried and found innocent of the embezzlement of public funds, demanded the thirteenth place on the NRP list for his collaborator Ben-Zion Reubin. When the demand was rejected, he left the party and established an independent list, Tami.

Tami, which jumped on the bandwagon just 24 hours before the deadline for submitting lists for the elections, was also a product of withdrawal from other parties. All of its leaders joined for different reasons, connected with dissatisfaction with the support they were receiving from their parties for themselves or for their viewpoints (*Yediot Aharonot*, 25 May 1982).

In all the examples given, a subjective feeling of being discriminated against, which can develop in any politician, was expressed in ethnic terms, with ethnic identity used as a resource for political bargaining. It was made possible because of the various supportive mechanisms outlined above.

## CONDITIONAL ETHNICITY AS AN IDEOLOGICAL PATTERN

In the absence of financial resources and efficient organizational tools, the enlistment of support for the ethnic lists manipulated one central resource — the symbols of ethnic identity.

It is customary to distinguish between political tactics used on the organizational level and those used symbolically. The organizational level tactics consist of bargaining over favors and services, and threat of sanctions. On the symbolic (ideological) level, symbols and feelings are manipulated. Policy, then, is more than bargaining of cold reason. Success does not depend solely on the ability to propose a better deal for enough people. Politicians also influence beliefs and feelings. Bargaining is not only over clear and defined interests of people, but also on what people perceive as their interests. Therefore, bargaining is also about the definition of the situation (Collins 1973, pp. 331-33). The ability to influence beliefs signifies power. If power is defined, in the Weberian sense, as the ability to influence someone else to act according to one's wishes (Weber 1968, p. 70), then the acceptance by others of one's definition of the situation as a basis for action means the accumulation of power. The principle behind the desire to control the definition of the situation received its classic expression in Thomas: "If people define a situation as real, it is real in its consequences" (Thomas and Thomas 1928, p. 572).

Scholars emphasizing organizational manipulation in their studies have not ignored the importance of control of the definition of the situation on the symbolic level, though they did not study this aspect. Duverger (1954) and in his wake Shapiro (1977), identify the dominant party not only as a majority party governing for a long period, but also as a party identified with the spirit of the times. It is also recognized as such by its rivals (Duverger 1954, pp. 307-8; Shapiro 1977, pp. 119-21); namely it has succeeded in defining the situation both organizationally and symbolically.

All parties operate on both levels. The differences between the parties lie only in the extent to which they use each of these tactics.

Recent students of organizations emphasize that the manipulation of symbols and feelings designed to achieve recognition is not exclusive to political organizations which it is customary to see as dealing in ideology. Scholars point out that one of the latent purposes of organizations is to legitimize their products and activities (Perrow 1970, p. 98). In Perrow's view the legitimacy of organizations is not automatic, and companies, like non-profit-making organizations, exist not only because of their efficiency and/or profitability, but because their products and methods of operation are accepted by an important part of their environment. In his opinion, even in the analysis of companies, one should not limit oneself to the understanding of simple market mechanisms. In reality giant companies operate by various means to guard their level of legitimacy (ibid., p. 101). This concept of legitimacy includes the environment as an important factor in understanding the organization. Legitimation is bestowed by others in mutual contact.

From this standpoint, the success of any organization, and a political organization as a specific case, does not depend only on the quality of the organization but on the extent it succeeds in gaining legitimation. In a situation of organizational weakness and lack of resources, the recognition of legitimacy can become a source of strength, or at least a starting point for political bargaining. The lack of good organization and financial resources enhance the importance of the tactics of symbolic manipulation.

The initiators of the ethnic lists transferred their struggle to the symbolic level by using ethnic identity and thereby forced the other parties, despite their organizational advantage, into this field of battle. The granting or withdrawal of legitimation became a subject for bargaining in the political arena.

One of the main subjects used by the initiators of the ethnic lists in symbolic manipulation was what was defined as the ethnic-social gap. The leaders of the ethnic lists presented themselves as representing a large, discriminated-against public, and the problem of this group as a problem of society as a whole. In this way they brought up for discussion a subject in which the ruling parties were not interested, and became a threat to all the parties by entering into competition for the votes of the Oriental voters.

In reaction, the parties tried to reduce the bargaining power of the ethnicity factor. They tried to do this, as I have shown, by means of various neutralizing mechanisms. But placation, partial solutions, the establishment of ethnic organizational frameworks within the parties, co-optation, and the allocation of resources to individuals and groups who had the potential for ethnic crystallization, all of which on the contrary, encouraged the continuation of ethnic organization.

Despite the support on the organizational level there was, however, a denigration of this kind of organization on the ideological level. The parties tried to define the ethnic lists as representing societally marginal conflict groups. The legitimacy of ethnic organization was continually questioned (Bernstein, 1976, p. 103; Herzog 1983; Lissak 1972, p. 275). The representatives of the large parties tried by every means to continue their control of the definition of the symbolic-values situation which supported unity and the melting-pot, which meant the merging of those of eastern origin into the dominant groups (Deshen 1976, p. 271). The ethnic basis for political organization was interpreted as opposing the idea of the unity of the nation and even of endangering it. The absolute denial on the ideological level of any independent ethnic-based organization began with the opposition to the Sephardic and Yemenite organizations in the Yishuv period, and continued in a refusal to recognize the legitimacy of any ethnic list in the period of the state.

As a result, most of the ethnic lists presented their ethnicity as temporary, or emphasized the fact that the meaning of the ethnic base was class or general social discrimination. This was the case, for example, with the justification for the establishment of an ethnic newspaper which served the Histadrut ha-Sepharadim (The Sepharadic Federation): "We do not aim at separation but at unity ... the full unity and ingathering of all the tribes of Israel ... but unity is not possible and will not occur before all sections of the Yishuv achieve full equality" (*Hamizrah*, 10 June 1942, pp. 1, 7). Many ethnic leaders emphasized their national identity, stressing that they were spokesmen for the masses, the workers, the discriminated-against, and not just for the Orientals. It was not accidental that the offshoots of the Black Panthers chose names like Blue-White Panthers or Zionist Panthers. These names were a reaction to the attempts of the parties to push ethnic organizations beyond the normative limits of Israeli society. Reuven Abergil, one of the leaders of the Black Panthers, said in a newspaper interview: "We wanted a name to get people angry and maybe even frightened ... not, God forbid, the same ideology..." (*Maariv*, 25 June 1971). Bernstein (1976, pp. 303-13), in analyzing the Black Panther phenomenon, emphasizes that the explanation given for the social conflict was not ethnic per se. Their question "Where is the pride of the Sephardis?" was not intended to nourish ethnic identity or ethnic separatism.

Most of the lists in the campaigns for the ninth and tenth Knessets which were defined as ethnic did not emphasize the ethnic element in their propaganda. For example, Mifleget Ha-Ihud (The Unity Party), led by Saadia Marciano and Mordechai Algrabli, in the tenth Knesset election campaign, called their list "the only social party" and their election poster did not mention ethnicity at all. Victor Tayar, who led the Amha (Your People) list, declared that although representing the distressed neighborhoods, his list was not an ethnic one (Yediot Aharonot, 31 March 1981).

An analysis of the way Tami presented itself to the voters in the 1981 election campaign reveals very nicely the ambivalent and conditional attitude of the initiators of eastern origin towards ethnicity as an ideological principle. In the first television interview (29 May 1981) of a representative of the list, the interviewer asked Eli Dayan: "Why an ethnic list?" and Dayan replied: "It is not an ethnic list, it is a list of authentic leaders, a list against the system, for national social ideas, appealing to the whole nation." Dayan, in the interview, emphasized a number of times that "we are not ethnic, we are for the brotherhood of Israel." At the same time, the propaganda used by Tami made use of the motto "Standing up straight," which indicated ethnic pride. But again, it was conditional pride, as worded in one of Tami's election posters: "No more ethnic discrimination, no more 'quotas' according to ethnic origin, no more two nations in one country. And I, Aharon Abu-Hatzeira, hereby promise, together with my comrades, that when the day comes and these divisions will not exist any more, I, Aharon Abu-Hatzeira, will be the first to take down the standard I have raised today..." (Yediot Aharonot, 2 June 1981). And after the elections, Abu-Hatzeira, in a television interview (1 July 1981) said: "Look, we are the only list that did not emphasize the ethnic aspect, in comparison with other lists." This sensitivity of the political initiators towards labelling them according to their origin stands out in view of the fact that throughout the years the general parties never refrained from using ethnicity as a basis both for organization and for symbolic manipulation, a process that perhaps reached its peak in the election campaign of 1981 in the struggle between the two large parties.

## SUMMARY — ETHNICITY 1981

As we have indicated, the "ethnic lists" in the 1981 elections were in the main no different from their predecessors. The character of the "ethnic lists" was influenced to a large extent by the nature of the relations between political entrepreneurs of eastern origin and the parties with which they negotiated.

The system of mutual relations which became institutionalized between various parties and ethnic political leaders served as a factor encouraging ethnic organization in temporary and factional patterns, leading to bargaining mainly in election periods. The ethnic lists did not crystallize as parties but as "factions" in the sociological meaning of the concept. They were conflict groups based on personal ties and loyalties between politicians and representatives of groups or pseudo-groups. From an organizational viewpoint, they were temporary and conditional alliances of political entrepreneurs.

This factionalism, I claim, is not a transition stage in political organizational development, but a product of the political structure in Israel. This political structure created mechanisms supporting temporary organizations which engaged in manipulation of ethnic identity as a political resource. Ethnic political identity was never an end but a means. Even when this identity was the focus of ethnic organization it was presented as temporary and conditional, because the dominant groups rejected ethnicity as a basis for independent organization.

The organizational history of the ethnic lists reveals that up to now no real political competition has developed between them and other parties, nor did they become a focus for ethnic political identity. The ethnic lists in their factional organizational pattern became tools for negotiations on political exchange. Their organizational character as well as their ideology are a result of the negotiations carried on in the political arena.

Tami, which seemed to the public to be a new organizational model, was in fact no different from the previous model of ethnic lists described. It had the advantage of having succeeded in obtaining some financial resources, and it could offer something to its supporters because of Abu-Hatzeira's involvement in the NRP's administrative apparatus. Most of the support for Tami came from Abu-Hatzeira's NRP supporters. Tami did not become a focus of identification for others of Oriental origin and it gathered almost no "Orientals" from other parties. Like other "ethnic lists," Tami was accepted with reservations because of the dominance of the "merging of the diasporas" ideology.

Nevertheless, it should be pointed out again that although in the course of the long negotiations in the political area for legitimacy, the ethnic political organizations and their various initiatives were pushed aside, this was not true for "ethnicity" as a political resource. It became accepted, common currency within the parties, for internal and external use.

The 1981 elections were characterized by political negotiations which made use of ethnic ideas. In the NRP the struggle was called the "Sephardic Rebellion," after representatives of the Oriental communities demonstratively left a meeting of the executive committee, while demanding that three out of the first ten on the list be of Oriental origin, as well as second place (*Yediot Aharonot*, 20 May 1981; *Maariv*, 21 May 1981). The large parties neutralized the eruption of ethnic demands by putting a candidate of Oriental origin as number two on the list: for the Labor Party — Shoshana Arbeli-Almoslino, and for the Likud — David Levy.

The "slip of the tongue" of the entertainer Dudu Topaz in a Labor Party election rally in which he used the popular name "צ'חצ'חים" for those of Oriental origin focused the Likud's election propaganda around the question of ethnic identification.

Analysis of voting patterns in the 1981 elections reveal an ethnic pattern (Arian 1981) in light of the fact that a larger percentage of Orientals voted for the Likud, and more non-Orientals for the Labor Party. Apparently, this may be claimed to be a growth of ethnic consciousness. In my opinion, the comparative lack of success of Tami and the vote for the Likud (which is identified as a national party) indicate the same trend pointed out regarding the lists identified as ethnic in the past: flight from the stigma of ethnicity and identification of those of Eastern origin as a separate category from Israel society as a whole.

This is attested to by the reservations toward ethnic lists shown by activists of Oriental origin in both the Labor party and the Likud (*Yediot Aharonot*, 29 June 1981). Those very active members who are identified in their parties as representing the Oriental communities refuse to be identified as *only* representatives of the ethnics, their identification as such reduced their ability to claim leadership of "society" as a whole, as do the other party leaders.

The mayors of development towns who have made their way to the Knesset (such as David Magen of Kiryat Gat and Meir Shitrit of Yavneh) see themselves as representatives of the south (*Maariv*, 21 May 1981), but refuse to be identified as "professional ethnics" (*Yediot Aharonot*, 7 June 1981; *Maariv*, 2 October 1981). Those of Eastern origin, like the initiators of "ethnic lists," formulate their claims in class terms and/or general social terms, speaking for the wage-earner, the housewife, young people, or the disadvantaged in general. They refuse to be labelled "ethnics."

At the same time attention must be paid to changes occuring in current politics. The tendency to construct social reality in Israel in ethnic terms results in more and more mobile and successful people of Oriental origin, in spite of their success, to see the ethnic party as a solution to problems of class and social distress. A striking recent example is that of Tat-Aluf (Colonel) Ben-Eliezer joining the Tami party. In a television interview (4 January 1982) Ben-Eliezer denied having met any ethnic discrimination in the army, in fact he praised the opportunities available there to anyone qualified. Nevertheless, he saw the social problems of Israeli society in ethnic terms, leading him to take an active role in an ethnic party.

Another development which calls for investigation is the fact that recently groups of intellectuals of Oriental origin have joined or expressed identification with ethnic-political groups and organizations. There is, for example, the group of intellectuals of Yemenite origin whose means of expression is the periodical *Afikim* (Horizons). This group cooperated with the politicians who formed the Beit Yisrael (House of Israel) list for the ninth Knesset. Another group is Merhav — writers, poets and university people of Oriental origin who joined Tami when it was formed. There are also university students who take part in the Peilei Tzibur (Public Activists) program and who identify with Tami.

Up to the present, these groups have not yet put their stamp on ethnic organization. The fact of their existence, however, and of their attempt to cooperate with politicians raise a number of interesting questions. One, a general question, is about the connections between intellectuals and politicians. The other, more specific, hints at the possibility of a change in the patterns and character of political organization based on ethnicity.

## NOTES

1. The analysis is based on data collected about all the ethnic lists since the elections to the first Asefat Ha-Nivharim (1920) up to the elections for the tenth Knesset (1981). The data were taken from various sources: archives, biographical and autobiographical material on the active leaders of the lists, newspaper articles, newspaper interviews of leaders, and secondary analysis of previous studies.

2. An exception was the Aliya Hadasha (New Immigrant) list, of people of German origin, which appeared in the elections to the fourth Asefat Ha-Nivharim (1944). This list was also dubbed "ethnic" at the time. On the local level, the term "ethnic list" is widely used to describe lists of Romanian or Hungarian immigrant origin, usually groups of Ashkenazis perceived as "discriminated-against."

3. Abu-Hatzeira, an NRP member, was Minister of Religious Affairs in the ninth Knesset. Uzan, a Mapai activist, was a former Minister of Agriculture in the Alignment government and one of the leaders of the Moshavim (rural settlements) movement. Eli Dayan was one of the leaders of Young North Africans movement called Oded and the Mayor of Ashkelon.

4. The development of political machines is also said to be connected with conditions of change and transition, in areas in which the traditional political and social order has not yet been replaced by political differences arising from the new class and social situation (Key 1949; Wilson 1973, p. 98).

## REFERENCES

Arian, A. (1981). "Election 1981: Competitiveness and Polarization." *The Jerusalem Quarterly* 21 (Fall):3-27.

Barth, F., ed. (1969). *Ethnic Groups and Boundaries*. Boston: Little Brown and Co.

Bernstein, D. (1976). *The Black Panthers of Israel 1971-1972: Contradictions and Protest in the Process of Nation-Building*. Unpublished Ph.D. Dissertation, University of Sussex.

Brichta, A. (1972). *The Social, Political and Cultural Background of the Knesset Members in Israel*. Unpublished Ph.D. Dissertation, Jerusalem (Hebrew).

Chambers, W.N. (1963). *Political Parties in a New Nation: The American Experience, 1776-1809*. New York: Oxford University Press.

Chambers, W.N., and Burnham, W.O., eds. (1975). *The American Party System*. New York: Oxford University Press.

Cohen, A. (1974). *Two Dimensional Man: An Essay on the Anthropology of Power and Symbolism in Complex Society*. Berkeley: University of California Press.

Cohen E.; Shamgar, L.; and Levi, Y. (1962). *Summary Report: Immigrant Absorption in a Development Town*. Jerusalem: Hebrew University (Hebrew).

Cohen, E. (1972). "The Black Panthers and Israeli Society." *Jewish Journal of Sociology* 14:93-109.

Collins, R. (1973). "Politics in Society." In Douglas Jack, ed., *Introduction to Sociology Situation and Structures*. New York: The Free Press, pp. 328-35.

Deshen, S.A. (1970). *Immigrant Voters in Israel*. Manchester: Manchester University Press.

————— (1974). "Political Ethnicity and Cultural Ethnicity in Israel during the 1960s." *ASA Monographs: Urban Ethnicity* 12:281-309.

————— (1976). "Ethnic Boundaries and Cultural Paradigm: The Case of Southern Tunisian Immigrants in Israel." *Ethos* 4:271-94.

Duverger, M. (1954). *Political Parties*. New York: Wiley.

————— (1972). *Party Politics and Pressure Groups*. New York: Thomas Y. Cromwell Co.

Eisenstadt, S.N. (1967). *Israeli Society*. London: Weidenfeld and Nicholson.

Etzioni-Halevy, E. (1975). "Patterns of Conflict Generation and Conflict 'Absorption': The Cases of Israeli Labor and Ethnic Conflict." *Journal of Conflict Resolution* 19:286-309.

Gluska, Z. (1974). *On Behalf of Yemenite Jews*. Edited by S. Greidi. Jerusalem: Ya'akov Ben David Gluska (Hebrew).

Graziano, L. (1973). "Patron-Client Relationships in Southern Italy." *European Journal of Political Research*, April: 3-34.

Herzog, H. (1981). *The Ethnic Lists to the Delegates' Assembly and the Knesset (1920-1977) — Ethnic Political Identity?* Unpublished Ph.D. Dissertation, Tel Aviv University (Hebrew).

————— (1983). "Ethnicity as a Negotiated Issue in the Israeli Political Order." In A. Weingrod, ed., book in preparation.

Hodaot Ha-Vaad Ha-Merkazi Le-Hitahadut Ha-Teimanim (Announcement of the Central Committee of the Yemenite Federation), 1923-1926, Tel Aviv.

Huntington, S.H. (1969). *Political Order in Changing Societies*. London: Yale University.

Key, V.O. (1949). *Southern Politics*. New York: Vintage Books.

Landau, J.M. (1981). "Alienation and Strains in Political Behaviour." In A. Layish, ed., *The Arabs in Israel*. Jerusalem: The Magnes Press, The Hebrew University, pp. 197-212 (Hebrew).

Lissak, M. (1972). "Continuity and Change in the Voting Patterns of Oriental Jews." In A. Arian, ed., *The Elections in Israel — 1969*. Jerusalem: Academic Press, pp. 264-77.

Nicholas, R.W. (1965). "Factions: A Comparative Analysis." *A.S.A. Monographs: Political Systems and the Distribution of Power*.

————— (1966). "Segmentary Factional Political Systems." In M.J. Schwartz, V.W. Turner, and A. Tuden, eds., *Political Anthropology*. Chicago: Aldine Publishing Co., pp. 49-59.

Nicholson, N.K. (1972). "The Factional Model and the Study of Politics." *Comparative Political Studies* 5:291-315.

Peres, Y. (1976). *Ethnic Relations in Israel*. Tel Aviv: Sifriat Hapoalim (Hebrew).

Peretz, D. (1960). "Reflections on Israel's Fourth Parliamentary Elections." *Middle East Journal* 14:15-27.

Perrow, C. (1970). *Organizational Analysis: A Sociological View.* London: Tavistock Publications.

Shapiro, Y. (1977). *Democracy in Israel.* Ramat Gan: Massada (Hebrew).

Smooha, S. (1978). *Israel: Pluralism and Conflict.* London and Henley: Routledge & Kegan Paul.

Thomas, W.I., and Thomas, D.S. (1928). *The Child in America.* New York: Knopf.

Weber, M. (1968). *Economy and Society,* vol. 2. Edited by Guenther Roth and Claus Wittich. New York: Bedminster Press, pp. 926-40.

Wilson, J.Q. (1973). *Political Organization.* New York: Basic Books.

Zamir, R. (1966). "Beersheba 1958-59: Social Processes in a Development Town." In S.N. Eisenstadt et al., eds., *The Social Structure of Israel.* Jerusalem Academon (Hebrew).

Zuckerman, A.S. (1979). *The Politics of Faction: Christian Democratic Rule in Italy.* New Haven and London: Yale University Press.

# 13

## The NRP in Transition—Behind the Party's Electoral Decline

### Menachem Friedman

#### Introduction

Since the establishment of the State of Israel (1948), the National Religious Party (founded by the Mizrachi and Hapoel Hamizrachi movements[1] has been characterized by relatively stable electoral support. In the Ninth Knesset elections (1977), voters "punished" not only the Alignment but also its traditional coalition partner — the Independent Liberals (Progressives.[2] However, despite the fact that the NRP had been part of virtually all Labor (Mapai) governments — and despite the party's "historic alliance" with Mapai in the Zionist Executive and "National Institutions," extending back to the 1930s — the NRP not only retained but actually increased its support in those elections.[3] In light of this impressive achievement, NRP circles expressed the view that party appeal had extended beyond its traditional stronghold — the national-religious public — reaching other sectors of the population who maintained positive attitudes towards the Jewish religion and traditions. Thus, the NRP might become a centrist party.

Following the elections, a new pattern of relations developed between the NRP and the Likud, unlike those which traditionally prevail between a small party and its dominant coalition partner. The NRP no longer considered its role to be protection of its own vital interests and those of its members from the major party (as it did in Mapai/Alignment governments), but rather as a partnership between two movements which have identical social goals and joint political objectives. This new relationship is reflected in the heretofore unparalleled proportion and significance of key ministries accorded to NRP members within the Likud-led cabinet.

This background underscores the significance of the NRP's electoral decline in Tenth Knesset elections (1981), after four years of coalition partnership with the Likud, a phenomenon which apparently resulted from severe internal crisis. A study of recent internal party affairs has revealed struggles for factional domination within the NRP and serious tension within the party leadership, as in the Young Guard's bid for control of the *Lamifne* faction and the all-out battles waged with *Likud Utemura*. There are even some signs of an ideological crisis, in light of growing religious extremism among certain population sectors and the "Greater Israel" issue (see below). We thus note that the NRP's decline indeed appears to be rooted in internal crisis. Yet there is still room for further speculation, as party history includes a series of similar crises which had never before affected NRP voting adversely. Until the Tenth Knesset elections, in fact, the party was characterized by virtually unconditional voter support. Hence we proceed to investigate the changes in voting patterns among traditional NRP supporters, analyzing the major processes they have undergone against the background of more extensive changes which took place within the party itself since the 1950s.

Analyses of the historic basis for social change may tend to adopt a positivistic approach; i.e. they may posit that the changes under consideration were the positive result of past processes. Hence we hasten to clarify our claim that the decline of the NRP is connected with processes of social change in religious society which have been taking place since the 1950s, as these processes are ultimately of dialectic character. In the final analysis, historical realities are ultimately determined by a combination of social circumstances which pertain to the development of Israeli society as a whole.

## The "Camp Party" as a Factor Promoting Stability

The issue of NRP electoral stability — up to the last elections — has been considered in a most productive and intensive analytical study (Don-Yehiya 1980). Don-Yehiya perceives of the NRP as a party with "essential stability" expressed on both the organizational and ideological planes. Don-Yehiya utilizes two concepts to explain the phenomenon: "camp party" and "institutionalized factionalism." The former term refers to "a party which represents a particular subculture within the population, distinguished by its values and life-styles and maintaining a comprehensive system of institutions and organizations reciprocally connected with the party" (*ibid.*, p. 26). The NRP, therefore, is a "camp party," as it represents a population with a specific religious lifestyle and culture, preserved and transmitted through a particularistic educational system whose protection, welfare and develop-ment are perceived as a primary obligation by the political leadership. In addition to these educational institutions, the party also maintains affinity for a wide variety of financial and mutual aid institutions which reciprocally link the party and its members. This definition of a "camp party" suits most political parties in Israel, primarily labor parties. Never-theless, Don-Yehiya justifiably contends that since the 1950s, the affinity between such parties and discernibly consolidated social groups within the population has been weakening steadily. All religious parties may essentially by considered as "camp parties"; according to Don-Yehiya, this fact at least partially explains the obligation of the "camp" to support its representative party at election time.

The concept of "institutionalized factionalism" explains the organizational stability of the party despite the variety of opinions and interests therein. This stability is fostered through "official recognition by party institutions and regulations of the status of factions as an integral part of the party system" (*ibid.*, p. 27). "Institutionalized factionalism" is thus institutionalization of the concept of "parties" within a single party. Don-Yehiya explains the phenomenon by way of a paradox: even though party factions generally threaten organizational stability, in the religious parties, which are "camp parties," institutionalized factionalism is function-al for this purpose. Such parties are characterized by social pluralism, which demands official expression within the various factions. Furthermore, institutionalized factionalism allows for expression of characteristic internal party tensions while maintaining an external appearance of solidarity.

These concepts undoubtedly enable evaluation of several internal processes within the NRP. It is doubtful, however, whether they suffice for explaining the key phenomenon of long-term organizational and electoral stability. Moreover, if these concepts are indeed capable of explaining electoral stability and the obligation of the NRP-voting public (the "camp") towards the party, the question of why this obligation was not preserved in the Tenth Knesset elections acquires increased relevance. Furthermore, a group maintaining a particular subculture — with discernible values and lifestyles and a comprehensive system of institutions and organizations — need not express itself on the political level within the framework of a camp party. Rather, it may defend itself and demand fulfillment of its unique needs within a party pressure group or through competition among various parties for its electoral potential. On the other hand, it would not be difficult to demonstrate that institutionalized factionalism may, under certain conditions, constitute the basis for splitting a party. We apparently do not yet possess a satisfactory explanation of why the religious parties — and particularly the NRP — were formed and consolidated as camp parties and under what conditions institutionalized factionalism is indeed functional for party solidarity.

Complete and detailed answers to these questions undoubtedly demand coverage of an area extending far beyond the scope of this article. We will perforce limit ourselves to key issues which account for past stability and attempt to explain the drop in NRP support in the last elections.[4]

## Erosion in Religious Life

Erosion in religious lifestyle is a phenomenon largely responsible for molding religious society in Israel and its relations with secular populations. The image of Jewish society has been constantly changing since the late eighteenth century. The disintegration of traditional Jewish society and processes of secularization have taken their toll and have created a new social reality: adherence to *Halacha* (Jewish religious law) according to its orthodox interpretation has become the lot of the minority, while the majority has somehow abandoned

the religious-traditional Jewish lifestyle.[5] This dynamic
process of alienation from tradition takes place against the
background of dramatic social changes in both overall and
Jewish society. Permeation of modernity expressed itself
in revolutionary technological changes which fundamentally
changed lifestyles and challenged the validity of tradition.
Among European Jews, the political and social changes
which came in the wake of technological advancement led to
steadily-worsening social, economic and political crises.

By the end of the nineteenth century, all of these factors
led to phenomena of uprooting and migration from rural to
urban areas, from villages to the large cities, from Eastern
Europe, which was still largely traditional, to Palestine,
Western Europe and the United States. The process of abandoning tradition has led to a severe *Kulturkampf* between the
guardians of tradition and the revolutionary social movements
which seek to change the character of Jewish society and the
role of the Jew in history. The result was that this *Kulturkampf* penetrated the family unit and set children against
their parents.[6] The rapid changes and their unambiguous
character with regard to affinity for tradition challenged the
security of the traditional world and created a feeling of
anxiety or even perhaps of extended trauma.

Anxiety — one might even say paranoia — over the actions
and intentions of the militant secular movements, over the
secular-modern culture and those who represent it, is apparently the dominant phenomenon which determined the relationship of orthodox religious society in all its variations towards
secular Jewish society. Vestiges of this approach persist to
this very day. As shown below, there was no uniform orthodox religious reaction to the challenge of modern culture.
However, irrespective of  attitudes towards modern culture
*per se,* anxiety over the secular social environment, over the
deeds and misdeeds of the secular socio-political movements,
was largely shared by all shades of orthodoxy. The historic
experience in Palestine only strengthened these feelings, as in
the battle over educational institutions in immigrant camps
during the first years of statehood.[7] For the orthodox, this
incident was a warning sign of what could happen to the entire
religious educational system if they do not maintain the
political power demanded *a priori* for protecting values, norms

and vital needs: It thus follows that public support of religious parties in Israel stems primarily from feelings of anxiety over the "secular environment" and the need to "protect" the traditional individual and public and provide them with their essential needs, especially in the area of education. We may indeed concur with Don-Yehiya's definition of religious parties as "camp parties"; however, party loyalty is not only a result of obligation to shared culture and lifestyles; rather, it results also from consciousness of a threat to the very existence of the "camp" by hostile factors which control society's chief financial and social resources.

Even when the "Yishuv" (Jewish community in Palestine) political institutions were first established (1917–1936), there was conflict between the religious and the secular Zionist political establishments (the Chief Rabbinate and the National Council and Zionist Executive, respectively), wherein the former felt anxious and threatened by the intentions of the latter. The Chief Rabbinate, which considered itself as representing religion and tradition, perceived a direct confrontation with a political system which it did not trust but upon which it was almost entirely dependent financially. From this point of view, intensification of the power and influence of Mizrachi/Hapoel Hamizrachi apparently helped restore balance and mutual trust between the religious and political establishments, a fact which ultimately enabled the autonomous *Yishuv* institutions to develop to their fullest extent (Friedman 1978, pp. 116, 385–388).

The link between the religious party and its "camp" thus also derives from the "threat" to the latter's vital interests, a dynamic variable which may define the intensity of affinity between "camp" and "camp party."

As the Zionist enterprise developed, the pioneering left was considered as representative of a militant anti-religious outlook, proposing alternative values for the newly-forming Jewish society in which there was no room for traditional Sabbath and Festival observance, dietary laws or even religious marriage and divorce.[8] The rise of Mapai to power within the *Yishuv* (1931) thus intensified the threat to the religious camp. The "historic alliance" between Mapai and Mizrachi/-Hapoel Hamizrachi, forged when the former was the dominant party in the *Yishuv* and Zionist movement (1931–1935), thus appears to be more of an act of defense — guaranteeing, through political partnership, that the basic needs and rights of the religious sector would be provided by the senior partner in government — than an ideological and methodological association (Bat-Yehuda 1979).[9] Despite this alliance, relations between Mapai and the two components of the Mizrachi movement were fraught with conflict over attacks upon religion and tradition — intentional and otherwise — on the part of various factors within the labor camp *ibid.*, pp. 429, 433, 444–448), which invariably reawakened feelings of hostility and mistrust. This led to a rather paradoxical situation: those very suspicions over the left's intentions towards religion and its institutions actually bolstered the historic alliance, as the religious camp realized that its dissolution was liable to cause them irreparable harm.

This is only one component of the complex relationship between the Mizrachi — and especially Hapoel Hamizrachi — movements and Mapai and the Labor Party. However, it is this particular aspect which acquired increasing significance as the parties became more estranged from their social and ideological roots and began turning into centrist movements — slightly to the left of center.

In summary: the consistent loyalty of the NRP voting public to its party was indeed based upon the existence of a subculture with discernible values and lifestyles. However, the need to express this culture on the political plane — as a party traditionally participating in government and struggling for allocation of power and financial resources in society — is connected with the feeling of anxiety over the continued existence of this very subculture in the face of dominant social forces. This anxiety was corroborated in the long historical experience of alienation from religion and tradition and of conflicts — chiefly with the socialist left — over preservation of religious and traditional values in the *Yishuv* and during the first years of Israel's independence. It thus stands to reason that when confidence in the existence and continuity of religion and its institutions is reinforced and when anxiety over the "threat from without" decreases, party affinity and electoral support is likely to diminish as well.

## The Generation Gap Within the NRP

The NRP has recently been characterized by generational conflict, expressed in the Young Guard's ambitions of attaining a dominant position within the party and accompanied by a religious-cultural change of delegitimization of the culture and political methods of the older generation. There are various manifestations of this change, including retreat from the principles of the *Torah Vaavoda* (Torah and Labor) movement and what has been termed "religious extremism." The topic merits extensive and intensive research far beyond the scope of this study, which will consider only those aspects which pertain directly to the issue at hand.

1. The dialectic character of relations between Mapai/Labor and the NRP (Mizrachi/Hapoel Hamizrachi) within the framework of the historic alliance necessarily bred tension within the latter. As the arrangement was a system of relations between unequal powers, it was only natural that compromise would be demanded, including turning a blind eye to various "sins of commission and omission" which the religious population perceived as injurious to Jewish tradition. Partnership in government demanded a practical policy and constant differentiation between the real and the ideal. This brought groups which felt more obligated by religious values, such as young people, into conflict with the senior partner, which is perceived as "dealing" in values and religious affairs. The greater one's self-confidence over facing the secular environment, the greater the basis for delegitimization of the veteran leadership and its historical path. On the other hand, once the State of Israel was established, Mapai was challenged as the representative of Labor movement values. Furthermore, once these values ceased to be of significance for most of the population, young NRP members — who did not experience the veteran's struggle for securing their special religious rights within the developing Israeli society — felt that another basis had been eliminated for justification of the NRP's historic path.

2. As indicated above, estrangement from religion and tradition has apparently been the main problem facing the orthodox religious establishment in recent generations. This

problem is seen to exist on two planes: *public* — i.e. religious society's obligation to impart its lifestyles to the coming generations and *individual* — i.e. parents' natural desire for their children to remain loyal to all that they cherish and hold sacred. Within the framework of religious Zionism (the Mizrachi movement), this problem was reflected on still another plane, the *national* plane, i.e. the religious-Zionist movement's obligation not only to impart religious and traditional values to the coming generations but also to participate actively in the construction of a modern Jewish society in Israel — hence the obligation to prepare the next generation for fulfillment of all roles within this society.

The Mizrachi movement consequently assumed responsibility for development and establishment of a multi-faceted educational system, including kindergartens, elementary schools, secondary schools and teachers' seminaries. The movement sought to redesign the traditional educational system to prepare the new generation in Israel to take part in modern society while maintaining loyalty to the orthodox lifestyle. Essentially, this system closely resembled the general educational system; even the curricula were similar, with the exception of religious studies.

Jewish studies were indeed accorded more time and significance in Mizrachi schools, but this in no way upset the balance among the various subjects. On the other hand, the absence of *yeshivot* (Talmudic academies) in this educational system was most prominent. During the *Yishuv* period, there were several attempts — most of which ended in failure — at establishing yeshivot in the spirit of the Mizrachi movement. It was only towards the end of this period that foundations were laid for a yeshiva high school (Midrashiyat Noam — 1944). At the time, however, it was considered only a marginal phenomenon.[10]

Mizrachi schools indeed strove for full integration in the renewing Jewish society in the Land of Israel, with affinity for both modern and special Jewish culture. However, it was particularly in the area of education that the Mizrachi movement — as a religious movement in which parents who sought to educate their children towards loyalty to religion and its values — had to face a most frustrating situation: a developing secular Jewish culture whose symbols, heroes and ceremonies attracted and unified Israel's youth and which Mizrachi educators could not combat successfully. No precise statistics are available concerning this phenomenon. However, members of the generation in question have declared that only a minority of Mizrachi school graduates remained loyal to religious principles (Bar-Lev 1977, pp. 83–87).

The "failure" of the Mizrachi school system served as yet another basis for delegitimization of the parents' generation, the founding fathers. The schools were perceived as shallow in terms of Jewish content and the parents' homes were unable to serve as models for full Jewish lives (a detailed explanation follows below).

3. Up to now, the term "erosion" was understood as overall abandonment of an orthodox religious lifestyle, wherein the individual considers himself to be "non-religious" and is defined as such by his environment. However, the concept of religiousness may also be defined as a continuum, such that any systematic and public diversion from *Halacha* and tradition would express erosion. It would be most productive to investigate the religious culture which developed in Israel among the population which identifies with the Mizrachi movement. Such research is currently only in its initial stages; nevertheless, we may claim that within this population sector – especially among members of Hapoel Hamizrachi kibbutzim – diversion from accepted traditions has been legitimized to some extent. Negation of Diaspora Jewish lifestyles not only led to changes in traditional clothing and appearances, but also to adoption of the Hebrew language in its Sephardic pronounciation for prayers, liturgy and religious studies. This enabled intermingling among immigrants from various countries and traditions into an overall religious community with a "neutral" religious culture. The rejection of key components of Diaspora religious culture could be accomplished only within the framework of a "holy war" (Fishman 1979, p. 21) against the Diaspora and all it represents. The religious culture represented by Hapoel Hamizrachi members on kibbutzim, moshavim and even in cities was generally less demanding and less restrictive – and therefore less "pious" (Bar-Lev, in press). There are numerous examples: relations between the sexes, institutionalization of the custom that married women need not cover their heads, less obligatory

attitudes towards public prayer, afternoon and evening services, ritual hand-washing, grace after meals, etc. In a general sense, we may define this phenemenon as "diminished piety," more lenient towards deviation from *Halacha* than the traditional approach.

As ideological justification could be found for the change in pronunciation of the prayers and in the language of religious study — which apparently were not legitimized by any senior rabbinic authority[11] — it is characteristic that the innovators did not require any Halachic opinions regarding the change. The strength of their Zionist experience and rejection of the Diaspora as a central component of their *Weltanschauung* were sufficient reasons for institutionalizing this decisive religious change. However, no such formal justification could be found for other deviations from religion and tradition. The institutionalization of such phenomena may be explained in light of the following factors:

a)    The experience of renewal and change resulting from a radical change in lifestyle was in constant conflict with traditional Judaism.

b)    Abandonment of religion and tradition, erosion and adoption of the values of democratic society, including the right to privacy. This atmosphere precluded meticulous social supervision of the deeds and misdeeds of every individual. Hence no obligatory organizational or individual conclusions could be derived.

c)    Individual and collective desire for minimizing external conflicts with the dominant culture, on the one hand and stressing the difference between the new religious culture and the traditional one, which was "Diaspora-like," non-pioneering and anti-Zionist, on the other hand. This implies that the modern religious society forming in Palestine was indeed united in its obligation to *Halacha,* although relative tolerance was displayed towards varying shades of diversion therefrom.

Such innovations and changes could not be instituted without arousing reaction. From the very outset, they exposed religious Zionism to criticism and delegitimization on the part of Agudat Israel. With the change in historical circumstances (which we will consider briefly below), they served as an additional basis for delegitimization of the parents' generation, wherein children contrasted their parents' lifestyles with the tenets of religious law.

In summary: Changes in conditions and circumstances exposed the founding fathers of religious Zionism in Israel to criticism from their children regarding three central issues:

a)    Over-subservience to the secular ruling party and political lobbying;

b)    Failure to halt erosion; lack of success in education;

c)    "Diminished piety."


## The Educational Crisis in the Religious Camp

The rise of the Young Guard faction within the NRP occurred against a background of comprehensive economic, religious and social changes which reshaped the image and character of modern religious society in Israel. The clearest expression of these changes focused primarily upon education, rather than politics: institutionalization of the yeshiva high school (and later the *Ulpana* for girls) as a dominant pattern of secondary education since the latter half of the 1950s (Bar-Lev, in press (b)). The yeshiva high school essentially supplanted the religious high school — a change whose comprehensive social significance cannot be exaggerated. This is a topic which demands a far more extensive and intensive study than can be provided here. Hence we relate to only a few of the most significant aspects of the phenomenon.

There are four principal reasons for the institutionalization of the yeshiva high school:

a)    *The Holocaust Crisis:*  The tragic and brutal disappearance of traditional Judaism in Eastern Europe and the destruction of centers of Jewish learning in Poland and Lithuania aroused guilt feelings among Jewish communities in Israel, particularly among movements for which "revolt" against the Diaspora was a central ideological component. As a result, there developed an increasing tendency to consider the once-derided traditional pre-war past in a positive, romantic light. Furthermore, religious Jews maintained the additional incentive of reestablishing the destroyed world of learning. Many of the founding fathers — who had "rebelled" but remained loyal to *Halacha* — sustained even stronger guilty consciences. The renewed post-Holocaust legitimization of the yeshiva was thus an expression of parents' desire to reconstruct, through their children, a bridge to a past world which no longer exists.

b)    *The "Failure" of the Religious High School:* The fact that the "erosion" of the second generation in Zionist religious society was not arrested during the entire Yishuv period pointed an accusing finger at the Mizrachi educational system — and particularly its high schools — as primarily responsible for the situation. It was claimed that teachers had little religious faith and that religious studies (Talmud) were not sufficiently covered in the curriculum (see opinion of R. Maimon (Fishman) in Bat-Yehuda 1979, pp. 482–483). However, it was not only the high school which was perceived as "guilty." The parents' generation effectively felt that it too had failed to transmit its religious heritage to the children. Moreover, the renewed legitimization of traditional Judaism necessarily implied at least partial delegitimization of the new religious culture which formed during the Yishuv period ("diminished piety"). This situation prepared parents for adoption of a new educational pattern, wherein responsibility for molding the children's Jewishness is transferred to other factors serving *in loco parentis* within the younger generation's primary agent of socialization. This is one of the main reasons that yeshiva high schools are generally boarding schools.

c)    *"Creeping Secularism":* Another factor which encouraged the rapid development of yeshiva high schools is the institutionalization of Western, urban secular norms in Israel. The 1950s also marked a period of crisis for militant secularist culture, that self-assured culture which constituted an alternative and a most outspoken critic of the old world in which tradition and religion played a major role. In its place, however, emerged a "creeping secularism" — i.e. day-to-day life which in-

cluded substantial contravention of religious conceptions
and *Halacha* without any premeditated or demonstrative
(i.e. spiteful) intention to harm religion or its adherents.
One key component of this secular culture is sexual per-
missiveness, as expressed in women's clothing, advertising, theater, cinema,[12] television and literature, in the
press, in parlor conversations, etc. In many respects,
this situation "frightens" the religious person more
than militant secularism. The latter is better-defined
and even more "legitimate," despite its rejection of
religion, as it suggests an alternative of social and national values. "Creeping secularism," on the other hand, is
"frightening" because it somehow characterizes a situation of anomie, attacking modern man on all fronts and
invading his home and bedroom. Furthermore, it offers
no alternative of social and national values, considering
daily life and pleasure within Western consumer culture
to be a legitimate objective. The religious Jew feels that
he has no choice other than to remove his children from
their home, where they are exposed to the attractions
of creeping secularism, and place them in a closed educational system which covers all hours of the day.

d)    *The Establishment of the State of Israel and the Rise in
      Standard of Living:* The steadily-rising standard of living
      in Israeli society aids parents in bearing at least part of
      the heavy financial burden of boarding school costs and
      maintenance. Other financial factors include:

1.    Western Diaspora Jews, whose financial status and
      sensitivity to the well-being of Israeli society has become
      a key factor in maintaining cultural and educational
      institutions in Israel.

2.    These schools (like other educational and cultural
      institutions) also benefit from the support of various
      governmental agencies, including the Ministry of Educa-
      tion and other national and public factors (the Ministry
      of Religious Affairs, the Jewish Agency, etc.)

Yeshiva high schools rapidly became the preferred path for
religious youth with affinity for the NRP. From these schools
there developed a new generation ("the knitted skullcap

generation") whose values and lifestyles indeed maintained continuity with their parents' culture. Even more prominent, however, was their revolt and criticism of the founding fathers regarding the issues indicated above. The development of yeshiva high schools signified halt to erosion. For the first time since the secularization process began, there were signs of generational continuity within the religious population, as feelings of self-confidence permeated its ranks. Regardless of whether this development is to be credited entirely to the yeshiva high schools or to other social-communal factors, the former are considered as primarily responsible for this historic change and are among its principal beneficiaries.

These comprehensive schools led to the development of a new religious culture, accompanied by inculcation of new political national conceptions. This was a comfortable framework for molding a new generation: the pattern of studies demanded constant confrontation between accepted lifestyles and the ideal presented in *Halachic* literature. The modern religious home necessarily emerged from this confrontation at a disadvantage. The political traditions of national-religious society were similarly put to the test. Thus, in parallel to the attenuation of ideological and militant secularism arose a new, self-assured religiousness which demanded the right to mold the image of the Jewish people not only in the narrow religious sphere but also in terms of its social-national character. This situation was accorded prominent expression after the Six-Day War (1967) and especially following the 1973 Yom Kippur War.

The development of yeshiva high schools was not initiated by the NRP political leadership. Rather, this solution to the severe problems facing national-religious society was provided through its youth movement (Bnei Akiva). Although the first yeshiva high schools did not officially belong to this movement, there is no doubt that Bnei Akiva helped transform them into select institutions for modern religious youth. To a certain extent, the atmosphere prevailing at these schools continues the romanticism of the youth movement. Most are connected with the "Bnei Akiva Yeshivot Center," although their financial dependence upon the NRP political establishment is marginal.

The young modern religious Jew, especially if of Ashkenazic origin, is thus educated today from kindergarten until his induction into the Army — and in certain cases even during military service (in the *Nahal* corps or *Yeshivot Hesder*) — within a special religious framework. At adolescence, he finds himself in a closed and comprehensive society together with his friends, most of whom are old youth movement acquaintances. Thus not only is his social and religious image formed, but also informal social frameworks which retain their validity for years afterward. Moreover, the school provides him with tools for playing an active role in the economic and professional components of modern society. From the 1960s on, we find young religious people attending institutions of higher learning and from there to continuing on to assume key positions in government, the economy and the free professions, thereby according them financial security. As participation in national institutions becomes more and more institutionalized, they feel increasingly more confident of their own capabilities, on the one hand and their non-dependence upon any party apparatus on the other.

In parallel to the development of yeshiva high schools, there emerged a process of "ghettoization" — i.e. an increasing tendency among the religious population to live in special residential areas. This phenomenon, too, is a result of "creeping secularism" and a rise in standard of living. "Creeping secularism" created a situation which makes it difficult for religious people to maintain primary friendship relations with non-religious persons as a result of the "secularization" of leisure-time activities and entertainment. In the past, acceptable entertainment and leisure-time patterns (social evenings, excursions and the like) were perceived as "neutral," at least by the modern religious Jew. Today, however, it is impossible for a religious family to spend time with non-religious persons, owing to potential violation of Sabbath or dietary laws, for example. This obligates the religious person to seek social outlets among people who resemble him. The new "ghetto" is thus not of a defensive character and does not express anxiety or inferiority. Rather, it fulfills a social need among people whose social and financial security in Israeli society generally does not require bolstering. These changes had an even more far-reaching social consequence: in contrast to the humdrum attitude induced by a decrease in ideological-Zionist tension — even within bodies which once stood for pioneering and self-sacrifice for Zionist objectives — there is a prominent display of national affinity, readiness for sacrifice and obligation towards Zionist ideology on the part of national religious youth. Such attitudes were easily expressed on an organizational plane, thanks to the social relationships consolidated through special youth movement education, yeshiva high schools, *Nahal* units, *Yeshivot Hesder* and the "ghetto."

In summary, the social changes which befell the national-religious "camp" — the rise of the yeshiva high school, halting of erosion towards the secular camp and processes of "ghetto-ization" — necessarily influenced religious and social patterns and increased self-confidence among modern religious individuals and the religious public as a whole within Israeli society. This implies a challenge to one of the fundamental components of the heretofore uncontested obligation to vote for the NRP. Once again, the "camp" has no essential need for the services and protection of the "camp party."

## The NRP Young Guard — Revolt and Continuity

The rise of the Young Guard within the NRP and the system of relations between them and the traditional party leadership constitutes yet another manifestation of the afore-mentioned processes. The changes which took place in NRP political platforms over the past few years accurately reflect the social changes which affected national religious society, represented on the political plane by the NRP Young Guard (see parallel discussion in Deshen 1978, pp. 115—158).

Historically, the leadership of the NRP Young Guard faction developed from the Young Guard organization, initially established not as a special ideological movement but rather as a means of providing leisure-time activity for young religious people who — upon returning home to the city following *Nahal* service — found themselves alienated from secular entertainment and activities. The organization ceased functioning within a few years; in the meantime, however, Young Guard leaders began to present themselves as an alternative to the veteran NRP leadership, acquiring incentive from young people's overall discomfort with the veteran leadership (see above discussion). The relatively facile and swift rise of the NRP Young Guard to the front lines of party leadership may thus be partially explained by feelings of failure among parents and their desire for their children's success.

From the very outset, the NRP Young Guard constituted an opposition to the traditional party leadership. Their criticism focused upon two key issues: (a) The system of internal party relations, based upon "institutionalized factionalism" and (b) the tactics and strategy of the party in all that pertains to partnership with Mapai (and subsequently the Alignment).

Don-Yehiya describes institutionalized factionalism as a mechanism which enables expression of internal differences of opinion while maintaining external party unity. Clearly, this mechanism is functional primarily within a "camp party" — i.e., one which senses that the "threat from without" is so great that sacrifices must be made to preserve unity, at least superficially, thus allowing for internal differences only. Furthermore, there is a virtual consensus among all factions regarding political issues on an overall, national scale, so that differences are considered "insignificant" in light of the impending "threat" to religion and religious society. However, "institutionalized factionalism" has other functions: it allows the veteran establishment to retain its status when threatened by a new factor and serves as a power base for party politicians, who attain their objectives through internal arrangements among the factions. According to our investigation, institutionalized factionalism indeed enabled the veteran factions to delay the rise of the Young Guard and to block several of their demands for long-term personnel changes. For example, consider the Young Guard's demand for a "beautiful NRP," the thrust of which was directed against Itzhak Raphael, then head of the *Likud Utemura* faction. Regardless of whether the accusations leveled against Raphael were true or false, it is important to note that the young NRP members presented themselves as standard-bearers of righteousness, as opposed to the "corrupt wheeler-dealers." Furthermore, we note that Raphael's status remained strong so long as his faction supported him. The Young Guard did not succeed in eliminating factional rule and itself became a faction among others.

Consequently, they did not have the means to oust Raphael except through his faction ("Oslo," in party jargon). However, it was this very act which intensified tensions within the party and created the backdrop for the crisis among young people in the second-large faction, *Lamifne*. Since institutionalized factionalism was not eliminated, the condition for normal party functioning was the relative security of faction leaders regarding "outside interfention" by other factions. The success of the Young Guard's initiative in causing a "court revolution" with the *Likud Utemura* faction necessarily fostered reform among *Lamifne* leaders anxious over challenge to their own status.

In the area of external relations, the NRP Young Guard played a decisive role in the party's rightward swing. This approach paralleled second generation discomfort over partnership with the Alignment and the ILP. By "rightward swing," we refer primarily to opposing territorial compromise and supporting the demands of Gush Emunim settlers. A far-reaching change occurred in the NRP's involvement in national political activity. Identification with Gush Emunim's principles led to overlap between the most important global overall national political question and the religious demands by which the NRP considers itself bound. This introduced some ferment with which institutionalized factionalism could not contend, as noted below. However, this approach did not lead to partership with the Likud until the latter became the largest party and was to form the government coalition (the "upheaval" of 1977).

It is against this background that we investigate the difference between the NRP's achievements in the 1977 (Ninth Knesset) and 1981 (Tenth Knesset) elections. In the former, the results — 12 mandates — were most impressive, while in the latter, the NRP sustained a mighty blow as their representation was cut in half. The reasons for these vastly different results may be explained in terms of the processes which have been described extensively above.

The processes which challenged the role of the NRP as a religious "camp party" were in effect during the Ninth Knesset elections as well. Nevertheless, the NRP was not hurt in those elections because it appeared highly probable that the Alignment would again form the government and that the NRP — not the Likud — would continue to be the main partner in   the coalition. Consequently, the NRP would assume the same obligation it had fulfilled in previous governments: prevention of relinquishing territory, primarily in Judea and Samaria. Greater Israel supporters among the NRP voters considered a vote for the Likud to be wasted, whereas the NRP represented the primary factor capable of preventing the Labor-headed government from relinquishing territory. A different situation confronted voters in 1981: prior to the elections, NRP leaders had already committed their party to joining a Likud coalition. On the other hand, the Alignment posed a threat to continued Likud rule. As a result, many of those religious voters who felt no obligation to the NRP, their "camp party" (see above), instead came to the aid of the Likud.

## The NRP, Gush Emunim and  the Techiya Movement

Perhaps the best proof of the theory presented above is the history of relations between the NRP and Gush Emunim and the establishment of the Techiya Party as a joint religious-secular movement. As indicated earlier, the political path of Young Guard is characterized by revolt and continuity. Gush Emunim, which became consolidated chiefly after the Yom Kippur War, is considered a more authentic expression of national religious youth, the yeshiva high schools, *Ulpanot* and *Yeshivot Hesder*. There is surely a need for an intensive and fundamental study of Gush Emunim as a religious, social and political phenomenon[13]. We do not propose to fill this gap herein, but rather to raise several ideas which pertain to the subject at hand.

Gush Emunim is based upon those very social frameworks which were consolidated in the yeshiva high schools, *Nahal* or *Yeshivot Hesder*. It subsumes continuation of the youth revolt, ideological commitment, youth movement romanticism and a desire to depart the "secular city" and live together in a small community. But Gush Emunim is more than this. It is a political-religious movement with a leadership which has unified and led the masses. Relations between the NRP Young Guard and Gush Emunim are complex in nature: initially,

the former considered themselves as the political patrons of
the latter. This necessarily led to tension between them, as
the NRP's central role in government demanded that it maintain political realism and condemn violations of the law,
whereas Gush Emunim is a religious movement, functioning
by the power of faith and internal fortitude, which is not
always prepared to consider "day-to-day" national regulations.
On the other hand, Gush Emunim does not want to be
identified with the NRP because it prefers recruiting a varied
political lobby comprising representatives of different parties
who recognize it as a pioneering, idealistic movement, pre-
paired to sacrifice itself for national objectives. However, it
would have been naive to posit that Gush Emunim would not
ultimately assume some form of political, parliamentary expression. The Likud's victory and partnership with the NRP
demanded such expression, as it was then that differences
emerged between the ideological-religious-messianic obligation
to Greater Israel and ideological commitment tempered by
practical considerations. Had the NRP been in opposition to
Likud government, it could then have served as a tool for
Gush Emunim's criticism of the government's reneging on
commitments to Greater Israel. Gush Emunim's political
activity thus laid the foundations for limiting its obligations
to the NRP. Furthermore, operating within the NRP as an
independent faction or together with the Young Guard was
irrelevant for another reason: Gush Emunim focused upon an
issue which was by nature religious but also politically significant from an overall, national point of view. Institutionalized
factionalism, as indicated above, could not cope with issues
in this dimension.

The establishment of the Techiya Party by a number of
Gush Emunim members and secular extremists from the
"Land of Israel" movement expresses a change which took
place among at least part of the NRP voters regarding their
obligation to vote for a religious party. Techiya had but
one political demand — the imposition of Israeli sovereignty
over Judea, Samaria and Gaza. This does not mean that
Gush Emunim members in Techiya reject or belittle the vital
importance of those social-religious needs which the NRP, as
a "camp party," is supposed to guarantee. On the contrary, a
significant portion of those who identify with Gush Emunim

are among the prominent representatives of the renewed "meticulous piety" trend ("extremism") in the NRP camp. Rather, such people do not anticipate any danger to these social-religious needs; they consider them to be ensured or assume that they are capable of defending their rights without the aid of the party. Once again, there is no need for a "camp party" because the basic and vital needs of the "camp" are guaranteed, in one way or another, by other factors.

### Religion and Ethnicity — Tami and the NRP

The resignation of Aharon Abuhatzeira from the NRP and the establishment of Tami just prior to the elections was one of the major factors leading to the drop in NRP electoral support. A brief glance at the election returns from a number of development towns in southern Israel reveals that the NRP was essentially "deserted" for Tami by entire party branches. However, it appears that not all Tami supporters formerly voted for the NRP; rather, Tami clearly attracted votes from the Likud and the Alignment as well.

Note that Tami is an ethnic party, primarily based upon religious and traditional observance, which has succeeded where others have failed. Paradoxically, religion and tradition were key factors in Jewish national unity throughout the period of Exile. This may be explained through a relatively simple sociological analysis: it was the geographic dispersion of the Jews that fostered development of local traditions expressed in daily life, in synagogue and in Jewish law. So long as there was dispersion, the unifying aspects of Judaism were emphasized over the differentiating factors (Katz 1979, p. 155). However, once groups of Jews with different traditions converge upon one place, it becomes clear that particularistic traditions make it difficult even for them to pray together; hence separate congregations are established.[14]. In the old Yishuv, these differences acquired powerful historical significance not only with respect to relations between Sephardim and Ashkenazim but also those among adherents of the various Ashkenazic traditions. These differences were so influential that it was impossible to organize a unified Jewish community in Jerusalem, for example. Research on

Agudat Israel's settlement attempts (*Mahane Israel* — 1924) reveals that one of the difficulties in   consolidating the settlers' society was rooted in the fact that they belonged to groups with different traditions (*Hassidim, Mitnagdim,* German Jews and *Yerushalmim*), which made intermingling difficult. On the other hand, abandoning the tradition of the country of origin, adoption of Sephardic pronunciation and instituting uniform versions of prayer and liturgy enabled the consolidation of Hapoel Hamizrachi training and settlement groups into a unified religious-social community.

The NRP, as a religious subculture, contributed decisively to the absorption of Sephardic (Asian and African) Jewish immigrants who maintained loyalty to *Halacha* (Deshen 1978, pp. 164–165). This culture included elements which the Sephardim could adopt without difficulty or loss of identity (such as the use of Sephardic pronunciation in prayer and religious study), as well as those which bridged the gap between religion/tradition and modern culture.[15]

However, none of this sufficed to create a uniform religious culture. No one synagogue was established which could express the existence of a single religious community. In order to implement this dramatic change, both sides had to continue the "holy revolt," but were unwilling to do so. The Sephardic Jews did not come to Israel through negating tradition; rather, the opposite was true. In the painful process of absorption, they were forced to give up an important part of their former lifestyles, such that the traditions of prayer and liturgy remain the major focus of their past and self-identity. For veteran Ashkenazim, as indicated above, the era of revolt has already passed and a new affinity for *Halacha* and Ashkenazic tradition ("meticulous piety") is developing. Furthermore, the social-demographic processes ("ghettoization") analyzed above have imposed additional difficulties on intermingling of ethnic groups and traditions. The processes of "ghettoization" are connected with the rise in standard of living and economic status, which itself creates a tendency towards isolation — even on an ethnic-religious basis. This situation also influences the ability to maintain reasonable integration in state religious schools.[16]

Latent ehtnic schism has apparently existed for some time within the NRP. The reasons behind its outbreak in the 1981 elections are certainly linked with various incidents within the party and Israeli society which created the appropriate atmosphere. The rise of the maturing young leadership and the fact that the synagogue, which is ethnic in nature, is the primary organizational base of the religious parties enabled Tami to commence operation successfully even without an independent organizational infrastructure.

In summary, we may obviously inquire whether Tami will become a permanent fixture in Israeli politics. The above analysis hints at an affirmative answer. However, it is difficult to predict at this stage, primarily because of the personal difficulties nad problems which face several key figures in the movement. Nevertheless, it is unlikely that we will witness a return to the NRP. It is more reasonable to assume that if Tami's infrastructure disintegrates, the majority of its supporters will prefer the Likud, which already has a strong nucleus of traditional Oriental Jews.

## Conclusions

The reasons for the drop in NRP support in the 1981 elections to the Tenth Knesset were shown to be linked with significant changes taking place in  the status of the national-religious "camp." A challenge was posed to the camp's traditional commitment to support the religious party. The religious voter's feeling of dependence upon the party because of the "threat" from the secular government to essential religious services and needs apparently diminished considerably. The social-economic and religious revolutions undergone by the NRP's younger generation led to delegitimization of their parents' ways and strengthened confidence in their ability to confront the various expressions of secularism and emerge "victorious" without needing the party and its institutions.

Nevertheless, it would not be correct to state that this weakening commitment *necessarily* led to the drop in the NRP support. The NRP could have obtained many votes because of its political stand on the issue of Greater Israel, as it apparently did in the 1977 elections. Rather, reduced support of the NRP resulted from the rise of the Likud to power. The two parties were rivals for voter potential, with the Likud

making inroads among some of the traditional NRP supporters. The Likud's attraction to such voters is reinforced by
their confidence in Menachem Begin as a traditional Jew. The
tendency of Sephardic voters towards the Likud is likely to
foster further abandonment of the NRP; moreover, Tami
voters formerly associated with the NRP are not likely to
return. The Likud's rise to power and partnership with the
NRP necessarily intensified differences between these parties
and extreme supporters of the Greater Israel concept within
Gush Emunim, forming the basis for the establishment of
Techiya.

In light of the above, it appears that an NRP comeback
will be possible only if there is a drastic change in the political
situation — one which is currently considered to be highly
unlikely — and Likud support drops to a level so low that it
cannot possibly form and head a coalition government.

## NOTES

1. Merged in 1956.
2. This party obtained 1.2% of the vote (20,384 votes) in the 1977
   elections, as compared with 3.6% (56,560 votes) in 1973.
3. Its strength increased from 8.3% (130,349 votes) in 1973 to
   9.2% (160,787 votes) in 1977.
4. From 9.2% (160,787 votes) in 1977 to 4.92% (95,232 votes) in
   1981.
5. This was expressed in the concepts of "old" and "new" generations in eastern Europe, wherein the former described traditional
   Judaism and the latter those who had abandoned traditional life.
   See also Note 7, below, as well as Friedman 1974, p. 457, n.7.
6. For example, consider the following representative quotation
   from *Hahavatzelet* (May 5, 1909): ". . . The anxious Jew . . . is
   struck a twofold blow: not only is he not given his rightful place
   among his people but he also suffers by seeing that his children
   do not follow the true path . . . He sees the new generation
   digging a grave for all of Judaism, for which he has sacrificed his
   very soul . . . Alas! How sad is this tragedy . . . He cannot defend
   his children and family. He has no weapons, he has no protection.
   What can he do? He can only weep bitterly . . . "
7. 1949–1950. See Friedman 1982, pp. 11–12.
8. The problem of observing Jewish holidays (including Passover
   and the Day of Atonement) and other traditional customs, particularly on leftist settlements, has not been crossed off the
   agendas of Zionist institutions. However, what particularly hurt

those loyal to tradition was the instituionalization of holidays and ceremonies of the Yishuv's "secular religion," based upon the traditional holidays and ceremonies. See Friedman 1978, pp. 319–320; Don-Yehiya & Liebman 1981.

9. Prior to their reaching an arrangement, relations between them were characterized by conflict over the right to work. See Shefatia 1977, pp. 165–176 and comments to bibliography.

10. The Bnei Akiva Yeshiva at Kfar Haroeh was indeed founded in 1939, but until 1950 it was not a yeshiva high school and its students were not trained for taking matriculation examinations. See extended discussion in Bar-Lev 1977, pp. 116–128.

11. R. Kook did not favor change in pronunciation of prayers. See Kook 1962, p. 243 (Letter 719).

12. The NRP newspaper, *Hatzofe* has instituted a self-imposed censorship of cinema advertisements over the past few years.

13. Research by Raanan (1981) is indeed an important study of this topic but still does not answer several fundamental questions. The study by Sprinzak (1981) considers the connection between Gush Emunim and youth in yeshiva high schools, but I do not believe that it sufficiently clarifies the nature, essence and roots of this link.

14. Good examples of this are the Sephardic and Ashkenazic communities of Venice, Hamburg, Amsterdam and London.

15. This was one of the reasons that these immigrants were not accepted in Agudat Israel, whose traditional Ashkenazic culture was dominant and whose spoken language was Yiddish.

16. This problem has recently been given increased attention. See Egozi 1975; Hen, Levi & Adler 1978; Schwartzwald 1978. pp. 107–122.

## BIBLIOGRAPHY

Bar-Lev, M.

1977          "Yeshiva High School Graduates in Israel: Between Tradition and Renewal." Unpublished doctoral dissertation, Bar-Ilan University, Ramat Gan, Israel (Hebrew).

in press      "And These Are the Generations — Fifty Chapters
(a)           of Action." *Bimeshoch Hayovel* (Jubilee publication of Bnei Akiva — 1929-1979) (Hebrew).

in press      "Bnei Akiva's Educational Institutions: The
(b)           Yeshiva, *Ulpana* and *Yeshivat Hesder,*" ibid. (Hebrew).

Bat-Yehuda (Raphael), G.
1979    *R. Maimon in his Generation.* Jerusalem, pp. 420-423. (Hebrew).

Deshen, S.
1978    "Israeli Judaism: Introduction to the Major Patterns." : Mossad Harav Kook, *International Journal of Middle Eastern Studies* 9, pp. 141– 169.

Don-Yehiya, A.
1980    "Stability and Change in a Camp Party – the NRP and the Youth Revolt." *Medina Mimshal Vihasim Benleumiyyim* (State, Government and International Relations) 14, pp. 25-52 (Hebrew).

& Liebman, C.S.
1981    "The Symbol System of Zionism-Socialism: An Aspect of Israeli Civil Religion." *Modern Judaism* 1, pp. 1-28.

Egozi, M.
1975    "Elementary School Pupils, by Origin and Size of Family – 1975 vs. 1972." Jerusalem: Ministry of Education and Culture, Planning Department, 1975 (Hebrew

Hen, M., Levi, A. & Adler, H.
1978    "Process and Result in Education: An Evaluation of the Contribution of Junior High Schools to the Educational System." Jerusalem: Ministry of Education and Culture (Hebrew).

Katz, Y.
1979    "Traditional Society and Modern Society." *Jewish Nationalism.* Jerusalem, pp. 155–166 (Hebrew).

Fishman, A.
1979    *Hapoel Hamizrachi: 1921-1935.* Tel Aviv: Teudot (Tel Aviv University) (Hebrew).

Friedman, M.
1974    "The Social Significance of the Sabbatical Year Debate." *Shalem* A, Jerusalem, pp. 455–480. (Hebrew).

1978    *Society and Religion.* Jerusalem: Yad Itzhak Ben-Zvi (Hebrew).

1982 "From the Trauma of Erosion to a Feeling of Confidence and Supremacy." *Migvan* (Spectrum) 63, pp. 9—14 (Hebrew).

Kook, Rabbi A.I.
1961 *Letters.* Jerusalem: Mossad Harav Kook (Hebrew).

Raanan, Z.
1981 *Gush Emunim.* Tel Aviv: Sifriyat Poalim (Hebrew).

Schwartzwald, Y.
1978 "As a Foreign Implant? Concerning the Oriental Religious Student in Well-Run Junior High Schools." *Iyunim Behinukh* (Topics in Education 19, pp. 107—122 (Hebrew).

Shefatia, D.
1977 "Hapoel Hamizrachi's Initial Battle for the Right to Work." *Sefer Hazionut Hadatit* (The Book of Religious Zionism) **B**, Jerusalem, pp. 165—176 (Hebrew).

Sprinzak, A.
1981 "Gush Emunim — The Iceberg Model of Political Extremism." *Medina Mimshal Vihasim Ben-leumiyyim* (State, Government and International Relations) 14, pp. 25-52 (Hebrew).

# Part IV

# THE SOCIAL BASIS OF POLITICS

# 14
## Generational Units and Intergerational Relations in Israeli Politics

*Yonathan Shapiro*

Israeli politics is unusual in that the politicians who came to Israel after reaching political maturity abroad have succeeded in retaining their places in the political elite until old age (in some cases — advanced old age), while the younger generation of native-born Israelis have been unable to take up the reins of power clutched firmly in their elders' grasp. Political elites in other democratic countries are generally characterized by a far greater heterogeneity of age and a more frequent changing of the guard. My paper is an attempt to explain this unusual phenomenon in Israeli politics on the basis of generation units and intergenerational relations.

Although sociologists customarily treat the generation as a social category, much as a class or an ethnic group, theoretical understanding of generational dynamics and intergenerational relations is still limited. Most research into groups defined on the basis of age has preferred other analytical units. One of the reasons seems to be the difficulty in defining the sociological generation.[1]

Intergenerational relationships in politics are different from those in other fields. In the scientific community, for example, scientists are generally agreed on the methods by which the validity of new ideas can be ascertained. Using these, the new generation of scientists can persuade their elders of the validity of a new approach. In contrast, political disputes cannot be resolved on the basis of agreed rules.[2]

Nevertheless, researchers who have investigated intergenerational relations are generally agreed on a number of points.[3] Firstly, the biological generation is not necessarily a sociological generation. A sociological generation exists when a biological generation crystallizes a world view that is uniquely its own. This world view may contradict that of the older generation, or complement it, but it has to be different. Secondly, the younger generation will develop this independent world view in their formative years, namely, the age at which they are capable of the abstract thought necessary for asserting a political world view, and at which they feel the need for such a view

— normally between seventeen and twenty-five.[4] Once they have passed the formative age and adopted their world view, it will be extremely difficult for them to change it.

Generally, the world view adopted is that of the older generation. A biological age group only becomes a generation when a central historical event occurring during their formative years undermines the world view that they were about to receive from their elders. This challenging of conventions leads the young to what Karl Mannheim called "spiritual destabilization." It liberates them from the world view held by their elders, and enables them to adopt new ideas. This liberation, which is crucial to the process, will enable the members of the new generation to develop an independent outlook that will become their natural world view.

According to Mannheim, not all the members of a new generation will develop a new world view. This task will usually be undertaken by a few nuclei groups, made up of peers with a common cultural and social background, who have undergone similar formative experiences. To the extent that the new ideas of the nucleus group express the life experience and aspirations of their contemporaries with similar cultural and social backgrounds and are adopted by them, generation units holding the same world view will take shape.

Lewis Feuer offers a slightly different view. Although he too regards the young people's rejection of their elders' world view as the critical stage in the creation of a generation in the sociological sense, he emphasizes that the behavior of the older generation may itself catalyze this process, undermining their authority over the younger generation and stimulating them to independent thought. He terms the process "deauthorization." Only then will they feel the need to adopt a new world view, and begin to organize for the struggle to impose their opinions and ideas on society as a whole.

Unlike Feuer, Mannheim does not consider ideological differences a cause of intergenerational conflict. According to Mannheim, the younger generation matures and takes on roles which were previously held by their elders. In doing so, they tend to adopt their elders' world view. Nevertheless, they retain something of the world view they crystallized in their formative period. Their behavior in later years can thus only be understood against the background of the developments which occurred in their youth. Eventually, the ideas which they crystallized in their formative period will come to influence the system, but this will be achieved gradually and without conflict.

I consider Mannheim's approach inapplicable in the realm of politics. In politics, an idea can only gain currency when it has strong organizational backing.[5] Verbal formulation alone cannot satisfy aspirations: a political organization must be set up in order to implement these ideas. The generation unit is thus only suitable for the analysis of intergenerational politics when it constitutes the basis for political organization. The new organization will be led by the nucleus group, which will recruit more members from its own generation unit. Together, they will form the backbone of the organization.

Naturally, a political organization of this kind, controlled by a vigorous young generation unit, will compete with the existing political organizations controlled by the older generation. This will bring about the intergenerational conflict envisaged by Feuer. However, it seems to me that intergenerational political conflict cannot be attributed entirely to conflicting world views. A generation unit may well organize for collective political action because its members have not found themselves roles that they consider suitable. As part of the struggle for such roles they will develop an independent world view anchored in their collective formative experience. In order to justify their demands and grant legitimacy to their separate organization. Thus, an explanation of intergenerational political struggles must take into account conflicts of interests as well as ideological differences.

In analyzing intergenerational relations in Israeli politics, I have identified a number of generation units that developed around different nuclei groups. As I have already explained, it is the generation unit, and not the generation as a whole, that formulates a world view and creates an organization that plays a part in the political system. I have also adopted Feuer's historical thesis on generational conflict, which argues that the formation of a new generation unit on ideological grounds will lead to intergenerational conflict over a prolonged historical period, until a new equilibrium is attained.

Feuer typifies the conflict that occurred among the Russian

intelligentsia between the middle of the nineteenth century and the Bolshevik revolution as one such sequence of intergenerational struggles. The intelligentsia began to develop as a social stratum in the middle of the nineteenth century. It detached itself from traditional society, and organized itself as a subculture around an ideology of progress and modernity. Many of its members organized themselves as generation units, and set up radical political movements to change the existing regime. But the change they sought was not achieved until the revolution of 1917. As they grew older, members of these generation units were forced to come to terms with reality and find employment in the developing government bureaucracy. Such compromises left them with strong feelings of failure, and members of younger generations who had witnessed their debacle refused to accept their elders' authority. They therefore established new generation units that crystallized their own world views, and organized themselves for the struggle against the regime. This process repeated itself until the outbreak of the revolution. Only the revolutionaries who finally took control of society succeeded, thanks to their success in revolution, in consolidating their authority over the young. Russian society thus returned to the situation in which youth accepts the authority of the older generation and adopts its world view.

Many of the immigrants from Eastern Europe who came to *Eretz Israel* (Palestine) before the Second World War had taken part in intergenerational conflicts abroad, and were already organized in generation units headed by nucleus leadership groups. The members of the first three *aliyot* (waves of immigration) underwent their formative periods in prerevolutionary and revolutionary Russia. Many of the members of the Fourth and Fifth *Aliyot* who came from Eastern Europe had taken part in the intergenerational conflict which continued, especially among the Jews, into the interwar period. The fact that many of the young immigrants cut themselves off from family and community to settle in *Eretz Israel* with members of their own age groups further reinforced peer-group solidarity after their immigration.

Most of the nuclei groups were in their twenties when they immigrated, in the middle of their formative period. Their new circumstances therefore influenced their world view. In crystallizing it, they set up new organizations. Members of their generation units arriving from abroad strengthened these organizations and reinforced the position of the original nucleus groups, many of whom continued to head the organizations they had founded for many years.

The new political system took shape and was institutionalized in the period between the two world wars.[6] The generation unit to which the founders of the new political system belonged was composed of members of the Second *Aliya*. These were people who had been born in Russia between 1885 and 1890, and immigrated in the wake of the pogroms of 1903–1906, the abortive revolution of 1905, and the ensuing repression. It was this unit which set up many of the structures uniquely characteristic of Israeli society: the *kibbutz* and *kvutzah*, the *moshavim*, the *Histadrut* with its economic and political institutions, and others.[7] This generation unit continued to lead the Jewish *yishuv* for many years. Its most outstanding leader, David Ben-Gurion, was the prime minister of the State of Israel until 1963. Many of the immigrants who arrived later, and were younger than the members of the Second *Aliyah*, accepted their authority completely.[8] Others, who and organized themselves as nuclei groups of generation units while still abroad, maintained their independence and distinctness after their immigration. During the 1920s and 1930s they played an active part in the creation of new structures in the political and settlement systems, placing themselves at the head of these organizations.

For the purpose of this essay I have identified five generation units from the Third, Fourth and Fifth *Aliyot*, each headed by a nucleus leadership group. We are in a position to trace the activities of these units after their arrival and assess their specific contributions to the political structures created.[9]

One such unit arrived in the country from Soviet Russia in the years 1919–1921. It was headed by a nucleus group of political activists from the *Zeire Zion* Socialist party (Z.S.), lead by Menachem Elkind and his associates. After the Bolshevik revolution, this party had decided to support the revolution and join the Soviets. Those of its members who left the Soviet Union after the end of the civil war also shared the euphoria of the victorious socialist revolution, and sought to realize it in *Eretz Israel* as well. They tried to attain hegemony in the labor movement, and were ready from the first to fight the established leadership in order to achieve it. Their intensive organizational and intellectual activity, coupled with the support they enjoyed from their numerous compatriots in the country, were sufficient to persuade the established leadership of the advantages of compromise. The older generation thus agreed to adopt a number of the newcomers' ideas. Some of the young politicians were satisfied with this, but others continued the struggle for hegemony. They failed in their attempt. Some then followed Menachem Elkind back to the socialist way of life in the land of the revolution which they had left only a few years earlier. It seems to me that one of the reasons for their failure was their inability to continue to adapt their ideas to the new reality. The euphoristic formative experience of socialist victory prevented them from making the necessary adaptation.

A second group of activists from the same party arrived in the country between 1923 and 1926. They were contemporaries of the first immigrants, but their formative experience in the Soviet Union included seeing their country transformed into a dictatorship, and their party banned. Their arrival in *Eretz Israel* followed underground political activity, imprisonment, and, finally, expulsion form the Soviet Union. As a result of this formative experience, they were less imbued with the sense of victory of the revolution than were their contemporaries in the party who had left the Soviet Union before them. On the other hand, they had learned to appreciate the power of the party, and the ability of the party machine to take control of society and to change it. They arrived after the liquidation of their own party in the Soviet Union. Apparently as a result of this experience they did not dare to dream of hegemony, but accepted the leadership of the older generation unit. Their most important contribution to the new social structure was within *Ahdut Ha'avodah* (the major political party of the laborers, which became *Mapai* in 1930). They organized the party machine, and recruited members of their generation unit to increase its power and its influence over the *yishuv* in general.

A third generation unit was composed of groups from *Hashomer Hatzair*, also contemporaries of the previous two units. They arrived from Galicia in 1920 and 1921. Many of them had been through the First World War together in Vienna. There they had been influenced by the German youth movements and the progressive views of the

Viennese intelligentsia, which was mainly Jewish. In *Eretz Yisrael* they succeeded in preserving the youth movement mentality which they had acquired abroad, and regarded the preservation of their organizational and ideological autonomy a prime objective. They preferred the role of the avant garde of the labor movement to that of official leadership.

The fourth generation unit was also from *Hashomer Hatzair*. Its members started arriving from Eastern Europe in 1929. Born in 1910 or thereabouts, their early formative experiences in the late 1920s had been influenced by the destabilization of European society at that time, both general and Jewish. Most of its members came from Poland, where they had witnessed the increasing polarization between the right-wing elements which had taken control of the state, and the left-wing opposition. The increasingly Marxist tendencies of *Hashomer Hatzair* in *Eretz Israel* during this period was largely due to their influence.

The fifth generation unit was composed of members of *Betar*, the representatives of integral nationalism in its Zionist version. Most of them came from the Baltic states and Poland. Born about 1915, they too reacted to the events witnessed by the Marxist *Hashomer Hatzair* members in their formative period, but they were influenced by the right-wing groups on the ascendancy in their countries. Under the influence of the latter, they emphasized the military character of their organization and attributed great importance to discipline, decorum, and smart external appearance. They also adopted an antisocialist world view and supported private enterprise. In *Eretz Israel* they provided the impetus for other groups to leave the *Histadrut* (General Federation of Labor) and join them in forming the National Labor Federation in 1934. It was they, too, who were responsible for the establishment of the *Irgun Zvai Leumi* (IZL — a dissident military undergound group), in 1937.

By the end of the 1930s the political system of the *yishuv* had taken shape. Many of its organizations were headed by the leadership nuclei of the various generation units. These recruited members of their own generation units to fill secondary roles in the organizations. The informal relations between the members of the generation units constituted the backbone of the organizations and reinforced the authority of the leaders. Outside this generation framework, the native-born had no place in these political organizations.[10]

This placed the native-born in an extremely difficult situation. Unlike the young Jews who had grown up abroad in confrontation with the older generation incapable of finding a solution to the Jews' worsening situation, the native-born found themselves confronting an older generation imbued with success at having accomplished its goals. They had established a flourishing new society in an underdeveloped and desolate country, and had won the administration of the native-born youngsters who had grown up in the new society and watched its rapid development. In consequence, these young people did not challenge the Zionist and socialist theses of the generations of the founders. The native-born youth were thus unable to crystallize into generation units with nuclei groups capable of adopting independent world views. However, when they grew up, they found that the organizational and political structures set up by their elders were closed to them. For lack of any other alternative, they were compelled to organize themselves but they were an abortive generation without an independent world view.

It may well be that the above description was characteristic of the first generation of native-born in every sphere, but in the field to which we have restricted ourselves here — that of the political system — this generation was indeed conspicuous in its weakness and sterility. In the period preceding the Arab riots which began in 1936, most of the youth were characterized by withdrawal into their personal problems and a pronounced indifference to the demands of their elders to embrace pioneering values and volunteer for national tasks. While the politicians called on them to go to pioneering agricultural settlements, most of the youth preferred individual economic and social advancement in the cities. A survey of the population of Jewish workers in 1937, for example, showed that about one-quarter of those born in the country to parents engaged in manual work found jobs in the bureaucracy and services.[11]

Among the youth of this period, however, there were also those who wished to take active part in politics. These young people sought ways of integrating themselves into the political system. One such group set up the Socialist Youth, which became the youth movement of the *Ahdut Ha'Avodah* party. Many of them had immigrated to

*Eretz Israel* after being active members of Zionist youth movements abroad. There they had begun to reject the spiritual authority of the older generation, which was already suffering from a sense of confusion and failure. This process was nipped in the bud with their arrival in *Eretz Israel;* they came up against generation units with a self-confident leadership not prepared to have its authority challenged by the younger generation. As Berl Katznelson, leader of the labor movement in *Eretz Israel* until his death in 1944, explained in his opening speech at the founding convention of the Socialist Youth movement:

> Whatever the foundations have already been laid — it is the duty of the younger generation to adhere to its basic principles. They may amend them or improve them, but they must accept them ... control and direction of the youth organization must remain in the hands of the mother-party ... our basic principles of our political movement cannot be questioned.[12]

The members of the Socialist Youth did not share the admiration and self-abnegation displayed by the native-born youth towards the generation units of their elders. Nevertheless, their bitterness at not being allowed to play a more active role in the party did not express itself in a challenge for the spiritual authority and leadership of the generation of the founders. They did not form generation units, and did not develop ideas of their own. Consequently, they did not possess the daring or ability to organize themselves as an independent political organization, or even as an independent faction within the party, and found their vocation in the civil service or the liberal professions.

As opposed to this group, their native-born contemporaries with political aspirations displayed an astonishing degree of sycophancy and self-depreciation vis-à-vis the older generation. They did not dare to demand a place for themselves in the political system. The local youth movements — the *Machanot Olim* and *Hanoar Ha'oved* — proclaimed their unquestioning loyalty to their leaders and their ideas. Yisrael Galili, one of the leaders of *Hanoar Ha'oved* and a leading member of the Labor party to this day, declared at the movement's convention in 1932:

> The *Hanoar Ha'oved* movement was born in the bosom of the labor movement and was nourished by it. It is not built on the

rejection of the adult labor movement. Its direction is not that of
an independent youth movement, its aim is rather to foster the
elements of good citizenship required of future members of the
labor movement when he grows up.[13]

Perhaps the behavior of these people can be explained by the absence
of any historical event that could have undermined their confidence
in their adult leaders? In such circumstances, the emergence of a
generation and the creation of generation units would have been
most unlikely. But this was not the case. In 1936, a series of events
commenced which could well have undermined youth's faith in the
authority and world view of their elders — the Arab general strike in
1936, the Arab riots which continued to the end of 1938, and the
British authorities' growing support for the Arab national movement.
This period also witnessed the persecution of the Jews by the Nazis in
Europe, a process which culminated in the murder of millions of Jews
in the gas chambers. We have proof of the influence of these events
on the youth who spent their formative period in *Eretz Israel*
during these years. The young people who found their way into
underground movements, according to Yisreal Galili who was a
few years their senior, "were strengthened by the shocking events
which commenced in the riots of 1936–38, the subsequent policy of
the British, the slaughter of millions in Europe, and the burning
insult of the slaughter and silence of the world."[14]

The rioting of the Arab gangs in 1936 surprised the *yishuv* and
its leaders, and found them unprepared. The older generation did
not know how to react to the attacks on the settlements and the
destruction of their fields. Many of the members of the Second and
Third *Aliyot* were already too tired for the kind of military activity
demanded by the new circumstances. The immigrants who had
come from Europe in the 1930s were also unaccustomed to
thinking in military terms, unlike their predecessors who had been
active in underground movements and in Jewish self-defence in
Russia.[15] There were, however, a few enthusiasts among the older
generation units who pressed for the setting up of an underground
military organization. They were the exceptions in the generation
— "forerunners" in Mannheim's terminology — who blazed the
trail for the native-born youth. One of them was Yitzhak Sadeh,

the legendary commander of the elite unit of the *Haganah*, the *Palmach*, and one of the men who laid the foundations for the Israeli Defense Forces (IDF). Sadeh was one of the leaders of the first generation unit mentioned above, the Z.S. group which immigrated to *Eretz Israel* after the Bolshevik revolution. The group itself disintegrated, and Sadeh remained a lone wolf. Others who devoted themselves to military activities were a group of the first class of graduates of the Herzliah Gymnasium in Tel Aviv, who had joined the *Ahdut Ha'avodah* party in 1919, and were a few years younger than the party leaders and activists.[16] But otherwise, the field of underground military activity remained wide open to the new generation of native-born Israelis. These seized the opportunity eagerly.

While the political activists of the older generation encouraged the youth in this activity, it appears that they did not envisage the wave of enthusiasm which swept them. Groups of high school pupils left school to volunteer for the underground, defying both parents and teachers, and astonishing the politicians, who naturally refused to restrain them.

Enthusiastic reactions to militarism may be found in many statements made by this generation. One such example is Yehiam Weitz, the son of a well-known Zionist functionary. Like many other sons of political functionaries, Weitz junior wished to play a role in public life, but was unable to adjust to the way of life on an agricultural settlement as advocated by the leadership. When he joined the *Haganah* he discovered in his new activity, as he wrote to a friend, "much skill, thought, new ways, and an abundant source of expression and realization; a collective consciousness acting and demanding its due even from so called 'loners,' so called 'individualists,' *luftmenschen* like us."[17] When the *Haganah* decided to cease its military activities during the Second World War for political reasons, many of the youth became impatient and joined the British army.[18] Their formative experience directed their national and public aspirations into military activity, and it was in this form of activity that they continued to find expression for their emotional and intellectual response to their experiences even as they grew older.

It seems to me that one of the explanations for the enthusiasm and zeal with which the native-born embraced military careers was their yearning for a role which preserved their subjection to the authority of their elders and their world view. The underground provided the youth with a role which corresponded to their formative experience, in that it required submission to the authority of the generation of the founders. So powerful was the authority of their elders among the native-born that no process of deauthorization took place among them during their formative period, even when the generation of the founders was confused and did not know how to react to the new reality. In the military underground, the native-born found a mission which demanded discipline rather than independence. This discipline attracted them no less than the military activity itself. The history of the *Haganah* and the *Palmach* reflect astonishing discipline and submission to leadership, a striking contrast to other military underground organizations, which were plagued by schisms and violent disagreements. The only schism which took place in *Eretz Israel* was between the *Haganah*, whose members referred to themselves as the "organized *yishuv*," and the IZL and *Lochamei Herut Yisrael* (LHY), collectively styled "dissidents." The latter organizations were founded by the members of the generation unit of *Betar* activists, led by their nucleus group. Sixty per cent of the commanders of the IZL and the LHY were immigrants who arrived in the country in the 1930s.[19] These *Betar* activists placed their faith in a political and social philosophy which differed widely from the Zionist-socialist ideology of the leaders of the *yishuv*. Yet the polemics of the commanders of the *Haganah* (90 percent of them native-born), against the heads of the IZL and LHY, centered mainly on the demand for obedience to the decisions of the chosen leaders of the *yishuv*.

The activities of the native-born youth in the military underground became part of their formative experience, and further reinforced their loyalty to the generation of the founders and to its world view. While their experiences during their formative period impelled them to military activity, this underground military activity itself further strengthened their submission to their elders' leadership. Discipline is the highest value in all military organizations, and membership in the military organization was the formative experience of one age group after the other. Submission to the authority of the older generation of politicians controlling the military arm of the organized *yishuv* thus became the supreme value of the native-born generation.

This does not mean that there was no tension between the generations. The native-born commanders of the *Haganah* were in continuous conflict with the political leadership. The former in most cases supported a more extreme line ("activist" as it was then called); the political leadership were more moderate. Even so, there were no severe breaches of discipline. It was only when a split took place in the veteran leadership that many of the commanders of the *Haganah* joined the group headed by Yitzhak Tabenkin and his colleagues from the *Kibbutz Hameuchad* movement. This activist group left *Mapai* in 1944 and set up a new party. Tabenkin himself was a member of the nucleus leadership group of the Second *Aliyah*. He and his associates among the political functionaries of the Third *Aliyah* provided the younger generation with authority figures. There was thus no challenge to authority in their enlistment in the new party, nor did they liberate themselves from the authority of the previous generation and crystallize an independent world view. Many of these commanders also supported *Mapam*, the Marxist Labor party which was founded in 1947 with the declared intention of providing an alternative to the rule of social democratic *Mapai*. Nevertheless, when the *Mapai* head of the provisional government, David Ben-Gurion, ordered the disbanding of the *Palmach* headquarters in the midst of the War of Independence, the order was obeyed although it was clear that one of the reasons for his order was *Mapam's* considerable influence in the *Palmach*.[20] I attribute this discipline and restraint more to the loyalty of the native-born commanders of the *Palmach* to the traditional leadership than to a sense of national responsibility on *Mapam's* part.

After the War of Independence, the native-born found new roles in the developing social, economic, and military frameworks. Some remained in the regular army, others found their place as senior officials in the governemnt bureaucracy, and others entered the private sector. The successful among them became the Israeli establishment. The establishment may be defined as the highest social stratum, whose members act in common social frameworks, possess a special life-style, and are also united by the similarity of their views on the structure of society and its system of values and norms. This is a social stratum with high prestige, which usually possesses sufficient economic resources to adopt a standard of living capable of impressing its prestige upon itself and upon the public at large. The power elite, on the other hand, is the group which makes the decisions about the important political problems facing the state.[21] The distinction is usually analytic, and we would not expect the establishment to be without influence on political decisions: in Israel, however, the two functions have become detached. This separation (which was not, of course, total) seems to be unique to Israel. One explanation for this exceptional phenomenon lies in the fact that the political elite with the power to make decisions about important political issues was made up of the generation units of the immigrants controlling the parties, while the Israeli establishment was for the most part composed of the younger generation of native-born Israelis. This establishment was continually augmented by new members drawn from the ranks of native-born ex-army officers, whose distinguishing characteristic continued to be their submission to the authority of the aging politicians born abroad.

While there have been attempts on the part of the younger generation of native-born Israelis to penetrate the power elite and take over the various parties, these attempts have ended in failure. In the incessant intergenerational conflicts which have taken place, for example, in the dominant party — *Mapai* — the reason for the younger generation's failure was only partly organizational. In addition to the fact that a cohesive and united generation unit was in control of the sources of power in the party, the younger aspirants to power were unable to liberate themselves from the authority of their elders and organize themselves for action as a generation unit. The native-born members of *Mapai* did not succeed in organizing themselves as a faction. They did not develop a counterideology, nor did they formulate a common plan of action. Their behavior was characterized by an unwillingness to challenge the authority of the older generation. Their hesitancy and lack of initiative in face of the solidarity of the older generation unit paralyzed their capacity for action.[22]

Only when Ben-Gurion declared war on the leadership of the party, then in the hands of the generation unit born in 1900, was he joined by the frustrated native-born. Only with his backing did they dare to defy the authority of the older generation that had been blocking their way to positions of power in the party for fifteen years. They were followed by many of the young native-born who had joined their abortive generation on leaving the army in the 1950s and 1960s. In 1967, 60 percent of the members of the new party founded by Ben-Gurion — *Rafi* — were under the age of thirty-five.[23] The story of *Rafi* is also one of the failure of the native-born generation. In the face of their aging leader's inability to lead them — Ben-Gurion was then eighty years old — the new party broke up within a few years. Even after they had founded a party of their own, this generation (headed by personalities like Moshe Dayan and Shimon Peres) did not achieve the true political independence that comes from the rejection of the authority of the older generation and the formulation of an independent ideology.

This conflict between the generations in the political system and the failure of the younger generation of native-born Israelis to reach positions of power had important consequences for the functioning of the system as a whole. The lack of turnover among the political decision makers prevented the penetration of new ideas. These decision makers had arrived at political maturity together and continued their political activity for many years as a closed and cohesive generation unit. they reinforced each other in their old ideas and prevented innovation. This made it difficult for the system to react to internal and external developments. A social structure must be constantly renewed in order to react both to the developments within the system and to external changes over which it has no control.

The native-born generation arrived at the political summit only after most of the members of the foreign-born generation units had grown old and died, and the remainder had been forced to resign their posts as a result of the October War. The first government was formed by the Labor party in 1974. This government was headed by ex-General Yitzhak Rabin. Its minister of foreign affairs was Yigal Allon, Rabin's commander in the War of Independence, and the most prominent figure to emerge from it. These were the members of the abortive generation which had not formed generation units with independent world views. They did not attain leadership as a united generational nucleus group like their predecessors in the leadership of the party and the state, but by a process of cooptation: each advanced along a separate course under the aegis of his patrons.[24] As a result, their government was weak, incohesive, and lacking in authority. Within three years, they had brought about the defeat of the party which had led the *yishuv* and the state for over forty years. It was replaced by another party still led by the remnants of the old *Betar* generation unit, headed by the ex-IZL commander, Menachem Begin. The new government also included many representatives of the younger native-born generation, but the almost unquestioned authority of Prime Minister Begin can partly be explained, in my opinion, against the background of the relations between the generations described in this paper.

It remains for me now to attempt to answer the question: how much longer will young people growing to adulthood in Israeli society continue to join the ranks of this barren generation? When may we expect the development of a new generation capable of cutting itself off from the adulation of the generation of the founders and its world view, and organizing itself as independent generation units? Theoretically, we will have to wait until Israeli youth in their formative period are exposed to an experience capable of undermining the world view and authority of the older generation.

The first native-born generation became an abortive generation without authority or an independent world view, and failed to give birth to generation units. In this case, we may have expected the crystallization of independent generation units among those whose formative period occurred after the founding generation had ceased to control the political system. The undermining of the authority of the older generation could have taken place after the mid-1960s, when Ben-Gurion founded a new party and embarked on a struggle against the heads of the generation unit which controlled *Mapai*. Or it could have taken place after the remnants of the same generation unit were compelled to resign their posts in 1974 after the October War, bringing the new generation to power despite themselves. Recent years have witnessed further historic events which could undermine the world view of the founders. In the wake of the last two wars with the Arab states, in 1967 and 1973, the balance of power in the Middle East has changed. Israel has been confronted with new circumstances. Sadat's historical visit to Jerusalem in 1977 could be a further catalyst to change. We already see signs of destabilization among the youth. They are raising doubts about fundamental elements in the world view of the founding generation, ideas that the abortive generation which followed never dared to challenge: doubts about the basic nature of Zionism, our right to *Eretz Israel,* the relations between Israel and the Jewish people, the nature of Judaism, and other vital issues.

The fact remains, however, that these young people have not yet crystallized an independent world view, not organized themselves as generation units. This may lead us to conclude that while spiritual destabilization is a necessary condition for the liberation of a generation, it is not sufficient for the crystallization of a world view and the creation of independent generation units.

A further factor which may possibly contribute to the crystallization of a generation unit is to be found within the structural sphere: the exclusion of the young from the political system, or their elder's interference with their advancement. This may well prompt them to organize for the collective struggle over their views and their place in the system. In politics, as I pointed out at the beginning of this discussion, ideas require an organization for their crystallization and promotion. Without an organization, the ideas current among the young in their formative period when they are in a state of destabilization will not mature and find their way into the political system.

However, in recent years, the political system in Israel has opened to the young without their having to organize for a struggle against the older generation. Following the departure of the generation of founders, the young have been able to enter the system and advance to positions of influence. The age composition of members of the government, *Knesset,* the *Histadrut* Executive

318 **Politics and Society in Israel**

and other institutions of the power structure is now far more heterogenous than previously. However, the fact that in the process of their advancement in the political system the young were absorbed into groups and organizations in which older people held central roles has also had its effect. Sociologists expect youth to oppose the older generation, but they also assume that the young will belong to groups and organizations in which their elders fulfil central roles and will dominate the young people and their views. Sociologists regard these cross-current relations as an important factor in the preservation of stability and conservatism in social structures.[25] The influence of the events of the past years on the youth presently growing up in the State of Israel will only become clear in the next decade.

## Notes

1. Martin W. Riley, Marilyn Johnson and Anne Foner, *Aging and Society* (New York: Russel Sage Foundation, 1972), vol. 3. chap. 4.

2. Lewis S. Feuer, *Einstein and the Generation of Scientists* (New York: Basic Books, 1974), p. 345.

3. Karl Mannheim, "The Problem of Generations," in *Essays in the Sociology of Knowledge* (London: Routledge and Kegan Paul, 1952), pp. 276–322; Lewis S. Feuer, *The Conflict of Generations* (New York: Basic Books, 1969).

4. Neal E. Cutler, "Toward a Generational Concept of Public Socialization," in *New Directions in Political Socialization*, ed. David C. Schwartz and Sandra Kenyon Schwartz (New York: The Free Press, 1975), pp. 254–88.

5. Samuel Barnes, "Ideology and the Organization of Conflict," *Journal of Politics*, 28 (1966): 522–23.

6. See Yonathan Shapiro, *Ha-Demokratia be-Israel* [Democracy in Israel], (Tel Aviv: Massada, 1978), chap. 2, [Hebrew].

7. *Ibid.*

8. Yonathan Shapiro, *The Formative Years of the Israeli Labor Party* (London and Los Angeles: Sage Publications Ltd., 1976), pp. 118–19.

9. The material on the five generation units for this essay was taken from the following books: Shapiro, *The Formative Years of the Israeli Labor Party*; Elkanah Margalit, *Ha-Shomer ha-Tzair — me-Edat Neurim le-Marxism* [Ha-Shomer ha-Tzair — from youth community to revolutionary marxism] (Tel Aviv University and Hakibbutz Hameuchad Press,

1971), [Hebrew]: Y. Ophir, *Sepher ha-Oved ha-Leumi* [The book of the national worker] (Executive Committee of the National Labor Federation, 1963) (Hebrew); David Niv, *Ma'arachot ha-Irgun ha-Tzvai ha-Leumi* [The struggle of the Irgun Tzvai Leumi], (Jerusalem: Klausner Institute, 1965), [Hebrew].

10. Shapiro, *Ha-Demokratia be-Israel*, pp. 170–171.

11. D. Weinreib, *Ha-Dor ha-Sheni ve-Darko ha-Miktzoit* [The second generation and its professional career patterns], *Metzuda* 7 (1954): 319, [Hebrew].

12. Socialist Youth Papers in Sharett Archive, File No. 1.

13. The 11th National Council of *Ha-Noar ha-Oved*, 4/3.32, *ha-Noar ha-Oved* Papers, *Labor Archive*, File No. 9.

14. *Sefer Ha-Palmach* [The book of the Palmach] (Tel Aviv: Hakibbutz Hameuchad 1957) vol. 1, pp. 62–63, [Hebrew].

15. Shapiro, *Ha-Democratia be-Israel*, p. 180.

16. Danny Zamir, *Aloufim ve-Politika be-Israel* [Generals and politics in Israel] Unpublished manuscript, 1977, [Hebrew].

17. Yehiam Weitz, *Michtavim* [Letters], (Tel Aviv: Am Oved, 1968), p. 217. [Hebrew].

18. Yehuda Bauer, *Diplomatia ve-Machteret be-Mediniut ha-Tzionit 1939–1945* (Diplomacy and the underground in Zionist policy, 1939–1945), (Tel Aviv: Sifriat Hapoalim, 1966), pp. 256–60, [Hebrew].

19. Dan Horowitz and Moshe Lissak, *The Origin of Israeli Polity* (Chicago: University of Chicago Press, 1978).

20. *Sefer ha-Palmach*, vol. 2, pp. 971–1009.

21. Shapiro, *Ha-Demokratia be-Israel*, pp. 164–65.

22. Yossie Beilin, *Ma'avak Bein Yechidot Dor be-Irgun Politi* [The conflict between generation units in a political organization] Master's thesis, Department of Political Science, Tel Aviv University, 1976; Peter Medding, *Mapai in Israel* (Cambridge: Cambridge University Press, 1972), pp. 246–85.

23. Medding, *Mapai in Israel*, p. 282.

24. I am indebted to my colleague Dr. Israel Sheffer for bringing this point to my attention.

25. Riley, Johnson, and Foner, *Aging and Society*, vol. 3, pp. 146; 445–46.

# 15

# Ethnicity and Legitimation in Contemporary Israel

## Erik Cohen

The principles of 'Absorption of Immigrants' (*Klitat ha'Aliyah*) and 'Ingathering of Exiles' (*Mizug ha'Galuyoth*), which informed the attitudes and actions of the Israeli institutions dealing with the new immigrants during the period of mass immigration, drew their justification from some of the basic value premises of political Zionism. The pioneering-socialist establishment, which dominated the *Yishuv* during the British Mandate and the first three decades of the existence of the State of Israel, employed these principles so as to achieve a *de facto* 'symbolic domination'[1] over the mass of immigrants streaming into the country in the late 1940s and early 1950s from Eastern Europe, the Middle East and North Africa. Such domination was, at the time, justified by the claim that it was a necessary precondition of 'absorption' and 'integration'; it was at least passively acquiesced to by the immigrants themselves. The leadership and staff of the absorbing institutions was composed primarily of veteran Israelis, most of whom were *Ashkenazi* Jews; but it also included some Oriental Jews, who were, in terms of their value orientations, attitudes and behavior, often indistinguishable from

An earlier version of this essay was presented to the seminar on 'Rethinking Israeli Sociology' at the Department of Sociology and Social Anthropology, Hebrew University of Jerusalem, in 1982. Thanks are due to S.N. Eisenstadt and B. Kimmerling for their helpful comments.
P. Rabinow, *Symbolic Domination: Cultural Form and Historical Change in Morocco*, Chicago (Univ. of Chicago Press) 1975.

the *Ashkenazim*. In the early stages of absorption of the mass immigration, these old-timers formed a distinct status group, faced by a motley of immigrants from different countries, all of whom were basically on an even footing.

The pace of 'absorption' and 'integration' of the various groups of immigrants, however, was not the same. The majority of European immigrants passed the process more quickly and successfully than those from the Middle Eastern and, particularly, North African countries; they generally identified with, and eventually joined, the veteran establishment. The fundamental division of the Jewish society in Israel thus gradually shifted from old-timers/newcomers to *Ashkenazim*-Orientals,[2] although within each sector marked distinctions of seniority (*vetek*) were preserved for a long time to come. The public at large and many researchers concluded that the absorption and integration of a sizable portion of Oriental – and especially North African – immigrants 'did not succeed'.[3] The economic, educational and power gap between the two categories remained remarkably persistent over a period of about thirty years.[4] While earlier Israeli sociology and historiography tended to ascribe the gap mainly to cultural factors, inherent in the background of the Oriental immigrants, a more recent 'revisionist' interpretation ascribes it to structural factors inherent in a situation in which a powerful elite 'absorbs' a mass of powerless immigrants.[5] The principles of 'absorption' and 'integration' are interpreted as an ideology which has permitted the exploitation of the immigrants, helped to perpetuate it, and – as they themselves internalized it – created a 'false consciousness' which led them to submit willingly to their predicament.

I leave open the question of interpretation of the period of mass immigration and of its consequences.[6] For my purposes,

[2]  Such a shift was clearly discernible in the early 1960s in the development towns. See e.g., E. Cohen, 'Development Towns: The Social Dynamics of "Planted" Urban Communities in Israel', in S.N. Eisenstadt *et. al.* (eds.), *Integration and Development in Israel*, Jerusalem (Israel Universities Press) 1970, pp. 605–6.

[3]  L. Weller, *Sociology in Israel*, Westport, Conn. (Greenwood Press) 1974, pp. 45–46.

[4]  The literature comparing the *Ashkenazi* and Oriental Jews on various levels over time agrees on the fact that considerable gaps prevail in all areas, even if authors differ in their interpretations. See particularly, Y. Peres, *Ethnic Relations in Israel* (Hebrew), Tel-Aviv (*Sifriat Hapoalim* and Tel-Aviv University) 1976, Ch. 4, pp. 83–134; S. Smooha, *Israel: Pluralism and Conflict*, London (Routledge and Kegan Paul) 1978; and the most recent publication on the subject, J. Bernstein and A. Antonovski, 'The Integration of Ethnic Groups in Israel', *Jewish Journal of Sociology*, 23(1), 1981, pp. 5–23.

[5]  See particularly, S. Smooha, *op. cit.*, and for a more radical version, S. Swirsky, *Lo Nechshalim ella Menuchshalim* (Orientals and *Ashkenazim* in Israel), Haifa (*Machbarot LeMechkar u'le-Bikoret*) 1981, and D. Bernstein and S. Swirsky, 'The Rapid Economic Development of Israel and the Emergence of the Ethnic Division of Labour', *British Journal of Sociology*, 23(1), 1982, pp. 64–85.

[6]  The period of mass immigration is currently under study by Professor M. Lissak at the Department of Sociology and Social Anthropology, the Hebrew University of Jerusalem.

however, it is important to note that the 'revisionist' approach resembles, and perhaps also reflects, the resentment of and animosity towards the veteran establishment and the ideology it represented, presently quite widespread among broad sectors of Oriental and particularly North African Jews in Israel. This indicates a trend towards some far-reaching changes in the ethnic consciousness of this Jewry, which, in turn, has some important implications for the future legitimation of the State of Israel. To understand this trend, we have to examine the value premises of political Zionism, their translation into practice and their implications for the Oriental immigrants to Israel.

### Tensions in the Value Premises

One of the salient features of political Zionism is that it purported to be not merely a 'nationalist' ideology, but strove to integrate two, in principle conflicting, value premises: the collective particularism of Jewish aspirations to an independent national state, and the universalism of modern Western civilization. The Jewish state was to be an enlightened one, in which the secular values of freedom, justice and equality for all citizens without difference of race, nationality or religion would be fully realized; though a national state, it was to be a fully democratic one, in which universalistic principles would govern the relations between all citizens. In the high expectations of Zionist idealists, it was to be an ideal state, a 'Light Unto the Nations'.[7]

Both sets of premises, the particularistic and the universalistic ones, became fundamental components of the legitimation of the State of Israel. In political practice, however, they necessarily clashed. One of the most acute conflicts between them emerged in an area which received relatively little consideration by the ideologues of political Zionism: the conduct of the state towards its Arab subjects. Owing to the imposition of a military government and other complications following the 1948 War of Independence, it took the Arabs of Israel many years to attain the status of formal civil equality; however, the problem of their status in the new state did not provoke a national political crisis, and by 1967 the ruling Jewish establishment evolved a policy based on the apparently technical, but in fact poignantly political concept of 'minority' which apparently reconciled the conflict between the particularistic and universalistic premises on which the state was established: while the Arabs were left free not to

---

[7]  Cf. G. Shaked's comment in his review of S. Friedlander's recent autobiography: 'Friedlander ... interprets the State of Israel as a sort of allegory of humanity's woeful course ... in and of itself the state is not enough for him and merits legitimation only if it fulfills a universal mission, something on the order of being a Light unto the Nations'. (G. Shaked, 'No Other Place', *The Jerusalem Quarterly*, No. 16, 1980, p. 85).

identify with the symbols of the Jewish state, they were asked to fulfill their civic duties and in return enjoy full civil liberties. They were expected to be able to lend allegiance to the state, precisely owing to the universalistic component in its basic make-up, while remaining neutral towards the particularistic Jewish component.

With the occupation of the Arab territories on the West Bank, the Gaza Strip and Golan Heights in the 1967 Six-Day War, the problem was seriously aggravated. Most politicians realized that the precarious balance between the universalistic and the particularistic components in Israel's legitimation could not be maintained if the occupied territories were formally annexed. A million and a half Arabs cannot be defined merely as a 'minority', and Israel would face the stark choice of either becoming a *de facto*, bi-national state, and thus forego its particular Jewish national character, or of preserving that character, at the cost of abrogation of its democratic nature, by denying the additional Arabs full civil rights and participation. The problem found a provisory solution in the introduction of a deliberately liberal permanently-temporary policy of 'enlightened occupation', which, however, became less liberal and less enlightened as it dragged on, provoking growing dissatisfaction and desperation among the occupied population.

The occupation thus exacerbated the tensions between the particularistic and universalistic premises of Zionism; in the ensuing polarization of public opinion in Israel, which cut across the established political parties, the particularistic tendency gradually gained the upper hand. This could be seen principally, in the growing conviction among many Jewish citizens that the whole of biblical *Eretz Israel* belonged to the Jews, to the exclusion of the rights of others; in the settlement of a growing number of Jews in the occupied areas; and in the hardening of the opposition to the return of those areas to Arab sovereignty.

The experience of shock and frustration following the Yom Kippur War of 1973 significantly reinforced the trend towards traditionalistic nationalism and away from the universalistic premises of Zionism; this embraced wide strata of the Jewish population, including, for different reasons, members of the established middle class, marginal Orientals and recent immigrants from the Soviet Union and the United States.[8] Concomitantly, a return to traditional Jewish symbols occurred among broad segments of the younger, Israeli-born *Ashkenazi*

---

[8]  With respect to American Jews, this point is saliently illustrated in a recent paper by K.A. Avruch, 'On the "Traditionalism" of Social Identity: American Immigrants to Israel', *Ethos*, 10(2), 1982, pp. 95–116. Avruch emphasizes that the identity of *olim* from the US undergoes traditionalization, expressed in a shift of emphasis from civil to primordial attachments; the principal expression of this shift is their conception of Israel as a 'family' or a moral community 'united by ties of blood' (p. 110).

generation, finding its fullest expression in a return of many to orthodox religion; complementary to these developments, there emerged an activist and militant nationalism among the previously predominantly dovish national religious youth, which found its most salient expression in the *Gush Emunim* movement.[9]

Another expression of the new nationalism is the change in the climate of political opinion which was one factor leading to the fall of the Alignment and the ascendence of the *Likud* in the 1977 elections; it now becomes increasingly clear that this was not a merely temporary political reversal, but an expression of a more fundamental change in the political orientation of broad strata of Israeli society towards a stronger emphasis on nationalistic values and away from the premises of the older pioneering-socialist ideology.

While the political change did not pose a serious threat to the democratic character of Israel within its pre-1967 boundaries, it certainly predisposed many Israelis to turn a blind eye to the hardening of the military rule in the occupied areas after the assumption of power by the Begin government.

The shift of emphasis towards the particularistic components of the Zionist ideology, which had already begun under the pre-1973 Alignment government, thus intensified dramatically in recent years. This shift, in turn, created a more comfortable background against which the Oriental Jews could reassert their ethnicity and their changing attitude to the nature of the State of Israel.

*'Absorption of Immigrants' and the Oriental Jews*

The conflict between the universalistic and particularistic components of the Zionist ideology found one of its most salient expressions in the controversy on the principles and practice of the so-called 'Absorption of Immigrants'. During the period of mass immigration in the early years of statehood, large numbers of immigrants reached the country without much prior ideological preparation. The absorbing institutions, reflecting the basic ideological premises of pioneering-socialist Zionism, conceived of 'absorption' not merely in specific technical terms – i.e., as assistance to the immigrants to perform autonomously basic occupational, civic, educational or cultural roles; rather, they conceived of it in broad ideological terms, as a complete re-education or re-socialization of the newcomer, who would in the process become a 'new man': in its most fundamental, secular-

[9]   See, e.g., K.A. Avruch, 'Gush Emunim: Religion and Ideology in Israel', *Middle East Review*, 11(2), 1979, pp. 26–31; Tz. Ra'anan, *Gush Emunim*, Tel-Aviv (*Sifriat Hapoalim*) (In Hebrew) 1980; J. O'Dea, '*Gush Emunim*: Roots and Ambiguities', *Forum*, no. 25, 1976, pp. 39–50.

religious sense, immigration was meant to be a spiritual 'ascension' (the literal meaning of *aliyah*) and absorption – a 're-birth'. Such a radical change of the individual in fact meant that he was expected to 'switch worlds',[10] and internalize a complete-ly new scale of values, including both the modern nationalistic as well as democratic ones on which the legitimation of the state and the national consensus were to be founded.

The re-orientation of the new immigrants' attitudes and behavior in the light of these values was the principal criterion according to which their 'absorption' had to be judged; on it were said to hinge their eventual acceptance and full participation in the new society. In the name of these same values, the immigrants were asked to forsake their past, including their particular diaspora values, attitudes and traditions. The Oriental immigrants were asked to adopt European culture; their own ethnic cultural heritages were denigrated as contemptible products of diaspora life, or as retrograde superstitions, unworthy of the new, modern Israeli. Veteran Israelis frequently denied that Oriental immigrant groups, such as the Moroccans, even possessed any culture at all.[11]

It is easy to see how such an approach – whether motivated by sincerely held beliefs or by covert interests – contained the seeds of a future controversy about the period of mass immigration. For this ideology, perhaps unintentionally, fortified and lent legitimacy to the complete ascendancy of the largely *Ashkenazi*, veteran establishment over the masses of new immigrants. That establishment wielded all the power and monopolized all the resources, material and symbolic; by inculcating its ideology into the immigrants, it moved them to consent, at least initially, to the denial of status to which they have been subjected and to their virtual reduction to the level of minors – i.e., people lacking an independent status and personal autonomy in the new situation. This state of affairs permitted an abuse of power on the part of the veteran functionaries, who often practiced a double standard – preaching universalistic criteria in the distribution of benefits and positions, but actually giving preference (*protektzia*) to their relatives, acquaintances or members of their own ethnic group, whether on their own initiative or in the wake of urgent demands made upon them by the needy immigrants. In any case, such double standards soon undermined the moral authority of these functionaries in the eyes of those immigrants – mostly of Oriental origin – who did not enjoy the protection and assistance of powerful patrons.

[10] P. Berger and T. Luckmann, *The Social Construction of Reality*, Harmondsworth (Penguin) 1966, p. 144.

[11] For the complaint that Israel is a Europocentric society, see N. Rejwan, 'The Two Israels: A Study in Europocentrism', *Judaism*, 16(1), 1967, pp. 97-108; for a more radical view, see M. Selzer, *The Aryanization of the Jewish State*, New York (Black Star Publn.) 1967.

Nominally, the new demands were made equally on all the immigrants, whether *Ashkenazi* or Oriental. However, in practice, the *Ashkenazi* immigrants, who were by background better prepared for the demands of the new situation and had better connections with the old-timers, generally succeeded in overcoming relatively easily and quickly the first stages of 'absorption', and established themselves independently in the new society. The Oriental immigrants were less successful in such efforts and remained dependent – far longer and in greater numbers – upon the absorbing institutions.

Initially, the Orientals in general consented – largely passively – to the requirement to relinquish most of their traditional culture and to confine their cultural life mainly to the sphere of religion, in which particularistic ethnic expressions were still tolerated. The submission was done in the belief – at times religious – that whatever had been appropriate for life in the diaspora is inappropriate or irrelevant for the new life in Israel. The submission was also supported by the hope that it would lead to the eventual acquisition of full and equal membership status and participation in the new society. This process, however, proceeded only slowly and partially, as many of the immigrants in fact failed – for whatever reason – to become satisfactorily 'absorbed'. And, as their sense of failure grew, their readiness to submit to the demands made upon them declined, though their resentment remained generally vague and politically or ideologically unarticulated for many years.

Here we come to the crux of the matter: the veteran, mainly *Ashkenazi* establishment, announced unequivocally that all Jews immigrating to Israel are to become full-fledged members of the new society, provided, however, that they successfully pass the process of 'absorption'. All immigrants, including the Oriental Jews from the most remote and 'retrograde' regions, were thus eligible for membership status. Formal membership, indeed, was quickly achieved: for example, all immigrants were given the right to vote a mere six months after their arrival. Informal status recognition and acceptance, however, was another matter. The criteria, based as they were on the basic but conflicting values of pioneering Zionism, frequently remained vague; and their application was the prerogative of the old-timers, who thus remained 'gate-keepers', deciding who was acceptable and who would remain more or less permanently marginal.

Again, the question if and to what extend these criteria were misapplied to the detriment of the Oriental Jews – i.e., whether there was deliberate discrimination against them, to ensure the preservation of power in the hands of the veteran *Ashkenazi* establishment – is a controversial one, but need not concern us here. For even if we grant that there was no deliberate discrimination, the fact remains that wide sectors of the Oriental

Jews were for a long time considered incompletely absorbed and judged incompetent to perform central roles in the emergent society. They were labelled 'backward', and relegated to a more or less marginal position in most spheres of life. Their marginality found expression not only in a generally lower status and more limited life-chances in comparison with the *Ashkenazim*, but also in their lesser participation in roles of national significance and lack of express symbolic recognition of their contribution to the realization of central national goals. Thus, for example, their participation in the Israel Defense Forces was peripheral in comparison with that of the veteran *Ashkenazim* and their sons, who predominated in elite units.[12] The new immigrant towns which were settled predominantly, but not exclusively, by Oriental Jews, (the so-called 'development towns'[13]) were for a long time denied symbolic recognition as 'pioneering' settlements, and never achieved the prestige of the early agricultural settlements.[14] The marginal status of Oriental Jews was inadvertently expressed in the continuing reference to them, even after a quarter of a century, as 'new immigrants', and to their settlements as 'immigrant settlements' – a poignant symbolization of the widely shared old-timer conviction that the Oriental Jews did not accomplish successfully the *rite de passage* into full membership of Israeli society and remained, socially, adolescents for life.

Gradually many Oriental Jews made individually the transition into Israeli society. The majority are at present economically well established. Whole sectors of the economy, particularly in the trades, technical services and small businesses are presently dominated by Jews of Oriental origin. However, the overall socio-economic gap between *Ashkenazi* and Oriental Jews changed little and appears lately even to have widened.[15] At the bottom of the status hierarchy, an Oriental Jewish ethno-class, commonly referred to as the 'Second Israel', of low socio-economic as well as ethnic standing, emerged;[16] a considerable portion of this ethno-class consists of second-generation Orien-

---

[12] D. Horowitz and B. Kimmerling, e.g., report that 'In... elite units, the number of members of *kibbutzim* and *moshavim* ... and of high-school graduates who are sons of old-timers and in particular of members of the pioneering elite groups is. far greater than the relative representation of these segments in the population', ('Some Social Implications of Military Service and the Reserve System in Israel', *Archives Européennes de Sociologie*, 15(2), 1974, p. 268).

[13] See E. Cohen, 'Development Towns', *op.cit.*

[14] See e.g., E. Cohen, 'The City in Zionist Ideology', *The Jerusalem Quarterly*, No. 4, 1977, pp. 126–144.

[15] On the gap see: Y. Peres, *op.cit.*, Ch. 4, pp. 83–134. In a more recent paper, Bernstein and Antonovski (*op.cit.*, p. 22) argue that there are signs '...that the achievements in closing the [ethnic] gap in earlier years may have come to a halt and in some cases may have been reversed since the early or mid-1970s'.

[16] D. Weintraub and V. Kraus, *Social Differentiation and Locality of Residence: Spatial Distribution, Composition and Stratification in Israel*, Working Paper, Settlement Study Center, Rehovot, 1981.

tals. Its precise size and the gravity of the socio-economic gap are hard to estimate, since the accepted indicators do not always tell the whole story, particularly in the economic sphere. Many Orientals of both the first and the second generation entered the interstices of the modernizing Israeli economy, forming a little-researched but important 'informal sector',[17] integrated with, but distinct from, the 'formal' sector of the economy. Such individuals advanced economically, often in semi-legitimate ways, much beyond what emerges from the official statistics. Others became politically active, some building spectacular careers leading right to the centers of power. But even if all this is granted, sharp differences persisted in all important areas of Israeli life; ethnicity remained a potent political issue, refuting the optimistic prognoses of some Israeli sociologists of the 1960s that 'the business of ethnicity is finished',[18] and that a transition from political to cultural ethnicity is taking place among Israeli Jews.

Oriental Jewish ethnicity, far from disappearing or becoming nostalgically 'museumized' through folkloristic preservation of 'interesting' and 'colorful' old customs, made a surprising political comeback in the early 1970s in the Black Panther movement.[19] This was the first significant protest movement of Oriental Jewish youth which challenged the premises of the dominant ideology concerning the 'absorption' of immigrants, emphasized the particular Oriental or *Sephardi* Jewish values and identity, and blamed the establishment's policy for the predicament of disadvantaged or 'backward' Oriental youths. Though the movement gradually vanished into insignificance, ethnic resentment, which continued to simmer beneath the surface during the difficult years after the 1973 October War, recently made a forceful comeback in Israeli politics, challenging the whole ideology of 'absorption of immigrants', and, at a more radical level, the fundamental values legitimizing the state. Its most salient expression was the formation, in 1980, of the distinctly ethnic *Tami* Party, headed by Aharon Abu-Hatzeira, scion

[17] The informal sector is composed of enterprises, occupations and types of employment which operate outside the formally recognized framework of the economy; it encompasses such activities as peddling, hawking, maintaining of unlicensed kiosks and steak-stalls, informal building contracting and subcontracting, etc. Many such activities remain unrecognized by the authorities, and are neither registered nor taxed. A study of these activities is presently under way at the Dept. of Sociology and Social Anthropology, Tel-Aviv University, under the supervision of Prof. E. Ya'ar.

[18] Sh. Deshen, '"The Business of Ethnicity is Finished!"?: The Ethnic Factor in a Local Election Campaign', in A. Arian (ed.), *The Elections in Israel, 1969*, Jerusalem (Jerusalem Academic Press) 1972, pp. 278–302; see also, Sh. Deshen, 'Political Ethnicity and Cultural Ethnicity in Israel During the 1970s', in A. Cohen (ed.), *Urban Ethnicity*, London (Tavistock) 1974, pp. 281–309.

[19] See E. Cohen, 'The Black Panthers and Israeli Society', *Jewish Journal of Sociology*, 14(1), 1972, pp. 93–109; Y. Peres, *op. cit*, Ch. 6, pp. 160–175; S. Smooha, 'Black Panthers – the Ethnic Dilemma', *Society*, 9(7), 1972, pp. 31–6.

of one of the most illustrious North African Jewish families, ex-mayor of Ramle and a minister in Begin's cabinet.

The re-emergence of the ethnic issue in Israeli politics was effected by a confluence between the political aspirations of the younger Oriental elite and the resentments of many disgruntled second-generation Oriental youths. The new Oriental leadership openly articulated the rejection by many Oriental youths of the accepted principles of the ideology of 'absorption of immigrants', according to which they appeared to stand no realistic chance of achieving fully recognized status and full participation in the wider society. They refused to accept the premise that, in order to become Israelis, they ought first to become Westernized. This resentment coincided with the wounded pride of the Oriental Jewish elite and with the threat which Europeanization posed to their identity. Their rejection of the universalistic component of the Zionist ideology, though stemming from quite different motives, converged with the growingly particularistic outlook in other sectors of Jewish society; in the post-October War period, these converging trends posed a powerful challenge to the basic legitimation of the state.

*The Challenge of the New Ethnicity*

The principal objection of the new ethnicity against the old, *Ashkenazi*-dominated establishment is that the ideology of 'absorption of immigrants' deculturated the Oriental Jews, even as they were precluded from full participation in the center of Israeli society, and thus engendered the emergence of a degraded and marginal 'second Israel'. The proposed remedy to this state of affairs consists of a radical redefinition of the status and role of Oriental Jews in the society, and, by extension, of the basic character of the state itself. The ideology of 'absorption of immigrants', according to which re-socialization is a basic precondition of full participation, is rejected in principle; it came to be seen not as an instrument to forge a new nation, but as a means to deny the Oriental Jews their heritage, as an expedient to safeguard the dominant position of the veteran *Ashkenazi* establishment, and the continued social, economic and political subordination to it of the Oriental 'new immigrant' Jews. It is denied that, in order to be Israelis, the Oriental Jews should first uncritically embrace Western values and abandon and denigrate their own culture. By implication, the right of the establishment to spell out the criteria of 'absorption' and to control access to the societal center is denied. It is claimed that Oriental Jews are entitled to gain such access – by sheer virtue of being Jews, and not because of some particular process of absorption and re-socialization. Thereby, however, the nature of the center itself is subtly, and perhaps inadvertently, redefined.

It is important to stress that even this new perspective does not amount to a demand for Oriental Jewish separatism; rather it is an attempt to redefine the criteria of access to full participation in the Jewish national collective and to deny the *Ashkenazi* Jews a monopoly over those criteria. While on the one hand emphasizing cultural pluralism – the basic equality of the many cultures of Jews from various origins – on the other hand, the new ethnicity emphasizes the common elements which traditionally unite all Jews and by virtue of which they enjoy the right to participate in the Israeli national community. In the past, merely to be Jewish was a necessary precondition for future participation, but in itself, it was not enough – one had also first to be 'absorbed'. Now mere Jewishness, rather than the internalization of any particular Zionist or 'Israeli' values, attitudes and patterns of behavior, becomes sufficient for participation. The saliency of the traditional, religious components in the Jewish national identity has been substantially heightened. Consequently, the various Jewish ethnic traditions, instead of something to be ashamed of and discarded, now become symbols of the rightful, unmitigated participation in Jewish nationhood. For, though these traditions are apparently divisive, it is emphasized that they are all equally Jewish. Under these circumstances, the Jewish religion, in all its particular manifestations, gains in importance as a unifying bond.

Beyond this, however, attempts are also made to extend the scope of symbols and landmarks of Israel's civil religion,[20] by incorporating into it elements from the history of Oriental Jewry; thus, e.g., the suffering of Oriental Jews at the hands of the Arabs are interpreted as a parallel to the Holocaust of European Jewry; and the contribution of Oriental Jews to the Zionist enterprise is presented as a counterpart to the well-known contributions of the *Ashkenazi* Jews. Appeals are constantly made to expand the teaching of the history of Oriental Jewish communities in Israeli schools. More attention is also paid to the literary, artistic and musical heritage of Oriental Jewry.[21] While the main effort of the new ethnic ideology is thus to establish Oriental Jewry as an equal but distinct partner with the *Ashkenazim* within the common frame of the Jewish nation, some of the more radical ethnics discard such pluralism as too moderate and advocate the formation of a new establishment, dominated by the Oriental Jews, and a new social center, based primarily on their culture, which will eventually supersede the present *Ashkenazi*-dominated establishment and the Western-oriented center.[22] The *Ashkenazim*

[20]  Cf. Ch. S. Liebman, 'Religion and Political Integration in Israel', *Jewish Journal of Sociology*, 17, 1975, pp. 17–27 and Ch. S. Liebman and E. Don-Yehiya, 'Israel's Civil Religion', *The Jerusalem Quarterly*, No. 23, 1982, pp. 57–69.

[21]  Cf. A. Shiloah and E. Cohen, 'The Dynamics of Change in Jewish Oriental Ethnic Music in Israel', *Ethnomusicology* (forthcoming, 1983).

[22]  Demands to this effect were voiced recently in the public debate accompanying the discharge of the *Ashkenazi* director of the National Insurance Institute, R.

would, under such circumstances, become a political and cultural minority, and Israel an essentially Oriental country. While such aims are presently shared by only a minority of Oriental Jewish intellectuals, they are indicative of prospective future trends and strains in Israeli society.

## Changing Patterns of Legitimation

The emergence of a new Oriental ethnicity has to be seen within the broader context of ideological change in Israel. This change is itself a consequence of the failure of the veteran Israeli establishment to live up to, maintain and realize the original Zionist synthesis: the creation of a modern, secular, Western, democratic but national Jewish state. While the aspired synthesis would possibly fail in any case, owing to the incongruence between its universalistic and particularistic components, the failure was expedited by the conditions which prevailed after the 1967, and especially the 1973 wars. The general shift towards particularistic, nationalistic or orthodox religious values can be at least partly explained by the disenchantment of wide strata of Israeli society – not all Orientals – with the basic premises of pioneering-socialist Zionism. The shift, on the one hand, weakened the moral strength of the argument that only 'well-absorbed' Jews are entitled to full participation in the social center. On the other hand, it facilitated an unexpected ideological rapprochement between some segments of the established *Ashkenazi* sector and the herefore marginal strata of Oriental Jewry: the new Oriental ethnicity turned out to be largely congruent with the wider trends of ideological re-orientation, even if its origins are of a very different nature: though it dwells upon its own particularism, it also claims to reflect widely shared particularistic Jewish values, and thus dovetails with the nationalistic and neo-traditional trends among *Ashkenazi* Jews. The emergent congruence between the outlook of such diverse social strata endowed Israeli politics and ideology with a novel twist. In politics, the congruence helped to produce an unexpected coalition of Orientals and *Ashkenazim* which adopted Begin as their charismatic leader and brought the *Likud* to power. In ideology, the shift was more subtle but is highly significant for the long run: it represents a retreat from the modern, universalistic component in the legitimation of the state, towards an almost exclusive emphasis of the particularistic component, i.e., Jewish nationalism. Israel is thus well on its way to becoming another merely nationalistic state, and to losing its 'enlightened' character, which was in the past construed as the 'redeeming'

---

Roter, and the appointment of a North African by the minister in charge of the Institute, who belongs to the *Tami* party; see e.g., the short piece entitled 'Salamat Roter' by the Jerusalem journalist Bardugo in *Kol Yerushalayim* of May 21, 1982 (in Hebrew).

quality of Zionism, and served as the basis of Israel's moral claims in the world.

The retreat to sheer nationalism is thus, to a large extent, a consequence of the failure of the Zionist program. Israel is, in a symbolic sense, undergoing 'de-modernization'. But this very process makes the claim of the new Oriental ethnicity for fully recognized status and full social participation on its own terms more legitimate and acceptable than it would have been in the past.

The shift to neo-traditional Jewish nationalism expresses the disappointment of many Israeli Jews with the state, in which such high hopes were placed upon its establishment. It is a throwback among both *Ashkenazi* and Oriental Jews, to an older symbolic level anchored in the still-farther past, which pioneering-socialist Zionism strove to supersede. Seen in this light, it is the peculiar Israeli variety of the effort to come to grips with the crisis of modernity, which most Western and developing societies are currently experiencing.

This regression to an older, pre-immigration symbolic level has many concrete manifestations on the contemporary cultural scene in Israel. One of its most poignant and interesting expressions among the Oriental and particularly North African Jews, is the revival of the cults of their diaspora saints and of the festivals (*hiluloth*) at the tombs and sites consecrated to these saints.[23] Significantly, these cults experienced a revival only many years after the immigration of their adherents, and today enjoy popularity not only among the older generation, but also among their Israeli-born progeny. While their re-emergence is not yet completely understood, one explanation for it ties up with our principal theme: when the immigrants came to Israel, the power of the Holy Land to which they 'ascended' was deemed to supersede that of their diaspora saints. The contempt and ridicule of 'religious superstitions' which they encountered on the part of the old-timers upon arrival, and to which, for a while at least, they submitted, helped to suppress the cults of the saints. However, the saints were not completely forgotten. With the frustration of the high hopes, both religious and secular, engendered by immigration and with the failure of many North African immigrants to become fully absorbed and accepted in the new society, old and young turned for succor to their traditional saints, whose tombs and sanctuaries often miraculously re-emerged at different locations of North African settlement in Israel, and particularly in the development towns. This re-emergence can be interpreted as a sign of a sym-

---

[23]    See e.g., Sh. Deshen, 'The *Hiluloth* of Tunisian Immigrants', in M. Shokeid and Sh. Deshen (eds.), *The Generation of Transition*, Jerusalem (Yad Yitzhak Ben-Zvi) 1977, pp. 110–121 (Hebrew); and I. Ben-Ami: 'Folk Veneration of Saints Among the Moroccan Jews', in S. Morag *et. al.* (ed.), *Studies in Judaism and Islam*, Jerusalem (Magnes) 1981, pp. 283–344.

bolic 'diasporization' of Israel: the country in its present state loses much of its precedence and special status as the Holy Land and universal center, and is increasingly seen as just another state, though governed by Jews. The spiritual life of the North African Jews is consequently re-assimilated to that which has characterized its diaspora past.

The re-orientation of Oriental Jews to Israel leads to a re-alignment of identities: the distance which in the past separated those Jews who 'ascended' to Israel and those who remained in the diaspora is reduced – and the ethnic Jewish bond is reaffirmed over the previous separation. The crisis of Zionism also helped to bridge the distance which existed in the past between the Oriental Jews and their orthodox *Ashkenazi* compatriots. Previously exclusively *Ashkenazi* political parties, such as *Agudat Israel*, now enjoy growing support among Oriental Jews. More generally, as the traditional element in the identity of Israeli Jews gained strength, religion increased in importance as a bond between all Jews, and as a symbol of the changing societal center. While the new ethnicity thus creates a deepening chasm between parts of the Oriental community and the secular veteran representatives of the pioneering-socialist Zionism which was dominant in the past, it also forges new ties between Oriental and *Ashkenazi* Jews.

I conclude on a somewhat pessimistic note. The foregoing analysis demonstrated that the present crisis of Zionism made it easier for Israel's Oriental Jews to re-assert their ethnic identity while claiming acceptance for themselves and their traditions by the wider Jewish society. However, a successful realization of their aims may significantly change the nature of Israeli society. In a sense, an Israel dominated by neo-traditional Jewish values will eventually become a 'Middle Eastern' country – an ironic realization of a hope which some Westernized Jews conceived in a quite different sense. The antagonism between Israel and its neighbors, and between Jews and Arabs within Israel, however, will be further exacerbated and perhaps even hopelessly extended by that change – because the exclusion of the universalistic component of Zionism from the values legitimizing the state will do away with a necessary precondition for both an ultimate accommodation with the Palestinians, as well as the full realization and future assurance of the civil rights of Israeli Arabs.

# 16

# Existing and Alternative Policy towards the Arabs in Israel

## Sammy Smooha

Today many countries are deeply split along cultural, ethnic or racial lines. Minorities that are culturally distinctive, living in a separate community and rejecting the dominant basic ideology, constitute a potential source for disruptive conflicts. Violent strife does in fact occur frequently. The question then arises as to what policies these states adopt to keep internal tranquillity.

### Theoretical framework

It is possible to classify policies towards minorities in terms of the three major ways to achieve stability in pluralistic societies. These are consensus-building, consociationalism and domination.

The policy of consensus-building is reflected in a sustained effort to do away with ethnic divisions, the weakening of primordial ties and the formation of common national culture and identity. The most important measures used to implement this option are the inculcation of shared core values, crosscutting affiliations and resource allocation according to merit. Based on the uni-cultural, uni-national ideal of the nation-state, the consensus-building policy usually takes the form of assimilation, either voluntary or imposed. Typical examples are the policies of Americanization and Russification as well as endeavours at nation-building by many new states (Eisenstadt and Stein, 1973).

In contrast, the policy of consociationalism intends to retain the ethnic division and to legitimize the ethnic cultures and identities. An attempt is made to secure political integration through crystallization of broad operative consensus, compromise in controversial issues while depoliticizing irreconcilable areas and cooperation among the ethnic elites. Rather than individual achievement, proportional group representation is practised to attain equal opportunity. Similarly, legal-cultural self-rule and sometimes territorial autonomy are granted to minorities instead of personal competition and ethnic integration. Consociationalism is carried out with considerable success in the Netherlands and Switzerland, with some headway in Canada and Belgium, but failed in Cyprus and Lebanon (Lijphart, 1977).

An alternative avenue to preserve social stability is via effective domination over the minority (Lustick, 1979). As in consociationalism, the ethnic division in culture, identity, organizations and resources is retained. However, ethnic stratification and cultural hegemony are institutionalized in lieu of consociational compromise and partnership. The majority dominates the state institutions, superimposes its culture, takes for itself a disproportionate share of resources and promotes its ethnic interests. It determines the living conditions of the minority and tends to disregard its needs. Domination relies on two mutually reinforcing mechanisms: *economic dependence* on the majority that deprives the minority of any independent economic base, and *political control* that prevents the minority from organizing itself independently and resisting the regime (van den Berghe, 1973: 965). While the minority's right to separate identity and institutions is acknowledged, institutional autonomy is withheld to avert cumulation of power. This method has proved itself with regard to blacks in the United States up until the 1960s, Catholics in Northern Ireland between the years 1921 and 1968, and the non-Amharic minority in Ethiopia for centuries. It has nevertheless failed in other periods and circumstances (e.g. the collapse of colonialism which was built upon domination).

None of these methods is universally effective for preserving internal peace. While domination is morally indefensible, it is not necessarily less efficient than consensual or consociational means. To cite but one example, South Africa has, for over a hundred years, been administering a growingly sophisticated, rigid system of domination over the non-white majority. Moreover, whenever these policies are successfully executed, they prevent social disorder but with differing costs and benefits for the minorities. In consensus-building, the minorities enjoy entering into the society, rights and power, but lose their identity. In consociationalism, they keep their separate existence, protect their interests and play a role in decision-making, but are trapped in a patchy stalemate. In domination, they are placed under control but safeguarded against persecution, bloodshed, deportation and chaos.

Reinforced by certain designs for policy analysis that are common today in the policy sciences (Greenstein and Polsby, 1975), this classification provides a handy framework for analysing policies and policy changes towards minorities. They should, however, be defined more broadly to consist of three major components (Lockard, 1975: 246–8). The 'manifest' component includes official resolutions, laws and regulations, whereas the 'latent' one contains informal discriminatory norms or practices. The third component is policy 'by default', i.e. the unwillingness to alter a policy that is ostensibly irrelevant to the minority but is in fact discriminatory (e.g. ignoring the unemployment problem although it mainly affects the minority). Comprehensive analysis of policy towards minorities requires, therefore, an examination of official and unofficial actions as well as inactions by dominant public bodies.

The existing policy

The question of Arab—Jewish relations in Israel, within its pre-1967 borders, is typical of many plural societies, i.e. accommodation between conflicting population sections. It is understandably experienced differently by Jews and Arabs. For the Jews the issue is primarily of what Rose (1971) in his study of Northern Ireland calls 'governing without consensus'. They regard themselves as an involuntary dominant majority who have to handle a dissident (i.e. dissenting from the unwritten state constitution of Zionism) and potentially disloyal minority, while remaining within the bounds of political democracy. Jewish suspicions are further augmented by feelings of insecurity and alienation in the broader Arab region. The Arabs, on the other hand, are an involuntary nondominant minority, which encounters the impasse of what de Tocqueville (1969: 250—4), in a classic treatise on the ante-bellum United States, identifies as the 'tyranny of the majority'. This is the inability to effect a radical change in their status in the face of an organized opposition of the majority.

Underlying the problematic status of Arabs in Israeli society are four factors that any public policy must come to terms with. The first is political democracy in which civil liberties and equal opportunities are supposedly granted to all. The second is the Jewish-Zionist character of the state, which casts different group statuses, with Jews being afforded preferential treatment and Arabs being regarded as outsiders. The third force of national security turns Arabs into a hostile minority, suspected of possible collaboration with the enemy. The last consideration concerns the features of the Arabs themselves as a small (14 per cent, excluding East Jerusalem), permanent, nonassimilating, westernizing, internally divided and socio-economically disadvantaged minority that is considerably vulnerable and manipulable. These four forces that shape Arab status constitute constraints and challenges for policies towards the Arabs.

The declared policy stresses political democracy as the decisive force and the attainment of equality and integration as the major objective. It is abundantly manifest in official statements. In the Declaration of Independence, Arabs were promised equality of social and political rights and full participation in Israeli society. Integration was a basic principle of all labour governments up until the changeover in May 1977: 'The policy of the Government of Israel will aim towards the complete integration of the minorities in Israel into all spheres of life in the State, while respecting their religious and cultural individuality' (Israel, Prime Minister's Office, 1977: 8). Prime Minister Begin spoke in this vein when presenting the Likud government: 'Jews and Arabs, Druzes and Circassians can live together in this country. They should live together in peace, with mutual respect and equal rights, in freedom and socio-economic progress' (Knesset Proceedings, 20 June 1977). In order to carry out the official policy of equality and integration, separate Arab departments operate in government offices, the Histadrut and major political parties. They officially aim to cater to the special needs of Arabs, to protect their rights, to help develop their settlements and expedite their participation in Israeli society.

The actual policy diverges, however, from the consensual or consociational spirit of the declared policy. It consists of quite different presuppositions, goals and means.[1]

*Presuppositions*

As a whole, the Jewish community in Palestine rejected the idea of a bi-national state and accepted the 1947 United Nations partition resolution that envisaged a Jewish state with an Arab minority. At the end of the 1948 war, Israel controlled a much bigger territory in which about 750,000 Arabs and 650,000 Jews lived in 1947. The mass exodus of Arabs and the mass immigration of Jews sharply reduced the Arab presence to a small minority. As a result, Israel was actually relieved of a large-scale minority problem and hence the top leadership and public at large did not develop an interest in the internal Arab question.

Moreover, the Arab question is considered temporary. While during the early years of the state the Arabs believed that Israel was ephemeral, many Jews expected Arabs to disappear so that they would not have to establish permanent relations with them (Lin, 1971: 313). Although both sides have become more realistic over the years, the idea that the Arab problem should be put in abeyance until the settlement of the Israeli–Arab conflict is ingrained. It exempts the authorities from a policy-making that will lead in the long run to peaceful Arab–Jewish coexistence and legitimizes present decisions that might shatter the chances of living together in the future. Lin, who was the chairman of the Arab Department of Labour Party until 1968, wrote: 'The general assumption was that all that should be done for the time being in this area till our relations with the Arab countries are made clear, is *to prevent fires or put them out*' (1971: 311). Toledano, the Prime Minister's Advisor on Arab Affairs between the years 1965 and 1976, said: 'as long as there is a state of war between Israel and the Arab states, there is no radical solution to the difficult issue of the Arab minority living in Israel. On the other hand, there is no doubt that it is possible to ease the situation and to hold it in check' (1975).

The idea that the Arab problem is transitory yet intractable has from the very beginning shaped the priorities in handling Arabs. The general guideline for decisions is the precedence of the Jewish-Zionist mission of the state and national security over political democracy. The Arab vulnerability makes it possible to rank Arab interest at the bottom with relative impunity. Policy-makers see Arabs as a threat and as an obstacle to the national goals of security, immigration, economic growth, settlement and population dispersion. Arabs also have to be contained in order to ensure the flow of their services to the dominant group.

Once these priorities are set, the authority for dealing with Arabs is delegated from the public to the regime. The Jewish public neither considers Arabs as part of the state nor does it perceive their problem as a national issue. Hence it grants the authorities a free hand in handling Arab affairs and renounces its right to intervene in policy-making. The gut feeling of the Jew in the street is that Arabs enjoy extra privileges, are exempted from duties and are afforded abundant educational and economic opportunities. It is also felt that Arabs, as a hostile minority, do not deserve such advantageous conditions, particularly when compared to the predicament of both Jews and Arabs in Arab countries.

The establishment itself has, nevertheless, neither the interest nor the time to deal with Arab matters. Since it has no positive expectations of them, such as Arabs becoming equal and active partners in Israeli society, it does not define this situation as a state concern that requires planning, allocation of resources and ongoing daily care. It is interested in localizing the problem in order to be free to attend to what are considered really important state affairs.

This attitude prompted an additional delegation of authority from the top decision-makers to the Arabists who head the Arab departments. These Jewish experts who have a knowledge of Arabic are  supposed to grasp the special needs of the Arab population and to intercede between the authorities and the Arabs. In fact, the existence of separate Arab departments of secondary rank is designed to keep the Arab issue permanently out of the policy-making agenda. Since the Arab departments were created as part of the arrangement for the delegation of authority, the Arabists' success in their duties is measured by their ability to preserve the status quo, to check the problem and to relieve the establishment and the general public from the necessity of responding to Arab needs. In addition, the separate frameworks for Arabs and Jews make it possible to practise a policy in the Jewish sector that differs from that in the Arab sector. They facilitate the use of double standards in education, housing, agriculture, regional development and other spheres.

For these reasons, the Arabists are not keen to propose innovative policies or to take risks in suggesting far-reaching changes. In order to usher in radical transformations, the active backing of the establishment and the general public must be gained. This would, nonetheless, amount to an infringement of the delegation of authority and the undermining of the status quo. The Arabists therefore prefer the strengthening of conservative forces in the Arab sector, compromises and piecemeal reforms.

*Goals*

According to the above conception of the Arab status in Israel, the existing policy is that of domination rather than consensus-building or consociationalism. The main objective is to institutionalize effective domination over Arabs for an unlimited period of time for the purpose both of averting the threat to Israel's national security and Jewish-Zionist character and of harnessing Arab resources on behalf of the Jewish majority. These are the general principles of the policy in reality that enjoy a broad consensus.

The more specific operative goals are four, each of which has two facets — achievement and avoidance:

1. *Loyal citizens.* In order to attain this goal, Arabs are afforded civil rights, including franchise and freedom of expression, organization and movement. Apart from laws which apply directly to the religious and cultural uniqueness of Arabs in Israel, the state endeavours to avoid any legal distinction between Arabs and Jews. For instance, even in the military service law there is no mention of national origin. In return for civil rights, Arabs are expected to maintain law and order.

Israel wishes to prevent the Arabs from becoming a security and political threat. Hostile Arab activity might entail espionage, sabotage, guerrilla warfare, the terrorizing of loyal Arabs, and political struggle internally or abroad, which is detrimental to Israel's international status (Alon, 1969: 332). In order to forestall such developments, Arabs are placed under surveillance — until 1966 openly by the ˙military government and since then by more subtle and covert means. Arabs (excluding Druzes) are also exempted from military service. Similarly, they are barred from sensitive places of employment so as to deny them access to confidential information. Their residence in separate settlements and quarters facilitates the ongoing security measures and effective control in the event of resistance with force. From the fulfilment of this specific goal, it is obvious that national security takes precedence over the egalitarian-democratic ethos.

2. *Minority members.* A suitable assessment of this specific goal requires a familiarity with some of the difficulties of its completion. It is not easy for Arabs to accept the reversal in their status from a numerical majority to a minority as a result of the creation of Israel. Yet although the Arabs became a minority in the state, they have remained a majority in the Middle East. It is also especially hard for Muslims, who constitute a majority among Arabs in Israel, to adapt to minority status. In addition, internal and external developments conducive to changing Arabs from a vulnerable ethnic minority to a powerful national minority are under way. These are serious obstacles in reconciling Arabs to a minority status in a Jewish-Zionist state. At the same time, the authorities want to prevent Arabs from becoming a strong force that might endanger Israel as a state with Jewish institutions, Jewish majority, preferred status given to Jewish citizens and the Zionist mission.

The threats against this supreme cause are many. The most salient are assimilation, biculturalism, institutional autonomy, state-wide leadership and regional majority.

a) *Prevention of assimilation.* The regime is heedful of reinforcing the Arab characteristics of Arabs in Israel as a powerful brake against assimilation. Arabs are accorded a right to separate identity. They are allowed to maintain separate institutions (such as schools, communications media and religious bodies) in order to preserve a separate existence. The religious marriage laws inhibit mixed marriages from evolving into acceptable social norms.

b) *Unilateral biculturalism.* Biculturalism means that individuals or institutions are bilingual and they adopt practices taken from both cultures. It has different meanings for Arabs and Jews. Although, as mentioned above, the establishment discourages Arabs' assimilation, it does undertake to infuse them with institutional and individual biculturalism. This is because biculturalism can ease their adaptation to life in Israel and diminish their alienation as an Arab minority in a Jewish-Zionist state.

On the other hand, biculturalism is viewed as inappropriate for the Jews. Institutional biculturalism might blur the Jewish nature of the state institutions, and individual biculturalism might weaken the hold against assimilation, a phenomenon which characterizes Jewish populations in industrialized countries the world over. Hence the establishment is diligent in scattering distinct 'Zionist culture' among Jews originating from different cultural backgrounds and in keeping them away from Arab–Jewish biculturalism.

c) *Denial of institutional autonomy.* Institutional autonomy means that Arabs control their separate institutions. While the regime allows institutional separation between Arabs and Jews, it does not grant Arabs institutional autonomy. Arab local authorities, like the Jewish ones, are under strict control of the Ministry of the Interior and their level of development is determined to a great extent by external forces. Arab education is controlled by Jews. The Arabic communications media, except the ones dominated by Rakah, are in Jewish hands. The heads and directors of the separate Arab departments are Jews. Jews exert great influence over the activities and staff of religious institutions and the Muslim Waqf (property endowment). The authorities are largely responsible for the lack of independent national Arab bodies like trade unions or a university. The establishment regards the existence of Arab-ruled institutions as exceedingly hazardous as they might impose a binational character on the state, constitute a power base for resistance to the regime and incubate an irredentist movement.

d) *Containment of state-wide leadership.* The authorities not only deny Arabs institutional autonomy, they also contain the emergence of state-wide national leadership. This is because leadership of such a type can win the support of the Arab masses and demand recognition as the legitimate representative of the 'Israeli-Palestinian national minority'. Operating in this spirit, university administrations refuse to officially recognize Arab student committees, although elected in democratic elections, and needless to say there is no official body which is ready to go along with the National Committee of Arab Students. This is also the main reason why the establishment declines to acknowledge the National Committee of Heads of Arab Local Authorities and the Committee for Defence of Arab Lands as authoritative representatives of Arabs in Israel. Rakah is not banned because, inter alia, it is a Jewish–Arab Communist party which does not vie for the throne of representative national Arab leadership. As long as the Sons of the Village Movement limits its activities mainly to the local level, it will not be declared illegal.

The government does not hesitate to issue administrative bans to stifle serious efforts to form a state-wide national leadership, best known of which are the outlawing of the Al-Ard Movement in the early 1960s and the banning by a military injunction on 1 December 1980 of the conference of Arab leaders ('the Arab Congress'), and on 12 April 1981 of the umbrella organization of nine radical action groups ('The National Coordinating Committee').

This policy towards the Arab leadership is well stated in the document 'Arabs in Israel – Policy', submitted to the political committee of the Maarakh (the labour alignment) in 1973: 'The formation of a *state-wide* Arab leadership must be prevented. Leadership on a local, sectarian, regional, or trade-union level should be encouraged. . . . Power should be split among Arab leaders in order to avert the concentration of political power by one or several leaders' (Israel Labour Party, 1973). Similarly revealing is the Minister of Justice's explanation that the outlawed Arab congress was considered subversive because its organizers 'hoped to establish a separate Arab entity in Israel and to set up a permanent forum that would eventually become the representative Arab body and serve as an address for the PLO when it attempted to harness the Israeli Arabs to its cause' (*Jerusalem Post International Edition*, 7–13 December 1980).

More positively, the deliberate policy has been to retain the traditional local hamula elders and to recruit a new corps of modern leaders – both affiliated and accountable to the Zionist establishment (for details on the cooptation techniques used, see Lustick, 1980: ch. 6).

e) *The undermining of a regional majority status.* For similar reasons the regime views with disfavour regions in which Arabs are or are becoming a demographic majority. It is maintained that the existence of a territorial power base constitutes above all a security hazard. However, many Jews consider the prevalence of Arab geo-cultural regions a flaw in the Jewish-Zionist character of the state. Consequently, the government launches programs to Judaize western and central Galilee, the northern Negev and to a lesser extent the Little Triangle. It is intended to ensure Jewish superiority in all regions.

3. *Suppliers of services.* Although the Zionist settlement of Palestine and national policies in Israel have pursued Jewish self-sufficiency, Arab involvement has always played some role. The Arab minority cannot simply be ignored, because it has the potential of rewarding Jews by furnishing services and of penalizing them by holding back or even by successfully competing with Jews for the available resources.

It is, therefore, a goal of the policy to assure that the present state of vulnerability will endure so that Arabs will not thwart the use of their services by the Jewish majority and will not organize themselves to strive for equal status in the state. Only if Arabs remain disorganized can they uninterruptedly provide the needed services and enable Israel to invest much less than the average in subsidies and developments in the Arab sector.

Arabs supply three major services:

a) *Labourers.* Arabs constitute 9 per cent of all employed Israelis. They make up, however, one-quarter or more of the labourers or low-status workers, especially in construction. There is a shortage of production workers that is increasingly filled by Arabs. The growing Arab economic integration provides non-European Jews with short-range social mobility, particularly to lower white-collar occupations in the Jewish economy that are closed to Arabs. Emigration, strikes, frequent absenteeism, or upward mobility by Arab workers can hurt the Israeli economy.

b) *Landowners*. Although over 90 per cent of the land in Israel is publicly owned, Arabs are the single largest private landowners. The national goals of land settlement and population dispersion necessitate the massive deterritorialization of Arabs (Rosenfeld, 1978: 400). Over 1.25 million dunams (one dunam is one-quarter of an acre) of Arab lands were expropriated since 1948, amounting to over half of all Arab lands and hurting close to two-thirds of all landowning Arab families. About two million dunams in the Negev and some lands in other areas are still disputed. These land losses have expedited Arab proletarization, have reduced Arab regional majority status and have boosted Jewish land settlement and population dispersion.

c) *Voters*. Arabs constitute one-tenth of the Israeli electorate and they definitely count in the highly competitive, multi-party Israeli system. Over the years about two-thirds of them have voted for the Zionist parties (by and large for the ruling labour and religious parties) and in the 1977 national elections 49 per cent so cast their votes. Arabs vote even in higher proportions for the Zionist dominant parties in the Histadrut trade-union elections.

4. *Israeli-Arabs*. The idea is to turn Arabs into a collection of new ethnic minorities with an Israeli Arab rather than a Palestinian identity. This objective has three complementary components:

a) *A mixture of minorities*. The intention is to divide the non-Jews into a large number of distinct minorities. The Druzes are granted religious status and are handled increasingly apart from other Arabs. The non-Arab traits of Circassians, Ahmedians, Armenians and others are stressed. Bedouin are differentially treated in the hope of the emergence of a separate political community. A similar attempt is made to strengthen the separate status of the Christians, and a recommendation to this effect appears in another confidential document of the Israel Labour Party: 'The Christian communities vis-à-vis the Moslem majority should be given special treatment and their distinctive character should be accentuated in order to prevent state-wide Arab organizations whose activities are determined by a nationalist Muslim spirit' (Israel Labour Party, 1974: 3).

b) *De-Palestinization*. An additional aim is to cut off, as far as possible, the cultural, nationality and identity ties of Arabs in Israel from the Palestinian population and, by so doing, to curb the development of Palestinian national consciousness among them. Although this aim has been in existence since the declaration of the state, it came to the fore only later, after the 1967 war, following the resumption of contact with the Palestinian people and the intensification of Palestinian nationalism.

c) *A new Israeli identity*. The new identity which the regime wishes to inculcate in Arabs in Israel is ethnic, religious or cultural but not national. It is feared that national (Arab, all the more so Palestinian) identity might make Arabs in Israel a unified national minority. An organized minority can demand institutional autonomy and collective rights and threaten the uninational Jewish-Zionist nature of the state. Prime Minister Rabin was unequivocally explicit on this point when he dismissed a memorandum by the National Committee of Heads of Arab Local Authorities advancing the idea of Israel as a binational state, declared that Arabs are a religious and cultural but not a national minority, and consequently refused to recognize this Committee as the authoritative representation of Arabs in Israel (*Maariv*, 20 June 1976).

The clearest indication of the intent to transform Arabs to a new Israeli ethnic minority is Arab education, which aims to distribute biculturalism yet is devoid of national Arab or Palestinian objectives. Another sign is the encouragement of 'Israeli Arab consciousness' and 'Druze consciousness'.

The specific goals and their components fall in order of priority. At the top ranks the goal of making Arabs loyal citizens because it directly relates to national security and law and order. Arab resignation to their minority status in a Jewish-Zionist state ranks next, followed by the goal of keeping the supply of Arab services. At the lower end is the goal of creating new ethnic minorities cut off from the Palestinian nation. Within the goals themselves, the negative sub-goals are more important than the positive ones. For instance, the refraining by Arabs from hostilities against the state is more highly regarded than their identification with Israel. By the same token, their noninvolvement in the Israeli–Arab conflict is more appreciated than their 'contribution' to the state in manpower and land.

The above four operative goals of policy towards the Arabs are far removed from the official goals of integration and equality. This is because equality and integration serve in practice as means rather than ultimate ends. The Jewish majority has neither an ideological commitment nor a willingness to invest the immense resources to shatter the institutionalized ethnic stratification (i.e. to close the gaps in education, occupation, material well-being and positions of power between Arabs and Jews). As much as measures are taken to promote equality (such as five-year development plans of Arab villages and dispensation of benefits during elections), they are directed towards achieving other goals, viz. to strengthen Arabs' loyalty to the state, to prompt them to resign themselves to their fate as a vulnerable minority and to keep them away from the Palestinian people. Allocation of resources to Arabs is not yet accepted as a basic right due to them as citizens. It is perceived rather as a favour or reward for the demonstration of loyalty, compliance and cooperation.

The same holds true for integration. Integration is not an aim in itself as it may lead to assimilation. It is instrumental in pacifying Arabs. Economic integration renders Arabs dependent on Jewish employers, suppliers and buyers. Political integration implies Arab reconciliation with the Zionist mission of the Jewish political parties. Other institutional integration staves off the rise of independent national Arab organizations.

### Means

It should be clear from the discussion of the operative goals that the present policy of domination, like any other policy of domination, rests on the two central mechanisms of economic dependence and political control. Since a detailed analysis of these mechanisms is made elsewhere (Lustick, 1980;

Smooha, 1980a), it will suffice here to indicate several major points.

1. *Economic dependence.* Economic dependence on Jews denies Arabs an independent economic base for a political struggle. Arabs rely on Jews as employers, providers of services and as decision-makers on the allocation of public funds. There is no separate Arab economy. The value of Arab agricultural production is marginal (only 7 per cent) in Israeli agriculture. While Arabs constitute one-tenth of the Israeli civilian labour force, the economic power (ownership, management, trade-union leadership) is concentrated in Jewish hands. Arabs lack a bourgeoisie which owns large industrial and commercial concerns and have no trade-unions of their own. They are devoid of external financial resources like the United Jewish Appeal. Being without a developed physical and social infrastructure, Arab settlements are unable to provide employment for members of the Arab intelligentsia who have leadership skills. Indeed, about half of the Arab college graduates work as teachers, who are civil servants, and most of the others depend in one way or another on Jews. The comprehensive material dependence of Arabs on Jews facilitates political control over them: since employed Arabs depend for their livelihood on Jews and Arab settlements rely on governmental subsidies, it is possible to offer concessions and to purchase peace inexpensively.

2. *Political control.* The constant political control over Israeli Arabs is intended to directly prevent a national struggle. The 1945 Defence (Emergency) Regulations (including the 1979 amendments), which are put into effect according to need, are the legal bases for control and for its smooth operation even without imposing a military government.[2] The dense spread of the security services in the Arab sector guarantees ongoing, deterrent, detecting and punitive surveillance. The efficiency of the security services is aided by the economic dependence (which generates a large reservoir of candidates for collaboration) and the hamula structure (which makes it possible to gain information and to exercise control through several local key persons only). There is a noticeable element of control in breaking territorial concentrations by land confiscations in Arab regions and setting up a network of Jewish settlements there. Similarly, control over existing Arab institutions in the educational and religious spheres aims to prevent them from becoming independent bases of power. For this reason, an effort is made to obstruct the formation of independent national Arab institutions, such as a party, a trade-union, a communications medium and a university. At the same time, the authorities encourage internal rifts, both sectarian and hamula, and try to foster the consciousness of ethnic (non-Palestinian) identity in each group. Additionally, support is given to 'positive' leaders, whether they are hamula heads or the educated or young who are willing to cooperate, but 'negative' leaders are discouraged. The reasonable and calculated use of power by the authorities and their avoidance of random terror contribute appreciably to the efficiency of political control.[3]

*Variations*

The domination policy towards Arabs is no doubt part of the operative national consensus, and as such it is accepted by the general Jewish public and the major Zionist parties (Maarakh, Likud and the National Religious Party). However, a controversy has raged for many years among makers and administrators of this policy concerning its more specific direction. Today it is possible to distinguish between liberal and hardline policy. Despite the tendency to overstate the differences between these two lines, they are in fact only variations on the agreed-upon domination policy. In other words, both sides accede to the goal of domination of Arabs in order to deter them from being a threat to national security and the Jewish-Zionist mission and to arrest their resources for the Jewish good. They also consent to the strategies of economic dependence and political control for achieving this goal. They disagree, however, on the emphasis, procedures, tactics and assessments of the situation.

1. *The liberal policy.* Toledano (1969, 1974, 1975, 1977) is considered the ideologist and implementer of the liberal policy, which was dominant in the years 1966–78. According to this line, domination should be based more on economic dependence than on political control. The Arab passive compliance is attainable by a conditional flow of resources for development, provision of employment for all in the Jewish economy, opening the civil service and other white-collar jobs to the Arab intelligentsia to facilitate its cooptation, and wide distribution of personal benefits. In this manner, the vested interests of as many Arabs as possible in the existing system are promoted.

As long as the Israeli–Arab conflict continues, Arabs in Israel will face the irresolvable dilemma of loyalty to the state as against loyalty to the Arab world ('My people fight my country,' as Zubi used to say). The policy should, therefore, be founded on realistic compromises. For the time being, a certain inequality in duties and rights between Arabs and Jews is unavoidable. Arabs should not be required to serve in the army or in its place to fulfil civil service duties. They should also not be required to demonstrate loyalty actively. Today, it is impossible to change the basic hostile attitude of Arabs towards the state, and they should not be prohibited from expressing verbal protest as long as their behaviour remains non-hostile.

The regime should refrain from detrimental and inessential measures (such as the land expropriation of 1976) and should make benevolent gestures (such as allowing the return of the displaced residents of Ikrit and Biram). It must also avoid as far as possible the exercise of power, keep ongoing security surveillance low-key, and educate the Jewish public to be more open to Arabs. The prime interest of Israel is to delay the anticipated confrontation between Arabs and Jews for as long as possible. It is worthwhile paying a rising economic price for internal peace. There is no substitute for reliance on economic means to dominate Arabs, as long as Israel wishes to preserve its democratic regime and the backing of the Western world, which is sensitive to civil and minority rights.

2. *The hardline policy.* Lin (1971) is regarded as the ideologist of the hardline policy. This line requires a shift of emphasis from economic dependence to political control. Under conditions of an improving material situation and increasing alienation from the state, economic means become less and less effective and hence the policy towards Arabs should rely mainly on political control.

For political control to be both just and efficient, the duties and rights of Arabs and Jews should in the first place be equalized. It is maintained that Arabs ought to do military service or alternatively civil service, to shoulder the burden of taxes equally, to construct buildings with permits only, not to squat on state land, to refrain from public identification with the enemy, etc. In this manner, a clearcut distinction will be made between 'positive' and 'negative' Arabs. This distinction is supposed to be the cornerstone in the policy even though most Arabs would opt to be 'negative' (including the young, the educated, Rakah members and sympathizers, and nationalist circles). The 'positive' Arabs would find the Jewish society open and enjoy definite advantages. At the same time, economic and political sanctions will be exercised against 'negative' Arabs, including dismissal from the civil service, expulsion from universities, confinement to their immediate localities, and being closely watched, harassed and brought to justice.

The hardline policy can block the Arab radicalization and strengthen the 'positive' camp. If it is applied consistently, it could delay the inevitable showdown between the 'negative' majority of Arabs and the Jews, in which Arabs would be hurt while damaging the state. Israel should act strongly to halt the radicalization in the Arab sector. It can do so mainly by using power against the 'negative' Arabs since they interpret the tolerance and patience of the regime as a weakness. A significant rise in the price Arabs have to pay for hostility would guarantee internal quiet.

The characterization of these two variations of the domination policy may help to distinguish between the policy of the labour alignment (Maarakh) and that of the right-wing Likud towards the Arabs in Israel. As expected, the Maarakh is closer to the liberal line, whereas the Likud is nearer to the hardline position. Despite the initial continuity of policy, it became evident by 1980 that the Likud government, as compared to the previous labour governments, (a) relies more on coercive legislation, restrictive orders, preventive measures and other political controls, (b) tends to be tactless and even antagonistic in pronouncements, (c) lacks an organizational base in the Arab sector and hence finds it more difficult to strike deals with the Arab population, and consequently (d) is perceived by Arabs as more rigid, alienated and hostile.

## Results

The question arises to what extent the policy towards Arabs has succeeded. An unambiguous answer is not easy to come by, because it depends largely on the specific criterion of success and the level of expectation from the policy. On the one hand, the policy can be presented as a failure. This is the attitude of the Jewish public during periods of strain in its relations with the Arab population. Severe criticism was levelled, for example, following the detection of sabotage rings in which Arab citizens participated, the ascent of Rakah to power in Nazareth and its gaining of half of the Arab vote in the 1977 national elections and the 1976 Land Day events. There is no doubt that the Arab public itself, to whom the policy is applied, is also not satisfied. In the 1980 representative national sample of Arabs, 55 per cent of the respondents held that the government policy widens the socio-economic gap between Arabs and Jews, 32 per cent said that it has no effect and only 13 per cent estimated that it narrows the gap.[4] Even from the establishment's viewpoint, the current policy is deficient. It does not accomplish its two official aims of equality and integration between Arabs and Jews. Furthermore, according to leading Arabists' forecasts, Arab—Jewish confrontation should be expected and the present policy can at best postpone but not preclude it.

On the other hand, it is possible to portray the existing policy as successful given its minimal operative goals and the constraints under which it operates. Its chief objective of neutralizing the Arab minority was obtained. Arabs have remained a passive and marginal element in Israeli society. They did not obstruct the implementation of the prime state aims in the areas of security, foreign affairs, internal order, economy, immigration and settlement. They neither engaged in civil resistance nor became a fifth column. They reconciled themselves with the policy which directly affected them adversely. One striking example is resignation to the military government, in the abolition of which they played little part. Another instance is their restrained response (prior to the Land Day of 1976) to the massive land take-overs.

These impressive achievements of the present policy were attained at relatively low cost. The extent of violence was negligible. With some exceptions (the Kfar Kassem Affair and the Land Day incidents), there were almost no casualties. Even the resources allocated for this purpose were quite meagre. At the same time, the limited investments in Arabs in Israel realized handsome profits in terms of added manpower essential to the economy, confiscated lands for which compensation was below the market value, and votes gained to strengthen the Zionist parties.

A realistic appraisal of the policy towards the Arabs should be founded upon a dynamic perspective. During the first half of the thirty-two years of statehood, the policy was effective. However, during the second half it has slowly been eroded following the formation of Rakah in 1965, the lifting of the military government in 1966, the Six-Day War in 1967 and the Yom Kippur War in 1973. Additional factors which add to Arab power include the rise of a new generation, the population explosion, the revolution of rising expectations, class differentiation, the formation of an elite and a leadership, the crystallization of sophisticated political culture, the emergence of the PLO and the Palestinization of identity. The erosion of the domination policy is, nonetheless, not an offshoot of this or other change in the Arab status. Domination of minorities is inconsistent with political democracy, an economy with full employment and rapid growth as in Israel, and therefore is bound to wear away. Under these circumstances the minority becomes stronger over time, and if direct repression is not enforced to halt the erosion, the machinery of domination is weakened.

## Reforms

In response to the deterioration of the domination policy, a number of plans to handle Arabs were submitted. The public proposals are usually supposed to ameliorate the present situation through continuing liberalization of the current policy. At the same time, several reforms purporting to reinforce domination became known.

1. *Liberal reforms.* There is little new in the series of liberal reforms to the existing policy suggested by various establishmentarian bodies. Equality and integration as the guiding principles of the official policy recurred in public commission reports during the 1970s. In addition, spheres in need of improvement were reviewed and recommendations were made. It will suffice to mention only a few of these plans. The Geraisy Committee (1973) detailed the backward Arab municipal services and called for equality in treatment and standards between Arab and Jewish local authorities. The Koversky Committee (1976) proposed legalizing the unlicensed buildings located within the boundaries of Arab local authorities and accelerating the preparation of master plans for Arab localities. Another study team documented the housing predicament in the Arab sector and put forward a plan of housing assistance (Kipnis, 1978).

In the area of education, the Peled Committee (1975) specified the means of bridging the educational gap between Arabs and Jews and set forth a modification in the goals of Arab education. Another commissioned study designed a decentralization scheme of the department of Arab education (*Haaretz*, 24 April 1978).

The Harel Committee (1976) surveyed the Histadrut activities in the Arab sector and made recommendations in four fields. With regard to organization, it urged completing the integration of Arabs on workers' councils, on labour committees and in departments in the Histadrut headquarters. As to participation in decision-making, the increase of Arab representation in the governing bodies was advocated. In the social-cultural area, more activities were advised. Economically, Hevrat Haovdim (the Histadrut service and industrial complex) was counselled to build plants in Arab settlements.

Three all-embracing programs were formulated in political parties but they are nationally oriented. One was advanced by Cohen (1976), the director of the Arab department of the Israel Labour Party, the second by Kol (1979), the former head of the Independent Liberal Party, and the third by Shai (1978), the Movement for Change and Initiative. The recommendations called, inter alia, for promoting equality in the living conditions of Arabs and Jews, greater participation of Arabs in state institutions, Arab incorporation into Zionist parties, a year of national service in lieu of military conscription, and the creation of permanent high-ranking state committees for Arab affairs. A similar approach was propounded by a team of experts, mostly Orientalists, who deliberated Israel's transition from war to peace (Neaman Institute, 1979).

The public pressures accompanying the Land Day strike eventually prompted the government to reconsider its policy in its meeting of 23 May 1976. Proposals were made to the government by the Inter-Ministerial Committee for Arab Affairs in which many of the above recommendations were included. The government neither announced any new policy nor put out its resolutions in a public document. The approved actions which were executed immediately were the formation of both a ministerial committee for Arab affairs and the Jewish–Arab Public Council. It was also resolved to enhance equality between Arabs and Jews in basic services, education and political representation as well as social integration (Jewish–Arab Public Council, 1976: 3–4).

The above reforms, although compatible with the existing domination policy, were only partially carried out because the Arab minority is not strong enough to thrust them upon the Jewish majority.

2. *Hardline reforms.* As compared to the well-publicized liberal reforms, the hardline ones tend to be confidential because of the democratic ethos, but some of them have been leaked to the press or surfaced during implementation. The 'Koenig Report' (1976) is, no doubt, the most detailed and definite proposal for consolidating the domination policy. This secret memorandum, which was submitted to the government by the Northern District Commissioner, called for the thinning out of Arab population concentrations, the harassment of radicals, the use of smear tactics against Rakah leaders, restrictions on the number of university graduates, tough law enforcement, expanded surveillance, the reduction of Jewish economic dependence on Arabs, and so on.

Other strong-arm reforms were legislated. In the summer of 1980, the Knesset passed an amendment to the 'Terror Act – 1948' which makes it a criminal offence to express public identification with a terrorist organization. It is directed against Arabs who declare their support of the PLO. In addition, an amendment to the citizenship law was enacted that may have a special implication for dissident Arabs. It authorizes the Minister of the Interior to revoke, without trial or right of appeal, the Israeli citizenship of a person who 'committed an action implying a breach of allegiance to the State of Israel'. Another law provided for the speedy expropriation of Bedouin lands, earmarked for a military airfield in the Negev, without allowing for a court appeal.

Among further stiff measures was frequent resorting to the military regulations for restricting the movement of radical Arab students, Rakah functionaries and other activists. In addition, the 'Green Patrol' was established to throw out and even sell Bedouin flocks, suspected of trespassing, without due process. About thirty 'Observation Posts' were also set up all over Galilee to monitor Arabs squatting on state land and to remove them. In April 1979, the Knesset Finance Committee issued a report attributing large-scale tax evasions to Arabs in general and Arab self-employed in particular and urged the government to take strong action in this matter (Israel, Knesset, 1979).

The implementation of the hardline reforms by the Likud government were accompanied by harsh declarations. To quote only two cabinet ministers, Minister of Agriculture Sharon said that 'national land is actually robbed by foreigners. . . . Although there is talk of the Judaization of Galilee, the region is regressing into a Gentile district. . . . I initiated strong action to prevent aliens from taking state lands' (*Maariv*, 9 September 1977). Arab citizens were referred to as aliens. Later, on the occasion of the ban on the Arab congress, Sharon also made an implicit threat of deportation: 'While we have no intention of displacing Arab citizens from Galilee, I would advise the Arab citizens in the area not to radicalize their positions in order not to bring about another tragedy like the one that befell the Palestinian people in 1948. Even if we do not want it, it may recur.' Another Minister scornfully remarked that Israel keeps an open door for any Arab citizen 'who does not like to live here. He can hire a taxi cab . . . to cross the [Jordan's] bridge. . . . We will even wave him goodbye' (*Haaretz*, 4 December 1980, quoted in the editorial).

### The alternative policy

Over against the reforms, some radical and comprehensive solutions for the Arab problem are proposed. They utterly disregard one or more of the above fundamental forces shaping Arab status and hence they are inescapably utopian. Included among these utopias are the Canaanite state (Ratosh, 1976), a secular-democratic state (Tessler, 1975), and population transfer (Kahane, 1977), in all of which the Arab question ceases to exist.

By presenting an alternative policy, it is not intended to suggest yet another reform or utopia. The intention is rather to outline an alternative policy which can guarantee a *modus vivendi* significantly different from the status quo. Broadly speaking, the alternative policy differs from the existing one in the shift of emphasis in Arab–Jewish relations from the present domination to coexistence marked by greater consent and partnership. The superordinate aim is to move away from a model of political integration based on domination over the Arab minority to a greater use of the voluntary mechanisms in the models of consensus-building and consociationalism.

### *Underlying assumptions*

The existing and alternative policies differ in a number of paramount ways. First, in order to keep the Arab problem manageable, Israel must give up the occupied territories, otherwise Arabs will reach unmanageable numerical proportions. A possible Arab majority will set up a vicious circle of Arab offensive and Jewish repression. While the present policy distinguishes between Arabs on the two sides of the Green Line, the retention of the territories will continue to antagonize the Arabs in Israel.

Second, the point of departure of the alternative policy is that Arabs are a stable minority and therefore a permanent, noncoercive settlement should be reached with them. The thirty-two years of statehood, which have seen many changes, have proved that Arabs are not a transient element. The frequent wars did not cause their flight, and their living standards in times of relative quiet did not push them to emigrate. Seventy-three per cent of the Arabs interviewed in 1980 expressed unwillingness to even consider a move to a Palestinian state were it to be established alongside Israel. The alternative policy assumes that the problem will not be resolved by the settlement of the Israeli—Arab conflict. National security is a constraint which makes the tackling of the question difficult, but it is not an insurmountable obstacle. Hence the exploration of a solution should not be delayed until overall peace in the Middle East is attained.

Third, the conception of the alternative policy requires a reconsideration of the imposed constraints. The idea is to raise the egalitarian-democratic ethos to head the value-scale concerning Arabs in Israel. In cases where there is no concrete and immediate danger to national security and the Jewish-Zionist character of the state, the alternative policy insists upon applying the rules of democracy and equality to Arabs. In other words, it regards security and the Jewish-Zionist state as constraints to be taken into account rather than superior goals which subordinate other considerations and warrant the fullest implementation. In contrast to the commonly held opinion that security is the gravest impediment in the way of Arab—Jewish relations, the alternative policy emphasizes the Jewish-Zionist mission of Israel as being an equally if not more serious barrier. Arabs suffer no less from the preference of Jews *qua* Jews and from the Judaization of policies and public institutions than from an unduly excessive sensitivity to security on the part of Jews. Hence any moderation of the Jewish-Zionist nature of the state would improve understanding between Jews and Arabs.

Forth, the alternative policy stresses the achievement of positive goals. As against the present policy, which takes the neutralization of Arabs in the state as a prime objective, it aims to strive for peaceful coexistence between Arabs and Jews. It recognizes the pluralistic structure of Israeli society as well as the Arabs' right, like any other community, to organize themselves as a pressure group. It regards equality as an operative target rather than a means to buy internal tranquillity.

Fifth and last, the alternative policy defines the situation of the Arab minority as a state concern and aspires to eliminate the practice of 'delegation of authority'. It aims to salvage the problem from the exclusive care of the Arabists and to reinstate it in the hands of policy-makers and the general public. The return of responsibility to the establishment is designed to contribute to a more fully comprehensive policy and to its firmer application. The Jewish public's sharing the responsibility for policy is intended to moderate its extreme stands on the Arab question. This is because extremism is partly due to lack of public involvement in this matter and to the transfer of authority to the regime. Besides, instead of unilateral policy-making and its imposition on the Arab minority, as is done today, the alternative policy advocates the recognition of the Arab public as a legitimate party and as a participant in the process of Arab policy formulation. The shared assumption of responsibility for the policy by decision-makers, the Arabists, the Jewish public and the Arab public itself is intended to engender an atmosphere of Arab–Jewish exchange in order to reach mutually acceptable arrangements.

## The alternatives

In principle, it is possible to discern various alternatives to the existing policy on the 'approachment–avoidance' spectrum between Arabs and Jews. Among these, three distinct ones are chosen for presentation below in order to throw into relief the gamut of possibilities.[5]

1. *Maximal incorporation.* The alternative of maximal incorporation aims to integrate as much as possible but without assimilating the Arabs as individuals into Israeli society. The Arabs will develop an Israeli Palestinian identity. They will regard themselves as an integral part of Israel, and the Jews, for their part, will see them as equals and partners. Although Israel will remain a Jewish-Zionist state, bilingualism and biculturalism will be fostered and common cultural patterns will evolve. Civil rights and duties, apart from the Law of Return, will be uniform and implemented irrespective of origin. To put it differently, military service will be imposed on Arabs in the same way as it is on Jews, the separate Arab departments will be phased out, free Arab entry to any economic or political sphere would be guaranteed, and even legal permission for mixed marriages for those interested will be granted. In addition, the formation of common social frameworks, such as bilingual schools and mixed neighbourhoods, will be encouraged. Similarly, great efforts to narrow the gaps in modernization and resources between Arabs and Jews will be made. A special law against discrimination will be enacted and determined steps for its enforcement will be taken. State institutions and other public bodies, such as the Jewish Agency and the Jewish National Fund, will avoid double standards or the use of national descent as a criterion in policy.[6]

2. *Status as a Palestinian national minority.* This option confers on Arabs the status of a Palestinian national minority. They will identify themselves as Palestinian Arabs and as part of the Palestinian nation living in Israel and will be recognized as a national minority by the state. They will control and manage their existing institutions of education, religion and culture and will head the Arab departments. They will also form new, national and independent organizations such as a political party, a trade union, communications media and a university. They will be given great investments for setting up Arab-owned and -managed industries, for bringing the standard of services in Arab settlements up to par with those of Jews, and for lessening the Arab–Jewish socio-economic discrepancies. As well as being a part of the Jewish-Zionist state, the Palestinian Arab minority will nurture the cultural and other ties with the Arab world.[7]

3. *A personal choice between integration and separation.* This possibility offers Arabs a personal choice between the above two options. By selective

implementation of elements from the two alternatives, the situation will arise where Arabs will be free to choose between considerable personal integration in Israeli society and equally considerable personal separation as members of a recognized Palestinian national minority. Arabs will be granted the same privilege as is enjoyed by religious Jews in Israel today, i.e. individual incorporation into the society at large or membership in communities having appreciable autonomy.

*An appraisal*

The three alternatives are similar in certain respects. They are assumed to be serious attempts to gain more harmonious coexistence between Arabs and Jews instead of the present situation of domination. All purport to preserve the Jewish-Zionist mould of the state. In each alternative, Arabs are endowed with better opportunities and rights than at present but not with totally equal status.

The three alternatives, however, differ significantly, particularly the first two. To sharpen the contrasts, the maximal incorporation option regards Arabs primarily as a cultural minority, whereas the other confers upon them full status as a Palestinian national minority. The first offers Arabs more equality but less expression for their Palestinian nationalism. It aims to individualize and neutralize Arabs as a national entity while the other option strives to pacify them with separate yet less equal status as a national minority. The two are dissimilar in the threat they present to the Jewish-Zionist nature of Israel. The first might blur the Jewish-Zionist mission of the state by rendering citizenship a central force and by creating an all-inclusive Israeli identity. The second, on the other hand, endangers the Jewish-Zionist character of the state by encouraging binationalism, transferring too much power to the Arabs and heightening the risk of an Arab irredentist movement.

As to the preferences of the Jewish majority, the three alternatives are not desirable because they diverge substantially from existing domination and thereby strengthen the Arab minority. Should the Jewish public be obliged to choose one of the three, it would opt for 'maximal incorporation' as the lesser evil. This is not because of a belief in integration but rather as a preventive measure against dangerous polarization commensurate with Palestinian nationalism. Were a Palestinian state established alongside Israel or were autonomy arranged in the administered territories, maximal incorporation of Arabs in Israel would furnish better safeguards against a resistance or irredentist movement than the conferring of Palestinian national minority status. On the other hand, it is possible that a new Palestinian entity would satisfy the national aspirations of Arabs in Israel so that they would resign themselves to living as a minority in a Jewish-Zionist state. In fact any move toward a settlement of the Israeli—Arab conflict will make Arabs and Jews in Israel more acceptable to each other because such a settlement will enhance the legitimacy of the state in the eyes of Arabs and will make Jews less defensively Zionistic and exclusionary. The peace treaty between Israel and Egypt has already had such an impact on the Arabs in Israel. The proportion of Arabs recognizing Israel's right to exist rose from 50 per cent in 1976 to 59 per cent in 1980, whereas those denying this right dropped from 21 per cent to 11 per cent (Arabs with reservations remained 29–30 per cent). Reconciliation is conditional, of course, on providing Arabs with fuller rights, greater access to state institutions and a more proportional share of national resources.

Arabs' enthusiasm for these alternatives should not be expected as long as they oppose Israel's Jewish-Zionist character. They would, nevertheless, prefer them to their present situation as a dominated minority. Of the three possibilities the open alternative of a personal choice between individual integration into predominantly Jewish institutions and life in an autonomous Palestinian community would gratify the largest number of Arabs, but most would reconcile themselves to maximal incorporation if such an option were instituted by the Jews. This is because this alternative is compatible with the orientation of two out of the three camps in the Arab population. Maximal incorporation is accepted by the accommodating Arabs (one-quarter of the population) who are already resigned to living in a Jewish-Zionist state if afforded greater opportunities. It will be also agreed to by the Arabs, constituting a majority of two-thirds, who belong to the 'reserved' camp. They acquiesce to the Rakah compromise of Arab–Jewish coexistence if equality is increased, if a Palestinian state rises alongside Israel so that Arabs can identify themselves with it and if the Jewish-Zionist features of the state are less prominent. Only the dissident camp (one-tenth) who reject in principle a minority status and aspire to a secular-democratic state instead of Israel will continue to resist this solution.

Findings of the 1980 national surveys of Arabs and Jews lend support to the above assessments. When asked what compromise settlement to the problem of Arabs in Israel they were willing to accept, 64 per cent of the Arabs opted for living as a people with equal rights in Israel, 4 per cent would move to a Palestinian state alongside Israel, 16 per cent wished such a state also to include Galilee and the Little Triangle where most Arabs live, and 16 per cent insisted that a secular-democratic state should rise in all of Palestine. The majority of Arabs willing to remain part of Israel is larger among the more accommodating Arabs, and, more importantly, all the Arab leaders affiliated with the Zionist establishment as well as the independent Front or Rakah leaders are committed to staying in Israel. Only the small dissident section of the population and the activists in the Sons of the Village Movement and the Progressive National Movement reject being part of contemporary Israel.

In response to a question about the policy that Israel ought to pursue towards the Arabs in Israel, only 6 per cent concurred with the present policy of control, 60 per cent desired equality and integration, 23 per cent wished Arabs to be allowed to organize independently and share power, and only 11 per cent demanded a separate legal status as in the autonomy plan. Feeling that they have poorer chances of achieving equality and integration under the existing circumstances, Arabs by a large majority opposed the Jewish-Zionist character of the state. To illustrate, 57 per cent were confident that Israel as a Jewish-Zionist state has no right to exist and 30 per cent were unsure about this right; 61 per cent viewed Zionism as racist and 24 per cent were unsure; 82 per cent thought that Israel should not retain a Jewish majority and 94 per cent favoured the repeal or modification of the Law of Return; etc. They were, however, evenly split on the question whether Arabs can live as equal citizens in Israel as a Jewish-Zionist state and identify themselves with the state.

These and other statistics show that Arabs are diametrically opposed to the present domination and are interested, instead, in either individual incorporation or moderate consociationalism. These preferences are evidenced in the desire for reducing institutional separation of neighbourhoods and schools, acquiring control of Arab institutions but short of regional autonomy, and having a representative leadership officially recognized by the state.

The majority of Jews, on the other hand, insist on continued domination. For 14 per cent of them the only acceptable settlement of the Arab problem is complete exclusion, 48 per cent would tolerate Arabs only if they were resigned to a minority status in a state designed for Jews, 34 per cent were willing to have Arabs as a national minority with equal rights and just 3 per cent consented to the idea of equal status in a non-Jewish state. Answering the question of policy towards the Arabs, 32 per cent were for the status quo, 41 per cent for the increase in surveillance, 22 per cent for equality and integration and only 6 per cent for allowing Arabs to organize independently or have autonomy.

It is thus clear that continuing control is the first choice of the majority of Jews whereas Arab individual incorporation or consociationalism are not considered viable alternatives. To cite only a little of the available evidence for this generalization, in a response to specific questions, 62 per cent of the Jews advocated the increase of surveillance over Arabs. Only 17 per cent agreed to let Arabs organize and pursue their vital interests in the same way as religious Jews in Israel do. Eighty-four per cent were certain that Israel should prefer Jews to Arabs and 57 per cent would give precedence to the Jewish-Zionist character of the state when it collides with the democratic-egalitarian ethos. Jews are so accustomed to domination that they do not mind working with Arabs, but only 30 per cent were prepared to have an Arab as a superior.

Another national representative survey of the Israeli Jewish adult population, taken in January 1980, reveals a similar picture (Tzemah, 1980). To quote only highlights, 67 per cent of the respondents agreed that Jews must show a favourable attitude towards minorities. Yet while 90 per cent held that Israel should wage a struggle on behalf of persecuted Jewish minorities, only 56 per cent thought the same with regard to persecuted non-Jewish minorities. At the same time, 48 per cent favoured equal rights for Arabs in Israel, and the proportion of those endorsing equal treatment for Arabs and Jews in specific areas ranged from 32 per cent regarding jobs in the private market or loans to agricultural development to 15 per cent regarding high posts in government offices. Whereas a majority of 72 per cent would oppose the admission to university of Arabs in Israel who openly express their dissatisfaction with Israel's existence but do not agitate to take actions against it, 74 per cent would not justify the denial of university admissions or jobs to Jewish candidates in Russia on grounds of anti-Soviet declarations or a wish to immigrate to Israel. For 76 per cent of the respondents, national security is a sufficient basis for imposing restrictions on Arabs.

Along with the majority that clings to the status quo of domination, there is a minority favouring equality, integration or partial consociationalism. These liberal Jews tend to be more leftist, dovish and educated than the average. But given their concern over Zionism and national security, they are sympathetic yet fall short of supporting an alternative policy. Lustick is right, therefore, in observing that there is no 'political base for a Jewish leadership committed to changing the fundamental terms of the relationship between Arabs and Jews in Israel', and that in the absence of such a constituency, 'the guided transformation of Israel toward a consociational or pluralist society will not take place' (1980: 271).

Conclusions

Over the past thirty years, Israel tried to cope, using varying mechanisms of domination, with the difficult problem of an Arab minority having culture, identity, community, resources and, above all, a non-Zionist ideology significantly differing from those of the Jewish majority. It managed to neutralize Arabs as a threat to national security and the Jewish-Zionist nature of the state as well as to harness their services in manpower, lands and other resources.

The conditions conducive to the use of domination instead of more voluntary means were disagreement on basic values, few cross-cutting affiliations, the lack of an objective need of Arab participation in the regime thanks to the existence of a permanent Jewish majority, a sense of threat among Jews, a belief that the control of the Arab minority will contain the danger and the special vulnerability of Arabs which makes possible the cheap and efficient administration of domination. Under these complex circumstances, domination is a more effective means of buying peace than the less practical ways of consensus-building and consociational partnership.

Since these conditions are still in effect today, it is not surprising that the domination policy has remained largely unchanged for years. It is reasonable to assume that as long as (a) no revision is made to the exclusionary ideology of a Jewish-Zionist state in which there is no real room for Arabs, (b) the Israeli—Arab conflict endures to sustain the basic Jewish mistrust and legitimizes the inferior and dominated status of Arabs in Israel and (c) the machinery of control continues to keep order at a low cost, no significant change in the present policy should be expected.

When the domination policy encounters difficulties the establishment responds by seeking to remedy it through different kinds of reforms. During the 1970s, many liberal reforms were suggested. As a whole, they do little more than tinker with the status quo in which limited steps to increase equality and integration are employed as a means of control. Most of the recommendations were, however, disregarded because they involve a higher economic price that Jews are not yet prepared to pay. This is witnessed by the resignation in January 1979 of the Likud-appointed Prime Minister's Advisor on Arab Affairs after he realized that the government was unwilling to discuss his policy reforms (Sharon, 1979). Since then, the Likud government has embarked on a strong-arm course implementing hardline reforms and resorting to a direct political regulation of Arab behaviour.

Given the great potential for disruptive conflict in Israel, there is a need for redirecting Arab–Jewish relations. It is hence vital to formulate alternative policies along lines of consensus-building and consociationalism. The three options presented here ('maximal incorporation', 'status of a Palestinian national minority' and 'personal choice between integration and separation') are not the only possibilities, and other alternatives can definitely be drawn. All of them take into account the constraints of a Jewish-Zionist state, security imperatives and the nonassimilating status of Arabs. It is granted that these options are not viable for the time being, but they may become so in the future.

The existing and alternative policy presents Israeli society with a number of difficult dilemmas. First, it raises the question regarding the nature of Israeli democracy. Shapira characterizes democracy in Israel as being formal in which certain procedures (elections, freedom of organization by opposition parties and freedom of expression) are regarded as supreme values and as the embodiment of representative government. Democracy is not, however, viewed as the care of individual and minority rights and as the restriction of state power to defend them (1977: 191). This critique holds true for the Jewish population, and is far removed from the drastic shrinkage of Israeli democracy vis-à-vis the Arab minority. As far as Arabs are concerned, in addition to the lack of protection of minority rights and the unrestricted powers of the regime, there is the problem of 'the tyranny of the majority' and the excessive use of state power to subdue the minority. All this done while abiding by the formal rules of free expression, freedom of organization and the right to vote. The Arab minority puts Israeli democracy to a critical test in which it does not greatly succeed, as evidenced by the institutionalization of the domination policy.

No less grave is the dilemma of Israel's national identity. If Israel is a Jewish-Zionist state, that is, an entity for serving Jews and a political instrument to achieve the goals of the international Zionist movement, the Arab status within it is not clear. There is no internal ideological answer to this question. The solutions of de-Zionization or population transfer are consistent but utopian. The way Israel handles the problem is by institutionalizing the Jewish-Zionist nature of the state, thereby forcing the Arab minority to pay the costs.

An additional dilemma concerns national security. The central question is whether security in Israel is so overriding as to warrant the neglect of painful internal problems and the delay of their treatment. The security hazard is still perceived as a sufficient ground for freezing the status quo of domination over a 'hostile' minority and for the unwillingness to seek more liberal relations. The question arises, however, whether internal peace, like external peace, can be acquired without risk-taking and without paying a price.

There is also a pragmatic dilemma. The critical question refers to the life expectancy of the machinery of control over Arabs in Israel. The authorities feel that the Arabs are a time bomb and that a showdown is inevitable. They act to postpone the explosion for as long as possible. The historical experience indeed shows that in domination situations a confrontation between a minority and a majority is endemic though not always violent. If successful, the process of peace-making in the Middle East, while it will remove some barriers for coexistence and boost mutual acceptance, will provide Arabs in Israel with legitimacy for their struggle against domination and for equality in rights and resources. If conflict is expected to intensify, why should Israel continue with a policy which is bound to exacerbate conflict further instead of trying another direction?

In this connection a political dilemma comes to mind regarding the special role of policy and leadership in shaping social processes. Is the status of the Arab minority really determined by external factors outside Israel's ambit which make policy change pointless? Is it not the great test of policy like that towards Arabs in Israel to cope with problems which seem intractable — whether because they are built in the very structure of the society, moulded by historical forces or protected by a wall of strongly vested interests? If leadership does not have a popular mandate for change, as is the case with the Jewish leadership, why not attempt to create a mandate? If politics is the art of the possible, how can the possible and impossible be disentangled before putting them to the test of reality? Do not deeply divided societies like Israel enjoy a wide margin of indeterminacy which provides policy with room for manoeuvre and opportunities for breakthroughs?

Last, but not least, is a sharp dilemma regarding the moral fibre of Israeli society. Domination over a minority for a long time and as an institutionalized machinery raises severe ethical queries. The question is especially grave concerning the Jewish people, who themselves have suffered for centuries from the status of a vulnerable minority and only in the last generation were the victims of a vicious scheme of extermination. The moral dilemma is even greater in the light of the continued peculiar situation of the Jews today, most of whom still live as minorities in many countries. Furthermore, Israel aspires to defend the Jewish minorities, to build a new Jewish society based on social justice and to fulfil the historical mission of setting an example to other nations.

## Notes

*The support of the Ford Foundation is gratefully acknowledged.
1.    Lustick (1980) offers the most thoughtful, systematic analysis of the policy towards Arabs in Israel. He discusses control of Arabs on three levels — structural,

institutional and programmatic – of which the last one concerns specific policies of the regime. This paper has gained in insight from Lustick's analysis.

2.    In this connection Toledano (1969) commented:

The deterrent capability lies in a wider use of the Defence (Emergency) Regulations and not in imposing a military government which is not a deterrent without the application of the Defence Regulations. It is possible to declare a curfew in an Israeli Arab village (as has recently been done in Kfar Sulam near Afula), to close areas and to ban entry, to arrest people, to restrict or confine them, to demolish houses and to lay down a policy of permits. All this can be done without reinstating the military government.

3.    The close link between the mechanisms of economic dependence and political control is explicit in the 'Policy of Reward and Punishment' which has underpinned the domination policy for many years. In one policy document some of the means used are specified as follows:

1. The dispensation of personal favours to positive elements and withholding them from negative ones. 2. The fostering of leaders in different ranks by allocating benefits through them. 3. The provision of preferential treatment to religious groups like the Druzes, Circassians and Christian sects or 'positive' villages in social and economic development according to the degree of their integration into the state. 4. The punishment of 'negative' persons and bodies by withholding benefits from them. (Israel Labour Party, 1973)

It is further stressed that 'the democratic character of the state does not allow an effective application of this policy without exposure to a public or judicial criticism'.

4.    The survey was based on a national interview sample of 1,185 Arabs representing all Arabs aged sixteen years and over living in Israel, within the pre-1967 borders (excluding residents of East Jerusalem). A parallel national representative sample of 1,267 Jews was also taken. The fieldwork for both samples, along with complementary interview samples of ninety leaders from each population, was completed in July 1980 and was funded by the Ford Foundation. Some findings from this study will be quoted below. For similar findings of an earlier survey, conducted in 1976, see Smooha, 1980b.

5.    These alternatives are taken, with some modification, from my book, 1978: 249–51.

6.    Two proposals along the lines of the alternative of maximal incorporation were published. One is by Kook and Merlin (1975) and is general but has weighty implications for the status of Arabs in Israel, and the second by Rosenzweig (1977), one of the leaders of the Shutafut (Partnership) Movement ('Union for Creating Conditions of Partnership between Arabs and Jews').

7.    Hilf (1979: 48) maintains that the provision of a separate legal status for Arabs in Israel is an integral component in the resolution of the Palestinian problem. Collective legal rights may include, inter alia, proportional representation in the Knesset, in the government and in the civil service, officially recognized Arab representation and institutional autonomy in certain areas. During the inter-war period, the League of Nations widely used a separate legal status as a means of tackling the rampant problem of national minorities in Europe. For instance, Polish Jews waged a struggle and to a large extent managed to gain official status as a national minority (Netzer, 1980). The policy of the United Nations since 1945 shifted the emphasis, however, from protection of minority collective rights to individual human rights because of the tremendous obstacles the previous policy had faced.

## References

ALON, YIGAL 1969 *Curtain of Sand.* (Hebrew). Tel-Aviv: Hakibbutz Hameuhad.
COHEN, RAANAN 1976 'The integration of Arabs in Israel'. (Hebrew.) *Migvan* 6 (May): 39–42.

DE TOCQUEVILLE, ALEXIS 1969 *Democracy in America.* Garden City, N.Y.: Anchor.
EISENSTADT, S. N., and ROKKAN STEIN (eds) 1973 *Building States and Nations.* Vols 1–2. Beverly Hills, Calif.: Sage.
GERAISY COMMITTEE 1973 *The Committee Report to Determine the Expenditures and Revenues in the Local Councils of the Minorities.* (Hebrew.) (Mimeographed.) Jerusalem: Ministry of the Interior.
GREENSTEIN, FRED, and NELSON POLSBY (eds) 1975 *Policies and Policy Making: Handbook of Political Science.* Vol. 6. Reading, Mass.: Addison-Wesley.
HAREL COMMITTEE 1976 *The Conclusions of the Committee on the Activities of the Histadrut in the Arab Sector.* (Hebrew.) (Mimeographed.) Tel-Aviv: Executive Committee of the Histadrut.
HILF, RUDOLF 1979 'The other dimension of peace'. *New Outlook* 22, 4 (May–June): 44–50.
ISRAEL, KNESSET 1979 *Tax Collection among the Self-employed in the Minority Sector: The Conclusions of a Sub-Committee of the Finance Committee.* (Hebrew.) (Mimeographed.) Jerusalem: Knesset.
ISRAEL LABOUR PARTY 1973 *Arabs in Israel – Policy: Issues for Discussion by the Political Committee of the Maarakh.* (Hebrew.) (Mimeographed.) Tel-Aviv: Israel Labour Party.
ISRAEL LABOUR PARTY 1974 *Arabs in Israel* (2) *– The Party Policy and Activities of the Arab Department.* (Hebrew.) (Mimeographed.) Tel-Aviv: Arab Department, Israel Labour Party.
ISRAEL, PRIME MINISTER'S OFFICE 1977 *Government Year Book, 1976–77.* (Hebrew.) Jerusalem: Government Printer.
JEWISH–ARAB PUBLIC COUNCIL 1976 *The Protocol of the First Session of 3 November 1976.* (Hebrew.) (Mimeographed.) Jerusalem: Bureau of the Prime Minister's Advisor on Arab Affairs.
KAHANE, MEIR 1977 'Emigration is the only solution'. *Judaism* 26, 4 (Fall): 393–404.
KIPNIS, BARUCH 1978 *Housing Assistance in the Arab Sector.* (Hebrew.) (Mimeographed.) Haifa: Hahevra Leyissum, University of Haifa.
KOENIG, ISRAEL (Northern District Commissioner, Ministry of the Interior) 1976 'The Koenig report: top secret: memorandum proposal – handling the Arabs of Israel'. *Journal of Palestine Studies* 6, 1 (Autumn): 190–200.
KOL, MOSHE 1979 *In the Struggle for Jewish–Arab Partnership.* (Hebrew.) Kibbutz Tel-Yitzhak: Forder Liberal College.
KOOK, HILLEL, and SHMUEL MERLIN 1975 'Proposal for a national debate'. *New Outlook* 18, 7 (October–November): 86–95.
KOVERSKY COMMITTEE 1976 *The Committee Report on Planning and Construction Problems in the Northern Region.* (Hebrew.) (Mimeographed.) Jerusalem: Bureau of the Director-General, Ministry of the Interior.
LIJPHART, AREND 1977 *Democracy in Plural Societies.* New Haven, Conn.: Yale University Press.
LIN, AMNON 1971 'Amnon Lin on the activity of the Israel Labor Party among the Arabs and Druzes in Israel'. (Hebrew.) Pp. 307–24 in Jacob Landau, *The Arabs in Israel.* Tel-Aviv: Maarakhot.
LOCKARD, DUANE 1975 'Race policy'. Pp. 241–303 in Fred Greenstein and Nelson Polsby (eds), *Policies and Policymaking: Handbook of Political Science.* Vol. 6. Reading, Mass.: Addison-Wesley.
LUSTICK, IAN 1979 'Stability in deeply divided societies: consociationalism versus control'. *World Politics* 31, 3 (April): 325–44.
LUSTICK, IAN 1980 *Arabs in the Jewish State: A Study in the Control of a National Minority.* Austin, Texas: Texas University Press.
NEAMAN INSTITUTE 1979 'Report of the Work Team on Arabs in Israel'. (Hebrew.) Pp. 124–70 in *Implications of Peace for the State of Israel.* (Mimeographed.) Haifa: Samuel Neaman Institute for Advanced Studies in Science and Technology, the Technion.

NETZER, SHLOMO 1980 *The Struggle of Jews in Poland for Their Civil and National Rights, 1918–1922.* (Hebrew.) Tel-Aviv: Tel-Aviv University.

PELED COMMITTEE 1975 *Report of the Committee on Arab Education.* (Hebrew.) (Mimeographed.) Jerusalem: Planning Project of Education for the Eighties, Ministry of Education and Culture.

RATOSH, YONATHAN 1976 Press Interview. (Hebrew.) *Maariv,* 13 August.

REKHESS, ELI 1977 *Arabs in Israel and the Land Expropriations in Galilee: Background, Events and Implications, 1975–1977.* (Hebrew.) (Mimeographed.) Sekirot No. 53. Tel-Aviv: Shiloah Centre, Tel-Aviv University.

ROSE, RICHARD 1971 *Governing without Consensus: An Irish Perspective.* Boston: Beacon Press.

ROSENFELD, HENRY 1978 'The class situation of the Arab national minority in Israel'. *Comparative Studies in Society and History* 20, 3 (July): 374–407.

ROSENZWEIG, RAHEL 1977 'Partnership'. *New Outlook* 20, 4 (June–July): 31–4.

SHAI, THE MOVEMENT FOR CHANGE AND INITIATIVE 1978 *Arabs in Israel – Basic Recommendations.* (Hebrew.) (Mimeographed.) Tel-Aviv: Party Headquarters.

SHAPIRA, YONATHAN 1977 *Democracy in Israel.* (Hebrew.) Ramat Gan: Massada.

SHARON, MOSHE (Prime Minister's Advisor on Arab Affairs) 1979 Press Interview. (Hebrew.) *Maariv,* 2 February.

SMOOHA, SAMMY 1978 *Israel: Pluralism and Conflict.* Berkeley and Los Angeles: University of California Press.

SMOOHA, SAMMY 1980a 'Control of minorities in Israel and Northern Ireland'. *Comparative Studies in Society and History* 22, 2 (April): 256–80.

SMOOHA, SAMMY 1980b *The Orientation and Politicization of the Arab Minority in Israel.* Occasional papers on the Middle East (New Series), No. 2. Haifa: The Jewish–Arab Centre, University of Haifa.

TESSLER, MARK 1975 'Secularism in the Middle-East? Reflections on recent Palestinian proposals'. *Ethnicity* 2: 178–203.

TOLEDANO, SHMUEL (Prime Minister's Advisor on Arab Affairs) 1969–1977 Press interviews. (Hebrew.) *Maariv,* 28 November 1969: *Maariv,* 22 November 1974; *Yediot Acharonot,* 15 December 1975; *Haaretz,* 28 January 1977.

TZEMAH, MINA 1980 *The Attitudes of the Jewish Majority in Israel towards the Arab Minority.* Research Report. (Hebrew.) (Mimeographed.) Jerusalem: Van Leer Foundation.

VAN DEN BERGHE, PIERRE L. 1973 'Pluralism'. Pp. 959–77 in John J. Honigmann (ed.), *Handbook of Social and Cultural Anthropology.* Chicago: Rand McNally.

# 17

# Civilian Control during a Protracted War

*Yoram Peri*

In spite of the many references to Israel and the IDF
in comparative works on civil-military relations, none
of the existing conceptual frameworks in the field appear to be fully applicable to the case of Israel. The
complexity and unique features of the case of Israel
against the background of relative poverty of conceptualization in most comparative works in the field
account for the tendency among students of civil-
military relations in Israel to focus on the characteristics of the case rather than engage themselves
in theorizing. [1]

This contention, however accurate, is unfortunately exces-
sively forgiving of the state in which the research of civil-military
relations in Israel finds itself today. The low level of theoretical
development on the one hand, and the limited scope and depth of
empirical research on the other, have brought about a distorted
presentation of political-military relations—even in the descriptive,
as opposed to the theoretical, sphere. This distortion is a result
mainly of the lack of distinction between the normative model and
the operative pattern.

Until recent years most researchers of the Israeli case described the operative pattern. However, they did not realize they
were using terminology borrowed from the normative model. This
was particularly evident in Perlmutter's article: "The Israeli Army
in Politics: The Persistence of the Civilian over the Military,"[2]
and even more in his book, <u>Military and Politics in Israel</u>—considered <u>the</u> textbook on the Israeli case.[3]

At the base of this conception, which is still accepted by the majority of researchers, the IDF is presented as an instrumental army. In other words: (1) the military is nothing but a tool that carries out government-approved policy, (2) as such, it is subordinate to efficient national supervision, and (3) it is completely separated from the party system.

David Ben-Gurion who, more than anyone else, molded the institutional pattern of the Israeli defense system, defined the role and status of the military on October 27, 1949, as follows:

> The military does not determine the policy, the regime, the laws and the government-rulings in the state. The army itself does not even determine its own structure, regulations and ways of operation, nor does it decide upon peace or war. The military is the executive branch, the defense and security branch of the Israeli government. . . . The government carries the full brunt of responsibility for the military before those elected to the Knesset; the military is subordinate to the government, and is no more than the executor of the political line and the orders received from the legislative and executive institution of the state: i.e., the Knesset and the cabinet. . . .[4]

Even Ben-Gurion's historical opponents credit him with this great achievement—the depoliticization of the armed forces, the elimination of the private military organizations, and the creation of a unified national army, that stands under the supervision of the national government and is disconnected from party politics. This perception of the "nationalized" IDF is commonly accepted to this very day by military personnel and politicians in Israel and, indeed, in the professional literature. Thus it is even possible to find in Safran's recent and acclaimed book the contention that "Israel's record has so far been clean of intrusion of the military into politics in any form."[5] Indeed?

Actually, this description of the relationship between the IDF and the political system stems from a more general conception of civilian-military relations in Israel. The first researchers of the Israeli case, during the early 1960s, were influenced by the academic climate of the time. What surprised the military sociologists and the modernization researchers was the fact that Israel, whom they believed belonged to the category of developing countries, did not experience what most of its neighbors did—military takeovers. The enigma the scholars were faced with was this: how was military infiltration into the various systems of the civilian sector avoided.

The multitude of answers posited all shared a common basic assumption: the IDF never became a praetorian army because the conditions for praetorianism never developed in Israel. Israel is a "nation in arms" and the IDF is a "people's army." In other words, the military does not reflect one group or social class, but rather the society as a whole. True, the military embodies a constant professional nucleus, with developed military capabilities; that nucleus is limited, however. Actually the entire army is based on general, obligatory conscription. This army is affected by the developed values of equality that characterize the civilian society; it is a professional army with antimilitarist values, and a strong ethical sense of public service. In short, the military service is an expression of good citizenship—of virtue.

The theoretical development in the field of modernization that took place in the early 1970s, and the Israeli empirical research done in the field, led to the realization that the concept of modernization is not appropriate as the accurate theoretical context for the analysis of Israeli civilian-military relations. The problem was now defined in terms of Lasswell's paradigm: What characterizes Israel is its state of protracted war, be it actual fighting or latent war.

The question that therefore arises is, what happens to a society that is perpetually in a state of siege? Is it possible that the existence of a large military establishment that absorbs respectable portions of national resources will not lead to the infiltration of the military and the military-mind into civil sectors not directly connected to defense? In other words, is it possible for a "society in siege" not to become a "garrison state"? Apparently, despite the different points of departure of research, the answer remained the same: while the centrality of security in Israeli society is the reality, a process of militarization of Israeli society has not occurred; Israel has remained an Athens and has not become a Sparta. Once again, for the same reason, Israel is a "nation in arms" and its army—"a people's army."[6]

Furthermore, one of the accepted conditions that induce military intervention in politics—in third world countries as well as in northern hemisphere societies—is the alienation of the army from civil society; alienation as a result of a high corporative level of the military establishment, stemming from antimilitary attitudes among sectors of the civilian elite, or due to the ascriptive draft base of the army (i.e., based on a specific social group, locale, class, ethnic group, etc.). Within a "nation in arms" such as Israel—a society in which, according to the definition of the IDF's second chief of staff, Yigael Yadin, "every citizen is a soldier on an 11 month leave"—it is impossible for alienation between the

people and their army to develop, and therefore development of
interventionist motivation among the military establishment is
unlikely.

Thus, a number of mechanisms that deepen the identification
of the army with civilian society reappear in every description of
the Israeli case. One of these is reserve service, that opens up
the professional cadre to civilian influence. Another is the rapid
rotation and early retirement of high command personnel, a phenomenon that prevents the creation of a corporate military establishment, a military interest group, or a military class.

In effect, the second generation researchers, like the first
generation researchers, committed a double error. First, their
contention that the IDF is disconnected from politics, and that the
IDF is a people's army—that is to say, that there is no categorical
distinction between these two inherently different sectors—is a
contradiction in terms. How are these two contradictory conten-
tions to be resolved? The second error was their acceptance
a priori of the assumption that military intervention in politics is
always a result of alienation, meaning a situation in which the
civilian and military sectors are separate from one another, and
there exists between them ideological tension or a struggle over
interests and resources. 7

Does there not, however, exist a danger of the expansion of
military roles into civilian functions in the opposite instance, when
the civilian society and the military overlap?

This inner contradiction in the description of the relationship
between the IDF and the political system results from a more basic
drawback in the analysis of civilian-military relations, an affliction
common to both generations of researchers. This relates specifically to their vision of the civilian sector as one monolithic, homogeneous unit, which it is not. The civilian sector must be seen as
a complex, pluralistic social system, that includes various analyti-
cally separate subsystems. It is imperative to differentiate the
nature of relations between the army and each one of these subsystems separately. Thus one will discover that in each society there
does not exist one type of civilian-military relation, but a combination of various types. One type exists between the army and one
subsystem, while another between the army and a different subsystem. What distinguishes each society is a different combination—
a different assembly of these types of relationships.

Luckham's development of the concept of boundaries may be
of help in this matter. 8 He distinguished between three types of
intersystem boundaries—integral, permeable, and fragmented—
according to two variables: (a) the degree to which the military
establishment supervises the interaction of military personnel with

the nonmilitary environment; and (b) the extent to which there is complete fusion, both in respect of goals and of organization, between the possessors of the means of violence and other social groups. The boundaries are permeable between the military sector and the civil sector while there is obfuscation or complete integration in terms of roles and organizational structure between those in society who control the means of violence, and other social groups. On the other hand, the boundaries are integral in a situation in which the interaction between the actors within the military hierarchy, and their social environment, is supervised by those who are responsible for the determination of objectives and operational goals of the military, that is, the military high command.

The third type—fragmented boundaries—are partially integral and partially permeable. The type of interaction between society and the military is characterized by fragmented boundaries when the military establishment does not succeed in efficiently supervising the contact of its personnel with high ranking civilian officials. Thus military officials, while interacting with their social and political environment, find it difficult to operate as one unit, with professional considerations only.

Luckham's contribution to the research of civilian-military relations was significant. Nonetheless, he erred by not distinguishing between the various institutional spheres of the civilian sector, and by categorizing them all under the rubric of "society." This is particularly evident with the lack of clarity between "social" and "political," and his indistinguishable use of the terms "civilian power," "socio-economic environment," and "political institutions" as parallel and identical terms.

Analysis of the Israeli case from a pluralistic point of view enables us to avoid the internal contradiction which those who attempted to define civilian-military relations in one all-inclusive definition got caught up in. The relations between the IDF and the legal subsystem, for example, are characterized by integral boundaries. It is possible here to distinguish between two separate sectors, with a high degree of autonomy for the military. (The IDF's opposition during 1980 to the Shamgar Committee that tried to open up the legal system of the IDF and subordinate it to the civil system is but one example.)

On the other hand, the IDF's interaction with the cultural subsystem is characterized by permeable boundaries and a high degree of penetration of the civilian sector into the military. Occasional attempts within the IDF to develop a value system or normative code different from those existing in the civilian sectors (i.e., strict authority patterns, "external" discipline, and formal behavior between officers and their subordinates) have been unsuccessful.

And what of the political field? Here we can locate a third
type of boundary with dual influence. The boundaries here are
fragmented and the influence is mutual. The military infiltrates
into the political subsystem, while the latter in turn infiltrates into
the army. In summary, it is possible to speak both of processes of
civilianization of the military, and militarization of civilian society
in Israel. The adoption of a pluralist conception, that divides the
civilian sector into subsystems, enables us to identify the seemingly
contradictory process that, in fact, exists side by side. [9]

The use of the pluralistic conception for the analysis of
civilian-military relations in Israel makes it possible to isolate,
for the purposes of discussion, political-military relations from
the military's other relationships with the various social subsystems,
so as to describe them more accurately. It will consequently become clear that the three assertions of the instrumentalists' thesis
are questionable. (1) The IDF does not only serve as the operational
army of the government's policy, but rather as a strong influence
upon policy formation; (2) civilian control over the military is not
effective enough. On the contrary, national supervision suffers
from weakness, and many of its control mechanisms are faulty;
and (3) the IDF is not separated from the party system, but on the
contrary, is strongly connected to it, influenced by it, and at times
even influences it. In conclusion, as opposed to the instrumentalist
model, we are now faced with a different model that can be defined
as a political-military partnership or political-military complex.

The organizational conception, according to which the public
servant's role is to deal solely with the implementation of policy
determined by the political echelon, is no longer accepted in contemporary organizational theory. Appointed officials and elected
politicians are no longer differentiated according to policy imple-
mentors and policy makers, but rather according to policy makers
and decision makers. This distinction means that while the formal
decision is made by the elected political echelon, the appointed
rank shares a large part of the responsibility for policy formation.
This is true concerning public service as a whole, including the
military. Huntington points out that, in addition to the classic role
of policy executor, there are additional roles which include representation and advising to the government. He contends, however,
that when the military transcends these roles by advocating government policy and by direct involvement in political issues that are
not related to defense, it strays from the normative framework of
a professional army. [10] For a realistic perception of the IDF one
must admit that it fulfills the function of advocacy and, to a certain
degree, that of direct involvement also.

A detailed description of the role of the IDF in the process of formulating national security policy necessitates a wide and separate analysis. We will raise here, in summary form only, a number of points that prove this contention:

1. Israel's defense policy is inseparable from its foreign policy (a symbolic expression of this is the joint committee of the Knesset for foreign and defense affairs, a unique case in Western parliamentarism). Moreover, foreign policy is perceived as mainly a function of defense policy—as in Dayan's saying: "Small countries have no foreign policy, only security policy." Consequently those responsible for defense enjoy the right to influence foreign policy directly. Since the definition of Israel's "defense" is very wide, this field of influence is very large. [11]

2. The IDF represents the cabinet's sole strategic think tank in national defense issues. Meager attempts made to place civilian strategists at the cabinet's side, whether from the foreign office or from the prime minister's office, have failed. The imbalance between the military and political arms has been raised a number of times even by government officials, but nothing has been done to alter the matter. One of the institutional expressions of that condition was pointed out by the Agranat Commission (in paragraph 22 in the interim report, April 1974); it noted that military intelligence was the only body in charge of preparing the national estimate. Despite the establishment of a research center in the foreign office and the committee's recommendations to strengthen the involvement of the Mossad, no change had taken place in military intelligence's monopoly.

3. Israel's military doctrine has created constraints upon the political aspects of strategic planning. [12] First, it has affected the world's conception of Israel's foreign policy. Since Israel was forced, for example, to compensate itself for a lack of strategic depth by adopting an offensive tactic (transferring the battle into enemy territory), it created the notion that it had an offensive security policy—while, actually, Israel's political-strategic posture was purely defensive.

Military doctrine has become a determinant upon the political process of decision making, and not only on the "image level." The influence of a rigid and static defense doctrine along the Suez Canal during the pre-Yom Kippur War period, to a large extent nurtured the political conception of nonwithdrawal from the water line without a formal peace agreement. Prime Minister Golda Meir's refusal to respond to the partial withdrawal interim agreement proposed in 1971 by Dayan, was partially affected by this doctrine. The general staff's recommendation on this particular issue strengthened the prime minister's decision to reject the proposal, which was backed by some cabinet ministers.

4. For years all of Israel's governments have avoided drafting a document that would clearly spell out Israel's war objectives. De facto, objectives have been determined on the eve of a war, or after it has broken out, and they have been formulated negatively, that is, "to foil the enemy's aggressive objectives." In other cases they have been defined partially and unclearly or, when the objectives were positive, retroactively. Consequently, partial results of some of the wars have not been predetermined by the political echelon, but rather were achieved in combat by the field commanders, according to what is known in IDF slang as "field developments."[13]

5. The structure of the general command of the IDF (which is a joint command of all three arms) and the integration of the functions of the general command (organization and preparation of forces during peace time and control over them during war) grants the Israeli chief of staff far more power than his colleagues in other Western armies. As the sole formal contact between the military and political ranks, his political power is strengthened. Since the roles of the defense minister and the prime minister were separated in 1967, the chief of staff has become a pseudo-minister. While he lacks formal voting power in the cabinet, he enjoys, de facto, as much influence as a senior member.

The chief of staff's participation in cabinet meetings, and not only in those that deal with defense matters, is but one manifestation of his special position. More important, however, is the fact that he is the only public servant able to overrule the decisions of the minister to whom he is responsible; indeed he does this quite frequently. This right evolved as a result of political struggles amongst the power elite. When the state was established, the roles of prime and defense ministers in Israel were placed in the hands of one person. They were separated later because of the need of one group within the elite to share its authority with another, so as to gain its political support. The separation of control over defense issues between the representatives of two groups, one the prime minister's and the other the defense minister's, has enabled the chief of staff to maneuver between both authorities, thus strengthening his political influence.[14]

6. When it was decided that the IDF would serve as the sole governmental authority over the territories conquered in 1967, the military government became responsible for purely civilian functions as well. The military became an active partner in the formulation of civilian policy in the territories in issues such as education, employment, health, or economy, in addition to direct

security issues. During different periods, the IDF has initiated policy in the territories (e.g., preparing plans for civilian settlements) and has even, at times, acted against the declared policy of the defense minister. The dismissal of officers in the territorial military administration and the unsuccessful attempt by Defense Minister Ezer Weizman in 1979 to dismiss the coordinator of activities in the territories, Major-General Dani Matt, was but one manifestation of the tension that existed between the military and political ranks—a tension that resulted from the military's institutional power and that contradicted the principles of an instrumentalist army.

The IDF's infiltration into the sphere of foreign and defense policy formulation is not only an inevitable product of the "state of siege" existence. It is also the result of the premeditated actions of the man whose influence upon the institutional pattern of the defense system of Israel was greater than anyone else's—Ben-Gurion. His fear of the perpetuation of the prestate Yishuv patterns, in which political movements controlled the military organizations and officers were loyal to particular parties, moved him to separate the defense sphere from the party system. Not only did he nationalize the military organizations, but he wanted to autonomize this field and separate it from the set of considerations, norms, and game rules that were common practice in all other public fields.

He did this in a number of ways. One was the professionalization of defense matters. While taking advantage of his full authority as national and movement leader, and as prime and defense minister, Ben-Gurion declared that the process of decision making in the field of defense would be different from that in the political system, where compromise, bargaining, searching for consensus and majority rule were accepted. In the sphere of defense, the decision would be one man's alone—his own. Moreover, professional considerations only, and not political ones, would determine defense policy, and defense matters would be under the jurisdiction of professionals only—the military high command—and not politicians. [15]

Ben-Gurion was not aware at the time that by acting in such a way, he was creating a problem. By placing defense matters in the hands of military personnel he indeed isolated the politicians from that field, but, on the other hand, he enabled the military to deal directly with politics; for ultimately, it is impossible to isolate defense matters from their political context. Thus, while preventing the politicians' influence over the specialists, he granted the specialists an almost free hand in the political ball game.

Had the political echelon held substantial means of control over the army, it would perhaps have been able to limit the span of the specialists' political activities. However, the system of national supervision over the military was built differently.

## THE WEAKNESS OF NATIONAL CONTROL

The 1976 Basic Law: The Army, was a direct outcome of the conclusions of the Agranat Commission, created to examine the events surrounding the Yom Kippur War. Paragraph 17, Chapter 3 of the Commission's interim report states: "We discovered that there is no clear definition of the distribution of authorities, obligations, and responsibilities in matters of defense, between the three authorities in charge—the government and prime minister, the defense minister, and the chief of staff—and of the relationship between the political leadership and the high command of the IDF. . . ."

The legislation of this law did nothing to alter the obfuscation surrounding civilian control over the IDF. The law determined only that the military was subordinate to the cabinet; yet, there had never been any doubt concerning the normative authority of the cabinet. The Yom Kippur War simply revealed a gap in the formal definition of this authority, and the new law came to fill this gap. Nonetheless, concerning the distribution of roles, responsibility, and authority between the various echelons—the situation remained the same. This is the case in the relationship between the prime minister and defense minister, and in relations between the political rank (the defense minister), and the military rank (the chief of staff).

Two events that took place a number of years following the legislation of the law prove this point quite well. At the beginning of May, 1979, during a cabinet debate between the prime minister, Menachem Begin and the defense minister, Ezer Weizman, the latter contended: "I am responsible for defense." The prime minister responded: "This table (i.e., the cabinet) is responsible for the IDF." Weizman assumed that the prime minister was attempting to weaken his position, since the Basic Law: The Army, clearly stated that the minister of defense had greater responsibility over the army ("The appointed minister in charge of the army is the defense minister" [paragraph 2(b)]. "The chief of staff is responsible to the cabinet, and subordinate to the defense minister" [paragraph 3(b)]). Weizman repeated his point at the next cabinet meeting, on the 18th of that month, and once again Begin retorted, "I still contend that you do not understand the constitution."[16] The public debate that took place following this affair is evidence of the confusion surrounding the topic, three years after the matter was supposedly determined by law.

The second incident concerns the distribution of roles and authority between the minister of defense and the chief of staff. It occurred in the autumn of 1979, and involved an appeal to the Supreme Court. The issue that stood before the court was whether the Arab lands of the West Bank village of Rujaib had been appropriated by the military government for purely defense needs, or to erect the settlement of Elon Moreh for political reasons. The distinction is important since, according to international law, the appropriation of land in occupied territories is legal only in the first instance. The minister of defense had made no secret of his view, that political and even ideological considerations (the historical right to the Land of Israel) were behind the act; the chief of staff, on the other hand, presented the Supreme Court with his opinion that the considerations were purely of a defense nature. This deep contradiction between the position of the elected minister and the appointed chief of staff, which should have been prevented by the Basic Law, did not escape the court's notice, and the acting chairman of the Supreme Court mentioned it in his verdict.[17]

The Elon Moreh affair brings to mind a different incident that took place before the Basic Law was legislated, and which demonstrated the pseudoministerial status of the chief of staff. When, in May 1974, a PLO unit infiltrated Israel's northern border, took over a school in Galilee and held students as hostages, Minister of Defense Dayan and Chief of Staff Gur were divided on whether and when to command IDF units to storm the school. The government, which discussed the matter, authorized both to decide. The "Horev Committee," later appointed by the prime minister to examine the consequences of the affair, was forced to contend with the government's peculiar decision to grant an elected minister and an appointed chief of staff equal authority on such an operative issue. It was not clear whose opinion would have carried the day had the two adopted differing points of view.[18]

A mechanism appears to exist that mediates the role and responsibility distribution among the chief of staff, the defense minister, and the prime minister. This "constitution" is in fact a working paper that determines which operative act necessitates cabinet authorization as opposed to prime ministerial authorization only or defense minister authorization, and which is simply left to the chief of staff, with no need for preliminary authorization. For returning fire over the border, for example, the chief of staff's authority is sufficient. On the other hand, an across-the-border operation requires ministerial authorization.

This document was first prepared in June 1967 when Moshe Dayan became defense minister. Since then it has been reformulated and approved with the advent of each new government. This "constitution," however, deals only with operational aspects, and leaves much room for misunderstanding. Indeed, this happened a mere two days after it was first signed in June 1967: Dayan directly ordered the Head of the Northern Command, Major-General David Elazar, to attack the Syrian front on the Golan Heights without previously receiving explicit approval from Prime Minister Levi Eshkol.

A statement made by Chief of Staff Mordechai Gur more than ten years later indicates the confusion that continued to surround even the operational aspect: "The authority of the defense minister is in political-strategic matters. The chief of staff's authority is over all matters of military tactics. There is cooperation between the two in the intermediary issues. The mutual influence between the strategic sphere and the tactical and political ones is what prompts misunderstandings and disagreements."[19]

Indeed a confusing definition. The "constitution" blatantly states that even in the tactical sphere, the chief of staff must receive clear-cut approval from the political rank. Furthermore, what is the meaning of "cooperation between the chief of staff and the minister in the intermediary issues?" Who defines the intermediary issues? Whose authority prevails in cases of disagreement? The commentary given by Chief of Staff Gur, according to this quote at least, openly contradicts the definitions determined in the "constitution." Did these remarks result from the fact that while he served as chief of staff he acted, in certain cases, on his own understanding of his authority?[20]

The weakness of national control over the military is, however, expressed not only on the operative level. Civil control mechanisms are weak in other aspects of political-military relations. So marginal is the authority of the Knesset Defense and Foreign Affairs Committee that a few illustrations will suffice. Not only do its decisions lack obligatory validity, but it lacks the power to force military personnel to appear before it. The influence of this committee, as well as that of the finance committee, over the defense budget, is minimal; it lacks the tools and the apparatus to deal with it. Since the state was established, the approved budget that emerged from the committee's chambers has been, in practically all cases, very similar to the proposed budget presented to it; and this is but one indirect expression of its passivity.

The government's influence over the defense budget is also marginal. In fact, the Israeli defense budget is basically determined by the military high command, and not by the civilian arm of the Defense Ministry. One institutional manifestation of this situation is the fact that, since 1956, the chief of staff's financial advisor serves also as head of the budget department in the defense ministry. Those personally acquainted with this issue testify that "since the head of the budget department is a military man—specifically the financial advisor to the chief of staff—his loyalty and obedience to the chief of staff are stronger."[21]

The following limited and random collection of statements testifies to the weakness of the civil control mechanisms: "Things are going on (in the defense sphere) that I do not hear about. I hear of the news on 'The Voice of Israel,' and later read it in the paper, without knowing its true background" (Prime Minister Moshe Sharett, 1954). "I haven't hid my passive cooperation in deceiving Prime Minister Sharett" (former Chief of Staff Dayan, 1960). "Despite the fact that the approval of the defense minister is needed for the appointment of military generals, in 99% of the cases, the minister accepted the chief of staff's position" (the military secretary to Dayan and Peres, 1979). "Civil control over the defense budget is fragile, since the Cabinet lacks the tools to check the budget" (Minister of Justice Chaim Tsadok, 1977). "The budgetary system in the defense ministry does not stand up to the essential demands necessary to function adequately. As a result, its effectiveness as a managerial tool and as a means of control and supervision is harmed" (State Comptroller's yearly report, 1967. Similar reports appeared for a few years consecutively). "Naturally we must rely on the general command when it tells us that there is a need for additional missiles or tanks, even if there is someone on the committee who thinks otherwise. Who are we to decide? We understand nothing in this matter" (Member of Knesset Israel Kargman, who was for many years chairman of the Knesset Finance Committee, 1977).[22] "During the War in Lebanon the Cabinet was always informed, but sometimes only after operations had been carried out" (Deputy Prime Minister Simcha Ehrlich, 1983).

These weaknesses of national control mechanisms over the military dialectically result from the depoliticization conception that guided Ben-Gurion when he established the defense system. In his desire to separate the IDF and the defense sphere from the political arena, he created integral boundaries not only between the military and the political parties, but between the military and public institutions. Due to Israel's political nature, however, the parties do have influence within certain national institutions: the Knesset, and even the cabinet itself. For this reason Ben-Gurion critically limited the Knesset's authority (the defense budget, for example, was not even brought before the Knesset during the early 1950s). For the same reason, he objected to the creation of a war cabinet or a ministerial

committee on defense. Indeed, when it was created, against his
will, he severely limited its actions (unlike his successor, Eshkol).

Ben-Gurion objected to the creation of an institutional civilian
control system such as Defense Minister Pinchas Lavon proposed
in 1954. A system with a bureaucratic basis would not only limit
the personal maneuverability of the prime minister and minister of
defense, but would inherently reflect the political culture and prevent the possibility of an autonomous defense sphere. In its stead,
Ben-Gurion preferred rather charismatic control: a pattern that
rests on his special status as prime minister and defense minister,
as national leader and leader of the ruling party. And indeed, the
system's faults became apparent at the time Ben-Gurion left his
post; the disappearance of the charismatic authority figure shattered
the entire control system.

Thus civilian control over the military, having been vested in
institutionalized charismatic authority alone, with no clear and
formal legal definitions, and with no strong mediatory mechanisms
between the military and civilian sectors, was not sufficient to ensure civilian control over the army. To that end, Ben-Gurion
needed an additional channel of control. This existed during the
pre-State Yishuv period, but Ben-Gurion supposedly did away with
it after the State was established. In reality, however, he did not:
during Ben-Gurion's entire term of office and even following his
resignation in the 1960s, this additional channel of civilian control
continued to exist; it was within the framework of the ruling party.


The Dual Control Pattern

One of the main differences between the pattern of civilian
control over the military accepted in communist countries, and that
in liberal democracies, revolves around the role of the political
party within the political system in general, and within political-
military relations in particular. While in Western regimes ruling
parties do not enjoy any status whatsoever in the institutional arrangements of control, the ruling communist party fulfills a crucial
role in civilian control: "The party must control the rifle, for the
rifle must never control the party," states the Maoist formulation
of the Leninist dictum.[23]

The founding fathers of the Israeli political system, who were
reared in the tradition of the revolutionary parties of Eastern Europe
at the turn of the century, accepted this principle and have acted
accordingly ever since the Haganah was established in 1920. Despite the fact that, during the entire period of the Yishuv, military
organizations were subordinate to the formal authority of broad-

based national institutions—in the beginning the Histadrut (Confederation of Labor), later on the National Committee (the representative body of the entire Jewish community in Palestine) and the Zionist Organization (which included all worldwide Zionist movements)—de facto, the authority and influence of the leaders of the ruling party, Mapai, was never eliminated.[24]

While formally Ben-Gurion spoke of eliminating the political parties' influence over the military, he was well aware that the influence of the party control channel had continued after the state was established. This influence was vested in a number of mechanisms, the first being the "enlisted department"—a special branch of Mapai headquarters. This body maintained a permanent staff, and was created as a kind of political department for the military command, whose political activities could not be as overt as those of the other party departments. The department recruited officers as party members, organized meetings in which the party political elite (i.e., the government) participated, and supplied written material to its members. During elections, active department members helped the party function within civil and military branches of the defense system.[25] When an officer-member was about to retire, he was aided by the department in locating civilian jobs and housing, and in solving material problems.[26]

Occasionally department heads were involved in officer appointments and advancement within the army. Often they took part in consultations concerning appointment of officers to specific positions, or acted as an indirect channel for officers who wished to conduct informal contact with the political elite. In some cases department personnel examined lists of candidates for advancement within the command system. Most important, the department created the feeling within the IDF that "an officer who wants to advance in the army must belong to the right party."[27] These were accepted norms of political activism in the 1950s and 1960s.

The difference between the department's activities and the control pattern of the commissar in the Soviet army is, of course, considerable. In the latter case, the party representative uses political control in the widest sense of the word—changing or limiting the behavior of an organization member to advance aims external to the organization or its goals.[28] Within the IDF there was no attempt to influence professional decisions at the officer rank. Since officers accepted their subordination to civilian authority, objective control within the IDF was, in Huntington's terms, clear-cut—the aim of the party control channel being to attain diffuse support among the officers for the political leadership. This was done by the participation of officers in joint meetings with the leadership, and not by direct control over them.

The 'enlisted department' was, in this sense, a tool that was aimed at arousing solidarity between those in uniform and party leaders; it was both a tension regulator and an integrational mechanism between the two groups. The political leadership sought to use this tool to strengthen its influence over the officer ranks, and to that end was prepared to enable officers to participate in the decision-making process. But the influence was, nonetheless, indirect and exercised through informal means, such as party meetings of a nonobligatory nature.[29] The weakness created by this pattern of party control, however, is easily apparent. It strengthened the military elite vis-à-vis the political elite, and obfuscated the relationship between the two at the national and party levels as well.

The second mechanism of party control was the political appointment of officers. This was formally possible due to the legal arrangement by which an appointment to the rank of colonel or above required the authorization of the minister of defense. In the early 1950s, Ben-Gurion blatantly limited the advancement of officers who either did not support his Mapai Party or were not at least politically neutral (in the spirit of the British Army). The low professional level of the IDF at the time, however, necessitated changes in the high command: a substantial limitation of the number of British Army veterans, and the advancement of officers who performed well during the War of Independence despite their political "disadvantage" (support of parties to the left of Mapai: Mapam and Achdut Haavoda). This was heartily encouraged by Moshe Dayan, then head of the Operations Branch. Consequently, Ben-Gurion and the prime ministers who followed him were careful to insure the appointment to other key military positions of officers who, in addition to their professional expertise, belonged actively or passively to Mapai. This touched on positions such as head of Manpower Branch, head of Personnel Department in charge of advancement and appointment of officers, chief of intelligence, chief education officer and others.

Of all these positions, the one with the greatest political significance was the chief of staff. Government sensitivity to the chief of staff's political orientation has continued to this very day. But for one exception, in which Ben-Gurion preferred a nonparty man with a purely instrumental approach (Major General Haim Laskov, a British Army veteran), all chiefs of staff have been identified not only with the policies of the political elite that appointed them, but have supported that elite's party. And even in the case of the one politically neutral chief of staff, the party channel was ensured by the appointment of a deputy who was a reknowned party man (Major General Zvi Zur).

Mapai's activities within the army contradicted its own "national army" banner, and for that reason it acted discreetly. That dominant party leaders took part, however, points to the fact that Ben-Gurion was not interested in integral boundaries, but rather in fragmented ones: impenetrable to other parties, permeable to Mapai; closed to public institutions, open to the elite of the ruling party.

The continued existence of party control can be seen, in this respect, as part and parcel of the national control package. The weakness in the national arm that resulted from charismatic control required additional mechanisms to ensure effective control. From the politicians' point of view, the creation of an additional control mechanism was necessary precisely because the military elite enjoyed such an honorable status in the national political system and the national decision-making process. Hence the additional party control framework that ensured three components of military loyalty to the civilian rank: personal loyalty to the national leader, organizational loyalty to the ruling party, and loyalty to the party's political policies. While an appraisal of this informal and noninstitutionalized control channel on the party level shows that it contradicted the formal principle of an instrumentalist army, one must admit that it also ensured harmony between the political and military ranks, and a coherent political approach by the military and political elites.

CONCLUSION: EXPANSION OF THE PERMEABLE SECTIONS

The early 1970s were characterized by a decline in the level of politicization of Israeli society, and a substantial decrease in the power of the ruling party apparatus. Parallel to this development, the postindependence war generation of officers entered the military elite. The officers did not go through intensive premilitary political socialization as had the founding generation, and many held professional military orientations. Consequently, the importance of the formal channel of party control declined. Thus, in 1971 a non-Mapai major-general was appointed, for the first time, as head of the Manpower Branch.[30]

However, the political upheaval that took place with the rise to power of the Likud coalition in 1977 brought about a resurgence of party politicization in the 1980s and this process was apparent in the military as well. These new developments proved, once again, that the party control channel had not been completely eliminated with the establishment of the state, and that the pattern of dual control remained intact.

On the other hand, over the years both the military's self-
image and its attitude toward its own relationship with the political
system, had undergone considerable change. Once the opportunity
to enter the political field was granted to the military establishment, it was no longer willing to limit the parameters of its activities and influence. As time passed, it became more and more an
interest group, with corporative interests. Consequently, it prevented the formulation of a clearer definition of the patterns of
civilian control. The permeable boundaries between the military
and the political system that were created at the beginning of the
1950s by the politicians to fortify their influence over the military—
now granted the military establishment more power than the political establishment.

This surfaced with the crisis following the Yom Kippur War.
The Agranat Commission that examined the military's failures and
omissions at the outset of the war avoided dealing with the responsibility of the political rank, and placed full responsibility upon
the military echelon. This created a feeling of resentment among
senior officers that the politicians were using them as scapegoats.
The high command, and especially the chief of staff, consequently
demanded more authority than it had had in the past.[31]

Thus, Mordechai Gur, the last chief of staff to serve during
the Labor Party government, as well as Rafael Eitan, the first
chief of staff to serve under the Likud, enjoyed respectable political
status in any matters concerning the formulation of national defense
and foreign policies. During an intermediary period in which the
roles of defense minister and prime minister were united once again
(this occurred in 1980 under Menachem Begin) the influence of
Chief of Staff Eitan was crucial.[32]

The strengthening of the military's influence was expressed
in the status of the chief of staff. But instances of the weakness of
civilian control on the administrative level as well, were not lacking. The military's opposition to changing the role distribution
between itself and the Ministry of Defense is but one example.

In September 1969, the incoming director-general of the
Ministry of Defense, Colonel (Res.) Yeshayahu Lavie, appointed a
committee to examine the ministry's organization, structure, and
activities. The committee was appointed with the blessings of
Defense Minister Dayan, who requested it to "concentrate on those
branches and units of the ministry that had the most contact with
the army and the social environment." To this end it had to deal
with IDF units. The chief of staff, Major-General Haim Barlev,
knew the director-general's conception of the desired relationship
between the two: that the ministry would serve as a tool of civilian
control over the army. In early October Barlev informed the

director-general of his opposition to the committee's dealings with
the IDF. "The committee's dealings are with the Ministry of Defense, and not with the arms, branches, and corps of the IDF."
Barlev then sent letters to the IDF's generals ordering them "not
to discuss with the committee any actual IDF organizational or
structural problems."[33]

In this instance, as in many others both before and after it,
the chief of staff had the upper hand, and the minister, who was
forced to decide between the director-general and the chief of staff,
ultimately supported the chief of staff. Shortly afterwards the
director-general was forced to resign.

In 1969 the director-general attempted, to no avail, to
strengthen civilian control over the military. In 1981, on the other
hand, a new minister of defense, Ariel Sharon, attempted to reform
the allocation of functions between the ministry and the military in
the opposite direction: according to his plan, the military was
destined to receive direct responsibility for additional areas which
were traditionally under the supervision of the ministry. Moreover, by merging certain ministry functions with units of the general
command—such as arms procurement, supply, and maintenance—
heads of the general command branches might serve also as heads
of civilian departments in the ministry.

The army, as expected, praised the proposed plan. No less
naturally, however, the ministry staff declared against the plan,
and warned against the danger of militarization of the civilian system. With the support of external political groups, they succeeded
ultimately in discouraging the minister from pushing his plan.[34]

The war in Lebanon of summer 1982 more acutely expressed
the relationship between the IDF and the political system that existed at the time. Israel's strategic concept in this war was conceived by the prime minister, the defense minister, and the chief
of staff. The national debate surrounding the legitimacy of the
war took place not only among the civilian population but within the
army as well. For the first time in the history of Israel's wars
there were expressions of passive protest, refusal to serve in
Lebanon on the basis of conscientious objection, and expression
by high-ranking officers of nonconfidence in the minister of defense.

During the war, the minister of defense contended that there
had never existed such close and positive cooperation between the
military and civilian echelons. But it was increasingly clear,
even to members of the ruling parties, that the Cabinet's real involvement in the process of central decision making was limited.
Once again, demands were voiced to strengthen the basis of civilian
control over the military. Again a public debate took place over
relations between the civilian and military echelons, over the

military's reporting procedures to the various civilian echelons, and over the distribution of authority and responsibility between the prime minister and the minister of defense. All these topics had previously been discussed as a result of the Yom Kippur War, and were supposedly resolved by the legislation of the Basic Law: the Army.

Corporate advantages for the military on the one hand, and the expansion of the range of the politicians' power maneuverability on the other, again prevented a clear definition of the boundaries between the military and the political system. Due to the lack of efficient mediating mechanisms between the two systems, the permeable sections of the fragmented boundaries were widened. Thus the obfuscation of the components of the Israeli military-political complex was deepened.

NOTES

1. Dan Horowitz, "The Israel Defense Forces: A Civilian-ized Military in a Partially Militarized Society," in Soldiers, Peasants, and Bureaucrats, ed. R. Kolkowicz and A. Korbonski (London: Allen & Unwin, 1982), pp. 77-100.

2. World Politics 20 (July 1968):606-43.

3. Amos Perlmutter, Military and Politics in Israel (London: Cass, 1968).

4. David Ben-Gurion, Singularity and Mission (Tel Aviv: Maarachot, 1971), p. 82 (Hebrew).

5. Nadav Safran, Israel, the Embattled Ally (Cambridge: The Belknap Press of Harvard University Press, 1978), p. 319.

6. See Gabriel Ben-Dor, "Politics and the Military in Israel during the 70s," in The Political System in Israel, ed. Moshe Lissak and Emmanuel Gutman (Tel Aviv: Am Oved), pp. 411-12 (Hebrew).

7. A blatant expression of this approach can be found in Dan Horowitz, "Is Israel a Garrison State?" The Jerusalem Quarterly, No. 4, 1977, pp. 58-75.

8. A. R. Luckham, "A Comparative Typology of Civil Military Relations," Government and Opposition, No. 6, 1971, pp. 5-35.

9. For an additional example of the use of boundaries to analyze the Israeli case, see Moshe Lissak, "The Defense Establishment and the Society in Israel: Boundaries and Institutional Linkages," an unpublished paper, prepared for the U.S. Conference, Chicago, October 23-25, 1980.

10. S. P. Huntington, The Soldier and the State (Cambridge: Belknap Press, 1957), p. 374.

11. See, for example, the IDF's struggle with the Foreign Ministry over responsibility for the armistice committees at the beginning of the 1950s; the Foreign Ministry's objections to the independent conduct of political operations in Third World countries by the Ministry of Defense and the military in the 1960s; the status enjoyed by the IDF surrounding diplomatic contacts with Egypt in 1978 (the Israeli delegation to Cairo was composed of military personnel and not foreign office personnel), and so on.

12. Dan Horowitz, "The Israeli Defense Forces," 1982.

13. Examples are the conquest of Eilat by infantry forces headed by Yig'al Alon following an expedition in the Arava during the War of Independence; the IDF's reaching the water line at the Suez Canal despite the minister of defense's opposition, or the conquest of the West Bank, both during the Six Day War; stopping at the Litani River during the "Litani operation" in 1978, etc. See Haim Benjamini, "Decisions, Coalitions, Consequences, The Six Day War, Israel, 1967: A Sociological View," unpublished research paper, University of Chicago, Department of Sociology, 1980.

14. For a detailed description of relations between the prime minister, minister of defense, and chief of staff, see chapters 6 and 7 in: Yoram Peri, Between Battles & Ballots: Israeli Military in Politics (Cambridge University Press, 1983). For example, the Barlev-Eshkol coalition versus Dayan. In effect, the appointment of Barlev to chief of staff was aimed at ensuring the prime minister's continued influence over the military, despite Dayan's appointment as defense minister. A similar situation existed in the coalition linking Prime Minister Meir and Chief of Staff Elazar against Dayan; and in the cooperation between Chief of Staff Gur and Minister of Defense Peres against Prime Minister Rabin, and between Chief of Staff Eitan and Prime Minister Begin against Defense Minister Weizman.

15. A blatant example of the attempt by the political echelon to transform a political problem into a "professional" military one and thus create a situation in which military personnel will decide on a political matter, is the request of the Biram and Ikrit villagers to return to their villages. See Baruch Kimmerling, "Sovereignty Ownership and Presence in the Jewish-Arab Conflict," Comparative Political Studies 10, 2 (July 1977):155-76.

16. See Ze'ev Segal, Maariv (Hebrew), May 27, 1979, and also Uzi Benziman, Haaretz (Hebrew), June 22, 1979.

17. Supreme Court of Justice Appeal 399/79, October 23, 1979. The court actually accepted the minister's version and criticized the chief of staff's opinion.

18. See entire report of the Horev Committee, Haaretz, July 11, 1974.

19.  Interview with Major-General Mordechai Gur, Maariv, April 14, 1978.

20.  For his statement upon his retirement from the IDF see interview in Hotam (Hebrew), May 10, 1978.

21.  See "Defense Budget" entry in Eitan Haber and Ze'ev Schiff, eds., Israeli Defense Dictionary (Guide) (Tel Aviv: Zmora Beitan, Modan, 1976), p. 551. (Hebrew)

22.  For detailed description and extensive additional evidence, see Peri, Between Battles & Ballots, especially chapters 8-10.

23.  Mao Tse Tung, Selected Military Writings (Peking: Foreign Languages Press, 1963), p. 272.

24.  See Yoram Peri, "Civil Military Relations in the Palestine Yishuv," The Wiener Library Bulletin, Vol. 34, No. 53/4, pp. 2-15.

25.  See conference protocols of the Labor Party Bureau, January 23, 1969.

26.  Interview with department head during the 1950s, Tzvi Tzafriri, on August 24, 1977.  During the 1960s and 1970s Tzafriri was a high-ranking official in the Defense Ministry and retired as deputy general director.  For additional evidence, see Peri, Between Battles & Ballots, pp. 64-70.

27.  The formulation is taken from a description by General (Res.) Matti Peled, Maariv, March 10, 1972.

28.  Timothy J. Colton, Commissars, Commanders and Civilian Authority, the Structure of Soviet Military Politics (Cambridge and London: Harvard University Press, 1979), pp. 4, 39.

29.  In 1969 the public discovered the existence of the department, and the party leaders were forced to close it down.  The editor of Davar, Yehuda Gothelf, illustrated their mood when he wrote that "in the future it is desirable to deepen the relationship between the officers and the Labor Party, for the good of both the popular character of the IDF and the democratic spirit of Israel," Davar (Hebrew), January 26, 1969.

30.  The allusion here is to Major-General Shlomo Lahat who, following his retirement from the IDF joined the Likud, and was elected Mayor of Tel Aviv.

31.  One of the clearest expressions of this conception was made by Yitzhak Rabin following publication of the Agranat Commission's conclusions.  See his autobiography, Pinkas Sherut (Tel Aviv: Maariv, 1979), pp. 413-15. (Hebrew)

32.  For details on this issue see Yoram Peri, "Political-Military Partnership in Israel," International Political Science Review 2, 3 (1981):303-15.

33.  The letter from Chief of Staff Barlev of October 7, 1970 was meant for the heads of the operations, intelligence, and

quartermaster branches and the commanders of the air force and
navy. This letter, additional correspondence on the subject, and
the committee's report are located in the Defense Ministry's
archives. Evidence of similar clashes from the 1960s and 1970s
concerning military-Ministry of Defense relations are also filed
there.

34. This conflict received extensive press coverage during
the summer of 1981.

# 18

# Materialism, Postmaterialism, and Public Views on Socioeconomics Policy: The Case of Israel

## *Avi Gottlieb* and *Ephraim Yuchtman-Yaar*

This article is concerned with public views in Israel on a series of socioeconomic and labor market issues. The empirical findings were analyzed with the aim of exploring the nature of ideological orientations and value hierarchies underlying these public views. The main findings are that there is a major concern with economic recovery, at the expense of sensitivity to humanitarian, civil, and social problems; that there appears to be a pronounced emphasis on the need for law and order that, along with related preferences, suggests a pattern of an authoritarian variant of rightism; that a majority of the public gives priority to materialist goals; and that individual level and collectivist material orientations, while moderately interrelated, produce different patterns of socioeconomic attitudes and preferences. At the aggregate level, these findings seem counter to the stereotyped preference of the Israeli public for socialist policies, and the multidimensionality of materialist value orientations may have major implications for other postindustrial nations as well.

## GENERAL CONSIDERATIONS

It is often assumed that socioeconomic policies correspond to specific sets of social values or sociopolitical ideologies. Consequently, discussions

Avi Gottlieb and Ephraim Yuchtman-Yaar, "Materialism, Postmaterialism, and Public Views on Socioeconomic Policy: The Case of Israel," *Comparative Political Studies,* Vol. 16, No. 3 (October 1983), pp. 307-335. Copyright© 1983 Sage Publications, Inc. Reprinted by permission of Sage Publications, Inc.

AUTHORS' NOTE: *Financial support from the Russell Sage Foundation, New York, and the Pinhas Sapir Center for Development, Tel-Aviv University, is gratefully acknowledged. We would like to thank the editor and the anonymous reviewers for their helpful comments. Address all correspondence to either author at the Department of Sociology and Social Anthropology, Tel-Aviv University, Tel-Aviv, Israel.*

of the interrelationships between ideologies and policies frequently revolve either around the role of dominant national ideologies in determining policies, or around the degree to which implemented policies in fact realize prevailing social values or underlying sociopolitical ideologies.

Social scientists have considered alternative classificatory schemes of value orientations relating to socioeconomic policies. The evolution of the welfare state, for example, has often been discussed in terms of leftist, liberal, or socialist ideologies, whereas rightist, conservative, or capitalist doctrines are viewed as inherently hostile to its expansion. The usefulness of applying these global concepts of ideological orientation to the study of socioeconomic policies is open to attack from several different perspectives; also, their analytic status is particularly problematic due to imprecise and inconsistent usages. On the other hand, the persistence of these terms over time, and their popularity among laymen and experts alike, suggest that what these concepts lack in elegance may be compensated for by relevance. For whatever reasons, the fact is that the study of socioeconomic policies in conjunction with these ideological labels has been central to students of industrial societies.

The recent debate over the future of the welfare state and the phenomenon of backlash against specific welfare programs have reemphasized the viability of ideological orientations, as indicated by the nature of social alignments around these issues. Thus, the antagonism between the idea of the welfare state and classical conservative (that is, also rightist and capitalist) ideology, is echoed in the writing of new-conservatives, like Bell (1975). His dismay with the welfare state stems from the conviction that many of the economic and social ills of the United States—such as high inflation and low productivity—are inevitably tied to its development. Perhaps the welfare state's most detrimental effect is the stimulation of insatiable levels of economic demands vis-à-vis the government—"the revolution of rising entitlements" (Bell, 1975).

*Fortune* magazine's editor, Robert Lubar, has recently echoed Bell's concern even more forcefully in his review of Thurow's *The Zero Sum Society:* "Government . . . [as opposed to the free market economy] produces nothing; the only way it can benefit anybody is by taking from

*acknowledged. We would like to thank the editor and the anonymous reviewers for their helpful comments. Address all correspondence to either author at the Department of Sociology and Social Anthropology, Tel-Aviv University, Tel-Aviv, Israel.*

somebody else" (1980). This neoconservative position adds another layer to the classical conservative opposition to the welfare state, based on the conviction that the economy should be dominated by market mechanisms, and on the belief in individual achievement and differential reward allocation.

Any analysis or even description in terms of the left-right, liberal-conservative, or socialist-capitalist ideological dimensions makes at least one of the following implicit assumptions: that there is a correspondence, or even a causal relationship, between predominant national ideologies and socioeconomic policies; that there is a correspondence between these ideologies and opinions regarding specific policy issues; and, not unrelatedly, that these specific opinions and attitudes are interrelated. Moreover, the latter two consistencies should be observable not only among sociopolitical elites, but in the general public as well. Yet, these are precisely the conceptual problems that have vexed analysts of political behavior for decades.

At the aggregate level, it is perhaps most interesting to note that the actual evolution and growth of welfare programs across nations may be affected very little by dominant ideologies. For example, Wilensky (1976) maintains, on the basis of his comparative empirical analysis, that economic growth and its demographic and bureaucratic ramifications are the sources of the emergence and progress of the welfare system. Wilensky states that

> in any systematic comparison of many countries over many years, alternative explanations collapse under the weight of such heavy, brittle categories as "socialist" versus "capitalist" economies, "collectivist" versus "individualistic" ideologies, or even "democratic" versus "totalitarian" political systems. However useful they may be in the understanding of other problems, these categories are almost useless in explaining the origins and general development of the welfare state [1976: XII].

Wilensky (1976) also points out that protagonists of sharply differing ideological orientations (such as conservatives and radicals) have attacked the welfare ethos of modern societies, albeit·with different motives and for different reasons.

There is not much more support for the second assumption referred to above—namely, the correspondence between ideological orientations and specific opinions. Hero (1969), for example, finds no relationship between the public's general ideological orientation and its support for specific welfare policies in the United States. In the same vein, Robinson et al. (1969) point out in their general discussion of political attitudes that terms such as "liberalism" and "conservatism" have relatively little meaning to the American public.

At the individual level of analysis, the correspondence among opinions on different policy issues, and the formation of internally consistent ideologies or "belief systems" (see Converse, 1964) has sustained a lively debate ever since Campbell et al.'s (1960) pathbreaking work. For example, Converse (1964) has reported that the public's identification with global ideological labels such as "conservatism" or "liberalism" fails to predict attitudes toward government policies in both socioeconomic and foreign affairs. While follow-up studies by Nie and his colleagues (such as Nie and Andersen, 1974; Nie et al., 1976) suggest that inter-attitudinal consistencies may have grown in recent years, both the empirical viability and the predictive power of ideological labels and self-identifications remains contested (see Smith, 1980; Hurley and Hill, 1980).

Why indeed is there so little evidence for consistent ideological orientations in the public? Before we decide to dismiss the importance of discussing socioeconomic policies in terms of conventional ideological concepts, we should remember that each ideological system may in fact represent, as Canovan (1981) has put it, "a family of related ideas." In other words, ideological orientations may well contain their own diversities and internal contradictions, rather than being definable as single, unidimensional entities. Converse (1964) was well aware of this view and its implications when he asserted the importance of recognizing,

> the degree to which our "normal" or a priori expectations in these matters are conditioned by sophisticated views of the parts that make up a coherent political ideology . . . . The fact that one issue reaction fails to fit into a larger organization of attitudes that seem appropriate for it does not mean that response is random or in any other sense "uncaused" [1964: 112-113].

The above commentaries suggest, then, that attempts to relate global ideologies to specific socioeconomic attitudes ultimately may not be as futile as some of the empirical analyses imply. The potential complexities of ideological orientations suggest that simplistic labels such as socialism or liberalism are unlikely to predict support or opposition to specific welfare policies in any straightforward manner. Yet, empirical knowledge of the prevailing attitudes in any such domain may lead to a better understanding of the actual configurations of ideas that make up distinct ideologies in different nations and groups, and among different individuals. For example, the public may well respond to a given set of socioeconomic issues or welfare programs in a way that seems inconsistent if we employ a priori notions about, say, the socialist ideological orientation; but in terms of the actual empirical construction of the socialist ideological stance taken by the public, these responses may be perfectly consistent.

While the long tradition of research on the relationship between political ideologies and policy preferences is still very much alive, different and more recently developed conceptualizations of social values have gained increasing attention among students of the public scene. Common to these perspectives is the assumption that the structural changes that have taken place in industrial nations necessitate new analytic concepts for understanding the nature of value systems and the bases for their organization. Implicitly at least, this approach rejects the conventional ideological typologies as inadequate for capturing the most meaningful dimensions of values mapping. The socioeconomic reality of modern societies presumably implies new levels of needs and opportunities that give rise to new constellations of value structures that must be explored and understood.

One of the influential propositions of this nature has been Inglehart's (1977; 1981) conceptualization of the materialist-postmaterialist dimension. The point of departure for this distinction is that, as societies move from a relatively primitive to a more advanced stage of industrialization, there is a fundamental shift in value orientation. The single most important structural factor underlying this transition is the affluence level reached by these societies, and the experiences of psychological and economic security facilitated by it. These experiences are conducive to the emergence of new value priorities among the publics in these nations: materialist (or "austerity" and "authoritarian") values are replaced by postmaterialist (or "hedonist" and "libertarian") values (Inglehart, 1982:1).

The assessment of materialist and postmaterialist value hierarchies is indicated by the priorities given to different goal alternatives on both the collective level (such as "maintaining a high rate of economic growth" or "fighting rising prices" reflecting a materialist outlook, versus "giving the people more say in important government decisions" or "progress toward a less impersonal, more humane society" representing post-materialist values), and the individual level (such as "having a good salary" or a "safe job", versus "having more to say on the job" or "doing an important job which gives a feeling of accomplishment"). Inglehart's theory has been tested empirically in both cross-sectional and cross-cultural research.

While Inglehart's argument has been disputed on both methodological and empirical grounds (see Flanagan, 1979, 1980: Milkis & Baldine, 1978), the basic idea underlying his approach generally has been accepted. In particular, Inglehart's findings support the unidimensionality of the materialist-post-materialist concept and testify to the existence of systematic differences in value preferences as predicted by the theory. Thus, Inglehart finds value differences as a function of age or cohort, socioeconomic and occupational status, and other social status and situs variables. On the other hand, there are few systematic variations in value preference among the eleven nations studied to date—nine European countries, the United States, and Japan. All are advanced, postindustrial economies, and all but one (Italy) publics show an approximately 3:1 ratio preference for materialist values.

Yet, and most significantly for our present purposes, in none of these cases is there any indication that value priorities at the individual and collective levels might be discrepant. Indeed, when presenting empirical data, Inglehart (1982) often uses these two levels interchangeably. It is precisely the possibility of such a discrepancy—that is, that material-postmaterial value preferences are *not* unidimensional—that makes Israel a most intriguing case for the study of socioeconomical value hierarchies.

In contrast to the condition of the nations studied by Inglehart in the 1970s—and perhaps in increasing congruence with the condition some of these nations may be approaching as a result of the current economic crisis—in Israel there exists a *fundamental and persistent discrepancy* between the economic malaise at the national level and the economic affluence generally prevailing at the individual level. This article is concerned primarily with the question of whether or not this discrepancy also entails a corresponding divergence between collective and individual values regarding socioeconomic issues. A brief discussion of the Israeli socioeconomic context may further clarify this matter.

## THE ISRAELI CONTEXT

The case of Israel is particularly interesting, with respect to the study of socioeconomic values, for four reasons. First, despite its modest position in the group of advanced industrial nations, Israel has gained a significant measure of success in establishing itself as a welfare state par excellence. The initiation and implementation of programs aimed at enhancing social welfare in Israel are part of a complex process, but undeniably were accompanied by a potent ideological orientation, at least in the early years.

Second, the Israeli public is and always has been assumed to be, characterized by particularly high levels of ideological commitment and involvement. This may not only explain the significant ideological component in the emergence of the Israeli welfare state, but it also predicts relatively stable attitudinal consistencies in the domain of present socioeconomic policies.

Third, the Israeli public has shifted gradually to the political "right" within the last decade, a shift evident in both voting behavior trends since 1969 and in public opinion polls (see Arian, 1973; Arian and Shamir, 1981). Yet, there has been no documented parallel shift of attitudes vis-a-vis domestic policies and socioeconomic issues. For example, while we know that for 20 years a constant majority of the Israel public identifies itself with a "socialist" ideology (Arian and Shamir, 1981), it remains unclear as to whether this socialist ideological label corresponds to specific socioeconomic attitudes, or whether a shift to the "right" has occurred in this sphere as well.

Fourth, and most importantly, the case of Israel puts Inglehart's conceptualization of the materialist-postmaterialist value orientation to a severe test. Ingelhart's research has so far been limited to highly developed and industrialized nations, characterized by a substantial convergence between national individual affluence. Israel, as already noted above, does not fit this pattern; national economic health and individual affluence are widely discrepant and continue to move in opposite directions,[1] leading us to suspect that materialism may in fact represent different continua on the collective and individual levels.

## METHOD

The data reported here were collected between October 1980 and March 1981. They reflect the replies of 132 respondents to a survey questionnaire that represents part of a more extended study entitled "Sociological aspects of socioeconomic policy in Israel." Of these respondents, 36 had taken part in one of seven group discussions[2] conducted on campus and consisting of 4 to 7 participants each; the remaining 96 participants were interviewed individually at their homes prior to filling out the questionnaire.[3] All discussion group questionnaires and some interview questionnaires were returned to the investigators personally or by mail; most interview questionnaires were administered immediately after the interview session. Three interviewees and four discussants failed to return questionnaires and are therefore not included in the analyses.

The sample included representatives of the adult Jewish population in the Greater Tel-Aviv area, and was obtained by a quota method of ecological sampling: an a priori contingency table reflecting the sex by socioeconomic status distribution in the adult Jewish population was generated, and interviewees were proportionately sampled in Greater Tel-Aviv areas populated by SES-matched income groups. The income distributions by areas were obtained from the 1979 Tel-Aviv-Yafo Municipality Statistical Yearbook (Table 7.26).

Despite these untraditional sampling methods dictated by considerations extraneous to the present concerns, the sample ultimately resembled closely the adult Jewish population as a whole. Males were slightly oversampled (54%), as was the younger age group of 20 to 30 years old (42.3% versus 33.0% in the population).[4] Of the sample, 60% were born in Israel (versus 55.9% of the population); the proportions of the Asia-Africa and Europe-America born were also well matched. Thus, the sample is quite close to being representative of the population in a number of important characteristics. Moreover, some of the findings cited below indicate a number of attitudinal trends that virtually match those obtained in surveys employing fully representative samples. Taken together, these features, while not ensuring a lack of bias, increase our confidence in the external validity of the findings.

Other characteristics of the sample—particularly those related to employment—include the following: The average occupational prestige rating, based on the Hartman (1979) scale was 5.25, with a standard deviation of 1.89; the scale ranges from 1 to 9. The sample included a wide range of blue-collar and white-collar occupations from all sectors of the economy, as well as housewives (6.7%)[5] and unemployed (5.4%, closely matching the 5.2% in the population). Finally, 17.2% were self-employed, and most of the rest (58.2%) were employed in the public rather than private sector.

The survey instrument included the following items and scales: Background items (sex, age, schooling, employment, and so on); general questions on the major problems, dilemmas, and possible solutions related to socioeconomic issues; items concerning unemployment, the role of the public and private sector in the economy, and tenure; attitudes toward the Israeli worker; preferences among work incentives; items probing for perceptions of equity and entitlements; evaluations of the effectiveness and trustworthiness of various social institutions; and measures of powerlessness (Neal and Seeman, 1962) and political alienation (Olsen, 1969). Data on perceived equity and entitlement, on the two social psychological measures, and on other selected items, will not be reported here. Completion of the questionnaire took approximately 30 to 45 minutes.

## RESULTS

### BASIC ORIENTATIONS: EFFICIENCY AND PRODUCTIVITY

Perhaps the most striking finding in this survey—a finding that permeates most if not all the individual questionnaire items—is the public's overwhelming concern with economic recovery, economic health, and efficiency. We should emphasize immediately that it is precisely such preoccupations that are indicative of a materialist value orientation at the *collective* level. As will be seen below, the attitudinal patterns formed by this emphasis on economic growth further elaborate this position.

The stress on economic recovery clearly supersedes the more traditional concerns with social equity and individual economic gains: in response to the question—"There are public discussions as to which socioeconomic goals Israel should try to achieve over the next years; please rank the following by order of importance"—most (64.4%) respondents ranked "economic recovery" first, as compared to only 22.7% who chose "a more equitable distribution of income and economic burden", and 10.9% who opted for "improving the standard of living".

Given the current state of the Israeli economy, this heightened sensitivity to economic recovery may not, in and of itself, be surprising. Yet, its juxtaposition with traditionally more highly valued issues, such as social and individual welfare is interesting insofar as it hints at a more general pattern of views that runs counter to the stereotypical conception of the Israeli public and its ideological outlook. This pattern or configuration, although not totally unequivocal or entirely consistent, is accompanied by, and possibly even reflects, several attitudes: an almost universal toughness in economic affairs and, particularly, in resolving economic and labor problems; a not entirely crystallized resistance to government intervention in the economy and to socialist solutions to socioeconomic problems; and a decidedly materialist outlook and set of values, particularly vis-a-vis workplace incentives.

The concern with economic recovery raises the question of attribution: who is to be blamed for the malfunctioning of the economy? In light of the central role of Israel's government in the planning, regulation, and supervision of economic affairs, one might expect that it would be the government that is perceived as detrimental to a well-functioning economy. While the public is indeed not complimentary about the economic performance of the government, there is also a pervasive tendency of "sharing the blame"—that is, an unfavorable view of the Israeli worker as a collectivity. Thus, in response to the question—"which of the following views of the Israeli worker are, in your opinion, correct, and which are incorrect?"—the majority of respondents (76.2%) concur that the Israeli worker is not highly productive, 79.5% that he cares only about what he can get from rather than what he can give to the workplace, and 82% that he does not, in general, invest sufficient effort. Not unrelatedly, the Israeli worker was also perceived as precipitous in announcing strikes (69.6%), unwilling to accept work discipline (56.7%), and having little or no sense of responsibility at the workplace (50.8%).

It is interesting to note that this set of attitudes virtually mirrors the findings from an earlier survey (Yuchtman-Yaar, 1976) based on a national probability sample of the Jewish labor force in Israel. This replication may be taken as one testimony to the apparent validity of the present findings. More importantly, the negative views that Israeli workers express about themselves as a collectivity evidently have prevailed for some years. Thus, the perceived economic malaise and the perceived need for recovery appear to be associated with the notion that the current normative climate discourages individual effort, productivity, and work morale.

If inefficiency and lack of productivity generate real and salient misgivings, it would be reasonable to expect that respondents should also advocate changes or mechanisms to surmount these problems—as indeed, they do. The relevant responses may be divided into two categories—the first dealing with efficacy at the workplace, and the second related to approaches to the unemployment problem.

The fact that respondents were willing to increase productivity and efficiency even at a (albeit not necessarily personal) sacrifice is evident in the 71.4% majority who either agreed or definitely agreed with the statement, "One should encourage the introduction of technological innovation even if it leads to the dismissal of workers." In a similar vein, only 26% expressed support for the present tenure system, whereas 64% advocated some change so as to make tenure contingent upon a set of criteria, and the remaining 10% suggested abandoning it altogether. It should be noted parenthetically that the tenure system is one of the pillars of labor relations in Israel, and that employees, who are usually tenured after 6 to 10 months, may be fired thereafter only with great difficulty and under high compensatory penalties to the employer. Any change would thus represent a major shift in labor relations. It is also of interest to note in this context that the Israeli labor union (Histadrut), which presumably promotes the worker's interests and protects him against disadvantageous changes, received correspondingly low performance X = 2.84) and trust (X = 3.02) ratings on a 5-point scale. Contrast this with the ratings of other social institutions, such as institutes of science and higher education (4.0 and 3.63, respectively), or the news media (3.81 and 3.62).

A similar pattern of giving priority to the resolution of the economic crisis—and here possibly at the expense of humanitarian concerns—is revealed in respondents' attitudes toward the problem of unemployment. First, this issue is ranked by far fewer (14.3%) as "the most significant problem in Israeli society today" than other and particularly more economic concerns, such as inflation (34.5%) and productivity (18.5%). Second, the prevailing interpretation of the unemployment problem appears to be an individualistic one: the blame is indirectly levied against the unemployed themselves, rather than against the structural factors of the market. Thus, 56.6% agreed that "the unemployed should be forced to join the labor force even if the jobs offered to them are undesirable," 67.7% that "unemployment benefits should be reduced since high benefits encourage people not to work," and 73.8% that "the low salaries paid in some sectors of the economy encourage people to collect unemployment benefits instead."

How is the unemployment problem to be resolved, and how is employment to be created? In addition to a small majority of respondents who still advocate direct government intervention by agreeing that "the government should create employment by establishing government-owned factories and businesses" (53.9%), we find an even larger majority (73.6%) supporting private sector initiatives indirectly stimulated by the government—"The government should create new employment by stimulating the private sector via tax reduction, credits, and so forth." In the same context, when indirect, direct, and no government intervention are literally juxtaposed as modes for resolving the unemployment problem, the former is preferred by a wide margin (57.8% versus 36.7% versus 5.5%, respectively).

Thus, though interviewees clearly preferred private sector initiatives over public sector expansion, they at the same time continued to advocate both alternatives. It appears reasonable to suggest, then, that the major emphasis is not on ideological purity in economic matters, but rather on the concern with economic recovery, as already suggested above. Both the government and the private sector are apparently seen as potential sources for economic stimulation. Since the government has continuously been in charge of the economic arena, however, there is a clear tendency to let the private sector play a greater role than heretofore, perhaps under the belief that the latter conforms more closely to the rules of efficiency.

To summarize the findings reviewed so far, there seems to be strong concern over economic health and economic recovery, probably coupled with a sense that the resolution of current economic problems is a matter of some urgency. The preferred source of economic intervention and change is the private sector, bolstered indirectly by concessions from the government. Even if the public still sees a direct role for government in the economy, this view is undoubtedly less motivated by a positive evaluation of the government's performance; rather, it appears to reflect the perceived need to resolve the current economic malaise urgently, and by any means.

But the most important implication of the findings presented so far is that they reveal a predominant pattern of public views that reflect a materialist value orientation at the *collective* level. The concerns with economic recovery (coupled with the blaming of lack of productivity on the worker and unemployment on individual motivation) and capitalist (that is, private sector) and technological solutions for major socio-economic problems—these concerns clearly run counter to postmaterialist concerns, such as equity, individual welfare, and even freedom.

This pattern of socioeconomic outlooks, presented so far at the aggregate level, is buttressed further in individual-level analyses. In fact, on this level we find a fairly consistent configuration of interrelated attitudes, suggesting a relatively well-integrated structure of "belief systems" (see Converse, 1964). Consider, for example, the majority of respondents (66.4%) who viewed economic recovery—as compared to the equitable distribution of the economic burden or improving the standard of living—as the most important socioeconomic goal. As might be expected, these individuals also exhibited a more negative attitude toward the Israeli worker: For example, they were more likely to agree that he does not invest sufficient effort (90.8% versus 69.2%; $X^2_{(1)} = 7.19$),[6] and so on.

Moreover, supporters of economic recovery as the primary socioeconomic goal were also more likely to agree to technological innovations even at the expense of layoffs (Table 1), and to prefer worker layoffs as a solution to labor and economic problems (41.7% versus 9.5%, $X^2_{(1)} = 5.10$). They were also more likely to advocate changing or abolishing the tenure system (80.8% versus 67.5%, $X^2_{(1)} = 5.47$), and tended to emphasize productivity and inflation above all other problems (like unemployment, but human relations as well) in Israeli society (59% versus 39.5%, $X^2_{(1)} = 3.15$, $p < .10$).

Further, supporters of economic recovery also exhibited consistent views regarding the unemployment problem and its solutions: They were more likely to agree that the unemployed should join the labor force even in undesirable jobs (81.5% versus 61.8%, $X^2_{(1)} = 3.95$), and that unemployment benefits encourage people not to work (80% versus 65.8%), although this difference is not statisticaly significant. In regard to the solution of the employment problem, they were less likely to support the government's role in creating employment (52.3% versus 78.4%, $X^2_{(1)} = 5.73$), and to favor direct versus indirect or no government intervention (Table 2); but all respondents were equally positively inclined toward private sector initiatives in this area (92.1% versus 90%, n.s.).

The other attitudes reviewed earlier in the agreement level analyses reflect similar attributional patterns, although the internal consistencies are not always as impressive. For example, the negative attitudes toward the Israeli worker transcend specific content, with inter-item congruencies fluctuating around 75% to 90%. Thus, among those agreeing that the Israeli worker invests insufficient effort at work, more than 90% also agreed that the Israeli worker is precipitous in announcing strikes, unwilling to accept discipline, has little or no responsibility, cares only what he gets and not what he gives, and is unproductive. On the other hand, attitudes toward the Israeli worker were not always consistent with other views in support of efficiency and productivity. Further, those negatively inclined toward the Israeli worker also tended to

## TABLE 1
## Major Socioeconomic Goals and Technological Innovation[a]

|  |  | Innovation | |
|---|---|---|---|
|  | Economic Recovery | For | Against |
|  |  | 67[b] | 8 |
|  |  | 89.3 | 11.0 |
| Goals | Improving Standard of Living | 8 | 4 |
|  |  | 66.7 | 33.3 |
|  | Equitable Distribution of Income | 18 | 8 |
|  |  | 69.2 | 30.8 |

[a]The relevant questions were: "There are public discussions as to which socioeconomic goals Israel should try to achieve over the next years" (first ranking of goals coded); and "one should encourage the introduction of technological innovation even if it leads to the dismissal of workers" (innovation, recoded 5-point scale).
[b]First entry is N (19 missing observations); second entry is percentage-row.
$x^2 = 9.86$    df = 2    $p < .05$

express stricter views about the unemployed—(for example, 80.9% of those agreeing that the Israeli worker does not invest sufficient effort and 85.9% of those agreeing that he does not care what he gives but only what he gets, also concurred that unemployment benefits should be reduced so as to discourage people from not working, $X^2_{(1)} = 4.10$ and $X^2_{(1)} = 8.69$, respectively. Attitudes toward the unemployed were internally consistent: Responses to the questions about whether the unemployed should be forced into undesirable jobs and whether unemployment benefits should be cut were highly interrelated ($r = .536$). Finally, preferences for public and private sector intervention in employment problems were uncorrelated, as one might expect if the major concern is indeed not with ideological principles but with economic recovery at virtually any price and within virtually any system.

## INDIVIDUALISTIC AND COLLECTIVIST VALUES
## AND MATERIALIST PREFERENCES

Up to this point, we have tried to establish that our respondents are preoccupied with economic efficiency and recovery, and that they blame

## TABLE 2
## Major Socioeconomic Goals and Government Intervention

|  | Intervention[a] | | |
|---|---|---|---|
|  | Direct | Indirect | None |
| Economic Recovery | 15[b] | 56 | 7 |
|  | 19.2 | 71.8 | 9.0 |
| Improving Standard of Living | 9 | 3 | 1 |
|  | 69.2 | 23.1 | 7.7 |
| Equitable Distribution of Income | 17 | 8 | 1 |
|  | 47.2 | 22.2 | 2.8 |

Goals

[a]The relevant question was, "Which of the following ways of combatting unemployment do you think is best?"
[b]First entry is N (15 missing observations); second entry is percentage-row.
$\chi^2 = 26.07$    $df = 4$    $p < .01$

the workers for inefficiency and the unemployed for their fate; and that they prefer the private over the public sector in solving socioeconomic problems. These views are by and large internally consistent, as evidenced by the individual-level analyses. We now turn to a second pattern, which is equally significant theoretically and equally evident in this survey—namely, a clear preference for extrinsic as opposed to intrinsic incentives at the workplace. This preference again has a number of ramifications for other economy and labor-related attitudes. In response to the question; "People look for different things in their jobs; please rank the following by order of importance," we find a distribution of first rankings as follows: High income (37.8%), job security (27.7%), an easy job (4.2%), promotion (3.4%), and a feeling of accomplishment (26.9%). In other words, the majority of respondents (69.7%) opted for extrinsic incentives—or in Inglehart's (1977) terminology, sustained materialist values—whereas only the minority preferred intrinsic incentives or postmaterialist values.[7] Note also that when we compare the distribution of Israeli responses to those in industrialized Western Europe (see Inglehart, 1982, Table 7), we find similarities on all dimensions—for example, "a good salary": Germany—38%, Belgium—34%, Italy—33%; and "a safe job": Germany—28%, Belgium—23%, Italy—29%; and so on.[8]

It may also be of interest to examine the extent to which respondents were consistent in their preferences for materialist values.[9] The vast majority of respondents (68.9%) consistently ranked materialist values as first (income-security, or vice versa), while only a small minority (7.6%) consistently chose postmaterialist values (feeling of accomplishment-promotion, or vice versa). The remaining 23.5% were mixed materialists or mixed postmaterialists, in Inglehart's (1982) terminology.

The differentiation among preferences for materialist and postmaterialist values has important implications for other socioeconomic attitudes as well. In particular, there is a consistent pattern of lessened preoccupation with economic efficiency and productivity among materialistically oriented individuals. Note that this pattern differs at least in principle from Inglehart's conception of the materialist—post materialist dimension. We shall return to this issue in the ensuing discussion; yet we should point out immediately that this discrepancy pertains only to the materialist orientation at the *individual level*, and *not* at the collective level.

Those ranking materialist values as most important at the workplace also placed somewhat less emphasis on economic recovery as the major socioeconomic goal (Table 3). Not unrelatedly, materialists expressed less negative evaluations toward the Israeli worker. For example, they were less likely to agree that the Israeli worker is unwilling to accept discipline (48% versus 72.7%, $X^2(_1) = 4.78$), tended to agree more that his productivity is high (70% versus 51.2%, n.s.), and less that he does not invest enough effort in his work (73.8% versus 57.4%, n.s.). Materialists were also more satisfied with the present labor market situation, indicating, for example, more agreement with the existing tenure system (31.7% versus 13.9%, $X^2(_1) = 3.23$, p $<$ .10), and less agreement that technological innovations should be adopted even at the expense of worker payoffs (78.5% versus 93.9%, $X^2(_1) = 2.79$, p $<$ .10). Finally, materialists were more likely to agree that the government should create employment (66.7% versus 40.7%, $X^2(_1) = 4.53$), and that the unemployment problem is best resolved by direct government intervention (46.2% versus 11.4%, $X^2(_1) = 11.40$). Note that while even those individuals who maintain materialist values continue to stress economic recovery and mechanisms that might ensure heightened efficiency and productivity, such emphases are clearly muted among these respondents.

An even clearer picture emerges when we compare among *consistent* materialists and postmaterialists (that is, those rating the corresponding

## TABLE 3
## Materialism-Postmaterialism and
## Major Socioeconomic Goals

|  |  | GOALS | |
|---|---|---|---|
|  |  | Economic Recovery | Other[b] |
| Materialism | Materialist[a] | 49[c] | 29 |
|  |  | 62.8 | 37.2 |
|  | Post Materialist | 28 | 7 |
|  |  | 80.0 | 20.0 |

[a]Based on the following item: "People look for different things in their jobs; please rank the following by order of importance." First rankings of "high income" or "job security" and "and easy job" are coded as materialists; first rankings of "promotion" and "a feeling of accomplishment" are coded as postmaterialists. For the phrasing of the "goals" item, see Table 1.
[b]Includes "improving the standard of living" and "an equitable distribution of income."
[c]First entry is N (19 missing observations); second entry is percentage-row.
$\chi^2 = 3.28$      df = 1      $p < .07$

work incentives consistently first or second in importance), and those evincing mixed patterns. Consistent materialists were more likely to agree to creating employment via government-owned businesses (72%) than either consistent postmaterialists (41.4%) or those exhibiting a mixed pattern (40%, $X^2_{(2)}$ = 8.66). Correspondingly, materialists showed only a slight preference for indirect or no government intervention to resolve unemployment problems (52.7%), whereas both nonmaterialists (84.4%) and those with mixed ratings (83.3%) were significantly more partial ($X^2_{(2)}$ = 10.82). Moreover, while all three groups agreed that technological innovations should be introduced even if they lead to the dismissal of workers, the intensity of this sentiment varied again according to the emphasis on economic efficiency identified above— consistent materialists 79%, both mixed and consistent postmaterialists 100%, $X^2_{(2)}$ = 7.12. Other patterns (such as attitudes toward workers and unemployed, positions of tenure, and so forth), while not always significant, point in the same direction.

Thus, (particularly consistent) materialists at the individual level (that is, regarding job incentives) are more satisfied with the current economic status quo, less preoccupied with enhancing efficiency and productivity, and more tolerant of the government's dominant role in the economy. In short, materialists at the individual level fail to exhibit materialist concerns at the collective level—a pattern distinctly at odds with Inglehart's conception of the materialist—postmaterialist value orientation.

Let us now examine one additional item that gives further insight into the pattern identified above: "In politics, it is not always possible to obtain everything one might wish. Rank the following goals by order of importance." The goals, by order of frequency of first rankings, were: "maintaining law and order" (45.5%), "fighting rising prices" (27.6%), "giving people more say in decisions of government" (13.8%), and "protecting the freedom of speech" (13%). In Inglehart's (1982) work, these options are supplemented by eight additional goals, which are distributed on differential points of salience along the materialist-postmaterialist continuum.[10]

Note that in contrast to the materialist-postmaterialist distinction based on work incentives (which reflects primarily goal-striving at the indvidual level), the present distinction clearly embodies an orientation toward more collectivist objectives. It should be clear that these two dimensions are both theoretically associated and empirically interdependent (in this study, $X^2_{(3)} = 8.42$); yet the two continua do not form the same attitudinal patterns and consistencies and, consequently, the conceptual distinction between individualist and collectivist goal orientation may indeed be an important one.

The emphasis on "maintaining law and order" by itself—chosen by the majority of respondents as the most important collective goal—is of considerable interest in its own right. This predilection may reflect an authoritarian tendency in the Israeli public today, which has already been documented in previous studies on both the sociopolitical (see Shamir, 1981) and the psychological levels of measurement (see Peres & Shemer, 1981). The present study, however, is the first to suggest that authoritarianism (as indicated by the emphasis on law and order) is significantly related to socioeconomic, rather than exclusively to political, attitudes. As can be seen in Table 4, there was a significant overlap between the emphases on law and order and on economic recovery. There was also several remarkable resemblances between these two orientations. For example, proponents of law and order were less interested in continuing the present tenure system (12.7% versus $X^2_{(1)} = 7.32$), and somewhat more willing to risk layoffs due to

## TABLE 4
## Major Socioeconomic Goals and Emphasis on Law and Order[a]

| | | Law and Order Emphasis | |
| | | Law and Order | All others[b] |
|---|---|---|---|
| Socio-Economic Goals | Economic Recovery | 39[c] <br> 76.4 | 37 <br> 56.9 |
| | Improving Standard of Living | 6 <br> 11.8 | 7 <br> 10.8 |
| | Equitable Distribution of Income | 6 <br> 11.8 | 21 <br> 32.3 |

[a]For the phrasing of the "goals" item, see Table 1. The "Political Goals" question, of which "maintaining law and order" was one response, was phrased as follows: "In politics, it is not always possible to obtain everything one might wish. Rank the following goals in order of importance" (first ranking coded).
[b]Others are, "fighting rising prices," "giving people more say in the decisions of government," and "protect freedom of speech."
[c]First entry is N (16 observations missing); second entry is percentage column.
$\chi^2 = 6.97$    df = 6    $p < .05$

technological innovations (88.9% versus 78.2%); somewhat more willing to force the unemployed into the labor market either by offering even undesirable jobs (79.1% versus 70.2%) or by paying lower unemployment benefits (83% versus 71.4%); and less agreeable to government-provided employment (44.7% versus 74.6%, $X^2_{(1)} = 8.63$).

But the most interesting findings from the present perspective emerge when we examine differences between *consistent* materialists and postmaterialists (as conceptualized and operationalized by Inglehart) on this level of *collectivist* value orientations. Whereas materialists on the individual level were most likely to be satisfied with the socio-economic status quo (contrary to what Inglehart would predict), materialists at the collective level, in conformity with Inglehart's model, were most likely to reject this status quo and to advocate increased efficiency and productivity.

Among our respondents, 44.6% conformed to the pattern of consistent materialists (that is, chose law and order and fighting inflation as the two most important goals); 12.1% were consistent postmaterialists (that is, chose citizen influence and freedom of speech as the two most important goals); the rest were mixed materialists or postmaterialists. In other words, on this collective level we find far fewer consistent materialists, and generally a greater predominance of mixed patterns than on the individual level discussed so far.

Table 5 presents the primary findings that differentiate consistent materialist and postmaterialist views on a number of socioeconomic issues. Individuals evincing mixed patterns were deleted for the purpose of these analyses. As the findings presented in Table 5 indicate, the two groups exhibit an internally consistent and distinct pattern of opinions; materialists regard economic recovery as the most important socioeconomic goal; disfavor direct government intervention in the economy and prefer more encouragement for private sector initiatives instead; endorse a tough stance vis-à-vis the unemployed (are willing to accept worker dismissals so as to enhance technological innovation and efficiency); and express generally negative opinions about the performance of the Israeli worker and about the tenure system. Consistent postmaterialists, on the other hand, exhibit the opposite pattern of views. Other differences between the two groups, such as other attitudes toward the unemployed and toward the Israeli worker, although not statistically significant, corroborate the material emphasis on efficiency at the expense of more quality-of-life or human-relations related concerns.

## DISCUSSION

As one might expect in research concentrating on socioeconomic attitudes, various subgroups within the sample responded differently to some of the issues raised in the survey questionnaire. The most consistent differences occurred among the three subgroups of socioeconomic status:[11] Based on the materialist-nonmaterialist distinction of consistent preferences for work incentives, we find that 71.4% among the low status respondents may be categorized as materialists versus medium—68.4%, and high status—42.9%, $X^2(_4)$ = 13.95). In line with these differences, low status respondents were less concerned with economic recovery and more with the equitable distribution of wealth less likely to make negative judgments of the Israeli worker; less willing to accept technological innovations at the expense of layoffs; and more favorable toward the role of the government in the economy. In short, they were both more materialistically oriented and more content with

# TABLE 5
## Pro-Efficiency Choices by Consistent Materialists and Postmaterialists[a]

| | Pro-Efficiency/Productivity Choice[a] | | Missing Cases | $\chi^2$ | df | p < |
|---|---|---|---|---|---|---|
| | Materialist | Post-Materialist | | | | |
| 1. Socioeconomic Goals | 32 (65.3)[b] | 4 (28.6) | - | 6.00 | 1 | .02 |
| 2. Government Intervention | 30 (63.8) | 4 (30.8) | 3 | 4.53 | 1 | .05 |
| 3. Encouragement of Private Sector | 38 (80.8) | 6 (46.2) | 3 | 4.96 | 1 | .05 |
| 4. Technological Innovation | 35 (77.8) | 5 (41.7) | 6 | 5.90 | 1 | .02 |
| 5. Workers' Insufficient Effort | 36 (78.3) | 6 (50.0) | 5 | 3.75 | 1 | .10 |
| 6. Workers' Acceptance of Responsibility | 28 (60.9) | 3 (25.0) | 5 | 4.92 | 1 | .05 |
| 7. Acceptance of Tenure System | 34 (69.4) | 5 (41.7) | 2 | 3.21 | 1 | .10 |

[a]Pro-efficiency and productivity choices are, respectively:
  (1) Economic recovery versus increased income *and* equitable distribution of income;
  (2) Indirect *and* no government intervention versus direct intervention in the economy;
  (3) Agreement versus disagreement that the private sector should be encouraged;
  (4) Technological innovation should be introduced at the expense of worker layoffs;
  (5) The Israeli worker does not expend enough effort;
  (6) The Israeli worker does not feel responsibility at his workplace; and
  (7) The present tenure system should be changed or abolished versus maintained.
[b]First entry is N; second entry is percentage. Total N = 63 (49 consistent materialists and 14 consistent postmaterialists).

the current socioeconomic status quo. Several of these differences also occurred between subgroups differentiated by age, education, and ethnic origin, although with far less pervasive consistency.

Yet, despite these fairly self-evident patterns, most of the between-group differences emerging in this study reflect divergences in the *intensity* or degree of similar opinions, rather than real differences in the *directionality* of views. For example, while low status respondents differed statistically from the other two groups on all items probing for attitudes toward the Israeli worker, a majority of low class respondents still expressed negative views on all these items except one—"has a sense of responsibility". Note also that these three groups did *not* differ in their attitudes toward unemployment and toward the role of the government in the economy.

Considering these findings, we may suggest that the three patterns identified earlier on the basis of their inter-attitudinal consistencies are pervasive insofar as they transcend most if not all of the individual and social position differences within the sample. These patterns—a preoccupation with economic health and efficiency at the expense of social and individual welfare, a preponderance of materialist versus postmaterialist values at both the individual and the collective levels, and an authoritarian tendency—are interrelated. The most representative configuration is an emphasis on both economic efficiency and law and order, coupled with a preference for postmaterialist values.[12] Yet, the relationships among these dimensions—and in particular the reversal in the attitudes of individual versus collectivist materialists toward socioeconomic issues—are not self-evident. It is this reversal that departs from what one would expect on the basis of Inglehart's (1977, 1982) theoretical analysis.

In sum, the present empirical findings identify a clear pattern of attitudes regarding socioeconomic issues among the Israeli public. On the collective level of goal priorities, the most salient concern is with the malfunctioning of the economy, coupled with an emphasis on the need for law and order. We might even venture the conjecture that these two concerns are not only empirically but also functionally related: The uncertainties and anxieties associated with the prolonged economic crisis may well have generated a longing for a stronger hand and a more tenacious direction of policy. In any event, the emphases on economic recovery and law and order stand in contrast to the deaccentuation of more humanitarian values of equality and political freedom.

Consistent with the hierarchy of such general goals are the attitudes toward more specific labor market policies, such as unemployment, technological innovations, and job tenure. The modal positions taken on these issues express less consideration for individual welfare than for the imperatives of production and efficiency. Finally, and still on this level of collective goals and national policies, we find a clear preference for the private as compared to public sector as the main vehicle for the recovery of the national economy—perhaps due to an appreciation of the superior performance of private enterprise.

Taken together, these findings depict a trend in the Israeli public that might best be labeled as an authoritarian version of rightist ideology. This conclusion is consistent with the voting behavior of the Israeli public since 1969, and with a series of studies on political identification (see Arian and Shamir, 1981) and on foreign policy opinions (see Arian, 1973; Arian and Shamir, 1981). Yet, and as we have already noted, this evident shift to the right has not previously been shown to manifest itself with respect to socioeconomic orientations. Quite the contrary, the Israeli public has consistently identified itself with a socialist ideology. Such identifications show only small variations of magnitude over time, ranging between 54% and 60% in the 20 years covered by pertinent surveys since 1962 (see Arian and Shamir, 1981).

At face value, our findings appear to be irreconcilable with this apparently predominant socialist ideology. Recall, however, that the sociological literature generally discourages any reliance on the assumption that specific opinions correspond to global ideological labels (Converse 1964; Hero, 1969). Indeed, Hero's (1969) work is perhaps most illuminating in this context: On the basis of scrutinizing a large number of public opinion surveys during several decades in the United State, he reached the conclusion that there hardly exists any relationship between the public's general ideological orientation and its support for specific welfare policies. The fact that most Americans oppose the general idea of "socialism," and the transformation of the American society into a "welfare state," is of little use in predicting aggregate responses to specific and concrete socioeconomic programs initiated by the government. Thus, "The general picture seems to be one of most citizens approving the specific welfare and economic programs of their national government, but opposing sharp shifts toward general or abstract socialist principles" (Hero, 1969:35).

It appears, then, that our findings depict a mirror image of those reported by Hero (1969): Among both the Israeli and the American publics, there is no correspondence between global ideological identifications and specific socioeconomic attitudes. However, while the American public rejects socialism as an ideological orientation but accepts specific socialist economic and welfare programs, the Israeli public continues to adhere to the socialist label but disapproves of socialist economic policies. In short, the shift to the "right" is not restricted to defense and foreign policy; it is reflected in socioeconomic orientations as well.

Unfortunately, our data do not permit us to determine what the term "socialism" means to those 60% of the Israeli public who choose this label for themselves; but we may be able to suggest at least what the term has ceased to mean for most. It appears that socialist ideology has lost support for the two of its classical foci: The requisite of a state-owned and state-regulated economy (the production aspect), and the priority of individual welfare over national strength and economic growth (the humanitarian aspect). It is less clear whether or not acceptance of the allocative aspect of socialism (that is, entitlement—the right of every individual to receive a share of the national pie should he be in need) has diminished as well. Given this impoverished version of socialism, we would suggest that this label—for those who identify with it—is essentially an ideological rhetoric, reflecting perhaps a superficial intellectual and emotional commitment to an idea nourished at an earlier time and at a younger age.

Turning now to the level of individual goals, the findings point to a clear emphasis on materialist rather than on postmaterialist needs, as indicated by the preference for income and job security as the most important job rewards. This utilitarian tendency seems to be consistent with the pragmatic approach to socioeconomic problems that we discerned at the macro level. The coherence revealed in the aggregate data, however, is not maintained at the individual level of analysis. Contrary to Inglehart's (1977) conceptualization, we find that it is the postmaterialists and not the materialists who advocate the importance of economic growth, individual productivity, and technological progress. In other words, those who personally pursue nonmaterialist values are *more* likely to stress material objectives for the national economy.

While any explanation for the discrepancy between these empirical findings and the theoretical conceptualization of the materialist-post materialist dimension must by definition be ad hoc, the pattern is too consistent and intriguing to be dismissed. We would suggest that Inglehart's original conceptions may overlook important national differences in economic stability and growth—differences that could explain the discrepancies between Inglehart's (1982) and our own findings.

Specifically, Inglehart's research so far has concentrated on the United States, Western Europe, and Japan—all countries in which conditions of both national economic stability and individual affluence either have prevailed until the very recent past or continue to prevail. Under such conditions, a preference for nonmaterial goals at the individual level is consistent with nonmaterialist concerns (such as "the quality of life", environmental concerns, and so on at the national level.

Israel, as we have seen, does not fit this pattern; while its economy has sufffered a persistent crisis, the affluence of its citizens has, if anything, burgeoned. Thus, the import-export ratio is constantly worsening monetary reserves have consistently diminished in the past 6 years, and the balance of payment has likewise worsened; all this in addition to the three-digit inflation and the growing financial demands of national security. At the same time, both real income and consumption continue to grow and are rapidly approaching the level of the most advanced industrial nations. Under such conditions, it is reasonable to hypothesize that those who have transcended materialist concerns are more likely to recognize the ultimate interdependence between national economic health and their own welfare; hence their greater sensitivity to economic recovery and their heightened support for system change. From a social psychological perspective, postmaterialists may well be characterized by a more collectivistic orientation. Conversely, those preoccupied with the provision of basic material needs may also be more satisfied with the current trend of growing individual affluence regardless of economic deterioration; hence, their heightened support for the status quo. The materialist orientation may thus best be described as individualistic. Note that the additional finding that materialists are both economically and educationally underprivileged is quite congruous with this line of reasoning.

Inglehart recognizes, of course, the ultimately *structural* nature of the variations in materialist-postmaterialist concerns. In fact, the central argument throughout his work has been that the shift toward postmaterialist values in postindustrial nations has been due to increased physical and economic security. Yet, it is because there was little variation in postwar affluence among these nations that Inglehart and others have mostly concentrated on social psychological explanatory variables, or on intergenerational or life-cycle changes in values. The case of Israel, however, appears to demonstrate that discrepancies between individual and collective value orientations may exist when there is a correspondent discrepancy between individual affluence and economic health.

Moreover, this discrepancy between individual affluence and the state of the national economy may have implications beyond the extension of Inglehart's model. To a considerable extent, the vitality and even the stability of the Israeli political system may depend on the continuing discrepancy between individual and national prosperity, in the sense that the government's repeated surrender to public demands for higher income and a higher standard of living may postpone the ultimate confrontation between the high level of public expectations—based on a long tradition of entitlement and welfare—and the government's inability to fulfill these expectations—due to the deteriorating state of the national economy. In other words, any impingement of the weak economy on individual welfare could lead to grievances, protests, and other forms of social unrest, which could threaten the very stability of the political system.

Most importantly, the discrepancy and its potential ramifications are not necessarily unique to Israel; they may even have some relevance to Western postindustrial nations. We are already witnessing tensions and unrest in both Europe and the United States as a response to the belt-tightening measures proposed to counteract the current economic decline. Much of the opposition to these measures emanates from quarters that which to preserve the existing and encompassing welfare system—that is to perpetuate individual prosperity under conditions of economic malaise. In sum, the discrepancy between individual level and collective socioeconomic values may be only one of the outcomes of this scenario.

## NOTES

1. This discrepancy between the welfare of the national economy and the economic welfare of individuals is evident from the following figures: during the last 5 years, GNP per capita has grown at annual rates of 1.0 to 1.5% and personal consumption per capita has increased by 6% annually. This improvement of individual affluence has been more than offset by an annual increase of $1.5 billion in the external national debt. Furthermore, while the rate of inflation exceeded 100% in each of the last 4 years, its

effect on individual welfare was minimized due to the various mechanisms of indexation with respect to wages, rent, savings, and social security transfers. These trends reflect a consistent attempt by the present Israeli government to protect and enhance the material well-being of citizens in spite of its detrimental consequences for economic growth and recovery. Such a policy must be understood in the context of Israel's highly centralized economy that enables the government to affect the internal political scene through the regulation of socioeconomic policies.

2. Two additional discussion groups involved only representatives of the political, academic, business, and labor elites. These individuals did not fill out questionnaires.

3. Analyses of these discussions and interviews are reported elsewhere. Interviews were conducted by four interviewers, all graduate students. Interviewers had no effect on questionnaire responses.

4. All population characteristics cited are from the 1981 Statistical Abstract of Israel.

5. Housewives were intentionally undersampled due to theoretical considerations.

6. Unless otherwise indicated, all chi-square values reported here reflect associations significant at the $p < .05$ level or beyond.

7. Indeed, as already noted, Inglehart uses these labels to refer to both intrinsic-extrinsic work incentives and goal priorities (Inglehart, 1982:7). We will suggest here that these two dimensions may in fact be distinct in certain empirically definable cases.

8. However, the pattern in the United States is strikingly dissimilar (for instance, "a good salary"—16%, "a feeling of accomplishment"—50%), a discrepancy that may be due to different dates of data collection or to more substantive differences.

9. Following Ingelhart, we define a consistent materialist as one who ranks *both* extrinsic incentives (income and security) first and second. The opposite pattern defines a consistent postmaterialist.

10. For example, the analyses preferred by Inglehart (1982) suggest that both law and order and fighting rising prices receive high factor loadings on the materialist dimension, whereas for the remaining two goals, the opposite is the case.

11. But recall that the measure of status is ecologically based; the findings should therefore be interpreted with caution.

12. We should caution, however, that these patterns may not necessarily pertain to periods other than that covered in this study. This is especially so as the study coincided with an unusual rise in the salience of national economic problems, along with a shift in government policies and a change of hands of the economic portfolio. Further research may establish the stability of these patterns over time.

# REFERENCES

ARIAN, A. (1973) The choosing People: Voting Behavior in Israel. Cleveland, The Press of Case Western Reserve University.
——and M. SHAMIR (1983) "The primarily political functions of the left-right continuum." Comparative Politics 15,2: 139-158.
BELL, D. (1975) "The revolution of rising entitlement." Fortune 91: 98-163.
CAMPBELL, A., P. E. CONVERSE, W. MILLER, and D. STOKES (1960) The American Voter. New York: John Wiley.
CANOVAN, M. (1981) Populism. New York: Harcourt, Brace, Jovanovich.

CONVERSE, P. E. (1964) "The nature of belief systems in mass public," in D. E. Apter (ed.) Ideology and Discontent. London: Free Press.

FLANAGAN, S. C. (1980) "Value cleavages, economic cleavages and the Japanese voter." Amer. J. of Pol. Sci. 24: 178-206.

——(1979) "Value change and partisan change in Japan: the silent revolution revisited." Comparative Politics 11: 253-278.

ETZIONI, E. and R. SHAPIRA (1977) Political Culture in Israel, Cleavage and Integration Among Israel Jews. New York: Praeger.

HARTMAN, M. (1969) "Prestige grading of occupations and sociologists as judges." Quality and Quantity 13: 1-19.

HERO, A. (1969) "Public reaction to government policies," in J. P. Robinson et al. (eds.) Measures of Political Attitudes. Survey Research Center, Institute of Social Research.

HURLEY, P. and K. HILL (1980) "The prospects for issue voting in contemporary congressional elections" Amer. Politics Q. 8: 399-425.

INGLEHART, R. (1982) "Changing values in Japan and the West." Comparative pol. Studies 14 (4): 445-479.

——(1977) The Silent Revolution: Changing Values and Political Styles Among Western Publics. Princeton, NJ: Princeton Univ. Press.

LUBAR, R. (1980) "Where zero sum politics came from." Fortune 102: 157-158.

MILKIS, S. and T. BALDINE (1978) "The future of the silent revolution: reexamination of intergenerational change in Western Europe." Presented at the annual meeting of the Midwest Political Science Association, Chicago. (unpublished)

Monthly Bulletin of Statistics 32 (1982) Jerusalem: Israel Center Bureau of Statistics.

NEAL, A. and M. SEEMAN (1964) "Organizations and powerlessness: a test of the mediation hypothesis." Amer. Soc. Rev. 29: 216-225.

NIE, N. H. and K. ANDERSEN (1974) "Mass belief systems revisited: political change and attitude structure," in R. G. Niemi and H. F. Weisberg (eds.). Controversies in American Voting Behavior. San Francisco: Freeman.

NIE, N. H., S. VERBA, and J. PETROCIK (1976) The Changing American Voter. Cambridge, MA: Harvard Univ. Press.

OLSEN, M. (1969) "Two categories of political alienation." Social Forces 47: 288-299.

PERES, Y. and S. SHEMER (1981) "Ethnic aspects of the 1981 elections in Israel." Tel Aviv University. (unpublished)

—— and J. L. SULLIVAN (forthcoming) "The political context of tolerance: a cross-national perspective from Israel and the United States." Amer. Pol. Sci. Rev.

SMITH, E. (1980) "The levels of conceptualization: false measures of ideological sophistication." Amer. Pol. Sci. Rev. 74: 685-697.

WILENSKY, H. (1979) The Welfare State and Equality: Structural and Ideological Roots of Public Expenditures. Berkeley, CA: Univ. of California Press.

YUCHTMAN-(YAAR), E. (1977) "The social psychology of the Israeli worker." (unpublished)

# Part V

# EPILOGUE: POLITICS AND SOCIAL CHANGE

# 19

# The Israeli Political System and The Transformation of Israeli Society

## S.N. Eisenstadt

In recent years the Israeli political scene has witnessed many far-reaching changes, although a continuity with the original political system, as a constitutional parliamentary democracy, has been maintained. The most obvious of these changes has been the "political upheaval" (*mahapach*) of 1977, ousting the Labor Party, for the first time since the mid-1930s, from its dominant position and changing its function from that of government to opposition. More recently, since around the 1981 elections, additional changes have taken place leading to mounting political turmoil, seen for instance in the rise of verbal, verging on physical, violence; growing divisiveness on ethnic issues, a deeper division between the religious and secular sectors and growing violence on the part of extreme religious groups; and the great divisiveness around the war in Lebanon and its aftermath. Other changes can be observed in the ambiance and tones of political debate; the increase in populism; the weakening of the rule of law; and the growth of extraparliamentary and extremist movements.

While it is too early to evaluate the full impact of these developments and while the democratic and constitutional framework has exhibited considerable resilience, there is no doubt that the Israeli political system has been affected—beyond the composition of the parties, the leadership, and the like—and with it Israeli life in its entirety has been transformed.

### The Changing Format of Political Life: Organizational Mobilization

To understand the above changes it is necessary to analyze the forces which shaped the initial mold of Israeli political life and produced its dynamics and transformations. The establishment of the State of Israel constituted not only a major political and historical event but also a turning point in the development of the *yishuv's* social structure. The establishment of the state transformed the former voluntary, pluralistic frameworks into a uniform framework based on political sovereignty; and the leaders of the various pioneering movements, organizations, and parties into a ruling elite —albeit of a constitutional parliamentary democracy.

Closely related to this political pattern there developed the very specific Israeli response to the continuous external security threat. This response did not give rise to a garrison state as had been often predicted, but resulted in the peculiar Israeli type of an "open civilian fortress." The major characteristics of this "open-fortress" society have been the development of a strong military and security ethos and an emphasis on being a society under stress as basic components of the emerging collective identity. The military image became one of the main elements of Israeli identity, and to a certain extent it took the place of the pioneering one, but was somewhat weakened after the Yom Kippur War. Concomitantly there developed, not unlike the Swiss pattern, a civilian reserve army together with a highly specialized and prestigious core of standing army composed mostly of officers. The army, together with a substantial military industrial base, has become one of the most significant achievements of modern Israel. At the same time, owing to the practice of releasing these officers at age forty-five to fifty, this core maintained a continuous orientation to the civilian economic and political sectors, and did not develop into a closed corporate unit or an autonomous political force. Although many generals (such as Dayan, Rabin, Sharon, Bar-Lev, Weizman, Gur, and others) entered the political arena, during the 1960s and 1970s they were dispersed among all major parties. In addition, the security establishment, presided over by the prime minister or minister of defense, provided a relatively strong civilian control over the army, although the military had a strong influence on political thought and security conceptions in the realm of national defense.

In the newly established political framework of the state the various movements and sectors—organized in the period of the *yishuv* in a semiconsociational pattern—were incorporated into a highly bureaucratized framework, with the new center becoming the principal locus of the power structure and the source of distribution of resources, as well as the focus of expanding and competing demands from the periphery. Underlying these changes was the weakening of the previously predominant pattern of a highly ideological polity in which bargaining and the allocation of resources were closely linked to sectoral issues, with a high degree of participation in each sector within a federative constitutional or semiconstitutional democratic framework.

The new format evidenced both several new directions and contradictions. First, broader universalistic premises developed. Second, contradictions arose between the old federative and new centralized aspects.

Third, tensions developed between the more universalistic and open premises and the strong regulative and paternalistic orientations of the ruling elite. These broader universalistic premises, together with a growing unification and centralization of services, developed within the framework of the newly established democratic state.

This weakening of the earlier pluralistic structure also strengthened the federative arrangements between the private sector, the Histadrut, the various political parties, and the newly emerging government sector. Similarly, the resources of the state and the Jewish Agency were channeled on a federative basis to the major political groups. The coalition basis of the government, resulting from an electoral system of proportional representation, ensured that ministries were controlled by different parties which acquired specific spheres of influence, as each tried to utilize its controlling power to gain support among the newly arrived, politically inexperienced immigrants.

Although such distribution according to federative arrangements and originating in the *yishuv* persisted and for some time was even reinforced by the creation of the state, crucial differences developed in comparison with the former period. Most of the parties or movements lost their independent access to outside resources—be they money or manpower—and these were channeled mostly through the organs of the state or the Jewish Agency, which mediated relations between these resources and the broader groups, sectors, and movements. This meant that relatively independent movements with autonomous access to the major centers of power and resources became dependent members of clientelistic networks. This gave rise for the first time in the history of the Jewish settlement to the emergence of a sharp distinction between center and periphery and shaped—at least initially—relations between the two into a clientelistic relationship on the basis of paternalistic policies. Economic expansion and the incorporation of politically inexperienced elements facilitated the development of such policies.

Closely related to this growing centralization of power in the hands of the state—but also in potential contradiction to it—was the development of the universalistic framework of the state based on premises of universal citizenship and a democratic form of government. Part of this development lay in the paradoxical process wherein the central leadership of the different parties ruling the state, and in particular that of the Labor Party, weakened the various sectarian tendencies and components of their parties and the autonomous access of these sectors to the centers of power and the control of resources. This fostered the development of clientelistic politics. Yet at the same time, these developments institutionalized more universalistic premises, which guided many state institutions.

The most important such institutional change was the establishment of general administrative services of the state, access to which was based on universalistic premises. While clientelistic intercessions also naturally developed within many parts of these bureaucracies, they could very quickly become dissociated from that of the parties. Moreover, the very multiplicity of such relations weakened not only any such single network, but also the whole clientelistic mode of politics. In a parallel manner, the state organs increasingly gained professional autonomy, developing more universalistic rules and orientations in such fields as housing, welfare, and the like.

The universalistic and civic orientations of the state were also continuously reinforced. One case in point is the continuous growth in prestige and strength of the legal institutions, especially the court system in general, and the Supreme Court in particular, when sitting as a high court of justice. The Israeli court system and particularly its Supreme Court have acquired an almost unprecedented prestige and standing—closely akin to that of the U.S. Supreme Court—as a place of appeal against government decisions in general and most critically those impinging on civil and political freedom.

A greater centralization of power occurred in all the political parties, but especially in those of the ruling coalition. This meant that the broader groups they represented had little access to the respective centers of power and to major decision making. The parties became organized around semioligarchic principles, restricted to small groups. The whole structure of the elite and leadership changed with the relative closure of the older parties extending to second- and third- level echelons of political professionals, who naturally became dependent on the center of the party.

Very few avenues of autonomous political expression and organization were opened up for many younger or new immigrant elements. The party elites tried to control most such activities, allowing little direct autonomous expression or organization. On the local level, they pursued a policy of cooptation. Later on, a policy of cooptation was applied also to more highly placed elements, such as the military, which usually had little political experience and little autonomous access to the political arena. Consequently most parties developed an atrophy of their internal political process in general and of the selection of the political leadership in particular, gradually weakening also the internal solidarity and even self-assurance of the leaderships of many parties.

Political mobilization became more and more based on some combination between cooptation and allocation of resources, with intensive bargaining over them. This bargaining over resources, which took place in various party and state channels, became dissociated from any ideological orientation, and it was indeed perceived as such by the broader strata of the population. Meanwhile, the central elites viewed the struggle for allocation as a technical matter, in service of the broad goals and ideology of the state.

The most extreme type of such allocation and bargaining could be seen in the initial stages of the absorption of immigrants—when votes were directly or indirectly bought through allocation or promise of allocation of work, housing, and so on. Later, more subtle mechanisms developed, although the growth of state services with their universalistic premises gradually weakened the influence and acceptance of many of these practices. The weakening of ideological orientations and the great striving for power gave rise to continuous struggles over the allocation of resources—a struggle manifesting itself in a wide variety of modes.

Within the parameters of such broad processes, new modes of political activity, bargaining, and political mobilization developed. The parameters were set by a number of factors: (1) the transformation of the older sectors into ruling elites, and of the political parties based on social movements into more oligarchic structures; (2) the tensions between the federative-consociational and the centralized aspects, and between the universalistic orientation and the regulative-paternalistic one. The processes which led to the new modes of political activity have continued till this very day.

Initially, probably the most visible such mode was the clientelistic one, based on the growing concentration of resources in the hands of the state and the parties, the granting of universal suffrage, and the weakening of autonomous access to the centers of power. The potentialities for the emergence of far-reaching clientelistic networks have naturally developed, above all, within the coalition parties (especially the Labor and religious parties), but also to some degree within the more oppositional sectors (those of the "bourgeois" parties and Herut). These clientelistic networks did allocate many resources, above all housing and work, and to a lesser degree education, in return for political loyalty.

The Israeli political system did not change into a purely clientelistic one due to the reactions against it. The constraints set by the development of more universalistic democratic features in the institutional premises and format of the state and the process connected with it, also militated against such relations. This was closely related to the growing social and economic differentiation and diversification of the social and economic structure, leading to intensive bargaining around specific issues which could not be integrated into existing ideological settings or party frameworks. The existing parties were unable to control or regulate these developments, and powerful lobbies cutting across parties—such as the agricultural lobby—developed. Within the parties there were subgroups and cliques contending in the various committees of the Knesset or in relation to different ministries. Most significant was the growing unruliness of such groups and the increasing difficulty experienced by the parties in their attempts to control them.

Political bargaining became clearly oriented toward safeguarding positions of power, guided by the internal dynamism of the various power groups and by continuously shifting interest groups and lobbies. Politics became much less influenced by ideological considerations oriented toward the realization of the initial ideology in whose name the elite claimed to be ruling, and the basic premises accepted by the new sectors of the population. These developments were accompanied by an increase in the importance of mass media, especially of television, as arenas of political debate and appeal—and this was closely related to the strengthening of populistic appeals.

## The Political Process and Transformation of Israeli Society

The processes of transformation which undermined the capacity of the Labor elite to rule have to some degree been shared by many post-revolutionary societies (e.g., Mexico, the Soviet Union), and societies which experienced some of the earlier "great revolutions," especially the United States.

The most important of these processes have been: first, the transformation of revolutionary groups from sociopolitical movements into rulers of states and the concomitant institutionalization of the revolutionary vision in the framing of the modern states; second, economic expansion and modernization with concomitant growing social differentiation; and third, the absorption, within the framework of such economic expansion, of relatively underdeveloped sectors of the population. These processes and the constant crystallization of different postrevolutionary institutional molds, of different patterns of modernity, varied in various postrevolutionary regimes.

The specific characteristics of Israel as a revolutionary society and of the processes of its transformation were shaped by several facts: its size as a small society, its geopolitical location, and last but not least, its being rooted in the Zionist vision and its rebellion against the Jewish life in the nineteenth-century European Diaspora. Jewish life in this period had three major facets: (1) the assimilationist one, predominant in Western and Central Europe: (2) the traditional Jewish society as it still existed in many parts of Eastern Europe; and (3) other Jewish collective movements that developed in Eastern Europe.

Israel, rooted in the Zionist vision, coped with seeming success with the perennial problems of settlement in Eretz Israel. Above all, it succeeded in demonstrating for the first time, after 2,000 years, the ability of the Jewish people to forge an independent political entity, encompassing all spheres of life, to enter history as an active agent, to face the civilizational challenges which were, as we have seen, inherent in its basic self-definition but which were only latent during the long period of the Exile.

Unlike the period of the Second Temple—the last time the Jewish people had such an opportunity—they were now more conscious of it. In many ways the Zionist movement was the epitome of this awareness, and unlike the period of the Second Temple, its civilizational orientation was directed not only to the political arena, but also to the social and institutional ones. Moreover, its relations to other civilizations were not necessarily as competitive and antagonistic as in the period of the Second Temple and in the long period of (especially medieval) *galut* (exile). The competition was, given the transformation of the civilizational visions in the modern world, more open and seemingly benign—although, of course, many of the antagonistic elements persisted in different ways.

The new institutional mold, rooted in the Zionist revolutionary orientation, went far beyond what the Jews could have developed in the period of dispersion in the countries of their settlement, in the networks of traditional *kehillot* and centers of learning, or the more dispersed and diversified organizations and ways of life in more modern times. It was not only the development of additional institutional arenas such as the political, military, or in the economic one of agriculture and of basic industries, but, above all, the fact that all these were brought together under the canopy of a new autonomous collectivity, an overall collective institutional framework, that was of crucial importance. This fact constituted the epitome of the Zionist revolution, the collective entry of Jews into history and into the international community.

Although this entry of Jews into history and the creation of the new institutional mold were rooted in a strong rebellion against the Jewish traditional and assimilationist molds, the rebellion did nonetheless not totally dissociate itself from many aspects or dimensions of Jewish history and tradition. On the contrary, this very rebellion against the concrete reality of Jewish life in the traditional and modern Diaspora not only reinforced and renewed themes and orientations that were latent in the earlier periods of Jewish history, but it also transformed them in the process; from being purely intellectual orientations, these themes have been realized and actualized in institutional areas and social frameworks. All the major themes and tensions of Jewish tradition and civilization—the tension between universalism and particularism, between internal closed solidarity and solidarity as a base for far-reaching social, ethical, and cultural creativity, between populist overtones and emphasis on excellence in different areas of such creativity—have merged in the construction and working of concrete institutional formats and the overall framework of the state. The same was true of the tension between the semi-Messianic future and the emphasis on the present which was no longer confined to the pages of the *halakha* (Jewish law) and of communal life. The different orientations to Eretz Israel and the *galut,* always latent, were now also related to the new reality.

This was true, too, of the basic themes and tensions of Jewish political culture—those related to the issues of solidarity mentioned above; as well as the tensions between the legal order and the strong antinomian and semi-anarchist tendencies in this culture. The emphasis on solidarity was no longer confined to communal arrangements and literary expressions. Rather, it became closely related to the working of overall political institutions, the army, and its civilian control.

Similarly, the emphasis on civility and of acceptance of the rule of law in tension with populistic political tendencies, with their emphasis on a "higher law," emerged from the narrow intellectual confines, to which it was limited in the medieval period, becoming inextricably interwoven with questions about the functioning of the framework of a full-fledged society and polity, with the different dimensions of its institutional format and political forces. The strong Jewish future orientation became connected with concrete institution building and hence with the exigencies of the present, giving rise to different forms of confrontation between the two perspectives.

The same was true of other specific Zionist themes—closely connected with the former, general Jewish ones—especially the tension between being a normal nation and being a *Jewish* nation to serve as a light to the nations; between the emphasis on territorial political dimensions and the orientations to institution building; between the conception of the State of Israel as a place of refuge and security, as against an arena of national renaissance.

All these tensions have found new literary and intellectual expression—but above all they have become inescapably interwoven into the overall institutional fabric of Israeli society. Consequently, the ways in which the general problems of postrevolutionary societies have crystallized within Israeli society became connected with the different perennial themes of Jewish life and existence in general, and with the major Zionist orientations and themes in particular.

The singular achievement of the initial institutional mold developed in Israel was not that it has obliterated these different orientations and tensions. On the contrary, all of them continued to exist within it, and their impact on social and political life was—given the fact that they have become inter-woven in concrete institutional settings—much greater. Rather, this achievement resided in the fact that the new institutional framework was able to contain these tensions, so that they both reinforced the working of the system and fostered continuous changes within it; thus opening it up but at the same time regulating the more anarchic potentials through the development and continuity of its central institutional frameworks, as well as by strong internal cohesion of the elites and their solidarity with the broader sections of the population.

The central focus of the postrevolutionary transformation in Israel developed around the possibility of incorporating both older and newer movements and sectors of the population into the more universalistic frameworks of the state. There was also emphasis on economic develop-ment and expansion within the framework of a mixed, heavily controlled economy. In the cultural sphere the aim was the construction of an old new nation by means of cultural renaissance and creativity.

## Disintegration of the Initial Institutional Mold of Israeli Society

To understand the full implications of the historical developments described, we must consider them in conjunction with the disintegration of the initial institutional mold of Israeli society, a process epitomized by the 1977 *mahapach,* but one which began earlier.

The trends uncovered in the initial institutional framework of Israeli society reflect the processes of transformation of revolutionary societies in general, seen in the change of the leaders of revolutionary groups into ruling elites, and the routinization of revolutionary visions and ideologies. These developments are also connected in all modern postrevolutionary societies with structural processes attendant on modernization and economic growth.

The increasing specialization of the elites in Israel and the increased segregation of these elites from one another changed the relationships among them. At the same time, a weakening occurred in common solidary frameworks, and relations in which they all participated. The nature of the connection between their respective spheres of activity and their relations to the center (the political elite) also changed, as seen in the growing dissociation of most elites from autonomous participation in the political process. The various elites, including large parts of the political one, came to overlap with the upper economic strata, developing a lifestyle stressing a continuous rise in the standard of living and a relatively high emphasis on conspicuous consumption. In this sense the elites became distanced from other strata and abandoned the pioneering vision, thus evidencing patterns of behavior in blatant contradiction with many premises of the very ideology through which they had legitimized themselves.

These structural developments were closely related to the transformation in the regnant labor-Zionist pioneering ideology. This was reflected in attempts by the central political elites, and in particular by Ben-Gurion, to free themselves from limitations that their national and social ethos, emphasizing egalitarianism, placed on them. The idea was to combine a democratic orientation with a tutelary-patronal attitude to the periphery. Another development was the rift between parts of the central political elite represented by Ben-Gurion on the one hand, and the older sectors in the movement on the other—the latter having developed into more routinized political machines. The first element tried to free itself from both the limitations and obligations of the sectarian dimensions of the movement and from its routinization, and to base its power on a more direct appeal to the broader strata of the population.

Ironically, the subsequent enormous institutional expansion characterizing Israeli society was accompanied by the exhaustion of the creative innovative component of the regnant ideology prevalent in the *yishuv* period. This gradually gave way to the perception of the environment as given to be "mastered," conquered, or adapted to, but not necessarily shaped anew.

Correlated with this, Israeli society shifted its self-definition to that of a society under constant threat and stress. This being the case, the society saw itself excused from further innovativeness except in technical and organizational aspects as responses to such pressures. Thus, there have been no great social or institutional innovations, like the kibbutz or the Histadrut, or the renaissance of the Hebrew language, which were characteristic of the former (prestate) *yishuv*. Many of the institutional frameworks and of the patterns of life that developed after the creation of the state do not differ significantly from those found in other Western societies. Very often they were shaped by orientations to various external models. At the same time there developed a growing dissociation between the normative specifications of the ideology and social and economic realities, leading to a feeling of delegitimation of the ruling elites.

The prevalence of the clientelistic mode of relations between the center and the periphery, and the attempts of the ruling groups to buy off the periphery, contravened many of the universalistic premises of the state services. Gradually, this gave rise to a situation of growing normlessness. The norm setters themselves often generated this in areas such as wage policy, labor relations, and taxation.

Since these attempts were seen as being part of the power games of the elites, a changed perception of the various aspects of the ideology by different sectors of the society arose. While to the new ruling elites this ideology and its relations to the developing institutional structure and its problems were perceived as natural and given, it was not perceived in the same fashion by the peripheral sectors. They tended to perceive these policies as being increasingly directed toward safeguarding the positions and power of the existing elite frameworks, and as guided more by the internal dynamism of the various power groups and less by the ideological concern and the national goals set by them.

As a result of these processes the regnant socialist democratic labor ideology became more and more identified by broader sectors of the population in general and by many of the new immigrants in particular as a mechanism for the maintenance of the power position of the ruling elites in a changing, more open society. The elite began to lose its claims to the commitment of broader sectors in the society. Unable to induce such commitments by means of continuously opening up the institutional frameworks, the quest for such commitments, albeit in renovated forms, has continued to be a very important ingredient among large sectors of the public, as well as in the self-portrayal and legitimation of the elites.

Thus these processes of transformation of ideology—as in the case of many revolutionary societies—acted against the basic ideological premises of the institutional system and, above all, against the basic legitimation and self-legitimation of the ruling elites and of the center. It undermined in many ways their self-image and the ways in which they presented themselves to the broader strata which they attempted to mobilize in a democratic manner. These processes have contributed to a growing disenchantment with the elites and their vision, and to the delegitimation of the ideology which they were portraying themselves as carrying and symbolizing.

In concluding our analysis of the institutional transformation and new political trends, we must stress the specific characteristics of the Israeli transformation of the revolutionary ideology and of its institutional implications—which are not found in other societies to such an extent. First, we discern the growing emphasis, rooted in the basic national Zionist orientations, on national solidarity and on the continuous recrystallization of the national tradition; and second, the strong emphasis on equality of participation in the new national framework. Third, and closely related to the former, yet perhaps a more astonishing aspect of this transformation, has been the rather widespread—even if often perhaps rather shallow— acceptance of democratic constitutional frames and practices in general, and of the rule of law in particular, as basic premises of the new institutional format.

This acceptance of the democratic ethic is indeed astonishing if we remember the sociohistorical roots of the original Zionist movements and especially the totalistic orientations prevalent in the different Zionist movements, the strong ideological sectarian element in Jewish political culture, and the more communal-solidary aspects of the traditional Jewish community. This parochial orientation in Jewish life is rooted in some very basic premises of Jewish culture historically, and persists, in a more articulated form, in the Zionist movement and in Israel in particular, and could have become intensified with the attainment of independence.

The democratic federative arrangements that developed in the Zionist movement and in the *yishuv* were not derived, as we have seen, so much from the ideological models set up in these movements, from the political culture inherent in them, but rather from the historical context of the emergence of the Zionist movement in Western and Central Europe; from the necessities of the different Zionist groups to live together in one common framework; from the relations between the *yishuv* and the Zionist movement in the Diaspora; and to some degree from the British model portrayed during the Mandate.

Yet these universalistic-democratic constitutional arrangements—together with a strong emphasis on the rule of law, even if undermined by the contrary sectarian and populist tendencies—did strike roots in the *yishuv* and the State of Israel. It is true that these arrangements aimed more to ensure the participation of different groups in the center than to uphold the rights and liberties of the citizens. Yet with all these many limitations such constitutional arrangements became, as we have seen, interwoven in the basic institutional framework of the state and became an important component, if not the only one, of its legitimation.

Parallel to the institutional transformation from the *yishuv* to a modern nation-state, the regnant ideology also underwent a transformation which weakened the participatory dimensions of the component groups in the *yishuv*. However, there was a marked continuity with the Zionist national vision and its initial constitutional democratic framework. In stressing both national solidarity and the ideology's universalistic aspects, this new ideological direction weakened the social institutional "constructivist" endeavors of the different elements. This also entailed the reconstruction of many components of the Jewish social and civilizational orientation and of the Zionist vision.

This unique combination of the transformation and continuity of ideology helps us understand both the decomposition of the initial institutional framework and the partial delegitimation of the regnant elite, as well as the repercussions and further developments that have been taking place in Israel. Given these specific characteristics of the Israeli scene, these developments have naturally become connected with the growing articulation, reformulation, and often "bursting out" of certain basic themes in the Zionist ideology, as well as of Jewish "traditional" political orientations, which in the earlier period of the State of Israel were encapsulated within the initial institutional framework. This articulation has first of all taken place on the ideological level but, needless to say, has far-reaching institutional implications, posing crucial questions as to the possibility of the crystallization of a new institutional mold in Israel, its direction, and viability.

# 20

## Politics and Society in Israel: Selected Bibliography

*David Glanz*
Assisted by *Grace Hollander*

### Introduction

Israel has just celebrated its thirty-sixth anniversary of independence at this writing. Over the years a considerable scholarly literature has grown up on the subject of Israeli politics. Yet to date, no systematic effort has been made to organize the material, particularly those scholarly works concerned with internal politics and social developments. This selected bibliography is both a supplement and a complement to the articles presented in this volume.

"Selected" is the key word for this first bibliography of books, essays, and articles on Israeli politics and society. Containing some 500 references, though not exhaustive, this listing is quite comprehensive of the English-language output in these fields.

Since the focus in this bibliography, as well as in the volume itself, is the internal political sociology of Israel as a whole rather than its external relations, we have excluded articles relating to international affairs, foreign policy, international law, and to Arab-Israeli conflict. Unpublished dissertations, theses, social science research reports, conference papers, encyclopedia articles, and nonscientific popular articles were also not included. In compiling the bibliography, the most basic and useful reference source was *International Political Science Abstracts,* which we scoured from its first issue in 1951 up to volume 33, number 6 (containing abstracts on publications as late as September 1983). Articles relating to legal or administrative questions or specific reforms were not included unless they

The editors gratefully acknowledge the considerable assistance of Grace Hollander in the compilation, editing, and technical preparation of the bibliography.

had a broader social significance. Journals publishing articles on this topic as late as mid-1984 were examined, and several anthologies on the 1981 elections and politics in Israel that we became aware of in the review process, and which have just been or are just about to be published, have been listed. In addition a computerized DIALOG search was made of the Public Affairs Information Service (PAIS) and Sociological Abstracts data bases. (Nothing appearing in the quasi-scholarly *Journal of Palestinian Studies* has been listed.)

The references selected here stem from the authors' point of view, which though rooted in a fundamentally sociological perspective, is grounded in a firm conviction of the sterility of drawing stringent lines of differentiation between political science and political sociology.

Political science has been described by one of its leading scholars, David Easton (1968), as "a discipline in search of its identity," and in the editorial introduction to the recently published *International Handbook of Political Science,* Andrews (1982) describes political science as a "rainbow science" still suffering from a "chronic identity crisis." Political sociology has been defined (Janowitz, 1968) as focusing generally on the social bases of power, and more specifically on the analysis of the organization of political groups, leadership, elites, public opinion, ideology, and political change. Yet Horowitz (1972) in his esssay "A Theoretical Introduction to Political Sociology" argues that the distiction between political sociology and political science is the former's concern with how basic sociological variables such as class, caste, religion, ethnicity, and the like, "intersect and interpenetrate" key political variables of power and authority, sovereignty and property. Horowitz contends that since political science sees the state as central, issues of power, interests, and elites occupy its attention, while for political sociology the stress is on civil society, social structure, and systems, and leads to focusing on normative behavior values and specific classes or publics.

Certainly no political scientist should ignore the perspectives and insights offered by political sociology and political anthropology to the study of politics—nor can the political sociologist disregard the findings and research of political scientists, if only as a point of departure for further work.

While we do not see this selected bibliography as a trend report on research on Israeli politics, it has been instructive to us in providing an overview of what has and has not been published in the field. With this in mind, we wish to point out those areas in which the material is meager and therefore offers fertile ground for future research. Especially worthy of attention is the field of political anthropology, where much work remains to be done. The social character of government bureaucracy and administration, in a country where the state is intimately involved in all aspects of public life, is another relatively neglected field. The relationship of politics to other institutional sectors, linkages, influences, decision making, and policy formation has barely been scratched. The interaction between politics and such areas as educational policy, resource allocation, settlement policy, the Zionist movement, religious legislation, and the like have yet to be explored.

We hope that readers of this volume, scholars, and students of Israeli society will find it an aid in mapping out the interaction between politics and society in Israel. Given the volatile character of Israeli life, a knowledge of the work of the past may not be the most perfect guide to the future, but it is still the best we have.

## References

Andrews, William
1982    "Freaks, rainbows, and pots of gold." In William Andrews, ed., *International Handbook of Political Science.* Westport, Conn.: Greenwood.
Easton, David
1968    "Political science." In D. Sills, ed., *International Encyclopedia of the Social Sciences.* New York: Macmillan.
Horowitz, Irving Louis
1972    *The Foundations of Political Sociology.* New York: Harper & Row.
Janowitz, Morris
1968    "Political sociology." In D. Sills, ed., *International Encylopedia of the Social Sciences.* New York: Macmillan.

### Selected Bibliography

Abramov, Zalman
1976    *Perpetual Dilemma: Jewish Religion in the Jewish State.* Cranbury, N.J.: Fairleigh Dickinson University Press.
Abu-Gosh, Subhi
1972    "The election campaign in the Arab sector." In A. Arian, ed.
Adles, H.A.
1970    "Local autonomy in Israel." *Public Administration in Israel and Abroad* 11:38-47.
Akzin, B.
1955    "The role of parties in Israeli democracy." *The Journal of Politics* 17:507-45.
1960    "The Knesset." *International Social Science Bulletin* 4:567-82.
1979    "The Likud." In H. Penniman, ed.
1980    "The Likud." In A. Arian, ed.
Albert, J.
1969    "Constitutional adjudication without a constitution: The case of Israel." *Harvard Law Review* 82:1245-65.

Antonovsky, Aaron
   1966       "Classification of forms, political ideologies, and the man in the
              street." *Public Opinion Quarterly* 30:109-19.
Arian, Asher (Alan)
   1966       "Voting and ideology in Israel." *Midwest Journal of Political
              Science* 10:265-87.
   1968       *Ideological Change in Israel.* Cleveland: Case Western Reserve
              University Press.
   1971a      *Consensus in Israel.* New York: General Learning Press.
   1971b      "Stability and change in Israeli public opinion." *Public Opinion
              Quarterly* 35:19-35.
   1972a      "Electoral choice in a dominant party system." In A. Arian, ed.
   1972b      "Stability and change in public opinion and politics." In A. Arian,
              ed.
   1973       *The Choosing People.* Cleveland: Case Western Reserve University
              Press.
   1975       "Were the 1973 elections in Israel critical?" *Comparative Politics*
              8:152-65.
   1977a      "Israeli elections: A mechanism of change?" *Jerusalem Quarterly*
              3:17-27.
   1977b      "The passing of dominance." *Jerusalem Quarterly* 5:20-32.
   1979       "The electorate: Israel 1977." In H. Penniman, ed.
   1980       "The Israeli electorate—1977." In A. Arian, ed.
   1981a      "Elections 1981: Competitiveness and polarization." *Jerusalem
              Quarterly* 21:3-27.
   1981b      "Health care in Israel: Political and administrative aspects."
              *International Political Science Review* 2:43-56.
   1983       "Political participation and ethnic conflict in Israel." In G. Mahler,
              ed.
   1984       "Political images and ethnic polarization." In H. Penniman and D.
              Elazar, eds.
Arian, Asher, ed.
   1972       *The Elections in Israel—1969.* Jerusalem: Jerusalem Academic
              Press.
   1975       *The Elections in Israel—1973.* Jerusalem: Jerusalem Academic
              Press.
   1980       *The Elections in Israel—1977.* Jerusalem: Jerusalem Academic
              Press.
   1983       *The Elections in Israel—1981.* Tel Aviv: Ramot.
Arian, Asher, and S. H. Barnes
   1974       "The dominant party system: A neglected model of democratic
              stability." *Journal of Politics* 36:562-614.
Arian, Asher, and Michal Shamir
   1983       "The primarily political functions of the left-right continuum."
              *Comparative Politics* 15:139-58.
Arian, Asher, and S. Weiss
   1969       "Split-ticket voting in Israel." *Western Political Quarterly*
              22:375-89.
   1972       "The changing pattern of split-ticket voting." In A. Arian, ed.

Aronoff, Myron J.
1972    "Party center and local branch relationships: The Israel Labor Party." In A. Arian, ed.
1973a   "Communal cohesion through political strife in an Israeli new town." *The Jewish Journal of Sociology* 15:79-105.
1973b   "The politics of religion in a new Israeli town." *Eastern Anthropologist* 26:145-71.
1974a   *Frontiertown: The Politics of Community Building in Israel.* Manchester: Manchester University Press.
1974b   "Political change in Israel: The case of a new town." *Political Science Quarterly* 89:613-25.
1974c   "Fission and fusion: The politics of factionalism in the Israeli labor parties." In F. P. Belloni and D.C. Beller, eds., *Faction Politics.* Santa Barbara: ABC-Clio Press.
1974d   "Ritual in consensual power relationships: The Israeli Labor Party." In S.L. Seaton, ed., *Political Anthropology and the State.* The Hague: Mouton.
1975    "The power of nominations in the Israeli Labor Party." In A. Arian, ed.
1976a   "Ritual rebellion and assertion in the Israeli Labor Party." *Political Anthropology* 1:132-64.
1976b   "Freedom and constraint: A memorial tribute to Max Gluckman. *Political Anthropology* 1:1-6.
1977a   *Power and Ritual in the Israeli Labor Party: A Study in Political Anthropology.* Assen: Van Gorum.
1979    "The decline of the Israeli labor party: Causes and significance." In H. Penniman, ed.
1980    "Center-periphery relations in the Israeli Labor Party." In E. Marx, ed., *A Composite Portrait of Israel.* London: Academic Press.
1982    "The Labor Party in opposition." In R. Friedman, ed.
1984    "Conflicting interpretations of Israeli reality." In M.J. Aronoff, ed.
Aronoff, Myron J., ed.
1984    *Cross-Currents in Israeli Culture and Politics.* New Brunswick: N.J.: Transaction.
Aronson, Shlomo, and Nathan Yanai
1983    "Critical aspects of the elections and their implication." In D. Caspi, A. Diskin, and E. Guttman, eds.
Avineri, Shlomo
1980    "Political trends under the Begin government." *Dissent* 27:27-35.
Avner, Uri
1975    "Voter participation in the 1973 elections." In A. Arian, ed.
Avruch, K.A.
1978-79  "Gush Emunim: Politics, religion, and ideology in Israel." *Middle East Review* 11:26-31.
Azmon, Yael
1975    "Some aspects of the Israeli political elite: Background characteristics in a comparative perspective." In A. Arian, ed.
1981    "The 1981 elections and the changing fortunes of the Israeli Labor Party." *Government and Opposition* 16:432-46.

Badi, Joseph
    1963        *The Government of the State of Israel.* New York: Twayne.
Bar-On, M.
    1967        "Education processes in Israel defense forces." In S. Tax, ed., *The Draft.* Chicago: The University of Chicago Press.
Barzilai, Gad
    1984        "Neutrality and nonalignment in foreign policy: Conflict and consent in the Jewish settlement during the period of World War I and after World War II." In S. Cohen and E. Don-Yehiya, eds.
Ben-Dor, Gabriel
    1975        "Politics and the military in Israel: The 1973 election campaign and its aftermath." In A. Arian, ed.
    1980        "Electoral politics and ethnic polarization: Israeli Arabs in the 1977 election." In A. Arian, ed.
Ben-Porat, A.
    1979        "Political parties and democracy in the Histadrut." *Industrial Relations* 18:237-43.
Ben-Rafael, Eliezer
    1982        *The Emergence of Ethnicity: Cultural Groups and Social Conflict in Israel.* London: Greenwood Press.
Ben-Sira, Z.
    1977        "A facet theoretical approach to voting behavior." *Quality and Quantity* 11:167-88.
    1978        "The image of political parties and the structure of a political map." *European Journal of Political Research* 6:259-83.
    1982        "The structure of stratification: A revised bimodal approach." *Quality and Quantity* 16:171-96.
    1983        "Instrumental and affective legitimization of party support." In A. Arian, ed.
Bernstein, Deborah
    1980        "Immigrants and society: A critical view of the dominant school of Israeli sociology." *British Journal of Sociology* 31:246-65.
Bernstein, M.
    1957        *The Politics of Israel.* Princeton: Princeton University Press.
    1959        "Israel's capacity to govern." *World Politics* 2:399-417.
Bhutani, S.
    1978        "Israel's ninth general election." *International Studies* 17:27-50.
Bilski, R., et al.
    1980        *Can Planning Replace Politics—The Israeli Experience.* The Hague: M. Nijhoff.
Birnbaum, Erving
    1970        *The Politics of Compromise: State and Religion in Israel.* Cranbury, N.J.: Fairleigh Dickinson University Press.
Boim, Leon
    1972        "Financing of the 1969 elections." In A. Arian, ed.
    1979        "The financing of elections." In H. Penniman, ed.
Bollen, K. and B. D. Grandjean
    1981        "The dimension of democracy: Further issues in the measurement and effects of political democracy." *American Sociological Review* 46:651-59.

Bowden, T.
1976    *Army in the Service of the State*. Tel-Aviv: University Publishing Projects.

Brecher, M.
1978    "Israel's political decisions, 1947-1977." *Middle East Journal* 32:13-34.

Brichta, A.
1972    "Social and political characteristics of members of the Seventh Knesset." In A. Arian, ed.
1974    "Women in the Knesset." *Parliamentary Affairs* 28:31-50.
1979    "The 1977 elections and the future electoral reform in Israel." In H. Penniman, ed.
1983    "Amateurs and professionals in Israeli politics." *International Political Science Review* 4:28-35.
1984    "Selection of candidates to the Tenth Knesset: The impact of centralization." In H. Penniman and D. Elazar, eds.

Brichta, A., and G. Ben-Dor
1974    "Representation and misrepresentation of political elites: The case of Israel." *Jewish Social Studies* 36:234-51.

Burnstein, P.
1976a    "Political patronage and party choice among Israeli voters." *Journal of Politics* 38:1024-32.
1976b    "Social networks and voting: Some Israeli data." *Social Forces* 54:833-45.
1978    "Social cleavages and party choice in Israel: A log-linear analysis." *American Political Science Review* 72:86-109.

Caiden, G.
1968    "Israeli administration after 20 years." *Public Administration* 8:9-29.
1969    "Coping with turbulence: Israel's administrative experience." *Journal of Comparative Administration* 1:259-80.
1970    *Israel's Administrative Culture*. Berkley: Institute of Governmental Studies.

Carmon, Naomi
1981    "Economic integration of immigrants." *The American Journal of Economics and Sociology* 40:149-63.

Caspi, Dan
1980    "How representative is the Knesset?" *Jerusalem Quarterly* 14:68-81.
1981    "The agenda-setting function of the Israeli press." *Knowledge* 3:401-14.
1983    "Following the race: Propaganda and electoral decision." In D. Caspi, A. Diskin, and E. Guttman, eds.

Caspi, Dan, Avraham Diskin, and Emanuel Guttman, eds.
1983    *The Roots of Begin's Success: The 1981 elections*. London: Croom Helm.

Caspi, Dan, and C. Eyal
1983    "Professionalization trends in Israeli election propaganda, 1973-1981." In A. Arian, ed.

Caspi, Dan, and Y. Limon
  1978    "How the Yom Kippur War affected Israeli legislative media exposure." *Journalism Quarterly* 55:474-80.
  1983    "The servants of two masters: The evaluation by the public and its representatives of the mass media in Israel." *Mass Communication Review*.
Caspi, Dan, and M.A. Seligson
  1983    "Towards an empirical theory of tolerance: Radical groups in Israel and Costa Rica." *Comparative Political Studies* 15:385-404.
Chetkow (Yanov) B., and Samuel Nadler
  1978    "Community social workers and political leaders in municipal settings in Israel." *Journal of Social Service Research* 1:357-72.
Cohen, Erik
  1972    "The Black Panthers and Israeli society." *Jewish Journal of Sociology* 14:93-109.
  1983    "Ethnicity and legitimation in contemporary Israel." *Jerusalem Quarterly* 28:111-24.
Cohen, S., and E. Don-Yehiya, eds.
  1984    *Comparative Jewish Politics, Vol. 2: Conflict and Consensus in Jewish Political Life.* Ramat-Gan: Bar-Ilan University Press.
Czudnowsky, M.M.
  1970    "Legislative recruitment under proportional representation in Israel: A model and a case study." *Mid-West Journal of Political Science* 14:216-48.
  1972    "Sociocultural variables and legislative recruitment." *Comparative Politics* 4:561-87.
Danet, Brenda
  1971    "The language of persuasion in bureaucracy: 'Modern' and 'traditional' appeals to the Israeli customs authorities." *American Sociological Review* 36:847-59.
Danet, Brenda, and H. Hartman
  1972a   "On *proteksia:* Orientations toward the use of personal influence in Israeli bureaucracy." *Journal of Comparative Administration* 3:405-34.
  1972b   "Coping with bureaucracy: The Israeli case." *Social Forces* 51:7-22.
Deshen, S.
  1970    *Immigrant Voters in Israel.* Manchester: Manchester University Press.
  1972a   "Ethnicity and citizenship in the ritual of an Israeli synagogue." *Southwestern Journal of Anthropology* 28:69-82.
  1972b   "The business of ethnicity is finished? The ethnic factor in a local election campaign." In A. Arian, ed.
  1974    "Political ethnicity and cultural ethnicity in Israel during the 1960s." In A. Cohen, ed., *Urban Ethnicity.* London: Tavistock.
  1976    "On signs and symbols: The transformation of designations in Israeli electioneering." *Political Anthropology* 1:83-100.
  1982    "Social organization and politics in Israeli urban quarters." *Jerusalem Quarterly* 22:21-37.

Diskin, Abraham
    1980    "The 1977 interparty distances: A three-level analysis." In A. Arian, ed.
    1982    "The 1981 elections public opinion polls." *Jerusalem Quarterly* 22:99-104.
    1983a   "The Jewish ethnic vote: An aggregative perspective." In D. Caspi, A. Diskin, and E. Guttman, eds.
    1983b   "Polarization and volatility among voters." In D. Caspi, A. Diskin, and E. Guttman, eds.
Diskin, Abraham, and Dan Felsenthal
    1981    "Do they lie?" *International Political Science Review* 2:407-22.
Diskin, Abraham, and M. Wolfsohn
    1978    "Strukturelle Veranderungen in den politischen Parteien Israels." *Jahrbuch de Offentlichen Rechts der Gegenwart* 27:455-99.
    1979    "Organizational and ideological evolutiom of the political parties in Israel." *Orient* 20:33-52.
Divine, Donna R.
    1974    "The modernization of Israeli administration." *International Journal of Middle Eastern Studies* 5:295-313.
    1979    "Political legitimacy in Israel: How important is the state?" *International Journal of Middle East Studies* 10:205-24.
Dominguez, Virginia
    1984    "The language of left and right in Israeli politics." In M. J. Aronoff, ed.
Don-Yehiya, Eliezer
    1975    "Religion and coalition: The National Religious Party and coalition formation in Israel." In A. Arian, ed.
    1981a   "Origins and developments of the Agudah and Mafdal parties." *Jerusalem Quarterly* 20:49-64.
    1981b   "The politics of the religious parties in Israel." In S. Lehman-Wilzig and B. Susser, eds.
    1984a   "Jewish orthodoxy, Zionism, and the state of Israel." *Jerusalem Quarterly* 31:10-30.
    1984b   "The resolution of religious conflicts in Israel." In S. Cohen and E. Don-Yehiya, eds.
    1984c   "Religious leaders in the political arena." *Middle Eastern Studies* 20:155-71.
Don-Yehiya, Eliezer, and Charles Liebman
    *See* Liebman, Charles, and Eliezer Don-Yehiya
Doron, Gideon, and Uri On
    1983    "A rational choice model of campaign strategy." In A. Arian, ed.
Dror, Yehezkel
    1977    "Are the Israel Labor Party and the alignment still viable?" *Middle East Review* 10:49-53.
Drori, M.
    1977    "Second municipal elections in Judea and Samaria under Israeli administration: Legislative change." *Israel Law Review* 12:526-40.
Dutter, Lee
    1977    "Eastern and Western Jews: Ethnic divisions in Israeli society." *Middle East Journal* 31:451-68.

Edelman, Martin
    1980a    "Politics and the constitution in Israel." *Statsvetenskaplig Tidskrift* 3:171-81.
    1980b    "The rabbinic courts in the evolving political culture of Israel." *Middle Eastern Studies* 16:145-66.
Eisenstadt, S.N.
    1956    "Patterns of leadership and social homegeneity in Israel." *International Social Science Bulletin* 8:36-54.
    1976    "Portrait of the *yishuv.*" *Jerusalem Quarterly* 1:28-35.
    1977    "Change and continuity in Israeli society." *Jerusalem Quarterly* 2:3-11.
Elazar, Daniel, J.
    1977    "The local elections: Sharpening trend toward territorial democracy." In A. Arian, ed.
    1979a    "Israel's compound polity." In H. Penniman, ed.
    1979b    "Zionism and the future of Israel." *Middle East Review* 11:19-24.
    1982    "Religious parties and politics in the Begin era." In R. Friedman, ed.
    1983    "Isreal's new majority." *Commentary* 75:33-39.
    1984    *"Israel: Building a New Society."* Bloomington: Indiana University Press.
Elboin-Dror, Rachel
    1981    "Conflict and consensus in educational policymaking in Israel." *International Journal of Political Education* 4:219-32.
Elizur, Judith
    1984    "The role of the media in the 1981 Knesset elections." In H. Penniman and D. Elazar, eds.
Elizur, Judith, and Elihu Katz
    1979    "The media in the Israeli elections of 1977." In H. Penniman, ed.
Elizur, Yuval, and Eliahu Salpeter
    1973    *Who Rules Israel?* New York: Harper & Row.
Elman, P.
    1975    "The Israel ombudsman: An appraisal." *Israel Law Review* 10:293-323.
Etzioni, Amitai
    1957    "Agrarianism in the Israeli party system." *Canadian Journal of Economics and Political Science* 23:336-75.
    1959a    "Alternative ways to democracy: The example of Israel." *Political Science Quarterly* 74:196-214.
    1959b    "Kulturkampf or coalition: The case of Israel." *Sociologia Religiosa* 3:7-28.
    1962    "The decline of neo-feudalism: The case of Israel." In Ready and Stokes, eds., *Papers in Comparative Public Administration.* Ann Arbor: University of Michigan Press.
Etzioni-Halevy, Eva
    1975a    "Patterns of conflict generation and conflict 'absorption': The cases of Israeli labor and ethnic conflicts." *Journal of Conflict Resolution* 19:286-309.
    1975b    "Protest politics in the Israeli democracy." *Political Science Quarterly* 90:497-520.
    1977    *Political Culture in Israel.* New York: Praeger.

1979     *Political Manipulation and Administrative Power—A Comparative Study.* London: Routledge & Kegan Paul.

Etzioni-Halevy, Eva, and Moshe Livne
1977     "The response of the Israeli establishment to the Yom Kippur War protest." *Middle East Journal* 31:281-96.

Eyal, Eli
1977     "The democratic movement for change: Origins and perspectives." *Middle East Review* 10:54-59.

Fein, Leonard
1967     *Politics in Israel.* Boston: Little, Brown.

Felsenthal, D.S.
1979     "Aspects of coalition payoffs: The case of Israel." *Comparative Political Studies* 12:151-68.

Fisch, Harold
1978     *The Zionist Revolution.* London: Weidenfield & Nicolson.

Freudenheim, Yehuda
1967     *Government in Israel.* New York: Oceana.

Friedman, Manachem
1983     "The NRP in transition: Behind the party's electoral decline." In D. Caspi, A. Diskin, and E. Guttman, eds.

Friedman, Robert, ed.
1982     *Israel in the Begin Era.* New York: Praeger.

Galnoor, Itzhak
1971     "Administrative secrecy in Israel." *Public Administration* 12:38-48.
1980     "Transformation in the Israeli political system since the Yom Kippur War." In A. Arian, ed.
1981     "Israel's polity: The common language." *Jerusalem Quarterly* 20:65-82.
1982     *Steering the Polity: Communication and Politics in Israel.* Beverly Hills, California: Sage.
1983     "The right to know versus government secrecy." *Jerusalem Quarterly* 26:48-65.

Gitelman, Z.
1979     "Baltic and non-Baltic immigrants in Israel: Political and social attitudes and behavior." *Studies in Comparative Communism* 12:74-90.
1982     *Becoming Israelis: Political Resocialization of Soviet and American Immigrants.* New York: Praeger.

Goldberg, Giora
1980     "Democracy and representation in Israeli political parties." In A. Arian, ed.
1981a     "The Israeli religious parties in opposition, 1965-1977." In Sam Lehman-Wilzig and B. Susser, eds.
1981b     "Adaptation to competitive politics: The case of Israeli communism." *Studies in Comparative Communism* 14:331-51.
1982     'The performance of women in legislative politics: The Israeli example." *Crossroads* 9:27-49.
1984     "The struggle for legitimacy: Herut's road from opposition to power." In S. Cohen and E. Don-Yehiya, eds.

Goldberg, Giora, and S. Hoffman
    1983    "Nominations in Israel." In A. Arian, ed.
Gonen, Amiram
    1983    "A geographical analysis of the elections in Jewish urban communities." In D. Caspi, A. Diskin, and E. Guttman, eds.
Goodland, Thomas
    1957    "A mathematical presentation of Israel's political parties." *Public Opinion Quarterly* 27:473-80.
Goren, Dina
    1979    *Secrecy and the Right to Know.* Ramat-Gan: Turtledove.
Goren, Dina, Akiba Cohen, and Dan Caspi
    1957    "Reporting of the Yom Kippur War from Israel." *Journalism Quarterly* 52:199-207.
Gottlieb, Avi, and Ephraim Yuchtman-Yaar
    1983    "Materialism, postmaterialism, and public views on socioeconomic policy: The case of Israel." *Comparative Political Studies* 16:307-35.
Greilsammer, L.
    1978    *Les Communistes israéliens.* Paris: Presses de la Fondation Nationale des Sciences Politiques.
    1981    "Les Groupes politiques marginaux en Israël." *Revue Française de Science Politique* 31:890-921.
    1984    "The Likud." In H. Penniman and D. Elazar, eds.
Gurevitch, Michael
    1972    "Television in the election campaign: Its audience and functions." In A. Arian, ed.
Gurevitch, Michael, and Alex Weingrod
    1978    "Who knows whom? Acquaintanceship and contacts in Israeli national elite." *Human Relations* 31:195-214.
Guttman, Emanuel
    1960    "The participation of citizens in political life: Israel." *International Social Science Journal* 12:59-69.
    1961    "Some observations on politics and parties in Israel." *India Quarterly* 17:3-29,
    1963    "Israel." *Journal of Politics* 25:703-17.
    1972    "Religion in Israeli politics." In J. Landau, ed., *Man, State, and Society in the Contemporary Middle East.* New York: Praeger.
    1979    "Religion and its role in national integration in Israel." *Middle East Review* 12:31-36.
Guttman, Emanuel, and Haim Landau
    1975    "The political elite and national leadership in Israel." In G. Lenczwoski, ed., *Political Elites in the Middle East.* Washington, D.C.: American Enterprise Institute.
Halevi, Nadav
    1968    *The Economic Development of Israel.* New York: Praeger.
Halpern, B.
    1961    *The Idea of the Jewish State.* Cambridge: Harvard University Press.
    1978    "To revamp a party system." *Jerusalem Quarterly* 8:127-44.
Harris, W. W.
    1980    *Taking Root: Israeli Settlements in the West Bank, the Golan Heights, and Gaza Strip, 1967-1980.* New York: Wiley.

Herzog, Hanna
 1983    "The ethnic lists in election 1981: An ethnic political identity?" In
         A. Arian, ed.
 1984    "Ethnic political identity: The ethnic lists to the Delegates'
         Assembly and the Knesset, 1920-1977." In A. Weingrod, ed.,
         *Studies in Israeli Ethnicity: After the Ingathering.* New York: Gor-
         don & Breach.
Hoffman, Steven
 1980    "Candidate selection in Israel's parliament: The realities of change."
         *Middle East Journal* 34:285-301.
Horowitz, Dan
 1977a   "More than a change in government." *Jerusalem Quarterly* 5:3-19.
 1977b   "Is Israel a garrison state?" *Jerusalem Quarterly* 4:58-75.
 1982    "The Israel defense forces: A civilianized military in a partially
         militarized society." In Kolkowicz and Korbonski, eds., *Soldiers,
         Peasants, and Bureaucrats.* London: George Allen.
Horowitz, Dan, and Baruch Kimmerling
 1974    "Some social implications of military service and reserve systems in
         Israel." *European Journal of Sociology* 2:64-89.
Horowitz, Dan, and Moshe Lissak
 1973    "Authority without sovereignty: The case of the national center of
         the Jewish people in Palestine." *Government and Opposition*
         8:48-71.
 1978    *Origins of the Israeli Polity.* Chicago: University of Chicago Press.
Horowitz, Ruth
 1979    "Jewish immigrants to Israel: Self-reported powerlessness and alien-
         ation among immigrants from the Soviet Union and North
         America." *Journal of Cross-Cultural Psychology* 10:366-74.
Ichilov, Orit
 1977    "Youth movements in Israel as agents for transition to adulthood."
         *Jewish Journal of Sociology* 19:21-32.
 1981    "Citizenship orientations of city and kibbutz youth in Israel." *Inter-
         national Journal of Political Education* 4:305-17.
Ichilov, Orit, and Nave Nisan
 1981    "The good citizen" as viewed by Israeli adolescents." *Comparative
         Politics* 13:361-76.
Iris, Mark, and Avraham Shama
 1983    "Political participation and ethnic conflict in Israel." In G. Mahler,
         ed.
Isaac, Rael J.
 1976    *Israel Divided: Ideological Politics in the Jewish State.* Baltimore:
         The Johns Hopkins University Press.
 1980    *Party and Politics in Israel: Three Visions of a Jewish State.* New
         York: Praeger.
Johnston, Scott D.
 1962a   "Election politics and social change in Israel." *Middle East Journal*
         16:309-27.
 1962b   "Party politics and coalition cabinets in the Knesset." *Middle
         Eastern Affairs* 13:130-38.

1965        "Politics of the right in Israel: The Herut movement." *Social Science* 40:104-14.
1967        "A comparative study of intra-party factionalism in Israel and Japan." *Eastern Political Quarterly* 20:288-307.
1968        "Campaigns and elections: The case of Israel." *Politico* 33:820-36.
1977a       "The prospects for a new Israeli politics." *World Affairs* 139:308-18.
1977b       "Reflections on Israeli electoral politics." *International Social Science Review* 57:3-12.

Kats, Rachel
1982        "Concerns of the Israeli: Change and stability from 1962 to 1975." *Human Relations* 35:83-100.

Katz, Alfred
1980        *Government and Politics in Contemporary Israel: 1948-Present.* Washington, D.C.: University Press of America.

Katz, E.
1971        "Platforms and windows: Broadcasting role in election campaigns." *Journalism Quarterly* 48:304-14.

Kennedy, K.A.
1976        "Impressions of Israel." *Administration* 24:425-67.

Keren, Michael, and Giora Goldberg
1980        "Technological development and ideological change." In A. Arian, ed., *Israel: A Developing Society.* Assen: Van Gorum.

Kieval, Gersen
1983        *Party Politics and the Occupied Territories.* London: Greenwood.

Kimmerling, Baruch
1974        "Anomie and integration in Israeli society and the salience of the Israeli-Arab conflict." *Studies in Comparative International Development* 9:64-89.
1977        "Sovereignty, ownership, and presence in the Jewish-Arab territorial conflict: The case of Bir'im and Ikrit." *Comparative Political Studies* 10:155-76.
1979a       *The Economic Relationship between the Arab and Jewish Communities in Palestine.* Cambridge, Mass.: M.I.T. Center for International Studies.
1979b       *Social Interruption and Besieged Society: The Israeli Case.* Amherst: State University of New York at Buffalo, Council on International Studies.
1979c       "Determination of the boundaries and frameworks of conscription: Two dimensions of civil-military relations in Israel." *Studies in Comparative International Development* 14:22-41.
1982a       "Change and continuity in Zionist territorial orientations and politics." *Comparative Politics* 14:191-210.
1982b       *Zionism and Economy: Sociological Explorations into a Case Study of Economic and Political Development.* Cambridge, Mass.: Schenkman.
1982c       *Zionism and Territory: The Socio-Territorial Dimensions of Zionist Politics.* Berkeley: Institute of International Studies, University of California.

Klein, C.A.
1978    "A Jewish state for Jews." *Jerusalem Quarterly* 7:37-47.
Knei-Paz, Baruch
1977    "Academics in politics: An Israeli experience." *Jerusalem Quarterly* 16:54-70.
Kraines, O.
1958    "Israel: The emergence of a polity, part 1." *Western Political Quarterly* 6:518-42.
1958    "Israel: The emergence of a polity, part 2." *Western Political Quarterly* 6:707-27.
1961    *Government and Politics in Israel.* Boston: Houghton Mifflin.
Krislov, Samuel
1983    "Mutual inolvement in electoral politics: The case of Israel and the United States." In. A. Arian, ed.
1984    "Mutual intervention in domestic politics: Israel and the United States." In H. Penniman and D. Elazar, eds.
Lahav, P.
1978    "Governmental regulation of the press: A study of Israel's press ordinance." *Israel Law Review* 13:230-50.
Landau, Jacob M.
1972a    *The Arabs in Israel: A Political Study.* Oxford: Oxford University Press.
1972b    "The Arab vote." In A. Arian, ed.
1983    "The Arab vote." In D. Caspi, A. Diskin, and E. Guttman, eds.
Lazar, David
1973    "Israel's political structure and social issues." *The Jewish Journal of Sociology* 15:23-43.
Lazin, Fred
1980    "The effects of administrative linkages in implementation: Welfare policy in Israel." *Policy Sciences* 12:193-14.
Lehman-Wilzig, Sam N.
1981    "Public protest and systematic stability in Israel, 1960-1979." In S. Lehman-Wilzig and B. Susser, eds.
1982    "The Israeli protesters: Attitudes, participation, trends, and prospects." *Jerusalem Quarterly* 26:127-38.
1983    "Thunder before the storm: Preelection agitation and postelection turmoil." In A. Arian, ed.
1984    "Conflict and communication: Public protest in Israel, 1950-1982." In S. Cohen and E. Don-Yehiya, eds.
Lehman-Wilzig, Sam N., and Giora Goldberg
1983    "Religious protest and police reaction in a theo-democracy: Israel, 1950-1979." *Journal of Church and State* 25:491-505.
Lehman-Wilzig, Sam N. and Bernard Susser, eds.
1981    *Comparative Jewish Politics, Vol. 1. Public Life in Israel and the Diaspora.* Ramat-Gan: Bar-Ilan University Press.
Leibowitz, Y.
1980    "State and religion." *Jerusalem Quarterly* 14:59-67.
Leslie, S.C.
1971    *The Rift in Israel: Religious Authority and Secular Democracy.* New York: Schocken.

Levite, Ariel, and Sidney Tarrow
    1983        "The legitimation of excluded parties in dominant party systems: A
                comparison of Israel and Italy." *Comparative Politics* 15:295-327.
Levy. S.
    1979        "The cylindrical structure of political involvement." *Social
                Indicators Research* 6:41-64.
Lewis, Arnold
    1979a       "The peace ritual and Israeli image of the social order." *Journal of
                Conflict Resolution* 23:685-703.
    1979b       *Power, Poverty, and Education.* Ramat-Gan: Turtledove.
    1984        "The ethnic factor in Israeli politics." In M.J. Aronoff, ed.
Liebman, Charles
    1975        "Religion and political integration in Israel." *The Jewish Journal of
                Sociology* 17:17-27.
    1977        *Pressure without Sanctions: The Influence of World Jewry in
                Shaping Israel's Public Policy.* Cranbury, N.J.: Fairleigh Dickinson
                University Press.
    1978a       "Myth, tradition, and values in Israeli society." *Midstream*
                24:44-53.
    1978b       "In search of status: The Israeli government and the Zionist
                movement." *Forum* 28-29:38-56.
    1984a       "History, myth, and tradition." *Jerusalem Quarterly* 31:3-9.
    1984b       "Attitudes toward Jewish-Gentile relations in the Jewish tradition
                and contemporary Israel." Occasional Papers, University of
                Capetown.
    1984c       "The 'Who is a Jew?' controversy." In S. Cohen and E. Don-
                Yehiya, eds.
Liebman, Charles, and Eliezer Don-Yehiya
    1981a       "Zionist ultra-nationalism and its attitude toward religion." *Journal
                of Church and State* 23:259-73.
    1981b       "What a Jewish state means to Israeli Jews." In S. Lehman-Wilzig
                and B. Susser, eds.
    1981c       "The symbol system of Zionist socialism: An aspect of Israeli civil
                religion." *Modern Judaism* 1:121-48.
    1982        "Israeli's civil religion." *Jerusalem Quarterly* 23:57-69.
    1983a       "The dilemma of reconciling traditional culture and contemporary
                needs: Civil religion in Israel." *Comparative Politics* 16:53-66.
    1983b       *Civil Religion in Israel: Traditional Religion and Political Culture in
                the Jewish State.* Berkeley: University of California Press.
    1984        *Piety and Politics: Religion and Politics in Israel.* Bloomington:
                Indiana University Press.
Likhovski, E.S.
    1971        *Israel's Parliament.* Oxford: Clarendon Press.
Lissak, M.
    1972        "Continuity and change in the voting patterns of Oriental Jews." In
                A. Arian, ed.
    1977        "The Israel defense forces as an agent of socialization and
                education: A research in role expansion in a democratic state." In
                M. R. Van Gils, ed., *The Perceived Role of the Military.* Rotterdam:
                Rotterdam University Press.

Lorch, Netanel, and Samuel Sager
1977      "Israel's parliament: The Knesset." *Parliamentarian* 58:172-76.
Lucas, Noah
1974      *The Modern History of Israel.* London: Weidenfeld & Nicolson.
1978      "A centenarian at thirty: The State of Israel, 1978."*Political Quarterly* 49:285-92.
Lustick, Ian
1980      *Arabs in the Jewish State.* Austin: University of Texas Press.
1982      "Israel's Arab minority in the Begin era." In Robert Friedman, ed.
Luttwak, E. and D. Horowitz
1975      *The Israeli Army.* London: Yoseloff.
Mahler, Gregory
1979      "Political consciousness and political events: A study of Israeli and Canadian members of parliament." *Political Science* 31:89-107.
1980a     "Political socialization and political interest in Israeli and Canadian legislatures: A comparative examination. *Political Science Review* 19:361-83.
1980b     "The effects of electoral systems upon the behavior of members of a national legislature: The Israeli Knesset—a case study." *Journal of Constitutional and Parliamentary Studies* 14:305-18.
1983      *"The Knesset: Parliament in the Israeli Political System."* Rutherford, N.J.: Associated University Presses.
Mahler, Gregory, ed.
1983      *Readings on the Israeli Political System: Structures and Processes.* Washington, D.C.: University Press of America.
Mahler, Gregory, and Richard Trilling
1975      "Coalition behavior and cabinet formation: The case of Israel." *Comparative Polititcal Studies* 8:200-233.
Marmorstein, Emile
1969      *Heaven at Bay: The Jewish Kulturkampf in the Holy Land.* London: Oxford University Press.
Mars, Leonard
1980      *The Village and the State: Administration, Ethnicity, and Politics in an Israeli Cooperative Village.* Westmead: Gower.
Marx, Emanuel
1975      "Anthropological studies in a centralized state: Max Gluckman and the Bernstein Israel Research Project. *The Jewish Journal of Sociology* 17:131-50.
Medding, P.
1970      "A framework for the analysis of power in political parties." *Political Studies* 18:1-17.
1972      *Mapai in Israel.* Cambridge: Cambridge University Press.
Medzini, M.
1971      "Censorship problems in Israel—the legal aspect." *Israel Law Review* 6:309-20.
Mendilow, Jonathan
1982      "Party-cluster formations in multiparty systems." *Political Studies* 30:485-503.
1983a     "Party clustering in multiparty systems: The example of Israel, 1965-1985." *American Journal of Political Science* 27:64-85.

1983b    "The transformation of the Israeli multiparty system, 1965-1968."
         In A. Arian, ed.

Michal, Shaul, and Abraham Diskin
1982     "Palestinian voting in the West Bank: Electoral behavior in a
         traditional community without sovereignty." *Journal of Politics*
         44:538-58.

Migdal, Joel
1978     "State and society in a society without a state." In G. Ben-Dor, ed.,
         *The Palestinians and the Middle East Conflict.* Ramat-Gan:
         Turtledove.
1980     *Palestinian Society and Politics.* Princeton: Princeton University
         Press.

Naamani, Israel
1972     *Israel: A Profile.* New York: Praeger.

Nachmias, David
1973     "A note on coalition payoffs in a dominant party system." *Political
         Studies* 21:301-5.
1974     "Coalition politics in Israel." *Comparative Political Studies*
         7:316-33.
1975     "Coalition, myth, and reality." In A. Arian, ed.
1976     "The right-wing opposition in Israel." *Political Studies* 24:268-80.
1977     "A temporal sequence of adolescent political participation: Some
         Israeli data." *British Journal of Political Science* 7:71-83.

Nachmias, David, and David Rosenbloom
1976     "Why exit the public bureaucracy? An explanatory study."
         *Administrative Change* 3:7-19.
1977     "Antecedents of turnover in public bureaucracy: The case of
         Israel." *Administration and Society* 9:45-81.
1978a    "Bureaucracy and ethnicity."*American Journal of Sociology*
         83:967-74.
1978b    *Citizens and Administrators in Israel.* New York: St. Martin's Press.

Ofer, Gur
1981     "Israel's Economy." *Jerusalem Quarterly* 20:3-16.

Oren. S.
1973     "Continuity and change in Israel's religious parties." *Middle East
         Journal* 27:36-54.

Osterweil, Zahava
1982     "The development of political concepts in Israeli schoolboys."
         *International Journal of Political Education* 5:141-58.

Paine, Robert
1984     "Israeli and totemic time." In M. J. Aronoff, ed.

Paltiel, K.Z.
1975     "The Israeli coalition system. *Government and Opposition*
         10:397-414.
1979     "The impact of election expenses legislation in Canada, Western
         Europe, and Israel." *Sage Electoral Studies Yearbook* 5:15-39.

Parzen, H.
1967     "A chapter in Arab-Jewish relations during the Mandate era."
         *Jewish Social Studies* 29:203-33.

Penniman, H., ed.
1979    *Israel at the Polls: The Knesset Elections of 1977.* Washington: American Enterprise Institute.
Penniman, H., and Daniel Elazar, eds.
1984    *Israel at the Polls: The Knesset Elections of 1981.* Bloomington: Indiana University Press.
Peres, Y.
1979    "Ethnic relations in Israel." *American Journal of Sociology* 76:1021-47.
Peres,Yochanan, and Sara Shemer
1983    "The ethnic factor in elections." In D. Caspi, A. Diskin, and E. Guttman, eds.
Peres, Yochanan, E. Yuchtman-Yaar, and R. Shafat
1975    "Predicting and explaining voters' behavior in Israel." In A. Arian, ed.
Peretz, Don
1970    "Israel's 1969 election issues: The visible and the invisible." *Middle East Journal* 24:31-46.
1974    "The war election and Israel's Eighth Knesset." *Middle East Journal* 31:251-66.
1977    "The earthquake: Israel's Ninth Knesset elections." *Middle East Journal* 31:251-66.
1979    *"The Government and Politics of Israel."* Boulder, Colo.: Westview.
Peretz, Don, and Sammy Smooha
1981    "Israel's Tenth Knesset elections: Ethnic upsurgence and decline of ideology." *Middle East Journal* 35:506-26.
Peri, Yoram
1975    "Television in the 1973 campaign." In A. Arian, ed.
1977    "Ideological portrait of Israeli military elite." *Jerusalem Quarterly* 3:28-41.
1977    "Political attitudes of Christian and Moslem children." *European Journal of Social Psychology* 7:369-73.
1981    "Political-military partnership in Israel." *International Political Science Review* 2:303-15.
1982    *Between Battles and Ballots: Israeli Military in Politics.* Cambridge: Cambridge University Press.
1983    "Coexistence or hegemony? Shifts in the Israeli security concept." In D. Caspi, A. Diskin, and E. Guttman, eds.
1984    "Civilian control during a protracted war." In Zvi Lanier, ed., *Israel's Security in the 1980s.* New York: Praeger.
Peri, Yoram, and Moshe Lissak
1976    "Retired officers in Israel and the emergence of a new elite." In G. Harris-Jenkins and J. van Doorn, eds., *The Military and the Problem of Legitimacy.* Beverly Hill, Calif.: Sage.
Perlmutter, A.
1968a    "The institutionalization of civil-military relations in Israel: The Ben-Gurion legacy and its challengers, 1953-1967." *Middle Eastern Journal* 22:415-32.
1968b    "The Israeli army in politics." *World Politics* 20:606-43.

1969    *Military and Politics in Israel.* New York: Praeger.
1977    "Cleavage in Israel." *Foreign Policy* 27:136-57.
1978    *Military and Politics in Israel, 1967-1977.* London: Frank Cass.
Pollock, David
1982    "Likud in power: Divided we stand." In R. Friedman, ed.
Pomper, G.M.
1982    "Ambition in Israel: A comparative extension of theory and data."
        *Western Political Quarterly* 28:712-32.
Rackman, E.
1955    *Israel's Emerging Constitution, 1948-1951.* New York: Columbia
        University Press.
Radian, Alex
1983    "The policy formation: Electoral economic cycle, 1955-1981." In
        D. Caspi, A. Diskin, and E. Guttman, eds.
Raphaeli, N.
1970    "The senior civil service in Israel." *Public Administration* 48:169-78.
Reich, Bernard
1979    "Israel's foreign policy and the 1977 parliamentary elections." In H.
        Penniman, ed.
Reisman, R.
1981    "Conflict in an Israeli collective community." *Journal of Conflict
        Resolution* 25:237-58.
Rolbant, S.
1975    *The Israeli Soldier: Profile of an Army.* London: Yoseloff.
Rosenbloom, D.H., and D. Nachmias
1974    "Bureaucratic under-representation: The case of Israel." *Adminis-
        trative Change* 2:23-33.
Rosenfeld, Henry
1978    "The class situation of the Arab national minority in Israel." *Com-
        parative Studies in Society and History,* 20:374-407.
Rosenfeld, Henry, and Shulamith Carmi
1976    "The privatization of public means: The state-made middle class and
        the realization of family value in Israel." In J.G. Peristiony, ed.,
        *Kinship and Modernization in Mediterranean Society.* Rome, Italy:
        The Center for Mediterranean Studies, American University Field
        Staff.
Rosenzweig, Rafael, and Tamarin Georges
1970    "Israel's power elite." *Transaction* 7:26-33, 38-42.
Roshwald, M.
1956    "Political parties and social classes in Israel." *Social Research*
        23:199-218.
Ross. J.A.
1979    "The relationship between the perception of historical symbols and
        the alienation of Jewish immigrants from the Soviet Union."
        *Western Political Quarterly* 32:215-24.
Rossetti, Michael
1955    "Israel's Parliament." *Parliamentary Affairs* 8:450-58.
Rubinstein, A.
1967    "State and religion in Israel." *Journal of Contemporary History*
        2:107-21.

Rubinstein, Elyakim
1979     "The lesser parties in the Israeli election of 1977. In H. Penniman, ed.
Sager, S.
1972     "Prestate influences on Israel's parliamentary system." *Parliamentary Affairs* 25:29-49.
1978     "Israel's provisional state council and government." *Middle Eastern Studies* 14:91-101.
Samuel, E.
1956     "Growth of the Israeli Civil Service, 1948-1958." *Revue Internationale des Sciences Administratives* 22:17-40.
Sandler, Shmuel
1981     "The national religious party: Towards a new role in Israel's political system?" In S. Lehman-Wilzig and B. Susser, eds.
1984     "The religious parties." In H. Penniman and D. Elazar, eds.
Schatzker, Chaim
1982     "The Holocaust in Israeli education." *International Journal of Political Education* 5:75-82.
Schiff, G.
1977     *Tradition and Politics: The Religious Parties of Israel.* Detroit: Wayne State University Press.
1978     "The politics of population policy in Israel." *Forum* 28-29:173-92.
Schnall, David
1977     "Native anti-Zionism: Ideologies of radical dissent in Israel." *Middle East Journal* 31:157-74.
1979     *Radical Dissent in Contemporary Israeli Politics.* New York: Praeger.
Segre, V.D.
1971     *Israel: A Society in Transition.* London: Oxford University Press.
Seliger, M.
1968     "Positions and dispositions in Israeli politics." *Government and Opposition* 3:465-84.
Seligman, Lester
1964     *Leadership in a New Nation: Political Development in Israel.* New York: Atherton.
Seligson, Mitchell A., and Dan Caspi
1982     "Arabs in Israel: Political tolerance and ethnic conflict." *Journal of Applied Behavioral Science* 18:(4).
Seliktar, Ofira
1980a    "Acquiring partisan preference in a plural society: The case of Israel." *Plural Societies* 11:3-19.
1980b    "Continuity and change in the attitudes toward the Middle East Conflict: The case of young Israelis." *International Journal of Political Education* 3:141-61.
1981     "National integration of a minority in an acute conflict situation: The case of Israeli Arabs." *Plural Societies* 12:25-40.
Shamir, Michal, and Asher Arian
1982     "The ethnic vote in Israel's 1981 elections." *Electoral Studies* 1:315-31.

Shamir, Michal, and John Sullivan
1983    "The political context of tolerance: The United States and Israel."
        *American Political Science Review* 77:911-28.
Shapira, Anita
1984    "The struggle for 'Jewish Labor' in the *yishuv* period: The concept
        and consequences." In S. Cohen and E. Don-Yehiya, eds.
Shapiro, Y.
1976    *The Formative Years of the Israeli Labor Party.* Beverly Hills, Calif.:
        Sage.
1979    "1979 Sabras in politics." *Jerusalem Quarterly* 11:112-27.
1980a   "The end of a dominant party system." In A. Arian, ed.
1980b   "Generational units and intergenerational relations in Israeli
        politics." In A. Arian, ed., *Israel—A Developing Society.* Assen:
        Van Gorcum.
Shargel, Baila
1979    "The evolution of the Masada myth." *Judaism* 28:357-76.
Sharkansky, Ira
1984    "Religion and state in Begin's Israel." *Jerusalem Quarterly*
        31:31-49.
Sharkansky, Ira, and Alex Radian
1981    "The Likud government and domestic policy change." *Jerusalem
        Quarterly* 18:86-100.
1982    "Changing domestic policy." In R. Friedman, ed.
Shashar, Michael
1979    "The state of Israel and the land of Israel." *Jerusalem Quarterly*
        17:36-65.
Sherman, Neal
1980    "The agricultural sector and the 1977 elections." In A. Arian, ed.
1982    "From government to opposition: The rural settlement of the Israeli
        Labor Party in the wake of the elections of 1977." *International
        Journal of Middle East Studies* 14:53-69.
Shimshoni, Daniel
1982    *Israeli Democracy: The Middle of the Journey.* New York: Free
        Press.
Shlaim, Avid, and Avner Yaniv
1980    "Domestic politics and foreign policy in Israel." *International
        Affairs* 56:242-62.
Shokeid, Moshe
1968    "Immigration and factionalism: An analysis of factions in rural
        Israeli communities of immigrants." *British Journal of Sociology*
        19:385-406.
1975    "Strategy and change in the Arab vote: Observations in a mixed
        town." In A. Arian, ed.
1976    "Conviviality versus strife: Peacemaking at parties among Atlas
        Mountain immigrants in Israel." *Political Anthropology* 1:101-21.
1978    "Israeli Arab vote in transition: Observation on campaign strategies
        in a mixed town." *Middle Eastern Studies* 14:76-90.
1980    "Political parties and the Arab electorate in an Israeli city." In E.
        Marx, ed., *A Composite Portrait of Israel.* London: Academic
        Press.

1984        "Ethnic myths and Israeli intellectuals." In M. J. Aronoff, ed.
Smith, Herbert
1972        "Analysis of voting." In A. Arian, ed.
Smooha, Sammy
1976        "Ethnic stratification and allegiance in Israel: Where do Oriental
            Jews belong?" *Il Politico* 41:635-51.
1978        *Israel: Pluralism and Conflict.* Berkeley: University of California
            Press.
1980a       "Control of minorities in Israel and Northern Ireland." *Compara-
            tive Studies in Society and History* 22:256-80.
1980b       *The Orientation and Politicization of the Arab Minority in Israel.*
            Haifa: The Jewish Arab Center, University of Haifa.
1982        "Existing and alternating policy towards Arabs in Israel." *Ethnic
            and Racial Studies* 5:71-98.
Smooha, Sammy, and Ora Cibluski
1978        *Social Research on Arabs in Israel, 1948-1977.* Ramat-Gan: Turtle-
            dove.
Smooha, Sammy, and Yochanan Peres
1975        "The dynamics of ethnic inequalities: The case of Israel." *Social
            Dynamics* 1:63-79.
Smooha, Sammy, and Don Peretz
1982        "The Arabs in Israel." *Journal of Conflict Resolution* 26:451-84.
Sprinzak, Ehud
1977        "Extreme politics in Israel." *Jerusalem Quarterly* 5:33-47.
1981        "Gush Emunim: The tip of the iceberg." *Jerusalem Quarterly*
            21:28-47.
Stone, Russel A.
1982        *Social Change in Israel.* New York: Praeger.
Swirski, S.
19756       "Community and the meaning of the modern state: The case of
            Israel." *Jewish Journal of Sociology* 18:123-40.
Tabory, Ephraim
1981        "Religious rights as a social problem in Israel." *Israel Yearbook on
            Human Rights* 11:256-71.
Tabory, Mala
1981        "Language rights in Israel." *Israel Yearbook on Human Rights*
            11:272-306.
Tartakower, Arieh
1964        "The state of Israel as a sociological phenomenon." *International
            Review of Sociology* 2:30-52.
Tokatli, Rachel
1975        "Image modification and voters' behavior." In A. Arian, ed.
Torczyner, J.
1972        "The political context of social change: A case study of innovation
            in adversity in Jerusalem." *Journal of Applied Behavioral Science*
            8:287-317.
Torgovnik, Ephraim
1972        "Party factions and election issues." In A. Arian, ed.
1973        "Election issues and international conflict resolution in Israel."
            *Political Studies* 20:79-96.

| 1975 | "The election campaign: Party needs and voter concerns." In A. Arian, ed. |
|---|---|
| 1976a | "Urban political integration in Israel: A comparative perspective." *Urban Affairs Quarterly* 11:469-88. |
| 1977 | "Local policy determinants in a centrist system." *Publius* 7:61-84. |
| 1978 | "Accepting Camp David: The role of party factions in Israeli policymaking." *Middle East Review* 11:18-25. |
| 1979 | "A movement for change in a state system." In H. Penniman, ed. |
| 1980 | "A movement for change in a stable system." In A. Arian, ed. |
| 1982 | "Likud, 1977-1981: The consolidation of power." In R. Friedman, ed. |
| 1984 | "Party organization and electoral politics: An analysis of the labor alignment and the 1981 election campaign." In H. Penniman and D. Elazar, eds. |

Torgovnik, Ephraim, and S. Weiss
1972    "Local nonparty political organization in Israel." *Western Political Quarterly* 25:305-22.

Webster, R.A.
1978    "Israel's political parties: The Zionist heritage." *Middle East Review* 11:5-10.

Weimann, Gabriel
1983    "Every day is election day: Press coverage of preelection polls." In D. Caspi, A. Diskin, and E. Guttman, eds.

Weingrod, Alex, and Michael Gurevitch
1977    "Who are the Israeli elites?" *The Jewish Journal of Sociology* 19:67-77.

Weinshall, T.
1982    "Toward the improvement of government administration in Israel." *Crossroads* 7:125-53; 8:51-96.

Weisburd, David, with Vered Vinitski
1984    "Vigilantism as rational social control." In M. J. Aronoff, ed.

Weiss, S.
1972    "Results of local elections." In A. Arian, ed.

Weiss, S. and A. Brichta
1969    "Private members' bills in Israel's parliament—The Knesset. *Parliamentary Affairs* 23:21-33.

Weiss, S., and Y. Yishai
1980    "Women's representation in Israeli political elites." *Jewish Social Studies* 40:165-76.

Weissbrod, Lilly
1981a    "From labor Zionism to new Zionism: Ideological change in Israel." *Theory and Society* 10:777-803.
1981b    "Delegitimation and legitimation as a continuous process: A case study of Israel:" *Middle East Journal* 35:527-43.
1982    "Gush Emunim ideology: From religious doctrine to political action." *Middle Eastern Studies* 18:265-75.
1983    "Economic factors and political strategies: The defeat of the Revisionists in Mandatory Palestine." *Middle Eastern Studies* 19:326-44.

1984a    "The rise and fall of the Revisionist Party, 1928-1935." *Jerusalem Quarterly* 30:80-93.
1984b    "Protest and dissidence in Israel." In M. J. Arnoff, ed.
Willner, Dorothy
1965    "Politics and change in Israel: The case of land settlement." *Human Organization* 24:65-72.
1969    *Nation Building and Community in Israel.* Princeton: Princeton University Press.
Witkonia, A.
1970    "Elections in Israel." *Israel Law Review* 5:42-57.
Wolf-Phillips, Leslie
1973    "The Westminster model in Israel." *Parliamentary Affairs* 26:415-39.
Wolfsfed, Gadi
1984    "Yamit: Protest and the media." *Jerusalem Quarterly* 31:130-44.
Yaacobi, Gad
1982    *The Government of Israel.* New York: Praeger.
Yanai, Nathan
1981    *Party Leadership in Israel: Maintenance and Change.* Ramat-Gan: Turtledove.
Yaniv, Avner, and Majid Al Haj
1983    "Uniformity or diversity: A reappraisal of the voting behavior of the Arab minority in Israel." In A. Arian, ed.
Yaniv, Avner, and Fabian Pascal
1980    "Doves, hawks, and other birds of a feather: The distribution of Israel parliamentary opinion on the future of the occupied territories, 1967-1977." *British Journal of Political Science* 10:260-67.
Yishai, Yael
1978    "Abortion in Israel: Social demand and political responses." *Policy Studies Journal* 7:270-89.
1979    "Interest groups in Israel." *Jerusalem Quarterly* 20:36-48.
1980    "Factionalism in the national religious party: The quiet revolution." In A. Arian, ed.
1981    "Factionalism in Israel: political parties." *Jerusalem Quarterly* 20:36-48.
1982    "Israel's right-wing Jewish proletariat." *The Jewish Journal of Sociology* 24:87-97.
Zaltzman, Nina
1981    "Restrictions on the freedom of expression of the state employees in Israel." *Israel Yearbook on Human Rights* 11:307-33.
Zamir, D.
1981    "Generals in politics." Jerusalem Quarterly 20:17-35.
Zelniker, S., and M. Kahn
1978    "Religion and nascent cleavages: The case of Israel's National Religious Party." *Comparative Politics* 9:21-48.
Zidon, Asher
1973    *Knesset: The Parliament of Israel.* New York: Herzl.
Zohar, D.M.
1974    *Political Parties in Israel: The Evolution of Israeli Democracy.* New York: Praeger.

Zucker, N.L., and N. Zucker
1973     *The Coming Crisis in Israel.* Cambridge, Mass.: The M.I.T. Press.

# Contributors

*Asher Arian* is professor of political science at Tel-Aviv University, Israel. He has published in the fields of political sociology, comparative politics, and Israeli parties and elections.

*Erik Cohen* is professor of sociology and social anthropology at The Hebrew University of Jerusalem, Israel. His areas of interest are sociology of strangers and tourism, sociology of Thailand and Israel, anthropology of art, relations between sociology and philosophy.

*Karl W. Deutsch* is professor of government and Stanfield Professor of International Peace at Harvard University. His main fields of interest are the theory of political communication and control, large-scale political communities, and the testing of political theories with the aid of quantitative data.

*Donna Robinson Divine* is associate professor of government at Smith College, Northampton, Massachusetts. Her fields of interest are Zionism, Israeli politics and society, Egyptian politics and society, Palestinian Arab social history.

*Eliezer Don-Yehiya* is senior lecturer in the Department of Political Studies, Bar-Ilan University, Ramat Gan, Israel. He is interested in religion and society, comparative politics, religious Zionism, and politics and education.

*S.N. Eisenstadt* is Rose Isaacs Professor of Sociology at the Hebrew University of Jerusalem, Israel. His major areas of interest are sociological theory, political sociology, comparative studies of civilization and modernization, and Israeli society—on all of which he has written extensively.

*Daniel J. Elazar* is president, Jerusalem Center for Public Affairs, and Senator N.M. Paterson Professor of Intergovernmental Relations at Bar-Ilan University, Ramat Gan, Israel. His major fields of interest are federalism, Jewish political studies, American politics, Israeli politics.

*Menachem Friedman* is senior lecturer in the Department of Sociology and Anthropology at Bar-Ilan University, Ramat Gan, Israel. His main fields of interest are the sociology of religion, extreme religious groups, the social structure of Israel, relations between religious and nonreligious people in Israel.

*David Glanz* is executive coordinator of the Bar-Ilan University—Brookdale Program in Applied Gerontology, and assistant editor of Studies of Israeli Society. He is a Ph.D. candidate at Bar-Ilan University, Ramat Gan, Israel. His interests include social gerontology, the sociology of religion, political sociology, and the sociology of organizations.

*Avi Gottlieb* is senior lecturer in the Department of Sociology and Anthropology at Tel-Aviv University, Israel. His main fields of interest are social psychology, attitudes and public policy, employment and crime, rehabilitation of delinquents.

*Hanna Herzog* is lecturer in the Department of Sociology and Anthropology at Tel-Aviv University, Israel. Her principal areas of interest are ethnic relations in a historical perspective, political organizations, voluntary organizations and their relationship to the political system.

*Dan Horowitz* is professor of sociology and political science at the Hebrew University of Jerusalem, Israel. He is interested in Israeli society and politics, communal conduct in divided societies, Israeli national security and defense policy, civil-military relations.

*Baruch Kimmerling* is senior lecturer in the Department of Sociology and Social Anthropology at the Hebrew University of Jerusalem, Israel. He has published extensively in the area of the sociology of the Zionist movement, the Jewish-Arab conflict, the military and war, as well as on social change and modernization.

*Charles S. Liebman* is professor of political studies at Bar-Ilan University, Ramat Gan, Israel. His interest is in political symbols, religion and society, Jewish identity, Israel-Diaspora relations.

*Moshe Lissak* is professor of sociology at the Hebrew University of Jerusalem, Israel. His main interests are military sociology, political sociology, social history.

*Yoram Peri* is lecturer on political sociology in the Department of Political Science at Tel-Aviv University, Israel. His principal areas of interest are civil-military relationships, Israeli politics.

*Michal Shamir* is lecturer in the Department of Political Science at Tel-Aviv University, Israel. She has done research in the areas of comparative politics, Israeli politics, and methodology.

*Yonathan Shapiro* is professor of sociology and political science at Tel-Aviv

University, Israel. His main fields of interest are political sociology and the social structure of Israeli society.

*Sammy Smooha* is senior lecturer in sociology at Haifa University, Israel. His main fields of interest are ethnic and racial studies, politics, social stratification, Near-Eastern societies.

*Yael Yishai* is senior lecturer in the Department of Sociology and Anthropology at Haifa University, Israel. Her areas of interest are domestic inputs into Israeli foreign policy, ethnic (Jewish) relations in Israel.

*Ephraim Yuchtman-Yaar* is professor of sociology at Tel-Aviv University, Israel. His main fields of interest are social inequality, the sociology of work and organizations, and social psychology.